The Argentina Reader

THE LATIN AMERICA READERS

a series edited by Robin Kirk and Orin Starn

Also in this series:

The Peru Reader: History, Culture, Politics

Orin Starn, Carlos Iván Degregori, and Robin Kirk, editors

The Brazil Reader: History, Culture, Politics

Robert M. Levine and John J. Crocitti, editors

LATIN AMERICA IN TRANSLATION/EN TRADUCCIÓN/EM TRADUÇÃO

Sponsored by the Consortium in Latin American Studies at
The University of North Carolina at Chapel Hill and Duke University

THE ARGENTINA READER

HISTORY, CULTURE, POLITICS

Edited by Gabriela Nouzeilles and Graciela Montaldo

DUKE UNIVERSITY PRESS   *Durham and London*   2002

© 2002 Duke University Press

All rights reserved

Printed in the United States of America on acid-free paper ∞

Designed by Amy Ruth Buchanan

Typeset in Dante by Tseng Information Systems, Inc.

Library of Congress Cataloging-in-Publication Data appear

on the last printed page of this book.

In memory of Charlie Feiling

Contents

i am thus in each of these ways
spanish french indian who knows
warrior farmer merchant poet perhaps
rich poor of all classes and of none
and well i'm an argentine

CÉSAR FERNÁNDEZ MORENO,
"Argentine to Death" (1963)

Acknowledgments

A book of this kind depends for its realization on the efforts and contributions of many people. Walter Mignolo and Orin Starn enthusiastically encouraged us to develop our project when it was still in its initial stages. With her professional experience and patience, Valerie Millholland, our editor at Duke University Press, accompanied us throughout the long editorial process.

There are many whose assistance enhanced our work. Four anonymous reviewers inspired us with their strong endorsement, insightful criticisms, and useful suggestions. Stephen Hiltner and Ryan Long carefully edited our introductions. John Kraniauskas's sharp editorial eye detected needed revisions. Mark Healey applied his knowledge and bilingual acumen to polish the final version of the manuscript.

Jon Beasley Murray, Desirée Martin, and Ruth Hill provided us with apt translations of often difficult pieces. With his extraordinary talent, William Rowe made Perlongher's and Juan L. Ortiz's poetry shine in a foreign language.

Our deep gratitude goes to Patricia Owen Steiner, the author of most of the new English translations included in the reader. No words suffice to acknowledge her dedication, hard work, and perseverance to achieve the best results, covering a very wide range of styles and historical periods.

For their generous permissions, we thank the many publishers, authors, and artists who acceded to our requests, including David Viñas, Beatriz Sarlo, César Aira, Vicente Palermo, Marcos Novaro, Tulio Halperín Donghi, David Rock, Marcela Nari, Jorge Palacio, Frank Graziano, Osvaldo Bayer, the Fundación Martínez Estrada, the Xul Solar Museum, Juan Carlos Distéfano, María Teresa Gramuglio, Nicolás Rosa, Carlos Alonso, Lily Berni, Daniel Divinski, Matilde Sánchez, Hebe de Bonafini, Graciela Speranza, Fernando Cittadini, Catherine Soriano, Johannes Wilbert, Javier Auyero, Rodolfo Rabanal, Horacio González, Juan Carlos Romero, María Moreno, Laura Ginsberg, Encarnación Ezcurra, Susana Lange, and Nora Kildal.

Two grants, one from Fundación Antorchas, from Argentina, and the other from the Duke University/University of North Carolina Center of Latin American and Caribbean Studies, eased the cumulative expenses of translations.

Nora Domínguez, Andrea Giunta, Marcos Mayer, Gabriel Pasquini, and Adriana Rodríguez Pérsico were invaluable in collecting information, contacting people and institutions, and being our representatives when we were unable to travel to Argentina. The librarians at the Archivo General de la Nación in Buenos Aires provided invaluable assistance in the process of identifying, gathering, and reproducing the photographs included in this book.

Finally, we would like to acknowledge our debt to our wonderful partners, Sergio Chejfec and Stephen Hiltner, for their unflagging support and love. And to Sofía and Anna for their sleeping habits.

General Introduction

"This is a land of exiles," the legendary writer Jorge Luis Borges would respond with a half smile when asked about Argentine identity. Aside from exhibiting his taste for eccentricity and puzzling his audience, in his answer Borges was in fact repeating one of Argentina's most powerful images: the idea that it is a modern country built from scratch through liberal economic and social policies and massive European immigration. Between 1880 and 1920, an enlightened elite of intellectuals and politicians purposely founded a nation modeled after Europe and the United States on the vast and fertile plains of the Southern Cone, relegating to the past the rebellious gauchos and nomadic Amerindians that until then had traversed the land. In 1845, Argentina's founding father, Domingo F. Sarmiento, described this process as an epic struggle between Western civilization and local barbarism. At the turn of the century, steady growth in export earnings, capital investments, modern technology, and labor supply at a favorable moment in the international economy helped turn a forgotten minor colony of the Spanish Empire into an earthly promised land. In 1910, one hundred years after independence from Spain, Argentina offered convincing proof that modernity could take root and prosper in postcolonial Latin America. The local elites had replaced a past of poverty, violence, and wastelands with a future of prosperity, cosmopolitanism, progress, and economic opportunity. In an essay celebrating the country's remarkable achievements, the Nicaraguan poet Rubén Darío expressed his conviction that Argentina would lead the rest of the former Spanish colonies along the path of progress. To the astonishment and applause of all the nations of the world, he contended, Argentina was already flourishing and would soon become strong enough to compete even with the big brother of the North, the United States. Nobody seemed to doubt that Argentines would eventually become the "Yankees of the South."[1]

Echoing this perspective, writers at home and abroad have repeatedly portrayed Argentina as a homogeneous and exceptional community, remarkably different from its Latin American counterparts. "The Argentines differ from most other Latin American peoples in many respects and from all of them in some important respects," the American historian Arthur P. Whitaker de-

Map of Argentina

clared in 1954. In his view, Argentina's superiority was worthy of many superlatives. Except for the people of Uruguay, the Argentines were culturally the most Europeanized and educated people in Latin America. Their literacy rate (about 90 percent) was the highest by far. Until 1945, the country boasted the highest per capita income on the continent, the most extensive urbanization, the largest middle class, as well as the best newspapers, universities, and publishing houses. Whitaker's numerous allusions to Argentina's "whiteness" also reveal a tendency, spoken or merely implied, to consider the country's racial stock a significant asset.[2] Thus, regretfully, praise has frequently bordered on declaring Argentina an oasis of Western civilization in a "darker" continent.

A look at Paul Theroux's unabashedly ethnocentric account of his journey from New England to the Southern Cone in 1978 attests to this. The Canadian writer remembers his sense of relief when entering Argentina from Bolivia and Peru by train. Suddenly, there were no Indians, he remarks. The faces on board had turned into reflections of his own. They were "the faces one might see on any train in the United States, or Europe for that matter. It was possible to enter a crowd in Argentina and vanish." Buenos Aires, the magnificent city embodying Argentina's exceptional sophistication, "is at first glance, and for days afterward, a most civilized anthill. It has the elegance of the old world in its buildings and streets; and its people, all the vulgarity and frank good health of the new world. All the newsstands and bookstores—what a literate place, one thinks; what wealth, what good looks." Theroux searches in vain for what he calls "seizable South American characteristics." After crudely depicting the social realities of countries like Colombia and Peru with the broad visual simplicities of underdevelopment—starvation, neglect, institutional chaos—he concludes that even the severe censorship imposed on the Argentine press by the then-ruling military dictatorship appeared unremarkable to him by comparison.[3]

Even less obviously biased perspectives convey a feeling of surprise. In an article written for the *Atlantic Monthly* in 1998, the journalists Benjamin and Christina Schwarz expressed their astonishment by comparing once again the experience of visiting Argentina with entering a world "out of place"—an isolated cosmopolitan society located at the "end of the world." In their description, however, one detects an unease that also characterizes other accounts. The feeling of sameness and familiarity is stubbornly haunted by the suspicion that something is missing, that the postcolonial mirror is cracked. "You feel as if you've entered a European Twilight Zone, a parallel universe where things are familiar and yet somehow skewed," they claim. In a very biased view of the country, V. S. Naipaul ties the "skewed" nature of Argentina to a colonial mentality that generates nothing but a hollow copy of the West. To be Argentine, he argues, is to inhabit a magical, debilitating world defined by painful contradictions. The artificiality of the society reveals itself, according to Naipaul, in the "absence of links between men and men, between immigrant and immigrant, aristocrat and artisan, city dweller and 'cabecita negra,' the poor man from a darker interior."[4]

Nowhere is this lack of cohesion more acutely reflected than in the cultural and economic schism between, on the one hand, the city of Buenos Aires and the eastern provinces — with two-thirds of the total population and more than half the country's resources — and, on the other, the provinces of the stagnant interior. At a gross level, one can speak of two Argentinas. One is cosmopolitan, developed, and markedly more wealthy, while "the other Argentina" is sparsely populated, backward, and chronically poor. The largest cities and industrial centers are concentrated in the fertile and well-watered lands of the pampean provinces, comprising Buenos Aires, Córdoba, Santa Fé, and some parts of Entre Ríos and La Pampa. In contrast, with 70 percent of the nation's land, the remaining seventeen provinces in the four regions of the interior (the Northeast, Northwest, Cuyo, and Patagonia) remain mostly rural, holding only a third of the country's population. With the exception of a few pockets of prosperity, the lack of resources in the interior and a deep inequality in their distribution has produced an economy with little potential for social progress.[5]

The image of Argentina as an incomplete being, an inauthentic reflection, or an unfinished product of modernity has often been seen as the inevitable drawback of its European genealogy. From this angle, Argentina appears to be a utopian dream that went awry. Its uneven modernity has led some abroad to portray the country as the lingering ruins of a stillborn great nation. In an unexpected twist on the colonial myth, international tourism is currently portraying Buenos Aires as a postmodern version of the fabulous hidden city. But this time, instead of the riches of lost civilizations, travel guides are promising to the American traveler a taste of old Europe in a peripheral setting. The introduction to Argentina in the Fodor's 1997 guide to South America warns: "Most travelers think they have stumbled on a long-lost European country when they get to Argentina. . . . A quick look at the people walking down the avenues of any Argentine city confirms the impression. But in spite of the symbiosis with Europe, the country has had a chaotic past, politically and economically."[6] As a new century begins, the international image of Argentina is a baffling one. It juxtaposes the paradox of a sophisticated and glamorous city attached to the Third World with the confusing stereotype of an underdeveloped country with European manners.

Someone fond of etymologies could intimate that the sense of a mirage was already sealed in the country's name. It is said that, in a rush of wishful thinking, the Spanish conquerors coined the name *Argentina* from the Latin word for "silver," expecting the region to be rich in the precious metal. None was ever found. Instead of collecting riches and glory, the story goes, most returned home empty-handed—when they did not suffer terrible deaths from starvation and violence. In modern times, disenchantment among Argentines has stemmed from the nation's political and economic missteps. Disillusionment has often been accompanied by a combination of melancholic pain and acute resentment. The essayist Martínez Estrada interpreted this pain as the experience of having to endure permanent exile and solitude, never able to settle down, always longing for a place closer to Europe, yet unable to return.[7] The suspicion that Argentina has never been a true national community has also arisen from the depths of this longing. "The soul of Argentina is an enigma," the historian José Luis Romero once said.

But, in contrast with the colonial version, in the modern tale of illusory silver failure is not a consequence of unfounded hope. For decades, high expectations fed on concrete achievements. In 1929, Argentina was among the ten most affluent countries in the world. Per capita income was the highest in Latin America, higher even than in several Western European countries. A substantial part of the population enjoyed prosperity and well-being. Even after the Great Depression, hard work and public education enabled most working families to move up the social ladder. It was not until the 1970s, when salaries dropped steadily and political dysfunction became pervasive, that pessimism took hold. Disenchantment grew out of the realization that modern Argentina was no longer capable of fulfilling its promises of democratic progress and economic opportunity for all, delivering instead a series of authoritarian political regimes and increasingly ineffective economic programs. Frustration reached unprecedented levels in the 1980s and 1990s. After enduring the bloodiest dictatorship in the country's political history, the majority found its standard of living shattered, first by hyperinflation, later by neoliberal policies and the extreme demands imposed by the IMF and the World Bank that plunged the country further into debt. Unemployment and pauperization have dumbfounded the children of formerly hopeful European immigrants. Echoing their state of disbelief, the popular rock singer Fito Páez exclaims, in biting lyrics, "I have no clue how I ended up in the Third World."[8]

In the past decade, perhaps the most difficult obstacle to overcome has been, along with economic uncertainty, the notable absence of powerful shared dreams. The promise of democracy has been tarnished more than once by pervasive official corruption and a perennial lack of equal opportunity and social security. Neither traditional populism nor revolutionary agendas have appeared to be a viable option. A pervasive, pessimistic viewpoint has seen this accumulation of failures as precluding any successful attempt to imagine a sustainable historical narrative. For those who distrust the IMF's recipes for development, the neoliberal state represents the end for visions of a liberating utopia. Even twenty years of stable constitutional government and more than a decade free of inflation have done little to give most Argentines the change for a better future.

As this book goes into production, Argentina's crisis has entered another, even more dramatic spiraling into the abyss. In December 2001, spontaneous riots and rallies brought down president Fernando de la Rúa's administration. The collapse of the economy and a run on the banks forced the new administration to default on the country's $141 billion debt. Economists, politicians, and experts of every stripe, at home and abroad, are deep in debate over the real causes and magnitude of the disaster. What all agree on is that there are no easy solutions at hand. Passive disenchantment has given way to a degree of civic activism not seen in years. In daily, peaceful demonstrations, resolute citizens are protesting against corrupt politicians and calling for an economic plan that takes into account not only the IMF's demands but also the well-being of the Argentine people. Heavily burdened by national and international pressure, President Eduardo Duhalde has called on all social and political sectors to find a way out of the current political impasse. Although no one can predict the outcome, through yet another transformation a new Argentina will emerge from the ashes.

The Argentina Reader aims to present to the American public a broader and more complex overview of the country's social, political, and cultural traditions that challenges the almost schizophrenic view of Argentina that still prevails today. Our goal is to offer an innovative and socially meaningful selection of texts and visual materials that is able to re-create the tensions and contradictions, as well as the continuities, that traverse Argentine history. Thus, we resist the prevailing perception that Argentina is the most European of all Latin American states — specifically, a predominantly white society that nearly succeeded in fulfilling the colonial dream of transforming the vast and wild continental lands into improved replicas of French and English cities. Instead, we choose to emphasize Argentina's heterogeneity and argue that, quite often, homogenization has been the result of authoritarian practices that suppress difference. Notably, imposed homogeneity is not just a local phenomenon. Creating uniform, cohesive communities has been one of the main requirements of modernization and is, therefore, a product of capitalism's global influence. Homogenization has thoroughly Westernized everyday practices, imposing a common identity that crosses national boundaries. Its unavoidable outcome has been that the histories and contributions of many have remained untold or misrepresented.

In an effort to reveal the diversity obscured by Argentina's official image, whenever possible we have incorporated the perspectives of those who spoke or speak from positions located outside the dominant perception and whose voices have at some point or another been marginalized or even silenced. The Amerindian and black communities have suffered such exclusion since colonial times. The Argentine cowboys—the gauchos—represent another case in point as they were rushed into modernity in the second half of the nineteenth century, forced to join the national army or to work for the landowning class. In this century, ethnic discrimination has primarily targeted the so-called *cabecitas negras,* the poor from the provinces who, to the dismay of the bourgeoisie, began migrating to cosmopolitan Buenos Aires in the 1940s in search of better jobs. By making room for alternative positions, we by no means promise to deliver a pristine, uncontaminated record of lost voices—"the real thing" buried by the hurricane of progress. In most cases, access to marginal cultures implies the mediation of a public figure who does not belong to that world—the ethnographer transcribing Tehuelches narratives, the writer ventriloquizing the voice of the suffering gaucho, the journalist giving an account of a clandestine execution of workers, and so on.

Ideologies, such as those that bolster a homogenous image of Argentina, are not complete lies. Their power stems from a capacity to emphasize certain facets of reality while leaving others unstated.[9] Despite being significantly deceptive, national myths always carry some element of truth. In pointing out cultural and ethnic difference, we do not wish to deny the transforming forces unleashed by massive European immigration and the incorporation of more than 3 million people into traditional Argentine society between 1875 and 1914. But acknowledging the obvious does not preclude stressing the varied impact of immigrants on the cultural and political fabric of Argentina. After all, the arrival of millions of European immigrants did not merely further the ethnocentric dreams of the local elite. As much as it helped consolidate a capitalist society, mass immigration was also responsible for the emergence of new forms of political participation and cultural expression that clashed with many of the old structures of economic and political power in the country. Neither the rise of a national industrial class nor the evolution of the Argentine Left and its revolutionary dreams of social change, for example, can be understood without taking into account the influence of European immigrant culture on Argentine society. In the last two decades, migration patterns have radically shifted. The new migrant workers come, not from Europe, but from neighboring countries with even harsher economic conditions. Poorer, less educated, and of mixed racial origin, they represent for many the persistence of a Latin American colonial legacy that Argentina had wished to leave behind and long denied. While Latin American heterogeneity returns to challenge cosmopolitan pride, dimmed hopes for a better future have prompted thousands of Argentines, mostly from the educated middle classes, to leave the country for Europe or the United States in search of opportunity.

Along with class and racial dynamics, gender has also played a major role in the construction of social identities and struggles for justice and equality. This is apparent in the symbolic figure of the female captive, who first embodied the complex relationship between the Spanish soldier and the Amerindian other during the conquest and later alluded to fears of racial contamination in the frontier policies of the national state. At different times, and from opposite sides of the political spectrum, women would question — with varying degrees of success — the predominantly male face of national politics. In the nineteenth century, Juana Manuela Gorriti diligently sought to give credit to women who contributed as caretakers and soldiers to the struggle for independence. As part of a prolonged battle to improve women's education, Victoria Ocampo made Virginia Woolf's complaint her own, demanding "a room of one's own" for all ambitious Argentine women. Our reader also shows that shared sexual identities do not necessarily imply common political agendas. The contrast between Eva Perón's extraordinary appeal to working-class women and the abhorrence her public persona aroused in upper-class ladies illustrates how being a woman does not make one invulnerable to class distinctions.

Besides questioning homogeneity, we also wish to present a more complex approach to Argentina's political history and its alleged institutional "aberrations." Our two emphases complement each other. By considering Argentina's unacknowledged plurality and the tensions that lie beneath its apparently uniform surface, American readers will be prepared to resist simplifications and reach a better understanding of puzzling political phenomena, such as Peronism. In accordance with this goal, readers will notice that our introduction to Perón's legacy avoids partisanship by providing a broad spectrum of contradictory perspectives. Without overlooking their flagrant authoritarianism, we call attention to the popular hopes and social frustrations that Perón and his wife, Eva, came to represent in the 1950s. As the historian Daniel James reminds us, Peronism's fundamental appeal lay in its broader notion of citizenship, one that claimed to take into account the social sectors that had been kept at the system's margins. Yet it would be misleading to consider Peronism a radical movement whose program was to destroy capital and drastically overturn social hierarchies. After all, the core of Perón's agenda was to mediate between different classes and seek a "third position" between opposing ideological projects —

American capitalism and Soviet communism; free market and protectionism; etc. In this respect, Peronism is not an isolated, anomalous phenomenon, but rather the latest and most enduring manifestation of Argentine populism. In 1916, the Radical leader Hipólito Yrigoyen, the first president elected by universal suffrage, was already applying populist strategies, creating political ties between the new middle class, the urban workers, and some sectors of the ruling class. Three decades later, taking Yrigoyen as one of his models, Perón expanded the scope of the populist call by giving an even greater portion of the marginalized population, including the long-forgotten provincial masses, access to the public sphere. A better understanding of this political tradition may also shed some light on the role that militarization has played in Argentina's recent history. The political scientist Guillermo O'Donnell has suggested that the increasing brutality of political repression after Perón's fall in 1955, up through the last dictatorship (1976–83), with its indiscriminate use of torture and kidnapping, can be interpreted as, among other things, an extreme effort to annihilate the radical forces unleashed by populism.[10]

Given the complexities of Argentine society, it should not come as a surprise that there has been an uninterrupted series of attempts to circumscribe the essence of Argentine nationality. For a country proud of its European heritage, Argentina has a remarkable tradition of writing about national identity. Since the country's independence from Spain in 1810, many intellectuals, politicians, and artists have pondered what it means to be Argentine in the global order of modernity. For intellectuals and politicians like Domingo Faustino Sarmiento, one of the nation's founding fathers, if Argentina was to become part of the Western world, local identity — and, with it, what Sarmiento saw as a national inclination toward rebellion — had to be tamed through compulsory public education while some popular traditions were preserved as symbolic reminders of a common past. For the nationalist writer Leopoldo Lugones, as for many others, the essence of Argentina resided in the countryside and its vanishing gauchos. Victoria Ocampo — an upper-class feminist — found Argentina's worth in its productive and cosmopolitan cultural elite. In his essays and fictional works, the writer Jorge Luis Borges contended that Argentine identity was an elusive and mobile frontier between conflicting cultural worlds. According to Atahualpa Yupanqui, a popular folksinger from the province of Santiago del Estero, a true national community would flourish only when all of Argentina's subaltern groups benefited from consistent standards of social justice. And the list goes on.

In our reader, we do not attempt to provide a definitive answer, thereby resolving this contentious discussion. Instead, we have chosen a range of materials that offer the reader a variety of responses to questions of national identity.

Following James Clifford, we maintain that culture is, not an organically unified or traditionally continuous entity, but rather a negotiated, ever-changing
process. Identity is always relational, never essential. If there is such a thing as
an essence, it is a tactical, political invention used to meet specific, local goals.
Strangely enough, Borges's reflections on Argentine culture somehow fore-
told Clifford's definition. According to Borges, if there was anything like an
"Argentine" peculiarity, this was not something with a specific content or form
but was instead a particular way of relating oneself to what was foreign. In
his opinion, Argentines' relationship with culture was akin to the attitude that
Jews maintained toward the Western canon. As in the Jewish tradition, Borges
argued, the Argentines simultaneously participated in and were external to the
cultures that they appropriated. This ambiguity allowed them enough flexibility to develop a voluminous cultural archive while maintaining an irreverent
attitude toward cultural authority.[11]

Borges's comments read as an accurate description of the ways in which
Argentine writers, artists, and intellectuals have used and transformed all kinds
of "foreign" materials. Although one can detect in their works the strong influence of the metropolitan values and ideas emblematic of high culture, it is also
undeniable that the same values and ideas have been transfigured and canni-
balized, becoming integral parts of newly created artifacts. Argentine cultural
dynamics can be portrayed as a gigantic translating machine that keeps betraying the original with endless digressions on national topics. As early as 1848,
the Romantic poet Esteban Echeverría celebrated what he saw as the healthy
strabismus of Argentine culture: "We will always have one eye fixed on the
progress of nations and the other focused on the heart of our own society." In
Facundo, an Argentine classic, Sarmiento adapted the accounts of European
travelers and presented himself as a sort of Tocqueville of the Southern Hemisphere proposing a new approach to Latin American democracy.[12] The avant-
garde sketches of Buenos Aires imagined by the painter Xul Solar in the 1920s,
Borges's combination of Western philosophy and the anonymous perspective
of a paralyzed gaucho in the 1940s, as well as the novelist Manuel Puig's interpretation of Argentina's social and political dilemmas through the plots of
Hollywood movies in the 1960s are clear instances of the same national tradition against intellectual purism.

Popular culture has operated in a similar fashion. Soccer, which originated
as an aristocratic form of entertainment for the British industrial elites, was
almost immediately embraced as the national sport by hundreds of thousands
of Argentines. In magazines, cartoonists such as Lino Palacio and Quino have
creatively used the comic strip to comment on the ever-growing middle class's
local lifestyle. Not even political traditions have escaped Argentina's translating

machine. The revolutionary agendas of the 1960s and 1970s centered around the question of how to adapt the Marxist creed to the nation's particularities. In every case, translation involved a set of transforming operations and creative transactions. Perhaps it was the poet Oliverio Girondo who best illustrated the notion of translation as cultural production through the image of a huge, omnivorous stomach with unlimited power to devour and digest. This voracious organ was not Argentina's exclusively but was shared with all Latin American nations. "As Latin Americans," Girondo says at the beginning of his *Twenty Poems to Be Read on a Trolley Car,* "we have the best stomachs in the world, the most free, eclectic stomachs, able to digest, and digest well, northern herrings or oriental couscous as well as a broiled small woodcock or one of those epic chorizos from Castilla."[13]

A special emphasis on multiplicity and multivocality guided our selection of texts and materials. In order to convey the cultural heterogeneity that in our view characterizes Argentine society, we have included different genres and styles, from scholarly analyses of political events to politically charged popular tango lyrics and folk interpretations of social oppression. By combining academic essays, journalistic reports, songs, paintings, photographs, comic strips, poems, and short stories, we hope to provide a complex set of cultural lenses through which the reader can gain access to a diversified view of Argentina. Perhaps those who may feel puzzled by such a mixture will find some reassurance in Walter Benjamin's reflections on history. "The chronicler," he once said, "who recites events without distinguishing between major and minor ones acts in accordance with the following truth: nothing that has ever happened should be regarded as lost for history."[14] Although, strictly speaking, our book does not belong to the field of history, its multilayered image of Argentina's past and present does acknowledge Benjamin's point by stressing the fact that a song, a tango step, or a short story can be as revealing as an official speech or a sociological analysis.

With a few exceptions, we have given priority to Argentine viewpoints. There were two main reasons for doing so. First, insofar as they exemplify instances in which Argentines sought to make sense of their place in history, pieces carrying immediate responses to current political and social events are favored. As a result, however, we were confronted with the problem that very often responses were so highly contradictory that the search for a unifying perspective became a futile task. In such cases, instead of hiding contradictions, we chose to let the texts speak for themselves. The tacit dialogue between texts will enable readers to consider the set of historical forces that were at play at a particular time while reminding them that history is never a straightforward path but rather a number of possibilities. Another reason for favoring local views lay in Argentina's solid and rich intellectual tradition, which includes many excellent scholars and writers who have at some point or another studied and commented on the country's historical and cultural profile. It would have been unthinkable not to have samples of such important works as Tulio Halperín Donghi's insightful historical account of Argentina's independence, David Viñas's revisionist approach to the epic vision of the Argentine frontier, or Guillermo O'Donnell's extensive research on Argentina's political practices. In order to bring the Argentine perspective to the American reader, we have included more than forty texts that have never before appeared in English as well as reproductions of translations that are no longer available elsewhere.

Because of their important contributions to understanding Argentina, the best and most relevant texts written by foreigners are also included in the reader. Travelers have profoundly influenced Argentina's self-perception. Imperial explorers such as Pigafetta provided the first European descriptions of the land and its Amerindian inhabitants. In the nineteenth century, scientific observers like Darwin and Ebélot witnessed the transformations that the country went through after independence. Prestigious writers like Darío and Gombrowicz developed opposing interpretations of Argentina's modernity. While Darío enthusiastically praised the country's fast development and its taste for European sophistication, Gombrowicz rejected the snobbism of its upper classes and preferred to applaud the sensual beauty of the lower classes. From the prolific and outstanding academic work done on Argentina abroad, we selected pieces that distinguished themselves both for their originality and for their insight. Rock's excellent reconstruction of the birth of the first modern political party and James's brilliant interpretation of Perón's populist strategies are just two obvious examples.

As for the reader's overall organization, there are ten main parts, each consisting of a set of representative texts and illustrations accompanied by introductory pieces written by the editors. The parts are arranged chronologically and according to what we consider the most meaningful themes and issues for understanding the social dynamics that have defined different Argentine historical formations. To provide readers with minimal tools to further their knowledge, the reader closes with a general bibliography including the best works on each period. Part I deals with the two stages of the Spanish colonial regime in the region from which Argentina would later emerge. Parts II–IV are devoted to the intense years of nation building from independence to the birth of modern Argentina. The remaining six parts focus on the twentieth century. Of these, parts V–VII trace the development of popular movements that made Peronism possible and that created the conditions for the revolutionary dreams of the 1960s and 1970s. Part VIII is devoted to the dark years of the last military dictatorship and the culture of terror and resistance that dominated the cultural production of the time. Finally, for parts IX and X, corresponding to contemporary Argentina, we have gathered a variety of texts that highlight the disconcerting tendencies unleashed by neoliberalism and the new global economy. This fairly traditional historical narrative, mostly anchored in political history, provides a basic framework so that readers who are not familiar with Argentina can navigate with the assistance of a reassuring compass. But, for those who wish to follow their interests and preferences, there are other maps available. We have left open the option of taking alternate routes off the main road that runs through the book—paths along which the adventurous reader can explore the issues of gender, political utopia, identity politics, and popular culture, to mention just a few possibilities. It is our hope that the basic map will evolve into a magnificent labyrinth promising at every turn, not frustration, but a richer view of Argentina and its people.

Notes

1 For Domingo Faustino Sarmiento's view of Argentina as the result of a struggle between civilization and barbarism, see "Civilization or Barbarism" in pt. II. For Darío's views, see "Argentina as Latin American Avant-Garde" in pt. IV.

2 See Arthur P. Whitaker, *The United States and Argentina* (Cambridge, Mass.: Harvard University Press, 1954), 4–22 (quote from p. 5).

3 Paul Theroux, *The Old Patagonia Express: By Train through the Americas* (1979; Boston: Houghton Mifflin, 1997), 354–55.

4 Christina Schwarz and Benjamin Schwarz, "Just as Other European Cities Are Getting Cold, Buenos Aires Is Heating Up," *Atlantic Monthly*, 1 September 1998, 4; V. S. Naipaul, *The Return of Eva Perón* (New York: Alfred Knopf, 1980), 117, 150–53.

5 See Larry Sawers, *The Other Argentina: The Interior and National Development* (Boulder, Colo.: Westview, 1996), 4–8, 141.

6 *Fodor's South America Guide* (New York: D. McKay, 1997), 43.

7 Ezequiel Martínez Estrada, *X-Rays of the Pampa*, trans. Thomas F. McGann (Austin: University of Texas Press, 1971), 109, 123–26, 135–43.

8 Fito Páez, *Tercer mundo* (1990, CD).

9 See Terry Eagleton's discussion of ideology and truth in *Ideology: An Introduction* (London: Verso, 1998), 9–19.

10 Guillermo O'Donnell, "And Why Should I Give a Shit? Notes on Sociability and Politics in Argentina and Brazil," in *Counterpoints: Selected Essays on Authoritarianism and Democratization* (Notre Dame, Ind.: University of Notre Dame Press, 1999), 86.

11 See James Clifford, *The Predicament of Culture: Twentieth-Century Ethnography, Litera-*

ture, and Art (Cambridge, Mass.: Harvard University Press, 1996), 273; and Jorge Luis Borges, "The Argentine Writer and Tradition," in *LabyrinthS: Selected Stories and Other Writings,* ed. Donald Yates and James E. Irby (New York: New Directions, 1964).

12 Esteban Echeverría, "Palabras simbólicas," in *Obras escogidas,* ed. Beatriz Sarlo and Carlos Altamirano (Caracas: Biblioteca Ayacucho), 254. Domingo Faustino Sarmiento, *Facundo: Civilización y barbarie* (Madrid: Ediciones Cátedra, 1997), 40.

13 Oliverio Girondo, *Veinte poemas para ser leídos en el tranvía,* in *Obras completas* (Colección Archivos, no. 38), ed. Raúl Antelo (Barcelona: Galaxia Gutenberg, 1999), 47.

14 Walter Benjamin, "Theses on the Philosophy of History," in *Illuminations: Essays and Reflections,* ed. Hannah Arendt (New York: Schocken, 1985), 254.

I

At the Margins of the Empire

How to begin? This was the question that we asked ourselves when deciding on the design and scope of the story that *The Argentina Reader* would tell. There were many beginnings at hand, all equally convincing and with the right historical credentials: the May Revolution against Spain in 1810; the declaration of independence in 1816; the definitive constitution of the state in 1880. Argentina's colonial past was not the most obvious choice. After all, there were no magnificent Amerindian empires to speak of, and, until the second half of the eighteenth century, the Spanish crown showed little interest in a region lacking in minerals and spices. Modern Argentina's persistent disavowal of its colonial origins made that era's relevance even harder to justify. By inaugurating our presentation with a section on Argentina's colonial history we are not indulging in archival curiosities. Our purpose is to call attention to continuities within profound transformations. Thus, even though we are aware that colonial Argentina might be considered a false beginning since, properly speaking, *Argentina* did not exist until after independence, we find it unquestionable that the country's colonial genealogy was fundamental in developing the style of its nation building.

Argentina's colonial past is rooted in the history of what used to be the provinces of Río de la Plata—an area that extended roughly from the Straits of Magellan to Asunción in Paraguay and from the Atlantic coast of Uruguay to the Andes. For most of the colonial period, this vast region was but a minor extension of the viceroyalty of Peru, sparsely settled and offering no clear military or economic value to the Spanish Empire. This was particularly true on the Atlantic side. Although its founding in 1536 marked the first Spanish settlement in the region, Buenos Aires and its hinterland remained peripheral to the Spanish colonial system until late in the eighteenth century. Most of the cities founded in the first wave of Spanish conquest were located in the interior. After Buenos Aires came Asunción, now the capital of Paraguay. In the 1560s, other cities were established in Tucumán in the Northwest and in Cuyo.

Salta, La Rioja, Córdoba, Santa Fé, Corrientes, San Luis, Jujuy, and Santiago del Estero followed soon afterward. All these cities' economies were subordinated to Spain's organizing principle for its South American colonies: maximizing the flow of silver from the mines of Potosí, in Bolivia, to Lima, Peru. Only when Portugal and England began to exert pressure on the Atlantic side did the crown create the viceroyalty of the provinces of Río de la Plata with Buenos Aires as its capital. The new administrative unit, founded in 1776, would not last long. Local discontent with Spain's commercial monopoly over local products, combined with the crisis of power produced by Napoléon's invasion of Spain, soon brought about the collapse of colonial rule. By then, Buenos Aires was already the most important commercial and economic center in the region, and the rivalries with a dependent interior had begun.

The Spanish viewed the American continent as a vacant, natural space, existing outside history, intended for the gradual spread of Christianity and European culture. Through the lenses of these ethnocentric ideals, America's native inhabitants appeared to be Spain's diametric opposite: peoples without civility, without religion, without history. Complicitous with this view was the use of two complementary functional operations to master land and people: the imposition of a new spatial order, through the elaboration of maps and the division of the territory into colonial administrative units, and the acculturation of the Amerindians through evangelization. The nomadic lifestyle of the Amerindian groups inhabiting the provinces of Río de la Plata—entailing as it did the lack of urban centers and roads and the near absence of agricultural activity—played into the imperial view, which tended to see nothing but emptiness.

To represent this first stage of the Spanish conquest, we have selected excerpts from some of the many travelogs and chronicles that fed the Spanish imperial archive with maps and catalogs of the conquered lands as well as with stories about European encounters with Amerindian difference. The repertoire of colonial images coming out of that incredible mass of writing would play a central role in Argentina's historical self-perception after independence from Spain. An important contribution of the geographic imagination of travelers and explorers visiting the area was the construction of emblematic zones—the littoral, the pampas, Patagonia, the frontier—and symbolic figures such as the woman captive and the savage Amerindian. Outside this collective core of ideas, disagreement was not uncommon. Father Strobel's celebration of the Guaraní people as ideal Christians in a letter to another Jesuit in 1729 demonstrates, for example, that, when it came to religion, the conquest was not a uniform enterprise and that there were competing agendas within the same imperial project. To help counter the predominant colonial perspective, we have included a Tehuelches mythical narrative as an example of the many Amerindian histories of the land that were silenced by colonial intervention. Its placement at the very beginning, before the Spanish and European sources, should not give the reader the impression that Amerindian narratives are mere souvenirs from a largely obliterated, prehistorical time. Not only did they survive four centuries of open conflict with dominant views, but many of them are still part of the cultural memories of the few Amerindian communities remaining in the country today. It is in this sense that they are also part of an unspoken present.

The remaining texts in this section were chosen because they reveal the emergence of economic and social forces that influenced Argentina's nation-building enterprise in the nineteenth century. First, they attest to the slow but uninterrupted formation of a Creole elite, consisting of people of Spanish origin but born in America who shared the same experiences and cultural roots and whose economic interests were repeatedly at odds with those of the Spanish crown. Their systematic exclusion from the colonial administration only deepened their sense of identity. Second, the texts attest to the emergences of the gauchos as a key force in local politics in the second half of the eighteenth century. The readings reveal the first signs of a complex and lasting antagonism that would come to define the relationship between these two groups. The ambiguous attitude that surfaces in Maciel's and Sánchez de Thompson's colonial pieces, in reference to the gaucho troops who defended the colony against non-Spanish imperial powers, would return during the process of national organization, when the gauchos became both the heroes and the victims of the newly created national state. Argentina's enduring and controversial association with England also originated in the last years of the colonial period. Sánchez de Thompson's unequivocally erotic admiration for the British troops entering Buenos Aires during the British invasion of 1806 presages the future role of England as Spain's imperial successor in Argentina's long romance with Europe.

The Deeds of Elal

Anonymous

The Western notion of history is by necessity ethnocentric in its interpretation of events. We must be willing, then, to imagine what has been left unsaid in the historical version that has prevailed. The outlines of what is now Argentina and the imperial notion of empty space that guided the imposition of the notion of Argentina on the landscape do not reflect the mosaic of conflicting territorial configurations that existed in colonial times. Jurisdictions created by the Spanish administration largely disregarded preexisting divisions historically maintained through the oral traditions of Amerindian tribes. Various and varied indigenous communities inhabited the region known as the provinces of the Río de la Plata under Spanish rule. On the plains were the Pampas, Charrúas, Guaraníes, Timbúes, and Kaigang; in the North the Matacos, Abipones, Mocobíes, and Tobas; in Patagonia the Puelches, Tehuelches, Araucanians, Selkman, and Yamanas; in Cuyo the Huarpes; and in the Center and the Andean Northwest the Comenchingones and Diaguitas. Each tribe perceived its relationship with the land in a distinct way. The following tribal narrative is one of many renditions of the story of Elal, transcribed by the Argentine explorer and naturalist Ramón Lista (1856–97) in 1894. Handed down through countless generations, it claims that Tehuelche territory is the product of holy arrangements that amount to biblical geneses. After subduing the animals and clearing the land of its terrifying monsters, the heroic god Elal created the Tehuelches and granted them Patagonia as their homeland.

Tradition has it that Elal arrived here from the east. But often this detail is passed over lightly, and the old ones believe that the god's baby cries were first heard in the mountains [to the west].

Nosjthej, Elal's father, killed his wife, cut her belly with a stone knife, and pulled out the fetus, which he was anxious to devour. But at this very moment he heard a strange noise coming from below the ground, and, when the earth began to shake, Nosjthej was so taken aback that he forgot all about the baby. A small field mouse [*térrguer*] [Elal's grandmother] appeared that snatched Elal and went to hide him in the most hidden place of his burrow.

Once recovered from his surprise, Nosjthej intended to carry out his abominable plan, his hands dripping with blood. The cave was deep and narrow. His face burned with brutish anger, and his thunderous outcries echoed through the Andes. However, all of this was in vain; the god was going to grow up in the protective shelters of the earth.

Now Nosjthej turned his deranged glance toward the bloody cadaver of his victim. But what a surprise: a sparkling spring of water was running from the mutilated belly. Even after so many years have gone by and centuries upon centuries, there it still is, outside of Teckel, on the road from Ay-aike to Senguer, the wonderful spring of Jentre in whose waters generations of Tzónek Indians bathed.

The first years of Elal's life passed unnoticed in the solitude of the desert. The rodent was his support: it taught him how to eat plant foods; it housed him in its nest of guanaco wool; and it showed him the paths through the forested land. Elal continued to grow; he invented the bow and arrow and soon started his roving travels. Every evening when he returned to the cave he would bring some bird that he had hunted with his magic weapon. "Be on your guard," said the rodent to him. "The wild beasts are the daughters of the dark." But Elal smiled.

One evening, as he walked along a winding stream, Elal was suddenly attacked by an enormous puma. He braced his bow, and his unerring arrow whistled through the air, wounding the beast in the side. The puma gave a frightful roar, and then a second roar answered the first one. Elal found himself between two wild beasts: one was wounded but still on its feet, and the other, even more frightening, was hidden in the thicket. Yet the hunter put a smile on his face; he did not even bother to ready his bow again but continued on his way until he came to a hilly place.

Going down into a valley, Elal went close to the edge of a river with much water. He picked a few stones from the riverbed and stepped back a little from the bank; then he began gathering kindling, shredding some of the sticks and breaking the others. And then fire flared up for the first time in this campestral solitude.

On another occasion Elal saw a condor standing on a hilltop. "Give me one of your wing's feathers for my arrow," said Elal. "Impossible," shouted the bird. "I need them; they are my coat, and I go through the air with them."

Elal insisted, begged, and threatened. But, "Impossible, impossible," said the condor, unfolding its wings and resuming its flight. The bird had almost disappeared in the distance when Elal carefully braced his bow and let fly. The air vibrated—and the bird came falling down in spiraling circles, shouting: "What feather did you want? What feather did you want?" It reached the ground with its talons half open. Elal took the condor by the neck, plucked its head, and said: "Return to the top of the hill."

The divine hero had already developed the strength and the muscles of a young man. There was no animal that could withstand him; the puma was humiliated; the fox accompanied him on his journeys; and the condor could not deny its feathers. Everything was subjected to his reign until, one day, Nosjthej reappeared.

"I am your father," he said. Elal took him to his cavern. He showed him his weapons, the bows and the arrows, his honed flints, and his sling. He also showed him his trophies, the puma skins, the shells of giant armadillos, and huge condor wings. Then Elal extracted the marrow from a bone and offered it to his father with an air of satisfaction.

Time passed while Nosjthej was the master and Elal his subordinate. But one day the hero revolted against his father's authority and fled to hide in the mountains. His father pursued and almost reached him. But Elal stopped for a moment, stamped his foot on the ground, and yelled with a strident voice. An entangled forest rose up before the raging father and grew to become an insurmountable barrier.

The earth had already become populated with people when a giant by the name of Goshge struck them with terror and desperation. Every night they found a child missing, and hunters who lost their way were devoured by the monster. Elal went in search of the giant and found him at the edge of the forest. However, the giant proved invulnerable, and the hero's arrows splintered and rebounded; Goshge was rightly held to be invincible. Victim after victim fell, and the terror knew no end.

Now Elal transformed himself into a horsefly and went out once more in search of Goshge. He skillfully entered the giant's throat and penetrated to his abominable stomach. There he bit fiercely. The giant contorted himself and uttered several powerful bellows such as had never been heard before. The wind carried them across the plain like the final vengeful wail of the monster.

After this, there followed a mysterious time of confusion; everything was contradictory and mixed up. It was a time of violent transitions during which the order of things was changed. Elal lost almost all his divine attributes. He adopted another name and held his hair with an Indian handkerchief across the forehead. He carried a stone axe and a spear in his hands, and his hut was made of interwoven branches. There appeared other beings like himself who accompanied him everywhere. He hunted guanaco and kept watch at night. He could be found at the edge of the forest as often as at the shore of the sea, eating game and fish.

In those days, Nosjthej went by the name of Tkaur, and the rodent was sleeping in his burrow. Then there appeared Sintalk'n, the powerful and keen-witted warrior. He engaged Elal in battle until their blood saturated the ground. Also, the ferocious animals returned to their destructive ways.

Reborn was Goshge, only in even more frightening dimensions, his forehead reaching higher than the highest mountains. Nature itself became unbalanced, the sun darkened, the earth throbbed in its crust, and the wind howled incessantly.

Elal no longer was a god; his mouth blasphemed, and in his heart churned the passions of mankind. Sintalk'n, Sintalk'n was the name that resounded between the shores of the ocean and the foot of the mountains. But, finally, the warrior was overcome, imprisoned, and eaten, and Elal became all-powerful once more.

He went to ask the Sun and the Moon to give him their daughter as a wife. However, the parents, afraid of opposing the union openly, employed a subterfuge to reject the request. They made a servant girl adopt their daughter's name and dress. Elal's emissaries conducted the girl to the side of the hero, who only later discovered the deceit. He raised his thunderous voice against the Sun and threatened him with his sharpest arrow.

Now the disgusted Elal withdrew from the world, where the things that he had created as god and hero continued to unfold themselves. But his mission was completed. He had created the first people and purged the earth of monsters that afflicted the world. He had planted the first seeds of right and wrong into the hearts of humans, taught them the secret of firemaking and the rudiments of toolmaking. Weapons, leather coats, and housing were among his gifts. He had removed for mankind all the obstacles of a harsh environment, telling them: "Go forth, then; yours is the horizon."

Finally, Elal transformed himself into a small bird, and, gathering his brothers, the swans, around him, he climbed onto the wing of the most spirited of them. The birds took to the air in a buzzing convoy eastward across the ocean, stopping to rest only on small islands that mysteriously appeared wherever Elal hit the waves with his invisible arrows.

Far away, where the steamboats go, there Elal and the swans vanished from sight.

That is how the old Papón told it.

Going Wild

Ulderico Schmidt

Ulderico Schmidt (1515–81), a German soldier and adventurer, joined Pedro de Mendoza's expedition fueled by a desire for riches. After twenty years, still poor, he returned to Europe, where he finally earned some money by publishing, in German, Voyage to Río de la Plata and Paraguay *(1554). In a tale filled with adventures and wonders, Schmidt presented a series of powerful images that would influence from then on all representations of the region as an ambiguous land, populated yet empty, fruitful yet threatening hunger and thirst, with Amerindians at turns indomitably savage and remarkably friendly. The hostile character of the region had the power to "barbarize" the European conquerors, transforming them into what they viewed as their natural opposite: the American cannibal. The following account of the initial founding and subsequent destruction of Buenos Aires (1535–41) is paradigmatic of Schmidt's imperial perspective.*

There we built a new town and called it Bonas Aeieres, that is, in German, *Guter Wind*.

We also brought from Hispania on board the fourteen ships seventy-two horses and mares.

Here, also, we found a place inhabited by Indian folk, named Querandíes, numbering about three thousand people, including wives and children, and they were clothed in the same way as the Charrúas, from the navel to the knees. They brought us fish and meat to eat. These Querandíes have no houses, but wander about, as do the Gipsies with us at home, and in summer they oftentimes travel upwards of thirty miles on dry land without finding a single drop of water to drink.

And when they meet with deer and other wild beasts, (when they have killed them) they drink their blood. Also if they find a root, called Cardos, they eat it to slack their thirst. This—namely, that they drink blood—only happens because they cannot have any water, and that they might peradventure die of thirst.

Hunger in Buenos Aires: Spanish soldiers practicing cannibalism (Ulderico Schmidt, 1554)

These Querandíes brought us daily their provision of fish and meat to our camp, and did so for a fortnight, and they did only fail once to come to us. So our captain, Pedro de Mendoza, sent to them, the Querandíes, a judge, named Johan Pabon, with two foot-soldiers, for they were at a distance of four miles from our camp. When they came near to them, they were all three beaten black and blue, and were then sent back again to our camp. Pedro de Mendoza, our captain, hearing of this from the judge's report (who for this cause raised a tumult about it in our camp), sent Diego Mendoza, his own brother, against them with three hundred foot-soldiers and thirty well-armed mounted men, of whom I also was one, straightway charging us to kill or take prisoners all these Indian Querandíes and to take possession of their settlement. But when we came near them there were now some four thousand men, for they had assembled all their friends. And when we were about to attack them, they defended themselves in such a way that we had that very day our hands full. They also killed our commander, Diego Mendoza, and six noblemen. Of our foot-soldiers and mounted men over twenty were slain, and on their side about one thousand. Thus did they defend themselves valiantly against us, so that indeed we felt it. . . .

Thus God Almighty graciously gave us the victory, and allowed us to take possession of their place; but we did not take prisoner any of the Indians, and their wives and children also fled away from the place before we attacked them.

At this place of theirs we found nothing but furrier-work made from marten or so-called otter; also much fish, fish meal, and fish fat. There we remained three days and then returned to our camp, leaving on the spot one hundred of our men, in order that they might fish with the Indians' nets for the providing of our folk, because there was there very good fishing. . . .

And when we returned again to our camp, our folk were divided into those who were to be soldiers, and the others workers, so as to have all of them employed. And a town was built there, and an earthen wall, half a pike high, around it, and inside of it a strong house for our chief captain. The town wall was three foot broad, but that which was built to-day fell to pieces the day after, for the people had nothing to eat, and were starved with hunger, so that they suffered great poverty, and it became so bad that the horses could not go. Yea, finally, there was such want and misery for hunger's sake, that there were neither rats, nor mice, nor snakes to still the great dreadful hunger, and unspeakable poverty, and shoes and leather were resorted to for eating and everything else.

It happened that three Spaniards stole a horse, and ate it secretly, but when it was known, they were imprisoned and interrogated under the torture. Whereupon, as soon as they admitted their guilt, they were sentenced to death by the gallows, and all three were hanged.

Immediately afterwards, at night, three other Spaniards came to the gallows to the three hanging men, and hacked off their thighs and pieces of their flesh, and took them home to still their hunger.

A Spaniard also ate his brother, who died in the city of Bonas Aieires.

Now our chief captain, Pedro de Mendoza, saw that he could not any longer keep his men there, so he ordered and took counsel with his head men that four little ships (called l'archkadienes) should be made ready, which must be rowed, and three more yet smaller ones, which are called podell or patt.

And when these seven little vessels were ready and equipped, our chief captain ordered all the people to assemble, and sent George Lauchstein with three hundred and fifty armed men up the river Paraná in order to find out the Indians and so obtain victual and provisions. But as soon as the Indians were aware of us, they wrought us the most abominable piece of knavery, by burning and destroying all their victual and provisions and their villages, and then all took to flight; in consequence whereof we had nothing to eat but three ounces of bread a day. One half of our people died during this voyage through hunger, therefore we had to return again to the said place, where was our chief captain.

Pedro de Mendoza desired to have a relation from George Lauchstein, our commander, as to the circumstances of our voyage, why so few of them had returned, since, they had only been absent for five months. To whom our commander answered thus: the people died for hunger, since the Indians burnt all the provisions, and then took flight, as has been related before.

After all this we remained still another month together in great poverty in the town of Bonas Aeieres, until the ships were prepared.

At this time the Indians came in great power and force, as many as twenty-three thousand men, against us and our town of Bonas Aeieres. There were four nations of them, namely, Querandíes, Charrúas, and Timbúes. They all meant to go about to destroy us all. But God Almighty preserved the greater part of us, therefore praise and thanks be to Him always and everlasting, for on our side not more than about thirty men, including commanders and ensign were slain.

And when they first came to our town, Bonas Aeieres, and attacked us, some of them tried to storm the place, others shot fiery arrows at our homes, which, being covered with straw (only the house of our chief captain, covered with tiles, excepted), were set on fire, and so the whole town was burnt down.

Translated by the Hakluyt Society (1891)

Monsters in Patagonia

Antonio Pigafetta

Antonio Pigafetta (1485–1534), an Italian nobleman, participated in Magellan's expedition in search of a new route to the Pacific Ocean from 1519 to 1522, contributing to the pragmatic consolidation of a hierarchical image of the world through imperial expansion and racial ranking. His travel journal, First Voyage around the Globe *(1524), provides the first impressions of a European encountering Southern Patagonia — a vast land that, together with the Río de la Plata, forms the core of Argentina's geographic imagination. The capture by deceit of two indigenous Tehuelches — named Patagonians after a medieval literary character of gigantic stature and monstrous appearance — for a collection of unusual specimens to be presented to the king of Spain belongs to a long imperial history of misunderstanding and abuse of non-European communities for the sake of Western civilization. It is likely that Shakespeare's famous character Caliban in* The Tempest *was modeled after Pigafetta's portrait of these two unfortunate native men.*

Leaving that place, we finally reached 49½ degrees toward the Antarctic Pole. As it was winter, the ships entered a safe port to winter. We passed two months in that place without seeing anyone. One day we suddenly saw a naked man of giant stature on the shore of the port, dancing, singing, and throwing dust on his head. The captain-general sent one of our men to the giant so that he might perform the same actions as a sign of peace. Having done that, the man led the giant to an islet into the presence of the captain-general. When the giant was in the captain-general's and our presence, he marveled greatly and made signs with one finger raised upward, believing that we had come from the sky. He was so tall that we reached only to his waist, and he was well proportioned. His face was large and painted red all over, while about his eyes he was painted yellow; and he had two hearts painted on the middle of his cheeks. His scanty hair was painted white. He was dressed in the skins of animals skillfully sewn together. That animal has a head and ears as large as those of a mule, a neck and body like those of a camel, the legs of a deer, and the tail of a horse, like which it neighs, and that land has very many of them. His feet were shod with the same kind of skins that covered his feet in the manner of shoes. In his hand he carried a short, heavy bow, with a cord somewhat thicker than those of the lute and made from the intestines of the same animal, and a bundle of rather short cane arrows feathered like ours and with points fashioned by means of another stone. The captain-general had the giant given something to eat and drink, and among other things that were shown to him was a large steel mirror. When he saw his face, he was greatly terrified and jumped back, throwing three or four of our men to the ground. After that he was given some bells, a mirror, a comb, and certain paternosters. The captain-general sent him ashore with four armed men. When one of his companions, who would never come to the ships, saw him coming with our men, he ran to the place where the others were, who came [down to the shore] all naked one after another. When our men reached them, they began to dance and to sing, lifting one finger to the sky. They showed our men some white powder made from the roots of a herb, which they kept in earthen pots, and which they ate because they had nothing else. Our men made signs inviting them to the ships, and they would help them carry their possessions. Thereupon, those men quickly took only their bows, while their women laden like asses carried everything. The latter are not so tall as the men but are very much fatter. When we saw them, we were greatly surprised. Their breasts are one-half *braza* long, and they are painted and clothed like their husbands, except that before their privies [*natura*] they have a small skin that covers them. . . .

A fortnight later we saw four of those giants without their arms, for they had hidden them in certain bushes, as the two whom we captured showed us. Each one was painted differently. The captain-general kept two of them—the youngest and best proportioned—by means of a very cunning trick, in order to take them to Spain. Had he used any other means [than those that he employed], they could easily have killed some of us. The trick that he employed in keeping them was as follows. He gave them many knives, scissors, mirrors, bells, and glass beads; and those two having their hands filled with the said articles, the captain-general had two pairs of iron manacles brought, such as are fastened on the feet. He made motions that he would give them to the giants, whereat they were very pleased since those manacles were of iron, but they did not know how to carry them. They were grieved at leaving them behind, but they had no place to put those gifts; for they had to hold the skin wrapped around them with their hands. The other two giants wished to help them, but the captain refused. Seeing that they were loth to leave those manacles behind, the captain made them a sign that he would put them on their feet, and they could carry them away. They nodded assent with the head. Immediately, the captain had the manacles put on both of them at the same time. When our men were driving home the cross bolt, the giants began to suspect something, but the captain assured them, however, and they stood still. When they saw later that they were tricked, they raged like bulls, calling loudly for Setebos to aid them.

Translated by James Alexander Robertson

Women Captives

Ruy Díaz de Guzmán

Ruy Díaz de Guzmán (1554–1629), a Spanish American mestizo soldier, was a relative of the conquerors Núñez Cabeza de Vaca and Irala. His Argentine History of the Discovery, Colonization, and Conquest of the Provinces of the Río de la Plata *(1612) is the first Spanish-language account of Spanish actions in the Río de la Plata from 1512 to 1573, written with the specific purpose of reminding the Spanish crown of the services rendered by the author's family in distant posts of the Empire. The chronicle includes one of the most famous versions of a classic topic in colonial historiography: the captive white woman as an object of dispute and negotiation between two antagonistic cultures. The captive, bound up in issues of frontier and identity related to the body, evoked fear of racial mixing and contamination. The story of Lucía de Miranda's fate contains all the elements that distinguished this colonial fiction. The passions that the beautiful Lucía unleashes in the Amerindian chief Siripo and his brother bring about both the destruction of the Spanish port of Sancti Spiritus, founded by Gaboto, and later the martyrdom of Lucía and her husband. As in other stories about women captured by Amerindians, Lucía is portrayed as a victim of the savages' alleged lasciviousness and of her own participation as instigator.*

. . . Captain Don Nuño tried to keep the peace with the natives living nearby, especially with the Timbúes Indians, easygoing people of goodwill. He had always enjoyed peaceful relations with their two most important chiefs. As was customary, they provided the Spaniards with food, which the Indians, being industrious, never lacked.

These chiefs were brothers, one named Mangoré, the other Siripo, young men of about thirty or forty years. Because they were courageous and skillful warriors, both of them, but especially Mangoré, were feared and respected by everyone. At this time Mangoré was attracted to a Spanish woman, Lucía de Miranda, who lived in the fortress with her husband, one Sebastián Hurtado, a native of Ezija. Mangoré gave this married woman many presents and helped her by bringing food; she, in grateful return, gave him affectionate attention.

The result was that the savage became so attached to her, and with such a wild love, that he determined to take her for his own in any way he could. Mangoré invited Hurtado to visit his village so that he could honor him and give him proof of his friendship. But Hurtado, suspecting something, showed good sense and declined the invitation. Seeing that he was not going to succeed that way, and feeling thwarted by the honorable behavior of the woman and the reserve of her husband, Mangoré began to lose patience and was overcome by great indignation as well as by mortal passion.

This led him to treachery and betrayal of the Spanish, all under the guise of friendship. It seemed to Mangoré that only in this way could he hope to take possession of the poor woman. Mangoré persuaded his brother to take part in his scheme, which they agreed to defer and keep secret until a better time came along. Just as Mangoré had hoped, it was not long before fortune offered an opportune moment. Because the fortress needed food, Captain Nuño dispatched Captain Ruiz García and forty soldiers to a brigantine. Their orders were to sail around the islands in search of food and to return as soon as possible with whatever they could gather. Sebastián Hurtado was among the group. Once the brigantine had set sail, Mangoré seized the advantage offered by this situation.

The Indian chiefs ordered four thousand Indians to assemble in a willow grove by the river, a mile or so from the fortress, from which position it should be easily captured. Mangoré led the way to the fort with an advance group of thirty robust young men bearing fish, meat, honey, butter, and corn. There, amid great displays of friendship, they shared the food, giving most of it to the captain and other officers and the rest to the soldiers. The natives were very well received and were made much of by everyone. Indeed, they were invited to spend the night within the fortress.

Once everyone was asleep, except for the men standing watch at the doors, the traitors struck. They signaled to the Indians lying in wait, who then crept up to the fortress walls. At that point the Indians outside, together with those already inside the fort, seized the guards and set the arsenal on fire. By this means they took command of the entrance to the fort, killing the guards and any Spaniards in their way. The frightened Spaniards who were in their rooms burst out onto the central plaza but were not able to resist successfully because the enemy force was so overwhelming. As other Spaniards were awakened, some here, some there, and some in their beds, the Indians beheaded them without much of a struggle, except for some few who fought valiantly. Especially Don Nuño de Lara, who ran out on the plaza with his shield and sword, ready to fight the great enemy force. He wounded and killed many of them. Some of the Indians, seeing that he might kill them, turned so cowardly that they did not dare approach him. Finally, the chiefs and the brave Indians who were outside the fort began to attack Nuño de Lara with arrows and lances. Bleeding and mortally wounded, but with a courageous spirit, he plunged into the thick of the enemy. Finding Mangoré, he stabbed him over and over, and the Indian chief fell to the ground, dead. Continuing to fight with all his might and valor, he killed many other chiefs and Indians. Finally, worn out and bleeding to death from his wounds, he too fell to the ground, where the Indians finished him off. A feeling of great satisfaction came over the Indians as they enjoyed their good fortune in the successful outcome of their attempt.

With the death of Don Nuño, the fortress was taken, and everything destroyed, leaving alive only five women and some children who were there. Among them was Lucía de Miranda. Their lives were spared, and they were taken captive as slaves.

The Indians piled up the booty so that they could share it with all the warriors, but it was the bravest and the chiefs and other leaders who had the advantage. They picked around and took the best for themselves.

Seeing his brother dead, and then finding the woman who had cost Mangoré so dearly, Siripo could not stop mourning. He realized the ardent love that he had for his brother, but he was also beginning to have feelings of desire for the Spanish woman. Thus, of all the spoils that were taken, Siripo wanted nothing for himself but the now-enslaved Lucía. Once in his power, Lucía cried bitterly and could not disguise her utter misery. Although she was well treated and waited on by Siripo's servants, she remained disconsolate, realizing that she herself was the property of a savage.

One day, Siripo, seeing her so afflicted, and hoping to console her, spoke to her in words of great love. "From today on, Lucía, you will not be my slave but my beloved wife, and you can be the mistress of all that I have and do whatever you like for all time. Not only that, but I give you the most important thing: my heart."

The sorrowing Lucía was greatly troubled, and a few days later things became even worse when Sebastián Hurtado was brought as a prisoner to Siripo. Hurtado, having returned to the fort with the other Spaniards from the brigantine, had discovered the fortress in ruins. Searching the devastated land with all the bodies, and not finding the body of his beloved wife among them, he resolved to let himself be captured by the Indians and so to become a captive with his wife, setting a higher value on that, although it might mean giving his life, than on living without her. Not telling anyone of his decision, he ventured down to the swampy land and the next day was taken prisoner by the Indians. They brought him, his hands bound, before their chief, who recognized him and ordered that he be executed. When his desperate wife heard of the sentence, she begged her new husband with tears not to have Hurtado killed. She entreated Siripo to let them both live so that they could remain in his service as real slaves—for which they would be forever grateful. To this Siripo agreed, for he wanted to please her. But he imposed one severe restriction: that, on pain of his indignation, and at the cost of their lives, they should not communicate with one another in any way. Siripo said that he would give Hurtado another woman who would serve him and with whom he could live. He also promised that he would treat him well, as if he were not a slave but a true vassal and friend. Lucía and Sebastián promised to comply with everything that Siripo ordered. For some time they restrained themselves without giving any trouble. But, as love cannot hide itself or keep the law, they began to neglect the savage's orders, and, now less afraid, they kept their eyes on one another whenever they could, like two lovers.

Behaving in this way, they were observed by some people there, especially by an Indian woman who had been Siripo's lover and repudiated by the Spanish. This woman, incensed by raging jealousy, told Siripo: "You are very happy with your new wife, but she is not yours because she thinks more of her own people and her old husband than of you. You had this coming to you. You abandoned the Indian woman to whom you were obligated by love, and instead you took a stranger, an adulteress, for a wife." Her words greatly disturbed Siripo, and no doubt he would have vented his full fury on the two lovers had he not waited until he could make sure that what the woman had told him was true.

Pretending that he was just wandering around, he tried to see if he could surprise the lovers together or, as they say, "red-handed." Finally, it happened, and, overcome by an infernal anger, he ordered a huge fire to be built so that Lucía could be burned at the stake. As the order was carried out, Lucía accepted it bravely, suffering the flames that ended her life like a true Christian, asking Our Lord to have mercy on her and to pardon all her sins.

Next, the cruel barbarian ordered Sebastián to be shot to death by arrows. Several youths brought him to Siripo with his hands and feet tied. They bound him to a carob tree, and those savage people shot at him again and again with arrows until his life came to an end. There were arrows sticking out all over his body, but his eyes were fixed on heaven. He had been praying to Our Father to pardon his sins, and it is to be believed that, through Our Lord's mercy, husband and wife are enjoying His holy glory. All of this happened in the year 1532.

Translated by Patricia Owen Steiner

The Jesuit Mission

Father Strobel

From their arrival in 1585 until their expulsion by royal decree in 1767, the Jesuits were the most influential religious order in the provinces of Río de la Plata. Distinguished cartographers, historians, ethnologists, naturalists, and educators were counted among their ranks. It would not be an exaggeration to say that their order helped define the cultural profile of colonial life in the region. In the northeast, their missions — Christian communities of Amerindians ruled by priests — were both powerful economic enterprises and religious utopias often in conflict with the interests of the Spaniards, the Creoles, and even the crown. The name of the current province of Misiones, on the frontier with Brazil and Paraguay, is an unmistakable reminder of the Jesuit missions that once prospered there. Until the end of the eighteenth century, the Jesuits dominated all institutions of advanced education. A significant portion of the colonial elite was educated at the University of Córdoba (founded 1622) and in the school of San Ignacio (founded 1661), both founded by the religious order. Even after the Jesuits were expelled, their large libraries provided fundamental philosophical readings for the revolutionaries. This letter to a priest in Vienna, in which a Father Strobel praises the self-sacrifice of the Jesuits in their evangelical mission and lauds the Christian fervor of the Guaraní people in contrast to the vices of Spanish settlers, illustrates the significant autonomy of the order's views on colonization.

Buenos Aires, 15 June 1729

I have already written Your Reverence two letters. The first, a short one, was sent before we sailed from Cádiz, Spain, on 7 December of last year [1728]. The other one was from Buenos Aires after we arrived here two months ago. I hope both these letters have reached you safely. This is my third letter, and with this I can tell you that once we missionaries arrived we soon separated. Following the orders of R.P. Provincial that we recently received, each of us went to our respective posts. Among the missionaries here are Fathers Innocencio Erber, José Brigniel and myself, and Francisco Limp as well as two fathers from

Upper Germany, two from Italy, two from Spain, two from Sardinia. There are twelve of us altogether, not counting a Bavarian brother who is learning to be a barber. We will go to the settlements where the converted Indians live on the banks of the Uruguay and Paraná Rivers. Within the next couple of days Father Orosz will undertake a trip to Córdoba de Tucumán with the remaining priests (all except for the two who will remain here in Buenos Aires). In Córdoba it will be decided who will stay there and who will be destined to go to the Chiquito settlements. The very estimable and holy Brother Martin Ritsch who came here from Austria in 1726 is now recuperating from a serious illness. He has the job of sexton and tailor for this college. There is also a father here from Upper Germany who has been so gravely ill that they have given him last rites. As I have completely forgotten my Latin, which is of no use with the Spaniards or the Indians, I am writing my letter in German so I won't entirely lose that too. . . .

The pagan Indians have mostly retreated South toward the Strait of Magellan for fear of being suppressed by the Spaniards, to whom they in no way want to submit. Those who remain in this region are living like gypsies. They wander around from place to place in bands and have a brutish life. They come to the city fairly often with horses and partridges, which they sell quite cheaply. Every hope of converting them is futile because all around them they see the scandalous example of the Europeans, whose wickedness is blamed on Christianity. . . .

In contrast, the honesty and extreme piety of the Christian Indians can hardly be exaggerated. A sizable group of them from Uruguay has arrived with twenty boats, and they will transport us to the various places we are going. Their innocence, their fear of God, and their sanctity so light up their faces that just looking at them lifts our spirits and fills us with abounding joy. I can't help but say quite frankly that not only the European Christians of Paraguay but also the religious community itself might try to emulate their irreproachable conduct. These Indians have so much love for the missionaries that, wherever we go, they follow us, even though we are ignorant of their language and can't talk with them. Through an interpreter we asked them why they went to such tremendous effort, following us everywhere, and the answer was that their greatest happiness was in contemplating us as their future fathers. Their dress is made up of shirt, pants, sash, jerkin, scapular, and something like a rain cape that hangs over their shoulders, the same as a monk's cape. Their clothes are a chestnut brown, made of cotton. Head and feet are bare, their hair short, smooth, and black. Their faces reflect their loyalty and holy simplicity. Their hands are covered by the scapular (especially when, according to custom, they kiss our hands) because their reverence for us and their way of thinking does

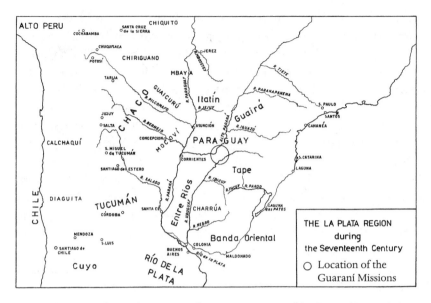

The La Plata region during the seventeenth century: Location of the Guaraní Jesuit missions

not permit them to touch even the hand of a priest. They call us *Cherubai*, "my father," and we respond *Charai*, "my son." In a word, one has to believe that God must take special pleasure in these thirty settlements that the company has built and maintains along the Uruguay and Paraná Rivers and that the entire community of Indians, with few exceptions, is inscribed in the Book of Life.

But their simplicity is not so limiting that they lack great intelligence. Indeed, their music and dance show how much they know about the arts. A few days ago musicians from the nearby Yapeyú settlement performed for us. There were various voices (two sopranos, two contraltos, two tenors, and two basses) accompanied by two harps, two bassoons, two tambourines, four violins, plus violoncellos and other instruments of that order. They sang vespers, the mass, and litanies as well as some canticles, all in such a way and with such art and grace that, if you had not seen them, you would believe that these musicians had come from India or from one of the best cities in Europe. Their music books brought from Germany and Italy; some are printed, some have been copied by hand. I have observed that these Indians keep the beat and rhythm much more accurately than Europeans do and that they also pronounce the Latin texts with precision, even though they have had no schooling.

Yapeyú dancers came here along with the musicians. Before they started to dance, they took off their cotton Indian clothes and put on rich vestments, made partly of silk and partly of velvet with gold trimming, as well as special stockings and shoes. They wore fine hats with gold-embroidered brims. Dancing in these costumes to the accompaniment of stringed instruments, they performed with such mastery that no teacher of European dance would be ashamed to recognize them as his students. . . .

Translated by Patricia Owen Steiner

A Gaucho Sings

the Victories of the Empire

Juan Baltasar Maciel

Portuguese pressure southward from Brazil was a constant threat to the political and economic stability of Spain in South America. In 1776, the Spaniard Pedro Cevallos led a successful military expedition to stop Portugal's expansion into the eastern territories of the Río de la Plata, mainly Uruguay. Cevallos's victory laid the basis for the foundation of a new viceroyalty whose administrative capital would be Buenos Aires. This military event generated a sense of political and cultural identity among the city's educated classes. The lawyer and writer Juan Baltasar Maciel (1727–88) gave voice to these new feelings in a poem in which a gaucho celebrates Cevallos's triumph. The poem, entitled "A Gaucho Sings in Rural Style the Victories of the Honorable Pedro de Cevallos" (1776), is the first example of gauchesque poetry, written by educated men who appropriated the language and style of the gauchos to give popular flavor to their own political agendas. The history of this type of literature symbolically mirrored the development of political alliances based mostly on the local upper classes' need to recruit the lower classes, first, to protect the integrity of the colony and, later, to fight for independence.

Here I begin to sing
beneath these thorny trees,
of the coolest of hands,
his feats and victories.
Of Lord Head Honcho,
who is a friend in need
of the well-heeled tall hats
who are never shy in deed.
A roughrider the fellow,
and may God bless his soul,

for having tanned their hides,
those studs from Portugal.
He has driven them like sheep,
into the prairies to scatter,
so by lassoes and by horns
they'll soon be part of our litter.
All in vain, my brothers,
your clucks and squawk.
After spotting Cevallos,
even People-eater balked.
Or better to say Cow-eater,
Pina Bandeira, Thy Don,
the bandit of Uruguay's trails,
who is always on the run
to one of many outposts,
like an ostrich en route,
though he'll lose the loot.
They'll never touch your snout,
the oranges or the potatoes
of Santa Catalina,
though you scream like cicadas.
Your colony flat as a line,
as the beach, and in your colony
when will you transform
the tiles into houses?
Mr. Cevallos, pardon me
my verse vulgar and woodsy
since the sisters of Apollo
don't live in the country.

Translated by Ruth Hill

The First British Invasion

Mariquita Sánchez de Thompson

Viceroy Cevallos's military and political skills made Buenos Aires the most important connection with the world overseas. A common market was created with Buenos Aires as its center, and export trade in bullion from Bolivia through the city's port was made legal. Within a few years, the insignificant provincial town became the promising capital of a vast region. The invasions of Buenos Aires in 1806 and 1807 represent a failed attempt by the British Empire to take advantage of the city's strategic location and open new markets for its products. Because of inefficient Spanish military organization, the task of defending Buenos Aries was left to its citizens, who recaptured the city with the support of the masses. In spite of this outcome, some Creoles had an ambiguous response to the brief British occupation because they considered the British superior to their Spanish counterparts and the local mestizo population or because of common commercial interests. A clear example of this ambivalence can be found in Mariquita Sánchez de Thompson's account in her diary of the first British invasion. Mariquita was an affluent Creole woman, married to a British merchant, who later actively supported independence from Spain. In her prejudiced comparison of the two armies, she confides to a woman friend her unabashed admiration for the Britons' looks — and their fair complexion — and the quality of their already famous industrial textiles.

I have given you a little idea of what Buenos Aires was like at the time of Beresford's arrival, and, although superior pens have written about it, I am going to give you my own opinion. The war has been blamed on our military establishment, but not persuasively. It is difficult to find another event such as this in history.

First of all, nobody ever imagined that there would be a war here. Old people had forgotten what war was, and young people were quite uninterested in war. (I have already told you what it was that kept them occupied.)

No one believed that a foreign squadron would be able to land here. No one had seen the huge ships at what are now called the outer beacon lights.

Nothing bigger than brigantines. When the port captain, Martin Thompson, warned Viceroy Sobremonte that sails had been sighted near Quilmes, people chose to believe that they belonged to smugglers, even though Thompson had said that they were the sails of a warship. . . .

What a night! How to describe the situation faced by the viceroy, he who was later blamed for all the confusion and for spending too much energy on trying to protect the king's treasure. A great deal has been written about this. I will only say one thing: that it is very difficult to explain why all the men charged with defending the city were so terribly surprised by what happened and why they felt it was impossible to save the country.

When the time came to think about surrender, our leaders were so bewildered that one of the judges, Don Joaquín Campusanos, who lived on Mercy Street in the house now owned by Don Tomás Anchorena, asked Don José Mila de la Roca, a businessman who happened to be in the fort, to go back to his house and find a *Mercurio* [a newspaper, something like a pamphlet, that came from Spain]. The *Mercurio* had a copy of the official surrender of Pansacola; this became the model for the terms of surrender.

With the plan for surrender in hand, our men came out of the fort ready to receive the English army, which arrived with their soft music, marching through the San Francisco district of Buenos Aires. Beresford said that he accepted our surrender plan and would stand by it. He entered the fort where the soldiers on guard yielded to him.

It was five in the afternoon. As the English troops marched in, a squadron stationed itself in front of the plaza and shot off a few volleys just to see how far they would go. At the moment the English flag was raised over the fort, the entire English squadron fired their weapons in salute, a custom that fortunately until then was unheard of in Buenos Aires. Between one scare and another, the people already were thoroughly thunderstruck.

Permit a digression. I am going to sketch for you these two military forces, one after the other. The militia from Buenos Aires: I have to confess that our people from the countryside are not beautiful. They are strong and robust, but dark skinned. Their faces are round and dirty. Some have jackets, others do not. Some wear tiny little hats on top of a handkerchief tied under their chins. The handkerchiefs are colored, some yellow, some bright red. In complete disarray, our men ride on filthy, poorly tended horses. Everything is most miserable and most ugly. Their weapons are grimy — it is impossible to give a full idea of these troops. When I saw them on that fateful day, I said to a close friend: "Unless the English are frightened to death by the sight of these men, there is no hope for us."

Now I am going to describe for you the troops that marched through the

"Creole Women in the
Street of Buenos Aires"
(William Holland, 1808)

Plaza: the Seventy-first Highland Regiment commanded by General Pack. The
most beautiful troops that you could ever imagine. The most poetic uniforms,
boots with red laces, part of the leg bare, a short skirt, hats of black feathers a
foot high with a band of plaid ribbon, and a plaid sash over a short bright red
jacket.

This exquisite uniform, on the most handsome youths with faces of snow.
Oh, the spotlessness of these admirable troops. What a great contrast!

Fijo's regiment from Buenos Aires was still wearing their old garb: long
burlap, blue jackets; all quite worn. The regiment of dragoons was more nearly
up-to-date. But everything of ours was in sad contrast to the appearance of the
English, above all the freshness of their uniforms and the cleanliness of their
weapons.

Everyone was stunned as they looked at the elegant enemy, and they cried
as they realized that they were heretics and that the king of Spain would lose
the Argentine jewel in his crown (this was the phrase). People cried, not for
themselves, but for the king and for religion. . . .

Translated by Patricia Owen Steiner

II

To Build a Nation

The struggle for liberty and its ideals did not by itself bring an end to the colonial order, as some historical accounts still contend. The principal catalyst for independence was instead the colonial authorities' loss of credibility in America after the French imprisoned Fernando VII, the Spanish king, and replaced him with Napoléon's brother in 1807. During those chaotic years, republican ideas gradually gained support in a society critically lacking in centralized, legitimate power. The belief that government should be an expression of the general will of the people found its strongest support among the citizens of Buenos Aires, who had twice initiated the defense of their city against British invaders. Years of hesitation, resistance, and political debates finally led to the revolutionary events of 25 May 1810 in Buenos Aires's central plaza, later to be named the Plaza de Mayo—a site that would become the central stage of Argentine political life. The ensuing armed struggle with the Spanish, successful despite great loss of life and enormous expense, ended with an official declaration of independence in 1816 by a congress in Tucumán, a provincial city in the Northwest.

Independence hardly guaranteed political harmony among the different regions that joined the new country. One of the main points of dissension lay in the disparity between the economic interests of the region of Buenos Aires—for which independence provided a more direct access to the world market—and the interests of older colonial enclaves of the former viceroyalty, like Mendoza and Salta, which had benefited from the protection that the colonial market guaranteed their products. Nor was there agreement concerning which political model would best suit national society. The endless vacillation on this issue led to a progression of different forms of government, which eventually escalated into civil war as several factions competed for political hegemony. The struggle came to a halt in 1835 with the surrender of all political power to the caudillo Juan Manuel de Rosas, marking the onset of Argentina's longest and most controversial dictatorship. Under Rosas, the nation's politics became reduced to the opposition between Federalists and Unitarists. Until then, the Federalists had supported a system that respected provincial autonomy, while the Unitarists placed Buenos Aires at the core of a more centralized system. Under Rosas's dictatorship, however, these distinctions weakened as the names of the two factions were given additional, more complex connotations. For example, Rosas's supporters came to consider a Unitarist someone who was bound to foreign interests, despised the lower classes, or was simply opposed to Rosas. Among Rosas's critics, Federalists became associated with the Spanish colonial past, religious fanaticism, and the tyrannical law of the caudillos and their semifeudal bond with their loyal gauchos.

This war of words was fought for high stakes: no less than the definition of an emerging national society. For many decades after independence, Argentina's identity remained a riddle fraught with enigmas. How realistic were a peripheral country's aspirations to modernity? Which kind of modernity could it be? How could the new nation compete in a world dominated by European powers? What segment of the economy, agriculture or cattle raising, offered the most promising future? Would the popular masses have a say in the debates on national organization, or would they be brought into the new national community by force? These questions are central to this part of the reader, which illustrates how each of the most influential political and cultural movements of the time sought to answer them during the years leading up to the definitive constitution of the state in 1880.

Halperín Donghi's historiographic essay and Moreno's petition complement each other and, taken together, provide an insightful introduction to independent Argentina's confusing beginnings, when the Creoles—who during colonial times had formed a fairly homogeneous group that defined itself by its opposition to the Spaniards—broke into several subgroups (landowners, the army, merchants), each with its own political agenda. Notably, not only did revolutionary times produce a divided society. The wars of independence against a common enemy also laid fertile ground for more democratic, even if limited, participation as well as a more inclusive notion of community. Military service gave some women and blacks a unique opportunity to claim a better position within the boundaries of the new nation.

Despite their disagreements, the different Creole factions were unified in their concern about repeated failures to organize the nation in the period following independence. There was no shortage of explanations for these failures. The independence hero José de San Martín and the liberal thinker Domingo Faustino Sarmiento argued that society's inability to achieve constitutional legitimacy stemmed from a lack of civic traditions. Rosas, while noting the absence of a ruling class with administrative experience, emphasized practical causes: a meager national treasury and the need for a stronger federal system with the ability to delegate political power to a national congress. Each diagnosis called for a different political solution.

During Rosas's dictatorship, two basic approaches to national organization came to the fore. Rosas resorted to the authoritarian practices of populism— a paradoxical political model that combined a strong alliance with the popular classes with an unwillingness to foster radical changes in social and economic structures; a system bolstered by a vigorous suppression of political dissent. The dictatorship flagrantly protected the economic interests of the landowning class, of which Rosas himself was a powerful member. At the other end of the political spectrum, the liberal opposition sought to turn the marginal former colony into a modern, secular society, propelled by a strong capitalist economy and modeled after Europe and the United States. Liberals dreamed of a country traversed by trains and steamboats, with urban centers scattered all across its surface, radiating laws, scientific ideas, and cultural sophistication. Agriculture and the work ethic that it inspired was their economic and cultural ideal. But for this program to succeed, they argued, the country's local customs had to be radically transformed. Public education would turn the popular classes into citizens and workers. And if education was not sufficient, massive European immigration would finish the job.

Customarily, Rosas and his time have been depicted in simplistic terms. The texts selected for the reader, however, show that easy explanations for the durability and strength of the dictatorship that focus exclusively on Rosas's proven thirst for power and control are, at the very least, insufficient. His extensive use of repression and censorship was undoubtedly instrumental in silencing the opposition, but his decisive strength lay in his extraordinary popularity among the lower classes. Such popularity was not accidental. Rosas's political apparatus revealed an awareness of popular desires that was sorely lacking in the opposing camp. Liberals like Sarmiento and Juan Bautista Alberdi deeply distrusted the popular classes, whom they mostly perceived as obstacles to progress. Politically speaking, they envisioned Argentina as a blank slate on which a modern republic must be designed from scratch, then built from the top down. Embedded within their dreams of civilization and progress was the colonial desire to turn the American continent into a better Europe.

The Revolution

Tulio Halperín Donghi

In one of the most comprehensive studies of archival material from the late colonial regime and the revolutionary period, the renowned Argentine historian Halperín Donghi masterfully analyzes the gradually increasing momentum of the struggle for independence that began in Buenos Aires. The loyalists, the military, various segments of the Creoles, and even the masses all jockeyed for influence as the Revolution took form. Resisting the allure of easy explanations, Halperín favors a more comprehensive interpretation of the Revolution. In his view, independence was not exclusively the work of a small elite of professionalized military officers, nor was it the natural outcome of popular will. Instead, massive militarization of society is what made secession a real possibility. Along with militarization, the city of Buenos Aires gave birth to national political life through the development of patriotic rituals, such as the commemoration of the May Revolution, and new forms of urban control that would serve as a guide for proper civil behavior.

The Revolution

The viceroy, Pedro Cisneros, was aware of the extent to which the local situation depended on that in Spain, and for this reason he tried to prevent the dissemination of the news that was beginning to arrive concerning the disastrous course of the war. He failed in this intention, of course. There were too many people who — in tones of the gravest consternation — were spreading from Rio de Janeiro and Montevideo news of the successive stages of the collapse of Spain. Meanwhile, some were beginning to take it for granted. From Upper Peru a zealous servant of the imperial system, José Vicente Cañete, wrote a prophetic analysis of the predictable effects of a military defeat and the best ways of attenuating these. He proposed that the viceroys should order a reorganization of Spanish America that would include the establishment of local representative institutions. Cañete was, however, well aware of the tensions against which he was proposing to build defenses that he himself did not consider sufficiently solid. The lack of internal cohesion in the social apparatus of the Indies, which he envisaged as threatened with breakdown because of the rivalry between the Spanish born and the Creole elite, made any optimism impossible. Even in the eyes of this defender of the established order, the latter had very limited chances of surviving the approaching storm. This fundamental pessimism also seemed to underlie the conduct of the last viceroy, who was prepared to do what he thought to be his duty right to the bitter end but not to anticipate the predictable crisis by risking a confrontation with those groups that, he knew only too well, had given him only provisional allegiance and were waiting for news from Spain in order to retract it.

. . . The entire course of the institutional crisis was decided between the advocates and the adversaries of a change in the system, the former group exercising constant pressure, but the latter group not regarding this as a good enough reason to abandon a struggle over the outcome of which they had few illusions. On the contrary, this element of coercion was either ignored or invoked to justify perseverance in the search for agreed solutions, which were poor disguises for the capitulation of one sector to the other. It was precisely the need to avert a greater evil (a violent confrontation) that was offered as an explanation for the gradual concessions made by those who, while opposed to change, really did very little to prevent it.

In opposition to them there was, in the first place, that military force of which Cisneros had not dared to transform the internal equilibrium. On it depended, in the last resort, the outcome of the crisis, and it was only when he was effectively disavowed by that force, when its leaders declared themselves to be incapable of maintaining order, that Cisneros realized that the only course open to him was to yield to the victors. Yet this decorous confession of impotence was not an exact reflection of the attitude of those officers who recognized the leadership of the commanding officer of the first regiment of Patricios,[1] Colonel Cornelio Saavedra. Rather than being remiss in the defense of the old order, they took an active part in its destruction. This was to happen in one turbulent week, from 18 to 25 May, against the same background and with the same characters as the clash of January 1809. The vast spaces of the central squares of Buenos Aires, overlooked by the fort, were filled only intermittently by a crowd—as to its size and degree of representativity, contemporary witnesses are in no closer agreement than are the historians. In the fort and the cabildo building flanking the squares, officials, cabildo members, dignitaries, eminent citizens, and officers of the new army, after months of the frozen equilibrium that Cisneros had been able to ensure, were again making, on the reduced local political chessboard, moves that they knew to be decisive.

Of those troubled days the protagonists appear to have preserved only a confused recollection. The first event was the official publication on the seventeenth of the bad news from Spain. Resistance to the French was continuing only in Cádiz Bay, and the Seville junta had been tragically suppressed by a mob seeking those responsible for the defeat. This news, deplorable though it was, seemed to be less so in comparison with the rumors with which it was competing for the attention of an incredulous public opinion. Its very publication was universally forgotten by the protagonists of the process, even by the viceroy who ordered it. As a precautionary measure, the troops of the mobilized regiments, which were still, as we have observed above, the successors of those that in January 1809 had supported Santiago de Liniers,[2] were confined to barracks, and in the name of their officers the viceroy was induced to resign his appointment, deemed to have lapsed as a result of the suppression of the supreme authority from which it was derived. In the name of the same officers, the cabildo was requested to take action in the emergency. On the twenty-first pressure was brought to bear in a less discreet manner. A small crowd of probably under a thousand in number, recruited from the lower classes by three efficient agitators, gathered in the square. The viceroy and the cabildo decided to deal with the situation by summoning a general junta of citizens, which included the most distinguished ones of the city, and, on his part, Colonel Saavedra offered the assistance of the troops under his command to ensure order during the meeting.

This Open Cabildo thus created an entirely new situation and offered the defenders of the existing order an opportunity to reassert themselves against the pressures being brought to bear on them. In contrast to the version of events perpetuated in a persistent myth, the selection of those invited to the junta was controlled by the cabildo, which was ill disposed toward the new movement, and the roll-call system of voting employed at the meeting excluded even the possibility of intervention by participants not included among those invited. But, of these, nearly half (200 out of 450) preferred to stay away. Among those who did appear, those prepared to defend the existing order found themselves, from the beginning, to be in a minority.

We shall not make another attempt to reconstruct—on the basis of an account of the proceedings that is hopelessly condensed and a mass of subsequent testimony that is excessively verbose—the arguments expounded at this meeting, which was opened by an appeal by the cabildo for moderation and prudence in the meeting's deliberations. It is enough to point out that the actual truth of the institutional crisis was never laid open to doubt, nor does there appear to have been any disagreement as to the legal bases of any solution. The possibility of a popular decision to fill, on a provisional basis, the vacant appointments in the sovereign authority was solidly based on legal texts, and, perhaps more to the point, the crisis of dissolution of the Spanish absolute monarchy had again conferred on such texts an unexpected relevance. The debate of 22 May was not, therefore, an ideological one but a legal dispute between rival groups that were trying to utilize a normative system whose legitimacy they did not question in order to inherit the vacant power. At this stage, there was no longer any fundamental discussion as to whether the authority of the viceroy had or had not lapsed according to the law. There was even less discussion as to whether the appeal to the popular will proposed as a means of creating a new authority was inspired by the principles of the Seven Partidas of King Alfonso the Wise or by the opinions of certain seventeenth-century jurists. What was of much greater interest was the question of who was going to fill the vacant posts.

To this question the reactions of the meeting were varied. The prudent absence of many people guaranteed a majority for the innovators, but it did not provide them with the cohesion they needed. Those who had been responsible for both pressure and agitation seem to have been ill prepared for the confrontation in the Open Cabildo. The very fact that voting took place in an order that took no account of the leadership structure already established within the innovating group would have made necessary an extremely strict voting discipline. The result was a decision that no doubt signified a break with the old order but left to the cabildo the task of establishing a new government. This solution had, in any case, been quite openly suggested in the cabildo's address at the beginning of the meeting.

Thus the cabildo was left as master of the field or, to be more precise, as master of the next move. It had only limited freedom of maneuver, and its ambitions had already been curtailed by the experience of 1809. The solution that emerged from its deliberations was obviously inspired by prudence. The viceroy was transformed into the president of a junta. Of its four members, two (Colonel Saavedra and Dr. Juan José Castelli) were the visible heads of the movement that was pressing for institutional change, while the other two (Canon Juan Nepomuceno Solá and the Spaniard José Santos Incháurregui) had on the twenty-second supported that center party that had simply wanted to leave power in the hands of the cabildo. The governing junta was, therefore, a faithful enough reflection, in its very incoherence, of the equilibrium of forces revealed at the Open Cabildo. The revolutionary leaders appointed do not seem to have hesitated to join the junta. But, on the very day (the twenty-fourth) that the cabildo handed over power to the junta it had created, the conflict broke out anew. The officers were ill disposed to leave the supreme military command in the hands of Cisneros, and those who represented them in the junta resigned from it. The cabildo tried to defend its creation but again received the solemn disavowal of the military leaders. The members of the junta established on the twenty-fourth, faced with the resignation of their president, do not appear to have thought that their own investiture was invalidated. On the morning of 25 May they requested the cabildo to designate a successor to Cisneros. Another day of disturbances led to a different outcome. The main square was once again the scene of popular agitation, and the crowd presented a petition that the cabildo hastened to accept: a more broadly based junta than that appointed on the twenty-fourth was to replace the authority of the viceroy. Its president was Saavedra, who thus at last received the supreme military power. Its members were Juan José Castelli and Manuel Belgrano, both lawyers and both veterans of the political discussion circles that had played such a big part in the preparation of these events, the cleric Manuel Alberti, the landowner and militia officer Miguel de Azcuénaga, and the Spanish-born merchants Juan Larrea and Domingo Matheu. The secretaries—who still had no voting rights—were the Doctors Juan José Paso (who on 22 May had drawn attention to himself by making an effective, though not very solidly based, defense of the right of Buenos Aires to take decisions on behalf of the entire viceregal area) and Mariano Moreno, who enjoyed the confidence of the cabildo and in 1809 had been one of the supporters of Martín de Álzaga's coup.

It is not easy to ascertain the origin of the idea behind the establishment of this body. A later testimony attributes it to a sudden inspiration on the part of one of the agitators who came to the fore on the twenty-first. This excessively simple version may be hard to believe, but it is difficult to replace it with another and more satisfactory one. It is, moreover, significant that, from Saavedra—whose behavior between the twenty-second and the twenty-fifth followed a less direct course than in the immediately preceding period—to Moreno, who was surprised at his own appointment, Belgrano, who declared that he "did not know how or from where" the new junta had arisen, and Azcuénaga, who before joining the junta decided to express his legalistic scruples about the matter, most of the members of the junta who have left us comments on their appointments agree as to their lack of any connection with the process that gave rise to the junta's establishment. One is, then, forced to admit that a movement firmly controlled in its early stages by a leadership that had a strong hold over it was superseded by a new and spontaneous movement, which was, moreover, destined to last only a short time. The establishment of the junta and the concentration of political and military power ensured the institutionalization of the same leadership whose efficacy was demonstrated in the clashes that occurred before the twenty-second.

However, although there may be some doubt as to the precise origin of the solution imposed on the twenty-fifth, there can be none as to the mechanisms by which that solution was imposed. It was, once again, the military leaders who delivered the city to those discontented with the junta created by the ca-bildo. The petitions presented to the latter body also bear the marks of having been elaborated within the context of the urban military organization. Can it be said, then, that the events that put an end to the colonial system were the result of the action of a small elite of professional military officers who were boldly prepared to take advantage of the passivity resulting from the disen-chantment not only of the representatives of the ancien régime but also of the mass of the urban population? This is the conclusion that some historians have thought fit to draw from facts that are well-known in their essential outlines and have been analyzed in detail by those same scholars, the most insistent representative of this school of thought being Dr. Marfany. But this conclusion does not necessarily follow from the facts expounded, and such writers per-haps oversimplify their task by postulating as the only alternative to a military revolution a popular one, which, to be worthy of that name, would have had to enjoy the support of the majority of the population, expressed by behavior that would enable present-day scholars to reach satisfactory conclusions, based on statistics, as to the real existence of that majority support. Is it necessary to point out that so exacting a definition makes the notion of a popular revo-lution completely untenable? One would, however, search the works of such writers in vain for an examination of the specific function of the military orga-nization in the political and social context of prerevolutionary Buenos Aires. In 1810 Buenos Aires had about forty thousand inhabitants living within the city limits and perhaps fifty thousand including the suburbs. There were three thousand soldiers and noncommissioned officers in the urban military units on 24 March 1810. This number, which was undoubtedly the lowest since urban militarization began in 1806, includes only soldiers and noncommissioned offi-cers quartered—more or less effectively—in barracks, and it shows that an unusually high proportion of the active population was still subject to military discipline. Their leaders were those who had arisen from the frantic organiza-tion of urban units that took place from 1806 onward. Few among them were living on the remuneration—which was very low but still represented a heavy burden on the hard-pressed treasury—assured them by their military activi-ties. Many of them still continued, despite their military duties, the activities that had occupied them in more peaceful times. And even among those who had found in the career of arms a new profession, in which they were to con-tinue after 1810, this change of activity was relatively recent and certainly did not separate them from the social sectors from which they had been so recently recruited.

But to suggest, as mutually exclusive hypotheses, a "military" and a "ci-vilian" origin of the Revolution is even more absurd if one remembers that it was only through militarization that the sectors of the Creole elite had assured themselves both an institutional organization and institutionalized channels of communication with the urban masses. The simple fact is that there did not then exist, for the sectors desirous of ending the colonial connection, any other organizational framework than that provided by militarization. But this militarization, so broad in scope, within the framework of which the organization of the sector that was to become revolutionary necessarily took place, permits one to define the Revolution as "military" only in a sense that makes this definition, if not inaccurate, only barely enlightening. The military revolution was at the same time the revolution of the entire Creole elite. The two terms, which might appear to be mutually exclusive, simply designate, in this context, two aspects of the same phenomenon.

It had been the solid support of the urban regiments that had ensured a transition without violence or flagrant scandal. The viceroy had signed the successive documents that bore witness to the gradual abdication of the old regime, but the Revolution still had to ensure the obedience of the entire territory that it aspired to govern. On 25 May, it was decided to send missions with military support into the interior, to spread the good news and crush any possible dissent vis-à-vis the new order. Neither the Revolution nor the war had dared to pronounce its own name, yet both were now established in the Río de la Plata region and were not to abandon the scene until they had thoroughly transformed it.

This transformation was felt, above all, in the sphere of politics and administration, not only because it put an end to the predominance of a Spanish-based bureaucracy, but also to the extent to which it affected the very group that replaced that bureaucracy. That Creole elite that the events of 1806 and after had endowed with local power had to create from within its own ranks a political class and a professional military apparatus that it still lacked; its new role as the protagonist of events therefore imposed on it profound changes, which could not take place without some upheavals. From it were to come men who were to follow what was called, most significantly, the "career of the Revolution," but as misfortunes accumulated it was to find it increasingly difficult to recognize itself in those men (whose audacity had somewhat perturbed it and whose necessarily arbitrary power was eventually to alarm it even more), who had identified themselves with an enterprise that at first had appeared easy and revealed itself as almost desperate — the Revolution. . . .

The Birth of Political Life

The events of the twenty-fifth had created a new focus of power, which was both the adversary and the heir of the one that had fallen. This new power intended to use the principle of legitimacy as its trump card. It not only used this as a legal argument to demand the obedience of the entire jurisdictional area subject to Buenos Aires, from the Atlantic to the plateau of Upper Peru, but from the very beginning it used this extreme legitimism as a somewhat unexpected but nevertheless vital element in its own revolutionary ideology. The adversaries of the new order were "rebels," and the authorities used this term in just as pejorative a sense as their predecessors had done. Even in late 1810, the poet of the new glories of Buenos Aires, Vicente López y Planes, celebrating the first revolutionary victories in the North, proclaimed:

> Glory to the great Balcarce; eternal glory
> to his warrior legion,
> which reddened its butcher's sword
> with rebel gore!

Like the poet, the Revolution suffered no qualms over the condign punishment of the rebels and did not hesitate to publicize it as a legitimate instrument of intimidation. Moreover, this legitimism also represented an attempt to halt the slide of the Revolution into civil war. As the heir to the old regime, the revolutionary government also inherited from it the sense of identification with the whole of colonial society, rather than with a particular sector of it, and the new power wanted to deal, not with whole groups, but with isolated individuals. Although the drift into war could not in the long run be avoided and the entire group of the Spanish born eventually became suspect and therefore subject to discriminatory legislation, at first this deliberate reluctance to be associated with a specific social base contributed to making the new political authority isolated. By preferring to base itself on a legitimacy that was in any case debatable rather than on an unambiguous identification with those sectors discontented with the old order it did not encourage the unreserved support of those sectors, whose members were, moreover, restrained by prudence.

The Revolution thus began as a strictly personal adventure on the part of some citizens of Buenos Aires, and they found the hesitations that they encountered on the part of others somewhat alarming. As late as January 1811, the *Gaceta* founded by the revolutionary government and intended to be its spokesman was to deplore "the silence of many educated men of our city (one cannot see for what reason) on the affairs of the day." Of course, the new order did have at its disposal the means of threatening people into obedience. The oath of loyalty, which at first was demanded only of the higher officials, was eventually made compulsory for all heads of families. Yet it was precisely the readiness of the adversaries of the Revolution to give it this obligatory allegiance that made the latter less significant. Neither friends nor enemies were deceived as to the value of such forced declarations; the Revolution appeared to find a surer method of calculating its sincere supporters by means of the monetary collections it sponsored. Of course, the voluntary character of the donations received does not seem to have been above all suspicion. It is, at least, suggestive that on 5 July a report of the donation of his only slave by the European-born friar José Zambrana emphasized that the donor had "a staunch character and could not be swayed by adversity or by flattery." However, the clearest indication of the voluntary nature of the donations was their very scarcity. A week after reporting the news of Father José's donation, the *Gaceta* observed, still without openly expressed alarm, that it was the poor who were most disposed to behave with generosity:

> The middle classes and the very poorest members of society are the first contributors and hasten eagerly to consecrate to the fatherland a part of their modest resources; the rich will begin to make contributions appropriate to their fortune and their zeal; but although a rich merchant may excite one's admiration over the large amount of his donation, he can no longer deny the poor man the merit of having been so prompt with his contributions.

But the rich showed no eagerness to engage in this onerous competition, and the flood of donations appears to have dried up. The reaction of the *Gaceta* shows how the holding of a census of adherents was not the least important of the aims of the collections of donations: "Knowing as we do that a high proportion of the most well-disposed people," we read in the number of 2 August, "decline to make a donation because their scarce resources do not permit them to give adequate expression to their noble ideas, we must point out that they should not feel the slightest embarrassment, for the smallest donations are accepted, and it is realized that these reflect the most sincere conviction and adherence to the just cause of unity, which is based on the sacred rights of our legitimate and august sovereign Don Fernando VII." However, without acquiring excessively numerous testimonies of allegiance, the collection campaign soon lost its original connotations. On the one hand, the increasing financial requirements of the new state led to the primary emphasis being placed on the revenue-collection aspect of this activity, and, on the other hand, donations seem to have become the most obvious way of ingratiating themselves with the regime on the part of its internal adversaries. When we read the overobsequious message that accompanied the donation of the Spaniard Francisco Antonio Molina, a native of Málaga, who offered five hundred pesos "with an expression of his allegiance to the present system and without words to express the gratitude that he quite justly feels toward these countries, where he had acquired the wealth he possessed as a result of his fortunate migration to them," and we remember that this eloquent testimony was offered at the moment when the discussion of fresh discriminatory measures against the European born occupied such a large part of the political activity of Buenos Aires, we may allow ourselves certain doubts. When we read the less effusive note sent by Archbishop Moxó of Charcas with six thousand pesos collected among the clergy of his archdiocese "for the army defending these provinces and for the public library" and we compare with his subsequent behavior the proclamation of his "fervent patriotism and unvarying love and gratitude . . . toward a country from which he has received so many favors," no doubt whatever is possible: the archbishop was not speaking sincerely and preferred to follow the dictates of prudence when giving this onerous proof of an allegiance that he was very far from feeling.

Thus, this more forceful manifestation of allegiance to the new order was not necessarily more sincere than the solemn oath. The fact was that the situation necessarily cast suspicion on the sincerity of any statement of allegiance that could not be refused without danger. It was to be the existence of an alternative danger — derived from the possibility of a return of the old order — that lent, if not a more sincere, at least a more definite character to certain expressions of allegiance to the new system. Yet even this regulating element was of only relative efficacy. Reconciliation with Spain, by way of submission, still seemed in 1815 to be a viable solution, and not only to secondary figures, but to prominent revolutionary leaders, and — as the studies of José María Mariluz Urquijo have shown — Spain itself had not abandoned the hope of regaining the allegiance of some who had explicitly sworn it to the Revolution in the Río de la Plata region. Even so, the fear of the reprisals that would follow any restoration was a valuable element in encouraging the cohesion of the revolutionary sector. The very notion of "commitment to the Revolution," that is to say, of an unequivocal allegiance that would make impossible any reconciliation with the old order, is a clear demonstration of the emphasis that, very early on, was placed on this element in the creation of revolutionary solidarity.

This element was made even more necessary by the fact that this solidarity was marked by hesitations, even among the leaders of the movement themselves. Even if there is no truth in the report that the very secretary of the junta, Mariano Moreno, approached the audiencia in order to allay his scruples before accepting the appointment, it is true that Miguel de Azcuénaga, a member who was later to distinguish himself by the zeal with which he persecuted the disaffected Spanish born, did just that, and, on a more private level, another member, Domingo Matheu, was able to write to his relations in Cádiz and express a remarkably detached attitude toward the political movement he was supposed to be leading. It is not necessary to move very far from the center of power to find hesitations — and even discreet opposition — that were ready to increase as soon as the first hardships were felt. This isolation, against the background of a public opinion that was either hostile or felt a sympathy tinged with skepticism, has been emphasized in his memoirs by Saavedra and makes it easier to understand the efforts made to identify the new order with complete legality and the representation of the whole of society — efforts that, as we have seen, the revolutionary leaders made at an early stage. Unsure of support from any particular sector, those leaders expected to save themselves only by avoiding direct confrontations and taking advantage for this purpose of the similar incoherence of the opposition that was beginning to rise up in their path.

Was the revolutionary power base really so isolated? Even though its leaders may have felt this, the evidence of those to whom their victory was repugnant tells a different story. The revolutionaries were masters of the streets, and their enemies prudently refrained from disputing this mastery. Behind closed doors, these angry witnesses hoped for the ruin of the victors, but they do not seem to have foreseen any concrete course of action capable of turning the tables. As masters of the urban army and of the entire administrative machinery and of the viceregal capital, where hostility abounded but did not dare to express itself openly, the revolutionary leaders did not have much to fear from Buenos Aires in the immediate future. Nevertheless, they had to consolidate their newfound power. The group that had stormed the stronghold of political power had been transformed by its very success into the titleholder of power, and this made it necessary for it to establish new ties with the entire subject population, which had been only partly affected by the military and political processes that had led to the rise of a revolutionary faction supported by a popular following. In establishing such ties, the authoritarian style of the old order was not to be abandoned. The prestige and the means of coercion derived from the traditional use of power proved to be definite advantages when dealing with those marginal sectors. In its dealings with them, the new government tried to use the church as a somewhat unwilling intermediary. An order to preach sermons on the political changes and the blessings deriving from them was given to all parish priests, in an atmosphere of increasing intimidation of those ecclesiastics who disagreed with the new order of things. Of even more importance as an instrument for controlling and disciplining the population was the police system inherited from the colonial regime: that of alcaldes and assistant alcaldes, who were part of the municipal organization. The new regime, which, from its commencement, enjoyed the wholehearted support of these people, as was shown by the voting of those of them who were present at the Open Cabildo of 22 May, used them as its agents for the application of the increasingly complex legislation of surveillance and repression. In August 1810 the alcaldes were ordered to keep records of people's residence and changes of residence and also

> to make sure, in the blocks under their supervision, that no suspect meetings were held. . . . If anyone were apprehended committing this crime, they were to be taken immediately, without consideration of rank or privilege, to the prison in the case of men or to the house of correction in the case of women.

The need for greater political vigilance was the explanation given for the stricter control of people's movements. A law passed in July decreed the confiscation of the property of those who abandoned the city without authorization, and all sorts of punishments, "including the death penalty," were decreed for those still hiding arms. The alcaldes were immediately made responsible for registering and licensing these. The same sanctions were threatened for those caught corresponding "with persons in other cities, causing political divisions, lack of confidence, or conspiracies against the present government." Of course, such fearful penalties were meted out only after careful consideration, and in any case the edicts providing for surveillance were often no more than the resurrection of other laws that had in theory been in force for a long time but had not been applied in practice. Nevertheless, it is undeniable that the Revolution made the authoritarian presence of the state felt among that marginal urban population that the colonial administrators had found it more prudent to ignore and that the new mechanisms of control would make themselves felt with increasing intensity among the sectors more closely integrated into urban society. But it was not only a case of seeking out and neutralizing dissent; what was also sought was to bring allegiance under disciplinary control. Here too, without showing any trace of originality, the new regime followed in the steps of the old one. It found it perfectly natural to control in an authoritarian manner expressions of public rejoicing, just as in colonial times religious and royal festivals had been closely regulated. Street illuminations arranged by enthusiastic citizens were subject to regulations laid down by the supreme power, which also decided how many days they were to continue. Here too, the alcaldes in each quarter played a decisive part, as organizers of the collective celebrations and controllers of the enthusiasm of those under their jurisdiction. It is easy to understand how in this atmosphere the external signs of allegiance to the new order were supported even by those who had strong private reservations about it. The logical consequence of this process was the situation described by the American Brackenridge in 1816. At that time, the European-born Spaniards who had not managed to obtain citizenship were immediately recognizable because they were the only people in the streets not wearing the revolutionary cockade.

By this time, however, the Revolution had become part of customary habits, and allegiance to it, though still universally attested, was accompanied by less external manifestations of fervor than in the past, when "this enthusiasm, like that of the French Revolution," had suffused the life of Buenos Aires. However, during those years of fervor, through the collaboration of an authority anxious to affirm itself and the sector of the population that supported it, a new revolutionary liturgy had been created. . . .

These festivals were a mixture—elaborated over a period of time—of the old and the new. In 1811 there were four nights of illuminations, "salvos of artillery, ringing of bells, fireworks, music, triumphal arches, and countless other amusements, such as masquerades and dancing. . . . The people were beside themselves with joy and thought of nothing but diverting themselves in a spirit of brotherhood." Behind all this spontaneous enjoyment was the discreet preparation and supervision exercised by the police: "The junta gave orders," wrote María Guadalupe Cuenca de Moreno, filled with rancor against those who had brought about the political ruin of her husband, "that the alcaldes in each quarter should tell the citizens to erect triumphal arches and other things, to show their patriotism, and to put up double illuminations besides their usual contribution. I haven't given anything." "So as to keep order," Beruti pointed out in his turn, "all the taverns were closed . . . and there were many patrols going the rounds of the city, with the alcaldes in charge of each district." Dances and masquerades were nothing new, nor were illuminations. Though not totally new, what was more important than in the past was the part played by the armed forces in the celebrations. In May 1811, on the pyramid that the Revolution had commanded to be built to its own glory and that was still unfinished, "on each of its four sides there was inscribed a ten-line verse celebrating the achievements and victories gained by the valiant troops of this immortal city. . . . Their flags and standards adorned the pyramid during the four days of the festival." Yet, here again, these innovations of style and content took place within the context of traditional rituals adapted to the new circumstances. The celebration of 25 May opened with the carrying past of the royal standard, borne, as always, by the royal standard-bearer of the cabildo.

The ceremony had formed part of the ritual of the vigil of the patron saint of Buenos Aires, Saint Martin of Tours, and had been incorporated into the new civic festival.

What notions and what beliefs was this celebration expressing and trying to disseminate? From very early on, the prevailing political instability made it impossible for the celebration to be an expression of support for a particular ruler or faction, although no doubt popular enthusiasm displayed at the festival might be interpreted as a sign of satisfaction with the prevailing political situation. Obviously, the importance attributed to the first anniversary of the Revolution was connected with the desire of the faction that had managed to displace its rivals among the revolutionary groups to see itself supported by popular fervor, and when María Guadalupe Cuenca — in contrast to other less biased witnesses — recorded that "the festival has been a poor thing, and the crowds have been small," she concluded with satisfaction: "It seems to me that the people are not contented." She too, therefore, was disposed to measure the political attitude of the city toward its government by the degree of enthusiasm displayed by the crowds during the celebration. Yet, although it is possible that extreme discontent might cast a cloud over the festivities, the latter were held in honor of the Revolution itself and not of its temporary leaders, who everybody knew were ephemeral. What precisely, in the Revolution, was being celebrated? In the first place, the city was celebrating itself. Intoxicated with its own glory, "immortal" Buenos Aires represented itself as the liberator of a whole new world. The second aspect was the celebration of the liberty of America, after centuries of Spanish oppression. In a spirit of opposition to the old metropolis, with which, however, the political connection had not been broken, the Indian past was reasserted as the common heritage of all Americans. In 1812, during the festivities with which the parish of Saint Nicholas, in Buenos Aires, celebrated the failure of the counterrevolutionary conspiracy led by Álzaga, the four children who "sang from time to time various songs in harmony" were dressed as Indians, and in the same year the first trench mortars cast in Buenos Aires were christened "Tupac Amaru" and "Mangoré." There is no doubt that this exaltation of collective pride in the political and military achievements of the emancipated city implied a new image of the political and social order, but in both aspects of this order the revolutionary creed contained an element of discretion. As regards the first aspect, the political transformation initiated in 1810 had certainly been very far-reaching, but it cannot be said that it had been too successful in solving the problems that the change itself had created. As regards the second aspect, the idea of equality, which was voiced in loud tones against the privileges — which had, in any case, lacked legal sanction even within the colonial system —

of the European-born Spaniards and also evoked to proclaim the end of the servitude of the Indians—who were conspicuous by their absence in Buenos Aires—was employed with very much more caution when criticizing the social hierarchy that actually existed and that, in any case, appeared to be explicitly confirmed by the revolutionary ritual. Thus, the alms distributed to celebrate the second anniversary of the Revolution appear to have been clearly directed toward different social categories. Three thousand out of the eight thousand pesos distributed were earmarked for giving dowries to "six girls, honorable, poor, and of good family," in other words, to guarantee suitable husbands for the offspring of the least affluent sector of the upper class (this, as we have observed above, followed a traditional practice), whereas only sixteen hundred pesos were assigned for "assistance to families known to be honorable but impoverished," one thousand pesos to war widows, and twelve hundred pesos to those wounded in action. In the same way, the largesse distributed by Beruti during his memorable celebration of the repression of Álzaga's mutiny took three different forms: a splendid dinner for the clergy and "various distinguished citizens"; a "big meal" of chocolate, biscuits, and spirits for more guests; and a distribution of money, thrown from the balcony to the crowd in the street below. On the same occasion, "money was thrown to the common people" by some enthusiastic patriots in the main square. . . .

This attitude marks the limits of the political mobilization that the Revolution was sponsoring. It is true that since May 1810 the presence of the lower classes had made itself felt to a greater extent than at any time in the past, and at certain times the desires of this new political clientele did affect the course of the internal crises of the revolutionary regime. Furthermore, as the Revolution came to appear to those popular sectors not merely as a faction in conflict with other factions, but as the state itself, and more disposed than its predecessor to make its presence felt, the mobilization of those popular sectors became easier and more broadly based. In early April 1811 it was the influence of the mob from the outlying suburbs, mobilized and controlled by their alcaldes, that saved the dominant faction from what seemed certain ruin. Yet that very experience provoked a fresh spirit of prudence among all the revolutionary leaders, even those who had directly benefited from this popular intervention, and perhaps the caution that was displayed in September in controlling the admittance of voters stemmed from the fearful possibilities revealed by the events of April. The threat of a permanent broadening of the sector fully incorporated into political activity was thwarted with surprising ease. This happened because the mobilization of the popular sectors, though impressive because of its massive character, was at the same time very incomplete. It was characteristic that the leaders of the events of April were not figures who had arisen from the mob itself but people appointed by the revolutionary authorities to control it.

Though limited, the politicization of the masses was a very real fact. The revolutionary government, which had no desire whatever to transform plebeian public opinion into an important element in the new political system (in particular, in the complex interplay of factions within the movement), did not, however, scruple to evoke it in its own favor. This happened for several reasons, of which the most evident one was that, since the revolutionary leaders occupied an unimportant place within the group that traditionally dominated society and administration, they had to seek support outside that group. It was the proclamation of the rights of all Americans that transformed those who had been in a disadvantageous position in the internal rivalries of the colonial elite into the leaders of what were to become new nations. However, as long as that newfound superiority did not encompass the destruction of their adversaries within the elite, and while, therefore, the war went on, the community of interest of all Americans was to have definable effects on the political equilibrium of the revolutionary party. There was a further reason: the war was to make necessary an increasing mobilization of the popular sectors and—as we shall see later, chiefly for economic reasons—principally of those that in the colonial era had remained rigidly excluded. It is true that in the case of these groups compulsion was used frequently, but some persuasion was necessary since the enthusiasm of the members of these marginal sectors recruited into the army does not appear to have been universal. Their aggressive responses found an increasingly wider scope after the Revolution, in the shape of the spread of banditry, which had to be harshly suppressed from 1812 onward.

The content of the revolutionary credo that it was intended to disseminate among the popular sectors was related to the function of controlled and unspontaneous support assigned to those sectors and with the aggravation of the military burden that the Revolution imposed on their marginal fringes. For both these reasons, patriotic and military motives received the principal emphasis. As for the political aspects of the revolutionary changes, it was preferable to leave these in the hands of a more restricted sector, which was thus not limited in its freedom of decision in this sphere by the demands of that broader public opinion that the Revolution was, however, making efforts to mobilize.

Even if one recognizes its limitations, however, it would be unwise to ignore the extent of popular mobilization, above all in the city, which did not wait for the events of May 1810 to find a new dimension, increasingly political in nature, to its collective life. The utopian character of the campaign of ideological clarification launched in 1810 by the more staunch revolutionaries, the most extreme manifestation of which was the attempt to make Rousseau's *Social Contract* a primary school textbook, has been emphasized by many writers. The meticulous care with which the more moderate sector, once it had rid itself of its embarrassing allies, put an end to those efforts gives one reason to suppose that some danger existed. Several witnesses have recorded the fact that in Buenos Aires the printed word was a means for the dissemination of ideas that was by no means restricted to a small minority. Printing presses multiplied after the Revolution and were kept busy, and indeed in 1818 it was difficult to find a ten-year-old boy who could not read. The progress of egalitarian sentiments is equally well attested, though not always with approval. If the "most eminent citizens" were not able to walk the streets of Buenos Aires without running the risk of being splashed with mud by a cart driver or jostled by a horseman, the reason for it—according to *La prensa Argentina* in its number of 11 June 1816—was that "that was one of the rights supposedly derived from equality" in the view of that "insolent rabble" that now felt itself to be "raised to the level of a common equality."

Popular mobilization, however, limited, could not, therefore, fail to have political consequences. This was recognized, in terms demonstrating substantial agreement, by the supreme director, Juan Martín de Pueyrredón, and an unsympathetic observer, the U.S. agent Thomas Bland. Summarizing the lessons derived from his experience of government, Pueyrredón observed that,

> since the natural talents of the people are almost in contact with the knowledge of the educated class, the people has followed closely in the steps of those who have led it; however, one can count on their docility only up to a certain point; they express their opinion by signs that admit of no ambiguity, and which no one has been able to oppose with impunity.

Similarly, Bland observed that, even though the revolutionary regime could not be considered as representative, "the sentiments and wishes of the people, as in all similar circumstances, have had considerable sway over this newly-created Government. There is a point beyond which it does not go; and a limit, as the numerous changes that have taken place clearly show, beyond which the forebearance of the people cannot be stretched." This limitation of their own freedom of action encountered by the revolutionary leaders became increasingly serious as their policies diverged from those that the Revolution had originally adopted. In fact, whereas the most favored tactics were direct confrontation and war was the instrument par excellence of this, the massive propaganda designed to imbue all the inhabitants of Buenos Aires with a proud consciousness of the political, economic, and military might of their city served the purpose of gaining support for the leaders among the plebeian opinion thus roused. However, when those leaders discovered, as a result of very painful experiences, the limitations of that power and adopted tactics more in accord with the really rather modest resources at their disposal, they despaired of their chances of diminishing the more extreme aspects of that somewhat blind optimism that they had been encouraging among their supporters for years. That did not mean, however, that they could ignore the existence of a body of public opinion that still believed with the same passionate faith in the invincibility of their city and their revolutionary enterprise. Thus the gulf increased between a political leadership that was privately perplexed and a mass of humanity that was advancing with blind assurance along the path opened for it by that very leadership. Although that hiatus did not make itself felt in the course of the war of independence, this was principally due to the fact that the intransigence of the enemy made the prosecution of the war the only possible course. But the wavering—and sometimes rather undignified—policy pursued by Buenos Aires toward Brazil and the Banda Oriental displayed for over ten years an oscillation between the cautious attitude of the leaders—which at times approached complete passivity—and the people's faith in a revolutionary war as a sure instrument of victory. When, in 1827, Lord Ponsonby reproached the ephemeral president, Bernardino Rivadavia,[3] for his concessions to the "wild spirit of the mob," his accusations, though exaggerated, were less absurd than they appeared if one bears in mind the essentially oligarchic nature of the political system then in force. Although it would be unjustified to maintain that plebeian faith in the invincibility of Buenos Aires ever determined the policies directed from that city, it is, nevertheless, undeniable that no government there could with impunity entirely ignore that factor.

Was this unflagging faith in the fatherland, which was at the same time the city and the Revolution, the only sentiment that underlay the limited political mobilization of the popular sectors? If one were to assert this, one would run the risk of ignoring the progress of egalitarian ideas. The very efforts to limit, even on a theoretical plane, the scope of the revolutionary notion of equality show that the possible consequences of its dissemination did not pass unnoticed. What made this even more evident was the very fact that, from the summit of authority, the allegiance of the popular sectors was now eagerly sought. This was perhaps a sign more indicative than any doctrinal pronouncement of the increasing weight that those sectors were recognized as possessing. In a less direct manner, the effects of the Revolution on the internal equilibrium of the Buenos Aires elite, where it provoked sudden collapses and declines and no less surprising rises to power, were bound to diffuse a less rigid image of the social order. . . .

Translated by Richard Southern

Notes

For references and notes, see the complete version of the chapters excerpted here: Tulio Halperín Donghi, *Politics, Economics, and Society in Argentina's Revolutionary Period* (Cambridge: Cambridge University Press, 1975), 150–69.

1 The "first regiment of Patricios" was a military unit in the Spanish colonial army.

2 Santiago de Liniers, Martín de Álzaga, and Juan Martín de Pueyrredón were the civil and military leaders in the defense and recovery of the city of Buenos Aires during the British invasion of 1806–7. In recognition of his military achievements against the British, Liniers was made viceroy of the provinces of the Río de la Plata.

3 Bernardino Rivadavia, the first president of Argentina under the constitution of 1826, was a fierce opponent of cattlemen's interests and an advocate of a strong central government, what was called at the time a Unitarist.

The Landowners' Petition

Mariano Moreno

The cattle and horses that the Spaniards brought to Río de la Plata prospered in the humid pampas, a perfect environment for their proliferation. From this serendipitous abundance evolved the estancia—a social and economic institution based on cattle raising—and a landowning class, the estancieros, whose power and influence over the gauchos would be pivotal during the military and civil wars that followed independence from Spain. Mariano Moreno (1778–1809), a lawyer from Buenos Aires, had a brief but very influential political career as a revolutionary leader. He served as an advocate for the interests of the estancieros, who by the end of the colonial regime ran the most profitable economic enterprise in the viceroyalty. In his petition to the last Spanish viceroy, written in 1809, Moreno clearly states that independence from Spain for the landowning sector meant, above all, access to free trade and additional economic advantages that would eventually grant the estancieros a dominant position in national politics. As a spokesman for a dominant social class, Moreno replicated the political position assumed by many other intellectuals during the struggles for political and economic power in Argentina and elsewhere in Latin America.

Most Excellent Señor:

He, whom the workers and landowners of the rural areas of Banda Oriental and Occidental of the Río de la Plata have empowered to confer with you about the expedient of opening up trade with England in order that the funds raised by the flow of imports and exports would be able to address the very grave emergencies of the public treasury, declares:

That, although it has been presented as a purely government matter, where all the people need to do is to carry out promptly the resolutions adopted by a superior governing body, the immediate interest of my constituents is that there be no frustration of the realization of a plan that can pull them out of the age-old misery to which their lives have been condemned.

The landowners have a legitimate right to be represented in advising Your

Excellency as to the means of reconciling the prosperity of the country with the needs of the treasury. We see the solution as removing the obstacles to trade, which is in line with the beneficial ideas with which your government has begun to distinguish itself.

The solemn proclamations with which Your Excellency has chosen to announce the zeal to be dedicated to the welfare of these provinces have aroused the once dying hopes of those I represent. They are justly persuaded that any profit gained from our land should immediately revert to its owners and cultivators. Their sense of confidence, buoyed now by new promises, has them anxiously discussing the changes that would bring about their own betterment. The memory of their previous impoverished state is still horrifying to them, but now a combination of extraordinary events has created valid rights for them such as had been denied them for a long time. In the suffering they were accustomed to, they had left it to the government to initiate various benefits that have now been recovered from the oblivion to which they had been relegated. Thank God that we no longer live in those dark centuries when the interests of subjects were separated from those of the sovereign, a time when the accumulated wealth of the treasury was one of such true opulence that the people themselves were left in poverty. . . .

Fortunately we live under a benign prince, born in enlightened times and accustomed to humane laws, who does not allow the growth of public funds at the expense of the fortunes and properties of individuals.

Your Excellency, basing his ideas on such luminous principles, had hardly taken supreme command of these provinces than he suppressed the new taxes that had been given the name of *patriotic contributions*. To have ever authorized those taxes on food and other necessities of the people displayed a gross shortage of clear thinking. When the present state of commerce and the nation made it possible to enrich the treasury and simultaneously to foster the prosperity of the provinces, Your Excellency was not insensitive to the public need, a need that has been identified as being intimately tied to the King's cause.

First, you tried to increase the royal profits by bolstering the welfare of the people. Now, as you try to implement the just enterprise of reconciling the welfare of the country with that of the royal estate, what could be more appropriate than to open the doors of trade to the goods that we do not have and to promote the export of products that we have in excess of our domestic needs but that people are prohibited from selling abroad?

There are truths so evident that it is intellectually belittling to have to demonstrate them. Such is the proposition that the country should openly import goods that it neither has nor produces and export those products that are so abundant as to perish because they cannot be sold. It is in vain that certain selfish interests, which are often opposed to the common good, clamor against a system that they fear will hurt them. And it is in vain that they misrepresent the motives of their opposition by distorting the intentions that motivate them. The truth that underlies the proposition will shine through all their sophistry.

If the government were to consult men of superior intellect and long experience to draft these laws, they would surely support our contention that nothing is more appropriate to the well-being of a country than for it to facilitate the free flow of both imports and exports.

In these days when the real and imagined needs of man have been elevated to the same level, it is the duty of the government to provide for the people's needs by easy methods that will satisfy them. If not, people will have to fulfill their needs for essential products (whose scarcity has led to exorbitant prices) by economizing on other goods in order to meet the increased cost of their purchases. People will suffer intolerable sacrifices just to buy a small amount of their needed goods. Only the freedom to import can save the populace from this continual privation, for, when abundance is assured, people can make purchases according to their needs and resources, without having to make the sacrifices that monopoly imposes in times of scarcity.

Those who see the abundance of foreign goods as an evil for the country surely are ignorant of the first principles of economics. Nothing is more beneficial for a province than the abundance of desired goods that it does not produce since they become cheap as their price goes down to one that is beneficial to the consumer and that can only hurt the [domestic competitors of] the importers. . . .

The removal of obstacles to the import of foreign goods will have to be accompanied in equal measure by the removal of obstacles to the export of goods. Fortunately, the products of this province are highly desirable, of ready availability, and most of them are absolutely necessary. Usually, too, they can be produced rather quickly. Our agriculture would be very rapidly stimulated if the doors to all exportable goods were open and the farmer could count on profitable sales. Those who plow timidly because of the uncertainty of sales would work with a zeal inspired by profit, and they would be protected from excess supplies by the demand for exports. Larger investments would be encouraged and would produce prosperity for the cultivators that would be accompanied by substantial deposits for the royal treasury.

The fields of our country annually produce a million leather hides, not counting other kinds of leather, grain, and fat that are so important to foreign trade. With our warehouses full, and lacking the opportunity to export, we have an enormous surplus. Such a surplus ties up capital and makes for an impossible situation where farmers are not able to make new purchases. Since they cannot figure on a good price for their products or find new buyers, the situation degenerates to the pitiful state we have today where agricultural producers fail and go so far as to give up their work. None of this compensates the farmer for his tremendous effort and all his expenses.

The freedom to export will bring about a rapid change of direction by stimulating demand. It will make new products increase in value and help labor by producing profits. Agriculture will flourish, ensuring the circulation of money to the benefit of those who are the source of the basic private investment in the province. Who has not seen the fresh vigor of the farm worker when, after a long war, there comes a peace that facilitates exports that had previously been prevented?

Only the new plan will let us achieve those happy results that peace with Great Britain failed to give us because of the sad events that from that time on have ruined the trade relations of Buenos Aires. . . .

When the perfidious ambition of France caused violent convulsions in Spain, which was forced to direct its energies to shaking off the yoke of its oppressor, the noble people of our nation rallied and began to develop plans and ideas that might bring prosperity to us despite the dreadful situation that destiny had inflicted on us.

One of the outcomes that was most just, most magnanimous, and most politically significant was the declaration that the Americas were, not a colony or a subservient entity, but an essential and intrinsic part of the Spanish monarchy. Because of this new status, and in just proportion to the heroic loyalty and patriotism that this nation has shown Spain in difficult times, our country has been called on to give itself national representation with both voice and vote in the government of these provinces.

This solemn proclamation, which will bring about the most brilliant era for America, has not been a fruitless ceremony that takes lightly the hopes of the people and reduces them to only the sterile pleasure of pompous titles that are incompatible with their welfare. The Spanish nation, which has never seemed grander than in the trying days that still afflict it, proceeded with honor when it declared a state of perfect equality between the European and the American provinces. It upheld the most sacred rights when it did away with laws that would have fostered the continued degradation of our country. With the magnificence of a great nation it rewarded our faithfulness and union to which it had so brilliantly given legitimacy. The Spanish monarchy worked with the prudence and political wisdom appropriate to an illustrious kingdom. But, owing to the distressing status to which its enemies had reduced it, the most it could do was to confer on this Spanish colony the longed-for dignity of being a self-governing body.

The first duty of a magistrate is to bring about the public welfare in every way possible. "Then," so says a wise Spaniard,[1] "the whole community as well as individuals will give thanks to the hand that made them happy. There is no doubt that the love of the vassals forms the most solid base for the throne. This reciprocity of interests then should encourage those who govern to renew their efforts to bring about general prosperity. The government will be consolidated by public gratitude, and the nation will enjoy the fruits of its work and vigilance." If the wealth of these provinces were calculated in the same way as a complicated business, a steady reserve fund would be necessary in order not to disturb the flow of commerce affected by dramatic changes in demand. Treating agriculture like big business will bring about our welfare. And, since it is our destiny to be cultivators of fertile fields, it is the only way that we will succeed in becoming wealthy.

If Your Excellency desires to promote our good, the route that leads to it is very simple: reason and the celebrated Adam Smith, who according to the Spanish philosopher cited earlier is the indisputable apostle of political economy, lead us to see that governments that want to provide for the general good should be limited to removing obstacles. This is the linchpin on which Jovellanos based the luminous structure of his economic report on agrarian law. The principles of these great men will never be refuted. May the chains restricting our business be broken, and may our shipping lanes be opened. Then the self-interest of our farmers will produce a flow of trade that will make our agriculture flourish — from which the only thing we should expect is our prosperity. . . .

Translated by Patricia Owen Steiner

Note

1 Moreno refers to Gaspar Melchor Jovellanos (1744–1811), author of the influential work on agrarian law, *Informe de la Sociedad económica de Madrid al Real y supremo Consejo de Castilla en el espediente de ley agraria* (1795).

The Good Citizen

José de San Martín

After independence was assured, the apparently solid military and civil union against the Spanish Empire collapsed. Multiple attempts to organize the territories of the former viceroyalty into a single, unified country ultimately failed. For some, the source of the problem lay in the lack of the democratic ethics of tolerance and mutual respect. General José de San Martín (1778–1850), the first national hero of Argentine history, was one defender of this view. After completing his education in Spain, he returned to the Río de la Plata and organized the ejército libertador, the liberating army, that defeated the Spaniards in the territorial domains of the soon to be Argentine, Chilean, and Peruvian republics. He subsequently rejected public life and remained in exile in France for the rest of his life. In 1825 he wrote a series of "maxims." Although originally dedicated to his daughter Mercedes as advice for the education of her own child, they had as their implicit audience the Argentine citizenry, who considered him the "father of the country." The maxims stress the need to strengthen civic virtues in the children of a new republic that, since the Revolution, had suffered the effects of continuous political violence and failed to achieve institutional legitimacy.

To Mercedes Tomasa de San Martín y de Escalada:

1st. Make her rich in humane qualities, sensitive even to harmless insects. As Sterne opened the window to release a fly, he said, "Leave, little one, the world is big enough for us both."
2nd. Inspire her to love truth and detest falsehood.
3rd. Inspire her to trust and friendship, combined with respect.
4th. Encourage Mercedes to be charitable with the poor.
5th. Respect for the property of others.
6th. Teach her to keep a secret.
7th. Inspire in her tolerance of all religions.
8th. Teach her to be kind to servants, the poor, and the elderly.
9th. Teach her to speak little and precisely.

10th. Accustom her to have formal table manners.

11th. Love of cleanliness and disdain of luxury.

12th. Inspire in her love of the Fatherland and of liberty.

Translated by Barbara Huntley and Pilar Liria

Women in the Fatherland

Juana Manuela Gorriti

Whereas "decent" women contributed to nation building by donating their jewels to support the national army, making flags, and educating the children of the elite, there were other women who dared to stake a more significant claim to a position in the new public sphere. Juana Manuela Gorriti (1818–92) combined a private life that was scandalous for the times with a prolific writing career. Married to a mestizo captain who later became president of Bolivia, she divorced him, had several legitimate and illegitimate children, and traveled extensively between various South American cities. During most of her life in Argentina, she earned a living teaching and writing. Her writings were addressed mainly to women, and she tackled a wide range of topics and genres, from culinary recipes to feminist essays. The selected text is Gorriti's commemoration of Juana Azurduy, a patriotic woman who fought in the independence wars commanding male divisions. Her homage to an eccentric woman fighting for the nation in male terrain reflects Gorriti's political struggle for a more inclusive citizenship.

1

Now that the softness of our way of life has destroyed woman's strength of character and made her the slave of pleasure with no other guiding enthusiasm than vanity, with nothing more to worship than her own beauty, it is entirely good and proper to recall extraordinary women of another time. Those women, who were guided by the precepts of the church and by the dictates of their own hearts, accompanied their husbands to all kinds of places, following them on the plains or in the mountains, on hillsides and on cliffs, solely because of loyalty to their country.

One of those heroines was Juana Azurduy, born in 1781 in Chuquisaca, Bolivia. Married at twenty-four to Manuel Ascencio Padilla, beautiful and brave, on her wedding night she arose from her nuptial bed to follow her husband, Manuel, in the terrible war that the patriots waged against the hardened Spanish troops of Upper Peru.

While, from the Río Grande to the Pilcomayo, Padilla was feared because of his courage and daring, Juana Azurduy herself, because of her virtue and goodness, was beloved in equal measure by all those who had dealings with her. Her husband's followers found in her an affectionate mother.

2

After Padilla's army was driven back from its surprise attack on Chuquisaca, which was defended by the Spanish leader Colonel de la Hera, Juana Azurduy was entrusted by her husband to guard the village of El Villar. There, with bullets flying in all directions, she inspired those around her, for she knew how to rout the royalist troops that had attacked them. It was she who personally grabbed the flag of the [Spanish] Center Battalion from the hands of its standard-bearer.

Days later, on 14 September 1816, she saw her husband fall at her side. Far from bending under that catastrophe that darkened her life, she buried her tears deep in her heart and recovered her spirit. Seizing the blue banner, she lifted high the symbol of free men and went on to lead her husband's troops in their most heroic battles.

When enemies besieged them for a month on an arid hillside, she suffered the horrors of extreme thirst and hunger, but she set an example of the most stoic selflessness.

Some of the caudillos among her troops became envious of the glory she had won in battle and turned against her. Their hostility disheartened her, and soon after she found a new leader for her troops and withdrew to the United Provinces of the Río de la Plata, where my father (who was in command in Salta at that time) received her with all the honors that are given to heroes.

There, in 1822, I, as a child, had the honor of knowing her. Praise for her great deeds floated before my eyes like clouds of incense encircling that extraordinary woman, shaping a halo around her. Memory of her is still vivid to me, and I can see her now in her long black robe with her serene, meditative countenance.

Padilla was one of the great leaders of that gigantic war. In those times, among soldiers, there was no higher rank than hero, and that is exactly what Padilla was. Later, the country made generals and marshals of some of the men who survived those deadly battles.

In 1824, when the Battle of Ayacucho brought freedom to Spanish America, Juana Azurduy left Salta to return to her own part of the world.

What became of her? She vanished like those stars that light up the skies and then become lost in the immensity of the universe.

Translated by Patricia Owen Steiner

The Caudillo's Order

Juan Manuel de Rosas

*Taking power after years of political turmoil, Juan Manuel de Rosas (1793–1877)—
landowner and popular caudillo—maintained, as governor of the province of Buenos
Aires, a rigid control over the provinces of Río de la Plata between 1829 and 1852. According to the British historian John Lynch, studying Rosas's populist politics of multi-
lateral alliances is fundamental to understanding the origins of political power in modern Argentina and to gaining insight into political and social institutions throughout
Latin America. Nevertheless, Rosas's public persona has thus far eluded the definitive
judgment of history. For liberals like Sarmiento and Echeverría, who considered him
a bloodthirsty dictator defying progress and modern democracy, Rosas was a monster. His followers, on the other hand, saw him as the defender of national interests
against imperial powers and as the leader and protector of the popular classes. His
resistance to the creation of a national representative body is what brought Rosas the
most criticism, even from his federalist allies. In this letter in response to an inquiry
by Facundo Quiroga, a caudillo from the province of La Rioja, Rosas explains why,
in his opinion, any attempt at national organization in 1834 could result only in a
return to anarchy. To the very end of his regime, Rosas set himself against the constitutional organization of Argentina and steadfastly defended an undefined confederation
in which Buenos Aires exercised de facto hegemony over the other provincial states.
Quiroga's assassination in 1835 may have been a consequence of this policy.*

San Antonio de Areco, 20 December 1834

My dear friend, Don Juan Facundo Quiroga,

. . . It seems to me that, as you seek peace and order, both disgracefully
missing now, the strongest argument, the most powerful rationale for you to
use with those governors and other influential people, whenever you have the
opportunity, is to emphasize the backward step that the nation has taken, sadly
distancing itself from the longed-for day of the great work of establishing a
national constitution.

Leaving everything else aside, let us consider the state of the republic today. You and I left it to the provinces to dictate their own individual constitutions so that, after they were written into law, we might begin to sow the seeds of a great national constitution. In this sense we exercised our patriotism and influence, not because we were guided by a positive conviction of having arrived at the truth, but because the republic was at peace and had demonstrated its need for a national constitution. For these reasons, and because we wanted to avoid even greater evils, we believed that we should proceed as we did. The outcome speaks eloquently of what happened, and of the scandals that ensued, and of the truly dangerous state of the republic, whose lugubrious condition leaves us little hope of remedy.

Given these causes and all that experience teaches and counsels, who would be such a fool as to believe that the solution is to rush in and create a national constitution? Permit me to make some observations about this, for, although we have always been in agreement on such significant matters, I want to entrust to your judgment a small part of the many thoughts that occur to me about this. I do so with tremendous anticipation and for whatever use it may serve.

No one is more persuaded than you and I of the necessity of organizing a national government or more convinced that it is the only way to give life and respectability to our republic. Who can doubt that this should be the happy result of the means used to achieve it? But who would aspire to a goal by marching in the opposite direction? Who, in order to create an orderly, permanent whole, would use disparate parts to compose it? Who would dream of forming an army made up of a group of men without a leader, without officials, without discipline, without hierarchy—a group whose members never cease ambushing one another and fighting among themselves, involving everyone else in their disorderly behavior? Who would think of putting together a living robust body with limbs that are dead or injured and riddled with the most corrosive gangrene? The life and strength of a new complex government cannot be more than it receives from its own members.

Our costly and sorrowful experience has made us see in realistic terms that a federal organization of the provinces is absolutely necessary. This is because, among other important reasons, we totally lack the resources needed to make a true government. Don't forget the past predominance in the country of a faction (the unitarists) who, deaf to the cries of the ultimate necessity of a federal system, destroyed the means and resources required to establish such a system. Thus this faction created unrest, clouded people's judgment, and turned citizens against one another. Further, because they propagated immorality and intrigue and splintered society, hardly any trace of our traditional sense of unity has been left in place. The unitarists in their fury even tried to disrupt our most sacred institution, the only one that might save us: the church. In this lamentable state we need now to create everything anew, working modestly at first, and then, gradually, introducing a general system that embraces everything.

Observe that a loose confederation of the provinces is the most illusory and disastrous entity that could be imagined. If the provinces are not well organized among themselves (because each province has preserved its own sovereignty and independence), the central government would have little power beyond the boundaries of the capital. Its principal authority would be as a mere spokesman for the provinces in their relations with foreign nations. Consequently, if there is no organization to maintain order in the individual provinces, the creation of a general representative government serves only to agitate the entire republic in a series of small disorders that would inflame the situation in any one province and spill over into other provinces. For such reasons the republic of North America has not admitted new states into the national government until they are in a position to be completely self-governing. Until such time, territories have no direct representation in the government of the United States.

We now see the present turbulent condition of the provinces: all of them are contaminated by unitarists, by political strategists, by aspiring officeholders, by secret agents of other nations, and by the Freemasons who have all of Europe in a frenzy. What hope can there be for the calm and tranquillity needed to enter into an agreement of federation, the first step that is needed to achieve a federal congress.

Considering the conditions of poverty that political upheaval has created in all the provinces, who will pay (and with what funds) for the creation and maintenance of such a congress, not to mention the general administration? What funds can we count on to pay the foreign debt, monies that have been invested in businesses in the republic and whose recovery will take top priority when such an administration is created? Besides that, if in all actuality there are hardly enough able men for the individual governments of each province, where will the men come from to lead the entire republic? Will we hand over the general administration to ignoramuses, to politicians on the make, to all kinds of vile people? Don't we know that a constellation of wise men did not find any better man to lead the previous version of a national government than Bernardino Rivadavia and that he was not be able to organize his ministry without asking the priest to quit the cathedral and without bringing Dr. Lingotes from San Juan for the Ministry of Estates? For we know that Rivadavia understands the administrative branch of government to the same degree as a man who has been blind since birth understands astronomy.

Finally, taking into account the lamentable picture that the republic now presents, which of the heroes of our nation would dare to take over a central government? Which one would be able to form a group of representatives and of intellectually promising federal ministers who would cooperate in such a way that he, with dignity, could finish his term with his post still intact and without having lost either his credibility or his reputation? There is so much to say on this subject that a whole tome would be necessary to cover even the most important basic points, and it could hardly be written in the space of a month. . . .

The men who want a central government right away must be persuaded of the potential harm that threatens our country because, if their plans become a reality, the entire republic would be involved in a most frightening catastrophe. I think that, unless you and I want to damage our reputations or blemish our glorious triumphs, we ought not, for any reason, lend ourselves to this madness until such time as all this disorderly chaos has come to an end and we can see clearly that the outcome will be beneficial to the entire nation. If we are not able to avoid these developments, then let us just stand back and let them happen in their own good time. But we must endeavor to make the public aware that we have not taken the least part in such atrocious activity and that, if we didn't stop it, it is because it was impossible to do so.

When it is no longer feasible to deter the people from their resolution to act, a leader must carefully guide them in their march if it is going in the right direction, even if they are proceeding precipitously and without any plan. If they are headed in the wrong direction, the leader must help them change direction without any violence and by leading them to their own realistic conviction that it is impossible otherwise to reach their goals. By doing this and nothing more, we will have fulfilled our duty. Earlier events have shown us beyond any doubt that the best course is to allow time for the seeds of discord in the provinces to self-destruct. When that happens, there will be a flowering of the spirit of peace and tranquillity in each of those governments. Then all through our country the cement of peace and friendship will make it possible to negotiate amiable relations between provincial governments — today one kind of support, tomorrow another — until things are in such a condition that, by the time a congress is formed, almost everything will be in place. Then there will be nothing more to do than to march straight along the path that destiny has set for us. This is a slow process to be sure, but it is necessary to pursue it, and it is the only way that I believe possible for us now that everything is destroyed and we have to start over from the beginning

Good-bye, good friend. May heaven have pity on us and look after your health and happiness in the discharge of your commission. For us both, and for our friends, may we find equal pleasures, so as to defend ourselves and save our compatriots from the very great dangers that threaten them.

Juan M. de Rosas

Translated by Patricia Owen Steiner

Civilization or Barbarism?

Domingo Faustino Sarmiento

Domingo Faustino Sarmiento (1811–88) was a central intellectual figure among those who fought against Rosas. As a journalist, educator, and politician, he is considered to be the founder of modern Argentina. While exiled in Chile, he wrote Facundo *(1845), a biography of the caudillo Facundo Quiroga (1790–1835) that was also a passionate diatribe against Rosas and local political traditions. To explain Argentina's long history of civil unrest, Sarmiento established the famous opposition between civilization and barbarism, forces that he saw as continuously at war with one another. European culture, republican values, and city life represented civilization, while barbarism took the form of colonial and indigenous customs, the law of the caudillos, and the lifestyle of the gauchos. For Sarmiento, Rosas's dictatorship was the inevitable outcome of a cultural struggle in which local barbarism was temporarily prevailing over Western civilization. This social and political aberration originated in the country's vast expanses of unexploited land. Borrowing the eyes of the imperial traveler, Sarmiento viewed the Argentine landscape as a dormant desert awaiting the invigorating seeds of Western capitalism. The only way to overcome the sterile tyranny of unused space was to bring the city to the countryside through sweeping modernization, massive immigration, and the reeducation of the gauchos. Sarmiento's postcolonial dilemma between European and local traditions starkly highlights the untenable position of a society situated at the crossroads of history—a country that in order to become modern must cease to be itself. The following excerpts from* Facundo's *first chapter bespeak Sarmiento's main ideas about geography and culture.*

PHYSICAL ASPECT OF THE ARGENTINE REPUBLIC, AND
THE FORMS OF CHARACTER, HABITS, AND IDEAS
INDUCED BY IT

The extent of the Pampas is so prodigious that they are bounded on the north by groves of
palm-trees and on the south by eternal snows.
—F. B. Head

Its own extent is the evil from which the Argentine Republic suffers; the desert
encompasses it on every side and penetrates its very heart; wastes containing no human dwelling are, generally speaking, the unmistakable boundaries
between its several provinces. Immensity is the universal characteristic of the
country: the plains, the woods, the rivers, are all immense; and the horizon is
always undefined, always lost in haze and delicate vapors that forbid the eye
to mark the point in the distant perspective, where the land ends and the sky
begins. On the south and on the north are savages ever on the watch, who
take advantage of the moonlit nights to fall like packs of hyenas on the herds
in their pastures and on the defenseless settlements. When the solitary caravan of wagons, as it sluggishly traverses the pampas, halts for a short period of
rest, the men in charge of it, grouped around their scanty fire, turn their eyes
mechanically toward the south on the faintest whisper of the wind among the
dry grass and gaze into the deep darkness of the night, in search of the sinister
visages of the savage horde, which, at any moment, approaching unperceived,
may surprise them. If no sound reaches their ears, if their sight fails to pierce
the gloomy veil that covers the silent wilderness, they direct their eyes, before entirely dismissing their apprehensions, to the ears of any horse standing
within the firelight, to see if they are pricked up or turned carelessly backward.
Then they resume their interrupted conversation or put into their mouths the
half-scorched pieces of dried beef on which they subsist. When not fearful of
the approach of the savage, the plainsman has equal cause to dread the keen
eyes of the tiger, or the viper beneath his feet. This constant insecurity of life
outside the towns, in my opinion, stamps on the Argentine character a certain stoical resignation to death by violence, which is regarded as one of the
inevitable probabilities of existence. Perhaps this is the reason why they inflict
death or submit to it with so much indifference and why such events make no
deep or lasting impression on the survivors.

The inhabited portion of this country—a country unusually favored by nature and embracing all varieties of climates—may be divided into three sections possessing distinct characteristics, which cause differences of character

among the inhabitants, growing out of the necessity of their adapting themselves to the physical conditions that surround them.

In the north, an extensive forest, reaching to the Chaco, covers with its impenetrable mass of boughs a space whose extent would seem incredible if there could be any marvel too great for the colossal types of nature in America.

In the central zone, lying parallel to the former, the plain and the forest long contend with each other for the possession of the soil; the trees prevail for some distance but gradually dwindle into stunted and thorny bushes, only reappearing in belts of forest along the banks of the streams, until finally, in the south, the victory remains with the plain, which displays its smooth, velvet-like surface unbounded and unbroken. It is the image of the sea on the land, the earth as it appears on the map — the earth yet waiting for the command to bring forth every herb yielding seed after its kind. We may indicate, as a noteworthy feature in the configuration of this country, the aggregation of navigable rivers, which come together in the east, from all points of the horizon, to form the Plata by their union and thus worthily to present their mighty tribute to the ocean, which receives it, not without visible marks of disturbance and respect. But these immense canals, excavated by the careful hand of nature, introduce no change into the national customs. The sons of the Spanish adventurers who colonized the country hate to travel by water, feeling themselves imprisoned when within the narrow limits of a boat or a pinnace. When their path is crossed by a great river, they strip themselves unconcernedly, prepare their horses for swimming, and, plunging in, make for some island visible in the distance, where horse and horseman take breath and, by thus continuing their course from isle to isle, finally effect their crossing.

Thus is the greatest blessing that providence bestows on any people disdained by the Argentine gaucho, who regards it rather as an obstacle opposed to his movements than as the most powerful means of facilitating them; thus the fountain of national growth, the origin of the early celebrity of Egypt, the cause of Holland's greatness and of the rapid development of North America, the navigation of rivers or the use of canals, remains a latent power, unappreciated by the inhabitants of the banks of the Bermejo, Pilcomayo, Paraná, and Paraguay. A few small vessels, manned by Italians and adventurers, sail upstream from the Plata, but, after ascending a few leagues, even this navigation entirely ceases. The instinct of the sailor, which the Saxon colonists of the north possess in so high a degree, was not bestowed on the Spaniard. Another spirit is needed to stir these arteries in which a nation's lifeblood now lies stagnant. Of all these rivers that should bear civilization, power, and wealth, to the most hidden recesses of the continent and make of Santa Fé, Entre Ríos, Corrientes, Córdoba, Salta, Tucumán, and Jujuy rich and populous states, the Plata alone, which at last unites them all, bestows its benefits on the inhabitants of its banks. At its mouth stand two cities, Montevideo and Buenos Aires, which at present reap alternately the advantages of their enviable position. Buenos Aires is destined to be some day the most gigantic city of either America. Under a benignant climate, mistress of the navigation of a hundred rivers flowing past her feet, coveting a vast area, and surrounded by inland provinces that know no other outlet for their products, she would ere now have become the Babylon of America if the spirit of the pampa had not breathed on her and left undeveloped the rich offerings that the rivers and provinces should unceasingly bring. She is the only city in the vast Argentine territory that is in communication with European nations; she alone can avail herself of the advantages of foreign commerce; she alone has power and revenue. Vainly have the provinces asked to receive, through her, civilization, industry, and European population; a senseless colonial policy made her deaf to these cries. But the provinces had their revenge when they sent to her in Rosas the climax of their own barbarism. . . .

I have indicated the circumstance that the position of Buenos Aires favors monopoly in order to show that the configuration of the country so tends to centralization and consolidation that, even if Rosas had uttered his cry of "Confederation or Death!" in good faith, he would have ended with the consolidated system that is now established. Our desire, however, should be for union in civilization and in liberty, while there has been given us only union in barbarism and in slavery. But a time will come when business will take its legitimate course. What it now concerns us to know is that the progress of civilization must culminate only in Buenos Aires; the pampa is a very bad medium of transmission and distribution through the provinces, and we are now about to see what is the result of this condition of things.

But above all the peculiarities of special portions of the country, there predominates one general, uniform, and constant character. Whether the soil is covered with the luxuriant and colossal vegetation of the tropics, or stunted, thorny, and unsightly shrubs bear witness to the scanty moisture that sustains them, or finally the pampa displays its open and monotonous level, the surface of the country is generally flat and unbroken — the mountain groups of San Luis and Córdoba in the center, and some projecting spurs of the Andes toward the north being scarcely an interruption to this boundless continuity.

We have, in this fact, a new element calculated to consolidate the nation that is hereafter to occupy these great solitudes, for it is well-known that mountains and other natural obstacles interposed between different districts keep up the isolation and the primitive peculiarities of their inhabitants. North America is destined to be a federation, not so much because its first settlements were independent of each other, as on account of the length of its Atlantic coast and the various routes to the interior afforded by the St. Lawrence in the north, the Mississippi in the south, and the immense system of canals in the center. The Argentine Republic is "one and indivisible."

Many philosophers have also thought that plains prepare the way for despotism, just as mountains furnish strongholds for the struggles of liberty. The boundless plain that permits the unobstructed passage of large and weighty wagons by routes on which the hand of man has been required to cut away only a few trees and thickets and that extend from Salta to Buenos Aires, and thence to Mendoza, a distance of more than seven hundred leagues, constitutes one of the most noteworthy features of the internal conformation of the Republic. The exertions of the individual, aided by what rude nature has done already, suffice to provide ways and means of communication; if art shall offer its assistance, if the forces of society shall attempt to supply the strength lacking in the individual, the colossal dimensions of the work will repel the most enterprising, and insufficiency of labor will be an obstacle. Thus, in the matter of roads, untamed nature will long have control, and the action of civilization will continue weak and inoperative.

Moreover, these outstretched plains impart to the life of the interior a certain Asiatic coloring, which we may even call very decided. I have often mechanically saluted the moon, as it rose calmly and brightly, with these words of Volney in his description of the ruins: "La pleine lune à l'Orient s'éleviat sur un fond bleuâtre aux plaines rives de l'Euphrate." There is something in the wilds of the Argentine territory that brings to mind the wilds of Asia; the imagination discovers a likeness between the pampa and the plains lying between the Euphrates and the Tigris, some affinity between the lonely line of wagons that crosses our wastes, arriving at Buenos Aires after a journey lasting for months, and the caravan of camels that takes its way toward Baghdad or Smyrna. The wagons that make such journeys among us constitute, so to speak, squadrons of little barks, the crews of which have a peculiar dress, dialect, and set of customs, which distinguish them from their fellow countrymen just as the sailor differs from the landsman. The head of each party is a military leader, like the chief of an Asiatic caravan; this position can be filled only by a man of iron will and daring to the verge of rashness, that he may hold in check the audacity and turbulence of the land pirates who are to be directed and ruled by himself alone, for no help can be summoned in the desert. On the least symptom of insubordination, the captain raises his iron *chicote* and delivers on the mutineer blows that make contusions and wounds; if the resistance is prolonged, before resorting to his pistols, the help of which he generally scorns, he leaps from his horse, grasps his formidable knife, and quickly reestablishes his authority by his superior skill in handling it. If any one loses his life under such discipline, the leader is not answerable for the assassination, which is regarded as an exercise of legitimate authority.

From these characteristics arises in the life of the Argentine people the reign of brute force, the supremacy of the strongest, the absolute and irresponsible authority of rulers, the administration of justice without formalities or discussion. The caravan of wagons is provided, moreover, with one or two guns to each wagon, and sometimes the leading one has a small piece of artillery on a swivel. If the train is attacked by the savages, the wagons are tied together in a ring, and a successful resistance is almost always opposed to the bloodthirsty and rapacious plunder of the assailants. Defenseless droves of pack mules often fall into the hands of these American Bedouins, and muleteers rarely escape with their lives. In these long journeys, the lower classes of the Argentine population acquire the habit of living far from society, of struggling single-handedly with nature, of disregarding privation, and of depending for protection against the dangers ever imminent on no other resources than personal strength and skill.

The people who inhabit these extensive districts belong to two different races, the Spanish and the native, the combinations of which form a series of imperceptible gradations. The pure Spanish race predominates in the rural districts of Córdoba and San Luis, where it is common to meet young shepherdesses fair and rosy and as beautiful as the belles of a capital could wish to be. In Santiago del Estero, the bulk of the rural population still speaks the Quechua dialect, which plainly shows its Indian origin. The country people of Corrientes use a very pretty Spanish dialect. "Dame, general, un chiripá," said his soldiers to Lavalle. The Andalusian soldier may still be recognized in the rural districts of Buenos Aires; and in the city foreign surnames are the most numerous. The Negro race, by this time nearly extinct (except in Buenos Aires), has left, in its zambos and mulattoes, a link that connects civilized man with the denizen of the woods. This race, mostly inhabiting cities, has a tendency to become civilized and possesses talent and the finest instincts of progress.

With these reservations, a homogeneous whole has resulted from the fusion of the three above-named families. It is characterized by love of idleness and incapacity for industry, except when education and the exigencies of a social position succeed in spurring it out of its customary pace. To a great extent, this unfortunate result is owing to the incorporation of the native tribes, effected by the process of colonization. The American aborigines live in idleness and show themselves incapable, even under compulsion, of hard and protracted labor. This suggested the idea of introducing Negroes into America, which has produced such fatal results. But the Spanish race has not shown itself more energetic than the aborigines, when it has been left to its own instincts in the wilds of America. Pity and shame are excited by the comparison of one of the German or Scotch colonies in the southern part of Buenos Aires and some towns of the interior of the Argentine Republic; in the former the cottages are painted, the front yards always neatly kept and adorned with flowers and pretty shrubs, the furniture simple but complete, copper or tin utensils always bright and clean, nicely curtained beds, and the occupants of the dwelling always industriously at work. Some such families have retired to enjoy the conveniences of city life, with great fortunes gained by their previous labors in milking their cows and making butter and cheese. The town, inhabited by natives of the country, presents a picture entirely the reverse. There, dirty and ragged children live, with a menagerie of dogs; there, men lie about in utter idleness; neglect and poverty prevail everywhere; a table and some baskets are the only furniture of wretched huts remarkable for their general aspect of barbarism and carelessness. . . .

The Argentine cities, like almost all the cities of South America, have an appearance of regularity. Their streets are laid out at right angles and their population scattered over a wide surface, except in Córdoba, which occupies a narrow and confined position and presents all the appearance of a European city, the resemblance being increased by the multitude of towers and domes attached to its numerous and magnificent churches. All civilization, whether native, Spanish, or European, centers in the cities, where are to be found the manufactories, the shops, the schools and colleges, and other characteristics of civilized nations. Elegance of style, articles of luxury, dress coats, and frock coats, with other European garments, occupy their appropriate place in these towns. I mention these small matters designedly. It is sometimes the case that the only city of a pastoral province is its capital, and occasionally the land is uncultivated up to its very streets. The encircling desert besets such cities at a greater or less distance and bears heavily on them, and they are thus small oases of civilization surrounded by an untilled plain, hundreds of square miles in extent, the surface of which is but rarely interrupted by any settlement of consequence.

The cities of Buenos Aires and Córdoba have succeeded better than the others in establishing about them subordinate towns to serve as new foci of civilization and municipal interests, a fact that deserves notice. The inhabitants of the city wear European dress, live in a civilized manner, and possess laws, ideas of progress, means of instruction, some municipal organization, regular forms of government, etc. Beyond the precincts of the city everything assumes a new aspect; the country people wear a different dress, which I will call South American, as it is common to all districts; their habits of life are different, their wants peculiar and limited. The people composing these two distinct forms of society do not seem to belong to the same nation. Moreover, the countryman, far from attempting to imitate the customs of the city, rejects with disdain its luxury and refinement; and it is unsafe for the costume of the city people, their coats, their cloaks, their saddles, or anything European, to show themselves in the country. Everything civilized that the city contains is blockaded there, proscribed beyond its limits; and anyone who should dare to appear in the rural districts in a frock coat, for example, or mounted on an English saddle would bring ridicule and brutal assaults on himself.

The whole remaining population inhabit the open country, which, whether wooded or destitute of the larger plants, is generally level and almost everywhere occupied by pastures, in some places of such abundance and excellence that the grass of an artificial meadow would not surpass them. Mendoza, and especially San Juan, are exceptions to this general absence of tilled fields, the people here depending chiefly on the products of agriculture. Everywhere else, pasturage being plenty, the means of subsistence of the inhabitants — for we cannot call it their occupation — is stock raising. . . .

Nomad tribes do not exist in the Argentine plains; the stock raiser is a proprietor, living on his own land; but this condition renders association impossible and tends to scatter separate families over an immense extent of surface. Imagine an expanse of two thousand square leagues, inhabited throughout, but where the dwellings are usually four or even eight leagues apart and two leagues, at least, separate the nearest neighbors. The production of movable property is not impossible, the enjoyments of luxury are not wholly incompatible with this isolation; wealth can raise a superb edifice in the desert. But the incentive is wanting; no example is near; the inducements for making a great display that exist in a city are not known in that isolation and solitude. Inevitable privations justify natural indolence; a dearth of all the amenities of life induces all the externals of barbarism. Society has altogether disappeared. There is but the isolated, self-concentrated feudal family. Since there is no collected society, no government is possible; there is neither municipal nor executive power, and civil justice has no means of reaching criminals. I doubt if the modern world presents any other form of association so monstrous as this. It is the exact opposite of the Roman municipality, where all the population were assembled within an enclosed space and went from it to cultivate the surrounding fields. The consequence of this was a strong social organization, the good results of which have prepared the way for modern civilization. The Argentine system resembles the old Slavonic sloboda, with the difference that the latter was agricultural, and therefore more susceptible of government, while the dispersion of the population was not so great as in South America. It differs from the nomad tribes in admitting of no social reunion and in a permanent occupation of the soil. Lastly, it has something in common with the feudal system of the Middle Ages, when the barons lived in their strongholds and thence made war on the cities and laid waste the country in the vicinity; but the baron and the feudal castle are wanting. If power starts up in the country, it lasts only for a moment and is democratic; it is not inherited, nor can it maintain itself, for want of mountains and strong positions. It follows from this that even the savage tribe of the pampas is better organized for moral development than are our country districts. . . .

Moral progress, and the cultivation of the intellect, are here not only neglected, as in the Arab or Tartar tribe, but impossible. Where can a school be placed for the instruction of children living ten leagues apart in all directions? Thus, consequently, civilization can in no way be brought about. Barbarism is the normal condition,[1] and it is fortunate if domestic customs preserve a small germ of morality. Religion feels the consequences of this want of social organization. The offices of the pastor are nominal, the pulpit has no audience, the priest flees from the deserted chapel or allows his character to deteriorate in inactivity and solitude. Vice, simony, and the prevalent barbarism penetrate his cell and change his moral superiority into the means of gratifying his avarice or ambition, and he ends by becoming a party leader. . . .

. . . Christianity exists, like the Spanish idioms, as a tradition that is perpetuated but corrupted, colored by gross superstitions and unaided by instruction, rites, or convictions. It is the case in almost all the districts that are remote from the cities that, when traders from San Juan or Mendoza arrive there, three or four children, some months or a year old, are presented to them for baptism, confidence being felt that their good education will enable them to administer the rite in a valid manner; and, on the arrival of a priest, young men old enough to break a colt present themselves to him to be anointed and have baptism *sub conditione* administered to them.

In the absence of all the means of civilization and progress, which can be developed only among men collected into societies of many individuals, the education of the country people is as follows: The women look after the house, get the meals ready, shear the sheep, milk the cows, make the cheese, and weave the coarse cloth used for garments. All domestic occupations are performed by women; on them rests the burden of all the labor, and it is an exceptional favor when some of the men undertake the cultivation of a little maize, bread not being in use as an ordinary article of diet. The boys exercise their strength and amuse themselves by gaining skill in the use of the lasso and the bolas, with which they constantly harass and pursue the calves and goats. When they can ride, which is as soon as they have learned to walk, they perform some small services on horseback. When they become stronger, they race over the country, falling off their horses and getting up again, tumbling on purpose into rabbit burrows, scrambling over precipices, and practicing feats of horsemanship. On reaching puberty, they take to breaking wild colts, and death is the least penalty that awaits them if their strength or courage fails them for a moment. With early manhood comes complete independence and idleness.

Now begins the public life of the gaucho, as I may say, since his education is by this time at an end. These men, Spaniards only in their language and in the confused religious notions preserved among them, must be seen before a right estimate can be made of the indomitable and haughty character that grows out of this struggle of isolated man with untamed nature, of the rational being with the brute. It is necessary to see their visages bristling with beards, their countenances as grave and serious as those of the Arabs of Asia, to appreciate the pitying scorn with which they look on the sedentary denizen of the city, who may have read many books but who cannot overthrow and slay a fierce bull, who could not provide himself with a horse from the pampas, who has never met a tiger alone and received him with a dagger in one hand and a poncho rolled up in the other, to be thrust into the animal's mouth while he transfixes his heart with his dagger.

This habit of triumphing over resistance, of constantly showing a superiority to nature, of defying and subduing her, prodigiously develops the consciousness of individual consequence and superior prowess. The Argentine people of every class, civilized and ignorant alike, have a high opinion of their national importance. All the other people of South America throw this vanity of theirs in their teeth and take offense at their presumption and arrogance. I believe the charge not to be wholly unfounded, but I do not object to the trait. Alas, for the nation without faith in itself! Great things were not made for such a people. To what extent may not the independence of that part of America be due to the arrogance of these Argentine gauchos, who have never seen anything beneath the sun superior to themselves in wisdom or in power? The European is in their eyes the most contemptible of all men, for a horse gets the better of him in a couple of plunges.

If the origin of this national vanity among the lower classes is despicable, it has nonetheless on that account some noble results, as the water of a river is no less pure for the mire and pollution of its sources. Implacable is the hatred that these people feel for men of refinement, whose garments, manners, and customs they regard with invincible repugnance. Such is the material of the Argentine soldiery, and it may easily be imagined what valor and endurance in war are the consequences of the habits described above. We may add that these soldiers have been used to slaughtering cattle from their childhood and that this act of necessary cruelty makes them familiar with bloodshed and hardens their hearts against the groans of their victims.

Country life, then, has developed all the physical but none of the intellectual powers of the gaucho. His moral character is of the quality to be expected from his habit of triumphing over the obstacles and the forces of nature; it is strong, haughty, and energetic. Without instruction, and indeed without need of any, without means of support as without wants, he is happy in the midst of his poverty and privations, which are not such to one who never knew or wished for greater pleasures than are his already. Thus, if the disorganization of society among the gauchos deeply implants barbarism in their natures, through the impossibility and uselessness of moral and intellectual education it has, too, its attractive side to him. The gaucho does not labor; he finds his food and raiment ready to his hand. If he is a proprietor, his own flocks yield him both; if he possesses nothing himself, he finds them in the house of a patron or a relation. The necessary care of the herds is reduced to excursions and pleasure parties; the branding, which is like the harvesting of farmers, is a festival, the arrival of which is received with transports of joy, being the occasion of the assembling of all the men for twenty leagues around and the opportunity for displaying incredible skill with the lasso. The gaucho arrives at the spot on his best steed, riding at a slow and measured pace; he halts at a little distance and puts his leg over his horse's neck to enjoy the sight leisurely. If enthusiasm seizes him, he slowly dismounts, uncoils his lasso, and flings it at some bull, passing like a flash of lightning forty paces from him; he catches him by one hoof as he intended and quietly coils his leather cord again.

Translated by Mrs. Horace Mann

Note

1 In 1826, during a year's residence at the Sierra de San Luis, I taught the art of reading to six young people of good families, the youngest of whom was twenty-two years old.

Rosas and Washington

Pedro de Angelis

After a respectable academic and journalistic career in Italy and France, Pedro de Angelis (1784–1859) moved to Buenos Aires in 1827 to help defend the liberal presidency of Unitarist Bernardino Rivadavia. For reasons still difficult to grasp, from 1833 onward he became an active collaborator in the Rosas dictatorship, writing and promoting state propaganda. In this short essay from 1843, de Angelis defends the dictator's public image against his enemies by comparing him to a classical American hero — George Washington — emphasizing his modesty and amicability. De Angelis's portrait adds to the already contradictory representations of Rosas's public persona by associating him with American democratic traditions and values, the political model advocated precisely by Rosas's enemies.

After the excesses of the French Revolution obliged Chateaubriand to abandon his home, he took pleasure in recalling his first journey abroad and his interview with General George Washington at his home. "When I went to present my letter of introduction," says the eloquent author of *The Martyrs*, "I encountered the simplicity of an ancient Roman. A small house in the English style, similar to adjoining ones, was the 'palace' of the president of the United States. There were neither guards nor servants. I knocked on the door; a girl opened it. I asked her if the general was at home. She answered that he was. I told her that I had a letter to give him. She asked me my name, but it is difficult to pronounce in English, and I didn't do it very well. Then she gently said to me: 'Come in, Sir, etc.'"

Anyone who has ever visited General Rosas will recognize him in this sketch of the illustrious founder of the North American confederation. At the height of power, surrounded by a grateful people eager to pay him homage, the governor of Buenos Aires has always cast aside the trappings of high office with as much firmness as others employ in pursuing them. *Without guards,* like Washington, without any sign of authority, in simple military dress, affable and courteous to everyone, we have seen him preside over the dinner table on his estate, casually offering seats to those who had come to visit him. The atmosphere of these gatherings was of complete freedom and the most intimate informality. Citizens, strangers, administrative assistants, office workers, all of them, if they had wanted to, could even have eaten with their hats on in front of him. The mighty leader, the great citizen, the supreme chief of the Republic, stripped away all authority save for his prestige, the one thing that it was not possible for him to forsake. This attitude was enough to win him the veneration and respect of his followers.

Such a habit is characteristic of General Rosas, a man who finds it more natural to come down to the level of his fellow citizens than to remain at the high level to which they have raised him.

He took command because he was compelled to by the call of public opinion and the force of events. He sought to resign several times, but without success. If he did not try harder, that was because no one would allow him to leave the helm of the ship of state in those stormy times.

Although he has resigned himself to continue as leader, he has relinquished all the honors that have been bestowed on him, even that of being called *Restorer of Laws,* his only reward for so much distinguished service. It was a title that, in the glorious moments of the Fatherland, his enemies heard with terror and his friends cheered with enthusiasm.

In his long public career, General Rosas has disagreed with his compatriots on only a single point: the greater the effort to raise him up, the stronger his resistance and his determination to keep to the common ways of other Argentines. General Rosas has rejected all those rewards that most men seek, even men who are not driven by passion or ambition. Rank, office, titles, honors, presents, he has wanted none of them, as he said, *so as not to abandon the republican principles that he had professed throughout his public life.* This is the way Cato and Cincinnatus spoke; we have to return to ancient times to find analogous examples of such heroic altruism.

We must add one further episode. General Rosas had the misfortune to lose, in the space of a few months, both his aged and respected father and his much beloved and estimable wife, Doña Encarnación Ezcurra de Rosas.

The Honorable Chamber of Providence ordered that their remains should be borne in all splendor to their last resting places. On these occasions, General Rosas lacked the will to oppose this flattering demonstration of appreciation. His sense of filial devotion together with the memory of his happy years with his virtuous and amiable life's companion calmed the cries of his republican heart. Deeply thankful, he permitted the honors that a benevolent public had ordered for these two people whom he both loved and respected.

Translated by Patricia Owen Steiner

The Black Girl

Anonymous

Many intellectuals and writers went into exile in neighboring countries during Rosas's dictatorship. Those who stayed, like de Angelis, collaborated with the official press or wrote propaganda praising Rosas's policies. Since the mostly illiterate popular masses in the countryside and in the city of Buenos Aires formed the political base of Rosas's regime, songs and poems, written to imitate popular styles, proved especially effective in disseminating Federalist ideals and attacking the Unitarist agenda. The Cancionero Federal (Federal song book) (1833), a collection of texts compiled by Manuelita, Rosas's daughter, contains several examples of propaganda literature. In "The Black Girl," an anonymous, educated writer imitates popular black language to celebrate Rosas's leadership among Afro-Argentines.

My name is Juana Peña,
And it's a point of pride
to be spread far and wide:
I'm a true Federalist black-girl.
A sister-girl who walks the talk,
not a sister-girl in fair weather.
Because I'm not of those sister-girls
who fly like a feather.

I'm the sister-girl at the dance parties
who starts and finishes in first.
And all had better disperse
when I get ready to dance.
But now that I've got the notion
to announce myself the pack,
I must show: I may be black,
but I'm a true patriot.

For rotten luck, I don't have

children, father, or man
whom I can command
to join this cause.
But I do have my countrymen,
brother and sister defenders,
who'll hear my bits of wisdom.
Patriots they are, and patriots with muscle,
with vim and verve, and with honor,
Defenders of the laws
and of their Restorer.

Only for Don Juan Manuel
will they kill and will they die.
And as for the rest,
"Yessum, General," they'll reply.
"At your service, General,"
they will say to the traitor
who wants them to fight
against their protector.
"Yessum, General,"
Juana Peña will tell him,
"At your service, General,"
this sister-girl from Buenos Aires.

Translated by Ruth Hill

Immigration as a Means of Progress

Juan Bautista Alberdi

Like Sarmiento, Juan Bautista Alberdi (1810–84) was one of the inventors of modern Argentina. Also an enemy of Rosas, he remained exiled in Montevideo, Uruguay, for several years. He openly supported Urquiza, a caudillo from the province of Entre Ríos, who finally defeated Rosas in the Battle of Caseros in 1852, opening the door to institutional change. In 1853, Alberdi wrote Las bases, *a detailed program for building a new modern nation out of the political ruins of Rosism. This text was a blueprint for the Argentine constitution promulgated in 1853, which remained in force for more than a century. Under the slogan "to govern is to populate," Alberdi proposed an aggressive immigration policy that would in time profoundly and permanently alter the cultural and ethnic profile of the Argentine population. In his utopian representation of the future, the immigrants are instrumental in the transformation of Argentine society. Teaching by their example, they would endow local men with a sense of discipline and responsibility, virtues that were essential for promoting progress. By marrying Creole women, they would breed a stronger national race.*

How and in what form will the reviving spirit of European civilization come to our land? Just as it has always come. Europe will bring us its fresh spirit, its work habits, and its civilized ways with the immigrants it sends us.

By the customs later communicated to our inhabitants, every European who comes to our shores brings us more civilization than a great many books of philosophy. Perfection that one cannot see, touch, or feel is poorly understood. An industrious worker is the most edifying of instruction manuals.

Do we want to plant and nourish the qualities of English liberty, French culture, and the industriousness of men from Europe and the United States? Then let us bring the living exemplars of these attributes to our shores and let those qualities take root here.

Do we want orderly, disciplined, energetic work habits to prevail in South America? Then let us fill our country with people who have a profound grasp of such habits. Those who are well acquainted with industrial Europe will soon form industrial South America. The plant of civilization is not propagated from seed (except very slowly). Rather, it is like a vineyard that takes root and spreads through its offshoots.

This is the only way that our America, uninhabited today, will become prosperous in a short time. To try to change without outside help is an extremely slow process. If we want to see our provinces be successful in short order, let us bring people from Europe whose good working habits are already well established.

Without large populations there is no flowering of culture, there is no substantial progress, everything is wretched and small. This is what happens to nations of only a half million inhabitants because of their limited population. They remain provinces and villages, and everything of theirs will always bear the stamp of a puny provincialism.

Important advice to men of South American countries: Primary schools, high schools, universities, are, by themselves alone, very poor means of progress without large manufacturing enterprises that are the fruits of great numbers of men.

Population — a South American necessity that affects all our other needs — is the critical measure of the capacity of our governments. The minister of state who does not double his state's population in ten years is inept and has wasted his time on bagatelles and trifles. He does not deserve the recognition of his country.

If we were to take the ragged homeless from Chile, our gauchos, the half-breeds from Bolivia — the basic elements of our masses — and let them experience all the transformations of our best system of instruction, we would not in one hundred years have made any of them into an English laborer who works, spends, and lives in a dignified and comfortable manner. Or try giving a million inhabitants (the average population of these republics) the best education possible, on as enlightened a level as the Swiss canton of Geneva or as the most cultured province in France. Would we then have a great and flourishing state? Certainly not: we are talking about a million people in a territory suitable for 50 million. Can they be anything more than a miserable population?

But so goes the argument: by educating our masses, we will have order; having order, population from overseas will come to our continent.

I tell you now that you are turning upside down the way progress works. You will not have order, or education for the general public, unless it is through the influence of immigrants who have firmly established patterns of order and good education.

Multiply our population of serious people, and you will see that foolish agitators (with their plans for frivolous revolts) will be unsuccessful and that they will become isolated from a world absorbed by concerns of real consequence.

How to achieve all this? More easily than by wasting millions on futile, trifling attempts to make endless improvements.

Foreign treaties: Sign treaties with foreigners in which you guarantee to respect their natural rights to hold property, their civil rights, their safety, their right to acquire wealth, and their freedom of movement. Such treaties will prove to be the most beautiful key to progress for those countries that choose to stimulate their growth through immigration. For such legal guarantees to be inviolable and lasting, sign treaties for an indefinite (and very prolonged) length of time. Don't be afraid to commit yourself to European order and culture. . . .

If there is the risk that immigration might introduce a barbarism or tyranny that would threaten us, don't be so afraid that you forsake the future of our industry and civilization. Fear of treaties is a bad habit left over from the early days of our Revolution. It is an old principle, outdated and misguided—a poorly executed imitation of the foreign policy that Washington counseled for the United States under circumstances and for motives that were totally different from those that we face. . . .

Plan for immigration: Spontaneous immigration is the source of true and great immigration. Our governments should promote it, not by piecemeal concessions of land fit only for bears, not in fallacious and usurious contracts (which hurt the immigrants more than they hurt the country being populated), not by mere handfuls of men or individual arrangements to do business with some influential speculator. That is all false, the face of sterile immigration. Only by the great, large-scale, disinterested system that gave birth to California in four years, by the lavish extension of freedom, and by concessions can we persuade foreigners to forsake their own country and instead to inhabit ours. We must try to make life and business here easier for them by eliminating restrictive measures so that they will achieve their legal objectives and their useful aspirations.

The United States is such an advanced country because it is now, and has been continually, composed of people from Europe. From the very beginning it received tremendous waves of European immigration. Those who believe that progress in the United States dates only from the time of independence deceive themselves. Under the colonial system, European immigration was as great and continuous as it was after independence. Legislators for the states tended wisely to promote immigration. One of the reasons for the perpetual disagreement of the United States with England was that England wanted to place barriers or difficulties in the way of this immigration, which they feared would turn its colonies into a colossus. Motives to settle in the United States are invoked in the colonists' Declaration of Independence. Take a look at that document, and then ask yourselves if mounting numbers of foreigners prevented the United States from winning its independence or from creating a great and powerful nation.

Religious tolerance: If you would like to have moral, religious settlers, don't encourage atheism. If you want families with their own individual ways, with their own special customs, then respect their religion and the tenets of their creeds. Reduced to Catholicism to the exclusion of other beliefs, Spanish America is a lonely and silent monastery. This is a fatal dilemma: either remain exclusively Catholic and sparsely populated; or populate and prosper by being tolerant in religious matters. To attract Anglo-Saxon peoples and settlers from Sweden and Switzerland and then to deny them the exercise of their religious beliefs is a form of hypocritical liberalism.

This is literally true: to exclude dissident religious sects from South America is to exclude the English, the Germans, the Swiss, North Americans who are not Catholics, that is to say, to exclude those settlers whom this continent needs most. To bring them here without their religion is to leave them without the features that help make them what they are. If people are not able to practice their beliefs, there is a real risk that they will become atheists.

Some intended policies violate common sense; one of these is to want population, families, and constructive mores and yet to make it difficult for settlers who are not Catholics to get married. To do so is to form an alliance between morality and prostitution. Since you are not able to destroy the invincible affinity of the sexes, what do you do about giving legitimacy to natural unions? Do you want to multiply concubines instead of wives, to destine our women to become the laughingstock of foreigners? To have babies born in America from such unions and be disadvantaged from the start is to fill our entire continent with gauchos and prostitutes. You would only promote sickness and impiety. This cannot be attempted in the name of Catholicism without insulting the magnificence of our noble church, a church that is capable of associating itself with all human progress. . . .

Inland immigration: Until now, European immigrants have settled along the coast, and from this fact comes the cultural superiority of the South American littoral over the interior provinces. . . .

The best way to introduce Europeans into the interior of our continent on a scale powerful enough to work a prodigious change in just a few years is by railroads, by navigable rivers, and by engaging in free trade. Europe comes to these distant regions on the wings of commerce and industry and is seeking the richness that our continent offers. Wealth, like population, like culture, is impossible when the means of communication are difficult, limited, and costly.

Wealth comes to our continent because of the opportunity offered by the ocean. Stretch out the ocean until it reaches the interior of this continent, by using steam engines on the land and on rivers, and you will have the interior as full of European immigrants as the coast is now.

Railroads: The railroad is the means of properly righting what colonizing Spain located upside down on this continent. She placed the heads of our states where the feet should be. To satisfy her aims of isolation and monopoly, that system made sense; for our expansion now, and for our commercial freedom, it is fatal. It is necessary to bring capital to our shores, to take the coast to our continent's interior. The railroad and the electric telegraph, which diminish space, bring about this marvel better than all the tycoons in the land. Railroads bring reforms and change the most difficult of situations, without either decrees or riots.

Railroads will unify the Argentine Republic better than all the congresses ever could. Congresses will then be able to declare the Republic one and indivisible. But, without a railroad system that extends to its remotest extremes, our country will always remain divisible and divided, despite all its legislative decrees. . . .

Without such powerful means of transportation you will not be able to bring to our provinces the kind of European stimulation that today regenerates our coastal regions. Immigrants are or will be to the local life of our territories what the great arteries are to the lower extremes of the human body, fountains of life. The Spaniards know this to be so; in the last years of their dominion over this continent they were seriously occupied with the construction of an interoceanic railroad across the Andes and the Argentine desert. Rivadavia was also deeply concerned by this same need and entertained the possibility of building a railroad.

Why do we regard as an impossible "utopia" the creation of a roadway that in another time preoccupied the Spanish government, so positive and parsimonious in its great works of improvements? . . .

Do we have insufficient capital for these enterprises? Then treat foreign capital as if it were our very own. Surround foreign capitalists with immunity from taxes and regulations, and give them privileges so that their money will be at home in our land.

South America needs capital as much as it needs population. An immigrant without funds is a soldier without weapons. Make pesos flow into these countries of future wealth and current poverty. But the peso too is an emigrant that demands many concessions and privileges. Grant foreign investors what they require; investment capital is the sure arm of progress for our countries. It is the secret on which the United States and Holland put such high value in order to give magic impetus to their industry and commerce. . . .

Interior navigation: Our great rivers, those moving paths, as Pascal called them, are another means of bringing the civilizing ways of European immigrants to the inner reaches of our continent. But rivers that are not navigated are like ones that do not exist. To keep them as the exclusive domain of our bands of impoverished and indigent peoples is to keep them unnavigable. For these rivers to fulfill their God-given destiny of populating the interior of this continent, we must establish the law of the seas, that is, waters where there is absolute freedom. God has not made our rivers great (like the Mediterranean Sea) just to be navigated by one family.

Proclaim the freedom of our waters. And, so that this may be permanent, so that the unstable hands of our governments do not take back today what they agreed to yesterday, sign perpetual treaties of free navigation. . . .

Do not be afraid either that our national identity will be compromised by the effect of numerous foreigners or that the national character will disappear. Such fear is meanspirited and preoccupied. A good deal of foreign blood has flowed in defense of South American independence. Montevideo, defended by foreigners, has deserved the name of New Troy. Valparaíso, made up of people who immigrated from other countries, is the luxurious Star of Chile. Of all nations, England has been the most conquered; all nations have tread on her soil and mixed their blood and race with hers. England is the product of all possible cross-breeding of castes, and, for just that reason, the English are the most perfect of men, and their nationality is so pronounced that it makes you believe that the common man is one integrated race.

Do not fear, then, the confusion of races and tongues. From Babel, from the chaos, there will emerge, some bright, fine day, the South American nationality. Our soil adopts men, it attracts and assimilates them and makes our land theirs. The emigrant is a colonist; he leaves the mother country for the country of his adoption. It was two thousand years ago that the words that form the motto of this century were first spoken: "Ubi patria, ubi bene." . . .

Victory will bring us laurels, but the laurel is a sterile plant for South America. A sprig of peace, which is golden, not in the language of poets, but in the language of economists, would be of more value. The epoch of heroes has passed; we are today entering into the age of good sense. The model of national greatness is not Napoléon; it is Washington. Washington represents, not military triumphs, but prosperity, exaltation, organization, and peace. He is the hero of the orderliness of freedom par excellence. . . .

To reduce a great mass of men to an eighth of its size in two hours by firing a cannon—that is the heroism of the past. In contrast, to multiply a small population in just a few days—that is the heroism of the modern statesman. The magnificence of creation in place of the savage magnitude of extermination. The population census will provide the measure of the accomplishment of the South American ministers of state.

Translated by Patricia Owen Steiner

III

Frontiers

As a political community, a nation is conceived as a delimited, horizontal comradeship, within which all its members should be considered equal. This emphasis on fraternity has prompted many authors to compare nations to large families, whose members willingly leave their differences aside for the sake of peaceful coexistence. Several of the texts in part II that advance utopian definitions of the Argentine nation draw parallels between family ties and national harmony. General San Martín's recommendations to his daughter and countrymen underscore this analogy by advising tolerance and respect for difference. In *Las bases,* Alberdi imagines modern Argentina as a contented family resulting from the loving union of immigrant men and Creole women. However, as history has repeatedly proved, political unity is always the result of brutal interventions. As much as it seeks to pull the scattered people of a given territory together, the creation of a national community inevitably releases strong centrifugal forces that strive to expel from society all that seems to challenge one or another group's dominant set of values and beliefs. Geographic as well as cultural frontiers are drawn and enforced largely by discriminatory practices ranging from the limitation of rights to total war. Complementing the readings of part II, which discuss different approaches to achieving a coherent national community, the readings in part III focus on the politics of the frontier as the basic mechanism controlling the violent movements of incorporation and exclusion—of territory, of people, of cultures and languages— that characterized the invention of modern Argentina.

The importance of the frontier to Argentine history is inextricably tied to the military campaigns that the state organized, first, to define its political boundaries with neighboring countries such as Paraguay and Chile that were also going through a process of nation building and, second, to take over the vast territories, like Patagonia, that were essentially controlled by rebellious Amerindian tribes. As was the case with the occupation of the West in the United States, conquering and developing frontier lands were deemed crucial for the economic future of a country that measured its strength by the size of its territory and the availability of natural resources.

According to the rationalist ideology driving territorial expansion — in many respects merely a modern version of colonialist arguments — the Amerindians, who were believed to embody racial inferiority, stood in the way of civilization and modernity. Argentina's nation builders perceived them as a people ignorant of how to exploit their land and burdened with a social organization that appeared utterly deficient compared to Western notions of society. The Amerindian tribes were therefore afforded no right to keep their territories. This implicit expansionist policy demanded their total surrender and, if necessary, extermination. Following his brief visit to the military frontier south of Buenos Aires, the British naturalist Charles Darwin rightly concluded that negotiating and signing treaties was often nothing more than an effective way for the central government to create discord among different Amerindian tribes and to obtain more time and resources for the national army. Colonel Lucio Mansilla's cynical account of his peace negotiations with the Ranquel Indians clearly illustrates that Amerindians found themselves in a very vulnerable position when forced to deal with a legal and cultural system that was not their own.

Frontier wars and the ideologically charged images of hideous Amerindian savages lying in wait just beyond the national border — images that legitimized state violence — suffused the debates on nation building during the nineteenth century. In this way, the frontier became the ultimate reference point for judging social conflicts in postcolonial Argentina. Insofar as literary fictions written at the time offer partial but insightful interpretations of social life, they confirm that frontiers existed, not only as lines on official maps marking political boundaries, but also as internal barriers separating the Creole elite from the local masses. In his political fictions, Esteban Echeverría ascribed to the gauchos and blacks that supported Rosas the same lack of civility and rationality attributed to Amerindian barbarism. For Echeverría, the half-breed gauchos were potentially dangerous hybrid monsters whose latent memory of the unredeemable savage waited to emerge and kill the innocent promoters of reason and progress. By denouncing the barbaric nature of the lower classes, literature tacitly urged their exclusion from the core of national society.

Written from a point of view sympathetic to the gauchos' cultural lifestyle, the poem *Martín Fierro* by José Hernández provides a compelling re-creation of how the gauchos might have experienced and reacted to frontier politics. Even though both the gauchos and the Amerindians were the target of persecutory state policies, the former were in a better position to negotiate than the latter. This meant that their resistance to state coercion did not prevent them from seeking out the advantages of citizenship. Thus, until they finally succumbed to the forces of assimilation, the gauchos variously occupied both sides of the physical and cultural frontier that gradually sealed the perimeter and homogenized the interior of the Argentine nation. Hernández's poem portrays the frontier as a mutable common space in which cultures at turns clash and intermingle. It was the unavoidable, albeit creative, tension within this contact zone that later on defined the essence of being Argentine in Borges's labyrinthine fictions.

The Slaughterhouse

Esteban Echeverría

Esteban Echeverría (1805–51) was a young Creole who, after five years of intellectual training in Paris, returned to Buenos Aires, where he promoted the social and aesthetic ideals of European Romanticism. Opposed to Rosas, he emigrated to Montevideo, Uruguay, during the dictator's reign. Echeverría's literary fictions, which exhibit the extreme contrasts and heavy strokes of his Romantic style, are powerful representations of the political, ethnic, and sexual tensions prevalent in Argentine society under Rosas. Through his fictions, Echeverría established the themes that would obsess many writers to come: the disgust and fascination provoked by the lower classes; the idea of the frontier as the limits of civilization; the racially and sexually charged body as a site of national controversy. Written in 1841 but published only in 1871, El matadero (The Slaughterhouse) is an explicit and passionate critique of the society that, according to Echeverría, grew out of Rosas's authoritarian and populist policies. In the selected passage, a violent horde of half-breed gauchos and black women, all fervent devotees of Rosas, torment and eventually murder a young, white, and educated Unitarist in a grisly scene reminiscent of rape. Fond of allegories, Echeverría makes a symbolic association between the animals destroyed at the slaughterhouse and the Unitarists who suffer through Rosas's repressive and violent reign. His emphasis on the race and gender of the Unitarist's persecutors reinforces the links that he establishes between barbarism and racial and sexual difference. Following its publication in 1871, El matadero became a national classic. The scene of gratuitous violence in which an educated man is humiliated by a savage torturer has reappeared time and again in a long series of interpretations ranging from Borges's philosophical fictions to popular comic-book images and stories.

. . . The Convalescencia, or Alto Slaughterhouse, is located in the southern part of Buenos Aires, on a huge lot, rectangular in shape, at the intersection of two streets, one of which ends there while the other continues eastward. The lot slants to the south and is bisected by a ditch made by the rains, its shoulders pitted with ratholes, its bed collecting all the blood from the slaughterhouse.

At the junction of the right angle, facing west, stands what is commonly called the *casilla,* a low building containing three small rooms with a porch in the front facing the street and hitching posts for tying the horses. In the rear are several pens of *ñandubay* picket fence with heavy doors for guarding the steers. In winter these pens become veritable mires in which the animals remain bogged down, immobile, up to the shoulder blades. In the *casilla* the pen taxes and fines for violation of the rules are collected, and in it sits the judge of the slaughterhouse, an important figure, the chieftain of the butchers, who exercises the highest power, delegated to him by the Restorer, in that small republic. It is not difficult to imagine the kind of man required for the discharge of such an office.

The *casilla* is so dilapidated and so tiny a building that no one would notice it were it not that its name is inseparably linked with that of the terrible judge and that its white front is pasted over with posters: "Long live the Federalists! Long live the Restorer and the Heroine Doña Encarnación Ezcurra! Death to the savage Unitarists!" Telling posters, indeed, symbolizing the political and religious faith of the slaughterhouse folk! But some readers may not know that the above-mentioned Heroine is the deceased wife of the Restorer, the beloved patroness of the butchers, who even after her death is venerated by them as if she were still alive because of her Christian virtues and her Federalist heroism during the Revolution against Balcarce. The story is that, during an anniversary of that memorable deed of the *mazorca,* the terrorist society of Rosas's henchmen, the butchers feted the Heroine with a magnificent banquet in the *casilla.* She attended, with her daughter and other Federalist ladies, and there, in the presence of a great crowd, she offered the butchers, in a solemn toast, her Federalist patronage, and for that reason they enthusiastically proclaimed her patroness of the slaughterhouse, stamping her name on the walls of the *casilla,* where it will remain until blotted out by the hand of time.

From a distance the view of the slaughterhouse was now grotesque, full of animation. Forty-nine steers were stretched out on their skins, and about two hundred people walked about the muddy, blood-drenched floor. Hovering around each steer stood a group of people of different skin colors. Most prominent among them was the butcher, a knife in his hand, his arms bare, his chest exposed, long hair disheveled, shirt and sash and face besmeared with blood. At his back, following his every movement, romped a gang of children, Negro and mulatto women, offal collectors whose ugliness matched that of the harpies, and huge mastiffs that sniffed, snarled, and snapped at one another as they darted after booty. Forty or more carts covered with awnings of blackened hides were lined up along the court, and some horsemen with their capes thrown over their shoulders and their lassos hanging from their saddles rode back and forth through the crowds or lay on their horses' necks, casting indolent glances on this or that lively group. In midair a flock of blue-white gulls, attracted by the smell of blood, fluttered about, drowning with strident cries all the other noises and voices at the slaughterhouse, and casting clear-cut shadows over that confused field of horrible butchery. All this could be observed at the very beginning of the slaughter.

But, as the activities progressed, the picture kept changing. While some groups dissolved as if some stray bullet had fallen nearby or an enraged dog had charged them, new groups constantly formed: here where a steer was being cut open, there where a butcher was already hanging the quarters on the hook in the carts, or yonder where a steer was being skinned or the fat taken off. From the mob eyeing and waiting for the offal there issued ever and anon a filthy hand ready to slice off meat or fat. Shouts and explosions of anger came from the butchers, from the incessantly milling crowds, and from the gamboling street urchins.

"Watch the old woman hiding the fat under her breasts," someone shouted.

"That's nothing—see that fellow there plastering it all over his behind," replied the old Negro woman.

"Hey there, black witch, get out of there before I cut you open," shouted a butcher.

"What am I doing to you, ño Juan? Don't be so mean! Can't I have a bit of the guts?"

"Out with the witch! Out with the witch!" the children squalled in unison. "She's taking away liver and kidneys!" And, with that, huge chunks of coagulated blood and balls of mud rained on her head.

Nearby, two Negro women were dragging along the entrails of an animal. A mulatto woman carrying a heap of entrails slipped in a pool of blood and fell lengthwise under her coveted booty. Farther on, huddled together in a long line, four hundred Negro women unwound heaps of intestines in their laps, picking off one by one those bits of fat that the butcher's avaricious knife had overlooked. Other women emptied stomachs and bladders and, after drying them, used them for depositing the offal.

Several boys gamboling about, some on foot, others on horseback, banged one another with inflated bladders or threw chunks of meat at one another, their noise frightening the cloud of gulls that celebrated the slaughtering in flapping hordes. Despite the Restorer's orders and the holiness of the day, filthy words were heard all around, shouts full of all the bestial cynicism that characterizes the populace attending our slaughterhouses—but I will not entertain the reader with all this dirt.

Suddenly a mass of bloody lungs would fall on somebody's head. He forthwith would throw it on someone else's head until some hideous mongrel picked it up as a pack of other mongrels rushed in, raising a terrific growl for little or no reason at all, and snapping at one another. Sometimes an old woman would run, enraged, after some ragamuffin who had smeared her face with blood. Summoned by his shouts, his comrades would come to his rescue, harassing her as dogs do a bull, and showering chunks of meat and balls of dung on her, accompanied by volleys of laughter and shrieks, until the Judge would command order to be restored.

In another spot, two young boys practicing the handling of their knives slashed at one another with terrifying thrusts, while, farther on, four lads, much more mature than the former, were fighting over some offal that they had filched from a butcher. Not far from them, some mongrels, lean from forced abstinence, struggled for a piece of kidney all covered with mud. All a representation in miniature of the savage ways in which individual and social conflicts are thrashed out in our country. . . .

Suddenly the raucous voice of a butcher was heard announcing: "Here comes a Unitarist!" On hearing that word, the mob stood still as if thunderstruck.

Can't you see his U-shaped side whiskers? Can't you see he carries no insignia on his coat and no mourning sash on his hat?"

"The Unitarist cur!"

"The son of a bitch!"

"He has the same kind of saddle as the gringo!"

"To the gibbet with him!"

"Give him the scissors!"

"Give him a good beating!"

"He has a pistol case attached to his saddle just to show off!"

"All these cocky Unitarists are as showy as the devil himself!"

"I bet you wouldn't dare touch him, Matasiete."

"He wouldn't, you say?"

"I bet you he would!"

Matasiete was a man of few words and quick action. When it came to violence, dexterity, skill in the handling of an ox, a knife, or a horse, he did not talk much, but he acted. They had piqued him; spurring his horse, he trotted away, bridle loose, to meet the Unitarist.

The Unitarist was a young man, about twenty-five years old, elegant, debonair of carriage, who, as the above-mentioned exclamations were spouting from these impudent mouths, was trotting toward Barracas, quite fearless of any danger ahead of him. Noticing, however, the significant glances of that gang of slaughterhouse curs, his right hand reached automatically for the pistol case of his English saddle. Then a side push from Matasiete's horse threw him from his saddle, stretching him out. Supine and motionless, he remained on the ground.

"Long live Matasiete!" shouted the mob, swarming on the victim.

Confounded, the young man cast furious glances on those ferocious men and, hoping to find in his pistol compensation and vindication, moved toward his horse, which stood quietly nearby. Matasiete rushed to stop him. He grabbed him by his tie, pulled him down again on the ground, and, whipping out his dagger from his belt, put it against his throat.

Loud guffaws and stentorian vivas cheered him.

What nobility of soul! What bravery, that of the Federalists! Always ganging together and falling like vultures on the helpless victim!

"Cut open his throat, Matasiete! Didn't he try to shoot you? Rip him open, like you did the bull!"

"What scoundrels these Unitarists! Thrash him good and hard!"

"He has a good neck for the 'violin' — you know, the gibbet!"

"Better use the Slippery-One on him!"

"Let's try it," said Matasiete, and, smiling, began to pass the sharp edge of his dagger around the throat of the fallen man as he pressed in his chest with his left knee and held him by the hair with his left hand.

"Don't behead him, don't!" shouted in the distance the slaughterhouse Judge as he approached on horseback.

"Bring him into the *casilla*. Get the gibbet and the scissors ready. Death to the savage Unitarists! Long live the Restorer of the laws!"

"Long live Matasiete!"

The spectators repeated in unison "Long live Matasiete! Death to the Unitarists!" They tied his elbows together as blows rained on his nose, and they shoved him around. Amid shouts and insults they finally dragged the unfortunate young man to the bench of tortures just as if they had been the executioners of the Lord themselves.

The main room of the *casilla* had in its center a big, hefty table, which was devoid of liquor glasses and playing cards only in times of executions and tortures administered by the Federalist executioners of the slaughterhouse. In a corner stood a smaller table with writing materials and a notebook and some chairs, one of which, an armchair, was reserved for the Judge. A man who looked like a soldier was seated in one of them, playing on his guitar the "Resbalosa," an immensely popular song among the Federalists, when the mob rushing tumultuously into the corridor of the *casilla* brutally showed in the young Unitarist.

"The Slippery-One for him!" shouted one of the fellows.

"Commend your soul to the devil!"

"He's furious as a wild bull!"

"The whip will tame him."

"Give him a good pummeling!"

"First the cowhide and scissors."

"Otherwise to the bonfire with him!"

"The gibbet would be even better for him!"

"Shut up and sit down," shouted the Judge as he sank into his armchair. All of them obeyed, while the young man standing in front of the Judge exclaimed with a voice pregnant with indignation:

"Infamous executioners, what do you want to do with me?"

"Quiet!" ordered the Judge, smiling. "There's no reason for getting angry. You'll see."

The young man was beside himself. His entire body shook with rage: his mottled face, his voice, his tremulous lips, evinced the throbbing of his heart and the agitation of his nerves. His fiery eyes bulged in their sockets, his long black hair bristled. His bare neck and the front of his shirt showed his bulging arteries and his anxious breathing.

"Are you trembling?" asked the Judge.

"Trembling with anger because I cannot choke you."

"Have you that much strength and courage?"

"I have will and pluck enough for that, scoundrel."

"Get out the scissors I use to cut my horse's mane and clip his hair in the Federalist style."

Two men got hold of him. One took his arms, and another his head and in a minute clipped off his side whiskers. The spectators laughed merrily.

"Get him a glass of water to cool him off," ordered the Judge.

"I'll have you drink gall, you wretch!"

A Negro appeared with a glass of water in his hand. The young man kicked his arm, and the glass smashed to bits on the ceiling, the fragments sprinkling the astonished faces of the spectators.

"This fellow is incorrigible!"

"Don't worry, we'll tame him yet!"

"Quiet!" said the Judge. "Now you are shaven in the Federalist style—all you need is a mustache. Don't forget to grow one!"

"Now, let's see: why don't you wear any insignia?"

"Because I don't care to."

"Don't you know that the Restorer orders it?"

"Insignia become you, slaves, but not free men!"

"Free men will have to wear them, by force."

"Indeed, by force and brutal violence. These are your arms, infamous wretches! Wolves, tigers, and panthers are also strong like you, and like them you should walk on all fours."

"Are you not afraid of being torn to pieces by the tiger?"

"I prefer that to having you pluck out my entrails, as the ravens do, one by one."

"Why don't you wear a mourning sash on your hat in memory of the Heroine?"

"Because I wear it in my heart in memory of my country, which you, infamous wretches, have murdered."

"Don't you know that the Restorer has ordered mourning in memory of the Heroine?"

"You, slaves, were the ones to order it so as to flatter your master and pay infamous homage to him."

"Insolent fellow! You are beside yourself. I'll have your tongue cut off if you utter one more word. Take the pants off this arrogant fool, and beat him on his naked ass. Tie him down on the table first!"

Hardly had the Judge uttered his commands when four bruisers bespattered with blood lifted the young man and stretched him out on the table.

"Rather behead me than undress me, infamous rabble!"

They muzzled him with a handkerchief and began to pull off his clothes. The young man wriggled, kicked, and gnashed his teeth. His muscles assumed now the flexibility of rushes, now the hardness of iron, and he squirmed like a snake in his enemy's grasp. Drops of sweat, large as pearls, streamed down his cheeks, his pupils flamed, his mouth foamed, and the veins on his neck and forehead jutted out black from his pale skin as if congested with blood.

"Tie him up," ordered the Judge.

"He's roaring with anger," said one of the cutthroats.

In a short while they had tied his feet to the legs of the table and turned his body upside down. In trying to tie his hands, the men had to unfasten them from behind his back. Feeling free, the young man, with a brusque movement that seemed to drain him of all his strength and vitality, raised himself up, first on his arms, then on his knees, and collapsed immediately, murmuring: "Rather behead me than undress me, infamous rabble!"

His strength was exhausted, and, having tied him down crosswise, they began undressing him. Then a torrent of blood spouted, bubbling from the young man's mouth and nose, and flowed freely down the table. The cutthroats remained immobile and the spectators astonished.

"The savage Unitarist has burst with rage," said one of them.

He had a river of blood in his veins," put in another.

"Poor devil, we wanted only to amuse ourselves with him, but he took things too seriously," exclaimed the Judge, scowling tiger-like.

"We must draw up a report. Untie him, and let's go!"

They carried out the orders, locked the doors, and in a short while the rabble went out after the horse of the downcast, taciturn Judge.

The Federalists had brought to an end one of their innumerable feats of valor.

Those were the days when the butchers of the slaughterhouse were apostles who propagated by dint of whip and poignard Rosas's federation, and it is not difficult to imagine what sort of federation issued from their heads and knives. They were wont to dub as savage Unitarists (in accordance with the jargon invented by the Restorer, patron of the brotherhood) any man who was neither a cutthroat nor a crook, any man who was kindhearted and decent, any patriot or noble friend of enlightenment and freedom; and from the foregoing episode it can be clearly seen that the headquarters of the federation were located in the slaughterhouse.

Translated by Angel Flores

Wars of Extermination

Charles Darwin

The opposition's frequent association of Rosas with the Amerindians was, besides being a derogatory commentary on his followers, also motivated by the feeling that Rosas was excessively lenient toward rebellious tribes, thereby significantly slowing the advance of civilization into the heart of the country. This perception was inaccurate. In Voyage of the Beagle *(1839), the British naturalist Charles Darwin describes some of the strategies that Rosas employed for confronting the Amerindians in the frontier wars. Following a method proved successful by the Spanish conquerors, Rosas took advantage of existing rivalries among the tribes by making selective deals with them. As a result of his policy, it was common to see Amerindians from one tribe serving as soldiers of the national army and persecuting Amerindians from an enemy tribe. Paradoxically, despite Darwin's revulsion at the excessive use of violence against women and children, his biological theories on racial war and the survival of the fittest would later lend legitimacy to the conquest and decimation of Argentina's last autonomous Amerindian tribes.*

During my stay at Bahía Blanca, while waiting for the *Beagle*, the place was in a constant state of excitement, from rumors of wars and victories, between the troops of Rosas and the wild Indians. One day an account came, that a small party forming one of the *postas* on the line to Buenos Aires, had been found all murdered. The next day, three hundred men arrived from the Colorado, under the command of Commandant Miranda. A large portion of these men were Indians (*mansos*, or tame), belonging to the tribe of the Cacique Bernantio. They passed the night here; and it was impossible to conceive any thing more wild and savage than the scene of their bivouac. Some drank till they were intoxicated; others swallowed the steaming blood of the cattle slaughtered for their suppers, and then, being sick from drunkenness, they cast it up again, and were besmeared with filth and gore.

> *Nam simul expletus dapibus, vinoque sepultus*
> *Cervicem inflexam posuit, jacuitque per antrum*

Angel della Valle, *The Return of the Indian Raid* (1892). Collection Museo Nacional de Bellas Artes.

Immensus, saniem cructans, ac frusta cruenta
Per somnum commixta mero.

In the morning they started for the scene of the murder, with orders to follow the *rastro*, or track, even if it led them to Chile. We subsequently heard that the wild Indians had escaped into the great pampas, and from some cause the track had been missed. One glance at the *rastro* tells these people a whole history. Supposing they examine the track of one thousand horses, they will soon guess by seeing how many have cantered the number of men; by the depth of the other impressions, whether any horses were loaded with cargoes; by the irregularity of the footsteps, how far tired; by the manner in which the food has been cooked, whether the pursued traveled in haste; by the general appearance, how long it has been since they passed. They consider a *rastro* of ten days or a fortnight, quite recent enough to be hunted out. We also heard that Miranda struck from the west end of the Sierra Ventana, in a direct line to the island of Cholechel, situated seventy leagues up the Río Negro. This is a distance of between two and three hundred miles, through a country completely unknown. What other troops in the world are so independent? With the sun for their guide, mares' flesh for food, their saddle-cloths for beds — as long as there is a little water, these men would penetrate to the land's end.

A few days afterward I saw another troop of these banditti-like soldiers start on an expedition against a tribe of Indians at the small salinas, who had been betrayed by a prisoner cacique. The Spaniard who brought the orders for this expedition was a very intelligent man. He gave me an account of the last engagement at which he was present. Some Indians, who had been taken prisoners, gave information of a tribe living north of the Colorado. Two hundred soldiers were sent; and they first discovered the Indians by a cloud of dust from their horses' feet, as they chanced to be traveling. The country was mountainous and wild, and it must have been far in the interior, for the Cordillera was in sight. The Indians, men, women, and children, were about 110 in number, and they were nearly all taken or killed, for the soldiers saber every man. The Indians are now so terrified, that they offer no resistance in a body, but each flies, neglecting even his wife and children; but when overtaken, like wild animals, they fight against any number to the last moment. One dying Indian seized with his teeth the thumb of his adversary, and allowed his own eye to be forced out, sooner than relinquish his hold. Another, who was wounded, feigned death, keeping a knife ready to strike one more fatal blow. My informer said, when he was pursuing an Indian, the man cried out for mercy, at the same time that he was covertly loosing the bolas from his waist, meaning to whirl it round his head and so strike his pursuer. "I however struck him with my saber to the ground, and then got off my horse, and cut his throat with my knife." This is a dark picture; but how much more shocking is the unquestionable fact, that all the women who appear above twenty years old, are massacred in cold blood. When I exclaimed that this appeared rather inhuman, he answered, "Why, what can be done? They breed so!"

Every one here is fully convinced that this is the most just war because it is against barbarians. Who would believe in this age, in a Christian civilized country, that such atrocities were committed? The children of the Indians are saved, to be sold or given away as servants, or rather slaves, for as long a time as the owners can deceive them; but I believe in this respect there is little to complain of.

In the battle four men ran away together. They were pursued, and one was killed, but the other three were taken alive. They turned out to be messengers or ambassadors from a large body of Indians, united in the common cause of defense, near the Cordillera. "The tribe to which they had been sent was on the point of holding a grand council; the feast of mare's flesh was ready, and the dance prepared: in the morning the ambassadors were to have returned to the Cordillera. They were remarkably fine men, very fair, above six feet high, and all under thirty years of age. The three survivors of course possessed very valuable information; and to extort this they were placed in a line. The two first being questioned, answered, 'No se' (I do not know), and were one after the other shot. The third also said, 'No se', adding, 'Fire, I am a man, and can die!' Not one syllable would they breathe to injure the united cause of their country! The conduct of the cacique was very different: he saved his life by betraying the intended plan of warfare, and the point of union in the Andes. It was believed that there were already six or seven hundred Indians together, and that in summer their numbers would be doubled. Ambassadors were to have been sent to the Indians at the small salinas, near Bahía Blanca, whom I mentioned that a cacique, this same man, had betrayed. The communication, therefore, extends from the Cordillera to the east coast.

General Rosas's plan is to kill all stragglers, and having driven the remainder to a common point, in the summer, with the assistance of the Chilenos, to attack them in a body. This operation is to be repeated for three successive years. I imagine the summer is chosen as the time for the main attack, because the plains are then without water, and the Indians can only travel in particular directions. The escape of the Indians to the south of the Río Negro, where in such a vast unknown country they would be safe, is prevented by a treaty with the Tehuelches to this effect — that Rosas pays them so much to slaughter every Indian who passes to the south of the river, but if they fail in so doing, they themselves are to be exterminated. The war is waged chiefly against the Indians near the Cordillera; for many of the tribes on this eastern side are fighting with Rosas. The general, however, like Lord Chesterfield, thinking that his friends may in a future day become his enemies, always places them in the front ranks, so that their numbers may be thinned. Since leaving South America we have heard that this war of extermination completely failed.

Among the captive girls taken in the same engagement, there were two very pretty Spanish ones, who had been carried away by the Indians when young, and could now only speak the Indian tongue. From their account, they must have come from Salta, a distance in a straight line of nearly one thousand miles. This gives one a grand idea of the immense territory over which the Indians roam: yet, great as it is, I think there will not, in another half century, be a wild Indian northward of the Río Negro. The warfare is too bloody to last; the Christians killing every Indian, and the Indians doing the same by the Christians. It is melancholy to trace how the Indians have given way before the Spanish invaders.

The Triple Alliance

Captain Francisco Seeber

The War of the Triple Alliance (1864–70), in which Argentina and Uruguay joined imperial Brazil against Paraguay, is believed to have been one of the bloodiest and most costly conflicts in the history of postcolonial Latin America. The ostensible reason for declaring war was the apparently urgent need to overthrow the Paraguayan dictator Solano López, who allegedly oppressed his people and displayed an aggressive international policy toward neighboring countries. But there was more involved than humanitarian concerns or the need for a counteroffensive. The terms of the secret treaty signed by Brazil, Argentina, and Uruguay in 1866 leave little doubt as to Brazil and Argentina's desires to extend their boundaries. Despite Argentina's territorial gains, the public's response at the war's end was mixed. It was true that the Paraná River became permanently open to international commerce and that the territorial dispute over the province of Misiones was eventually decided in Argentina's favor. But the great loss of lives and the immense drain on economic resources were never forgotten. The war had never been a popular one. The troops' poor training and a lack of clear national interest caused many desertions and drew a wave of harsh criticism from many prominent national figures. From 1866 to 1867, in a series of letters to his friend Santiago Alcorta, Captain Francisco Seeber wrote a detailed and ambivalent account of the front. The letter reprinted here is about the disaster at Curupaytí, a battle on 22 September 1866 in which more than two thousand Argentine soldiers and officers died. Seeber blames the massacre on the outdated weapons of the Argentine army, the strategic errors made during the counteroffensive, and the miscommunication between Brazilian and Argentine commanding officers. Horrified by the slaughter, he denounces this nonsensical war between countries that should have been partners, not enemies.

Camp Curuzú, 28 September 1866

Dear Friend:

You must already know about the great disaster we suffered on the twenty-second, but not in all its sad details. The losses for the Argentine army are 5 commanding officers, 27 other officers, and 666 troops, all dead; 11 commanding officers, 97 officers, and 1,044 troops wounded; 1 commanding officer, 23 officers, 151 troops slightly wounded; and 155 dispersed. In all, our casualties come to 2,078 men. The Brazilians have had more or less the same losses. On the other hand, their naval squadron did not lose more than 21 men. López, the Paraguayan tyrant, took his revenge for Tuyutí, where he had lost 15,000 men. He caused the allies to lose 3,600 men there, although in the assault he lost less than 100 men.

As in all battles, there have been acts of heroism, but our soldiers have been pistol-whipped because they were unable to overcome the difficulties that the enemy set on us. Mostly our problems were due to the special conditions of the terrain. A lot of time was lost in the attack, and this permitted the enemy to reinforce its defenses. Once more the grave disadvantage of a divided command was evident: the Brazilian naval squadron operated on its own, and Admiral Tamandaré neither obeyed nor debated the orders of the general in charge of the allied forces. The squadron is composed of thirty vessels, among them four battleships with 101 guns. The plan was to undertake the attack with twenty thousand men after the naval squadron had stilled the fire of the fifty cannons (which were defending Curupaytí) and opened breaches. It was a sensible plan and one that should have brought results.

Admiral Tamandaré promised to carry out this work in two hours, but few believed him. When Tamandaré had made similar promises in Country Pass, Field Marshal Osorio always doubted what he said. On land we made the mistake of not having, between the Brazilians and the Argentines, more than twenty-four pieces of small-caliber cannon. Once again the defeat was due more to our own error than to the very capable actions of the enemy. Before giving you the dreadful details of this doomed attack, I have to tell you about some small matters of importance.

On the thirteenth we disembarked, leaving Tuyutí after the peace negotiations initiated by López broke down. On the tenth, the dictator, López, had asked General Mitre for a meeting, and it took place the twelfth in Yataity-Cora, in the presence of General Flores. It seemed strange to me that Polidoro was not there. Apparently, the Paraguayan López intended to make peace advances, but I believe, as does General Flores, that his real intention was to gain time in order to fortify Curupaytí. After Curuzú was taken, he must have suspected an attack.

Accompanied by a grand cortege, López arrived on a white horse, wearing a bright red poncho with gold fringe. General Mitre was dressed in his general's uniform and cap, and General Flores, for the first time in the campaign, put on his uniform and a tall fur hat. López tried to make a deal with the Argentines and the Uruguayans so that they would let him fight only with the Brazilians. To General Mitre he announced: "If you leave me alone with the Brazilians, I'll make mincemeat of them." It is not surprising that this ostentatious tyrant, who has wanted to dominate in the South American balance of power, would like to conquer Brazil, a rich and more civilized country that has ten times the population of Paraguay. General Mitre answered López that he would not listen to any peace proposals except under conditions that would recognize the treaty of the triple alliance of Argentina, Brazil, and Uruguay.

López refused to enter into any such arrangements. He assured General Mitre that he would keep on fighting the war, that it would be very long, and that he was governing a fanatic people who would resist until the extreme end. Mitre brought the conference to a close by exchanging a whip with him. Mitre also proposed to General Flores that he exchange something with López, but Flores answered: "I want to exchange nothing with the field marshal." "A cigar maybe?" replied López. "I smoke my own," was the dry and perhaps ungracious reply of this experienced warrior who, although lacking in formal education, abounded in sagacity and perspicacity. Perhaps there was some resentment because López accused him of being the cause of the war.

López took precautions. Fearing that his enemies might ambush him, he hid troops near the entrance. His men detained Major Díaz, the attorney for the Argentine army, as well as another lawyer, and they tortured them until they eventually died. Then López's troops tracked down a number of Paraguayans who were in the allied army and killed them brutally. . . .

The assault on Curupaytí would have taken place the seventeenth. This was combined with a demonstration in Tuyutí by Field Marshal Polidoro and an attack by General Flores on the Paraguayan left flank and rear guard. Distances, although not enormous, were interrupted by immense stands of trees and wide, deep streams. The engineer Chodasewitz told me that it was possible to communicate from lookouts with banners by day and Bengali lights at night. I understand that, by means of the banners and by using the river, there existed a low level of communication.

The morning of the seventeenth we were all in position with the ammunition that soldiers have to carry in their knapsacks. We were waiting for the order to advance, but then we were ordered to retreat. The squadron signaled that it couldn't begin the bombardment because of the cloudy weather and the threat of rain. At eleven o'clock the order to advance was given, and we once again took up our arms. It was a reconnaissance mission, not yet a general attack. This decision surprised me: a reconnaissance had recently been made, before the suspended attack. After we had been walking for a short while there was a torrential downpour, as only these regions know. There wasn't a dry shred of clothing among us, and our knapsacks were caked with mud. Even the cartridges in our defective cartridge belts got soaked. . . .

On the night of the twenty-first we found ourselves in front of Roseti's tent in the company of Majors Fuentes and Lora, Captains Morel and Garmendia e Iarraguirre, and Lieutenant Solier. Roseti told us in so many words: "Companions, tomorrow we are going to be routed. The Paraguayans are heavily entrenched, they have a battery of fifty cannons, the front is defended by tree trunks interlaced with spiny branches, the terrain is swampy for the most part, there are scattered deep holes, and the hills and escarpments are very steep. Our artillery is weak and insignificant. The enemy positions have not been sufficiently explored, and, above all, trenches have not been dug so that we can approach them without incurring unfortunate losses. The squadron will not be able to maneuver efficiently because the banks of the river are very high. I have the premonition that I will be one of the first to fall and that they will shoot me down with a bullet to the stomach. I have already told Major Fuentes to be prepared to replace me."

You can imagine how unpleasant these predictions were, and all the more so when the next day, before the attack, we were told that Major Laprade, the brother-in-law of Colonel Santa Cruz, had told Colonel Arredondo that he had found out that the Paraguayans were ensconced behind a barricade of dry corn kernels. He concluded that we ought not to attack without first trying to destroy those obstacles that would be fatal to us, in fact, even for the best army in the world.

Beginning early in the morning of the twenty-second the thunder of cannon from the squadron and the Paraguayan batteries was heard. It appears that Admiral Tamandaré had agreed to hoist a red and white banner when he had determined that our side had caused the enemy sufficient damage that the infantry could launch an attack. . . .

The Argentine troops in general were well dressed. The commanding officers and other officers were in full dress. With their flaming colors, their gleaming decorations, right down to their shoes of white glove leather, they were making a show of their courage and impatiently waiting for the signal to attack.

At twelve noon Admiral Tamandaré, after infernal cannon fire from both sides, raises the banner. It was supposed that the fire of enemy batteries would have been somewhat silenced. With shouts of frenetic enthusiasm, the Brazilians and the Argentines impetuously plunge into the charge. Their legendary valor makes them think little of their own lives; they are thinking of the honor of their country and the glory of their banner. The brilliance of their eyes lends confidence to the dream of victory.

The commanding officers and the line officers outdo one another in their

ardor for battle, and they lead their troops along the shortest route to conquer the enemy. The obstacles that they encounter, however, are greater than
predicted. The fifty enemy cannons don't cease firing for a single instant; our
bombardment has not managed to demolish even one of them. Well-placed
grain fields have broken up the unity of the attackers, the smoke of smoldering
grasslands has reduced visibility to zero, the water in the streams has made
the march impossible, and the fire of three thousand enemy infantry bring
numerous and continuous casualties.

Despite all this, we reach the first trench, and the enemy retreats to the second one. Part of our forces advance to the second wide trench, which was deep
and full of water. They want to use ladders, but these do not work for the most
part. They are fiercely beaten back hand-to-hand. Man after man falls, but the
sacrifice becomes totally useless.

After a bloody struggle of two hours in which enemy grenades, shrapnel,
and cannon balls have decimated our troops, sweeping away entire companies
and severely thinning our ranks, the order to retreat came. But a few moments
later the order was given to renew the attack. Rivas and Arredondo consulted
together, and they looked at each other in confusion because disaster seemed
a sure thing. But they carried out the order without hesitation and in a military
fashion. . . .

The orderly retreat of our troops, in a state of complete exhaustion after four
hours of bloody combat and with so many men sacrificed without inflicting
any damage on the enemy, finally took place. . . .

Those who were close to this Homeric battle described in somber colors
the spectacle that they observed with their own eyes: the ground was stained
with blood; the water had a rosy tint because of the blood that was running
from the bodies of thousands of dead and wounded men. The cries of the men
in intense pain, the incessant thunder of enemy cannons (which only increased
the number of our fallen), and the decimated, worn-out batallions gave the
whole scene a terrifying look.

At this point General Paunero approaches and is shocked to see a young
man of some eighteen years with the cap of a lieutenant colonel. It was Lieutenant Sebastián Casares who put the cap of the dead Alejandro Díaz over
his own hat. "Here they are, General, the four banners." He is accompanied
by only sixty men. General Paunero, so serene at moments of great danger,
cannot help reacting with emotion when he sees those batallions with their
glorious traditions in such a devastated condition. Would that the blood of
so many heroes, spilled so cruelly, might have the virtue of Ajax's blood and
make hyacinths grow and serve as a lesson for all Latin Americans, who should
be living quietly in peace and harmony, devoting themselves to the work of

Cándido López, *After the Battle of Curupaytí* (1893), detail. Collection Museo Nacional de Bellas Artes.

making productive their extensive land that is as fertile as it is unpopulated and uncultivated. . . .

After evening prayers we all retired to our encampments profoundly moved. In the beginning we had expected to be covered with the laurels of victory; now our only feeling was the anguish of defeat, the painful remembrance of the heroes who had lost their lives, and the eternal suffering of the friends who valiantly succumbed. Our sole consolation for such misfortune was that military honor had been maintained throughout the battle, in all its proud splendor.

On 24 May we committed the same error as the Paraguayans by attacking the enemy's most vulnerable positions. Also we did not observe the fundamental principles of the art of war concerning locations and attacks on fortified positions. Nor did we establish the necessary lines to facilitate the attack and to cut off any reinforcements that the enemy might be expecting.

The Argentine medical corps lent its humanitarian services, establishing, as was the custom, its ambulances right under enemy fire. Doctors Bedoya, Molina, Biedma, and Golfarini cared for the numerous wounded with ability and devotion. Biedma and Golfarini accompanied the wounded aboard the steamship *Jupiter;* the care of General Rivas was entrusted to Golfarini.

After we retreated, Juan Francisco Vivot was given the dangerous assignment of taking the shortest route to communicate to Polidoro the details of our defeat. A Paraguayan soldier showed him a path through the stand of trees. The darkness of night saved him, for there were moments when he passed so close to the Paraguayans that he could hear their voices quite clearly.

Before the horror of a new "banquet of beef jerky," Martín, José María Bustos, and I boarded the National Guard ship, where we had the chance to see wounded friends who were aboard, and we were given a splendid meal by Amancio Alcorta and Pepe Murature, which in a campaign is a very important matter.

Yesterday I asked General Mitre for permission to go down to Buenos Aires for urgent family reasons. While I was in Corrientes and despairing of almost all hope, I had refused to go down to the city, despite the insistence of my noble friend Dr. Caupolicán Molina. So it bothered me at first when the general denied me permission. But he was right because I did not present myself properly, and, besides, the way things are going now (by giving permission for so many others to leave), the army will be left without any officers.

Translated by Patricia Owen Steiner

One Hundred Leagues of Trench

Alfred Ebélot

A constant worry of the Argentine central government was how to secure most effectively the frontier along the southern line of settlements. Among the many official means to "solve" the so-called Amerindian problem, surely the most extravagant was conceived by Adolfo Alsina, a minister in President Avellaneda's administration. His plan was to dig a trench, two and a half meters deep and three meters wide, that would extend six hundred miles from the Atlantic coast to the Andes. As a demarcation of the limits of civilization and a barrier to the Indians, Alsina saw the ditch as an effective way to protect the frontier. In 1870, he hired Alfred Ebélot (1839–1920), a French engineer who headed Alsina's project throughout the military campaign against the Indians that extended from 1876 to 1880. Ebélot wrote a series of articles for the Revue des deux mondes *on his experiences in Argentina that were later published together as a travelog. In his account, Ebélot depicts the digging of the trench as a symbolic enterprise that allowed him to study Argentine social customs and the vicissitudes of frontier life in a country struggling toward modernization.*

The new tactics adopted by the Argentine Republic toward the Indians have turned out well. A campaign abandoned twenty years ago has finally come to a close with little expense. It called only for more energy than sacrifices; moving the frontier was exactly the right thing to do. The popular imagination, which so enjoys theatrical effects, at first exaggerated the difficulties but later found nothing better than the exaggerated results.

It was after the basic triumph over the Indians that the unpleasant and laborious enterprise of excavating a defensive trench began. To construct defense works that would protect the new frontier, and to enable the cavalry to compete in speed with the Indians, was more difficult than merely to be daring and to penetrate into little-known regions and occupy open positions that the Indians were not able to hold against our firearms. For there appeared to be obstacles much greater than the Indians' long lances and their rough rudiments of military organization. The construction of a defensive trench presented several problems: raising scarce money, finding well-mounted cavalry, struggling against detestable but inveterate habits that formed part of the national character. If the beginning of the excavation of the trench demanded solidity of purpose, its completion called for even more patient and meritorious strength of will.

The trench that the government planned to excavate along the new frontier would extend for four hundred kilometers, with an opening 2.60 meters wide and 1.75 meters deep. The slope of the trench had been determined to conform with the land so as to avoid any crumbling of the earth. The width at the bottom would be 0.5 meters. Above the trench would be an adobe parapet 1 meter high, against which some of the earth that had been removed would be packed. This parapet would form a barrier that would be covered with a thick barricade of spiny bushes. Wherever the floor was covered by rocks, the trench would be reinforced by a terreplein supported by two adobe walls.

Although the trench might not prevent the Indians from crossing over into Argentine territory, it was enough to prevent them from escaping with the sheep and horses that they had stolen, and without horses the Indians would not be mad enough to attempt an invasion.

Considering the vastness of this grassy frontier, it was difficult work to engineer the digging of the defensive trench that its planners considered necessary. Armies of excavators had to be sent to the heart of the desert in order to accomplish the work of removing 2 million cubic meters of earth. But, alas, the appropriation voted by Congress, not just for the trench itself, but for all the expenses involved in its construction, did not exceed 700,000 francs. That was all the money that could be provided because a state of economic crisis continued to assault the country. The government, feeling more pinched all the time, was living on loans from the Provincial Bank, which a little while earlier had suspended the conversion of its currency. But this did not make the excavators invest less courage in the construction of the trench; the men charged with reorganizing the frontier were convinced that it was important to begin the work. They reasoned that you can never reach your goal unless you make a start.

In order to begin the construction of the trench and its foundations, a citizens commission was immediately named, a requirement for all public works. The Argentine Republic does not have a well-organized public administration: it is supplied by volunteers. This has both its good and its bad sides. The government appoints a certain number of reputable people who are charged to work as directors of the projected works and to do this without compensation, for reasons of patriotism and vanity. Once such commissions are in place, they carry out the projects according to their own ability. They approve contracts, buy materials, keep accounts for the contractors. Such commissions are made up of large landowners, representatives of established businesses, wealthy ranchers living in the city, important dealers in leather, and buyers of raw wool. Their great wealth is considered to be a sufficient guarantee of their honesty, and their commercial acumen is taken as a token of their ability. . . .

The frontier commission was full of zeal and rectitude, but that did not stop it from choosing strange employees from time to time. One of those, bolstered by patronage from high places, quietly established a country store in one of the settlements that began to grow up around the main encampments. From the counter in this store, he directed the work under his charge. Some of the articles he sold were the same as those he should have provided free to the workers as part of their rations. No guarantee except his conscience assured that the property of the store would not be confused with the state's property. Evidently, he overstepped the bounds of tolerable audacity, and the state should have deprived itself of the services of a man who showed such a decided dedication to his business. But, while actually quite indignant, the commission as a whole basically looked the other way: the man was protected by one of its members. The commission tried to make him resign but left it up to him. He took his time and just increased his activities when his first profits permitted him to expand. Their sad philosophy seemed to be that one has to be savvy to become wealthy.

Among the Argentines, lucky speculations are a good thing. Making money is for them an avid ambition. But they certainly do not hoard it; honestly or dishonestly earned, money is tossed around with equal disregard. They use the excuse that they are not preoccupied with money. And yet their anxiety in managing money is so great that on certain occasions it clouds their ideas about the limits between the just and the unjust. Their familiar language expresses this in a blatant way. It uses euphemistic words to describe manipulations of business that our old society, raised on saner traditions, would have treated with a less benign epithet. . . .

It has to be said that this indulgence of speculators does not prevent one from finding people who love probity as cats do cleanliness, for its own sake. The Argentine Republic gives great importance to a high level of education and has had the wisdom on two consecutive occasions to elect as its leaders presidents who called themselves educators rather than politicians. Education, which is free in all grades, has been for ten years the major preoccupation of the chiefs of state. But, as this widely diffused system of education attempts to obliterate ignorance, it needs to have its goals and must react against the despicable aspirations of the mercantile class. The driving passion to make money, and the morality that this encourages, can produce the material prosperity of an agglomerate of merchants, but it does not promote the virtues that are the pride of the people and their true strength.

The frontier commission began its work bursting with enthusiasm, and from the beginning it found ways to accomplish a great deal with little money. It decided to employ four regiments to work on the trench, that is, about eight hundred men from the national guard who were mobilized explicitly for this project. The national guard is one of the most notable innovations of South American republics. Everyone is part of it, and in just a few days it can put a nation on its feet. The object is to place a nation's institutions and territory under the protection of its citizens. Nothing seems more democratic or more protective of the people's security — in the beginning. In application, it deserves a closer look.

Initially, the national guard was an instrument of continual disorder, and it was in vain that the constitution surrounded the consolidation of rural militias with precautions. An audacious act, illegal though frequent, allowed an ambitious person in a province to take control of a vast machine. To accomplish this, it was enough just to have battalions running through the fields brandishing their lances and proclaiming some kind of political program.

This was jokingly called a *patriada,* a show of patriotism, either because of the abuse done by long discourses about the country and patriotism or because it also referred to the roughshod confiscation of horses from neighboring properties. The horses instantly lost half an ear; this mutilation was to *patriar* the horses, that is, to consecrate them, most decidedly, to the service of the country and to transform them into those melancholy old nags that the soldiers, with daring ellipsis, called *patrias.* Such was the most current result of that "raising of shields" or, to also use a local expression, that "raising of ponchos" that happily belonged to ancient history.

During the war against the Indians, the regular army, which the government had intended to disband, acquired a practical importance. Although this importance was prematurely negated in theory, it will prevail until the political education of Argentina is completed. For now it offers the Congress, the regulator of the complicated mechanism of the autonomous provinces, the means of making them obey its decisions.

The ways of the *patriada* have now passed, together with the hope of seeing the national guard disbanded once and for all after months and months of galloping skirmishes. But the national guard has not ceased being an indirect instrument of tremendous power in the hands of the political parties. It is the influence that throws its weight, first one way, then another, in each of the elections. No one would have suspected that this visible and armed institution, which was voted in by citizens, would actually serve to strip citizens of their right to vote. But that is how things happen.

With a certain frequency, contingents were raised with the idea of legal and regular service, for example, to guard the frontier, to support frontline troops with a reserve detachment, and even to take part—as in the case with which we are concerned here—in military works of excavation and terrepleins. This last activity is the most unexpected; perhaps a student of ethics, with the constitution in one hand, would be able to raise doubts as to the validity of a decree that imposed such work on the national guard. In reality it is one of the easiest things that the government has had to do in some time.

Besides the pay provided by the provincial government, workers on the trench received a salary of thirty francs per month, and, a rare thing, they were paid regularly. The frontier commission in charge of their maintenance made it a point of honor that the trench workers wanted for nothing in regard to equipment and food. In the annals of the national guard that also is a rare phenomenon. But, in reality, almost always detachments that are ordered to far-off places by indebted, distracted provincial governments are abandoned and must look after themselves as best they can. After months, sometimes years, of that fatalistic resignation that the Argentines have inherited from their Moorish ancestors, such detachments solve their problems by desertion. After a time the corps melts away like snow; the time varies according to circumstances and, above all, depending on its leader. If they are apprehended, the deserters are sent to the front line as a punishment. But few are captured. A gaucho on his horse on the open plains is almost impossible to overtake, and he can count on discreet hospitality from any ranch. The wealthy bourgeoisie applies the law in its own way and understands that the fugitive has good reason to be escaping from some iniquitous and unjustified corporal punishment. . . .

Eight hundred men were reduced to six hundred before they ever got to the trench, for in this type of business you have to expect losses. At the time the national guard left for the frontier, some of the soldiers were freed because a highly placed individual had recommended their release. Others were freed on their own because of desertion. Of those who got as far as the trench site, two-thirds worked on excavations and the rest on military operations or diverse camp duties. Many of the men were used for the personal service of military officers.

The members of the national guard excavated more than a kilometer of trench a day. In the beginning they showed great repugnance for the work that was so contrary to that to which they were accustomed. They considered it "standing" work, that is to say, servile, and fine for foreign manual laborers who were incapable of getting back on a horse after being thrown or of skinning a wild horse. Soon, however, they began to take to the work, and, because they realized that they were being well treated, they went on with it quite happily. They were not difficult to please since few of them have ever been treated well. The regularity of their pay and rations was a pleasant surprise. They had country stores and very luxurious accommodations, and, at night, around a fire fed by dried dung, savoring their mate and accompanied on the guitar, they would improvise songs about their happy life (long ballads roughly versified with joyful words, a pitiful rhythm, and insufferable monotony). This was for them, aside from the times when they were drunk, the truest expression of their happiness.

Furthermore, these men have done a greater service to the frontier than simply embellishing it with a deep trench. They contributed significantly to keeping the Indians under control at the same time that they were working. Divided into two corps, to the north and south of the line, these militarily organized workers were on guard as in a campaign and frequently went off to the desert on reconnaissance missions. Covering a vast front, they reduced the amount of territory that the regular troops had to protect. This permitted the line troops to focus their attention and force on the most vulnerable places. Because of their location, the workers were able to drive back the Indians and, with threatening swords, make them turn around just as they were intending to cross the frontier.

Its equal has never been seen. The cloud of savage horsemen with all their agility had always made fun of the army's vigilance and persecution. Only when an Indian invasion was disturbed by the animals that they were herding was it possible for the army to reach its goal and take prisoners. The success of the new frontier policy is all the more notable since, realizing that they were fighting for their survival, the Indians redoubled their forces, their daring, and their courage. Recently, not only have they relentlessly explored the frontier from one end to the other to take advantage of the least relaxation of vigilance, but they have also tried to penetrate the frontier by using truly strategic operations, cleverly conceived and effectively carried out.

During this past month of April, the Indians decided to attack the southern coastal section of the frontier and deployed a sizable group of warriors against Puan, the principal encampment. They were hoping that, thanks to this diversion, the bulk of their warriors could invade territory farther away. The attacking group was destroyed. The detachment of Indian warriors that was stealthily advancing with a force of eight hundred lances was about to be cut in two and had to escape to the pampa. But it defended itself with such tenacity that some fifty Indians were left dead on the field, and there must have been considerably more who were wounded.

Hardened frontline troops would not have fought with greater furor.

The savages' ways of fighting are not the same as in earlier times. They no longer charge with deafening shouts. Their combat is silent; only the voice of the leader is heard and the trumpet that sounds the orders. The few deserters who have taken refuge with them, plus the reinforcements who have had experience with white men who have fought in open country, have no doubt helped teach the Indians the strategy of warfare. But it is misery, above all, that has so rapidly perfected their military education. To stop them from plundering is to cut off their livelihood. Poor devils! They do what they can.

Translated by Patricia Owen Steiner

Gauchos in and out of the State

José Hernández

Martín Fierro, *by José Hernández (1834–86), is a long poem in two parts,* The Gaucho Martín Fierro *(1872) and* The Return of Martín Fierro *(1879). Although the author was highly educated, the poem assumes the voice of a gaucho, Martín Fierro, a rural worker who narrates in verse his misadventures at the hands of arbitrary and cruel state officials during the years of political and economic modernization that followed Rosas's fall. In the first part of the poem, Fierro is an outlaw who rebels against the state's biased legal system, which curtailed the gauchos' freedom by tricking them into military service. Disillusioned with modern law, Fierro eventually defects from the bondages of civilized society and joins the Amerindian tribes just beyond the frontier. In the second part, he comes back to find the country transformed by progress. On being reunited with his sons, Fierro changes his attitude toward the state and advises them to obey the law and assimilate into modern society. According to the Argentine critic Josefina Ludmer, the contradiction between the first and the second parts of the poem may explain why it eventually became a national classic. Given the plurality of interpretations that it allows, different readers could identify with the most disparate political messages. The popular classes found an argument that protested the violence that the modern state inflicted on the poor by forcing them to work for others or to risk their own lives fighting in the army. The educated classes also saw themselves represented in the poem, particularly in the second part. In celebrating a gauchesque world that, however heroic, must capitulate to modernization,* Martín Fierro *endorsed the supremacy of the bourgeois values preached by Argentina's ruling classes.*

THE GAUCHO MARTÍN FIERRO

IX

So for many a day I roamed around;
To a house I never went in;
I sometimes drew near a ranch by day,
With my eyes well skinned for a getaway,

In case the police should be hiding there —
For I knew they were after my skin.

Like a hunted fox the gaucho lives,
That has got himself into a scrape,
Till some day he's off his guard, or rash,
And the dogs are on him like a flash;
For no matter how well a man can ride,
From a fall he'll not escape.

At the peaceful hour of the afternoon,
When everything seems to doze;
When the winds lie down on the prairie's breast,
And the whole wide world seems to turn to rest;
To some swamp or brake, with his load of care,
Ucho goes.

By the side of the white and woolly sheep,
The lamb bleats as it goes;
From the tether rail the calf calls out
To the cow that's grazing round about;
But the gaucho has never a friendly ear
To list to his tale of woes.

So when evening fell I would take me off,
And some resting place I found me;
From where the puma can make its den,
A man can hide from his fellow men,
And I knew if they caught me beneath a roof,
The police would soon surround me.

And although they're only earning their pay,
And doing their duty no doubt,
Yet I and they, we don't agree;
Their law for them, and mine for me —
And true-bred gaucho doesn't fight
Where there's womenfolk about.

. . .

Between earth and sky on the open plain,
Without either road or goal,
Like a lonely ghost, with his load of woes,
In the darkness the outcast gaucho goes,

And he puts his trust in his prairie craft,
To cheat the police patrol.

His prairie craft and his own stout heart,
He plays his life upon;
If he's sore beset and is forced to fly,
His trusty horse is his sure ally;
No shelter has he but the heaven above,
No friend but his keen *facón*.

. . .

Here windy words are nothing worth,
Nor doctors of high degree;
Here many think that they know a lot,
Would find their wits tied in a knot;
For this is a door with a different lock,
And the gaucho has the key.

Tis dreary out on the desolate plain
Alone all night to be
To lie awake on the chilly ground,
And watch the starts of God go round,
With only the silence and the beasts
To keep one company.

As I've told, one night on the open plain
I was dozing with one eye skinned,
While I brooded over my mournful lot,
When I pricked my ears up like a shot,
For from not far off the *chajá's* call
Came echoing down the wind.

As flat as a worm I laid me out,
And I stuck my ear to the ground,
And soon in the still of the night I caught
The thud of hoofs at a steady trot.
That they were a tidy bunch I knew,
For I counted them by the sound.

. . .

They were coming so soft that it was plain
They weren't just taking the air;
They had tracked me with their dirty spies,

Gauchos generally viewed the state as an oppressor threatening their way of life. Here, a group of rebel gauchos, participants in one of the last provincial uprisings against the central government, pose after being captured by the national army in 1863. Courtesy Archivo General de la Nación.

And were coming to take me by surprise.
It isn't a gaucho's way to run,
So I started to prepare.

. . .

I wound my sash, and I fixed it tight,
My drawers at the knee I tied,
I slipped my spurs, to free my feet,
For I knew I'd have to step quick and neat,
And on a clump of prairie grass
The edge of my knife I tried.

My horse I tethered to the grass,
To have him quick to hand,
I tightened his girth; and to know my ground,
I tried with my foot three paces around;
And then with my back against him there,
I quietly took my stand.

. . .

"You are a gaucho outlaw," said one of them,
"And we've come to settle your score;
You killed a nigger at a dance,
And a gaucho in a store;
The sheriff here has a warrant signed
To lay you in jail tonight;
And we'll lift your stakes, by the holy Jakes,
If you're fool enough to fight."

"Don't come to me," I said to him,
"With a lot of dead men's tales;
The thing we're going to settle now,
Is if you can get me, and when, and how;
You make me tired with your silly talk
Of the law, and police, and jails."

I had scarcely spoke when they tumbled off,
And all in a heap came on.
Six paces off they opened out,
Like a pack of dogs they ringed me about;
I called on the saints to give me help,
And I whipped out my *facón*.

Then close in front of my eyes I saw
The flash that a musket made;
But before the fellow could curse his luck
At missing me, I leapt and struck—
And as one spits a sardine, there
I lifted him on my blade.

Another was cramming a bullet down,
But little it did avail;
With a single thrust I made him squeal—
Than he gave one jump, and made for home,
Like a dog when you step on its tail.

. . .

As luck would have it, the dawn just then
Began to tint the sky,
And I said to myself: "If the Virgin now,
Get me out of this scrape, I'll take a vow

That from this day on, till the day I die,
I'll never harm a fly."

Then into the thick of the lot I leapt,
While they scattered all around;
I curled up there like a ball of string,
With my muscles all set to make my spring,
And in front of two that first came on,
I whetted my knife on the ground.

The one that was eagerer of the two,
Came in with a chop and a thrust;
I parried once and I parried twice —
If I hadn't he sure would have killed my lice,
And then before he could come again,
I filled his eyes with dust.

To follow up I wasn't slow —
I was into him like a flash.
He hadn't got over his surprise,
He was rubbing the dust from his blinking eyes —
"God help you!" I said, and I laid him out
With a single backhand lash.

Just then I felt along my ribs,
A sword point tap my juice;
It was only a flesh cut, I could feel,
But I went real mad at the couch of steel,
And from that moment among the bunch,
With a vengeance I cut loose.

The man with the sword near had my life
Before I could prevent him;
I gave ground quick — then I firmed my heel,
And point and edge I gave him steel —
He twisted his ankle in a pit,
And to the Pit I sent him.

The heart of the gaucho among them then,
A saint must have made rebel;
Above the rest he shouted loud:
"God damn your souls for a cowardly crowd!

Before you kill a man like that,
You'll have to kill Cruz as well!"

And in a jiffy he was afoot,
And into the fight he sprung.
I saw a chance, and in I ripped,
Between us two we had them hipped,
And the fellow Cruz was like a wolf
When you try to take its young.

The two that faced him he sent to hell
With thrusts to left and right.
The ones that were left began to wheel,
You could see they were sick of the sight of steel,
And when we rushed them they scuttled off
Like bugs when you strike a light.

The ones that had stretched their muzzles out,
All stark and stiff they lay;
One rode off swaying from side to side,
While Cruz looked after him and cried,
"You'd better send out some more police
To cart their dead away."

I gathered together their remains,
And I knelt and said a prayer;
I hunted around for two little sticks,
And then I asked God to forgive my soul
For killing so many there.

We left the poor fellows in a heap
Out there on the prairie lone;
We didn't think it wise to stay —
I don't know if they were carted away,
Or whether perhaps the *caranchos* came
And picked them bone from bone.

And as we went, between the two
We passed the crock of gin;
It's times like that, I always think,
That make you glad you've saved a drink;
And Cruz, I could see, didn't spare his throat,
When it came to filling his skin.

. . .

"I'm off, my friend," I said to Cruz,
"Where Fate may beckon me;
To stand in my path if anyone dare,
For heap of trouble they'd best prepare;
For a man is bound to follow his fate,
Whatever his fate may be.

"For many a day my luck's been out,
Not a roof can I call my own;
I'm poorer now than when I commenced—
I haven't a post to rub against,
Nor a tree to shelter me—little I care,
I can face the world alone.

"Before I left with the army draft,
I had cattle and home and wife;
But when from the frontier I came back,
All I could find was my ruined shack;
God knows my friend, when we'll see the end
Of all this sorrow and strife."

THE RETURN OF MARTÍN FIERRO

XXXII   *Counsels of Martín Fierro to His Sons*

When a father gives counsels to his sons,
He's a friend and father too;
As a friend, my boys, then hark to me:
In everything you must wary be,
You're never aware just when and where
Some enemy waits for you.

The only schooling I ever had,
Was a life of suffering;
Don't be surprised if at the game,
I've made mistakes—that's not my shame—
It's mighty little a man can know,
If he's never learnt anything.

There's heads with books stuffed chock-a-block,
Every breed and brand and style,

Though I'm not expert in such mysteries,
I've picked up enough to teach me this:
That better than learning no-end things
Is to know a few things worthwhile.

There's nothing you do will profit you
If no teaching it has dispensed you;
A man at a single glance should know
Just how things stand, and why they're so;
And it's worth a mint not to need a hint
When you're setting folks against you.

Don't pin all your hopes on any heart
Although you may think it's true;
When under the feet of Fate you're trod,
Hold firm your faith in Almighty God,
Of men set your trust in only one,
Or at very most in two.

The defects of men are common ground,
They've got no boundaries;
In the very best some fault you'll find,
So this advice take well in mind:
There's none so good that for other folks
Shouldn't make some allowances.

If your friend's in need, be his friend in deed,
Never leave him in the lurch;
But don't ask him for what you lack,
Or load your troubles on his back.
The truest friend that a man can have
Is a name that's got no smirch.

Don't fear to lose; don't scheme to gain —
That won't get you anywhere —
However much you may thraw and threep,
The goods you get you can't always keep.
Don't go with a gift to a rich man's door,
Or refuse with the poor to share.

Even infidels will treat you well
If you give every man his due;
Don't be too ready to get annoyed,

And extra trouble you'll thus avoid;
Don't put on airs among timid men;
With the brave let your words be few.

To work is the law, since the human kind
Must be clothed and housed and fed;
Don't let yourselves fall on evil days,
By lazing around in slipshod ways,
The heart is sore that from door to door
Has to beg for its daily bread.

By the toil of his hands man gets his bread
And salts it well with weeping,
For poverty doesn't lose a chance
To take advantage of circumstance;
Want lies in wait outside every gate
And slips in if it finds you sleeping.

Don't threaten a man, for there's never one
Won't turn if too hard you goad;
Don't talk big words, to intimidate —
Or maybe you won't have long to wait
To find you've one quarrel on your hands,
And another one on the road.

To front a danger or come off clear
From the traps of evil chance —
I tell you this from experience:
Your best standby is self-confidence;
To trust yourself is a surer arm
Than any sword or lance.

A moderate bit of mother-wit
All men that born possess,
Though without it no man could get very far,
I've noticed this queer particular:
That the same mother-wit that makes one man wise,
Turns others to craftiness.

When a chance comes by, the man that's spry
Takes hold of it on the spot;
Remember well what I'm telling you,

You'll find this picture of Chance is true —
Like the iron that's on the anvil laid,
It's got to be hit while hot.

There are many things that are lost and found
In the daily affairs of men,
But one of the lessons I've learned is this —
And fix it well in your memories —
If you lose your shame, it's lost for good,
For you won't get it back again.

To stick to your brother's a good old law
That'll help you in many dangers;
Remember this boys, and hold together
In fair as well as in stormy weather,
When a family fight among themselves
They're soon eaten up by strangers.

Respect gray hairs, for to mock at age
Is no matter for admiration;
Whene'er among stranger folk you be,
Take care how you choose your company,
For a man that picks up with a scurvy crowd
Gets an evil reputation.

When the stork grows old its sight gets dim
Till at last its eyes go blind;
Its little ones keep it in the nest,
And to care for its age they do their best.
Consider the storks, and learn from them
This lesson for humankind.

If a man offends — though you treat it light,
And the quarrel you don't pursue,
Be on your guard and keep well alert,
For whatever happens one thing's a cert:
The man that's done you an evil turn
Will always talk bad of you.

The man that lives at another's beck,
Can't expect to live in clover;
If he does his job with a haughty air,

He'll get worse treatment and harder fare,
The brisker the hand that's underneath,
The lighter the hand that's over.

To lose his time, or to lose his shame
Are the marks of a worthless man,
Your wits about you always keep,
And look round well before you leap,
And remember this: there was never a vice
That ended where it began.

Of all the birds that live by prey,
The hook-beaked bird is chief;
But the man that would keep a straight backbone
Never takes a copper that's not his own,
You may be poor—that's no shame for sure—
But it's shameful to be thief.

Keep your hand if you can, from the blood of man,
Never fight for sheer devilment,
Let my misery a mirror be,
And measure yourselves by what there you see;
To know how to hold yourself in hand
Is a thing that's most excellent.

You'll carry the guilt of the blood you've spilt
In your heart till death has stilled it,
The sight of that blood will haunt you so—
To my brief alas this truth I know—
That it falls like drops of burning fire
On the soul of him that spilled it.

Wherever you go, you'll find a foe
Worse than drink, to stir up trouble;
I'm telling you this, boys, for your good,
And I hope you'll remember it as you should:
For a crime that's done by a drunken man,
The punishment should be double.

In a general brawl and a "free-for-all,"
Get out first—it's the only sense;
Don't carry yourselves with too high an air,
Although you've got right on your side to spare,

And the man is wise that his knowledge buys
By other's experience.

If ever a woman you give your heart
This counsel I recommend:
Don't do her a turn that will leave her sore,
Or she'll serve you some day far worse, and more;
For a woman that's wronged won't soon forget,
And she'll ruin you in the end.

If you want to be singers, feel it first —
And you won't have to watch your style;
Don't ever tune up your strings, my boys,
Just to hear yourselves, and to make a noise,
But get in the habit, that when you sing,
It's always of things worthwhile.

These counsels true I give to you,
To learn them has cost me dear;
I've pointed you out the way to go
So you'll never say that you didn't know,
But to give you the grit to follow it
Is not up to me — that's clear.

Of the lessons I've learnt in my lonely days
These things that I've told are some;
In all this advice that I've given to you,
There's nothing that tested you won't find true;
It's out of the mouth of the hoary-head
That the wisest counsels come.

Translated by Walter Owen

An Expedition to the Ranquel Indians

Lucio V. Mansilla

Lucio V. Mansilla (1831–1913), military officer, diplomat, and writer, was a typical fin de siècle Argentine gentleman from the Buenos Aires elite. Educated in Europe but with strong ties to the landowning class (he was Rosas's nephew), he felt at home whether riding a horse for days across the pampas or listening to opera surrounded by members of high society. An Expedition to the Ranquel Indians (1870) bears the stamp of his bicultural upbringing. Written while Mansilla commanded a military mission to make peace with the Ranquel, the book is both a geographic and an ethnographic treatise as well as a cynical reflection on the notions of identity and national frontier. The following passage, in which Mansilla relates a discussion between him and the Ranquel council on the meaning of being "Argentine," exposes Mansilla's duplicity. He brags to a friendly reader, as sophisticated as Mansilla himself, about how for lack of other weapons he was able to manipulate and deceive the Ranquel council through his superior command of words and Western logical reasoning. At the same time, because of his ability to see through accepted truths, Mansilla undermines the authority of his own judgment by exposing the fallacies of power.

Mariano Rosas demanded that I reread the articles stipulating how many mares, how much tobacco, sugar, and mate, etc., would be allotted. He wanted all the Indians to hear for themselves what sort of peace treaty was going to be signed. This last phrase, *going to be,* considering that the treaty was already signed, ratified, and exchanged, was a truly original Ranquel touch. I had heard it not once but several times, and it did not sit well with me at all. The mood of the Indians was not at the moment a favorable one for me to score oratorical points. Moreover, the council appeared to be turning into a meeting to approve or reprehend the chief's conduct. I gathered as much from something he said several times. "I am now going to tell my Indians," he said, "what we have settled on, and whatever they decide, that is what will be done."

I had been warned of this the night before.

I conceded, reading yet again those articles of the treaty of greatest concern and interest to them.

Food will ever be a primordial chapter for the human race.

"Not enough! Give more!" shouted several voices in Araucan. I knew what they were saying because certain Christians then said it in Spanish, provocatively, and added a few yeahs to back it up. Noting this, Mariano Rosas lectured me on the poverty of the Indians, demanding more mares, mate, sugar, and tobacco.

The Indians are poor because they do not like to work, I countered. They would be as rich as the Christians if they could learn to love work. I also told them I could not commit to more than the amount agreed on, which was not a little but a lot.

"Too little! Not enough!" several of them shouted.

"Now do you see?" said Mariano Rosas, no longer using a brotherly tone of voice with me. "They say that what you are giving is little."

"I can see that," I said, "but it is not a little. On the contrary, it is very much."

"More, more, more," cried several voices together, more numerous than before. I addressed them, reading yet another time the articles detailing the allotment of mares, etc. I compared it with what Calfucurá's Indians were to receive and thus proved to them that they would be getting more.

"Tell me this isn't true," I said, when no one contradicted me. Then, seizing my opening, I loosed oratorical thunderbolts on Calfucurá.

"He has broken the peace," I said. "He is a real bandit who does not fear God and works in bad faith. He found out that Mariano Rosas is receiving more through this peace treaty than he and so has again become the Christians' enemy, claiming that the Ranquel Indians have been given preference. But all that is just to see if he can get as much from this treaty as my brother Mariano Rosas and I have arranged for *his* Indians to get."

I laid as much stress on the word *brother* as I could and looked in Mariano Rosas's direction. "So you can see," I shouted with all the volume I had and in my best Indian mimicry. I wanted them to hear me and felt my style was winning them over. "So you can see that the Ranquels are preferred over Calfucurá's Indians."

Mariano Rosas asked me how many mares the Indians were allotted by the treaty. He was actually asking when the treaty had gone into effect. Evidently it was and was not a treaty. I answered that the Christians were bound by the treaty from the day the president of the Republic had signed it. He said he thought it began the day on which he returned it to me signed. I said no. He then asked when the president of the Republic had signed it. I gave him his answer, whereupon he added up the days and told me how much we owed

them. At this point I explained what I had already gone over with him in Leu-
buco, namely, what the president, Congress, and budget are. I said that the
government could not immediately furnish everything agreed on. In order to
provide the money, Congress must first decide if the treaty was right for them.
I was complying with my orders in explaining all this, not that it was a simple
task to make these barbarians understand our complicated constitutional apparatus. At any rate, I continued along those lines.

"Some things will be furnished to you on a running account," I said. "The
rest will come when Congress approves the treaty. This is the president's way
of showing the native inhabitants that he means them well."

It dawned on me as I made these observations that there was a perfect similarity between the Indians' discourse and my own. Mariano Rosas, I reasoned
as my voice went on working, has signed the treaty. I, too, thought that was
the end of it. Now it turns out that this council can nullify it. Precisely the
situation with the president and the Congress. An identical case, is it not? The
extremes meet.

I expected an appeal from Mariano Rosas, but several Indians beat him to it.

"What if Congress does not approve the treaty?" they asked. "Will that
mean no peace?"

Put yourself in my shoes, Santiago, and tell me you would not have been
lost for an answer. I told them that would not happen. The Congress and the
president are very good friends, and the Congress is bound to approve and give
him all the money he needs.

"But Congress can disapprove, can't it?" asked Mariano Rosas.

I didn't dare admit this was true because I would risk confirming their suspicion that the Christians were only trying to gain time. I resorted to oratory and
mimicry, gave an extensive, fiery, sentimental, and emotional speech. I do not
know if I was inspired, but then I must have been (or they did not understand
me), for I noted certain currents of approval.

Eloquence has its secrets.

I always recall, when I see a crowd moved by resonating, euphonic, dazzling diction, a certain preacher from Catamarca. He was giving a sermon
on Good Friday. There was a boy hidden under the pulpit who was whisper-
ing it to him. The priest had reached the most touching part, the moment
when the Redeemer is about to expire, the Pharisees having finished him. The
martyr's agony had begun to wrench tears from the congregation. Bitter sobs
resounded in the temple vault. The preacher was moved as well and lost his
train of thought. He looked under the pulpit to find that the boy had fallen
asleep. He could not possibly continue speaking, so he turned to mimicry.

Quasi sermo corpis, Cicero has said, and this time it proved true. Sorrow rose in the church like a tide. With a little help, the crisis could be induced, and the picture would be complete. Lost for words, the preacher put his arms and lungs to work. He gestured and shuddered and gave out wrenching cries. Panting and overexcited and lost in their own moaning and groaning, the congregation could hear nothing else. They could see, feel, and reason that the preacher had reached a sublime peak, and they drowned him out with wailing and lamentation. The sacred effigy bowed its head for the last time, all shuddered under the wave of sorrow, and the preacher disappeared.

At a recent banquet given for journalists by King Leopold, it was the man from *La liberté* of Paris who garnered the most applause. "Let *La liberté* speak," they called out over and over, and so he rose to his feet. The lights, the wine, the laborious digestion of a sumptuous meal, and the conversations had left everyone somewhat light-headed. This was a smart young writer, I should add. "Gentlemen," he said in *sa majesté*'s presence, "let's have a round of applause!"

Which was as far as they let him get. He began to move his head, wave his arms like oars, and the applause and the hurrahs grew.

"Liberté!" he said, and there was more applause, more hurrahs.

"Egalité!" Twice the applause, twice the hurrahs.

"Fraternité!" Triple the applause, triple the hurrahs.

There are certain ploys one must not abuse. I tried not to exhaust mine. When I saw that my audience was convinced that the president and Congress would not be likely to fight over a pittance, nay over a million or more, I turned the meeting over to Mariano Rosas, who proceeded to ask me by what right we had occupied the Río Quinto. This had always been Indian land, he said. His fathers and grandfathers had lived near the Chemecó, the Brava, and the Tarapendâ lagoons, along Plata Hill, and in Langhelo. The Christians, he added, are still not satisfied. They want to stock up (his exact words) on more land. These accusations and appeals found an alarming echo in the crowd. Several Indians tightened the circle and moved in closer to hear my answer. I felt it cowardly to silence my conscience and sentiments, even before an audience of barbarians. With my elbows resting as always on my thighs, my face in my hands, and my eyes turned downward, I began to answer. The land, I told them, does not belong to the Indians but to those who make it productive by working it. The chief stopped me right there.

"How can you say it is not ours? We were born here."

I asked him if he thought the land where a Christian was born belonged to that Christian. He said nothing, so I continued.

"Government forces have occupied Río Quinto for the greater security of the border. However, those lands do not yet belong to the Christians. It is everyone's land and no one's. Someday when the government sells it, some one or two or more people will own it, and they will raise cattle on it and grow wheat and corn. Are you asking me by what right we stock up on land? I would ask you by what right you invade us to stock up on cattle."

"It is not the same," several of them said, interrupting. "We do not know how to work. No one has taught us how to do this like the Christians. We are poor. We have to go on our raids to live."

"But you steal what is not yours," I said, "because the cows and horses and sheep you bring back with you are not yours."

"And your Christians take our land away from us," they said.

"That is not the same," I answered. "In the first place, we do not recognize that land as yours, while you do recognize that the cattle you rob is ours. In the second place, you cannot live off the land unless you work it."

"Why haven't you taught us to work after you took away our cattle?" observed Mariano Rosas.

"That's right! He's right!" yelled a number of voices. A dull murmur floated along the circle of human heads. I looked quickly and saw more than one face glowering at me.

"It is not true that the Christians have ever stolen your cattle from you," I said.

"It certainly is true," said Mariano Rosas. "My father has told me there were many animals roaming the Cuero and Bagual lagoons in other times."

"They came from the Christian cattle ranches," I countered. "You are all ignorant and do not know what you are talking about. If you were Christians, if you could work, you would know what I know. You wouldn't be poor, either; you would be rich. Listen to me, barbarians. I have something to say. We are all children of God, all Argentines. Are we not all Argentines?" I asked, looking at some of the Christians. The word pierced the tender fibers of patriotism and drew my audience out like magic.

"Yes, we are Argentines," they said despite themselves.

"And you are Argentines, too," I told the Indians. "And if not, what are you?" Now I was shouting. "I want to know what you are. Answer me. What are you? Will you say you are Indians? Well, I too am an Indian. Or do you think that I am a gringo? Listen to what I have to say. You know nothing because you cannot read. You do not have books. You only know what you have heard from your fathers and grandfathers. I know many things that have happened before this time. Hear what I say so that you will not live in error. And don't tell me that what you are hearing is not true, because if I ask any of you the name of your grandfather's grandfather, you will not have an answer for me. Yet we Christians know these things. Hear now what I have to say.

"Many years ago the gringos disembarked in Buenos Aires. In those days the

Indians lived where the sun rises, on the shores of a very big river. The gringos who came were all men. They brought no women. The Indians were simple. They did not know how to ride horses because there were no horses here. The gringos brought the first mare and the first horse, and cows and sheep. What do you think of that? See how you know nothing?"

"That's not true," some of them shouted. "Him not tell truth."

"Don't he barbaric, don't interrupt me, listen to me," I said, pressing on.

"The gringos took the Indians' women from them, had children by them, and that is why I say that all those born in this land are Indians, not gringos.

"Hear me well.

"You were very poor then. The sons of the gringos, who are the Christians, us, Indians like you, taught you a number of things. We taught you to ride horses, to rope and hunt with the bolas, wear a poncho and a *chiripá* and breeches, heavy boots, spurs, and silver trim."

"That is not true," interrupted Mariano Rosas. "There were cows and horses and everything else here before the gringos came, and it was all ours."

"You are wrong," I said. "The gringos, who were the Spaniards, brought all those things. I will prove it to you. You call the horse *cavallo*, the cow *uaca*, the bull *toro*, the mare *yegua*, the calf *ternero*, the sheep *oveja*, the poncho *poncho*, the lasso *lazo*, the herb tea *yerba*, sugar *achúkar*, and many other things just as the Spaniards did. And why is it that you do not call them by some other name? Because you didn't know these things until the gringos brought them. If you had known them before, you would have given them another name. Why do you call your brother *peñi?* Because before the fathers of the Christians came you already knew what a brother was. Why do you call the moon *quien* and not *moon* as the Christians do? For the same reason. Before the gringos came to Buenos Aires, the moon was in the sky, and you knew her."

Faced with this irrefutable ethnological argument, an irascible Mariano Rosas asked me what all this had to do with the peace treaty.

"When did I ask you to tell me these things?" he said.

"And what do all your questions have to do with the peace treaty, which you have already signed? Do you suppose I came to the council for you to approve it? You already have approved it, and you have to abide by it."

"And will your people abide by it?" he asked.

"Yes, we will," I said. "You have our word of honor as Christians."

"Then why if the Christians have word of honor did Manuel Lopez have two hundred Indians' throats cut when he was at peace with them? Why if Christians have word of honor did your uncle Juan Manuel de Rosas order 150 Indians' throats cut at the Retiro barracks when he was at peace with the Indians?" (I am quoting him almost verbatim.)

"Yeah, what about that! What about that!" shouted several Indians. The council was beginning to look for all the world like a popular uprising, and I was no longer the ambassador but the accused.

"Don't ask me to settle those scores," I said. "Other men did those things. The president we have now is not like others that we have had before. I haven't asked you about the slaughter of Christians that the Indians have committed whenever they could." Then I threw the ball back into Mariano Rosas's court. "What does the slaughter that Lopez and Rosas ordered have to do with the peace treaty?" I gave him no time to answer. "You," I went on, "have killed more Christians than Christians have killed Indians." I made up every slaughter imaginable and added them to the ones I could actually remember.

"*Winca! Winca* lying!" cried several of them, and here and there around the circle a sort of clamor began.

This was the worst symptom.

Several of my assistants had retired to the shade of a carob tree. The sun was burning like fire, and the talk had been going for several hours now. There was no one left with me except the Franciscans and my adjutant, Demetrio Rodríguez. Clearly the situation was growing more dangerous. I looked at my compadre Baigorrita, who sat there like a statue. I could not draw his attention. I looked around for other familiar faces to ask them with my eyes to quell the restless spirit of the mob. They all sat there speechless. If they looked at me at all they did not see me. . . .

Then, whether it was the horses spooking, whatever it was—I don't know —but I felt something like a shudder go through the crowd. I will confess I feared an attack. Redoubling my energy, I continued.

"I am the representative of the president of the Republic here," I said. "I can promise you that the Christians will not go back on their word. If you keep your part of it, the peace treaty will be honored. You can back out of your part of the commitment, but sooner or later you will come to regret it, as will the Christians if they deceive you. I have not come here to lie. I have come to tell the truth, and the truth is what you are hearing from me. If the Christians should abuse the good faith you show them, then you would be right to take revenge for their false-heartedness. In the same way, if you do not show me and those accompanying me due respect and consideration, if you do not allow me to return or you kill me, the day will come—mark my words—when the army will put you all to the sword for being traitors. And in these immense pampas and these lonely forests there will be no memory, no sign that you ever lived here."

Camargo came over to me at that moment.

"Talk about what they will be getting with the treaty," he mumbled in my ear.

"And what else do you want the Christians to do?" I said. "Are you not getting two thousand mares to give out to your poor? And sugar, tobacco, paper, firewater, clothing, oxen, plows, seeds to plant, and money for the chiefs and captains? What more do you want?"

After a long silence, Mariano Rosas addressed the gathering.

"We are all set then," he said, "but we want to know how much of each thing you are going to give us. Go ahead and speak, brother." And turning to the Indians he said, "Now listen closely."

Once more I enumerated the provisions of the treaty. At last, calm was reestablished, and the council appeared to be coming to an end. I took the renewed mood of goodwill as an opportunity to dispel any and all motives of future resentment, explaining that my presence there did not ensure peace. I was a representative of the government and a subaltern of my superior officer, General Arredondo, with whose permission I now sat before them. They must not think, I said, that because another officer should replace me the peace was thereby altered. No, that officer would have to abide by the treaty and carry out the orders that the government gave him. I told them they often mistook the officers with whom they had their dealings for the government. At no time was my absence from the frontier to be the basis of any complaint or of a refusal to observe the agreement faithfully. Be they near or far, I told them, they would always have a friend in me, one who would do everything in his powers on their behalf if they deserved it.

Mariano Rosas rose from his place.

"It is over, brother," he said with the friendliest smile in the world.

Translated by Mark McCraffey

Letter to the President

Chief Manuel Namuncurá

The Amerindians knew all too well the disadvantages of signing peace treaties with the national government. Through the treaties, they waived the rights to their lands without becoming effective citizens of the nation. The excessive violence that characterized some of their raids and attacks was, among other things, an expression of their discontent and frustration. Besides waging war, some Amerindian chiefs tried to save their people from utter disaster by negotiating with the state on its own terms, that is, through the obscure mechanisms of bureaucracy. The difficulties of such a task were almost insurmountable. To demand a signed treaty's actual fulfillment, the Amerindian chiefs had to be able to address the government both in writing and in Spanish, neither of which they mastered. In this telling letter of 1877, written in hesitant Spanish to President Avellaneda, chief Namuncurá asks for the material compensations promised to his people in the treaties and demands the right to political representation in the national government.

Salinas Grandes, 7 December 1877

To His Most Excellent President of the Republic of Argentina:

Happily we have arranged with His Excellency, the Governor of the Nation, our treaties that are a guarantee of the tranquillity of our families; and at the same time, of the settlers, which is to say: the tranquillity and well-being of everyone. But today it is absolutely necessary to stand behind those treaties all the more, to call to the attention of the Most Excellent Governor certain events that we consider of high importance so as to avoid abuse and a true scandal.

We are referring to the following: before now, that is, when we celebrated other treaties, the distribution of rations was conducted in an irregular way. The supplier and the lawyer did as they pleased: a mare with its newborn colt was delivered as two animals when it shouldn't count for more than one animal.

Portrait of Chief Manuel
Namuncurá. Courtesy
Archivo General de la
Nación, Buenos Aires.

When at that time we stayed in the town of Azul, they gave us a mare as
a ration, but they skinned it first; that is to say, they gave us only the animal's
meat, and the supplier and the lawyer took the leather for their own use. The
result is, Most Excellent Señor, that it is said that the Indian goes around steal-
ing from people, and they add, unjustly, that he does not comply with the
treaties he signs and to which he is legally obligated.

Another thing: The tobacco that was given to us was damp so that it was
impossible to smoke it, to such a point that we got it only to abandon it and
throw it away. The same thing happened with the quality of the tea and sugar
that was distributed to us. . . .

Meanwhile, the supplier and the lawyer made fat profits, and all at the expense of the nation and our interests. And why? No doubt because the national
government is unaware of these events and others that we omit out of respect
for the treaties that we lately celebrated.

So as to avoid repeating these deeds today, we see the essential necessity of naming our beloved compatriot and friend, D. Damasio Tapia, to be our representative in the capital, and we appoint his son, D. Catalino Tapia, to be our general counsel in the same capital. They themselves should be the ones to take charge of the supplies and to receive the rations. They are the ones to check on the quality of the rations; they can reject or accept them according to their standards. They will keep an account of everything that is received, and, finally, they will represent our tribes before His Excellency in the best possible way.

We also want the supplier, D. Damasio Tapia, to watch over what happens at times on the frontier. It often happens that some kinds of scandal occur among the Indians. Almost always, and for no reason, they take one of the Indians prisoner, on the commandant's orders, with the preconceived plan of taking his horse. Nobody has observed until today this iniquitous procedure, the Indian's true exploitation. Why does the chief of the frontiers commit this injustice? Is it because we are not civilized like the rest? Justice alone should protect our desire to consolidate the peace treaties. . . .

It is entirely just that we ask to be given four thousand animals as semi-annual rations to be distributed to the tribes by our three Indian representatives in the national government. We also ask for a set salary for these three generals and for the other chiefs and subchiefs, and four generals' uniforms, with four flags, four trumpets, and four swords, and four complete saddles outfitted with silver, and gold-trimmed chaps, and four saddle pads to shine on the horses of the four generals. Also a quantity of articles of food and drink and more tea and tobacco, clothing for each chief and subchief and the captains who are on the list attached here. Still other presents that are requested for the families of the generals, that is, for we who represent all these tribes. As generals in command, we demand the value of the land that was taken from us, encompassed by the frontiers of Puán, Guaminí, Carhué and Chipilafquén, in the amount of 200,000 pesos — in national currency. We are authorized to represent and collect for all of the chiefs who are listed here on the attached page.

Signed: Manuel Namuncurá, Bernardo Namuncurá, Alvarito Reumay, Manuel Freire, secretary.

Translated by Patricia Owen Steiner

IV

Splendor and Fin de Siècle

There are ends of which everyone is aware, endings that arrive charged with symbolic and historical meaning as people speak of them with metaphors of death and rebirth. The nineteenth-century fin de siècle is one of those famous conclusions. In France, where the expression *fin de siècle* was coined, the century's end was largely associated with apocalyptic images of social and cultural decadence. In Argentina, the change of centuries elicited mostly feelings of completion, of dreams coming true, of patriotic pride and triumphant rejoicing. It was then that the powerful myth of Argentina as a modern nation built from scratch was born. Through a historical transformation that had elements of a fairy tale, a marginal ex-colony was managing to become a prosperous and promising country, finally moving forward after a long interlude of civil revolts and economic languor.

The Argentine fin de siècle begins in 1880, the year during which many formidable obstacles to national progress were overcome, and closes on a spectacular note in 1910 with the splendid celebrations marking a century of independence from Spain, when Argentina's affluence was displayed against the backdrop of a recently remodeled Buenos Aires city. Argentine historians have generally defined 1880 as the year when the process of national organization was consummated. This was the year when General Julio A. Roca, the "hero of the desert," won the national elections and became the president of Argentina (1880–86). Portrayed by some as the originator of economic dependency and a murderer of innocent Amerindian women and children, he has also been seen as a champion of order and progress. Each of these views contains an element of truth. As David Viñas demonstrates in the piece opening this part, violence and exploitation have been the unacknowledged tools of Western modernization. As commander, Roca led the military campaign that brutally subdued the last rebel Amerindian tribes in Patagonia, subsequently claiming their lands for the state, and openly mimicking the westward expansion of the United States. Also in 1880, Roca's troops managed to crush the last armed insurrection in Buenos Aires, whose political class had been reluctant to yield to the legal requirements of national organization. Immediately thereafter, the city of Buenos Aires was federalized and declared the capital of Argentina. Roca's expeditiousness and political success were linked to the scale and cohesiveness of the coalitions that he helped build. With the unconditional support of the national army, the League of Governors, and an important segment of the landowning class, he strengthened the central government and placed the reins of power firmly in the hands of the presidency. His administration paved the way for oligarchic Argentina's fin de siècle grandeur.

For three decades, Argentina was governed by the so-called oligarchy — an educated, progressive, and arrogant elite composed of liberals anxious to advance Argentine prosperity through massive immigration, urbanization, and public education. They were writers and thinkers committed to the scientific and materialistic values of Social Darwinism and Positivism and closely associated with landowning interests and British capital. Under their rule, Argentina would go through a sweeping process of economic growth and modernization that before long turned it into the most developed country in Latin America.

An agricultural revolution in the pampas, spurred by the need to improve the quality of meat for export, lay at the core of all these developments. A quick look at numbers immediately reveals the astonishing speed of economic growth. Between 1872 and 1895, cultivated acreage expanded fifteenfold. Exports climbed from 30 million gold pesos in 1870 to over 150 million by 1900. Argentina became a major producer of wheat, with annual exports topping 1 million tons in the 1890s. A second economic boom from 1904 to 1912 provided even greater incentive for the agricultural exploitation of the pampas. By 1910, the value of exports reached thirteen times the export trade of 1870.[1] The increase in population caused by massive waves of immigration was equally impressive. Between 1871 and 1914, more than 3 million immigrants settled in the country. The majority came from Italy and Spain, along with smaller numbers from France, England, Central Europe, the Balkans, and the Middle East.

The city of Buenos Aires came to embody the new Argentina. Architects, builders, and artists converted what used to be a *gran aldea* — a sprawling village — into one of the world's most sophisticated and cosmopolitan metropolises, the Paris of South America. Its boulevards and lavish mansions, the refinement of its upper class, its new sanitary system, all spoke to the country's modernity. When the independence centennial was celebrated there in 1910, politicians and writers alike were convinced that the national utopias dreamed of by Sarmiento and Alberdi were becoming a reality. It was then that the Nicaraguan poet Rubén Darío, excited and inspired by the occasion, wrote the essay in which he praised Argentina as a role model for the rest of Latin America. Many immigrants concurred with Darío's optimism. In letters to his expectant family back in Italy, the immigrant Oreste Sola saw in the ebullient movement of people and money the signs of a land full of economic opportunities. In a less secular mood, hopeful Jews like Alberto Gerchunoff thought that they had finally found the promised land.

But progress was not as widespread or as smooth as the celebratory tone of the centennial would lead us to believe. Compared to the newfound prosperity in the pampas, the economies of the interior remained relatively unchanged. Tucumán in the Northwest and Mendoza in Cuyo greatly benefited from the new railroad and protective tariffs against foreign sugar and wine. In Patagonia, fruit farms prospered in the valley of Río Negro, and rich oil deposits were discovered in Chubut and Neuquén. Extensive logging became a source of revenue for the provinces of Santiago del Estero, Catamarca, Chaco, and Formosa. But the rest of the interior was either bypassed by the economic boom or lost ground.

Besides being uneven, modernity had its social costs. As the historian James Scobie shows, South America's Paris had a darker side, one of crowded housing and poor health, of resentment and economic exploitation, of prostitution and delinquency. Socialists like José Ingenieros interpreted these phenomena from a Marxist point of view and encouraged the exploited to organize against a corrupt bourgeoisie. Many among the powerful saw these social ills as the natural outcome of unrestricted immigration and faulty policing. They argued that, far from being the industrious, strong men whom Alberdi had imagined, the actual immigrants were illiterate, malnourished, and vicious. Some even showed the unmistakable signs of inherited physical and mental diseases. The Social Darwinist Ramos Mejía offered a short catalog of sociobiological stereotypes as a practical tool for identifying and weeding out the degenerate immigrants hidden in the modern crowd. The future of the Argentine race, he believed, depended on discriminating between the bad and the good seeds that were intermingling in Argentina's vibrant melting pot. This surprising xenophobia nourished a form of nationalism that sought to strengthen national identity by instilling a sense of belonging based on the same local traditions that the government had previously tried so hard to eradicate. Lugones's celebration of gauchesque poetry and gaucho blood, when the gauchos as a cultural group were almost gone, must be read in this light.

Out of the ethnic, cultural, and social promiscuity that so many found alarming grew one of the most remarkable and powerful cultural traditions of modern Argentina. Argentine tango, Simon Collier contends, emerged from the contact between the splendid and the darker sides of Buenos Aires. In the dim rooms of the bordellos or under the glow of streetlights in the city's outskirts, Creole gentlemen entwined their bodies with those of the immigrant or mestizo prostitute, the Italian worker, the black dancer, and the urbanized gaucho or *compadrito,* following the beat of a music that itself combined diverse sounds from Africa, Europe, and colonial Latin America.

Note

1 James R. Scobie, *Argentina: A City and a Nation* (New York: Oxford University Press, 1971), 115–21.

The Foundation of the National State

David Viñas

With the aid of Remington rifles and telegraph lines, the last military campaign into Amerindian territories achieved what years of fragile treaties and defensive forts had not. By destroying the last rebel Amerindian tribes and seizing their lands, Roca's army opened a vast new area for economic exploitation and the expansion of estancias, railroads, and settlements. In this groundbreaking essay, published in 1982, the Argentine writer and cultural critic David Viñas, a forerunner of postcolonial studies scholars, highlights the historical ignominy that lies at the foundation of the modern Argentine state: the butchering of the Amerindians and the destruction of their lifestyle. By equating their conquest to a genocide not very different from the killings of innocent people carried out by the military dictatorships of the 1970s in Latin America, an angry Viñas denounces a crime that until then not even the most radical intellectuals had officially acknowledged.

In the glorious year of 1879 a series of happy events began and ended the great work with the following results: the pacification of the desert regions to the south of the Republic; the conquest of twenty thousand leagues of fertile land handed over to civilization; the submission and regeneration of savage populations; the liberation of several hundred captives; the conclusion of the century-old war against the Indians.
—Manuel J. Olascoaga, *La conquista de la pampa* (1881)

The Roots, the Trajectory, and the Problem of the Liberal State

For official Argentine history, 1879 marks the end of the conquest of Patagonia and the final subjugation of the Indians. At the same time, 1879 was the basis— and the blueprint—for institutionalizing the conservative republic that ruled until 1916, built on an understanding gradually reached between the army and the oligarchy. In 1930, this social alliance managed to make an ambiguous reappearance that lasted ten years. Even today, a century later, it still stubbornly tries to extend—with that growing harshness evident all along the underside of its victorious ascent—the life of an arrangement that yielded its greatest benefits long ago and now manages to reveal only its limits, its exhaustion, and its profound contradictions. The most obvious of these contradictions of liberal Argentina is, to get right to the point, its acts of bone-chilling repression.

This is a repression that has been notable for its capacity, not only to surface at moments of crisis, but also to produce a peculiar silence, managing to deny the violence that made the liberal state possible and to censure any debate about its origins. It is as if the liberal Argentine state had foreseen back then that any close look at the genesis of its power might place its power in question and therefore hid its traces.

Since I think we should examine these blind spots, I want to pose some questions. Especially now, in 1982, when the army has expanded to fill the entire stage of history, I want to ask, What did the Army *really do* in Patagonia more than one hundred years ago? When army discourse made use of spectacular gestures, was it denying the numerical importance of the Indians? Was that the strategy? Did they just reduce the numbers so that what they did would not count as "mass murder"? Or did they try to deny their responsibility by claiming that, because the dead were so few in number, this was no genocide but at worst a "massacre"? And those who did it, were they part of the military structure?

Because I am not interested just in the deals they made with the land they took from the Indians, a topic that has been treated, even by the Left, with the sort of bleeding-heart benevolence that those "gentlemen of 1880" were already using back then to speak of the gauchos they had crushed. And I am not interested just in how the liberal elite used Indians as servile manual labor. These things interest me, absolutely; but what interests me more is what has been hidden. What everyone has avoided. What is most disturbing.

Taking a look at our canonical historians, we can ask, Did they say anything about that silence, or did they collaborate in erasing any of the traces all this violence left behind? They did not cry out, these professional historians: were they hoarse, or were they accomplices? If "the voice of the conquered Indians" has been heard in other Latin American countries, why not in Argentina? Doesn't Argentina have anything to do with the Indians? And what about the Indian women? Do we have nothing to do with them? Nothing to do with Latin America? Why do we never speak of Indians in Argentina? What does it mean that Indians have been pushed offstage, relegated to ethnology and folklore or, even more sadly, to tourism and local color pieces in the press?

I stubbornly insist on asking questions: Do Indians have no voice of their own? Was sex an illness for them? Or was silence their illness? Might this be a matter of, paradoxically, a discourse of silence? Or might the Indians be the "disappeared" of 1879? Especially now, all these questions demand answers. I will do my best. Because, to be honest, I am not at all persuaded by the official answers liberal Argentina has given, from 1879 to now.

In the years between 1879 and 1930, and even more between 1930 and 1980, the crisis of the liberal imagination has become evident within the "republic of the proper," owing to a series of shifts that made it clear that the elite is, not only a hollow power, but also a hollow class.

But, more than a hundred years ago, that elite was aiming to make a qualitative leap forward, thanks to the catalyzing push of several long-standing factors. First, there was the indiscriminate consolidation of centralized power in Buenos Aires, then the final consolidation of the project based on the cattle ranches, which had been important since a century before. This project shaped a community and a space around a unique and homogeneous market for export production — cattle — and tied that community and market into the global project of capitalism.

This transformation already had a protagonist, a man who was clever and cautious, a gentlemanly positivist: Julio Argentino Roca, the thirty-six-year-old minister of war. Roca was the point man for the interlocking alliance of provincial oligarchies that was coming together in the National Autonomy Party and the key link in the oligarchy's close alliance with a discreet but increasingly powerful chorus: the army. By chance, Roca gave that hidden god of modern Argentine politics its first maxim: military might leads to political might. That was how the "the conquistador of the desert" in 1879 became "the conquistador of the city" in 1880; the general was half knowingly reproducing an Argentine precedent (Rosas) and a generic myth.

Within this context, a huge open-air mass was held for the Argentine army on 25 May 1879 on the island of Choele-Choel where the Río Negro widens and is bordered by trees that set it apart from the desolate remainder of Patagonia. The painter Juan Manuel Blanes needed an enormous canvas to paint the scene in proper heroic style. The solitude of the place, the silence of the wind, and the metallic sheen of the sun all added to the glory of this spectacle before four thousand dusty and patriotic men. As far as the precarious site allowed, nothing about the ceremony had been left to chance, down to the smallest details.

Above all, Roca stood out as the hero, strategist, spokesman, and architect of this act. Not only is he a figure of equal stature — owing to his military career, his avid pragmatism, and his social support — to Porfirio Díaz of Mexico, Justo Rufino Barrios of Guatemala, Piérola of Peru, Santa María of Chile, or Field Marshal Floriano Peixoto of Brazil. He was also, after the death of the popular leader and ex–minister of war Adolfo Alsina, one of the strongest candidates to succeed President Nicolás Avellaneda, whose term came to an end the very next year.

In the proclamation on 18 April 1879 that opened the campaign, Roca said, "The United States is one of the most powerful countries in the world, and yet until now it has not been able to solve the Indian problem, even though it has tried all kinds of strategies, has spent millions of dollars annually, and has dispatched numerous armies. You, the Argentine army, are now going to solve that problem at the other end of America, with a small expenditure of your labor."

Thus, the Argentine military campaign was undertaken with a clear vision of what the U.S. model of war against the Indians implied. Roca's allusion to the United States made clear the project's meaning and its similarities and differences with other situations across the continent. Liberal bourgeois civilization, described and summarized thirty-five years earlier in Sarmiento's *Facundo,* was rolling forward with devastating force over "the empty spaces." This was part of the worldwide task that Kipling would describe as "the white man's burden."

Roca was determined to improve on Alsina's strategy, which had relied on the old system of frontier forts and been widely criticized for pinning down troops, harming soldiers, and costing too much. Aware of how his action represented both a continuation of previous policy and a dramatic shift from it, a qualitative leap, Roca gave the order to cross the defensive line against the Indians drawn during Mitre's regime (1852–74). While the act was historically significant because it went beyond the old colonial boundaries, it proved effective because it took the traditional dominance of the Buenos Aires landowning elite very much into account. So, if Roca's project crossed over the known lines that defined the province of Buenos Aires, its outline was drawn by the expansionary drive of Buenos Aires ranchers.

Oligarchy and Expansion

I will not abandon Carhué to the white man.
—Calfucurá, *Testamento* (1873)

The ranchers were shaped by their alliance with England even in the gradual way they warmed to this modern Argentine leader who was in agreement with the new policies cattle exports demanded. When the steamship the *Refrigerator* landed in 1876, one look told cattle ranchers they urgently needed more land. "Further and further south," wrote one of their representatives. And, inescapably, the ranchers also needed a more stable place to raise their cattle. They needed protection, especially from Indians—"those enemies of all of us, Greeks and Trojans alike," as the gentleman doctor and historian Eduardo Wilde scribbled down in his history.

Roca was part of that background and the commander of the army's First Division. To be the hero, he had to be present at the crucial moment the attack was launched. "Because he is a first-order soldier," Wilde commented slyly. His generals, who imitated him even in his punctuality and his dandyism, were put in charge of the other divisions: Levalle, with his biblical beard, commanded the Second Division, marching from Carhué; Racedo, with the pomp of an ambassador of the French Third Republic, led the Center Division, advancing from Villa Mercedes; Uriburu, because of his ties with the foremost clan in Salta, was given the Fourth Division and moved south through Neuquén; the Fifth Division, under Godoy, departed from Guaminí. Another group, led by Lagos, with his shades of Grant in Tennessee, left from Trenque-Lauquen.

In its overall scope, Roca's expedition needed to retrace Rosas's itinerary of 1833. For, if he was extending the frontier on behalf of the cattle interests of Buenos Aires Province, he was also aiming to overcome those interests. And, if the control of land had partially shifted, overall it was unchanged. And the central justifying argument for the campaign against the Indians was the same one repeated time after time: formulated by the colonial viceroy Vertiz, picked up by Rivadavia, reiterated by Rosas, and hardly even altered by Mitre. "Eliminate the Indians," theorized Estanislao S. Zeballos, "but in an orderly manner."

The major change by April 1879 was that Patagonia was no longer the mythological land Pigafetta had glimpsed during Magellan's voyage around the world. Even in the first half of the nineteenth century, Darwin had felt Patagonia to be "the darkest origins of the universe," but then the power of the great chieftain Calfucurá had come to rule from the Andes to the Atlantic coast, and the adventurer Auguste Guinnard had crossed the continent between 1856 and 1859, inspiring Jules Verne in *The Sons of Captain Grant*.

But the other novelty was the emergence of a historically mature elite, who were ironic to the point of being sarcastic, distant to the point of being harsh, and lucid to the point of being ruthless. This elite had already learned some lessons and had assumed their share of the responsibility for earlier political failures. For it was the political exile experienced by their fathers, the generation of 1837, that was the imaginary wall that these gentlemen, the Wildes, Canés, and Avellanedas who made up the generation of 1880, leaned up against.

On top of these factors, the tactics of attrition pursued by the Argentine military—ready for action after the Paraguayan War (1865–60), the end of the 1873–77 economic crisis, and the defeat of the last gaucho militias led by Varela and López Jordán—had borne fruit. These tactics were key to the success of

Roca's "foray": relentless daily attacks; early, repeated, and systematic attrition; attacks, skirmishes, and "white raids" that were less swift but far more
cruel than those of the Indians. What were called "prior cleansing actions"
worked like this: "if those Indians have struck us," Olasconga decreed, "we
should strike back two or three times as hard."

This is why the wars against the Indians of Patagonia (and of the Chaco)
should be seen as the completion of the war against the Paraguayans and
the caudillos of the interior. That series of wars not only ratified the liberal-
bourgeois project of homogenizing the political scene — within which the Guaraní Indians of the Chaco, the gaucho militias of the interior, and the Pampa
Indians of Patagonia all seemed equally "naked, primitive, and racially un-
fit" — but also advanced the project of greatly strengthening centralized power.
That power saw Paraguayan Marshal López, the Entre Ríos caudillo Varela, or
the Indian chieftain Calfucurá alike as decentralizing forces that had to be destroyed and was finally legally confirmed by the formation of the federal district
of Buenos Aires in 1880. This process aimed to make Buenos Aires a continental gateway on the new world map as important as Shanghai or Singapore and
along the way also enhanced the military career of Roca himself.

The Tactics of Positivism

Today Namuncurá admits that the country belongs to the nation, and he no longer insists
on his ridiculous claims.
— General Levalle to Colonel Luis María Campos (1878)

Roca won his initial prestige thanks to Sarmiento's support when he was president (1868–74), gained his first promotions after fighting the "barbarous Guaraníes" at Tuyutí and Humaitá, and earned his later ranks battling the gaucho
militias in the Northeast, especially in Ñaembé, facing down "that mob of men
in tatters." Seen clearly, Roca's most notorious characteristics are those of an
officer of a civilizing army, the man who knew how to properly put down "barbarism." He was a true positivist leader: if he had been Mexican, he would
have fought the Yaqui; if he had been American, he would have started out
as a lieutenant in the Civil War to become a general fighting Geronimo in
Apache Territory; if he had been English, he would have faced the Mahdi in
the Sudan; and if he had been French, he would have sung "The Marseillaise"
before the ruins of Madagascar. By the second half of the nineteenth century,
military models could no longer remain just national. "In whatever latitude a
military leader finds himself, he should demonstrate his ability to act and, if

possible, his good manners," Sir John Seeley wrote in his work *The Expansion of England*. . . .

Roca's greatest achievement in 1879 was carried out in the space between an unobjectionable facade and a sordid back alleyway, through an eclectic series of politically measured actions. Overcoming a frozen policy that had been limited to the province of Buenos Aires, he finished his military career with a flourish and with an eye to the presidency. Roca marched south, driving before him the Indians broken by his subordinates and taking their lands, as per a prior agreement with export landowners in Buenos Aires. At the same time, Roca also mounted a diplomatic offensive to the north, realigning the coalition of provincial oligarchies around two axes: Tucumán (his native province) and Córdoba (his wife's native province, then under the control of his brother-in-law Juárez Celman). "Roca would bring the coast and the interior to agreement," Wilde noted. That was his first achievement. And the second was bringing the army into line with this easy and trumped-up campaign. With the generous distribution of Indian women as pantry or patio maids. With the vouchers for land given as prizes to officers, noncoms, and soldiers — vouchers "that would be sold to the tavernkeepers for four pesos," noted the implacable Wilde. And naturally with the payment — or firm promises of payment — of all back pay.

These last orders by Roca were intended, in the larger map of Latin America, to suggest his military power to Chile, a country that was, like Argentina, dominated by an oligarchy and that was advancing decisively on Peru and Bolivia in the War of the Pacific (1879–83) and drawing dangerous and persistent designs for Patagonia. At the same time, within Argentina, they were designed to make felt his growing political prestige against the other major candidate for the presidency. His rival was Carlos Tejedor, a Buenos Aires politician, an intimate ally of Mitre's, and a member of the generation of 1837 — which Wilde described as "so pompous, so ineffective, and so different from our own."

By crowning his conquest of Patagonia with that monumental outdoor mass at the edge of the Río Negro, Roca killed several birds with one stone. His positivism was evident, above all, in his severe "economy of tactics": monopoly control of lands taken from the Indians, exploitation of the polished prestige he had obtained thanks to the horrors of his subordinates, centralization, modernizing conservatism, ferocious "racial homogenization," strong state control, dutiful agreement with the rites of global capitalism, making national the provincial oligarchies and the army as opposed to local militias, reaffirming the borders and articulation of railroads, telegraph wires, and the single port of Buenos Aires into a unified system. In fact, Roca reshaped power as far as possible in keeping with the ideas of the modern bourgeoisie at the end of the nineteenth century.

And, at the same time, he launched oligarchic Argentina. Or, more exactly, that "republic of the proper" driven by the genteel, traditional style of the generation of 1880—Miguel Cané, Carlos Pellegrini, Estanislao Zeballos, Eduardo Wilde, Lucio Mansilla, Barros, Lucio V. López, Paul Groussac—riding the first economic "miracle" of agro export to a peak whose limits would be marked only by the first antiliberal laws of Roca's second presidency, between 1898 and 1904. Or by the availability of new lands, shrinking down to the vanishing point by 1914.

The Shifts and Reverses of a Program

Therefore, 1879 and 1880 should be read as the fulfillment of Sarmiento's *Facundo* and Alberdi's *Las bases*. The words of those liberal programs have been "put in action." Sarmiento and Alberdi even sat down to tally up the balance of their proposals in, respectively, *Conflict and Harmony among the Races in America* (1883) and *The Argentine Republic Consolidated in 1880 with the City of Buenos Aires as Capital* (1881). But the programs of the two greatest theorists of liberal Argentina were carried out with a peculiar pragmatism, which distorted them tremendously from the very beginning. The way Roca distributed and settled the land directly contradicted the best and most legitimate part of Sarmiento's proposal, and the way Roca made Buenos Aires into a federal capital did not "decentralize power"—as Alberdi had recommended—but instead quickly and massively concentrated it. . . .

This betrayal should be kept in mind. Because this double *alteration* of Sarmiento's and Alberdi's Romantic liberal programs is the root of the worst things about the victorious oligarchy. It is the root of the oligarchy's own later skepticism when faced with the limits and insurmountable conflicts of their model. And it is the root of that mind-set that has come to characterize this social group whose present-day creativity is defined by repression and whose real ideology, today, is the opposition to thought. Back then, when this mind-set was forming, it was a sign that, at long last, the Romantic nation had become the liberal state.

For these reasons, 1879, 1880, and Roca's first administration should be taken to be the *classic* moment of the liberal Argentine elite—especially because of the broad agreement reached around a core of ideological concerns. This agreement was reached precisely because the Indians were taken to be the number one "enemy of all of us." Put another way: if the primordial core of the philosophy of the generation of 1880 was this fear of Indians, the literary leit-motiv of the generation was a persistent discomfort at not being considered European. This is the point at which a set of circumstances combined to turn this generation's ideas into the "highest form" of Argentine conservative thinking and to turn Roca's actions into the most coherent and ruthless expression of them.

Translated by Mark Alan Healey

The Paris of South America

James Scobie

Modernization would change the urban geography of Buenos Aires forever. Sumptu-
ous mansions rose along French boulevards; parks and plazas were built for leisure
and exercise; paved streets shone with electric lights; and public transportation moved
people around smoothly and inexpensively. This was the city that by 1910 even Pari-
sians would claim as the Paris of South America. But, alongside affluent neighbor-
hoods, there were the crowded rooms and the filthy corridors of conventillos. *These*
cheap tenements, most of which were located in the city center, sheltered approximately
one-quarter of the city's population — the new working classes and the unemployed
who paid the price of economic expansion without always enjoying its benefits. In a
superb reconstruction, the historian James Scobie creates a verbal map of these two
contradictory faces of Buenos Aires, skillfully tracing the ways in which their social
and ethnic worlds defined urban space.

In the *gran aldea*, the Plaza de Mayo and adjoining blocks formed the center of
commercial, financial, social, and intellectual activity. Persons with wealth and
power sought to live in this center, and a pattern developed in which one's prestige roughly equated with one's proximity to the plaza. Thousands of laborers
who had come from Europe also sought to live near the Plaza de Mayo, in order
to be close to work and to save on transportation. By 1910, despite vast expansion — there had been a sevenfold growth in population — the center around
the Plaza de Mayo still remained the heart of the city, the residence of the
powerful as well as the home of the newly arrived laborer. . . .

Throughout the period of rapid population growth, all services important
to the activities and comfort of the city's merchants, politicians, and professional men remained concentrated in the blocks immediately adjacent to the
Plaza de Mayo. By 1910 the two blocks of Bartolomé Mitre (known before 1906
as Piedad) between 25 de Mayo and San Martín served as the focal point for
banking, exchange, and credit operations. A number of banks also appeared
on Reconquista and San Martín, in a block on each side of Bartolomé Mitre.

Buenos Aires, 1866: Street scene. A simpler existence soon to be transfigured by sweeping modernization and immigration. Courtesy Archivo General de la Nación, Buenos Aires.

This location for the city's financial institutions had been set in 1862, when the Bolsa de Comercio, the stock exchange, opened its doors on the west side of San Martín, between Cangallo and Cuyo. Two decades later, in 1885, this prestigious focal point for the financial and commercial community moved back toward the Plaza de Mayo, establishing its offices in a handsome two-story edifice that fronted both on the Plaza de Mayo and on Piedad (Bartolomé Mitre). The collapse of the Banco Nacional during the crisis of 1890, and its replacement by the Banco de la Nación, reinforced the shift toward the plaza. The new national bank occupied the edifice of the Teatro Colón on the plaza. Other major banking institutions preferred Piedad: the Banco de Italia y Río de La Plata, established in 1872; the Banco de Londres y Río de La Plata, which moved to that street in 1867; the Banco Carabassa, which opened offices here in 1880, only to be absorbed by the Banco de Londres in 1891; the Banco Inglés y Río de la Plata, until it moved to Reconquista in 1884; and the Banco de Comercio, which opened in 1884.

Concentration of the city's commercial activity took place in similar fashion around the Plaza de Mayo. By the 1880s the value of land and buildings on the north side of the plaza had increased slightly over that of those on the south side, but the sharpest decline of real estate values could be seen as one move away from the plaza in any direction. This same pattern appeared in the number and liquid assets of commercial establishments recorded by block.

Buenos Aires, 1865: Past and future. The city's first railway station rises behind the covered wagons that used to traverse colonial Argentina. Courtesy Archivo General de la Nación, Buenos Aires.

The hotels, restaurants, and shops frequented by the elite remained close to the Plaza de Mayo, particularly on the Perú-Florida axis. Gathering places for *porteño* notables were the Rotisserie Francesa and the Confitería del Águila on Florida, the Café de Paris on Cangallo, and hotels such as the Hotel de Londres and the Casa del Señor Leloir on Piedad, the Hotel de la Paz, Hotel de Provence, and Hotel de Roma on Cangallo, and the Hotel Argentino on Rivadavia. More and more of the clothing and retail establishments that catered to the city's upper class — among them Sastrería Parenthou (1870), Sombrería de A. Manigot (1853), and the Peluquería Ruiz y Roca (1876) — moved to choice locations along Florida. There was also a cluster of expensive stores along Perú and Victoria, just west of the Plaza de Mayo, including Zapatería de J. Bernasconi (1855), Imprenta y Librería de Mayo (1853), A la Ciudad de Londres (1873), El Progreso (1875), and Mueblería de París (1851).

Social clubs selected the Perú-Florida axis for their facilities. The first two gathering spots for the elite, the Club del Progreso (1852) and the Club del Plata (1860), opened just off Victoria, on Chacabuco and Perú, respectively. The Sociedad Rural Argentina (1866), the exclusive club of the country's livestock growers, established its headquarters at Perú 35. By the 1880s the elite clubs were choosing Florida for their centers: the Jockey Club (1881), the Club Naval y Militar (1881), and the Club de Gimnasia y Esgrima (1885). The elite of the foreign communities showed a similar preference for this same area. The Club Español (1866) was located in the section just west of the Plaza de Mayo, while the Club de Residentes Extranjeros (1841), the Club Francés (1867), the Circolo Italiano (1880), and the English Literary Society (1876) had their headquarters north of the plaza. The theater district, originally centered on the Plaza de Mayo—the old Teatro Colón, completed in 1855, and the Teatro Victoria, just west of the plaza—had begun to move northwest with the opening of new establishments such as the Odeón, Opera, San Martín, and Comedia. This outward move along Cuyo and Corrientes received dramatic confirmation in 1908 with the opening of the city's new opera house, named the Teatro Colón after its predecessor on the Plaza de Mayo. It occupied a whole block at the corner of Cerrito and Tucumán. Several new establishments—Apolo, Politeama Argentino, and Nuevo—also appeared farther out on Corrientes, while the famous Teatro Victoria moved five blocks farther west. . . .

After 1880 the burgeoning of the country's agricultural exports and the accompanying commercial-bureaucratic expansion of the city brought a marked change in upper-class housing styles and construction. Wealthy residents of Buenos Aires, many of them successful politicians and merchants from the provinces, saw modest income from lands, goods, and agricultural produce blossom into veritable fortunes. At the same time, increasing travel abroad, along with the admiration for progress and science engendered by the rising tide of positivist thought and philosophy that swept through Argentine educational and elite circles, filled the country's ruling classes with shame for their humble colonial origins and Hispanic background. Nouveau riche in spirit if not in origin, the *porteño* elite sought to remake their city in the style of the most modern of Europe's capitals. Alvear's dramatic reuniting of two plazas to form the Plaza de Mayo, and the plans for the Avenida de Mayo, merely highlighted the elite's admiration of Georges Haussman's design for the great Parisian boulevards.

The *porteño* upper class turned quickly from a taste for the Italianesque to a wholesale acceptance of currents emanating from the world's leader in architectural design, the École des Beaux-Arts in Paris. Italians were replaced by French-trained architects led by such figures as Carlos Agote, Alejandro Christophersen, Julio Dormal, Jacques Dunant, Pablo Hary, and Eduardo María Lanús—all of whom had studied in either France or Belgium. Supported by a few German and English architects, they remodeled the city into the Paris of South America. The crisis of 1890 and the ensuing depression years slowed but did not stop the trend toward more ornate and sumptuous styling, both in public and in private edifices. With the boom of 1905–12, the elite became eclectic, although the French influence, with its grand entrances, foyers, and vestibules, sweeping command of space, and harmonic balancing of lines, predominated. Italian-oriented architects, however, regained some popularity with their exuberant and exaggerated ornamentation of facades.

The impact of the École des Beaux-Arts on housing for the upper class, along with increasing land values at the city's center, stimulated the move toward Barrio Norte at the same time that it encouraged construction of the three- and four-story *palacio,* or "mansion," and the *petit hotel.* The elongated lot, so effectively used in patio-style construction, could not serve the French style, which demanded space. Although the narrow lot was still used for the new houses being built in the suburbs, the wealthy who moved from Florida toward Plaza San Martín and Barrio Norte acquired square lots, often a quarter of a city block, or at least rectangular lots with a depth not more than three times the width.

In its most pretentious form, the new style gave birth to mansions and *palacios* that occupied an entire city block. One of the most striking, the *palacio* of José C. Paz on the Plaza San Martín, completed in 1912 and still used in the 1970s as the social center for the Círculo Militar, took up a wedge-shaped block. The design for the building was drawn up in France by a leading French architect, Louis Sortais. Similarly, René Sergent sent prepared plans from Paris for the Errázuriz family's fabulous mansion, built in 1911 on Avenida Alvear (renamed Libertador General San Martín in 1950); today that building serves the city as the Museo de Artes Decorativas. Two years earlier the mansion of Mercedes Castellanos de Anchorena had risen on the Plaza San Martín — an entire block highlighted by a striking oval reception hall at its center. The tone of such stately, baroque mansions had already been set by the Ortiz Basualdo/Peña families, whose *palacio* was also located on the Plaza San Martín. This three-story house, winner of the municipality's architectural prize in 1904 and at that time valued at 500,000 pesos, or roughly a quarter of a million dollars, came from the drawing board of Julio Dormal.

Not only the exterior of these dwellings, but also the rich and ornate interiors, expressed the spirit, ambitions, and values of an upper class eager to parade its wealth and accomplishments and emulate the world's most current fashions. The mosaic billiard rooms, the mirrored and ornate salons, the special rooms set aside to exhibit art collections, suggest how much the elite's environment and attitudes had changed from the era of the *gran aldea.*

The new styles and tastes also affected those members of the *porteño* upper class who could not afford the sybaritic level of the *palacio* or the *petit hotel.* The chalet type of construction that appeared increasingly after the turn of the century appealed to families of comfortable means. Typical was the chalet

Elegant Buenos Aires, 1907. An elegant gathering of upper-class women and children at a festival. Courtesy Archivo General de la Nación, Buenos Aires.

described in an advertisement in 1906: "Attractive chalet in Belgrano. . . . First floor: salon, study, large dining room and antechamber, powder room, magnificent entry hail, kitchen and toilet, washroom, and a garden for vegetables. Mezzanine: one bedroom and two rooms for servants. Second floor: three bedrooms, charming drawing room, bathroom. Recently built, gas and running water installed."

Further down the scale, yet within grasp of modest professional men, were houses such as this one, advertised in 1907: "New . . . 10 by 27 yards. First floor with hall, study, living room, two bedrooms, dining room, bath, kitchen; upstairs a servant's room. Gas, running water, and sewers." In this case not too much had changed from the patio-style design, except that this was a more compact type of housing. . . .

The wealthy of Buenos Aires for a few decades at least sought to have the best of two worlds—proximity to the compact downtown area centered on the Plaza de Mayo yet the enjoyment of spaciousness, elegance, and luxury, which they could attain by moving out toward the Plaza San Martín and Barrio Norte. The outward push by the well-to-do thus came in more muted form and at a much later stage in Buenos Aires than in many commercial, industrializing urban areas. After 1920 the upper classes, assisted by the automobile, tended to follow the earlier lead of many of the foreign-born upper class— notably the English and Germans. Increasingly, they spread out into Belgrano, Villa Devoto, and Flores and beyond the Federal District to the north into

Vicente López, Olivos, La Lucila, Martínez, Acassuso, and San Isidro. But Barrio Norte retained its attraction for the upper class; even today it is the most concentrated and prestigious place of residence for the *porteño* elite.

Despite the elite's preference for the Plaza de Mayo area, most of those who lived in the city's center were manual laborers, artisans, skilled laborers, small shopkeepers, and clerks. Many had only recently arrived in Argentina. Since the demand for manual labor in the urban center was great and the streetcar fare was expensive until after 1900, these newcomers congregated in downtown *conventillos,* cheap boardinghouses, and apartments. Consequently, their working and living conditions formed the other part of changing patterns around the Plaza de Mayo. . . .

Working conditions—in addition to fluctuations in wages and living costs —affected urban laborers and European immigrants. The most common type of employment, and one that absorbed large numbers of recently arrived Europeans, consisted of the lifting and carrying associated with the waterfront, the construction sites, the railroad stations, or the wholesale and retail outlets. Dockworkers were hired each morning between 5:00 and 6:00 A.M. in gangs as employment opportunities presented themselves. This work might involve twelve trips an hour down a gangplank, unloading 220-pound bags of sugar, or 150 trips a day from ship to shore, balancing unwieldy, 130-pound stacks of lumber on one's shoulders.

Skilled and semiskilled workers—especially carpenters, blacksmiths, mechanics, masons, and painters as well as those who clothed and fed the urban populace (butchers, bakers, tailors, shoemakers)—also found ready employment. These men worked in small groups. Rarely did construction jobs or artisan shops employ more than ten persons. The fact that laborers were accustomed to working alongside their *patron,* or employer, and the relative absence of large industrial plants helped postpone development of working-class consciousness. Twelve- and fourteen-hour days were common, and jobs tended to be labor intensive rather than machinery oriented. There were, however, fewer industrial hazards and more healthy surroundings in Buenos Aires than there were in most European and U.S. cities.

In order to supplement family incomes, women and children often worked as long hours as men, frequently in cramped, unhealthy surroundings. Most children in the city attended the first grades of elementary school, but those from poorer families went to work at the age of nine or ten. Producers of cigarettes, matches, hats, buttons, and burlap bags invariably turned to cheap labor —women and children. These shops, which employed anywhere from a dozen to several hundred workers, also saved on light, ventilation, and space. Rarely did women and children, as marginal wage earners, effectively protest such economies. In addition, piecework from garment stores, as well as the city's laundering and ironing, afforded thousands of women employment at home, in the crowded patios and rooms of *conventillos* and apartment houses. . . .

Housing—even more than working conditions, cost of living, or wages— was a mark of the way of life of the nonelite groups that resided in the center of the city. Although, according to the municipal censuses of 1887 and 1904, *conventillos* sheltered only one-quarter to one-third of the population in the central city, the living conditions in this type of dwelling were in most respects the same as those of all of the nonelite who lived in the downtown area. The 60–70 percent of the population who did not live in *conventillos* or in individual family units—in the city's center such units were usually reserved for the upper classes—occupied boardinghouses, small apartment buildings, or narrow two-story houses that accommodated two to four families.[1] But life in these dwellings differed little from that in the *conventillo* in size of rooms, crowded conditions, or facilities. Indeed, the number of inhabitants sheltered in one building—usually over thirty—seems to have been the *conventillo*'s principal distinction. The large number of inhabitants also gave the *conventillo* visibility in contemporary sources—a visibility not shared by other housing for nonelite groups. Such visibility substantially facilitates examination of the *conventillo*.

Conventillos had first emerged in the city in the 1880s, when the shells of deteriorating patio-style homes south of the Plaza de Mayo were turned into multiple dwellings. Crowded tenement housing returned high income on increasingly valuable commercial land near the center of Buenos Aires, and *conventillos* thus competed with office and wealthy residential utilization of that land. Such profits added to the pressures that were bringing changes within the plaza area. Plaster-covered adobe or brick walls of patio-style homes frequently showed considerable deterioration after forty or fifty years. These older buildings, often with only slight interior remodeling, brought substantially higher profits for owners as tenement rentals than as housing for the affluent classes.

Outright construction of tenements also added to the supply of *conventillos* in the plaza area. One of the earliest recorded instances concerned a group of Italian merchants who, in 1867, leased a number of vacant lots along Corrientes and Lavalle on twenty-year contracts and put up cheaply constructed tenements. By the end of that year two newly built *conventillos* on Corrientes between Talcahuano and Uruguay had been filled. Each had thirty large rooms measuring six by sixteen feet. The initial monthly rental, four gold pesos per room, was a real bargain since it approximated only 20 percent of a common laborer's monthly wages. The construction of new *conventillos* led *La prensa* to comment, early in 1871: "The practice has now become general to build in a

Conventillo scene (1910). Courtesy Archivo General de la Nación, Buenos Aires.

small area a great number of rooms made with cheap materials and under conditions that they produce a monthly profit of 3–4 percent; at the same time, because of the low rent these rooms are within the reach of day laborers and persons who do not care how they live, packed together like animals without any concern for morals or health." By 1880 nearly three hundred of the two thousand *conventillos* in the city were new construction built expressly as rental property.

Whether remodeled from older housing or built new for speculation, the *conventillo* conformed to the elongated rectangular house lot that characterized the patio-style home and the subdivision of blocks generally in Buenos Aires. Thee *conventillo*'s depth, therefore, was three to six times as big as its width. The usual frontage was ten *varas* (18.4 feet), especially in the plaza area, where streets and blocks dated from the seventeenth century. Building materials and size of rooms varied somewhat, according to location and time of building; a *conventillo* also might consist of a single story or be a "double-decker." But the outline and structure of the *conventillo* was remarkably consistent during the entire period from 1870 to 1910. The framework of the patio-style building remained, with a single street entrance, a number of rooms opening off interior patios, latrines at the rear of the building, and no exterior windows except for the few barred ones on the street. Rooms usually measured twelve by twelve feet, with ceiling heights of fourteen feet common in the older buildings but a general decline toward nine feet by 1900. Since every square foot had value, patios often shrank until they were little more than corridors.

At the same time, by crowding as many as 350 persons into a building that formerly had accommodated twenty-five family members and servants, tenement housing sharply reduced individual rents. By this means alone, the newcomer to the city frequently closed the gap between his living costs and his wages. Single men banded together in groups of six or seven to share a room. Families of five or six members rented a single room and often took in a few additional relatives or compatriots to share expenses.

In these surroundings, life certainly never lacked for activity, commotion, and proximity to one's fellows. Each unit or room afforded some privacy as long as the door remained closed and a curtain covered the single window that opened on the patio. Community kitchens existed only rarely in *conventillos,* and most groups did their cooking on a charcoal brazier placed on a box or shelf at the entrance to, or occasionally inside, the room. Other boxes at the entrance might hold a basin for washing or serve as receptacles for collecting garbage. Furnishings were sparse. A double bed or some iron cots might accommodate a number of sleepers during the course of a twenty-four-hour period, especially among a group of single men. A pine table, a few benches or chairs, some old trunks, perhaps a sewing machine, and more boxes completed the furnishings. In summertime, light came from the open door and window; in other seasons, and at night, one relied on an oil or a gas lamp or sometimes on a bare electric lightbulb. Pictures of popular heroes, generals, or kings torn from magazines, an image of the Madonna and of a couple of saints, perhaps a faded photograph of family members still in Europe, appeared on the once-whitewashed walls.

The average day began early—at 4:30 in the summer and at 6:00 during the winter—as the men left quietly, often without breakfast in order not to wake the children in these cramped quarters. Shortly thereafter the women and older children began to stir: they put water or milk on the brazier, went to market, or haggled in their doorways with street vendors selling bread and meat. By 9:00 the children were off to scour the streets for odd jobs; those aged seven or eight might attend the first or second year of primary school. The women were long since at their piecework—sewing, rolling cigars, ironing, or doing laundry. At 11:30 the men returned for a hasty lunch of watery *puchero* or some cornmeal pudding. Afternoon brought the bedlam so often associated with *conventillos.* Despite all the landlords' precautions against taking in large families, half a *conventillo*'s population usually was under fifteen years of age, and fifty to one hundred shrieking, fighting, playing youngsters were the rule in any *conventillo* patio. Men returned from work by 6:00 or 6:30; a dinner of stew was eaten shortly thereafter; by 10:30 nearly everyone was in bed. Religious or patriotic holidays provided a break in this routine. Then accordions, violins, and guitars playing Old World dances enlivened the gray surroundings. A bottle of wine or, occasionally, *caña* injected warmth into tired bodies, and the *conventillo* acquired for a moment a vivacity and sparkle it usually lacked.

The *conventillo* and housing in general for nonelite groups in the downtown core served to condition great numbers of newcomers to the *porteño* environment. Over this bridge many European-born poor crossed into Argentina permanently. Only the 1887 census distinguished the native born from the foreign born among *conventillo* dwellers, registering 72 percent as foreign born in the central city, while for the city as a whole the figure stood at 66 percent. An examination of *conventillos* from Census District I (bounded by Paseo de Julio, Rivadavia, Maipú, and Córdoba) in the 1869 manuscript census suggests even greater foreign-born domination of *conventillo* population. Of the 707 individuals registered in eight *conventillos*, 468, or 66 percent, were foreign born. If one adds, however, the 180 children under fourteen years of age who were born to immigrant parents, the "foreign" component increases to 92 percent. . . .

Paralleling the predominance of the foreign born and the clustering of those from the same ethnic background was the similarity of occupations among *conventillo* dwellers. Of the 111 employed women (roughly half the adult female population) in this district all except one — a cigarette vendor — were occupied as washerwomen, seamstresses, or house servants. All the men worked with their hands. Day laborers, peons, and servants constituted a little over half the male workforce; the remainder were carpenters, masons, shoemakers, tailors, and store clerks. . . .

The Plaza de Mayo was a powerful magnet, pulling both the poor immigrant and the wealthy *porteño* toward the center of the city. The *conventillo* dweller was drawn to the plaza by the proximity of employment, and he was kept there by his inability to pay the high cost of transportation to outlying suburbs. The wealthy, although shifting his residence from the plaza's south side to its northern approaches, also refused to abandon the plaza for the suburb. The high concentration of social, economic, and political institutions around the plaza, as well as the powerful tradition that equated residential proximity to the central plaza with prestige, bound the upper class to the city's center.

The *conventillo* and the *palacio* typified the evolution of the Plaza de Mayo's environs. The *conventillo* provided the most identifiable and striking sort of worker housing in the center of the city. It constituted a principal shelter for new arrivals, and many of its aspects reappeared in other types of housing available to nonelite groups in the downtown area. The *palacio* gave exuberant expression to the materialism and conspicuous consumption that overtook the city's upper class in the economic booms of 1884–89 and 1905–12. Those who could not afford a *palacio* sought to emulate its opulence on a smaller scale in chalets and individual family dwellings.

The thrust away from the plaza was made by other groups. The boom years brought not only demographic growth, but also expanding opportunities. For the worker acclimated to the *porteño* environment and possessed of skills or savings, the road upward led toward the suburbs. The sons and daughters of immigrants thus sought a plot of land and a home on the outskirts. After electrification and unification of the streetcar system, low fares powerfully supported these efforts and moved the common man outward.

Notes

For additional references, notes, and tables, consult the complete version of this chapter in James Scobie, *Buenos Aires: Plaza to Suburb, 1870–1910* (Oxford: Oxford University Press, 1974), 114–59.

1 Some individual family units not belonging to upper-class families were owned by shopkeepers. Especially in the buildings on the small, square lots at the corners of blocks, which often housed food stores—*almacén, panadería, frutería, carnicería*—the owner and his family lived in a back room or an upstairs loft.

The Modern Crowd

José María Ramos Mejía

José María Ramos Mejía (1849–1914) was a physician, sociologist, and politician whose ubiquity attests to the authority given to positivism and scientific knowledge during this period. He wrote essays for the press and was very active in every sphere of the medical profession. In 1888, he became a congressman and, between 1892 and 1898, ran the Department of Public Health. Probably his most lasting and decisive influence was his writing in the fields of psychiatry and social psychology. In Argentine Crowds (1899), a book rife with ideas from Social Darwinism and the works of the French social psychologist Le Bon, Ramos Mejía develops a biological history of Argentina. He conceives of Argentine society as a collective organism that has undergone a series of racial and psychological metamorphoses from colonial to modern times. In the chapter selected, Ramos Mejía focuses on the effects that massive immigration had on Buenos Aires's racial profile. Despite the unstable identity of the modern crowd, he predicted that a future Argentine race would emerge from the combination of all the biological and cultural forces that were converging in the country. Yet he also questioned the optimism implicit in the idea of the melting pot, which foresaw the peaceful and smooth amalgamation of different ethnic backgrounds into a single, national heritage. Ramos Mejía's writings show an unmistakable anxiety about the democratization of customs and the mixture of bodies. Fear compels this Social Darwinist to identify and classify those immigrants who seem to threaten the natural hierarchies of the oligarchic order by trying to join the higher strata of local society or by disseminating among the people values foreign to the national character that was promoted by the elite. As in many literary and sociological works of the period, the ability of the "undesirables" to pass as true Argentines is the focus of Ramos Mejía's Creole paranoia.

We can see in Argentine history two powerful social forces that come from the coast and the interior and always flow toward this immense capital, Buenos Aires. Although still mercilessly mercantile and heterogeneous, this city is the foundry where the bronze of the great statue of the future is being molded, perhaps too hurriedly, and where a new race is emerging.

There slowly emerges a certain unity of political feeling between the metropolis and the rest of the Republic; the multitude that is formed in the capital will have traces of national traits. For it is in this center of Argentina's circulatory system that blood is refreshed and later sent out to the most humble of the nation's capillaries. The poisoned blood of the entrepreneurs of misery, of political pretensions, or of local grievances flows toward the great lung to be converted into the red globule providing the support of morality or the promise of a cure that is spread by the great heart. (But this works well only when the blood is not made toxic by some bit of that self-interest that exists in all the vineyards of the Lord.)

The well-known comparison of the capital with the brain is vulgar, although it is accurate. All sensations and impressions come to it through the channels of its circulatory system. The capital will be the kinesthetic center of the whole political being, of the confluence of all vital functions, and the vague conscience of that entire body. It is the center for intellectualizing about the subtle shadings of philosophical questions; it is the organ of reflection that sends back messages transformed into movement, light, ideas, and will. All these sensations are distributed throughout the entire territory by the communications system of the mail, the telegraph, and the press.

Thus, a person who wants to study the modern Argentine multitude and takes as a genuine representative type the populace that has been formed [under certain circumstances] in the capital is not being led astray.

When I was studying the admirable progression adopted by nature as it slowly developed organic types (from our modest Silurian ancestor, to the primitive fish, right up to man), it seemed reasonable to me that in the formation of this society something analogous must have happened. That at a certain stage in its development the first embryo, the immigrant, must have given the social order something like the anatomical structure of fish, later that of amphibians, and finally that of mammals. By that I mean that the immigrant would have followed a similar series of transformations in perfecting his intellectual and moral development.

The truth is that the analogy between the immigrant and the human body was seductive because it gave the intellect an easy and convincing means of interpreting society. And also because, in effect, there are social types in the evolution of our society that could be explained, with a little goodwill, by illustrative, though remote, comparison.

Any numskull is more intelligent than the immigrant who has just landed on our shores. The newcomer is rather amorphous, even "cellular," in his feeling of complete estrangement, in terms of his mental processes, from everything that is moderately progressive. His is a slow brain, like that of the ox, at whose side he has lived; he is myopic when it comes to physical sharpness, awkward and obtuse in everything that has to do with the easy, spontaneous acquisition of images by the great cerebral senses. . . .

That country bumpkin is in a twilight, and in a certain sense larval, state of psychic development, but, when he first begins to walk on our land, he is, in part, the vigorous protoplasm of the new race. We must convince ourselves that this unpolished peasant does not feel as we, the Creole elite, do. . . . But the environment works marvels on the moldable submissiveness of his almost virgin brain. . . .

I am amazed by the docile pliability of the Italian immigrant. He comes to Argentina a shapeless protoplasm and accepts with prophetic tameness all the ways that necessity and legitimate ambition imprint on him. He is everything in the life of the cities and the countryside, from wandering musician to priest. With the same hand that he gives the benediction, using the comic solemnity of a man who does it as a job rather than as a vocation, he turns the handle of the hurdy-gurdy or pulls around the vegetable cart; he offers us cheap umbrellas when it is sprinkling, he makes the clever monkey dance on a tripod, and he digs in the earth that he has conquered with his doggedness and has made fertile with his toil. Since there are so many immigrants, they inundate everything: second- and third-rate theaters, free promenades in the square, and the churches (because Italians are devout and peace-loving people). They fill the streets, the plaza, the asylums, the hospitals, the circuses, and the shops. They take on work in all jobs and professions, although their behavior is a little awkward and elemental. They are chauffeurs, after a sorrowful learning period of violent run-ins and crashes with other cars, of violations and fines that only sharpen their wits. They are trolley-car "coachmen" with extravagant, picturesque ways of manipulating the reins; they are drivers and conductors. Even the spicy wisecracks of urban gangs and city slickers burst forth from their lips with a certain exotic grace for a brain like theirs, still rough and watery. They are, in sum, everything that offers a livelihood and that promises a future that may be remote but appears to be secure.

In certain kinds of work they have even displaced the gaucho. These days, when you penetrate a little further inland, a strange kind of burlesque centaur startles your eyes. For there, riding by on a straggly horse, is a nervous figure swinging his legs up and down to the disjointed jostling of a tired old cob. . . .

In our country, which is still in its formative stage, the children of immigrants, the most genuine fruit of our national environment, give us a first vague manifestation of our future nationality as it is in modern Argentina. . . .

If you observe him in his most insignificant actions and in situations where his feelings manifest themselves in some way, however puerile, you will see that he is beginning to reveal his future passion, especially in whatever the Fatherland considers to be its overt, sensorial culture. The street urchin, made Argentine little by little by his environment and inheritance, focuses his affection on the land of his birth. . . .

This curious vagabond, an eternal occupant of the streets, is the one who applauds with most enthusiasm the cadets who, with enchanting gravity, parade by on national holidays. He is the one who cheers with fierce vigor the ragged banner of some old and glorious battalion, the one who always enlists, the one who gets involved in the most innocent and sincere debates about all popular matters having to do with the national flag and uniforms. . . .

The first generation is often deformed and rather ugly up to a certain age; it seems to be the product of some crude mold, the result of the first attempt at working a noble metal still full of the imperfections and sharp edges that later polishing will correct. There is a certain percentage of short noses and thick lips: his morphology has not yet been modified by culture's chisel. In the second generation you can already see the improvements that show he is living a more civilized, more cultured life than the one the immigrant laborer brought with him. The change in diet, the effect of the good air, and the relative calmness of spirit due to the ease with which he can provide himself with the necessities of life all work their transcendental influence. . . .

From the immigrant thus imperfectly modified, there emerges, as if by social epigenesis, all those products of evolution with whom we rub elbows daily and who form a peculiar but complete order of human beings. . . .

In social paleontology, the *guarango,* a crude offshoot of immigrant forefathers, represents one of those vertebrates that future sociologists will look on with curiosity in their attempt to establish the chain of successive types in our evolution. He is artistic, with homosexual leanings. Like similar men with the same sexual instincts, he reveals his doubtful potency in his outrageous appetites. He needs vivid colors and screeching music, just as he warms to the eroticism of the intense smell of flesh. He favors bizarre combinations without any sense of taste. He is given to twisted posturing and indelicate carryings-on intended to satisfy the particular idiosyncrasies of his sensibilities.

In music, he has the atavism of the hurdy-gurdy that his fathers followed in their misery. As to art, he has in his retina the screaming colors of the oil painting that surprised his eyes in their first contact with an art gallery on the outskirts of some frontier settlement. . . . You will see all these tendencies mixed together in revolting combinations: in his baroque clothes; in the decoration of his home; in the extravagant abundance of knickknacks; in his literary tastes; in his innocent fiestas; in the flourishes he adds to his signature; and in unusual perfume shops. Finally, he reveals himself even in his burial, which is characterized by his compromising insecurity and hence by an excess of mourning browns, lugubrious tapestries and hats, and horses of luxuriant black that go trotting along with great solemnity and frisk around with all the horses whose sex offers any doubts. . . .

He has received the benedictions of instruction in the habitual form of university injections; but he is a beggar when it comes to culture. In his outward appearance he is still too crude because of his proximity to his immediate ancestor, the rustic peasant, and therefore he resists the cultural varnish that comes from a decent home or, in its absence, from a college education that is not merely professional and practical. For this reason, even when he becomes a doctor, a lawyer, an engineer, or a journalist, you will note from a league away that slight sharp smell of the stable . . . that he gives off from head to foot. . . .

The *canalla* [riffraff] is the *guarango* who has climbed the ladder by dressing well or having money. But his soul is still full of atavisms. At the risk of overusing a medical analogy, I would say that he is like a liver that pours its poison into the heart instead of dumping it into the intestines. Through the long years of domestication that the beast in him has experienced, there is something that escapes the benefits of time and instruction, something that remains permanently in his soul, like a birthmark remains on the skin, despite its constant renovation. It is something that, in imitation of the coarseness of Heckel's classification, I would call "the appendix of the riffraff." . . .

The *huaso* is a *guarango* of a more grotesque kind. He has the moral skin of an elephant and scrapes together money through his astute contacts. Shaped by this and by his environment, he emerges as a "hustler," a spirited but restrained *huaso* tempered by his associations and his constant work on the street. All of this gives him daily contact with all classes of people.

There is another variety of *guarango* who differs from the *huaso* because he is less of an exhibitionist in his lifestyle. He is an essential type and excessively conservative, of a certain cautious modesty that comes from avarice and the tone set by the large fortune that he has amassed, perhaps at the cost of his health. He represents the bourgeoisie, the improvised millionaire born of the magical ways of the lottery. Thanks to his devoted work, he springs forth from the immense seeding ground of our country or from a steaming pile of fertile land. But, once he has taken his place in life, he has no other program than to protect his money, to defend it from charity and from the patriotism that sometimes knocks at his door. He presses his money close to his chest so it won't show, watering it with the milk of turnovers through repeated sales and reissued mortgages. Finally, his money is stuck to the nipples of usury that keep at a distance the tuberculosis of fortunes and is the saving comfort of bankruptcy and grief. Having arrived at that exalted level, he buys, naturally for little money, a title. Sometimes it is in high commerce. As his goals are now set high, you will see him bearded and solemn. Without being very scrupulous about the failings of good government, he can be seen docilely following Juan Manuel de Rosas, admiring García Moreno, or smiling on Santos and Melgarejo; the immigrant bourgeois's soul is lacking in magnanimous ideals; despotism or freedom are all the same to him, as long as he hangs on to his money. But woe to the authority whom he suspects of being disrespectful of the foreign coin! Then the wealthy man will rise up heroic in the revolution to give his life . . . before parting with his money. He is the one who at this passive level becomes the butt, and perhaps the incubator as well, of all the political jokes that the daily media distributes as journalistic literature.

This golden burgher will, as a man, be a terrible influence if national education does not modify him with the brush of culture. What he needs is the infiltration of other ideals than the ones to which he now clings in his precipitous ascent to political office in the capital.

Translated by Patricia Owen Steiner

Making it in America

Oreste Sola

*The millions of European immigrants seeking a better future in Argentina encoun-
tered a country full of promises but with few economic opportunities outside the urban
centers along the eastern coast. Since there was no land available, the only option
left to them in the countryside was to work for the traditional landowners as tenant farmers. As a consequence, large masses of immigrants concentrated in the cities,
particularly in Buenos Aires. Although most immigrants had a common background,
their experiences are hard to classify. Some managed to enter the local upper classes,
but the majority joined the developing working class. When they did not find what
they had hoped for, they returned to their homelands — as soon as they had gathered
enough money. The correspondence between Oreste Sola and his family in Italy offers
a glimpse of some of the experiences the newcomers shared. Like many, Oreste had
to change jobs and residences many times before achieving some degree of economic
autonomy. It is telling that he ended up in the construction business, working on the
urban projects that were transforming Buenos Aires into a modern city. He was among
those who would eventually form the powerful, large middle class characteristic of
Argentine society. Although Oreste's history is certainly illustrative, one must keep in
mind that his situation was not representative of the majority. Oreste was literate and
fairly well educated. Such skills gave him an advantage in his pursuit of fortune that
less educated immigrants certainly lacked.*

Buenos Aires, 17 August 1901

Dearest parents,

I have been here since the fifth of this month; I am in the best of health, as
are my two companions. As soon as we got here, we went to the address of
Godfather Zocco, who then introduced us to several people from Valdengo
who have been in America for some years and are all doing well more or less.
The language here is Castilian, quite similar to Spanish, but you don't hear anyone speaking it. Wherever you go, whether in the hotel or at work, everyone

speaks either Piedmontese or Italian, even those from other countries, and the Argentines themselves speak Italian.

This city is very beautiful. There is an enormous amount of luxury. All the streets—they call them *calle* [*sic*] here—are paved either with hard wood or in cement as smooth as marble, even too smooth since the horses, tram horses as well as carriage horses, which run here, keep slipping constantly. It is not unusual to see twenty or more of them fall in one day.

There are some buildings beautiful beyond words, only five stories high, six at the most, but with ornamentation the equal of which you won't find in all of Turin. The most beautiful building is the water reservoir, built by the English, and, what is surprising, it is all marble for half its height but with certain small columns sculpted and decorated with exquisite workmanship. The other half of it is also enchanting; it occupies ten thousand square meters.

The Piazza Victoria [Plaza de Mayo] is also beautiful, where all around on two sides there are only banks. They are of all nations: English, French, Italian, Spanish, North American, etc., etc. On another side is the government building where the president of the Argentine Republic resides. He is Italian, Rocca by name, the third Italian president in a row who sits on the Argentine throne. There is also the railway station of the south, which is something colossal. With workshops, offices, and the station itself it will cover 1 million square meters. Now they are at work on a government building for the Congress [Parliament]. The architect was an Italian, as is the chief contractor, who is supervising all the work. It is a job that in the end will cost more than 700 million lire. It will occupy an area of a block that is ten thousand square meters and will be surrounded by a square, which, along with the building, will constitute an area of about 100,000 square meters. This work will be better than the first (the railway station), but perhaps I shall not be able to see it finished.

All of this is inside the city, but if you should go outside for a few hours, it's worse than a desert. You find only houses made solely out of mortar, with only a ground floor and a door you have to enter on all fours. Outside you don't see a plant; everything is desert. The plains stretch as far as the eye can see; it takes hours on the train before you come to the mountains. There are a few tracts of land, sort of green, where they may let a few horses loose to graze. Here they let the animals go out no matter what the weather might be. Here you can't find a rock, though you pay its weight in gold for it. All the ground is black like manure, thick and muddy. When it doesn't rain, it gets hard, and if you try to dig, it shoots out as if it were rock.

The food here is pretty good, but it doesn't have much flavor. This is true for all Argentina.

All the guys here are jolly as crazy men. In the evening when we get together before going to bed we split our sides laughing. They would all like to go back to Italy, but they don't ever budge. Perhaps I will do the same. Here we eat, drink, and laugh and enjoy ourselves; we are in America.

Good-bye. You too should be happy as well as Mom that I am in America. Give a kiss to Narcisa and another to Abele. Tell him to study hard, that one who studies and is knowledgeable is greatly respected and sought after here.

Take one last loving kiss and hug from your always loving son,

Oreste

Mendoza, 18 September 1901

Dearest parents,

I am still in good spirits and happy that I am in America. I am now at Mendoza instead of Buenos Aires. I didn't like Buenos Aires too much because you don't get good wine there; and then every day the temperature changes twenty times, and I was always chilly. Otherwise it was fine.

One day I got the idea, knowing that Secondino's brother-in-law and sister were in Mendoza. Since the boss advanced me the money for the trip, I made up my mind to come here, where you see nothing but hills and mountains in the distance, like at home. You drink very well here; the wine costs half what it does in Buenos Aires and is pure and delicious. I am living here with Carlo and his wife and a man by the name of Luigi Ferraro from Chiavazza who has been here for seven years traveling around in America. There are few people here from Biella, but there is no shortage of Italians. I still haven't learned a word of Castilian because, everywhere you go, they speak Italian or Piedmontese.

I am better off here than in Buenos Aires. I am only sorry to be so far from my friends — they didn't want to come — and from Godfather and the rest. This city is ugly; it never rains even though it is close to the mountains. I have written a friend to send me the address of my schoolmate Berretta and might just go and see him in Peru; it takes four days or more on the train. From Buenos Aires to Mendoza takes two nights and a day on the railroad without ever changing trains or getting off. The longest stop is a half hour. In the entire journey you don't see a plant. [There are] two or three rivers about four hundred meters wide. They are all in the plain, so calm that you can't tell which way the water is going, and yet they flow on in an imperceptible way.

Throughout the journey one meets only horses, cows, and goats, none of which have stables. On the rail line you don't see a house for three hours or more, and everything is like that. The first night an ox was sleeping on the tracks; the train hit it so hard that it knocked it for a distance of more than fifty meters. It gave a long bellow and then died. There are also ostriches in great number. You find carcasses of other animals who have just died; the owners of these vast tracts don't go looking for them. They leave them there to rot as food for the vultures, which are abundant. All of Argentina is like that. From Mendoza it takes fifteen hours by mule to get to Chile. My trip cost me more than thirty scudos. Everyone, Carlo, Cichina, and Luigi, gives their regards to you. Tell Secondino to come and see America, to drink and eat and travel.

Time is pressing since I have to work every evening until ten. I work at home after work.

You should write me at: El Taller del Ferro Carril G.O.A., Mendoza.

Good-bye everybody. Kisses to Abele and Narcisa. Tell Abele to study hard and to learn to work. Send him to the technical schools; I imagine he has been promoted. Good-bye, Mom and Dad. Be in good spirits as I am.

Yours always,

Oreste

Buenos Aires, 3 May 1903

Dearest parents, brother, and sister,

As you will see from the heading, I am once again in Buenos Aires. Yesterday evening, while I was visiting Godfather Zocco, he showed me Dad's letter, indicating that you were already thinking ill of me because for some time now I haven't written. Actually you are not far wrong.

I am fine here, in excellent health; business is also good. As I had written you from Santa Teresa, [it is just] that I had to keep on the move. I left there toward the end of February and went straight to Santa Fé, where I had to take a job with a French railway firm. I worked a few days, but then, since Frenchmen and Italians don't get along with each other, I went on my way. The next day I left for San Cristóbal [San Cristóforo]. I stayed there for only three days since they are still all Negroes, and I headed straight for Tucumán, where I had an excellent job. But since there is malaria in that area—they call it *chucho* [*ciucio*]—and at that time there was also smallpox, and it seemed to be spreading, I got scared and took off again. I would have liked to go to Bolivia, but since I was rather far away from the big cities, it was not convenient for me. So I headed for the capital. Almost two days and three nights on the train. I assure you that I am tired and have had my fill of traveling.

Now for about a month I have been here and have been employed in the work on the Congreso Nacional, which is under construction; the work will last at least a half dozen years. I am doing very well here, and if I did not have to do my military service, I would stay on to the end. That would be of great advantage to me.

Meanwhile for this year I am not coming to Italy to be in the army. Since I have a good job, I have a firm desire to stay put until next year so that then I would do only one year of military service.

In a few days I'll pay a visit to the Italian consul, just so I won't be declared a draft dodger, though I have time up to the age of twenty-six. For this year then, unless something special happens, it will be difficult for us to see each other again. I had come here to the capital with the intention of coming back home, but since I have hit the mark nicely, it's better that I stay here.

The day before yesterday we celebrated May Day, but there wasn't much of a crowd, however. We talk a lot about the celebrations in Italy. Some time ago Sasso arrived, and he gave me news about you.

I imagine that Abele will be making progress in his studies and that soon he will become a Marconi or something like that [and that] Narcisa will continue to work and to sing. I'll accompany her from here. [I imagine that] Mom will be in good health, as well as Dad, and so you will last a hundred years, just as I think I will keep on going.

All our fellow countrymen here are in excellent health. Zocco and my travelling companion Pierino give their regards to all of you.

Keep in good spirits, and stay healthy, and don't worry about me so much. I manage all right wherever I am.

Best and heartfelt kisses and hugs from your ever-affectionate son and brother,

Oreste

Translated by John Lenaghan

The Jewish Gauchos

Alberto Gerchunoff

The first Jewish settlements in Argentina were agrarian communities in the eastern provinces. Some of the towns that these settlers founded are still standing today, like the traditional Moisesville in the province of Santa Fé. Jewish settlers built their own libraries, published newspapers in Yiddish, and observed their own religious and cultural ceremonies. In The Jewish Gauchos *(1910), the Jewish writer Alberto Gerchunoff (1883–1950) yields to the integrating drive of Creole nationalism by depicting the first Jewish settlers as a virtuous and persistent people, willing to join national society and to blend their own ancestral customs with those of local rural traditions in exchange for a better life free from persecution and ostracism. Gerchunoff's tales of reconciliation emphasize the variety of social forces that shape the assimilation process: the immigrants' hopes for a better life and their children's desire to fit in; the strong institutional pressure to create a common national culture coming from the state and public schooling; and, equally important, the cultural intersections that increasingly began to define cosmopolitan Argentina. As later events would unfortunately corroborate, xenophobic nationalism and anti-Semitism would make integration more difficult for the Jewish community than its members originally expected.*

The morning the new immigrants were expected, some two hundred people went to the station at Dominguez. The immigrants were expected on a ten o'clock train, and their colony was to be established outside San Gregorio and close to the forest where, according to local legend, cattle thieves and tigers abounded.

Spring was coming everywhere, and the green fields of the meadows were already well dotted with daisies.

The station was crowded, and the people speculated about the new arrivals from Russia, especially about the rabbi from Odessa, an old, learned talmudic scholar of the Vilna Yeshiva who had been to Paris, it was said, and had been very courteously received by Baron Hirsch, the father of the colonies.

The chief and the sergeant of the Villaguay constabulary had come to the station to assist in the arrival and were talking quietly together. Other gauchos were there, playing jackstones while a number of the Jewish colonists watched.

The shochet of Rajil had drawn the shochet of Rosch Pina into a discussion in the hope of confusing him before so many people. They were talking about the rabbi among the expected immigrants, and the shochet of Rosch Pina was telling some things about him. He had known him in Vilna, where they studied the sacred texts together. The new rabbi was a fine person, and he knew the Talmud almost completely by memory. He was a member of the group that had gone to Palestine to purchase lands before Baron Hirsch had thought of launching this project in Argentina.

The man had never practiced as a rabbi, the shochet said. After he finished his studies, he had become a merchant in Odessa, but he often contributed to *Azphira,* a periodical, written entirely in ancient Hebrew.

Later, the two shochets debated a complicated point of domestic law, and the shochet of Rajil quoted an idea of the divine Maimonides on the sacrifice of bulls.

Awaiting the new arrivals recalled deep and lasting memories for most of the crowd. Many remembered the morning on which they had fled the unhappy realm of the czar. Then they recalled their arrival in this promised land, in this new Jerusalem they had heard proclaimed in the synagogues and had read about in the circulars carrying little verses in Russian, praising the soil of this country:

To Palestine, to the Argentine,
We'll go — to sow;
To live as friends and brothers;
To be free!

"Don Abraham," the sergeant said to the shochet, "here comes the train." A sudden rush of talk spread. Behind the hills, in the clear morning, the thread of the engine's smoke was seen.

When the train puffed in, the immigrants descended from two coaches. They looked drained and miserable, but their eyes shone with bright hope. The last to descend was the rabbi. He was a tall, broad old man with a pleasant face and a thick white beard. The colonists gathered around him; he was overwhelmed with greetings and wishes of welcome. The shochet of Rajil, Don Abraham, worked his way to the rabbi's side and took charge. He led him away from the station. They were followed by the colonists and the long line of immigrants, with their bundles and their children. The immigrants seemed to be losing some of their misery as they moved in the soft morning air and stared at the beautiful countryside.

When the lines had moved a little away from the station, Don Abraham mounted the stump of a tree and made a speech of greeting—well interspersed with Hebraic quotations. The new rabbi answered for the immigrants with the quotation of a short verse from Isaiah. He spoke about czarist Russia then, telling of the horrible sufferings of his people there.

"Here," he said, "we shall work our own land, care for our own animals, and eat bread made from our own wheat." The rabbi was filled with a thrilling enthusiasm, and he made an imposing and prophet-like figure with his great beard waving in the wind. When he stepped down from the stump, the rabbi embraced the sergeant and kissed him warmly on the mouth.

Then, in the full warmth of the morning sun, the caravan started for San Gregorio.

Translated by Prudencio de Pereda

The Birth of Tango

Simon Collier

Between 1865 and 1895, various musical traditions blended and eventually formed what would later be identified as tango. The habanera, the Andalusian tango, and the milonga—an Afro-Argentine form of popular dance related to candombe—all came to influence the early rhythmic development of the musical genre. In its early stages, the Argentine tango was mainly the dance and music of the urban poor, the socially unacceptable, and the disinherited of Buenos Aires's suburbios (working-class neighborhoods). In the dance academies and bordellos, young upper-class men joined the lower classes in their appreciation of the tango. Everybody seemed to find a source of satisfaction in its egalitarian embrace. For the upper classes, it was a means of escaping social restrictions. For the less fortunate, tango lyrics expressed the alienation of urban life, while the dance's sharply tangled steps provided a form of release.

From well before the start of her great economic boom, Argentina had established close commercial links with Europe and had imported from the Old World not only textiles, machinery, and luxury goods, but also a host of new cultural trends, among them fashions in music and dance. It is these, of course, that had a vital bearing on the invention of the tango, so it is essential to ask what was being danced in Buenos Aires in the years before the tango came along.

The first new European dance to reach Argentina in the nineteenth century, roughly at the time of Independence (1816), was the waltz. This was followed in the mid-century years by the polka, the mazurka, and the schottische (spelled *chotis* in Spanish). Also in the mid-century came the immensely popular habanera, danced to the Spanish-Cuban rhythm perhaps best remembered today from its appearance in Georges Bizet's opera *Carmen*—a habanera Bizet borrowed from the Spanish composer Sebastian Yradier.

As its name suggests, the habanera evolved in early-nineteenth-century Havana, Cuba, from where it traveled both to Spain and to Argentina. (Its mild syncopation was to become altogether less mild in the extraordinary wave of dance rhythms that emanated from Cuba one hundred years later.) On its Spanish side, it derived from the contradanza, the Spanish adaptation of the French contredanse of the eighteenth century, itself derived in part from the English "country dances" (few, if any, of which were genuinely rural) of the seventeenth. The contredanse was itself introduced into Cuba by French planters fleeing from the slave rebellion in Saint Domingue (Haiti) in the 1790s.

The habanera and the polka in particular seem to have played a part in stimulating the emergence of the local Argentine dance known as the milonga, a dance evidently very popular by the 1870s among the *compadritos* of Buenos Aires and sometimes referred to, significantly, as "the poor man's habanera." The milonga had originated as a form of song and was a variant of the lengthy improvisations (with guitar accompaniment) that were the hallmark of the *payadores,* the folk singers of the pampa, who had played an important part in the now vanishing world of the gaucho. Once in the city, the milonga, its tempo simplified, acquired steps of its own. We do not know enough to describe them in any detail, but they appear to have been strongly influenced by the new dances imported from overseas.

There has never been any real doubt about the importance of the milonga and the habanera in the tango's immediate ancestry. It seems fairly clear that the milonga actually *was* the embryonic form of the tango before the new dance was finally given a name. It is at this point, however, that the issue becomes complicated, not only because of the lack of precise contemporary descriptions of what was happening in the *arrabales* of Buenos Aires in the 1870s and 1880s, but also because of confusion over the term *tango* itself. Where, in fact, does this term come from? Answering this question will help us to get closer to the tango's moment of conception and birth.

The etymology cannot be traced completely. It is possible that the word is straightforwardly African in origin, a theory strongly supported by the Argentine historian Ricardo Rodríguez Molas, who notes that in certain African tongues the word *tango* means "closed place" or "reserved ground." (On the map of Africa today, Tango can be found as a place-name in both Angola and Mali.) An alternative possibility, not to be dismissed too quickly, is that the term derives originally from Portuguese (and therefore from the Latin verb *tangere,* "to touch") and that it was incorporated, evidently in some kind of slave-trading connection, into a kind of pidgin Portuguese used on the island of Sao Tome (in the Gulf of Guinea), an important center for the slave trade. If this second derivation is correct, the word was picked up by African slaves from their captors. But, whether African or Portuguese, it seems highly probable that it reached the Western Hemisphere with the slave ships and on the lips of slaves. A third theory sometimes invoked — that *tango* is simply onomatopoeic, representing the sound of a drumbeat, *tan-go* — seems on balance to be less convincing.

In many parts of the Spanish-American Empire, the word *tango,* whatever its origin, acquired the standard meaning of a *place* where African slaves (or free blacks, of whom there were always more in the Spanish colonies than in the British Empire) assembled for the purpose of dancing. In Argentina, as elsewhere in the Spanish-speaking world, *tango* also sometimes came to be applied, though at a later stage, to black *dances* in general. It was in this sense that the word eventually reached Spain, as a name for African American or African-influenced dances of transatlantic provenance. The habanera itself was sometimes called a *tango americano.* (Isaac Albéniz's "Tangos for Piano" are in fact habaneras.) A Spanish variation of the habanera was given the name *tango andaluz* (Andalusian tango), and this, too, became well-known in Argentina in the second half of the nineteenth century, though as a form of popular song rather than as a dance. In the 1880s and 1890s both the sung habanera and the tango andaluz (sometimes just called a *tango*) were popularized in Buenos Aires by visiting Spanish theater troupes. Many habanera songs and tangos andaluces became hits, hummed and whistled all over the city, and domestic versions, often with local color added, soon went the rounds.

It can be seen from this that the name *tango* had been in use for a long time and was very familiar to the inhabitants of late-nineteenth-century Buenos Aires. It could easily be appropriated by — or attached to — a rising new music-and-dance tradition. And in due course it was. . . .

At this critical point in the story, it is necessary to take account of what seems to be the only coherent eyewitness description of the birth of the tango. This striking piece of evidence was brought to light by José Gobello, one of the wisest and most knowledgeable writers on the history of the tango and *lunfardo* and the moving spirit of the Academia Porteña del Lunfardo (the main body that studies the traditional popular culture of Buenos Aires) since its creation in 1962. It is contained in an article printed on 22 September 1913 in *Crítica* — Buenos Aires's first mass-circulation popular newspaper, itself founded only a few days earlier. The author signed himself Viejo Tanguero (Old Tangoer): he has never been definitely identified, but on the evidence of the piece he was an educated man who knew what he was talking about. Although the article was written thirty years after the events it describes, its testimony is impossible to ignore.

Viejo Tanguero's most serious claim is that in the year 1877 the African Argentines of Mondongo (an area on the western side of the centrally located barrio of Monserrat) improvised a new dance, which they called a *tango* — that name again! — and which embodied something of the style and the movement of the candombe. Couples danced it apart rather than in an embrace. Groups of *compadritos,* who apparently had the habit of visiting African Argentine dance venues and then parodying the gestures and movements they saw there, took this "tango" to Corrales Viejos—the slaughterhouse district—and introduced it to the various low-life establishments where dancing took place, incorporating its most conspicuous features into the milonga. From Corrales Viejos, according to Viejo Tanguero, this new way of dancing the milonga spread rapidly to other districts. At this distance in time, we have no way of corroborating his claim, but an interesting confirmation that something like this *was* going on may be found in a book by Ventura Lynch (1850–88)—a noted *contemporary* student of the dances and folklore of Buenos Aires Province—published in 1883. According to Lynch, "the milonga is danced only by the *compadritos* of the city, who have created it *as a mockery of the dances the blacks hold in their own places*" (author's italics). Moreover, Lynch further testifies to the popularity of the milonga at the time when it was undergoing this obviously important modification.

> The milonga is so universal in the environs of the city that it is an obligatory piece at all the lower-class dances [*bailecitos de medio pelo*], and it is now heard on guitars, on paper-combs, and from the itinerant musicians with their flutes, harps, and violins. It has also been taken up by the organ grinders, who have arranged it so as to sound like the habanera dance. It is danced too in the low-life clubs around the . . . [main] markets and also at the dances and wakes of cart drivers, the soldiery and *compadres* and *compadritos*.

So at the beginning, what was soon to become the tango was simply a new way of dancing the milonga—and probably, José Gobello suggests, also the mazurka in districts closer to the docks. It was not yet a new dance as such. The distinctive features of the new dance form came entirely from the *compadritos'* parodistic borrowings from the African Argentine tradition—in particular the so-called quebradas and cortes. The quebrada was simply an improvised, jerky, semiathletic contortion, the more dramatic the better, while the corte was a sudden, suggestive pause, a break in the standard figures of the dance, not in itself a particular movement so much as the prelude to a quebrada. The true novelty, as the embryonic tango slowly took shape, was that cortes and quebradas were incorporated into dances in which the partners danced *together,* not, as in the African Argentine "tango," apart. It is understandable that high society in Argentina, some sections of which frowned on dances like the mazurka and habanera as inherently lascivious, should have found the "Africanized" milonga-tango wholly unacceptable. Its lower-class, semidelinquent origins made it doubly so.

1903. Men dancing tango. In its beginnings, tango belonged to a masculine, transgressive world that dispensed with social conventions. Courtesy Archivo General de la Nación, Buenos Aires.

For the social milieu in which the tango was gradually improvised into existence by the *compadritos* and their women (and the many who were drawn into their world) was essentially that of the outer barrios and *arrabales*. It is possible only to sketch the kind of places where the vital experiments occurred—at impromptu Sunday gatherings under the trees, in rudimentary dance halls (some with earth floors, some in tents), and, above all, in and around the brothels and in those other, more numerous, establishments that were probably often no more than thinly disguised brothels: the so-called *academias* ("academies," from "dance academy") and *perigundines*. (There is some dispute about which term was used first.) These were shady cafés, bars, or dance venues where the waitresses could also be hired as dancing partners and in many cases, no doubt, as whores. Drunkenness and casual violence (typically in the form of knifing) were common in the *academias*—which ran the constant risk of being closed down by the police.

It was in such places, mostly on the poor southern side of Buenos Aires, that the tango's murky and unchronicled prehistory was lived out. Both the dance and its music were gradually refined through improvisation, by trial and error. It seems fair to assume that there was constant interaction between the music and the dance—the musicians fitting rhythm and melody (rather less in the way of harmony: that came later) to the complex and often unpredictable movements invented and repeated by the dancers themselves. The music, at this early stage, was entirely improvised, the musicians themselves untrained. The first instruments to accompany the dance seem to have been the flute, violin, and harp, with guitars and clarinets soon making an appearance. . . .

As with jazz in New Orleans a few years later, the connection between the tango and the brothel is inescapable. But prostitution ran right through the social scale, and the tango soon found its way into high-class bordellos (some close to the center itself) as well as into those of the outer barrios. Two legendary upmarket *clandestinos* at the end of the nineteenth century, and for some years beyond, were those of María la Vasca (María Rongalla)—the house was still standing in the 1970s—and Laura (Laurentina Montserrat), the latter virtually in the center itself and an establishment, by all accounts, of some luxuriousness. As Mario Battistella's tango lyric of 1931 has it: "You were king of the dances at Laura's and La Vasca's. . . ." The local police chief was always a welcome visitor at Laura's and had a tango written in his honor by the *clandestino's* celebrated pianist, Rosendo Mendizabal—a key figure in the early musical development of the tango and another African Argentine.

There were many other ways in which the new dance moved outward from its original base in the *arrabal*. The well-heeled sons of the *porteño* oligarchy, like their counterparts all round the world, were not averse to "slumming"— or to taking part in the occasionally bloody skirmish with *compadritos*, a tradition that extended itself into the early twentieth century. Viejo Tanguero, thirty years later, could remember "many young men with well-known surnames," dedicated frequenters of the brothels, who by 1913 occupied "high positions in the national government." These fun-loving young bloods of the 1880s took the new dance from its disreputable surroundings and introduced it into their *garçonnières*—the apartments they rented for their amorous ventures. Though the upper class—like the respectable middle class and much of the respectable immigrant working class—might disapprove strongly of the "reptile from the brothel," as the writer Leopoldo Lugones was later to call the tango, it harbored a subversive fifth column within its own ranks almost from the beginning.

And in fact, though the tango was long tarred with the brush of its semi-delinquent origins, it did not remain confined to the outer barrios for long. The new dance has sometimes been seen as a form of "Creole" protest against the immigrant influx—but the newcomers themselves, or some of them, soon took it up with enthusiasm. In the course of time, it became popular in dance halls patronized by Italian immigrants, such as the Stella de Italia and later the Scudo de Italia, which were more centrally located than many of the *academias* and which catered to a relatively poor but much less raffish clientele. Here the wilder and more aggressive cortes and quebradas were somewhat toned down, and what became known as the *tango liso* (smooth tango) emerged. This "Italianization" of the tango, as it has been called, also meant the introduction of new instruments—accordions and mandolins complementing the harps, violins, and flutes of the earlier groups. Professional dancers are known to have worked in these dance halls—a further sign that the tango was taking on a life of its own, gradually disconnecting itself from the world of pimps, ruffians, and whores.

This early division of dancing styles was fraught with significance for the future: the "smooth" tango was undoubtedly the forerunner of the ballroom tango of the twentieth century, while the fierce, lubricious aggressiveness favored in the outer barrios eventually faded away—though reconstructions of it, in "performance tangos," can still be seen to spectacular effect in shows such as the *Tango Argentina* of the 1980s.

Note

For complete references and notes, see Simon Collier et al., *Tango! The Dance, the Song, the Story* (New York: Thames and Hudson, 1995), 40–51.

Bourgeois Snakes

José Ingenieros

Modernity also brought with it fresh and daring political theories of what the future should be like. There were many men among the immigrants with a history of political activism in the revolutionary movements that were already shaking the foundations of European societies. Soon, Marxist and socialist ideas gained support among workers and intellectuals. The paper La montaña *(The mountain), whose only twelve issues were published between 1 April and 15 September 1897, gave voice to the beliefs and demands of the socialist agenda. One of its editors, José Ingenieros (1877–1925), the son of an Italian socialist, and a writer and physician who would leave an indelible mark on the history of Argentine scientific and political thinking, wrote several pieces for the paper that harshly criticized modern Argentina's economic order. In "Bourgeois Snakes Go to the Sanctuary," written in a style that combines the complexities of modernist prose with frank vulgarity, he targets the hypocrisy of a selfish bourgeoisie hidden behind public displays of religious and patriotic feelings. The article's subversive message was so unsettling that the government confiscated the issue in which it appeared.*

This is the Age of Enlightenment and of miseries. We live oppressed, beaten down by all the cursed culmination of mediocrity that guarantees, to anyone who knows how to compromise with baseness and villainy, the whole arsenal of petty satisfactions that these corrupt republics can offer to the inept, incompetent, rapacious mob of its citizens who are blinded by their passion for the filthy money of embroiled banks and by their desperate longing for the pound sterling.

The frightening whirlwind of life enervates hearts and consciences; everything contaminates it, everything infiltrates it. There is not one single sane organ, a single immaculate atom, in this social cadaver. There couldn't be because bourgeois purulence has infected all of it, fertilizing it with its germs that pulse through all its social arteries like sap saturated with leprosy of a new kind—a leprosy of the soul that lowers a man and gnaws at his backbone, threatening to make the stigma of subservience an inherited defect.

Our social life has assumed a special form and introduced a unique way of moving: slithering.

In the bourgeois dung heap to slither is to live.

Luján and visits to the national sanctuary, wretched symbol of nationality, give a perhaps pallid idea of the immorality that surrounds and asphyxiates us. This will remain so until the socialist revolution reduces it to rubble.

Luxurious trains leave an opulent station to the beat of profane music. They head for the sanctuary, but before they do young girls in heat ardently press the hands of their boyfriends. These young men then get into different cars and, through their perforated pockets, satisfy with convulsive hands the appetites of the human beast awakened by the provocative attention of their pilgrim girlfriends.

The spiritual father meanwhile leads the prayers. Even he is not free of the stimulation that pervades those railroad cars where the atmosphere is saturated by the smell of noxious cosmetics and evaporating fluids secreted through the toxic pores of those visitors to the Lord, in whose faces everything shines through except devotion.

When the train arrives in Luján, the tourists put on a masquerade that bores them as they march along in procession to the sanctuary. As they walk they hum songs of doubtful religiosity, and they tell lies as they say their prayers, all the while exchanging glances with the male pilgrims who parade along the sidewalk making signs, in no way sacred, and, in fact, overtly graphic.

The farce continues inside the sanctuary. Christ on his cross is obliged to contemplate all this corruption and hypocrisy and realizes that the moral level of Pilate and Judas Iscariot was not so low compared with this crowd of bourgeois tourists. For her part, the Virgin of Luján doubtless laments from her altar that she herself is not one of the young girls being pursued by the syphilitic or tuberculosis-ridden young men.

Besides couples in love, even bigger reptiles come on our pilgrimages. The thieves from the big banks; the rogues who speculate on the stock exchange; grand merchants who import women from Poland and Hungary so they can sell them at public auction; senators and deputies who sell their votes to any labor union that knows the ropes; the judges who deliver verdicts by commission; secretaries of state who rip off ministries; presidents who put their signatures on any project that guarantees them a cut in the take.

Here are some more of these reptile pilgrims: Juan Agustín, a minister under Juárez Celman, who suffers from unnatural depravity; Don Francisco, who has no scruples about holding a candle in the left hand while with the right one he masturbates. Don Luis, that disgraceful, useless old man who was president until they got rid of him when he sullied the papers he signed with his slimy dribble; and Don José Evaristo, titular servant of the Republic and victim of this new torture of Tantalus that doesn't allow him to enjoy the benefits of being indolent, thanks to the good offices of the puppeteers who manage him.

They all go to the sanctuary as if acknowledging that the Virgin was a virgin before she gave birth, during birth, and after it. They then stopped being plunderers of the public treasury. The great bank robbers and the despicable politicians, who commercialize a country they don't even believe in, pretend to impose their fake adoration on the people who pay with a thousand drops of their blood for each one of the bricks in the basilica. And, of course, they have never been able to make this pilgrimage.

The time has now come to question the efficacy of sanctuaries to wash clean the stains on the skin of the bourgeois elephants. The public is beginning to doubt the effectiveness of those indulgences, those fastings, those purgatories and infernos that are so easily bought or avoided by offering money (more or less well robbed) to a Virgin who doesn't even blush when she becomes an accomplice to so many miseries and such vast corruption.

And, let us be up-front about it: we present here the most moral aspects of the legion of bourgeois reptiles. Here come the big bankers, merchants, charity organizers, professors, members of parliament, and other orders of the reptile class whose immorality should be demonstrated to the public so that it can see, in all their nakedness, the ravenous pirates who, in their slithering, work on the budget with axes, knowing that they will partially satisfy their insatiable appetites.

We will do that while Leopoldo Lugones with his formidable paw engraves on the foreheads of this country's politicians the life story of each one of them, citing their subservience and their shamelessness.

Will it be possible for us to do this?

As we begin the demolition we are not unaware that we run the risk of being crushed by debris.

Translated by Patricia Owen Steiner

Argentina as Latin American Avant-Garde

Rubén Darío

The official celebrations of the centennial exhibited a splendor that nourished the general perception that Argentina was bound to lead the rest of Latin America along the path of progress. Many famous writers and poets wrote pieces applauding the country's impressive achievements. The Nicaraguan poet Rubén Darío (1867–1916), considered at the time one of the most important intellectual figures on the continent, found in the Argentine cultural environment the kind of cosmopolitan and modern spirit that his poetry had been seeking. In his essay "Argentina," included here, Darío expresses his conviction that Argentina would become Latin America's guiding force, by acting both as a political and economic model to be emulated and as a restraining force against what many Latin Americans saw as the mounting imperialistic ambitions of the United States.

Among the events that history must celebrate in the early years of the twentieth century is the emergence of "the new and glorious nation" of which the Argentine national anthem sings. This is not a hymn about the free and independent political life of the country; instead it praises the life of its remarkable people for their work and peaceful prosperity. On the balance scales of the American continent, it is the Argentine Republic that gives us the counterweight to Yankee power. This is the country that will rescue the spirit of our race and put an end to present and future imperialist ambition. Today, for these reasons, the world looks to this great country of the South. With its 7 million inhabitants, it rivals, in more than one agricultural or financial enterprise, the other great country of the North, with a population surpassing 80 million. A people formed from Spanish fathers who inherited all the qualities and defects of the conquistadors, together with a collection of new ingredients, initiated its independence with epic deeds, suffered through consequent disturbances and the revolts of a state in its testing stages, endured the winds of pampa anarchy, and bled profusely in civil disputes. It found out about the weight of lead and iron tyrannies and revolted against them. Little by little, it began lighting up its own soul, the soul of the people, and learned the true difference between civilization and barbarism. Argentina takes good care of its schools and universities, spreads culture and progress, raises up the parliamentary system, and sees that its greatest riches lie in the heart of the country. It is preoccupied by economic matters that are vital. By elimination and by cross-breeding, it is beginning the formation of a brilliant race. It takes in living blood and useful muscles from the four points of the earth. It casts into oblivion the harmful inquisitorial judgment of the Spanish and the Hispanic American evil of revolution. Flourishing under, and protected by, policies of economic growth, Argentina is becoming strong. It is making great nations look on it with fondness and celebrating the fete of its first century to the applause and astonishment of all the nations of the world.

For this reason an illustrious Argentine, Joaquín V. González, can say with just pride: "The Argentine people are one of those peoples of the Americas who had to overcome major difficulties in order to establish a social state of freedom and a common home for all men. They can offer the kind of actual and potential work that is more common in countries that have enjoyed longer periods of peace and order. Their major merit, in the opinion of their contemporaries, will be the absolute consecration of their labor and superior energy to the cultivation of prosperity and material wealth. Such dedication does not make them impervious to ideals and beauty, nor does it confine them within their own homes like birds in their cages, but rather it offers, for the benefit of all men, a communion banquet of fraternity and universal solidarity."

Few countries, it could be said, are more secure in their future. Relatively speaking, Argentina's national prosperity has no equal. For the men of the North are frightening. The Argentines are more aware of the lessons of the past, and, even during the most inflamed political struggles, all the political parties, all the officials, have been supremely mindful of national dignity and exaltation. The wave of progress has swept clean tremendous errors; the uncertainties of yesterday have fertilized the working fields of today.

The country has had to make itself strong in order to make itself respectable, although, according to Norberto Piñero, "Argentina's historical role is the creation of a race and a civilization founded on peace and pacific means." It has sustained its traditional culture despite its positive, practical development. "From the literary perspective," a French author wrote more than forty years ago, "Buenos Aires takes first place among the cities of old Spanish America."

The Argentine press is today the first in the Spanish language for its richness, for its incomparable vitality, and for its universal nourishing nature. Progress has been enormous and widespread in just a few years. Argentina's public instruction and its pedagogical institutions must be envied. Indeed, it has much to show, with just pride, to any country in the world.

To the ancient political romanticism that is noble and generous in its ideals, evolution is adding a deeper, firmer concept of national purpose and a sense of the country's future. All this is happening without diminishing the human fraternity, by offering work and homes to all comers.

And that is not just some idle lyrical phrase. I have inhabited Argentine soil, and I have seen how grandly the doors of the Republic are opened to all foreigners, how sincere and skillful is the hospitality extended to all useful immigrant workers. The native program could be proclaimed in two words: *work* and *culture*. With it comes independence and freedom. Who is more in control of its future than such a people? C. O. Bunge writes: "The seed spread so impressively by the hand of the Revolution on the fertile soil of Argentina has germinated, developing into a gigantic tree, exuberant with flowers, many of which now turn into the richest of fruits. If we are now deservedly proud of our present culture, largely the work of our national educational system, there is much more to be hoped for in the future. The future is ours!"

That future, which will result from Argentine effort and foreign collaboration, is defined in the words of Edmundo d'Amicis in his meticulous study of immigration. It is his prediction that the Argentine people and foreigners will always live as brothers "and that they will advance together on the pathway of goodness and work, maintaining that full, fertile sense of tolerance, of benevolence, of patriotism without arrogance, of fraternal love without jealousy, that can make of ten pueblos a single pueblo or turn various races into a single state. This, he says, will produce a marvelous generation, taking many forms, that will see an Argentina that is transformed and powerful—just the way the amiable fierceness of its sons and the sincere gratitude of its guests desire it to be.

Translated by Patricia Owen Steiner

National Identity in a

Cosmopolitan Society

Leopoldo Lugones

By 1910, at least half the population living in Argentina was of immigrant origin. Faced with a society that was becoming more and more heterogeneous, the traditional elite became increasingly alarmed. In 1913, in a nationalist response to social diversity, Leopoldo Lugones (1874–1938), the most prestigious poet at the time, gave a series of lectures at the Odeon Theater in Buenos Aires that were later compiled in a book entitled El payador. *President Roque Sáenz Peña was among those attending. In these famous lectures, Lugones canonized Hernández's gauchesque poem* Martín Fierro *as well as the vanishing gaucho as symbols of Argentine identity. The return to a tradition so persistently rejected by the nation's intellectual leaders must be read as a fairly obvious political maneuver to resist cultural heterogeneity. Giving voice to the anxieties and fears awakened by the threat of ethnic pluralism that the immigrants represented, Lugones resorted to biological reasoning to prove that the essence of the Argentine people lay in the racial vigor of the gauchos. The universalization of gauchesque poetry that associated the gaucho versifier or* payador *with the Homeric bard was part of the same strategic move.*

I have named this book for the ancient wandering singers of ballads and laments who used to roam our countryside, for it was they who played the most significant role in forming our race. Just as happened with other peoples of Greco-Latin origins, the formation of our race began here with a work of beauty. Its earliest manifestation was poetry. As the new race invented a fresh language to express the emerging spirit of its soul, this poetry brought forth our country's fundamental distinguishing characteristics. For since the country is an animated being, the soul, or the *spirit*, is its most essential part. . . .

The only thing that could effectively control Argentine barbarism was an element that, though participating itself in the local barbarity, would also bring

Gaucho breaking in a horse. The epic image of a gaucho dominating nature came to embody national identity after the 1910 centennial. Courtesy Archivo General de la Nación, Buenos Aires.

a civilizing influence. This is the gaucho, the picturesque product of that very conflict between civilization and barbarism.

The Indian raid, in effect, gave the Indians almost permanent contact with the frontier Christians, who, belonging to the white race, had the double advantage of its progressive character and its great capacity to adapt. In turn, the experience of repeatedly repelling the surprise attacks that the Indians waged gave the frontier people the experience of the desert, faith in the horse, and a sense of nomadic life. For the Spaniards who had recently come from the crossroads of Arabic culture, finding a life so similar to the one of their desert ancestors rekindled in them the tendencies of their Arabic inheritance. The intermingling of the Spaniards with the nomads of the pampa accentuated their peculiar characteristics.

Because they brought no Spanish women with them, the conquistadors had taken as their own the indigenous women of the tribes that they conquered. But, since the pure-blooded Indians, with the exception of those who retreated to the shelter of the Andes and the surrounding desert, were exterminated, Spanish blood predominates in the mixed breeds [*mestizos*], who in turn were given the names of their fathers. But Indian blood persisted, for it had not been completely purified; and so its traits survived in the dark skin and hair and in the passionate nature of the gauchos.

The conquest of La Plata happened so rapidly that very soon white women came to Argentina, and before long a sense of social difference was established that obliged the mixed breeds to unite among themselves. However, there was still a shortage of women in frontier populations. For a long time white women were a booty of war, and mixed breeding became more common on the frontier.

Another no less significant development was also taking place there. The conquistadors, incapable of dominating the Indian, often felt the necessity of making peace treaties with him, ceding him land located not many leagues from Buenos Aires. This pattern lasted until the first half of the eighteenth century, when the conquistadors began to violate the treaties so they could take back fields that had by then become valuable. In revenge, the Indians responded by pillaging. This then served as the pretext to try to expel the Indians — willy-nilly. Field Marshal Juan San Martín was the instrument of that attempt. Until then the white man and the Indian, despite latent hostility, had been friends and even allies against the most indomitable savages, the Araucanos. But the killing by San Martin, as he tried to exterminate the tribes, completely changed this situation. Indian raids, which had been sporadic until then, were transformed into the great war of the pampa that began with San Martin's expedition of 1788. This war against the Indian dragged on for 141 years until the conquest of the desert, executed by Roca.

The mestizos were not able to find work in the cities; Negroes held the available jobs in domestic service, and there was no industry to give employment. The mixed breeds then moved to the frontier, and it became their natural habitat. This is where a transitional national subrace, typified by the gaucho, began to be formed. . . .

. . . If one reflects on the essential ingredients of this study, it will be easy to find in the gaucho the prototype of the present-day Argentine. I am thinking of our best family qualities, like our great love for our children; the contradictory and romantic nature of our character; our sensitive reaction to music (so curious when first contemplated, especially in a country where aesthetics used to be considered a contemptible quality); the faithfulness of our wives; the importance we attach to courage; a tendency to boast and an inclination to be fickle; a lack of scruples when it comes to acquiring material things; and an ability to spend lavishly.

There can be no doubt: we are not gauchos. However, strong traces of the gaucho do remain in the Argentine of today, who, with his confused racial appearance, is so different from the gaucho and yet is himself a product of the present interbreeding. When this interbreeding has finally run its course, gaucho traits will still survive, and, because there is no other living incarnation of the gaucho, the poem [*Martín Fierro*] that typifies him will acquire a fundamental significance.

The gaucho was the country's most genuine actor when our sense of nationality was being shaped. It was he who gave our country's poetry its most characteristic traits. And so we accept him wholeheartedly as our ancestor, believing that we can hear an echo of his songs in the pampa breeze every time it whispers in the grass, as if the cords of some ancient guitar were being lightly strummed. . . .

. . . Included in our concept of beauty is the idea that, through the greatest expression of his spirit, man may live in a superior manner and that, by so doing, he can infuse material things with spiritual meaning. This idea of beauty, or *freedom* you might properly call it, was the aspiration of those innumerable ancestors of ours. By sustaining this ideal we give life to the gaucho. We are the vehicles of the immortality of the race that still lives in us. Thus, the ideal of beauty is like immortality, and this perpetuation of life liberates human beings from the material fatality of the law of force that is the foundation of all despotism.

Beauty, life, and liberty are positively the same thing. These concepts give us compassion so that we may work for the betterment of the spirit. It is the same compassion that, according to the mysterious Christian legend, Jesus showed to us mortals when he returned to earth to console humanity. But, by withholding justice and allowing silence to surround our indebtedness to the gaucho, we darken our own souls and appear to be cowardly, despicable people. It is the gauchos who effectively endure this horror of silence, with no other hope than our negligent sense of justice. We should correct this situation and should compensate the gaucho with our belated recognition of the glory that he conferred on the future Argentina. And that, though it transpires in the shadows, he still confers on us.

By thinking about the gaucho, about how he expressed himself and his ideas, and by transforming the gaucho language, the obligation of civilization and the country will be fulfilled. We must study the tradition of the race, not to become encrusted in it, but rather to discover the law of progress that will reveal to us the best way to live our lives in ways that are by degrees superior: by exalting peculiar virtues, not out of egotistical pride, but in order to make of the best Argentine of today the best man of tomorrow; and by practicing the ideals of beauty and freedom that are for our race the motives of the heroic life and the permanent condition of a superior humanity. We must struggle without rest until death because the quiet life is not a heroic life but a hollow one, the shadow of a hole that is open but that is without a cause, a hole that the viper then takes over as a hiding place.

To shape language is to cultivate that robust tree trunk of the forest, to civilize it so as to convert it into a fruit tree, not to amuse ourselves by carving a fragment of wood. The wiser and more beautiful that tree is, the better men will understand us, and our spirit will have expanded all the more. The beauty of our country should not resemble a sack of pearls but should be like the sea where the pearls swim and where everything is open to all the pearl fishers. To be stuck in one's own garden, however lovely it may be, is to abandon our country to others who march to different drummers. The same singer (Martín Fierro), about whose exploits we commented earlier, gives us an example of how we should proceed. Neither suffering, nor exile, nor loneliness, ever drove the source of poetry from his lips. For, in the serenity of the night, the gaucho raised his eyes to the heavens to foretell the direction of the next day's journey, and there he found, too, the inspiration for his verses that the golden vineyard of the stars distilled in drops of poetry and pain.

Translated by Patricia Owen Steiner

V

Modern Times

During the first decades of the twentieth century, the great expansion of Buenos Aires, the arrival of millions of immigrants, and the democratization of political institutions created in the pampean region a culture that was both dynamic and cosmopolitan. A modern public space took shape, defined by the speed and manners of urban life. On its frivolous side, city life meant fashion, elegant promenades, and mercantile exhibitionism. In political terms, the organization of public space and the consolidation of urban identity were heavily influenced by the urban masses that organized themselves to demand broader political representation. The crowds that in the fin de siècle appeared chaotic and uncohesive to Ramos Mejía were now collective civic bodies aware of their common ties and their combined strength, both of which translated into political power.

The phenomenal economic growth sustained by exports created the conditions for unprecedented upward social mobility. One important consequence of this process was the formation of a large middle class—the largest of its kind in Latin America—which gradually gained access to the public sphere and developed a remarkably strong cultural identity. Escalating pressure from the middle and lower sectors of society would soon force the long-dominant conservative party, whose programs had shaped modern Argentina, to share political power. Seeking to prevent widespread electoral fraud and boost popular participation, Congress in 1912 made voting mandatory and secret for all men. With promises of social progress and institutional honesty, the Unión Cívica Radical (UCR) won the presidential elections of 1916. The historian David Rock's penetrating analysis of Argentina's first attempt at truly representative democracy focuses on the complexities and contradictions of Argentina's first party of the masses and its charismatic leader, Hipólito Yrigoyen.

Democratization and the expansion of political participation came quickly, but not without tension. Alfonsina Storni, a feminist and writer, translated into articles and poems the dissatisfaction of women, who had remained quietly on the margins through most of the modernizing process. In their struggle for better wages and working conditions, workers clashed with their employers and, at times, with the government, igniting the fury of the most conservative sectors of society. From these sectors emerged the Argentine Patriotic League—a xenophobic, anti-Semitic, and anti-Communist alliance formed by youths from the traditional upper classes that carried out violent attacks against immigrants and leftist organizations. Among leftist militants, no other activists incited more virulent reactions than the anarchists who dominated the unions between 1905 and 1915. Although small in size and comparatively moderate in approach, Argentine anarchism would leave a lasting impression on the country's political imagination. Osvaldo Bayer's essay introduces one of the most enduring anarchist myths in Argentina, established around the figure of Simón Radowitzky, who at age eighteen became a powerful icon of popular rage after killing the chief of police, who had brutally repressed a 1 May demonstration. Despite its enduring political allure, Radowitzky's radicalism was not representative of labor activism. The strikes and demonstrations organized by the workers were aimed less at revolution than at negotiating the conditions for social mobility and an opportunity to prosper in a consumerist society. Excepting a few key issues, even the anarchists, the most reluctant to relinquish their revolutionary goals, were willing to negotiate. Ideological moderation was the tone of the times. Far from questioning the overall direction of the economy, the middle-class-oriented UCR limited its "radical" character to constitutional matters. Although to the left of the UCR, with only 5 percent of the general vote, the Socialist Party also avoided extreme agendas, favoring instead a reformist approach to labor legislation and public education.

Cultural developments in the 1920s paralleled the modernizing and democratizing trends in the political realm. A diverse, cosmopolitan society found ways to "nationalize" political and cultural themes. Universal public schooling and a uniform curriculum contributed significantly to the formation of a national community whose members shared a cultural identity. The education system molded the children of immigrant families and the poor of the interior alike according to homogenizing conceptions of nationality and literate citizenship. More spontaneous forms of identification sprung concurrently from the rituals of popular culture, as Roberto Arlt's urban chronicle demonstrates.

Buenos Aires became the stage for an original artistic avant-garde, complemented by a fast-growing culture industry. Oliverio Girondo's poems render vivid sketches of local everyday life in the experimental style of the European avant-garde, but seasoned with the impertinence of an art that "went to the streets." After seducing the elegant salons of Paris, the tango went from a type of music initially associated almost exclusively with the marginal sectors to the musical style of the city of Buenos Aires as a whole. Although it was highly popular throughout the city, each social group appropriated tango in its own way. While high society enjoyed the dance in private clubs, the lower classes adopted tango's sentimentality as a tool for political protest. "Cambalache," an irreverent tango by Enrique Santos Discépolo that would eventually reach the status of an alternative national anthem, is representative of the genre's steady politicization.

In 1930, the first military coup in Argentine history shattered the euphoria of the first decades of the twentieth century that had been the result of urban growth and democratization. General Uriburu's subsequent presidency was particularly pernicious, not only because of its authoritarianism, but also because it was unable to deal with the economic crisis unleashed by the 1929 Wall Street crash. While tango writers infused their lyrics with the disillusion and helplessness felt during those years, highbrow writers also explored the sense of tragedy that permeated national society. In *X-Ray of the Pampa,* Ezequiel Martínez Estrada outlined a pessimistic diagnosis of the country's condition in 1933 and argued that Argentine historical achievements were predominantly hollow, superficial accomplishments. Echoing Spengler's bleak prophesies for Western civilization, Martínez Estrada saw more simulacra than realities. Disenchantment characterized the social and political experiences of the decade that followed Uriburu's military coup, which were years of authoritarianism, corruption, and conservative social policies.

Simón Radowitzky

Osvaldo Bayer

The establishment's willingness to tolerate the increasing popularity of the Unión Cívica Radical (UCR) reflected its desire to counter a more threatening political move-ment, one that had gained remarkable strength during the first years of the twenti-eth century: the radical Left. Anarchism, a doctrine that rejects private property and regards the absence of all direct and coercive government as the indispensable con-dition for full social and political liberty, was among this radicalism's most feared manifestations. Although its practitioners seldom went beyond the organization of rallies, blockades, and strikes, there were some anarchists who employed direct, violent means to undermine what they saw as an unjust and corrupt political system. Simón Radowitzky, a nineteen-year-old immigrant from Russia, made history when he killed Colonel Falcón, the chief of police who on 1 May 1909 had ordered the brutal repression of a popular demonstration in the streets of Buenos Aires. Radowitzky would spend the next twenty-one years of his life in prison, in almost complete isolation. Although it was difficult to justify his crime, his idealism and endurance earned him the admi-ration and devotion of activists and workers. Simón Radowitzky became a legend. In 1918, anarchists from Chile and Buenos Aires made an unsuccessful attempt to free him from prison by boat. In 1930, after years of vacillation, and most likely as an effort to appease popular discontent, President Yrigoyen pardoned Radowitzky with the con-dition of permanent exile. The pardon outraged the establishment. Soon afterward, Yrigoyen's elected government was overthrown by the first military coup in Argentine history. In this account of Falcón's assassination and its aftermath, Osvaldo Bayer, an expert on the history of the Argentine radical Left, re-creates the events that prompted Radowitzky's glorification with an openly sympathetic view of his political motives.

That first day of May in 1909 dawned cold but sunny; later, around noon, it would become cloudy as if foretelling a storm. A storm, not of thunder and lightning, but of bullets, blood, and hatred.

The newspapers didn't have much news except for the birth of Juliana, the princess of Holland, and the opening performance at the Odeon of *Pater-*

Radical railroad workers pose in front of a portrait of their intellectual hero, Karl Marx (1904). Courtesy Archivo General de la Nación, Buenos Aires.

nal Home with Emma Grammatica as the leading lady. But more than one reader will have read, with a little anxiety, two small items that seemed to have gunpowder on each of their letters. Two workers' actions were reported: one organized by the General Union of Workers (socialist) that will take place at 3:00 p.m. where A. Mantecon and Alfredo L Palacios will speak; the other is the FORA [Federación Obrera Regional Argentina] organization (anarchist) that appeals to readers to come to a meeting in Lorea Plaza for the purpose of marching down Avenida de Mayo to Florida as far as Plaza San Martín, and from there along Paseo San Martín, and then on to Paseo de Julio and Plaza Mazzini.

Nothing is going to happen to the socialists, that's understood, but . . . the anarchists?

Internally, the country is going through a rather tough time. Figueroa Alcorta rules over a foundering world and an uncontrollable eruption: the mass of the new Argentine race, the wave of immigrants and their descendants. The bombs, the worship of science, the economic ideas, everything has repercussions in a Buenos Aires that gets more and more stirred up and seems more and more like a European city. Right after the noon hour Lorea Plaza begins to fill with strange people: lots of mustaches, caps, kerchiefs around necks, patched trousers, many blonds, some with freckles, many Italians, many Russians, and plenty of Catalans. They are the anarchists. The first red flags arrive: "Death to the bourgeois!" "War on the bourgeoisie!" are the first shouts. Then come red standards, usually with gold lettering. They are the different anarchist associations. By 2:00 P.M. the plaza is already pretty crowded. Everyone is enthusiastic. There are shouts, vivas, songs, and a murmuring undercurrent that begins to grow like a wave. The culminating moment comes with the arrival of the anarchist association called Light to the Soldier. Its members seem to be the most contentious. They have come along Entre Ríos Avenue, and, according to the police making their rounds, they have broken the glass storefronts of bakeries that didn't shut their doors in support of May Day. They have clubbed guards and trolley-car conductors, and they have smashed coaches in the plaza and freed the horses.

But the flint necessary for starting the fire is still missing. Quite by surprise a coach is stopped at the Avenida de Mayo and Salta Street. It carries Colonel Ramon Falcón, the chief of police. "Down with Colonel Falcón!" "Death to the Cossacks!" "War on the bourgeoisie!" All the while, standards wave in agitation.

Falcón sits there ramrod straight. His impassive face measures the crowd. It is a gesture neither of cynicism nor of friendship. He is measuring the enemy forces, like a general in battle. Falcón is a military man of the old school, a priest of law and order. Severe, intrepid, incorruptible. "He's a dog," the lazy

General strike, Buenos Aires, November, 1902. Bystanders outside a closed fruit market during a general strike. Courtesy Archivo General de la Nación, Buenos Aires.

slackers under his command would say. But they said it with fear. Once, as the only response to a repeated request by police sergeant majors, Falcón gathered them all together on the patio of the central department offices, grabbed the ringleader by the epaulets, and shoved him out into the street in a way that guaranteed that he would never come back. That's Falcón. He's a widower with no children; he has neither vices nor luxuries.

He never talks about himself. Only once in a while does he mention that he is a descendant of Moors and that his surname is doubly warlike: the *falcon* is a kind of cannon used in ancient times, and it also means "hawk."

There is the lean, hard man, face-to-face with that mob that in his judgment is foreign and undisciplined, without tradition or origin, anti-Argentina.

Insults fall on Falcón like a sprinkling rain; they hardly dampen him. There are officials who are biting their lips in rage at not being able to turn on the crowd with clubs. Falcón speaks briefly with Jolly Medrano, chief of the security squad, and then he retreats. The clash comes minutes later. As always, there are contradictory accounts. The police say that they were attacked by the workers, and the workers say that the repression began without warning. What is certain is that the result is one of the worst tragedies of our street fighting. Someone lights the first match by firing a shot. The shooting is now unleashed. They fire point blank. The cavalry attacks. The workers flee. But not all of them; there are some who don't retreat at all. They don't even seek the shelter of a tree. They fight face-to-face. This is a time when there are many working men who want to be martyrs for ideas. After half an hour of fierce fighting the plaza is empty. The pavement is littered with caps, hats, walking sticks, handkerchiefs . . . and thirty-six puddles of blood. Three bodies and forty seriously wounded men are gathered up. The dead are Miguel Bech, a Spaniard, seventy-two years old, who lived at 932 Calle Pasco, a peddler; José Silva, a Spaniard, twenty-three years old, of 955 Santiago del Estero, a store clerk; and Juan Semino, an Argentine, nineteen years old, an apprentice bricklayer. Hours later Luis Pantaleone and Manuel Fernández, a Spaniard, thirty-six years old, a trolley-car collector, will both die. The wounded are almost all Spanish, Italian, or Russian.

The city is in tremendous commotion. Falcón does not sleep; he immediately has sixteen anarchist leaders detained, and he locks up all local men of anarchist leanings. The police report especially singles out the actions of the Russian "elements" that make up some of the cosmopolitan crowd of workers. The police summary also mentions manifestos "written in a Hebrew that embodies extremely violent propaganda." According to the police, these manifestos called for assassination and looting the public. To make their claims more believable, official reports contain assertions like the following: "No one was

National guard (1908). Soldiers guard a train station after a terrorist attempt.

able to take a statement from Jacobo Bescroff, a twenty-two-year-old Russian, because he did not know any Spanish."

The workers also react: the socialists join with the anarchists and declare a general strike of indefinite duration. They will lift it only if Falcón revokes his repressive orders interring anarchists. The entire workers' protest is focused on the chief of police. That Sunday, the people await the next day with foreboding. They say that terror will reign in the streets, that the anarchists will not allow anyone to work at their jobs.

But on Monday morning hope is born: newspapers appear, despite the fact that the Printers Federation of Buenos Aires has complied with the general work stoppage. That is to say, the government has already succeeded in breaking the united stance of the movement.

As the hours go by, it is noted that the strike is only partially successful. Acts of violence occur: trolley-car conductors are attacked and seriously injured, and a foreman at the bull ring is killed by the strikers. At 3055 Cochabamba Street, the Vasena factory is attacked by a group of workers, but they are driven back. Five thousand people gather in front of the morgue to recover the bodies of the dead anarchists. President Figueroa Alcorta responds to the workers' request that Falcón renounce his actions with bruising words: "Falcón is going to resign on 12 October 1910, on the day that I conclude my term of office."

The police announce that "nine Russian nihilists" have been detained, and *La prensa* relates in pathetic terms the words of the wife of the anarchist Fernández who was killed in Lorea Plaza. Antonia Rey de Fernández says that three years ago she had separated from her husband because of "his violent ideas."

As the days go by the general work stoppage begins to collapse. The anarchists demonstrate that they are anarchists right down to their organization. But, even so, the politicians and upper- and middle-class people are surprised by the extraordinary manifestation of sorrow expressed by a column of sixty thousand workers who accompany the remains of their fallen comrades to the cemetery.

It is fitting that the second act of this drama takes place coming out of a cemetery—none other than Recoleta. Colonel Falcón is returning in his four-wheel carriage from the funeral of his friend Antonio Ballvé, director of the national penitentiary and an old political ally. Falcón is saddened, but he is not a weak man. Rather, he is thinking about the report that he has just presented to the minister of the interior based on an investigation by the commissioner of social order, José Vieyra. Subject: anarchist activities. The report notes the investigation undertaken to anticipate and prevent the criminal acts that the anarchist Pablo Karaschin tried to perpetrate in the chapel of Carmen. Just as he was going to deposit a bomb in the central nave, he was apprehended by Fernando Dufraichou and Rafael Grisolia. Falcón learns that Karaschin—who lived with his wife and two daughters in the cleaning company The Spanish Maid, at 971 Junín Street—is the leader of a group of terrorist activists. For that reason Falcón is seriously considering submitting to Minister Avellaneda a series of measures that he believes must be taken to prevent similar acts.

The coach advances slowly. Presently it turns onto Quintana Avenue. Driving it is the Italian Ferrari, a good coachman who entered Argentina in the 1898 contingent. Beside Falcón sits Alberto Lastigau, twenty years old, the only male in a family of nine children, a young man whose father made Falcón's private secretary so that at Falcón's side he might "become a man."

Ever since the tragedy of Lorea Plaza in May there have been many threats hovering over Falcón. The anarchists have targeted him as their chief enemy. And everyone knows that anarchists do not squander their threats. But Falcón is not afraid. He goes everywhere without bodyguards. And he is always in the most dangerous of places.

But this time he is worried about the Karaschin group. Will they be quiet now that their leader is behind bars? Or will they seek revenge with a sensational attack?

The coach now turns the corner onto Callao Avenue, heading south. And it is at that moment that two men—José Fornes, who is driving a car behind Falcón, and his orderly, Zorilo Agüero of the War Ministry—spot a young man who looks awfully foreign starting to sprint after Falcón's coach. There is something in his hand.

What's going on? Has something fallen out of the coach that he wants to return? Why doesn't he shout to get someone's attention? But here lies the truth. As the coach turns the corner, the unknown man runs up to it and throws the package inside. A half second later there's a terrible explosion. The terrorist looks all around and begins to run toward Alvear Avenue. After his initial surprise, Fornes gets out of his car and, together with Agüero, starts to run after the unknown man, who is about seventy meters ahead of them. They shout wildly, and more people join them in pursuit, among them the police officers Benigno Guzmán and Enrique Muller. The young man is running desperately; he burns up all his energy just to keep a step ahead. He knows very well that they will lynch him or shoot him. He can already taste a desire for death on his tongue and in his exhausted lungs. He turns down Alvear Avenue and sees construction work going on. He heads in that direction as if he had found a refuge, a nest where he can at least hide his head. He stops. Now his pursuers have almost caught up to him. He pulls out a revolver and begins to run again. And so, as he is running, a shot is fired at his right breast, and he falls onto the sidewalk. . . .

Falcón does not lose consciousness. Lying back on the pillow, he signals with an authoritative gesture that they should first attend to "the young Lastigau." He answers the onlookers by saying, "It's nothing. Are there any other wounded?" He is losing great amounts of blood. While they are waiting for the ambulance, two or three people try to use headbands and pieces of sheets to bandage up his shredded legs. They take Lastigau to the nearby Castro Hospital; he has lost consciousness.

When they come for Falcón, it is touching to see all those men trying so hard to lift the pillow with the wounded man and put him into the ambulance. In the emergency room the doctors see no other recourse than to amputate his left leg. But it is now too late; Falcón is almost drained of blood. He does not survive the traumatic shock of the operation and expires at 2:15 in the afternoon.

The young Lastigau is in better shape to fight back. His wounds are not as deep as Falcón's, but the doctors have also had to amputate a leg, and the loss of blood has been decisive. He holds out until eight o'clock in the evening.

The two men lie in state in the central police office. Seldom has Buenos Aires witnessed such a tremendous expression of sorrow, with delegations of police from all over the country and beyond. The Argentine army and the police have taken the incident as an affront. And, for that reason, for them there will be no pardon for the assassin. Many years will pass, but the rallying cry is always firm: we will not pardon Falcón's assassin. It is a rallying cry that will succeed in breaking only one stubborn man: the future president Hipólito Yrigoyen.

The terrorist has also fallen down on the street. But they yank him up by his hair and his clothes. They turn him over and leave him lying, face up, in the sun. He is disagreeably pale with a small, rather wispy, reddish mustache, bony features, the jaw of a boxer, watery eyes, and large lampshade ears. Undoubtedly he is a Russian, an anarchist, a worker. He is stretched out there on the street, panting like a filthy wild boar, surrounded by dogs. They insult him. They call him "a worthless Russian" and something more. His eyes are wide open, frightened, waiting for the first boot to hit his face. He is lost, and for that reason he doesn't ask for forgiveness but shouts twice, "Long live anarchism!" When the police officers Muller and Guzmán say to him, "Now you're going to see what's going to happen to you," he responds in broken, nasal Spanish: "I don't care. But I have a bomb for each of you."

These are the final bites of the cornered animal.

But the police make an exception. They don't comply with the unwritten law to avenge the death of one of their own. Assistant police chief Mariano T. Vila of the Fifteenth Precinct appears and gives the order to take the terrorist in an automobile to Fernández Hospital because he is losing a lot of blood from his right breast.

As they make a list of the terrorist's clothes, they find another weapon: a pistol that he has around his waist. Also a shiny belt loaded with twenty-four revolver bullets plus four automatic pistol cartridges, each with nine bullets, each powerful. The man had left prepared for anything.

In Fernández Hospital the doctor on duty examines the terrorist. The diagnosis: slight wound in the right pectoral region. Now bandaged, the prisoner is sent to the Fifteenth Precinct jail, where he is kept in rigorous solitary confinement. There are several interrogation sessions, but the terrorist does not talk. He says only that he is Russian and that he is eighteen years old. He will say nothing more. The police report notes the clothes he was wearing: "a navy-blue jacket, black trousers, calf boots, black broad-brimmed hat, a green tie, a red shirt with a turned-back collar." There are no papers on him to give away his identity.

A sense of uneasiness looms over the government. The president, the ministers, and high military officials all have guards so that they won't be the victims of the next attack. Figueroa Alcorta invokes martial law and categorically keeps from the newspapers any information about the prisoner and anarchist activities.

After several days of feverish work, the police succeed in identifying the terrorist. He is Simón Radovitsky or Radowitzsky, a Russian, living in the *conventillo* located on 194 Andes Street. He arrived in Argentina in March 1908 and was employed as a mechanic in the factory making railroad cars. Later he returned to Buenos Aires to work as an ironworker and mechanic. Argentine embassies are asked to inquire about his past history. The then ambassador in Paris, Dr. Ernest Bosch, reveals that Radowitzky took part in disturbances in

Kiev, Russia, in 1905 and was sentenced to six months in prison. In those disturbances he received wounds whose scars still remain. The report contains something else, which is very interesting. It points out that Radowitzky belongs to the anarchistic group led by the intellectual Petroff, together with the known revolutionaries Karaschin (who attacked the funeral of Carlos de Borbón), Andrés Ragapeloff, Moisés Scutz, José Buwitz, Máximo Sagarin, Iván Mijin, and the lecturer Matrena. These are names, all of them, designed to make all the hair of tranquil *porteños* of the day stand on end.

Once the prisoner was identified and confessed to his crime, it only remained for him to wait for the day and hour of his execution. No one can believe that he is only eighteen years old. Being eighteen means that he is a minor. And all the newspapers, without exception, argue that Radowitzky is more than twenty-five years old. No one defends him. Not even *La protesta,* the anarchist paper, which has been silenced by some young men from the upper class.

On Monday, the fifteenth, those same people forced the doors of the shop on 839 Libertad Street and systematically destroyed everything that the anarchists were doing. There is no one in influential circles who raises his voice to call for Radowitsky not to be treated with severity. The military, politicians, and officials are all in favor of exemplary punishment. And no one hesitates to say that applying the death penalty in this case does not require taking into account the age of the offender.

The opinion of the prosecuting attorney, Dr. Manuel Beltrán, was abundantly clear about what should be done with the prisoner. "Simón Radowitzky," said the attorney, "belongs to that caste of wretches who vegetate on the Russian steppes, dragging along their miserable life between the inclemency of nature and the harshness of their inferior condition." And there was no forgiveness for the foreigner: "During his first investigation, the arrested man stood before the haughty judge and persisted in resisting all questioning about his personal identity. He refused to answer the questions they put to him, but, in contrast, he hastened to confess that he, indeed, did commit the crime they are investigating. He boasted about his origins and exulted in the fact that Lastigau had also died."

Dr. Beltrán made this uncouth ironworker seem like a subtle, refined assassin: "We note the cold blood and arrogance with which Radowitsky excuses himself and his pose as a fanatic in the first confession where his pride in his heroic feat visibly struggles with his fear of punishment. For that reason he brags about this act, which he can neither deny nor hide. But, at the same time, he holds back any information about his personal history, believing that this will hamper the investigation."

And that was a tremendous contradiction for the attorney. Because Radowitzky was telling the truth: he was eighteen years old. But there's more: he admitted sole responsibility for the crime, hiding a companion who was on Callao Avenue and Quintana Avenue at the time of the attack but whose identity he would never divulge.

The attorney's report continued: "The physical appearance of the assassin has morphological characteristics that demonstrate with pronounced accents all the infamous marks of the criminal. Excessive development of the lower jaw, prominence of the zygomatic arch in his skull and his eyebrows, his receding forehead, his stormy look, the slight asymmetry of his face, these all make up the physical features that give him away as a delinquent type of person."

The attorney saw a born criminal in Radowitzky, like those who murder just to steal. He did not recognize that he is a child of desperation, born in a land where slavery and the whip reigned over the poor, where punishment was terrible for those who didn't obey the absolute rule of the czars. Although the attorney has some mitigating words for the racial origin of the prisoner, he offered them with profound disparagement and disgust: "Pariahs of the political absolutism of that environment, forced to yield to the discretionary powers of the boss, pursued and massacred by the ignorance and fanaticism of a people who see the Hebrew people as enemies of society, they at last emigrate, as Radowitzky did, after being condemned for the sole act of professing subversive ideas." That last phrase of Dr. Beltrán's did not agree with what he went on to demand. He asked that, "to the ends of social prophylactics," the trial be oral and swift.

Dr. Beltrán concluded his presentation by asking for the death penalty for the anarchist. The only difficulty was the "small" inconvenience of Radowitzky's age. At the time, there was no death penalty for minors, women, and the elderly in Argentina. But Dr. Beltrán discovered an original way around the problem. He calculated the prisoner's age by relying on "medical experts." Some of them figured that the offender is twenty years old, others twenty-five. Then the attorney said: "$20 + 25 = 45$, and one half of that is 22.5." That is, he was old enough for the firing squad. With total tranquillity Beltrán gave his verdict: "I should reveal that, although this is the first time that I have had the opportunity to ask for the ultimate penalty for a delinquent, I do so without misgivings or irrelevant vacillations. I do this with the firmest of consciences that I am doing my duty. For I realize that nothing is more counterproductive in the social or judicial order than the exaggerated sentimentality of a poorly understood philanthropy."

And, to put the final touches on a zeal that might have faltered at times, Beltrán added at the end: "Considering the social defense, we should see in

Radowitzky an unadaptable element whose frightening characteristics directly support the crime perpetrated and are able to inspire only the most extreme aversion to the ferocity of a proven cynicism that has led him to boast about that crime to this very day and to recall it with gloating pleasure."

Everything was going badly for Radowitzky. Nobody wanted to believe that he was eighteen. The press, influenced by the powerful, sought the death penalty. Things followed their course until one fine day a singular character appeared, a man with the air of the rabbi or a secondhand clothes dealer about him. He said that his name was Moises Radowisky and that he was the terrorist's cousin.

He produced a document, warpped up in a toilet-paper roll, that completely turned around the judicial process. It was the birth certificate of Simón Radowitzky. A strange document, written in Cyrillic script.

When providing the information, the then-popular magazine *Caras and caretas* commented that "Radowitzky is younger every day. At the first they attributed twenty-nine years to him, and from there they lowered the count to the essential age for the firing squad: twenty-two. He always claimed that he was eighteen, and he did not seem disposed to change his age, but who would believe him? Not even the anarchists. It was logical to suppose that Radowitsky would try to pass for a younger age. Has the point about his age finally been clarified? Mr. Vieyra, the inspector commissioner, has just received the document that we reproduce here in facsimile and that, judging from its appearance, is a faithful copy of Radowitzky's baptismal certificate. According to Vieyra's translators, that document, with so many scribbles and bizarre characters, purports to say that Simon Radowitzky was born in the village of Santiago, in the province of Kiev, on 10 November 1891. According to which Radowitzky would now be eighteen years and seven months old."

But the Russian baptismal certificate was not recognized by the judges because it was not a legal document. Yet it had a direct effect on the judges' minds; they were not motivated to send a minor to his death. They applied the criterion of "reasonable doubt," and Radowitzky was saved from being shot. But he was condemned to a slow death: in prison for life, in solitary confinement with bread and water for twenty days every year as the date of his crime drew near.

The long night was beginning for the boy anarchist. All his youth behind bars and silent walls. He spent twenty-one years there — and ten of them in solitary — among the dregs of society: child murderers, bloodthirsty individuals who kill without batting an eyelash just to rob someone, thieves, degenerate criminals. He passed nineteen of those years in Ushuaia, on the southern tip of Argentina, a penitentiary that didn't need any adjectives to instill fear.

But Radowitzky did not disappear from public opinion. On the contrary, as the doors of the prison closed tight, the second chapter of his life, of his life's adventure, began. A chapter that has the flavor of *The Count of Monte Cristo.*

But what does indeed close forever is the chapter of the assassination of Falcón and the young Lastigau. Radowitzky never again spoke of it. Who inspired it? Was it his own idea? Did he make the bomb? Did his companions perhaps order him to make the attack because he was a minor and that would save him from the death penalty? Five years later a similar attack occurred that marks the beginning of World War I. Gavrilo Princip—also a minor—was the man behind the tragedy at Sarajevo. All of his friends were shot, but not him, because he was not yet twenty-one years old. But he died of tuberculosis in an Austrian prison three years later. Radowitzky, on the other hand, endured all kinds of tortures, a near-starvation diet, cold, and unsanitary conditions—yet he managed to envision freedom, whose first glimmerings he spotted scarcely fourteen months after he was imprisoned.

On 6 January 1911, there is only one topic of conversation in Buenos Aires. Fourteen convicts from the national penitentiary have escaped through a tunnel constructed under the prison wall. Two famous anarchists were able to escape: Francisco Solano Regis (condemned to twenty years in prison for having made an attack on Ex-President Figueroa Alcorta) and Salvador Planas Virella (with a penalty of ten years for having attempted to kill President Quintana). The other eleven escapees are common prisoners. There is one more anarchist in the penitentiary who was not able to escape: Simón Radowitzky, who was taken to the prison print shop only a few minutes before the breakout.

. . . That same year his fate was decided, and the anarchist was transferred to the penitentiary of Ushuaia. It will be the last time that he will ever tread on land in the province of Buenos Aires. He will never again be able to return to his room at the *conventillo* on 194 Andes Street (today José Evaristo Uriburu Street) from which he departed that morning in November 1909 in order to commit the attack on Falcón.

Translated by Patricia Owen Steiner

The Unión Cívica Radical

David Rock

Organizing the national state according to republican principles changed Argentine politics forever. The new order brought with it a hesitant but steady democratization of public life that, in spite of multiple obstacles, created new spaces for political participation. In the 1890s, a new, effective political force emerged that later took the name of Unión Cívica Radical (UCR) — a centrist party still active today. From then on, political power struggles were fought out and negotiated through institutional mechanisms such as general elections and party membership. Since the UCR's public banner was democratization with social justice, it was soon perceived as the party of the urban masses. Led by Hipólito Yrigoyen, twice president (1916–21, 1928–30), the UCR paved the way for the first national populist movement. In the chapter selected, the British historian David Rock identifies the political bases of Yrigoyen's appeal during his first administration.

The general course of Argentine politics after 1916 was shaped by the relationship between successive radical governments and the conservative elite groups that they replaced. The election victory won by the UCR in 1916 appeared initially a reflection of the capacity of the traditional ruling class for retrenchment and self-preservation. Although the original objective of creating a majoritarian conservative party along the lines laid down by Pellegrini and Sáenz Peña had failed and direct control over the administration had passed into new hands, there was no reason to believe that the real power of the elite had disappeared or diminished in any significant way. The army and navy had the same commanders as before 1916. The major lobby associations representing the elite's interests, such as the Sociedad Rural, were still intact. Also, powerful members of the elite still retained their positions of close contact with the foreign business groups.

The Radical Government in 1916

In many respects the oligarchy appeared to have merely changed its form. In Yrigoyen's first cabinet in 1916, five out of the eight ministers were either cattle-owning landowners in the province of Buenos Aires or closely connected with the export sector. The minister of finance was Domingo E. Salaberry, who was involved in exporting, banking, and real estate. The minister of agriculture, who later became minister of foreign affairs, was Honorio Pueyrredón, a major landowner and patrician from the province of Buenos Aires. The minister of marine was Federico Alvarez de Toledo, who also possessed large areas of land in Buenos Aires and in the province of Mendoza. Pablo Torello, the minister of public works, was, like Pueyrredón, a major landowner. Yrigoyen's first minister of foreign affairs, Carlos Becú, was a person with similar background. He and Pueyrredón had until comparatively recently belonged to parties opposed to the radicals. Becú was a political protégé of Estanislao Zeballos, who was Roca's foreign minister in his second term. Pueyrredón had remained a member of General Mitre's Party, the Unión Cívica, until after 1912. The other ministers, Ramón Gómez, the minister of the interior, Elpidio González, the minister of war, and José P. Salinas, the minister of education, came from more humble backgrounds. They owed their rise to their control of the radical party machine in different key provinces, Gómez in Santiago del Estero, González in Córdoba, and Salinas in Jujuy. The vice president, Pelagio Luna, who died in 1919, was also chosen because of his provincial connections in Salta.

Under these circumstances the influential groups within the elite, which had finally become resigned to a change of government, were encouraged to believe that they had simply delegated their former direct power to the new government. The radicals seemed in many respects to have the same general objectives as themselves and to be worthy of carrying on where Sáenz Peña had left off.

Radicalism still largely retained its more conservative features. For example, many of the leaders of the new administration, most particularly Yrigoyen himself, were more markedly clerical than most of their predecessors, many of whom were Freemasons. In 1918, *La vanguardia* declared: "Never has the influence of the church been greater than at present . . . the government is pursuing a Christian Democrat policy with the help of the church, a paternalistic protective attitude toward the workers, so long as they remain submissive and resigned."

Also Yrigoyen had failed to win control by force. He had obtained the presidency as much by courtesy of Sáenz Peña and his successor, De la Plaza, as by his own efforts. In 1916 the radicals won little more than the office of the presidency. They were still in opposition in most of the provinces, and they were also still a minority in the national Congress. There the government managed to win a majority only in the popularly elected Chamber of Deputies in 1918. In the Senate, whose members enjoyed the lengthy term of nine years and were normally elected by the provincial legislatures, the conservatives continued to hold a majority until 1922 and beyond. In addition to their other prerogatives, the conservatives therefore kept control over government legislation.

In 1916 Yrigoyen's position was thus still relatively weak, and his policies were sharply conditioned by his relationship with the elite. His mandate was the achievement of two general objectives. First, he was bound by the need to uphold the economic interests of the landed groups. Second, he had to establish a new relationship with the urban sectors, which had been the main source of political instability since the turn of the century. In many respects these two objectives seemed contradictory and incompatible. The principal reason why the conservative groups themselves had failed to organize a mass party was because they had been unable to adapt their position as producer interests to the need to offer something concrete to the urban groups. Only the radicals had been apparently able to surmount this difficulty. They had become "inorganic." They had avoided drawing up a specific program. They had cloaked their objectives in a veil of moralistic rhetoric and their real commitments with a deceptively generous effluence of paternalism. On this had been superimposed continual hints at wider access for the middle-class groups to government offices.

This principle of mediating between elite and urban interests shaped the character of political conflict after 1916. It was not so much that the new government was impelled consciously into attacking the elite's economic interests directly. Like their predecessors, the radicals evaluated their own successes in terms of their ability to expand and consolidate the primary export economy, rather than attempt to change it. At the end of Yrigoyen's term in 1922, it is difficult to point to any significant change in the deeper texture of Argentine society. In 1922 the export sector still dominated the country's economy as it had done before 1916. The currency, taxation, tariff, and land systems also remained the same, and the connections with the British were still as strong as they had been before. The net achievements of the radical government were very few indeed, and these either complemented what had gone before or were mere tamperings that could easily be reversed.

The radicals were unable to develop any wider commitment to more substantial change at this point because they themselves, as a coalition of landowners and nonindustrial middle-class groups, were immediate beneficiaries of the primary export economy as producers and consumers. Their objectives were redistributive, rather than structural in implication. What they were primarily aiming for was to democratize estanciero society by rationalizing and improving the system of social and political relations that had emerged from it. These objectives are aptly captured in the following statements, which are taken from the year 1920:

> [The country's "social constitution"] will be unobtainable until governments appreciate their inescapable duty to provide the means for justice to extend its benefits to every social rank. . . . Democracy does not simply consist in the guarantee of personal liberty: it also involves the opportunity of everyone to enjoy a minimum level of welfare.

> In assiduous and direct contact with the people and with the progressive activities of the nation, President Yrigoyen, the true democrat, has managed to win something that the presidents of class were never able to win—the love and confidence of the citizenry.

The dual emphasis on *welfare* and *contact* also indicates that the radicals were aiming to achieve political integration and a state of class harmony. They intended to maintain the existing socioeconomic framework but promote institutionalized political participation outside the traditional ruling class. These objectives involved the government with two key groups, the "dependent" professional middle class, which already before 1916 had become an important component of radicalism, and, second, with the urban working class. The government's contacts with these two groups shaped its relationship with the elite and beyond it with foreign capital. The final quadruple relationship that emerged came to occupy a dominant place in Argentine politics up to 1930.

The central problem stemmed from tendencies on the part of the radical government to move too closely into line with the interests of the urban groups. This triggered dangerous expressions of political conflict, when it began to threaten the elite's relationship with foreign capital and overseas markets. Each of the major crises of the radical government, in 1919 and in 1930, was directly related to a process of this sort. At the same time the inclination toward the urban sectors underlay the survival of conservatism during these years and the eventual failure of the elite to delegate the supervision of its interests to the radicals.

The Techniques of Popular Leadership

In one respect the advent of the radical government marked a revolutionary change in the style of Argentine politics. The staid, closeted atmosphere of the oligarchy was swifly swept away in a wave of popular euphoria. When Yrigoyen was sworn in as president, his coach was dragged through the streets by his supporters from the party committees in the federal capital. Yrigoyen himself, through his dependence on novel methods of leadership, and through his control over a mass party with ramifications throughout the country, came to occupy a very different position from that of his predecessors. Although with Roca, Juárez Celman, Figueroa Alcorta, and at an earlier date with Rosas there had been a tendency to personalize policies and issues, with Yrigoyen this became one of the central stylistic elements of Argentine politics. It became the accepted convention for the radicals to prefix their actions and statements with lengthy panegyrics to their leader. Equally the opposition reserved its most biting attacks for the president himself. In Buenos Aires there was one newspaper, La mañana (which became known as La fronda in 1919), which discussed nothing else but the alleged failures and shortcomings of the peludo, as Yrigoyen now universally became known:

> Sr. Irigoyen is a simple boss, wise and supple in the maneuvers of the committee. The great orator, writer and thinker! He is nothing more than a legend of mystification, who after thirty years of obscurity, has suddenly exploded into the government, as the exponent of ignorance, regression, and brigandry.

At the same time there was always a great deal of fascination with Yrigoyen's personality. In spite of their distaste for his methods and their jealousy of his political acumen, many members of the opposition betrayed more than a touch of incredulity at the manner in which the new president defended and manipulated his position. A leader of the conservative opposition, Rodolfo Moreno, declared in 1918:

> A man incapable of facing public debate, because he lacked the necessary gifts to do so. A man who relied for his prestige on surrounding himself with a veil of mystery. What popular fantasy could have created a statesman out of a man who has never delivered a speech, written a book, traced out a program, obtained a university degree, and has never taken part in conventional social intercourse . . . and who, in a word, possesses none of the qualities that stand out in a democracy, an ability to discuss matters, and subject himself to free examination.

Yrigoyen was indeed something of a strange novelty in Argentine politics. Even when he became president he still refused to make public speeches. During his period of office the practice of delivering the presidential address at the beginning of the congressional sessions in person was abandoned, much to the chagrin of the staid elements of the conservative opposition. Instead Yrigoyen would write a rambling preamble to the message, most of it unintelligible to the average politician (often intentionally so), which the vice president or his deputy would read. He appears to have spent much of his time in confabulation with his party collaborators, not in the presidential palace, the Casa Rosada, but in his modest and run-down home near the Plaza Constitución. His public appearances were still very limited, and often the only time he would be seen was while attending the funeral of some apparently minor party dignitary. The opposition parties called this necrophilia, though it can be explained in terms of the high premium placed by Yrigoyen on loyalty to his political friends and his emphasis on personal relationships in administering and supervising the party.

The president was also known as something of a sexual adept. Although he never married, he produced at least a dozen children by a succession of mistresses. Later in life — in the late 1920s during his second presidency — cabinet ministers would complain of being kept waiting for days at a time while Yrigoyen entertained bevies of young widows who had come as claimants for state pensions. Until he became president in 1916 photographs of him were extremely rare. On the occasion of his brother's funeral in April 1916, press photographs of the event unmistakably revealed his tall frame, although his face was intentionally covered by a hat. He was said to object to photographs because of his Kraussian principles, which forbade the reproduction of his "soul." More likely this was all a little ploy to exploit the curiosity of the population. When he discovered the importance of the mass media for election purposes, these petty idiosyncrasies swiftly disappeared. By 1919 his portrait was plastered from one end of the country to the other. A union organizer from the period recalled a journey he had made around 1920 to the yerba mate plantations in the northern territories of Chaco and Misiones in search of recruits for his union. His efforts met with very little success. The Indian laborers proclaimed that their sole loyalties were to the "Father of the Poor," Hipólito Yrigoyen, whose effigy they treasured on small alloy brooches given to them by radical agents.

The mystery and adulation surrounding Yrigoyen can be further illustrated by anecdotes and reportage. An example, given currency by an opponent in 1919, comes from the province of Mendoza. It refers to Yrigoyen and to the radical leader of the province, José Néstor Lencinas. It seems that notions like this were sometimes put about, and the semi-Hispanicized population of areas like Mendoza were encouraged to see their national leader, and explain the vagaries of his policies, in its anarchically apocalyptic terms:

About three years ago, the present governor of the province of Mendoza, Dr. José Néstor Lencinas, whose friendship with the president of the Republic is well-known and appreciated throughout the country, suddenly began to express dissent with several aspects of his policy. But in reply to my protests against the iniquities of the national government, the governor made known to me a personal revelation.

He said to me, "I also used to stand in protest against Yrigoyen, but four nights ago, as I lay asleep, there spoke in my ear the voice of a dearly loved soul — that of my brother Santiago — which said to me in an ethereal, magnetic tone: "President Yrigoyen is not Hipólito Yrigoyen. Our teacher, friend, and apostle is at present tending a flock of sheep in the Guaminí district." On 12 October 1916, he completed the mission set for him by his party and his motherland. On that same day, transmuting himself into Yrigoyen's human form there arrived from India Joaquín Chrisnamurty, also known as Alcione, a young man twenty-eight years old and a veritable fountain of scientific knowledge, which he had set down in a book in eight days at the age of fourteen in the University of Oxford — a feat that would have demanded three thousand years of labor from any other person. This Chrisnamurty is a second God. "You can believe me," added Dr. Lencinas, "that whatever he may do from the presidency will be for the happiness of each one of us. He may destroy the country, but surely will rebuild it better. It is possible that the present generation may not comprehend his labors, but when in two thousand years time humanity studies the history of Argentina, it will possess a true insight into this miraculous leader."

Such bizarre extravagances were rare, although it was not infrequent even in Buenos Aires to find party stalwarts in public meetings frenetically crying "Yrigoyen es un dios" (Yrigoyen is a god). This purely symbolic appeal may have played some part in mobilizing support for the radicals in the more backward zones of the country, but generally in the cities the attempt to recruit allegiances was based on something more concrete and material than this. . . .

The new popular style of politics was also accompanied by a much greater political involvement on the part of the urban groups, which had been relegated to only an occasional or indirect role before. The radicals viewed this as symptomatic of a new spirit of democracy. The opposition groups, on the other hand, including the socialists, frequently described it as mob rule. They referred to the radicals' supporters in the committees as the *chusma,* the "rabble," whose distinguishing traits were an inordinate venality and an insatiable appetite for corruption.

Nevertheless, the presence of these groups served to accelerate the slow transformation that had been taking place among the political parties since the 1890s. At every level of politics it injected new patterns and styles of contact between the politicians and the electorate. Electioneering, apart from in the remote subsistence areas of the interior, ceased to be a matter of simple bribery and evolved fully into a problem of mass organization. There was a parallel revolution in the art of political propaganda, and a new style of popular journalism appeared. Finally, as a reflection of the much greater range of articulated demands within the political system, the process of government decisionmaking, and the span of government activities, began to acquire new, complex dimensions.

Radicalism itself remained a hybrid conglomeration. The regional and class disparities it enshrined, but had failed to conquer, prevented it further from acquiring the "organic" forms the reformers of 1912 had aspired for. In many ways it remained an offshoot of the "personalist" parties of the past, with many of the same authoritarian features as the governments of the oligarchy. The heterogeneous environment in which it operated, and the conflicting demands to which it was subject, preserved an impression of improvisation and confusion in the party. In 1919 one of the leading opposition conservative newspapers, *La nación,* declared:

> The Radical Party lacks any concrete concepts of government. It would be unable to define a fully integrated and precise strategy. Its ideals are nebulous, and its aspirations reveal themselves only in the vague claim of unlimited self-virtue. Its sense of common identity is no more than a torrential impulse of the memory of its days of opposition, which are negative by self-definition. The only thing it has . . . that is positive is the person of its chief, Señor Yrigoyen. He is the exclusive past and present point of reference.
> . . . .

The Government's Political Strategy

In 1916 the effects of inflation on the urban consumers put the radical government in a rather difficult position. It was committed to ending political tension between the elite and the urban sectors and consolidating its own position with the electorate at a moment when, as a result of inflation, the interests of the two groups were diverging sharply. The government could not afford to prevent the landed interests from profiting from the wartime boom in primary food products. On the other hand, unless it attempted at least to mitigate the effects of inflation it ran the risk of forfeiting its links with the urban groups. This would leave the way open for its competitors like the Socialist Party, which was more explicitly linked with urban interests. It was thus necessary to find some way of appeasing the urban groups without simultaneously alienating the elite.

So far as the urban middle-class groups were concerned, the only practicable way of doing this, it was found, was by increasing the supply of bureaucratic and professional positions. The readoption of the traditional mechanisms of political patronage, and its long-term effect on patterns of state spending, eventually became the central feature of relations between the urban middle class and the conservative elite and the basic condition governing the radicals' ability to maintain their middle-class support. Of course the use of such expedients did not mean that the whole of the voting native middle class obtained a job in the bureaucracy. Offices were used primarily to establish and maintain the nexus between the government and the party committees, and in turn the committees operated as the main device for the mobilization of the electorate, often using more conventional techniques. . . .

However, the patronage system did not develop immediately. The main short-term problem in 1916 was that any increase in state spending to expand the bureaucracy would require an increase in taxation. In the absence of reforms to the country's taxation system, this could be achieved only at the cost of the urban sectors themselves. The bulk of state revenues came from tariffs on imported goods and was thus levied on consumption. To change this, the only conceivable major modification to the taxation system would be a tax on land. Such a tax was difficult to envisage. It would be a direct attack on the landed elite, and, apart from anything else, it would endanger the coalition character of radicalism itself. But it was equally very difficult to increase tariffs when already the prices of imported goods were so high.

Before 1919, when imports and revenues began to pick up, the government proved unwilling to increase public spending by any dramatic amount. It was able to justify this up to a point by invoking some of its principles from its years in opposition. Although few, least of all the urban middle classes, had taken them seriously, the radicals had claimed before 1916 that once in power they would end the traditional spoils system, as part of the program of "moral regeneration" they had taken on themselves. Consequently the patronage system was rather slow in developing. Most of the appointees of previous administrations, at least in the national government, were allowed to keep their positions.

Instead in its first two years of office the government attempted to promote a number of mild reform schemes in Congress that were aimed mainly at the rural tenant groups. There was a proposal for the creation of an agricultural bank to help with colonization schemes. Also an attempt was made to impose a temporary tax on agricultural exports to relieve destitute farmers and to promote a public works scheme to help cope with the urban unemployment problem. Another piece of projected legislation aimed for the purchase of shipping, which could be used to reduce freight charges on the Atlantic run.

These measures are best interpreted as an attempt by the government to consolidate its grip over the rural sectors in the pampas area and to win control over the provincial administrations of Buenos Aires, Córdoba, and Entre Ríos. This was also plainly the reason why the conservative opposition refused to consider such legislation. One of Yrigoyen's later most prominent opponents, Federico Pinedo, described the measures in the following terms:

> When Yrigoyen became president in the style of a Messiah and his redemptory legislation was being awaited after its twenty years of preparation and gestation, he produced a grotesque balloon of nonsense in the shape of four bills. The only outstanding quality of these was their laughable childishness. In one of his messages he announced his intention of reforming the agrarian sector by means of a state-controlled colonization scheme. This, it was said, was necessary to correct the evils of private enterprise. In fact the proposal consisted of an authorization to the executive to employ the ridiculously high sum of 30 million pesos in loans to farmers for such different things as buying private or public land, housing construction, or the purchase of livestock. The allocation of all this money was to be decided exclusively by government officials, without the law saying anything about the recipients or the conditions of the loans. Everything was left to the government's whim.

The opposition groups in Congress refused to accept these tax changes because of their apprehensions that the revenues from them would be employed for openly partisan purposes. Without being unfair to the government, there is no reason to believe that the opposition was wrong. The radicals were in a weak position in the Congress and in many of the provinces in 1916 and were seeking means to consolidate their position.

Another of the government's proposals was that it should be authorized to negotiate a loan with a number of New York banks to consolidate the public debt. This again illustrated its financial orthodoxy at this point, its unwillingness to increase public spending, and its initial search for alternatives to a patronage system based simply on increased state spending. Similar legislation had been attempted in the past. The only real novelty was a proposed income tax scheme introduced in 1918. However, none of these projects prospered except, some time later during the export boom, the temporary tax on agricultural exports.

The export tax was finally passed by Congress on 18 January 1918, soon after a major grain deal at guaranteed prices had been negotiated with the Allies. Its acceptance by Congress at this point reflected the opinion that the burden of the tax would fall on either the Allies or the exporters, and not on the producers. The income tax scheme was extremely mild and can hardly be instanced as more than a token measure to reverse the effects of inflation on the distribution of income. Working-class and middle-class incomes between 2,500 and 10,000 pesos per year were to be taxed at 0.75 percent per year, with the rate progressively increasing to 7 percent for incomes over 150,000 pesos. The estimated revenue from the tax was 30 million pesos, a sum that would not have solved the revenue problem. Nevertheless this measure was more than the conservatives had attempted.

The Development of the Patronage System

In spite of not unwarranted conservative fears that any change in the tax system would be used by the radicals as subsidies for their election campaigns, the failure of this legislation illustrated the extreme unwillingness of the conservative majority in Congress to back the reforms they had made in 1912 with further tangible concessions. Under these circumstances of political impasse, in 1918 and 1919, the government's resort to cruder patronage techniques became marked. By 1919, as imports picked up again after the war, the revenue position also improved. Also by 1919, as will be seen later, there were signs that middle-class support for the government in the city of Buenos Aires was beginning to crumble.

Between 1919 and 1922 the use of government offices for political purposes developed into the principal nexus linking the government with the middle-class groups. Yrigoyen made administrative posts available to the party's local bosses in the committees, and they applied them to establish firm bridgeheads of support among the native-born electorate. During these years Yrigoyen's personal position as leader of the government and the party came to rest almost exclusively on his ability to manipulate state patronage. The following remarks by *La vanguardia* in 1922 are a bitter, though substantially accurate, comment on the importance the system had acquired by this time:

> Affiliation to the Radical Party is becoming a kind of passport or safe-conduct for all kinds of posts. This system owes its origin to the need to reward the nepotistical hordes of the "Cause" with public offices. It has con-

verted each of the national and municipal administrative departments into asylums for degenerates.

The major recipients of these benefits were the urban "dependent" middle-class groups of immigrant extraction in Buenos Aires and to a lesser extent in the other important cities near the Atlantic coast. These were the core groups of the Radical Party's committee organization, who had joined the party in increasing numbers after 1900. On the other hand, the system discriminated against the immigrants, who had no vote to be won. Equally it did not benefit the working class and the entrepreneurial groups, both of which were largely beyond the lure of jobs in the administration. Not surprisingly, the system was strongly opposed by the Socialist Party. It gave their main followers very little.

The main result of the growth of the patronage system was the great expansion of the links between Yrigoyen himself and the middle-class *caudillos de barrio* in the party committees. As the system became more established, these representatives of the urban middle-class groups began to appear among the upper reaches of the bureaucracy and to compete with members of the party's traditional leadership for candidatures for elective offices.

Another of the leading features of Yrigoyen's government was thus a struggle for control over the party between the middle-class groups and the elite wing, which had supported radicalism since the early 1890s. This division had been foreshadowed in the disputes over Yrigoyen's candidature in 1916. Afterward it put increasing strain on the cross-class character of the party. Opposition to Yrigoyen on the part of the party's aristocratic wing crystallized in the form of an attack on presidential "personalism" and in a demand for the separation of the party and the government. The aim of this was to check Yrigoyen's power by rupturing the direct link between him and the middle-class groups. At the end of 1918 the elite wing, which was still a majority in the official, but increasingly powerless, organs of the party such as the National Committee and the Committee of the Federal Capital, issued an important manifesto. It provides a convenient summary of the dissidents' objectives and illustrates their growing disenchantment with Yrigoyen:

> Public opinion has no reason to see in our party any more than what it is today: a movement with no further program beyond that of supporting the government. . . . Let us proclaim therefore the need to react against the spineless instinct of unconditional support, against "personalism," the lack of ideas, the predominance of mediocrity. . . . Radicalism ought to continue to be an independent association of the citizenry, resolving to direct its actions by its own deliberations and by its own will. All interference or outside influence, especially of the "personalist" kind, contradicts the defi-

nition of democracy. . . . The party ought to define its position on the most urgent and important political problems. . . . On indicating the need for such a program, we do not mean to invest the party with an encyclopedic collection of abstract principles. The radical ideal, which most interests the electorate, is to assure good public administration. This ideal depends for its realization on the qualities of the individual, on known competence, intellectual capacities, and on the behavior of both functionaries and governors. Radicalism will fulfill its mission if it criticizes those who do not fulfill these conditions. . . . It is necessary to make a just assessment of the values of individuals to put the party into the hands of the most competent and capable.

In 1918 and 1919 the party was brought very near to a major split on this issue. Yet in spite of the pressure of the "Blue Group," as it became known, attempts to control or reverse the trend of Yrigoyen's increasing involvement with the middle-class groups and with the precinct party bosses were unsuccessful. The elite group failed to obtain control of the party because it lacked access to the sources of party patronage and consequently the means to construct a popular following. Its members depended themselves on Yrigoyen for their political careers. Ultimately they were forced to accept either his leadership or a position of irredeemable political isolation. When in 1919 the opposition movement finally collapsed, the relationship between Yrigoyen, as the source of patronage, and the party committees, as the source of electoral support, became the party's dominating feature. . . .

Radicalism and the Working Class

The main source of friction between the radical government and the elite before 1922 came from another quarter. The most dramatic of the radical government's innovations was its attempt to go beyond the middle-class groups and to include in its project of political integration a new relationship between the state and the urban working class. Its experience in this field provides the best illustration of the character and the overall results of the political changes introduced in 1912. It also expresses some of the central characteristics of radical populism and highlights the precise nature of the relations between the elite and the urban sectors.

Before 1916 the radicals paid scant heed to the working-class problem. Their few references to it were made in a pro forma fashion simply as a means of adding to their more general complaints against the oligarchy. Also, when they did so, their complaints were phrased very much in terms of orthodox liberal conceptions. There was very little in their position that could be described as a reformist orientation. One charge against the oligarchy, for example, was that its authoritarian control had led to the growth of class sentiments. The implication was that these should be avoided at all costs: "The vices and complications of the old [European] societies have been reproduced here. The working classes, finding even their just petitions ignored, consequently represent an element of economic disruption and are creating grave problems that the government ought to foresee and resolve more opportunely."

An antipathy toward the notion of class was one of the salient features of the party's doctrines and ideology, which continued beyond 1916. In 1919 Francisco Beiró, one of Yrigoyen's close collaborators in the National Chamber of Deputies, declared:

> Nor do we accept class differences or that there should be any classes in the Argentine Republic. . . . We do not fail to see that there are conflicts between capital and labor, but we do not accept that there is a proletarian or a capitalist class, even if 95 percent of the Argentines were to fall into what in Europe is called *the proletariat*. Nor is it right to bring into our new America, here where new ideals of human solidarity are being formed, such sentiments of hate on account of differences of race, religion, or class.

Similarly, before 1916, the radicals condemned the repressive legislation used by the oligarchy against the anarchists, not because it was an instrument of oppression, but simply because it violated liberal notions of the due process of law: "The workers have seen their claims ignored, or they have been met with armed violence and with a body of repressive legislation that grants the police the extraordinary faculty of banishing abroad, as a dangerous criminal, anyone who protests against them. This being done without any clear reason being given and without due process of law."

Another of the leading features of radicalism at this time was its reactionary, almost paranoid, attitude to anything that might seem like "socialism." Its antipathies to Justo's Socialist Party were in many ways even more marked than those of the oligarchy:

> But how can the maximum or the minimum programs [of the Socialist Party] be accepted and at the same time the principle of private or public property be maintained intact? . . . Socialism implies the denial of many, if not all, of the inherent faculties of property. And since Proudhon, its originator, uttered the celebrated phrase, "Property is robbery," each one of the claims to which the party subscribes in its programs is a menace to the very foundations of property.

Accompanying this was an exaggerated and dogmatic assertion of the opportunities there were in Argentine society for social mobility. The following quotation is taken from the year 1920:

> Here all that is required to win through is health and strength of will: to go from laborer to employer from employer to tycoon. . . . Because the air we breathe here is that of democracy. There have never existed in this country titles of nobility, nor privileges, nor classes, nor any kind of aristocracy. . . . What does exist is nobility of sentiment, generosity, the liberty of healthy ideas, and reasonable human fraternity. This is the meaning of true democracy, so far superior to what is called "socialism."

To judge from this, and in spite of the Radical Party's cross-class aggregative character, there was no reason why the radical government should have displayed the interest in the working class that it did. What primarily forced it to do so were electoral considerations and its struggle after 1916 for congressional supremacy. The vote of the native-born workers, who had been enfranchised by the Sáenz Peña Law, was, despite their being a minority in terms of the working class as a whole, one of the major keys to the political control of the city of Buenos Aires.

The search for political control over the working class was one of the most significant effects of the widening of the franchise from 1912 onward. Yrigoyen was not alone, nor the first, to be propelled in this direction. There are a number of interesting parallels elsewhere. The policies of President José Batlle y Ondoñez in Uruguay were an important precedent. This may have been a model for Yrigoyen. It would be interesting to compare Batlle and Yrigoyen at more length and to show why reformism had so much more success in Uruguay than in Argentina. Batlle was always in a much stronger position than Yrigoyen after his defeat of the conservative National Party in 1904. Yrigoyen's revolt of 1905 failed, and eventually he came to power with the position of the conservatives still largely intact. The scope of Batlle's measures in Uruguay, which included advanced welfare legislation and went much further than the Argentine radicals ever proposed, possibly reflected Uruguay's need to compete with Argentina for immigrants. In the early twentieth century the Uruguayan landed interests around Montevideo, which Batlle's Colorado Party represented, were attempting to diversify from pastoral production into agriculture but found this difficult because of labor shortages. Batlle's reforms may have been partly inspired by the need to attract more immigrants. In other respects there were close parallels between him and Yrigoyen. Both aimed to eliminate the threat of anarchism, and both sought ties with the working class through the trade unions.

There were also precedents for Yrigoyen's policies in the province of Santa Fé. In 1912 after the first election held under the Sáenz Peña Law, a radical administration was elected, led by Manuel Menchaca. Here a determined attempt began to exploit control over the administration to win support among the workers. The main example came during a strike of tramwaymen in Rosario in 1913, when the provincial authorities intervened in the dispute to help the men. Later this led to accusations against the radicals in Santa Fé that they had bribed local union leaders to support them. In Santa Fé, as later in Buenos Aires, electoral considerations were uppermost in prompting attempts to create this relationship.

In Buenos Aires the search for working-class support was also a means to halt the growth of the Socialist Party and to prevent it from expanding outside the federal capital into the other major cities of the pampas region. In the federal capital in the congressional elections of 1912, 1913, and 1914 the Socialists won a succession of victories. At that moment it seemed that they were about to become a serious threat. They were united and were obviously also winning middle-class support in the federal capital. They were helped by Figueroa Alcorta's purge of the anarchists in 1910. This removed the main obstacle to their expansion.

In 1915, however, the socialists lost one of their most influential leaders, Alfredo L. Palacios, in a party split. For the next few years he led a separate party, the Argentine Socialist Party, in the elections. In 1916, in the presidential elections, the radicals for the first time made the winning of the working vote one of their principal objectives. Their campaign was organized along the conventional lines of ward boss paternalism and committee charity activities. Such "services" to the community were contrasted with the "false promises" of their opponents. The following newspaper précis of a streetcorner speech during the election campaign amusingly captures the flavor of the propaganda techniques they invoked:

> In the seventh ward alone . . . there had been sold at reduced prices and on a daily average 855 kilos of bread, 298 liters of milk, and 3,200 kilos of meat, which represented a daily economy of 900,400 pesos. This figure multiplied by the number of wards in the city yields an average daily saving of 18,000 pesos, or 6,588,000 annually, equivalent over fifteen years to 98,820,000 pesos. Over the same period, the socialists, making the same rigorous calculations, would have gushed forth 117,992,000 words, from which the working classes have obtained not the least benefit.

The socialists replied in kind. When it was announced just before the elections in March 1916 that Yrigoyen intended donating his emoluments to charity in the event of being elected, *La vanguardia* declared: "Do not let Sr. Irigoyen think that he is going to conquer the will of the electorate by laying bare a Christian and charitable soul, offering it the protection of asylums and hospitals, in order to deceive it, as the Roman emperors used to do, with bread and circuses."

This was the measure of the acute rivalry that developed between the two parties in years to come. For the first time in 1916 the radicals won an election in the city of Buenos Aires. Their share of the vote increased from 33 percent in 1914 to over 40 percent. But this was still a minority vote, and, in spite of all their efforts, the radicals failed to make any decisive headway in capturing the working-class vote. Although they increased their support in working-class areas of the city, they were still a long way behind the socialists. What gave them victory in 1916 was the disappearance of their conservative rivals from previous years. In 1914 two conservative parties, the Unión Cívica (the vestige of General Mitre's following from 1890) and the clerical Constitutional Party, had taken part in the election and had together won almost a third of the votes. The radicals had won another third. The other third in 1914, a slight majority, had gone to the socialists. In 1916 the Unión Cívica made way for the Progressive Democrat party, which had expanded into Buenos Aires from the province of Santa Fé. The church party affiliated with the radicals. In 1916 the Progressive Democrats won a mere 8 percent of the total vote. The two socialist parties, led by Justo and Palacios, however, won 50 percent of the vote, a proportion considerably higher than in 1914. The evidence was thus clear enough that the radicals gained only at the expense of the conservative groups and that it was only because the socialists were split that they managed to win the elections.

The election of 1916 suggested an imperviousness on the part of the working-class electorate to the committee charity style of electioneering adopted by the radicals. It showed that the committees were best suited to the middle-class groups, among which there was a higher degree of social atomization, a relatively low degree of class identification, and a prevalence of individualized aspirations for social mobility. If the radicals were to be successful in their efforts to capture the working-class vote, they would have to approach the problem in a different fashion. During a period of acute inflation, which affected the working class more than other groups, it was necessary to offer something in the way of benefits more durable and substantial than charity.

It was thus that the radical government embarked on its attempt to win working-class support by establishing close ties with the trade union movement. In 1916 the unions were an obvious target for the new government. They were the only remaining bulwark against the influence of the Socialist Party among the working class. Second, as class institutions, they had a certain stand-

The right-wing Nationalist Alliance of the Patriotic Youth patrols the streets during a wave of riots and strikes in 1919. After some hesitation, in an attempt to pacify the political right, Yrigoyen gave the order to repress the workers. Courtesy Archivo General de la Nación, Buenos Aires.

ing and legitimacy in the eyes of the workers themselves. Benefits that came through them had a much better chance of being accepted than anything that came from the committees. They were in principle an ideal substitute nexus through which contacts with the workers could be established. Third, and most important of all, the union movement itself was changing significantly. There would have been little hope of the radicals winning working-class support had the anarchists still been in a position of dominance. Soon after Yrigoyen became president, *La protesta* asked:

> Can a government, or a president, however democratic he may be, stand frankly and decidedly on the side of the workers? . . . The democratic ideals of modern rulers, the ideal made manifest through the "altruism," the "simplicity" of a president, which has become incarnate in the figure . . . of a misanthrope like Hipólito Yrigoyen, is only a temporary form of government in tune with the present moment of historical time. . . . The struggle, comrades, should be decidedly revolutionary, without admitting the influence of anyone, nor asking favors of the government.

But the anarchists were now in decline, and their influence was being rapidly superseded by the syndicalists. With them gradually declined the extreme anti-state stance adopted by the unions. The new role of the syndicalists meant that the unions had come under the control of a more moderate current, interested less in confrontation with the state than in improving the economic position of the workers.

During the election campaign in 1916 there were already signs that the radicals were beginning to appreciate the importance of the unions. In August 1915, the committees organized a workers' propaganda group, which they called the Federación Obrera Radical "Alberdi." This title was chosen because its initials, FORA, were the same as those of the major federations. The aim was to lure as many as possible unsuspecting union affiliates into contact with radical propaganda. There were several other petty schemes like it.

Yet, while the radicals now had a strategy with which to approach the working-class problem, they were still confronted by the question of the scale of benefits they would be able to provide. The syndicalists were interested in wages and were unlikely to be attracted by merely token gestures. Also the radicals were strongly committed in principle to laissez-faire. But here too there was a certain coincidence of approach. Neither they nor the unions were particularly interested in legislation, and they were both committed to preserv-

Military coup against President Yrigoyen (September 1930). Police prevent crowds from entering the Plaza de Mayo during the military coup against President Yrigoyen—the first in a series of military interventions that from then on would repeatedly disrupt Argentina's democratic institutions. Courtesy Archivo General de la Nación, Buenos Aires.

ing free market conditions for labor. The syndicalists saw legislation as either an attempt to institutionalize the subordination of the workers, as had been apparent with the abortive Labor Code introduced some years earlier by Joaquín González, or as capable, like the socialist measures, of providing only marginal benefits, which avoided the basic question of wages. Almost by virtue of their adherence to laissez-faire, the radicals escaped the difficulty of the socialists, who could be portrayed as trying to convince the workers to accept measures they did not particularly want.

The central problem with the question of benefits for the unions and the workers stemmed from its potential effects on the position of the conservative elite. In part the reforms of 1912 had been carried out to bring the workers sufficiently into the political system to undercut the position of the unions and the "foreign agitators." However, the railway strike of 1912 had shown that the elite still remained strongly opposed to an attempt to buttress working-class political participation by any material concessions. It was unable to do this because of its own vested interest in maintaining a supply of cheap labor and because of its links with foreign capital. In attempting to make changes, the radicals therefore ran up against the opposition of the elite. More than any other factor, this complex conflict of interests and objectives between the government and the elite shaped the character and the fate of the first radical government.

Note

For complete references and notes, consult the original version of this chapter in David Rock, *Politics in Argentina, 1890–1930: The Rise and Fall of Radicalism* (Cambridge: Cambridge University Press, 1975), 95–124.

Poems to Be Read on a Trolley Car

Oliverio Girondo

With the political democratization of the 1920s came cultural modernization, as well. Public education increased literacy levels and hastened the cultural integration of the children of European immigrants into nationhood. In the process, a new generation of writers and artists who enthusiastically embraced avant-garde aesthetics was born. Irreverent and playful, they opposed the homogenizing effects of modern culture while simultaneously transforming Argentina's local artistic traditions. Most representative was the group associated with the journal Martín Fierro (1924–27), where writers like Jorge Luis Borges, Raúl González Tuñón, Leopoldo Marechal, and Oliverio Girondo (1898–1967) published their texts. Important painters, such as Xul Solar, illustrated its pages. These two poems from Girondo's Twenty Poems to Be Read on a Trolley Car (1924) are written in the experimental and fragmentary style of a poetry that mimics the fast pace of modern life and the cultural fusions of a cosmopolitan society. Through interrupted images, they respectively portray the tumescent desires of working-class girls ("Exvoto" [1920]) and the entangled bodies of couples dancing to the violent rhythm of a milonga, a faster variant of tango, from the dizzying perspective of a passing cubist eye ("Milonga" [1921]).

EXVOTO
To the girls from Flores

The girls from Flores, have sweet eyes, like sugar almonds from "El Molino," and they wear silk jumpsuits that sip their rumps like fluttering butterflies.

The girls from Flores, walk together arm in arm, broadcasting their trepidation, and if anyone looks them in the eye, they press their legs together, for fear their sex will fall out on the sidewalk.

As darkness falls, they hang their innocent breasts over the iron branches of their balconies and their clothes turn purple, feeling them naked, and at night, towed by their mamas—armored frigates—they go out and promenade on

Xul Solar, *Jol* (1926). Private Collection.

the plaza, so that the men can ejaculate words in their ears, and their phosphorescent nipples will light up and fade away like fireflies.

The girls from Flores live with the anxiety that their buttocks will go rotten, like apples that are past their prime, and their desire for men is so suffocating that they would like to be free of it, as from a corset, but they don't have the courage to cut their bodies into pieces and toss them out to all the men who pass them on the sidewalk.

Buenos Aires, October 1920

MILONGA

On the tables, beheaded bottles of "champagne" with white clown sashes, nickel buckets that replicate the skinny arms and backs of "cocottes."

The *bandoneón* sings with the yawning stretches of a stupid worm, it contradicts the rug's red hair, it magnetizes nipples, the pubes and pointy shoes.

Males whose bodies rupture in a ritual court, their heads sunk low between their shoulders, their lips thick with coarse remarks.

Trolley in Buenos Aires's downtown. The trolley brought speed and a new urban experience to the people of Buenos Aires. Courtesy Archivo General de la Nación, Buenos Aires.

Females with their nervous rumps, bits of foam at their armpits and their eyes looking much too oily.

Soon the sound of shattering glass, the tables rise up, bucking, and end with four feet in the air. An enormous mirror and its pilaster come crashing down with all the people reflected in it; and, amid a breaking wave of arms and backs, a burst of fists and punches, seeming like a Bengali pinwheel.

The violet draped dawn, together with the lone policeman, enters the scene.

Buenos Aires, October 1921

Translated by Patricia Owen Steiner

Modern Women

Alfonsina Storni

*Although the steady pace of modernization opened careers such as teaching and jour-
nalism to women, Yrigoyen's move toward political democratization did not grant
women equal rights. Alfonsina Storni (1892–1938), a writer and journalist with feminist convictions, fought actively for women's political and civil rights—particularly
for sexual freedom and the right to vote. Her commitment to a feminist agenda permeates her writing. In "An Old Story," an essay appearing in La Nota on 25 April 1919
as a response to a cynical article by Carlos Gutiérrez Larreta on women's committees,
Alfonsina condemns the marginal status of feminism in Argentine society and the resistance that it encountered even among the educated men whom Alfonsina befriended.
Alfonsina was an unwed mother and an off-center poet who belonged neither to mod-
ernism nor to the experimental avant-garde. Always an outsider, she committed suicide
in 1938. Her place in Argentine cultural history remains ambiguous. Her memory,
crafted after the myth of the rebellious woman, has been celebrated on television and
in popular music, but her contributions as a serious thinker with a feminist agenda,
and as a writer whose aesthetics were at odds with dominant literary trends, have not
been sufficiently acknowledged.*

AN OLD STORY

There was a time when I had no intention of writing a serious word about
feminism. It seemed to me that to talk about an accomplished fact was a waste
of time.

But then I came across an article by Carlos Gutiérrez Larreta entitled
"Women's Committees," which appeared in the previous issue of this journal.
It has snapped me out of my torpor and is inducing me to commit the millionth
foolish act of my life.

I believe that my kind friend has written the article just the way he usually
recites his certainly magnificent madrigals and sonnets.

He has smoked two or three Turkish cigarettes, read his favorite poets, and then taken a few brightly colored billiard balls and caromed them around with a gold pen.

These caroms are his article.

But in life the brilliant little billiard balls the writer plays with are weighty worlds, and the billiard cue that moves them is subject to formidable laws. As we contemplate the implications of these laws our whole being trembles; our faces fall, our tears flow, and we are suddenly saddened and confused by this inescapable, inexplicable thing.

Only by making a carefree game cunning can one speak of feminism in terms of chivalrous pardon for feminine mischievousness.

I believe that feminism deserves much more than flippant gallantry because it is as important as a complete collective transformation.

I would even dare to assert that so-called feminism is nothing more than man's managerial failure to achieve by legal means the necessary equilibrium of human happiness.

If every chief of state and every head of the family were capable of knowing, and then satisfying, all the needs of the people under them, there would be an end to all modern problems, including the now-famous problem of feminism.

But life is not an equation perceivable by the eyes of man. However much one looks ahead, one will never see the intimate spiritual depths of each individual whose longings, unsatisfied, become the very struggle required for evolution.

Of this permanent discontent, of this thirst, of this expectation, of this endless movement eternity is made.

To say man is superior to woman, woman is equal to man, etc. seems to me no more than words, words, words.

To speak of feminism and to separate it from everything like an isolated entity, with no relationship and merely as an arbitrary expression of feminine caprice, seems utter nonsense to me.

To think that "woman wants this despite the fact that we are advising her otherwise" is not to think at all.

What does woman want?

Are thoughts and collective aspirations like mushrooms that sprout up whenever or wherever they feel like it?

Did men dictate that nails would emerge on their fingers?

To poke fun at feminism, for example, seems to me as curious as to poke fun at a finger because it ends in a nail. To arrive at what we call *feminism*, humanity has followed a process as exact as the one that an embryo follows to become a fruit or that a fruit follows to transform its elements from an embryo, each in their successive steps.

There is as much truth in the embryo as in the stem, in the stem as in the leaves, in the leaves as in the flower or any other stage of its development.

Clearly we have the right to express an opinion about which moment of that transformation appears to us to be more harmonious, more complete.

The writer we mentioned finds that the [ancient] Greeks, such exalted beings, had no feminism.

But this does not have to be the reason for the sublimity of Greece. By following such criteria we would come to believe that it was enough for a population not to have feminism for it to demonstrate its equilibrium.

I could point out to him that the Middle Ages, which did not have feminism, is an example of a barbarous period characterized by its humiliation of feminine dignity under the pretext of a stupid chastity and a religion that was as depressing as it was avaricious.

But in truth we have nothing in the past that can enlighten us about a movement like the present one, the fruit of our own days.

If the time in which we live is compared to some luminous periods of the past, such as [ancient] Greece, for example, it is seen as a setback, and we cannot attribute this setback to feminism.

On the contrary, feminism stems from this setback by seeking for "its" support, "its" ray of light, in troubled waters where nothing is visible. And, for that seeking, women want to use their own eyes.

Let me make myself clear: Catholic dogma is bankrupt; civilization is bankrupt; everything that has been built up in the last twenty centuries is crashing down with a deafening roar, its balance destroyed, its center of gravity out of kilter.

Men, after repeating the same old things for a long time, are bored with themselves and are demanding new actions, new words, new life.

This is as old as the sun.

We go now from unity to the parts.

Power is distributed, knowledge is distributed, responsibility is distributed. Man does not know what awaits him when he loses his protectorate, but he wants to free himself from it. Today every human cell wants to feel responsibility.

To disperse, to separate, to divide.

This is what things say.

Nonexistent or ineffectual dogma, a hard economic life, imperfect justice — for whom is woman now waiting? What holy word or perception of human justice leads her to accept the idea that she always comes out the loser, without daring to say, "I want to try doing this for myself"?

I understand perfect submission when the hand directing one's life is perfect, when that hand has taken care of and foreseen everything, for then obedience is sweet, slavery a pleasure.

But, while everything is changing and an infinity of laws and customs from earlier times are being modified, a group of women, protected by neither state nor man, are taking up the struggle against the new laws and customs.

These are the women who have had to earn their own living, those who are in a position to talk about the bunches of flowers that masculine piety tosses at their feet lest their delicate soles get hurt.

In the struggle for existence there is no truce, no sex, no pity, no flowers. Oh, poet! It's every man for himself. The first one gets the prize, and often the one arriving second, if he's stronger, snatches it away.

At least that's the pattern I personally experienced in my hard apprenticeship.

It is in great part this ruthless aspect of life that has broken woman's submission and that now tries her will, tries her ideas, tries her personality.

She doesn't part company with man, but she has stopped believing in the divine mission that dogma assigned him.

She doesn't turn against man, for, as she struggles, she thinks about her son, a man. But she distrusts the state's protection, she distrusts man's justice, and she tends, as I said before, to exercise her responsibility.

It is true that this way of living separates her somewhat from her instincts, but who says that instinct is an end and not simply a means?

Isn't it perhaps true that choice is one of the capabilities that characterizes humankind?

Only the egotism of the species can lead man to believe that he is the one uniquely qualified to make choices. I firmly believe that feminism today is a question of justice.

This way of thinking to which woman aspires, in fact, goes hand in hand with the condition of being born free that belongs to both woman and man — the right to exercise free will.

Naturally, in the course of developing her general abilities, woman will do as many foolish things as man has done, and goes right on doing, despite his long experience in directing affairs.

I believe also that perfection is unattainable and that woman and man, as they try to reach it, will both make the same kind of mistakes that have already been made.

But in the feminine exercise of this aspiration to responsibility there is no other justification than the unknown law that governs us, the law that has provided man with all his downfalls and consequently with all the changes through which he manages to survive.

None of us knows where this movement we call *feminism* is heading, but nothing will detain it.

Meanwhile, before long, women will obtain the suppression of the laws and concepts that have a shameful impact on feminine dignity, laws that a number of stalwart women have already rendered null. To transform words like *shame, pardon,* and *error* into *right of the woman, right of the mother,* and *right of the human being* will be one of the inevitable and invaluable triumphs of feminism.

As for the rest, woman's increased development implies a refinement of her femininity, a greater spiritual grace, a harmony that is restored only by controlled instincts.

This may seem a contradiction to my earlier paragraph, but it is not.

Instinct controlled by clear, conscious reasoning is a very different thing from instinct harshly suffocated because of dogma. Putting instincts in proper balance will be another of feminism's victories.

And if Christ, according to my kind friend Gutiérrez Larreta, had woman mapped out for a different direction, he will see, once again, that neither women nor men now succeed—nor ever will succeed—in comprehending that direction. For, although it may be opportune to present myths in articles and essays, these myths are ultimately indigestible for humankind because humankind is so weak, so trusting in an infinite divine goodness that, despite all the gospels, allows mankind to kill, rob, or commit "rosy, silky little sins," in the words of Rubén Darío, who, without Christ's permission, must have been quite a feminist. . . .

Translated by Patricia Owen Steiner

X-Ray of the Pampa

Ezequiel Martínez Estrada

In 1933, Ezequiel Martínez Estrada published X-Ray of the Pampa, *a long, melancholic essay on Argentine identity. In the chapter entitled "The Spider's Web," he analyzes the layout of the train system and its influence on Argentina's social and economic organization. The railroads were built with British capital during the final decades of the nineteenth century. A symbol of progress, they were also evidence of economic dependency on foreign investment. Centered in Buenos Aires — a city that felt closer to Europe than to the Argentine hinterlands — the tracks radiated like the strands of a spider's web to most of the provinces without making any links between the provinces themselves. Like a ravenous spider, prosperous Buenos Aires slowly devoured the rest of the country, which was left to languish in its isolation. Almost one hundred years after the publication of Sarmiento's* Facundo, *in* X-Ray of the Pampa *Martínez Estrada reexamined the persistent schism between Buenos Aires and the Interior.*

The railroad extended the national territory and then fractured it, leaving it reduced to a lineal sketch of its lines of track. The embankments of the railroad created a frontier: Europe was the railroad track; America was the rest. That which is not at the very foot of the embankment is at an unmeasurable distance, economically beyond the world of commerce. The railroad makes possible the exploitation of mines and forests; metals and lumber cannot reach the factories without substantially diminishing in value in transit. Whole forests and mines are not worth the transportation charges. The steam transportation cartel also makes impossible the existence of dirt or asphalt roads; it is interested that there be none and, if there must be some, that they be exclusively for tourism, for the simple reason that their trains are providing tourist services along two-thirds of the routes. The ruinous competition that trucks and buses are giving the railroads in North America, England, and France will never exist here because the roads are ours but the rail lines belong to others. In order to have thirty-eight thousand kilometers of iron ways, we have had to renounce hundreds of thousands of kilometers of paved roads. The extent of roads ought to be twelve times greater than that of the rail trackage, but it is scarcely more than half of it. Without highways an auto is a gas-driven dragon that sticks in the mud, like a diabolic artifact that the horse, pulling a sulky, contemplates without fear when he passes.

As a corollary to the dissolution of the interior into the economic distance, the railroad sharpened the umbilical destiny of Buenos Aires: progressively and irredeemably it made it into a head severed from the body. The iron ways were a dream of the metropolis, and they stretched out its predatory tentacles across the pampa. All political history from the time of the colony aimed at this, and the train secured it, settling forever an old dispute because trains are centralizing.

To understand the destiny of South America it is enough to look at the map of railroads. In spite of its marginal location, Buenos Aires forms the center of a circle—a design that one finds in *Argirópolis*. That network best resembles a spider's web. The fundamental problem of our economic life is transportation because the fundamental problems of our existence are distances, quantities, sizes, and solitude. When the government, which is unexcelled as a deformed structure, participated in the construction of communications, it was to show that its ideas were molded on old concepts. It is not accidental that the allotments of postal and telegraphic communication and those of the state-owned railroads were at the mercy of the whims of the government and were indices of its downfall. The government has laid out luxury lines for tourism under the pretext of development, and these have been extended into regions that are sterile not only geographically but also politically and economically. The epitome of astrological concepts in this regard is the branch line to Huaytiquina, the only straight nonstop route to Trapalanda. It can be considered the appendix to the conquistador's horoscope. Because Huaytiquina is a political, cultural, religious, and demagogical program, it symbolizes an entire epoch of coarse arrogance of progress. A branch line to nowhere, on constantly shifting alluvial lands, it transports only families of passengers with free passes and paid traveling expenses. The closure of the tunnel and the return to transportation by muleback on this stretch has an air of the most nonsensical obfuscation. Thus the state pays in order that its functionaries may admire a lunar landscape without putting out any money. This myopia obeys the politico-military concept that determines for the Argentine leaders the overall view of Argentine problems. Huaytiquina is more logical than one hundred dirt roads, just as three submarines are more rational than one merchant ship. Dreadnoughts and submarines at anchor are ready to sail out on the route of the caravels—and they never set sail. They are not war machines, thanks be to God; they are sentinels and escorts for the trains, placed where the trains link up with the transatlantic liners and America with Europe. Our railways are copies of the old strategic lines, but they are not mercantile or commercial, nor are they concerned with agriculture or cattle. We possess lines that are responses to panic, products of the eagerness for greatness and the fear of losing it.

Every day the trains follow the same routes as did Rondeau, Belgrano, San Martín. It could be said that they follow their footsteps at a distance of one hundred years and that they are one hundred years slower than those men. For-eign capital—which came to serve that old politicomilitary need, not the true economic need—further demanded material guarantees of the interests on its loans and did so in clauses that were accepted in the face of the urgency to lay rails where there were no roads. The terms of the concessions condemned us to perpetuate our original condition as a colony. The railroads demanded the grant of a league to extend on both sides of the tracks along the entire route or a settlement to consist in a set number of leagues. What we call *progress* is what has been produced within a league on each side of the railroad lines. Land again fulfilled the role of a substitute for money, of an insurance policy good for redemption tomorrow, of a troglodytic money. On the other hand, it was a precaution analogous to the three years of prepaid interest that the firm of Bar-ing and Company extracted when making us the first loan in 1824. With their leagues of land the railroads also established on their flanks a certain kind of natural frontier between the rich land of the company with its iron channel and the poor roadless land of the country. Since that league of width was the area of greatest value, the increase in value of the land that the railroad produced served, not the country, but the company. The area beyond the two leagues was fallowness, loneliness, and ignorance. From far away the lord of the land and the settler watched the train pass; but they raised their rents, speculating on the distant benefit. From that moment the train was a hindrance, a system imprisoned within its net like the fish inside a basket: a captive train. It stimu-lated the greed of the landlord, who raised his rental charge, and it stimulated the obfuscation of the settler, who ventured too far. The company assumed the direction of cattle raising and agriculture and exercised it to the benefit of capital that was in London—not beside the rails. The company also gave value to the land according to a fantastic standard as if the locomotive were something fantastic; it hastened the lawyer's and the politician's eagerness to plunder as if the locomotive were something immoral. The government fell headlong before the mirage of this false valuation; it believed that to extend the rail lines was to populate, without taking warning that the contrary could be the truth. And, when the government had thirty-six thousand kilometers of track, it said that the Republic was at peace and that culture had come to the depths of country life. In the depths of the countryside there was misery and ignorance, and that is the truth and not the lie.

Viewed from the train, all this truth appears to be a game of words, but it must be seen with the eyes of those who remain when the train goes. One should contemplate the railroad from the outside and realize that it is a living three-dimensional body and not a net of black lines on a white background as it appears on the maps. That white background is our countryside; full of truth and life, it is the guts and the source of the children of tomorrow. The progress of the Republic opposed to the interest of those who made it prosper, and no progress can be achieved until this relationship is changed. It will happen when the entire body is in a state of health and not just the euphoria of a severed head.

Translated by Alain Swietlicki

Soccer and Popular Joy

Roberto Arlt

*Roberto Arlt (1900–1938) was a prolific writer and journalist who forged his litera-
ture from the marginal discourses and cultural practices of modern Buenos Aires in
the 1920s and 1930s. The son of poor immigrant parents, completely self-taught, his
literature and public persona represent the plebeian side of cultural modernization,
in contrast with the artistic avant-garde. In his writings, popular culture is always
linked to utopian revolution and political contestation. Besides several fictional works,
he wrote a significant number of urban chronicles for the daily press that he called
aguafuertes porteñas. In the following aguafuerte, "Yesterday I Saw the Argentines
Win," Arlt portrays the popular joy and sensual excess of an afternoon at a crowded
soccer stadium, at a time when sports were becoming a democratic source of civic
identification that went beyond social differences by creating a national community
of (male) fans.*

You will say that I am the most extraordinary liar in the whole world from
what I am going to tell you:

Yesterday was the first soccer game I ever saw in my twenty-nine years of
existence, if you don't count as soccer the games that kids play with tiny balls
and that all of us, when we were younger, took a try at to the detriment of our
shoes and clothes.

Yes. The first game. So don't be surprised by the silly rubbish I'm going
to write. . . .

A rotten orange smashed a crazed fan on the head. Forty thousand handkerchiefs whirled around in the air, and Ferreyra, with his magnificent kick,
made the first goal. Not even a bunch of machine gunners could have made
more noise than those eighty thousand hands that were applauding the Argentine success. So many people were clapping for the Argentine success. So many
people were applauding behind my ears that the wind created by their hands
buzzed by my cheeks. Then the enthusiasm died down, and I began to take
notes. Here goes — so you'll see how a journalist works who doesn't half under-

Soccer stadium (1930). An afternoon at the soccer stadium. Courtesy Archivo General de la Nación, Buenos Aires.

stand *football* (I think that's the way the British refer to it) does his job. Here's what I saw.

A poor man selling a broken umbrella to shade out the sun. A whole regiment of young boys selling bricks, boxes, tables, oranges, apples, soft drinks, newspapers, pictures of soccer players, caramels, etc., etc.

An Argentine player fell down. Cherro missed a goal; immediate applause. And, from the box seats, applause galore. The "Little Bull from Mataderos" was passing by a section of admirers. Behind me a voice shouts: "That Evaristo is center stage all afternoon." (And it was Evaristo who made the second goal with Ferreyra.)

Another rotten orange burst open on the head of the same crazed fan. Hundreds of rascals look on and laugh.

Cherro misses another goal, and some guy who is hiding behind his mustache goes out of control to the rhythm of the worst of words.

The stands are packed with spectators. Over these forty thousand *porteños* some mysterious hand continuously sends flying missiles that fall between the air and the sun with the brilliance of silver leaves. Uruguayan and Argentine players are circled around a player who is lying on the ground. It was a kick to the neck. There's no point in talking about it; sports are wholesome.

Yet another rotten orange lands on the head of the same crazed fan. Ferreyra prances around, happy. There's no point in discussing it; he's the best player on the team besides Evaristo. "Ferreyra is number one!" shouts someone in the stands. And another: "What a scientific game."

From a Rooftop

South of the stadium of San Lorenzo of Almagro, on La Plata Avenue, there is a building with a pointed roof and various skylights. Suddenly, people began to look over there, and, from the two skylights, just like ants, curious spectators navigating on four legs were going to install themselves on the ridge of the roof. Something like in the movies.

With this the first half ended. Then, from behind the wire fence that separates general admission from the reserved seats, I saw the fellow who had gotten hit with the rotten oranges leaving. The back of his neck was dripping with rotten garbage, his face was worn out from clinging to the fence for so long, and he sank down on the cement walkway. To the great satisfaction of the hurler of all those oranges. Now the ground became a gypsy encampment. I began to walk around.

There was one thing that got my attention, and that was the water that continually fell from the top of the stands. I asked a spectator why they were doing all that watering, and the spectator answered me that they were Argentine citizens who, within their constitutional rights, answered Nature's call from the heights. I also saw a formidable thing, and it was a bunch of young kids hanging from the iron structures that supported the stands, that is to say, from the back sides where only the feet of the spectators could be seen. All these boys competed with each other in grabbing the legs of spectators, to whom they were invisible. . . .

I left the playing field a few minutes before Evaristo made the second goal. All the gates on La Plata Avenue were decked out with magnificent young girls. Boy are there beautiful girls on this La Plata Avenue! All at once a thunder of applause burst from the crowd; from high in the stands an arm with a signal flag made a mysterious sign on the celestial background, and all the girls suddenly raised their voices in a shout:

"The Argentines won: 2 to 0."

It's been a long time since the *porteños* could play with courage and decisiveness.

The Uruguayan players gave the impression of developing a more harmonious game, but the Argentines, even if they were rowdy, worked with the only thing that brings success in life: enthusiasm.

Translated by Patricia Owen Steiner

Cambalache

Enrique Santos Discépolo

Enrique Santos Discépolo (1901–51) conceived his 1935 tango "Cambalache" as a hymn of popular protest against the nation's lack of economic opportunity and social justice. Written during the depression that followed the global economic crash of 1929 and the military overthrow of Yrigoyen's government in 1930, "Cambalache" denounced the inversion of the social and moral values that ought to prevail in an honest society and affirmed that neither honesty nor hard work had any value in modern Argentina. The ironic lyrics, decrying the predominance of bad faith and corruption, would lend themselves to the bitterness and enraged pessimism of subsequent generations. Even in the 1980s, its subversive tone remained so powerful that the most recent military dictatorship (1976–1983) banned all broadcasts of "Cambalache."

That the world's always been rotten,
don't remind me, it always will be.
In the year 506 and 2000 too!
There've always been crooks,
men, and those who pretend to be,
the content, the sad,
pickpockets, and Machiavels.
But this twentieth century
has put insolent
evil on show, and that,
no one can deny.
Floundering in the mess,
we're rolling about in the mud,
manhandled all . . .
Today no one gives a damn
whether you're straight or bent . . . !
Ignorant, scholar, crook,
kind or con . . . !
Whatever! No matter!

Great professor or dunce,
who cares!
No lessers, no betters,
the immoral have made us the same.
If one lives by pretense
and another steals in his ambition,
you might just as well be a priest,
mattress maker or king of clubs,
scoundrel or cop . . .
What lack of respect,
what disregard of all reason!
Anyone a Lord!
Anyone a thief!
Alongside Stavisky goes Don Bosco
and his mistress, the tart,
Don Chicho and Napoléon,
the boxer Carnera and San Martín . . .
There's no respect in the windows
of the secondhand stores
where life's all been mixed up
and where leaning up against a heater
you can find the Bible weeping
wounded by a wrecked sword.

This secondhand twentieth century,
feverish and problematic . . .
in which everything's for sale.
Those that don't cry don't feed,
and those that don't steal are fools.
On, on! More! So what!
We're all going to burn in hell!
Stop thinking, step aside.
'Cause no one cares
if you were born honest.
And, like a mule,
you may work night and day,
but you're just the same
as the man who lives off others,
the man who kills, who cures,
who lives by breaking the law.

Translated by John Kraniauskas

VI

Populism and New Nationalism

Twentieth-century Argentine history was divided in two by the eruption of Peronism onto the political arena. Following the military coup against President Yrigoyen in 1930, the newly installed military dictatorship called a halt to the process of political democratization that had begun in the 1890s. But, once Colonel Juan Domingo Perón took command of the Ministry of Labor in 1943, the dynamics of the political game were irrevocably altered. Taking advantage of a favorable economy, with strong national credit from wartime sales to the United States and England and postwar demands for agricultural products, Perón's authoritarian populism sustained a policy of public assistance that was rejected by both the conservative elite and the radical Left, but that would grant him unparalleled popularity. In just two years, Perón progressed from a minor behind-the-scenes figure to become the most influential politician in the country's history. When general elections were restored in 1946, he won with 56 percent of the popular vote against a coalition that included all the established political parties. Besides playing an instrumental role in negotiating salary increases, he and his wife, Eva Duarte, inaugurated and developed a state system of pensions and health services that would benefit most Argentines. The Peróns' welfare policies and attention to the needy won the affection and the almost unconditional support of a wide majority.

For years, a skeptical historiography interpreted Perón's appeal among the working classes as the result of ideological manipulation and populist measures calculated to seduce politically naive workers, especially those from the interior who had moved to Buenos Aires in search of better jobs. According to this perspective, severe limitations on democracy and the absence of political parties able to provide an adequate response to workers' sentiments and needs combined to make some sectors of the lower classes easy targets for a clever demagogue who had offered them a modicum of political participation. In the 1970s, however, a more complex, less partisan view of the Peronist phe-

Perón and Evita. In reinventing politics in Argentina, Perón and Evita made public appearances a key element in establishing their popularity. Courtesy Archivo General de la Nación, Buenos Aires.

nomenon began to develop. Scholars now generally agree that Peronism was, not only a working-class movement, but a class alliance that included some sectors of the army and small industrialists. In striking contrast with President Hipólito Yrigoyen's populist alliances, in many respects similar to Perón's, much of Peronism's political strength came from the interior. More important, the idea of a populace helplessly manipulated by a Machiavellian leader has been abandoned in favor of a more balanced approach that takes into account the influential role of the unions and the political and economic victories that they were able to achieve under Perón.

But the strength and endurance of Peronism cannot be attributed solely to improvements in working conditions or to populist coalitions. If Peronism was able to redefine the social and political identity of important sectors of Argentine society, it was mainly because it created a powerful political culture that continued to function even during Perón's enforced exile from 1955 to 1973. According to the historian Daniel James, it was by expanding the meaning of *citizenship* that Peronism built a new political subject, the Argentine *pueblo* (the people), which included unionized workers, the urban poor, the migrant workers from the interior, as well as members of the lower middle class looking for greater political participation and social progress. This bedrock identification of the term *the people* with the most marginal sectors of society accounts for Perón's repeated references to the *descamisados* (literally, "the shirtless") when addressing his followers. Thus, when it comes to explaining Peronist appeal, words and symbols are as important as economic and political factors.

Peronism's major strength lay perhaps in its ability to create a common language. In order to build consensus, Peronism developed and sought to impose a series of myths, symbols, and public rituals designed to generate public support. From the very beginning, Perón resorted to amassing enormous crowds of people who would overflow downtown Buenos Aires in order to show loyalty to their leader. The political meaning of these political rituals was obvious to everyone. In a tacit competition for public space, the populace was taking possession of a city whose devotion to high culture and bourgeois sophistication had always excluded them. Since then, the image of dense crowds chanting Peronist slogans in the Plaza de Mayo, responding in rapture to the inspiring words of Perón standing on the balcony of the presidential palace, has become a fundamental component of Peronist iconography. As Tomás Eloy Martínez's novel *Saint Evita* (1995) masterfully shows, "Evita," as Eva Duarte de Perón was affectionately renamed by her admirers, has been Peronism's most enduring myth. In part a mask that Eva Duarte created for herself, in part a spontaneous creation of popular devotion, Evita's ambiguous but powerful public persona evoked images of the caring Virgin, the protector of the poor, and the faithful companion of a great man, with the charisma of a movie star whose stage presence and melodramatic speeches captivated the masses.

The compulsive need for public consensus also revealed Peronism's darker side. After winning the presidential elections in 1951, the movement sought to establish itself as the only legitimate political force. Although their modus operandi was to create multiple alliances, neither Perón nor Evita could accept political dissent. Those who questioned their wishes soon found themselves in trouble. Labor leaders who opposed government policies ended up in prison; court officials and representatives were forced to resign. Radio stations were taken over and used as outlets for government propaganda. Schoolbooks became filled with eulogies of Perón and Evita as the nation's saviors. Employing all available means, Peronism sought to impose a highly homogeneous national culture of which Peronist values were the ultimate expression.

Marginalized by the Peronist propaganda machine, the cultural elite took an openly anti-Peronist stance rooted both in long-standing social and ethnic prejudices and in their sense of having lost their cultural hegemony. Many writers and intellectuals found refuge in *Sur*—a prestigious and sophisticated literary journal founded by Victoria Ocampo in the late 1930s. Resisting both Perón's cultural populism and the ascendancy of the mass media, under Ocampo's direction *Sur* promoted Western high-cultural traditions and financed the translation of many European and American modernist works.

Ocampo's circle displayed an almost visceral contempt for Peronism, which many saw as a reincarnation of Rosas's popular dictatorship and the grip that it held on the ignorant masses who supported him in the nineteenth century. Others equated Peronism's totalitarian tendencies with the evils of European fascism. Both indignation and fascination led writers like Borges and Cortázar to produce some of Argentina's most peculiar and complex literary works. In his curious short story "House Taken Over," Julio Cortázar described the invasion of a house by an uncanny presence to express the misapprehensions that the new assertiveness of the masses awoke among the educated. At the same time, in his playful essays and fictions, Jorge Luis Borges advanced a more flexible, ambiguous notion of Argentina's cultural traditions in opposition to the confining definitions of national identity that prevailed at the time.

The constant clashes between the seemingly separate worlds of the people and the social elites affected all forms of cultural production. High or low, from comics to philosophical reflection, everything was marked in some way by this unsolvable social contradiction. In the comic strip "Ramona," the cartoonist Lino Palacio brought out the humor of the daily misunderstandings between a maid and her employers. In his *Diaries,* Witold Gombrowicz, an exiled Polish writer who witnessed the transformations brought about by Peronism, took sides against the snobbism of the local upper classes and celebrated the sensual irreverence of the common people. In beautiful but gloomy verses, Juan L. Ortiz registered in his poetry the human despair that pervaded an abandoned countryside.

Perón's strongly corporatist approach to politics and his nearly absolute power over the lower classes met with escalating, passionate resistance from the educated middle classes and some sectors of the armed forces. An unexpected confrontation with the Catholic church, which had until then approved of the conservative character of Peronist cultural nationalism, combined with a tapering off of the economic bonanza the country had enjoyed during Perón's first administration, precipitated the end. In September 1955, a coup removed Perón from office, and a military junta assumed power. The ensuing eighteen-year-long proscription of Peronism from political life only deepened the social schism that would undermine so many subsequent administrations. Rodolfo Walsh's portrayal of an illegal execution of Peronist workers by a military firing squad in 1956 reconstructed a moment that marked the end of the first Peronist era and the advent of a second stage, when the educated Left began to look at Peronist activism with more sympathetic eyes.

Perón and the People

Daniel James

In 1945, Colonel Juan Domingo Perón, then secretary of labor, who had introduced several social reforms that benefited the lower classes, was arrested by the reigning military government. On 17 October 1945, thousands of workers gathered in front of the government house in the Plaza de Mayo to demand Perón's immediate release. This protest sealed a political alliance that, in spite of substantial obstacles, would remain vigorous until the 1970s and whose aftereffects are still felt in today's Argentina. Overwhelmingly popular, Perón would be elected president on three occasions — in 1946, in 1951, and, after an exile of eighteen years, in 1974. In one of the most innovative studies on Peronism and the Argentine working class, the historian Daniel James outlines the political forces that transformed Perón into a popular leader between 1945 and 1955, bringing to the fore the novelty and appeal of his political vision.

"Speak freely. What is the problem? You speak, Tedesco. The colonel will understand you better." Well. . . . "You are Tedesco? Son of Italians, no?" Yes, colonel. "I thought so. What's up Tedesco?" Very simple, colonel; a lot of work and very little cash. "That's clear. Where?" We work on the night shift in. . . . They pay us three pesos and thirty centavos each night. "That's a disgrace! We'll fix that immediately. I will call the owners of the factory so that they sign a contract with you people. How much do you want to earn?" We would settle for three pesos and thirty-three cents, but the just wage would be 3.50 a night. "Everything will turn out all right. It's impossible that they still exploit workers in this way." Thank you colonel. "Tedesco, you stay. The rest can go and rest easy."
—Mariano Tedesco, founder of the Asociación Obrera Textil

Well look, let me say it once and for all. I didn't invent Perón. I'll tell you this once so that I can be done with this impulse of goodwill that I am following in my desire to free you a little of so much bullshit. The truth: I didn't invent Perón or Evita, the miraculous one. They were born as a reaction to your bad governments. I didn't invent Perón, or Evita, or their doctrines. They were summoned as defense by a people who you and yours submerged in a long path of misery. They were born of you, by you and for you.
—Enrique Santos Discépolo

Organized Labor and the Peronist State

Under the guidance of successive conservative governments the Argentine economy had responded to the world recession of the 1930s by producing internally an increasing number of manufactured goods it had previously imported. While generally maintaining adequate income levels for the rural sector, and guaranteeing the traditional elite's privileged economic ties with the United Kingdom, the Argentine state stimulated this import substitution by a judicious policy of tariff protection, exchange controls, and the provision of industrial credit. Industrial production more than doubled between 1930–35 and 1945–49; imports that in 1925–30 accounted for almost one-quarter of the Argentine GNP had been reduced to some 6 percent in the 1940–44 quinquennium. From importing some 35 percent of its machinery and industrial equipment in the first period, Argentina imported only 9.9 percent in the second. In addition the Second World War saw a considerable amount of export-led industrial growth as Argentine manufactured goods penetrated foreign markets. By the mid 1940s Argentina was an increasingly industrialized economy; while the traditional rural sector remained the major source of foreign exchange earnings, the dynamic center of capital accumulation now lay in industry and manufacture.

Changes in the social structure reflected these economic developments. The number of industrial establishments increased from 38,456 in 1935 to 86,440 in 1946. At the same time the number of industrial workers proper increased from 435,816 to 1,056,673 in 1946. The internal composition of this industrial labor force had also changed. New members were now drawn from the interior provinces of Argentina rather than from overseas immigration, which had effectively ceased after 1930. They were attracted to the expanding urban centers of the littoral zone, in particular to the Greater Buenos Aires area outside the limits of the federal capital. By 1947 some 1,368,000 migrants from the interior had arrived in Buenos Aires attracted by the rapid industrial expansion. In the overwhelmingly industrial suburb of Avellaneda, across the Riachuelo River from the capital, out of a total population in 1947 of some 518,312 over 173,000 had been born outside the city or province of Buenos Aires.

While the industrial economy expanded rapidly the working class did not benefit from this expansion. Real wages declined in general as salaries lagged behind inflation. Faced with concerted employer and state repression, workers could do little to successfully improve wages and work conditions. Labor and social legislation remained sparse and sporadically enforced. Outside the workplace the situation was little better as working-class families confronted, unaided by the state, the social problems of rapid urbanization. A survey of 1937 found, for example, that 60 percent of working-class families in the capital lived in one room.

The labor movement that existed at the time of the military coup of 1943 was divided and weak. There existed in Argentina four labor centrals: the anarchist Federación Obrera Regional Argentina (FORA), now simply a rump of anarchist militants; the syndicalist Unión Sindical Argentina (USA), also considerably reduced in influence; finally there was the Confederación General de Trabajo (CGT), which was divided into two organizations, a CGT No. 1 and another CGT No. 2. The influence of this organizationally fragmented labor movement on the working class was limited. Perhaps some 20 percent of the urban labor force was organized in 1943, the majority of them being in the tertiary sector. The great majority of the industrial proletariat was outside effective union organization. The most dynamic group to attempt to organize in nontraditional areas were the Communists, who had some success in organizing in construction, food processing, and woodworking. However, the vital areas of industrial expansion in the 1930s and 1940s — textiles and metalworking — were still virtually *terra incognita* for labor organization in 1943. Of 447,212 union members in 1941 the transport sector and services accounted for well over 50 percent of membership, while industry had 144,922 affiliates.

Perón, from his position as secretary of labor and late vice president of the military government installed in 1943, set about addressing some of the basic concerns of the emerging industrial labor force. At the same time he set about undermining the influence of rival, radical competitors in the working class. His social and labor policy created sympathy for him among both organized and unorganized workers. In addition, crucial sectors of the union leadership came to see their future organizational prospects as bound up in Perón's political survival, as traditional political forces from both Left and Right attacked his figure and policies in the course of 1945. The growing working-class support for Perón that this engendered first crystallized in the 17 October 1945 demonstration that secured his release from confinement and launched him on the path to victory in the presidential elections of February 1946.

While there had been many specific improvements in work conditions and social legislation in the 1943–46 period, the decade of Peronist government from 1946 to 1955 was to have the most profound effect on the working class's position in Argentine society. First, the period saw a great increase in the organizational strength and social weight of the working class. A state sympathetic to the extension of union organization and a working class eager to translate its political victory into concrete organizational gains combined to effect a rapid increase in the extension of trade unionism. In 1948 the rate of unionization had risen to 30.5 percent of the wage-earning population, and in 1954 it had reached 42.5 percent. In the majority of manufacturing industries the rate was between 50 and 70 percent. Between 1946 and 1951 total union membership increased from 520,000 members to 2,334,000. Industrial activities such as textiles and metalworking, where unionization had been weak or nonexistent prior to 1946, by the end of the decade had unions with membership numbering in the 100,000s. In addition a large number of state employees were also unionized for the first time. Accompanying this massive extension of unionization there was, for the first time, the development of a global system of collective bargaining. The contracts signed throughout Argentine industry in the 1946–48 period regulated wage scales and job descriptions and also included a whole array of social provisions concerning sick leave, maternity leave, and vacations.

The organizational structure imposed on this union expansion was important in molding the future development of the union movement. Unionization was to be based on the unit of economic activity, rather than that of the individual trade or enterprise. In addition, in each area of economic activity only one union was granted legal recognition to bargain with employers in that industry. Employers were obliged by law to bargain with the recognized union, and conditions and wages established in such bargaining were applicable to all workers in that industry regardless of whether they were unionized or not. Beyond that, a specific centralized union structure was laid down, encompassing local branches and moving up through national federations to a single confederation, the Confederación General de Trabajo (CGT). Finally, the role of the state in overseeing and articulating this structure was clearly established. The Ministry of Labor granted a union legal recognition of its bargaining rights with employers. Decree 23,852 of October 1945, known as the Law of Professional Associations, which established this system, also established the right of the state to oversee considerable areas of union activity. Thus, the legal structure assured unions many advantages: bargaining rights, protection of union officials from victimization, a centralized and unified union structure, automatic deductions of union dues, and the use of these dues to underwrite extensive social welfare activities. It also, however, made the state the ultimate guarantor and overseer of this process and the benefits deriving from it.

While the massive expansion of union organization assured the working class recognition as a social force in the sphere of production, the Peronist period also saw the integration of this social force within an emerging political coalition overseen by the state. From labor's point of view the precise nature of their political incorporation within the regime was not immediately apparent. The general contours of this political integration emerged only in the course of Perón's first presidency, and they were to be confirmed and developed during the second. The first period, from 1946 to 1951, saw the gradual subordination of the union movement to the state and the elimination of the old-guard leaders who had been instrumental in mobilizing the support of organized labor for Perón in 1945 and who had formed the Partido Laborista to act as labor's political expression. Their notions of political and organizational autonomy, and the conditional nature of their support for Perón, did not combine well with his political ambitions. Nor, it must be said, did their insistence on the principle of labor autonomy match the dominant perceptions of the rapidly expanding union membership. Moreover, the weight of state intervention and the popular political support for Perón among their members inevitably limited the options open to the old-guard union leadership. Increasingly the unions were incorporated into a monolithic Peronist movement and were called on to act as the state's agents vis-à-vis the working class, organizing political support and serving as conduits of government policy among the workers.

As the outline of the justicialist state emerged in the second presidency, with its corporatist pretensions of organizing and directing large spheres of social, political, and economic life, the role officially allotted to the union movement in incorporating the working class into this state became clear. The attractions of such a relationship were great for both leaders and rank and file. An extensive social welfare network was in place operated through the Ministry of Labor and Social Welfare, the Fundación Eva Perón, and the unions themselves. Labor leaders were now to be found sitting in the Congress; they were routinely consulted by the government on a range of national issues; they entered the Argentine diplomatic corps as labor attachés. In addition, concrete economic gains for the working class were clear and immediate. As Argentine industry expanded, impelled by state incentives and a favorable international economic situation, workers benefited. Real wages for industrial workers increased by 53 percent between 1946 and 1949. Although real wages would decline with the economic crisis of the regime's last years, the shift of national income toward workers was to be unaffected. Between 1946 and 1949 the share of wages in the national income increased from 40.1 to 49 percent.

While there were demonstrations of working-class opposition to aspects of Peronist economic policy, there was little generalized questioning of the terms of the political integration of labor within the Peronist state. Indeed, a crucial legacy of the Perón era for labor was the integration of the working class into a national political community and a corresponding recognition of its civic and political status within that community. Beyond that, the experience of this decade bequeathed to the working-class presence within that community a remarkable degree of political cohesion. The Peronist era largely erased former political loyalties among workers and entrenched new ones. Socialists, Communists, and radicals who had competed for working-class allegiance prior to

Perón had been largely marginalized in terms of influence by 1955. This marginalization was partly due to state repression of non-Peronist politicians and labor leaders. Principally, however, it reflected the efficacy of Perón's social policy, the advantages of state patronage, and the inadequacies of non-Peronist competitors for working-class allegiance. For socialists and radicals Peronism was to remain a moral and civic outrage, a demonstration of the backwardness and lack of civic virtue of Argentine workers. This position had determined their opposition to the military government of 1943–46, their support of the Unión Democrática, and their consistent hostility to Perón throughout the following decade.

The Communist Party attempted to adopt a more flexible position than its erstwhile allies. Soon after the election victory, the party changed its characterization of Peronism as a form of fascism, dissolved its union apparatus, and ordered its militants to enter the CGT and its unions in order to work with the misguided Peronist masses and win them over. Yet it, too, was never able to recover from the political error of supporting the anti-Peronist coalition, the Unión Democrática, in the 1946 elections; nor was it able to offer a credible alternative to the clear gains to be derived from integration within the Peronist state. While at the local level some of its militants were able to maintain credibility and lead some important strikes, politically the party could never challenge the hegemony of Peronism among organized labor. The importance of this legacy of political cohesion can be clearly appreciated if we also bear in mind the relative racial and ethnic homogeneity of the Argentine working class and the concentration of this working class within a few urban centers, above all Greater Buenos Aires. Together these factors helped give the Argentine working class and its labor movement a weight within the wider national community that was unparalleled in Latin America.

Workers and the Political Appeal of Peronism

The relationship between workers and their organizations and the Peronist movement and state is, therefore, clearly vital for understanding the 1943–55 period. Indeed, the intimacy of the relationship has generally been taken as defining the uniqueness of Peronism within the spectrum of Latin American populist experiences. How are we to interpret the basis of this relationship and, beyond that, the significance of the Peronist experience for Peronist workers? Answers to this question have increasingly rejected earlier expanations that saw working-class support for Peronism in terms of a division between an old and a new working class. Sociologists like Gino Germani, leftist competitors for working-class allegiance, and indeed Peronists themselves explained worker

Peronist demonstration at the Plaza de Mayo (1955). Courtesy Archivo General de la Nación, Buenos Aires.

involvement in Peronism in terms of inexperienced migrant workers who, unable to assert an independent social and political identity in their new urban environment and untouched by the institutions and ideology of the traditional working class, were *disponible* (available) to be used by dissident elite sectors. It was these immature proletarians who flocked to Perón's banner in the 1943–46 period.

In the revisionist studies working-class support for Perón has been regarded as representing a logical involvement of labor in a state-directed reformist project that promised labor concrete material gains. With this more recent scholarship the image of the working-class relationship to Peronism has shifted from that of a passive manipulated mass to that of class-conscious actors seeking a realistic path for the satisfaction of their material needs. Political allegiance has, thus, been regarded, implicitly at least, within this approach as reducible to a basic social and economic rationalism. This instrumentalism would seem to be borne out by common sense. Almost anyone inquiring of a Peronist worker why he supported Perón has been met by the significant gesture of tapping the back pocket where the money is kept, symbolizing a basic class pragmatism of monetary needs and their satisfaction. Clearly, Peronism from the workers' point of view was in a fundamental sense a response to economic grievances and class exploitation.

Yet it was also something more. It was also a political movement that represented a crucial shift in working-class political allegiance and behavior and that presented its adherents with a distinct political vision. In order to understand the significance of this new allegiance we need to examine carefully the specific features of this political vision and the discourse in which it was expressed, rather than simply regard Peronism as an inevitable manifestation of social and economic dissatisfaction. Gareth Stedman Jones, commenting on the reluctance of social historians to take sufficient account of the political, has recently observed that "a political movement is not simply a manifestation of distress and pain, its existence is distinguished by a shared conviction articulating a political solution to distress and a political diagnosis of its causes." Thus if Peronism did represent a concrete solution to felt material needs, we still need to understand why the solution took the specific political form of Peronism and not another. Other political movements did speak to the same needs and offer solutions to them. Even programmatically there were many formal similarities between Peronism and other political forces. What we need to understand is Peronism's success, its distinctiveness, why its political appeal was more credible for workers—which areas it touched that others did not. To do this we need to take Perón's political and ideological appeal seriously and examine the nature of Peronism's rhetoric and compare it with that of its rivals for working-class allegiance.

WORKERS AS CITIZENS IN PERONIST POLITICAL RHETORIC

Peronism's fundamental political appeal lay in its ability to redefine the notion of citizenship within a broader, ultimately social, context. The issue of citizenship per se, and the question of access to full political rights, was a potent part of Peronist discourse, forming part of a language of protest at political exclusion that had great popular resonance. Part of the power of such elements in Peronist political language came from a recognition that it formed part of a traditional language of democratic politics that demanded equal access to political rights. This tradition had found its principal prior embodiment in the Unión Cívica Radical and its leader, Hipólito Yrigoyen. The Radical Party prior to 1930 had mobilized the urban and rural middle classes and a not inconsiderable section of the urban poor with a rhetoric permeated with symbols of struggle against the oligarchy and with a traditional language of citizenship, political rights, and obligations. Peronism was certainly eclectic enough to lay claim to, and absorb elements of, this Yrigoyenist heritage.

In part, too, the force of such a concern for the rights of political citizenship lay in the scandal of the *década infame,* the infamous decade that followed the military overthrow of Yrigoyen in 1930. The *década infame,* which stretched in fact from 1930 until the military coup of 1943, witnessed the reimposition and maintenance of the conservative elite's political power through a system of institutionalized fraud and corruption. It was the epoch of "Ya votaste, rajá pronto para tu casa" (You've already voted, get along quickly to your home!), enforced by the hired thugs of the conservative committees. In Avellaneda Don Alberto Barceló controlled Argentina's emerging industrial center with the aid of a police force, a political machine, the underworld, and votes from the dead, much as he had done since the First World War. In the province of Buenos Aires Governor Manuel Fresco coordinated a similar machine of clientelism and corruption. The only island of relative political rectitude was in the federal capital, where fraud was rarely practiced. Political corruption set a tone of social degeneration of the traditional elite, epitomized in the seemingly endless series of scandals involving public figures and foreign economic groups that was to furnish the emerging groups of nationalists with many of their targets.

Beyond that, such institutional corruption bred a broader public cynicism. In the words of one author "this was a corruption which gave lessons." The political and moral malaise embodied in this situation clearly engendered a crisis of confidence and legitimacy in established political institutions. Peronism could, therefore, draw political capital by denouncing the hypocrisy of a formal democratic system that had little of democracy's real content. Moreover, the weight of Peronist claims to this heritage was reinforced by the fact that even those parties formally opposed to the fraud of the 1930s were perceived to have compromised themselves with the conservative regime. This was particularly the case with the Radical Party, which after a period of principled abstention between 1931 and 1936 had, under the leadership of Marcelo T. de Alvear, reentered the political fray to act as a loyal opposition in a political system it knew it would never be allowed to dominate. The crisis of legitimacy extended, therefore, far beyond the conservative elite itself and was a constantly reiterated theme of Peronist propaganda in 1945 and 1946. As the organ of the Partido Laborista expressed it during the run-up to the 1946 elections: "The old traditional parties, for many years passed, have ceased to be voices of the people in order to act instead in small circles of clear unpopular character, deaf and blind to the worries of that mass whose aid they only think to call on when elections come around."

Nevertheless, Peronism's political appeal to workers cannot be explained simply in terms of its capacity to articulate claims to political participation and a full recognition of the rights of citizenship. Formally the rights associated with such claims—universal suffrage, the right of association, equality before the law—had long existed in Argentina. The Sáenz Peña Law of 1912, the law of universal suffrage, continued in operation in Argentina throughout the *década infame*. Similarly there existed in Argentina a long-established tradition of representative social and political institutions. Peronism's articulation of democratic demands was, therefore, a claim for a reestablishment of previously recognized rights and claims. Moreover, Perón had no monopoly of this language of political exclusion. Indeed it was a language that his opponents in the Unión Democrática used against him, accusing him of representing a closed, undemocratic system, and it was a discourse that would continue to form the basis of political opposition to Perón throughout his regime and after his fall from power. Finally, it was, in the sense that it addressed the general issue of citizenship, not an appeal directed specifically at workers but, by definition, at all voters whose rights had been abused.

Perón's political success with workers lay, rather, in his capacity to recast the whole issue of citizenship within a new social context. Peronist discourse denied the validity of liberalism's separation of the state and politics from civil society. Citizenship was not to be defined any longer simply in terms of individual rights and relations within political society but was now redefined in terms of the economic and social realm of civil society. Within the terms of this rhetoric to struggle for rights in the sphere of politics inevitably implied social change. Indeed, by constantly emphasizing the social dimension of citizenship Perón explicitly challenged the legitimacy of a notion of democracy that limited itself to participation in formal political rights, and he extended it to include participation in the social and economic life of the nation. In part this was reflected in a claim for a democracy that included social rights and reforms and in an attitude that treated with skepticism political claims couched in the rhetoric of formal liberalism. This was most starkly apparent in the election campaign of 1946. The political appeal of the Unión Democrática was almost entirely expressed in a language of liberal democratic slogans. In the political manifestos and speeches there was virtually no mention made of the social issue. Instead, one finds a political discourse entirely framed in terms of a rhetoric of "liberty," "democracy," "the constitution," "free elections," "freedom of speech."

Perón, in contrast, constantly reminded his audiences that behind the phraseology of liberalism lay a basic social division and that a true democracy could be built only by doing justice to this social issue. In a speech in July 1945 in which he responded to growing opposition demands for elections he said: "If some ask for liberty we too demand it . . . but not the liberty of fraud . . . nor the liberty to sell the country out, nor to exploit the working people." Luis Gay, the secretary general of the Partido Laborista, echoed this perception in a speech at the formal proclamation of Perón's presidential ticket in February 1946:

Political democracy is a lie on its own. It is only a reality when it is accompanied by an economic reconstruction of the economy that makes democracy possible on the terrain of practical happenings. They are lying who don't agree with this concept and only speak of the constitution and of that liberty that they defrauded and denied right up to the coup of 3 June 1943.

It seems clear that this kind of rhetoric struck a deep chord with working people emerging from the *década infame*. Manuel Pichel, a delegate of the CGT, stated in the first official demonstration organized by the CGT to back Perón against the mounting opposition attack in July 1945: "It is not enough to speak of democracy. We don't want a democracy defended by the reactionary capitalists; a democracy that would mean a return to the oligarchy is not something we would support." Mariano Tedesco, a textile workers' leader, recalled some years later that "people in 1945 had already had a belly-full. For years they had seen the satisfaction of their hunger delayed with songs to liberty." In a similar vein, the skepticism with which the formal symbols of liberalism were met is forcibly evoked in an anecdote Julio Mafud recalls from the year 1945. Mafud remembers a group of workers responding to a questioner who asked if they were worried about freedom of speech if Perón were to be elected in the upcoming election. They had replied, "Freedom of speech is to do with you people. We have never had it."

More fundamentally still, Perón's recasting of the issue of citizenship implied a distinct, new vision of the working class's role in society. Traditionally the liberal political system in Argentina, as elsewhere, had recognized the political existence of workers as individual, atomized citizens with formal equality of rights in the political arena, at the same time as it had denied, or hindered, its constitution as a social class at the political level. Certainly, faithful to the liberal separation of state and civil society, it had denied the legitimacy of transferring the social identity built around conflict at the social level to the political arena. Rather, any unity, social cohesion, and sense of distinct interests attained in civil society were to be dissolved and atomized in the political marketplace where individual citizens sought, through the mediation of political parties, to influence the state and thus reconcile and balance the competing interests that existed in civil society.

Radicalism, for all its rhetoric of "the people" and "the oligarchy," never challenged the presuppositions of this liberal political system. Indeed, its clientelistic political machine, built around local bosses, was ideally placed to act as the broker of the individual citizens' claims in the political marketplace. Peronism, on the other hand, premised its political appeal to workers on a recognition of the working class as a distinct social force that demanded recogni-

tion and representation as such in the political life of the nation. This representation would no longer be achieved simply through the exercise of the formal
rights of citizenship and the primary mediation of political parties. Instead,
the working class as an autonomous social force would have direct, indeed
privileged, access to the state through its trade unions.

The uniqueness of this vision of working-class social and political integration in the Argentina of the 1940s becomes apparent if we examine the distinctive way Perón addressed the working class in his speeches both during
the election campaign of 1945–46 and after. In contrast to the more traditional
caudillo or political boss Perón's political discourse did not address workers as
atomized individuals whose only hope of achieving social coherence and political meaning for their lives lay in establishing ties with a leader who could
intercede for them with an all-powerful state. Instead Perón addressed them
as a social force whose own organization and strength were vital if he were to
be successful at the level of the state in asserting their rights. He was only their
spokesman and could only be as successful as they were united and organized.
Continually Perón emphasized the frailty of individuals and the arbitrariness
of human fate and hence the necessity for them to depend on nothing but
their own will to achieve their rights. Those rights and interests would have
to be negotiated with other social groups. Within this rhetoric, therefore, the
state was not simply an all-powerful dispenser of desired resources that distributed these — through its chosen instrument, the leader — to passive individuals.
Rather, it was a space where *classes* — not isolated individuals — could act politically and socially with one another to establish corporate rights and claims.
Within this discourse the ultimate arbiter of this process might be the state and
ultimately the figure of Perón identified with the state, but he did not on his
own constitute these groups as social forces; they had a certain independent,
and irreducible, social, and hence political, presence.

Clearly there were strong elements of a personalist, almost mystical caudi-
llismo attached to the position of both Perón and Evita Perón within Peronist
rhetoric. Partly this resulted from the different political needs of Perón and
Peronism at different times. From a secure position of state power the need
to emphasize working-class organizational autonomy and social cohesion was
evidently less than in the period of political contest preceding the achievement
of that power. Indeed such an emphasis would soon conflict with the new demands of the state. Even during the pre-1946 period the personalist elements
of Perón's political appeal were present, as witness the consistent, overwhelming chant of "Perón! Perón!" that dominated the mobilization of 17 October
1945. Nevertheless, even at the height of the adulation of Evita and the growing
state-sponsored cult of Perón's personal power during the second presidency,

this personalist element was not present entirely at the expense of a continued affirmation of the social and organizational strength of the working class.

This affirmation of the workers as a social presence and their incorporation directly into the affairs of state evidently implied a new conception of the legitimate spheres of interest and activity of the working class and its institutions. This was most evident in Perón's assertion of the workers' rights to be concerned with, and to help determine, the economic development of the nation. It was within the context of this new vision of the working class's role in society that the issues of industrialization and economic nationalism, key elements in Peronism's political appeal, were to be situated. Peronist rhetoric was open enough to absorb existing strands of nationalist thought. Some of these went back, once again, to the Yrigoyenist heritage, particularly his conflict with foreign petroleum companies in his last years in office. Other elements were absorbed from the groups of nationalist intellectuals that emerged in the 1930s and whose ideas were influential among the military. Thus, for example, terms such as *cipayo* and *vendepatria* became incorporated into the political language of Peronism to refer to those forces that wished to maintain Argentina within the economic orbit of the United States or the United Kingdom as a provider of agricultural and pastoral products. Such a language became symbolic of a commitment to industrialization overseen and guided by a commitment to *Argentina potencia* in contrast to the *Argentina granja* of Peronism's opponents.

The success of Perón's identification of himself with the creation of an industrial Argentina and the political appeal of such symbolism did not reside primarily in programmatic terms. Given the evident concern of an emerging industrial workforce with the issue of industrialization and Peronism's strenuous self-identification with this symbol and later monopoly of the language of economic development, it would be tempting to explain such a success in terms of a unique attachment on the part of Perón to such a program. Yet, in terms of political programs and formal commitments, the association of Peronism with industrialization and of its opponents with a rural, pastoral Argentina was scarcely accurate. Emphases varied greatly, and the commitment was rarely consistent, but very few of the major political parties in Argentina denied by the 1940s the need for some sort of state-sponsored industrialization. The most articulate sector of the conservative elite had affirmed their recognition of the irreversibility of industrialization with the Plan Pinedo of 1940. The Radical Party had also increasingly adopted a proindustrialization stance, and the Yrigoyenist wing of the party adopted in April 1945, with the Declaration of Avellaneda, an economic blueprint every bit as industrialist as that of Perón. The Left, too, in the form of the Communists and socialists, had consistently used an anti-imperialist rhetoric throughout the 1930s.

The real issue at stake in the 1940s was not, therefore, so much industrialization *versus* agrarian development or state intervention *versus* laissez-faire. Rather it was the issue of the different potential meanings of industrialism, the social and political parameters within which it should take place that were at stake. It was Perón's ability to define these parameters in a new way that appealed to the working class and his ability to address this issue in a particularly credible way for workers that enabled him to appropriate the issue and symbol of industrial development and make it a political weapon with which to distinguish himself from his opponents.

The success of this appropriation was partly a matter of perception. Certainly, the association of Perón's political opponents in 1945 and 1946 with the bastions of traditional rural society, the Sociedad Rural and the Jockey Club, weakened the credibility of their commitment to industrialism. In a similar way, their close association with the U.S. ambassador did not strengthen belief in their devotion to national sovereignty and economic independence. In terms of image making the identification of Peronism with industrial and social progress, with modernity, was an established fact by the end of the presidential election campaign of 1946. It was not, however, solely a matter of images and public relations. More fundamentally the working class recognized in Perón's espousal of industrial development a vital role for itself as an actor in the greatly expanded public sphere that Peronism offered to it as a field for its activity. Indeed Perón consistently premised the very notion of national development on the full participation of the working class in public life and social justice. Industrialization within his discourse was no longer conceivable, as it had been prior to 1943, at the expense of the extreme exploitation of the working class. In a speech delivered during the election campaign Perón had affirmed: "In conclusion: Argentina cannot continue to stagnate in a somnolent rhythm of activity to which so many who had come and lived at her expense had condemned her. Argentina must recover the firm pulse of a healthy and clean living youth, Argentina needs the young blood of the working class." Within Peronist rhetoric social justice and national sovereignty were credibly interrelated themes rather than simply enunciated abstract slogans.

A BELIEVABLE VISION: CREDIBILITY AND CONCRETENESS
IN PERÓN'S POLITICAL DISCOURSE

The issue of credibility is crucial for understanding both Perón's successful identification of himself with certain important symbols such as industrialism and, more generally, the political impact of his discourse on workers. Gareth Stedman Jones, in the essay to which we have already referred, notes that to be successful "a particular political vocabulary must convey a practicable hope of a general alternative and a believable means of realising it such that potential recruits can think in its terms." The vocabulary of Peronism was both visionary and believable. The credibility was in part rooted in the immediate, concrete nature of its rhetoric. This involved a tying down of abstract political slogans to their most concrete material aspects. As we have already seen, in the crucial years 1945 and 1946 this was clearly contrasted with a language of great abstraction used by Perón's political opponents. While Perón's rhetoric was capable of lofty sermonizing, particularly once he had attained the presidency, and depending on the audience he was addressing, his speeches to working-class audiences in this formative period have, for their time, a unique tone.

They are, for example, framed in a language clearly distinct from that of classic radicalism, with its woolly generalities concerning national renovation and civic virtue. The language of "the oligarchy" and "the people" was still present but now usually more precisely defined. Their utilization as general categories to denote good and evil, those who were with Perón from those against, was still there, but now there was also a frequent concretizing, sometimes as rich and poor, often as capitalist and worker. While there was a rhetoric of an indivisible community — symbolized in "the people" and "the nation" — the working class was given an implicitly superior role within this whole, often as the repository of national values. "The people" frequently were transformed into "the working people" (*el pueblo trabajador*): the people, the nation, and the workers became interchangeable.

A similar denial of the abstract can be found in Peronism's appeal to economic and political nationalism. In terms of the formal construction from the state of Peronist ideology, categories such as *the nation* and *Argentina* were accorded an abstract, mystical significance. When, however, Perón specifically addressed the working class, particularly in the formative period, but also after, one finds little appeal to the irrational, mystical elements of nationalist ideology. There was little concern with the intrinsic virtues of *Argentinidad* nor with the historical precedents of *criollo* culture as expressed in a historical nostalgia for some long-departed national essence. Such concerns were mainly the province of middle-class intellectuals in the various nationalist groups that attempted, with little success, to use Peronism as a vehicle for their aspirations. Working-class nationalism was addressed primarily in terms of concrete economic issues.

Moreover, Peronism's political credibility for workers was due, not only to the concreteness of its rhetoric, but also to its immediacy. Perón's political vision of a society based on social justice and on the social and political integration of workers into that society was not premised, as it was, for example, in leftist political discourse, on the prior achievement of long-term, abstract structural tarnsformations, nor on the gradual acquisition at some future date of an adequate consciousness on the part of the working class. It took working-class consciousness, habits, lifestyles, and values as it found them and affirmed their sufficiency and value. It glorified the everyday and the ordinary as a sufficient basis for the rapid attainment of a juster society, provided that certain easily achievable and self-evident goals were met. Primarily this meant support for Perón as head of state and the maintenance of a strong union movement. In this sense Peronism's political appeal was radically plebeian; it eschewed the need for a peculiarly enlightened political elite and reflected and inculcated a profound anti-intellectualism.

The glorification of popular lifestyles and habits implied a political style and idiom well in tune with popular sensibilities. Whether it was in symbolically striking the pose of the *descamisado* (shirtless one) in a political rally or in the nature of the imagery used in his speeches, Perón had an ability to communicate to working-class audiences that his rivals lacked. The poet Luis Franco commented cryptically on Perón's "spiritual affinity with tango lyrics." His ability to use this affinity to establish a bond with his audience was clearly shown in his speech to those assembled in the Plaza de Mayo on 17 October 1945. Toward the end of that speech Perón evoked the image of his mother, "mi vieja": "I said to you a little while ago that I would embrace you as I would my mother because you have had the same griefs and the same thoughts that my poor old lady must have felt in these days." The reference is apparently gratuitous, the empty phraseology of someone who could think of nothing better to say, until we recognize that the sentiments echo exactly a dominant refrain of tango — the poor grief-laden mother whose pain symbolizes the pain of her children, of all the poor. Perón's identification of his own mother with the poor establishes a sentimental identity between himself and his audience; with this tone of nostalgia he was touching an important sensibility in Argentine popular culture of the period. Significantly, too, the speech ended on another "tangoesque" note. Perón reminded his audience as they were about to leave the Plaza, "Remember that among you there are many women workers who have to be protected here and in life by you same workers." The theme of the threat to the women of the working class, and the need to protect their women, was also a constant theme of both tango and other forms of popular culture.

Perón's use of such an idiom within which to frame his political appeal often seems to us now, and indeed it seemed to many of his critics at the time, to reek of the paternalistic condescension of the traditional caudillo figure. His constant use of couplets from *Martín Fierro,* or his conscious use of terms taken from *lunfardo* argot, grates on modern sensibilities. However, we should be careful to appreciate the impact of his ability to speak in an idiom that reflected popular sensibilities of the time. In accounts by observers and journalists of the crucial formative years of Peronism we frequently find the adjectives *chabacano* and *burdo* used to describe both Perón himself and his supporters. Both words have the sense of "crude," "cheap," "coarse," and they also implied a lack of sophistication, an awkwardness, almost a country bumpkin quality. While they were generally meant as epithets they were not descriptions Peronists would necessarily have denied.

Indeed this capacity to recognize, reflect, and foster a popular political style and idiom based on this plebeian realism contrasted strongly with the political appeal of traditional working-class political parties. The tone adopted by the latter when confronted by the working-class effervescence of the mid-1940s was didactic, moralizing, and apparently addressed to a morally and intellectually inferior audience. This was particularly the case of the Socialist Party. Its analysis of the events of 17 October is illustrative of its attitude and tone:

> The part of the people that lives its resentment, and perhaps only for its resentment, spilt over into the streets, threatened, yelled, trampled on and assaulted newspapers and persons in its demon-like fury, those persons who were the very champions of its elevation and dignification.

Behind this tone of fear, frustration, and moralizing lay a discourse that addressed an abstract, almost mythical working class. Peronism on the other hand was prepared, particularly in its formative period, to recognize, and even glorify, workers who did "threaten, yell, and trample with a demon-like fury." Comparing Perón's political approach to that of his rivals one is reminded of Ernst Bloch's comment concerning Nazism's preemption of socialist and Communist appeal among German workers that "the Nazis speak falsely but to people, the Communists truthfully, but of things."

Perón's ability to appreciate the tone of working-class sensibilities and assumptions was reflected in other areas. There was, for example, in Peronist rhetoric a tacit recognition of the immutability of social inequality, a common-sense, shrug of the shoulders acceptance of the reality of social and economic inequities, a recognition of what Pierre Bourdieu has called "a sense of limits." The remedies proposed to mitigate these inequities were plausible and immediate. Perón, in a speech in Rosario in August 1944, had emphasized the apparently self-evident reasonableness of his appeal, the mundaneness behind the abstract rhetoric of social equality: "We want exploitation of man by man to cease in our country, and when this problem disappears, we will equalize a little the social classes so that there will not be in this country men who are too poor nor those who are too rich."

This realism implied a political vision of a limited nature, but it did not eliminate utopian resonances; it simply made such resonances — a yearning for social equality, for an end to exploitation — more credible for a working class imbued by its experience of the *década infame* with a certain cynicism regarding political promises and abstract slogans. Indeed the credibility of Perón's political vision, the practicability of the hope it offered, was affirmed on a daily basis by its actions from the state. The solutions it offered the working class did not depend on some future apocalypse for confirmation but were rather directly verifiable in terms of everyday political activity and experience. Already by 1945 the slogan had appeared among workers that was to symbolize this credibility: "Perón cumple!" (Perón delivers).

The Heretical Social Impact of Peronism

Peronism meant a greatly increased social and political presence for the working class within Argentine society. The impact of this can be measured in institutional terms by reference to such factors as the intimate relationship between government and labor during the Perón era, the massive extension of unionization, the number of union-sponsored members of Congress. These are factors that are clearly demonstrable empirically and often measurable statistically. There are, however, other factors that need to be taken into account in assessing Peronism's social meaning for the working class — factors that are far less tangible, far more difficult to quantify. We are dealing here with factors such as pride, self-respect, and dignity.

THE MEANING OF THE *DÉCADA INFAME*:
WORKING-CLASS RESPONSES

In order to assess the importance of such factors we must return to the *década infame,* for it was clearly a benchmark against which workers measured their experience of Peronism. Popular culture of the Peronist era was dominated by a temporal dichotomy that contrasted the Peronist present with the recent past. As Ernesto Goldar has noted in his analysis of Peronist popular fiction this dichotomy was accompanied by a corresponding contrast of values associated with the *hoy* of 1950 and the *ayer* of the 1930s. Some of these evaluative contrasts referred to the concrete social changes associated with better social welfare, improved wages, and good union organization. Yet others spoke to a wider, more personal social realm outside improvements in the world of the production line, the wage packet, or the union. These suggest strongly that the *década infame* was experienced by many workers as a time of profound collective and individual frustration and humiliation.

While we lack a comprehensive account of the elements that made up the social universe of the working class in the pre-Perón period, the evidence of anecdote, personal testimony, popular cultural forms, and working-class biography nevertheless can provide us with suggestive fragments of a whole picture. The harsh conditions and discipline attested to by most observers of the period evidently had an impact in the wider working-class community. Cipriano Reyes notes, for example, in his memoirs of his organizing experiences in the meatpacking plants of Berisso in the 1930s and 1940s that "the company was the master of the lives and dwellings of its workers . . . when a workman didn't pay his debts the tradesman went to see the personnel chief of the *frigorífico* and the offender was fired or suspended. The vigilance was incredible; everything was controlled."

This sort of control was probably most fierce in working-class communities dominated by a single large concern, such as the meatpacking plants. Nevertheless, the wider social implications arising from such a situation of employer dominance were not confined to the extreme case of the company town. Angel Perelman remembers leaving school at ten in order to enter a metalworking workshop in the federal capital where he worked "without any fixed hours . . . the time we finished was fixed by the boss . . . the sum total of happiness for a working-class family consisted in keeping your job." The 1930s were, he remembers, "the era of the desperate, the ingenious, and the petty theft." Another writer, commenting on the wider implications of the labor situation in the same era, observed that: "Fear of unemployment in this period led to humiliation. You had to be quiet, not talk. The lack of elemental defensive actions led to a moral decline, to cynicism. Within the factory the worker was alone, deprived of all social consciousness." Although such sweeping generalizations about moral decline and cynicism being characteristic of working-class attitudes in the 1930s need to be treated with caution, there is other evidence that tends to point in a similar direction.

Some of the most suggestive of this evidence is to be gleaned from popular cultural forms and in particular the tango. The social universe depicted in the tangos of the 1930s was universally bleak. The traditional themes of tango are still present—the betrayal of love, the nostalgia for a simpler past centered on an idyllic recreation of the barrio or *arrabal,* the affirmation of the virtues of valor and courage—but to this has now been added, in some of the most popular and significant tangos, a wider social context. In the tangos of Enrique Santos Discépolo, in particular, the impossibility of a meaningful relationship between a man and a woman has come to symbolize the impossibility of any social relationship that is not based on greed, egotism, and a total lack of moral scruples in a world based on injustice and deceit. A crucial figure in many of Discépolo's tangos is the *gilito embanderado*—the naive little man, humiliated by poverty and society, who still has illusions that he can survive in the world while being morally honest and decent or, more ingenuously still, that he can effect some change in an unjust world. The object of the tango then becomes to disabuse him of his illusions by confronting him with a reality where "Not even God saves those who are lost." The tone is one of bitterness and resignation. The popular wisdom about social life embodied in the narrative recommends an adoption of the dominant values of egotism and immorality. At its most extreme this implied an understanding, if not approval, of the attraction for the poor of the logic of the *mala vida*—prostitution, pimping, and crime. The alternative was a resigned acceptance or "an obstinate silence" for those who could not conform to this dominant social ethos.

Now evidently care must be taken in drawing conclusions about working-class attitudes from tango and other popular cultural forms of the period. Tango, for example, was increasingly a commercialized art form whose connection with the working-class barrio was very tenuous by the 1930s. What reached the general public was largely determined by record companies, and commercial success and failure depended on the reception in the wider consumer market and the theaters and music halls of downtown Buenos Aires. It seems likely, too, that the bohemian element that had always been a crucial part of tango was given greater prominence as tango lyricists came more and more from the urban lower middle class. Certainly, the desperate lament of Discépolo's great tango, "Cambalache," written in 1935, that "Everything is equal, nothing is better; it's the same to be a jackass as a great professor," rings with the educated middle class's disenchantment with society's failure to recognize true merit. The lyrics of the *década infame* lack, too, some of the optimism and social engagement found in some of the tangos of an earlier era. Yet the immense popularity of these tangos among the working class of Buenos Aires seems to attest to the fact that whatever the manipulations of the culture industry, whatever the caveats we place on the reading of working-class consciousness directly from the lyrics of tango, they did respond to certain attitudes and experiences re-created in tango that they recognized as authentic to themselves and their experience.

However, even if we recognize the suggestiveness of such evidence we must also recognize that cynicism, apathy, or resignation were not the only responses available to workers. Luis Danussi, who would become, after 1955, a leader of the print workers' union found when he first arrived in Buenos Aires in 1938 a city that was "tumultuous and possessed a frantic union activity, offering a broad field for action; national congresses, zonal, municipal congresses of workers and unions," according to his biographers. The militant working-class culture characteristic of an earlier epoch was still present. This culture was centered around the existence of "unions, atheneums, libraries, the distribution of pamphlets, papers, reviews, leaflets, and books; demonstrations, committees for the release of political prisoners, theater groups, cooperatives, communities, and attempts at a solidarity life style. Also campaigns were carried out against alcoholism, tobacco, picnics were organized, lectures discussed, and the spirit of mutual aid inculcated." Elements of this sort of traditional militant culture shared by socialists, Communists, anarchists, and syndicalists alike still flourished. They found an expression in the numerous committees formed in the 1930s to aid the Spanish republicans, and they were still a living presence in unions such as the print workers, which Luis Danussi entered.

Danussi himself had an anarchist background before arriving in Buenos Aires, but workers from outside this culture could be attracted by it and use it as a channel to express their resentment at exploitation and as part of their search for political solutions. Angel Perelman notes, for example, that:

> I learned about capitalist exploitation and class struggle first in that factory rather than in the books . . . at the age of fourteen, and with already four years as a worker I couldn't help but be interested in politics. How could I not have been interested? There were many demonstrations by the unemployed. Some left-wing parties protested against the reigning misery. Union meetings . . . brought together the most militant and determined workers. I began to attend all sorts of meetings and acts.

Other evidence, too, suggests an increase in union activity and attendance at union meetings in the late 1930s and early 1940s as unemployment decreased, industry expanded, and the union movement recovered somewhat from the decline of the years following the coup of 1930. Union membership responded to an improved national and international climate, increasing by some 10 percent between 1941 and 1945.

Yet this positive organizational and collective response to the conditions of the pre-1943 period does not seem to have been the predominant one. Evidently there was a wide spectrum of working-class experience and response. The working-class militants themselves recognized, however, that the militant culture of the union or ideological grouping touched only a minority of the working class. Danussi's biographers stress that "to open up the road for union organization was enormously difficult, in many respects because of police and employer repression, but what represented an almost insuperable obstacle to overcome was the indifference and disbelief of the workers themselves, reluctant to organize in defense of their own interests."

Something of the feeling of impotence and resignation that we may suggest characterized the response of many workers to the experience of the pre-1943 period can be found in the personal testimony of the nonmilitant. The following two excerpts from such testimony are offered in an attempt to convey the essence of this feeling. The first comes from a worker who had worked in the ports along the Paraná River, particularly in the port of Rosario:

Question: What were the 1930s like for you?

Don Ramiro: Well life was very hard back then . . . working people weren't worth anything, and we got no respect from those who controlled everything. You had to know your place and keep in line. I used to vote for the radicals in the 1920s, but after 1930 things got really bad. The conservative bosses ran the whole show. On election day I would go down to the town hall to vote, but I couldn't get in. . . . You see I was known as someone they couldn't trust, so they would stop me voting. By law they couldn't but that was a joke, what was the law back then? There would be a group of them, heavies, paid by the local conservative committee . . . everyone knew them . . . and they would block the doorway when you wanted to go in. You could see their guns bulging under their jackets.

Question: You mean they would use force to stop you voting? They would threaten you?

Don Ramiro: No. They never did that openly . . . not to me at least, they didn't have to . . . you knew you would have to pay for it somehow if you went against them. It was a sort of game for them.

Question: So what did you do?

Don Ramiro: What could you do? Nothing. You'd go home. Complain maybe to your friends about those bastards. If you made a fuss, they would get you one way or another, and it wouldn't do any good anyway. You were nothing to them. But later with Perón that all changed. I voted for him.

Question: How did it change?

Don Ramiro: Well, with Perón we were all machos.

The second excerpt comes from a younger worker from Buenos Aires who entered the workforce in the late 1930s:

Laurato: One thing I remember about the 1930s was the way you were treated. You felt you didn't have rights to anything, everything seemed to be a favor they did for you through the church or some charity, or if you went and begged the local political boss he'd help you get medicine or get into a hospital. Another thing I remember about the 1930s is that I always felt strange when I went to the city, downtown Buenos Aires—

like you didn't belong there, which was stupid but you felt that they were looking down on you, that you weren't dressed right. The police there treated you like animals too.

Question: Were unions or politics important to you at that time?

Lautaro: Well, I voted for the socialists usually. My brother was more interested in them, though I always thought that they were at least honest. But I never thought that it would do any good. The same really with unions. We didn't have a union in the shops where I worked—it must have been in the early 1940s, before Perón. We had plenty to complain about, but I don't recall that we thought seriously about the union. That was just the way things were, you just had to put up with it . . . with everything, their damn arrogance, the way they treated you. Some of the activists my brother hung out with wanted to change that, but they were exceptions I think. Not many workers thought of being heroes then.

Note

For references and notes, consult the complete version of this chapter in Daniel James, *Resistance and Integration: Peronism and the Argentine Working Class, 1946–1976* (Cambridge: Cambridge University Press, 1988), 7–30.

Saint Evita

Tomás Eloy Martínez

Eva Duarte de Perón (1919–52), Perón's second wife, had a brief but significant political career. During her husband's first administration, she moved beyond the traditional duties of a first lady and worked for social reforms through a charity foundation bearing her name. As the "champion of the poor," Eva Perón — renamed "Evita" by her admirers — led a broad campaign of public assistance that benefited Argentine society's poorest sectors. Although her critics accused her, not without cause, of being despotic and encouraging political clientelism, Evita helped incorporate into the public and political spheres the demands of the descamisados *(literally "shirtless") and the illiterate, many of them rural-born mestizo workers seeking jobs at new factories in Buenos Aires. Her strong will also appealed to working-class women who felt that she understood and represented their views. At official celebrations and public parades, Evita's charisma had a bewitching effect on the crowds. Trained as an actress, extremely attractive, and of humble origin, she performed the role of a vengeful Cinderella, able to harness the masses' unconditional love. At the peak of her popularity, Eva Duarte died from cancer in 1952. Her funeral extended for four days so that thousands of mourners could say farewell to their heroine. In this passage from* Santa Evita *(1995), Tomás Eloy Martínez re-creates the complex, quasi-religious relationship that the lower classes sustained with a woman that appeared to them as the embodiment of hope. Her popularity provided Evita with the status of a saint whose miraculous powers would overcome and outlast even death.*

Huge figures, millions, were always the aura that surrounded her name. In *My Mission in Life* the reader comes on this mysterious phrase: "I think that many men together, rather than being thousands and thousands of separate souls, are instead a single soul." Mythologists caught the idea on the fly and transformed the thousands into millions. "I will come back, and I will be millions," Evita's most celebrated phrase promises. But she never spoke that phrase, as is readily noted by anyone whose attention is attracted for an instant by her posthumous perfume: "I will come back" — from where? — "And I will be mil-

Eva Perón (1948). Eva Perón during a public ceremony in honor of the blessing of the Virgin of Luján.

lions"—of what? Despite the fact that it was often proved to be apocryphal, the phrase still appears at the bottom of the posters commemorating each of her anniversaries. She never said it, but it is true.

Until her sanctity little by little, with time, became dogma. Between May 1952—two months before she died—and July 1954, the Vatican received nearly forty thousand letters from laymen and laywomen attributing various miracles to Evita and urging the pope to canonize her. The prefect of the Congregation of Rites answered all the petitions with the usual formulas: "Any Catholic knows that in order to be a saint the person must be dead." And later, as she was being embalmed: "The trials for sanctification take a long time, hundreds of years. Be patient." The letters gradually became more and more peremptory. They complained that Maria Goretti had waited only forty-four years to be a saint and Theresa of Lisieux just a little over twenty-five. The case of Saint Clare of Assisi was even more striking, they said; the impatient Innocent IV wanted to canonize her on her deathbed. Evita deserved better: only the Virgin Mary surpassed her in virtues. The fact that the supreme pontiff should take so long to acknowledge such obvious sanctity was—I read in the papers—"an affront to the faith of the Peronist people."

During those same years, all the impoverished adolescents of Argentina wanted to look like Evita. Half the girls born in the provinces of the Northeast were named Eva or Maria Eva, and those who weren't named that copied the emblems of her beauty. They dyed their hair peroxide blond and wore it tightly swept back and caught up in one or two plaited chignons. They wore flared skirts, made of fabrics that could be starched, and shoes with ankle straps. Evita was the arbiter of fashion and the national model of behavior. That sort of skirt and shoes never came back in style after the end of the 1950s, but hair dyed blond appealed to the upper classes and became, in time, a distinctive feature of women of the northern section of Buenos Aires.

In the first six months of 1951, Evita gave away twenty-five thousand houses and almost 3 million packages containing medicine, furniture, clothing, bicycles, and toys. The poor started lining up before dawn to see her, and it was not until dawn the next day that some of them finally managed to do so. She questioned them as to their family problems, their ailments, their work, and even their love affairs. In that same year, 1951, she was matron of honor at the wedding ceremony for 1,608 couples, half of whom already had children. Illegitimate children moved Evita to tears because her own illegitimacy had been a martyrdom to her.

In the remote town of Tucumán, I remember, many people believed that she was an emissary of God. I have heard that on the pampas too and in the villages along the Patagonian coast country people often saw the outlines of her face in the heavens. They were afraid she would die because the world might end with her last breath. Simple folk often tried to attract Evita's attention so as to attain some manner of eternity thereby. "To be in the Señora's thoughts," said a woman stricken with polio, "is like touching God with a person's own hands. What more does anyone need?"

A girl of seventeen who went by the name of "pretty Evelina," and whose real name nobody ever found out, wrote Evita two thousand letters in 1951, at a rate of five or six a day. All the letters had the same wording, so that all that pretty Evelina had to do was copy it and deposit the envelopes in a mailbox in Mar del Plata, the city where she lived, once she'd come up with the money for the stamps. In those days, Evita was the victim of frequent epistolary effusions, but she did not ordinarily receive letters that were also little works of art:

> *My dere Evita, Im not going to aks you for anathing the way everbody else around hear does, cause the ony thing i want is for you to rede this leter and remember my name, I no that if you keep my name in yore mine even if its just for one little minate nothing bad can hapen to me and Ill be happy and not have any ailments or misries. Im 17 and I sleep on the matress you left at my house for a present last Chrismas. I love you lots. pretty Evelina.*

Female workers at a pantyhose factory (1940). Eva Perón would pay special attention to the welfare of working-class women. Courtesy Archivo General de la Nación, Buenos Aires.

When the rumor spread that Evita might be the candidate for vice president of the Republic and that the generals, indignant at the prospect of taking orders from a woman, would be opposed, pretty Evelina sent one last letter to which she added three words: "Long Liv Wommen." She immediately put herself on exhibit in the show window of a furniture store, lying in a large chest, with the intention of fasting until the generals changed their attitude. So many people came to see her that the store windows broke and the owner put a stop to the show. Pretty Evelina fasted for one night in the rough weather out on the sidewalks, until the socialist mayor of the city agreed to lend her one of the tents on Bristol Beach that were no longer in use because the season was over. At the entrance to the tent, Evelina hung a sign with her motto, LONG LIV WOMMEN, and began the second stage of her fast. Six notaries took turns as witnesses to the fact that the rules were being strictly observed. The fasting girl was allowed to drink only one glass of water in the morning and another at dusk, but after the first week Evelina accepted only the latter. The news came out in the papers, and people said that Evita would pay a visit to Mar del Plata to have a look. She was not able to come because she was suffering from pains in her abdomen, and the doctors made her stay in bed. The candidacy for the vice presidency was stalled, and pretty Evelina, whom nobody now called *pretty,* seemed doomed to a perpetual fast. The curiosity of the first days was lessening. When the autumn rains started, visitors to the beach disappeared, and the notaries began to drop out. The only person to take pity on pretty Evelina was a girl cousin of her own age, who regularly appeared every night to bring Evelina her glass of water and left the tent weeping.

The story had an unhappy ending. On the eve of Holy Week a violent storm came up that kept people at home and tore trees up by the roots. When it died down, not a single tent nor the slightest trace of pretty Evelina was left on Bristol Beach. When it announced this news, the daily *La razón* commented sarcastically: "The Bristol Beach episode clearly proves that the climate of Mar del Plata is inhospitable to fasting."

Pretty Evelina's sacrifice was not in vain. Thousands of imitators soon appeared, trying to force their way into Evita's imagination, though at less deadly risk. Two workers in a factory that made tin-plate artwork, who also backed her candidacy for the vice presidency, beat the world record for continuous work by turning out decorations for facades for ninety-eight hours in a row, but they had almost no chance to savor their feat because seven foremen from another factory beat them by assembling and polishing cylinders for 109 hours without stopping. The daily *Democracia* published on its front page a photograph of the seven of them, overcome by sleep at the foot of a huge column of tubing.

Evita's life was meanwhile sinking deeper and deeper into misfortune. She was obliged to give up her candidacy before a million people who wept and paraded past the presidential box on their knees. A month later she was hospitalized with fulminating anemia, another symptom of her cancer of the uterus. Almost immediately thereafter she went through two terrible operations in which she was gutted and scraped till they thought she was free of malignant cells. She lost more than forty pounds, and an expression of sadness that nobody had ever seen there before, not even in her days of hunger and humiliation, was now engraved on her face.

Nor did all this earn her the pity of her enemies, who also numbered in the thousands. Argentines who thought of themselves as the depositaries of civilization saw in Evita an obscene resurrection of barbarism. Indians, blacks with no morals, bums, hoodlums, pimps straight out of Arlt, wild gauchos, consumptive whores smuggled into the country on Polish ships, party girls from the provinces: all of them had now been exterminated or confined to their dark cellars. When European philosophers came on a visit, they discovered a country so ethereal and spiritual that they thought it had evaporated. Eva Duarte's sudden entry onstage ruined the pastel portrait of cultivated Argentina. That vulgar chick, that bastard B-girl, that little shit—as she was called at cattle auctions — was the last fart of barbarism. As it wafted by, you had to hold your nose.

All of a sudden, the champions of civilization learned to their relief that the knife blades of cancer were slashing into the uterus of "that woman." In *Sur,* the review that was the refuge of the Argentine intelligentsia, the poet Silvina Ocampo foresaw, in emphatic rhymed couplets, the end of the nightmare:

May the sun no longer rise, nor yet the moon
if tyrants like these sow more misfortune,
by conning the country. May these be the last days
of that creeping species, that accursed race.

On the walls that lead to the Retiro railway station, not very far from the presidential residence where Evita lay dying, someone painted an ill-omened slogan, LONG LIVE CANCER, and signed it PRETTY EVELINA. When the radio announced that Evita's condition was extremely serious, the opposition politicians opened bottles of champagne. The essayist Ezequiel Martínez Estrada, covered from head to foot with a thick black crust that the doctors identified as neuromelanoderma, was miraculously cured and began to write a compendium of invective in which Evita was referred to in these terms: "She is a sublimation of what is morally vile, despicable, abject, monstrous, vengeful, ophidian, and the people see her as an incarnation of the infernal gods."

In those same days, confronted with the certainty that Evita would go to heaven at any moment, thousands of people made the most exorbitant sacrifices so that, when it came time for her to account for herself to God, she would mention their names in the conversation. Every two or three hours, a believer would establish a world record for work without stopping, whether by assembling safety locks or cooking noodles. Leopoldo Carreras, the billiard champion, hit fifteen hundred caroms in a row in the atrium of the basilica of Luján. A professional named Juan Carlos Papa danced tangos for 127 hours with the same number of partners. The *Guinness Book of World Records* was not yet published in those days, and unfortunately all these records have fallen into oblivion.

The churches were full to overflowing with petitioners offering their lives in Evita's stead or else praying to the celestial courts to receive her with the honors due a queen. Records were made for glider flights, distances walked carrying sacks of maize slung over one shoulder, delivering bread, horseback rides, parachute jumps, walking across a bed of hot coals or barbed wire, outings in a sulky or on a bicycle. The taxi driver Pedro Caldas covered the distance between Buenos Aires and Rosario, almost two hundred miles, by running

Wake for Evita's death (1952). A portrait of Eva Perón rises over her grieving admirers during the twelve-day mourning period following her premature death at thirty-three. Courtesy Archivo General de la Nación, Buenos Aires.

backward on an oil barrel; the seamstress Irma Ceballos embroidered an Our Father three-eighths of an inch square in thirty-three different colors of silk thread, and, when she finished it, she sent it to Pope Pius XII, threatening to renounce her obedience to him as a Catholic if the Sacred Heart of Jesus did not immediately restore the health of "our beloved saint."

But the most famous of all the undertakings was that of the saddlemaker Raimundo Masa, along with his wife, Dominga, and his three children, the youngest of which was still nursing. Masa had just delivered a couple of saddles in San Nicolás when he heard some mule drivers talking about Evita's serious condition. That same day he decided to go on a pilgrimage with all his family to the Christ the Redeemer in the Andes, six hundred miles to the west, promising to return on foot as well if the sick woman recovered. At the rate of twelve miles a day, the journey there was going to take almost two months, he calculated. He loaded a few tins of powdered milk, jerky, hardtack, filtered water, and a change of clothes into knapsacks and wrote a letter to Evita explaining his mission to her and announcing that he would visit her on his return. He asked her not to forget his name and, if possible, to mention him in a speech, if only in code: "Just say regards to Raimundo, and I'll get the message."

He stopped on the endless plain with the whole family to recite the rosary, without taking his eyes off the trail and with an expression of inconsolable grief on his face. Dominga was carrying the nursing baby in a basket hung around her neck; the other two were tied with cords to Raimundo's waist so they wouldn't wander off and get lost. Every time they went through a town the parish priest, the pharmacist, and the ladies of the social club in their Sunday dresses just taken out of their nests of mothballs turned out to welcome them. They offered them cups of chocolate and hot showers, which Raimundo firmly refused so as not to lose time, paying no attention to the despair of his two older sons, who couldn't stand their diet of jerky any longer.

After forty days they went into the dreary desert between the cities of San Luis and La Dormida, where a hundred years before Juan Facundo Quiroga had escaped from the talons of a jaguar by climbing to the top of the one carob tree that grew in those desolate expanses. There seemed to be no end to the inhospitable landscape, the sun beat down mercilessly, and, owing to his lack of experience, Raimundo had allowed his children to drink up all the water. He turned off the main road and took the shortcuts laid down at the beginning of the century to confuse army deserters. The older boys fainted, and the father had to leave his knapsacks with the provisions behind so as to carry the two children on his back. On the third day he lost heart and was afraid he was going to die. Sitting at the entrance of a dusty cave, he prayed that all his mortifications had not been in vain and God would restore to Evita the health she had lost. It troubled Dominga, who was suffering in silence, that at this crucial hour her husband seemed to be giving no thought to the fate of his family.

"We are who we are, nobodies," Raimundo pointed out to her. "If Evita dies, though, those left without hope will number in the thousands. There are people like us everywhere, but there is only one saint like Evita."

Translated by Helen Lane

Ramona's Revenge

Lino Palacio

The 1930s and 1940s witnessed a flowering of graphic humor. With the profusion of newspapers and magazines, the popularity of comics reached unprecedented heights. Drawing from urban life, writers and draftsmen poked fun at different social groups by satirizing their customs, beliefs, and prejudices. Ramona, a comic strip by Lino Palacio that appeared in the newspaper La razón, *chose for one of its main targets the conflicts between middle-class families and their female domestic servants. In Palacio's formula, wit sparks from the extreme naïveté of the main character, an almost illiterate maid called Ramona. In following their requests and orders literally, Ramona takes revenge on her employers' sense of superiority and inadvertently exposes their petty values to a progressive readership.*

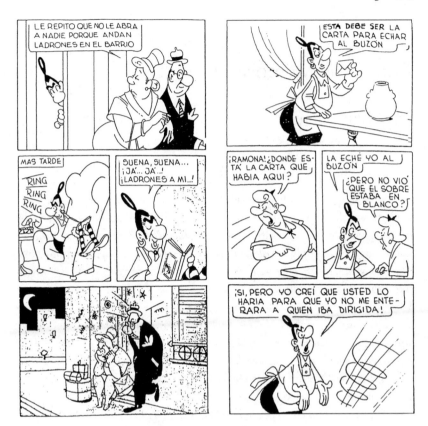

(above left)

Miss X: "I am telling you again. Do not open the door to anybody. There have been robberies in the neighborhood."

Later. "Ring, ring, ring."

Ramona: "Keep ringing!! Ha, ha!! No thief is gonna fool me!"

(above right)

Ramona: "This must be the letter to drop in the mailbox."

Miss X: "Ramona! Where is the letter I left here?"

Ramona: "I put it in the mailbox already."

Miss X: "But DIDN'T YOU SEE that the envelope did not have anything written on it?"

Ramona: "Yes, of course, but I thought that it was because you didn't want me to see to whom it was addressed!!"

Translated by Gabriela Nouzeilles

Funes, the Memorious

Jorge Luis Borges

Among the many issues that Peronism helped reconfigure, national identity was a particularly sensitive topic. The massive waves of unskilled workers who migrated from the countryside to the eastern cities reawakened the old antagonism between the more autochthonous, ethnically mixed interior and cosmopolitan, European Buenos Aires. This long-standing divide sparked yet another debate on the meaning of being Argentine. When Perón's administration launched programs giving the majority of people better access to cultural production, it clearly favored those works considered more local and closer to popular lore. This emphasis on the national popular was further stressed by propaganda. There was hardly any room for plurality or ambiguity. Jorge Luis Borges's stand on cultural identity was at odds with these Peronist cultural preferences. In "The Argentine Writer and Tradition" (1951), an essay that openly defied all narrow definitions of Argentinism, he contended that Argentine culture was not limited to one tradition but open to all; if there was anything one could call Argentine, it was the complex intermingling of all sorts of cultural heritages. "Funes, the Memorious" (1942) sharply conveys Borges's cultural poetics. Both a metaphor for insomnia and a philosophical digression on perception and memory, this short story is also a reflection on the relation between local and Western traditions. According to Borges, gauchos need not to be limited to one-dimensional caricatures of nationalistic mythologies; they could also be the bearers of universal obsessions around the concepts of time, space, and subjectivity.

I remember him (I scarcely have the right to use this ghostly verb; only one man on earth deserved the right, and he is dead), I remember him with a dark passionflower in his hand, looking at it as no one has ever looked at such a flower, though they might look from the twilight of day until the twilight of night, for a whole life long. I remember him, his face immobile and Indian-like, and singularly remote, behind his cigarette. I remember (I believe) the strong delicate fingers of the plainsman who can braid leather. I remember, near those hands, a vessel in which to make mate tea, bearing the arms of the Banda Oriental;[1] I remember, in the window of the house, a yellow rush mat, and beyond, a vague marshy landscape. I remember clearly his voice, the deliberate, resentful, nasal voice of the old Eastern Shore man, without the Italianate syllables of today. I did not see him more than three times; the last time, in 1887. . . .

That all those who knew him should write something about him seems to me a very felicitous idea; my testimony may perhaps be the briefest and without doubt the poorest, and it will not be the least impartial. The deplorable fact of my being an Argentinian will hinder me from falling into a dithyramb—an obligatory form in the Uruguay, when the theme is an Uruguayan.

Littérateur, slicker, Buenos Airean: Funes did not use these insulting phrases, but I am sufficiently aware that for him I represented these unfortunate categories. Pedro Leandro Ipuche has written that Funes was a precursor of the superman, "an untamed and vernacular Zarathustra"; I do not doubt it, but one must not forget, either, that he was a countryman from the town of Fray Bentos, with certain incurable limitations.

My first recollection of Funes is quite clear, I see him at dusk, sometime in March or February of the year '84. That year, my father had taken me to spend the summer at Fray Bentos. I was on my way back from the farm at San Francisco with my cousin Bernardo Haedo. We came back singing, on horseback; and this last fact was not the only reason for my joy. After a sultry day, an enormous slate-gray storm had obscured the sky. It was driven on by a wind from the south; the trees were already tossing like madmen; and I had the apprehension (the secret hope) that the elemental downpour would catch us out in the open. We were running a kind of race with the tempest. We rode into a narrow lane which wound down between two enormously high brick footpaths. It had grown black of a sudden; I now heard rapid almost secret steps above; I raised my eyes and saw a boy running along the narrow, cracked path as if he were running along a narrow, broken wall. I remember the loose trousers, tight at the bottom, the hemp sandals; I remember the cigarette in the hard visage, standing out against the by now limitless darkness. Bernardo unexpectedly yelled to him: "What's the time, Ireneo?" Without looking up, without stopping, Ireneo replied: "In ten minutes it will be eight o'clock, child Bernardo Juan Francisco." The voice was sharp, mocking.

I am so absentminded that the dialogue which I have just cited would not have penetrated my attention if it had not been repeated by my cousin, who was stimulated, I think, by a certain local pride and by a desire to show himself indifferent to the other's three-sided reply.

He told me that the boy above us in the pass was a certain Ireneo Funes, renowned for a number of eccentricities, such as that of having nothing to do with people and of always knowing the time, like a watch. He added that Ireneo was the son of María Clementina Funes, an ironing woman in the town, and that his father, some people said, was an "Englishman" named O'Connor, a doctor in the salting fields, though some said the father was a horse-breaker, or scout, from the province of El Salto. Ireneo lived with his mother, at the edge of the country house of the Laurels.

In the years '83 and '86 we spent the summer in the city of Montevideo. We returned to Fray Bentos in '87. As was natural, I inquired after all my acquaintances, and finally, about "the chronometer Funes." I was told that he had been thrown by a wild horse at the San Francisco ranch, and that he had been hopelessly crippled. I remember the impression of uneasy magic which the news provoked in me: the only time I had seen him we were on horseback, coming from San Francisco, and he was in a high place; from the lips of my cousin Bernardo the affair sounded like a dream elaborated with elements out of the past. They told me that Ireneo did not move now from his cot, but remained with his eyes fixed on the backyard fig tree, or on a cobweb. At sunset he allowed himself to be brought to the window. He carried pride to the extreme of pretending that the blow which had befallen him was a good thing. . . . Twice I saw him behind the iron grate which sternly delineated his eternal imprisonment: unmoving, once, his eyes closed; unmoving also, another time, absorbed in the contemplation of a sweet-smelling sprig of lavender cotton.

At the time I had begun, not without some ostentation, the methodical study of Latin. My valise contained the *De viris illustribus* of Lhomond, the *Thesaurus* of Quicherat, Caesar's *Commentaries,* and an odd-numbered volume of the *Historia naturalis* of Pliny, which exceeded (and still exceeds) my modest talents as a Latinist. Everything is noised around in a small town; Ireneo, at his small farm on the outskirts, was not long in learning of the arrival of these anomalous books. He sent me a flowery, ceremonious letter, in which he recalled our encounter, unfortunately brief, "on the seventh day of February of the year '84," and alluded to the glorious services which Don Gregorio Haedo, my uncle, dead the same year, "had rendered to the Two Fatherlands in the glorious campaign of Ituzaingó," and he solicited the loan of any one of the volumes, to be accompanied by a dictionary "for the better intelligence of the original text, for I do not know Latin as yet." He promised to return them in good condition, almost immediately. The letter was perfect, very nicely constructed; the orthography was of the type sponsored by Andrés Bello: *i* for *y, j* for *g.* At first I naturally suspected a jest. My cousins assured me it was not so, that these were the ways of Ireneo. I did not know whether to attribute to impudence, ignorance, or stupidity, the idea that the difficult Latin required no other instrument than a dictionary; in order fully to undeceive him I sent the *Gradus ad Parnassum* of Quicherat, and the Pliny.

On February 14, I received a telegram from Buenos Aires telling me to return immediately, for my father was in no way well. God forgive me, but the prestige of being the recipient of an urgent telegram, the desire to point out to all of Fray Bentos the contradiction between the negative form of the news and the positive adverb, the temptation to dramatize my sorrow as I feigned a virile stoicism, all no doubt distracted me from the possibility of anguish. As I packed my valise, I noted that I was missing the *Gradus* and the volume of the *Historia naturalis.* The *Saturn* was to weigh anchor on the morning of the next day; that night, after supper, I made my way to the house of Funes. Outside, I was surprised to find the night no less oppressive than the day.

Ireneo's mother received me at the modest ranch.

She told me that Ireneo was in the back room and that I should not be disturbed to find him in the dark, for he knew how to pass the dead hours without lighting the candle. I crossed the cobblestone patio, the small corridor; I came to the second patio. A great vine covered everything, so that the darkness seemed complete. Of a sudden I heard the high-pitched, mocking voice of Ireneo. The voice spoke in Latin; the voice (which came out of the obscurity) was reading, with obvious delight, a treatise or prayer or incantation. The Roman syllables resounded in the earthen patio; my suspicion made them seem undecipherable, interminable; afterwards, in the enormous dialogue of that night, I learned that they made up the first paragraph of the twenty-fourth chapter of the seventh book of the *Historia naturalis.* The subject of this chapter is memory; the last words are *ut nihil non iisdem verbis redderetur auditum.*

Without the least change in his voice, Ireneo bade me come in. He was lying on the cot, smoking. It seems to me that I did not see his face until dawn; I seem to recall the momentary glow of the cigarette. The room smelled vaguely of dampness. I sat down, and repeated the story of the telegram and my father's illness.

I come now to the most difficult point in my narrative. For the entire story has no other point (the reader might as well know it by now) than this dialogue of almost a half-century ago. I shall not attempt to reproduce his words, now irrecoverable. I prefer truthfully to make a résumé of the many things Ireneo told me. The indirect style is remote and weak; I know that I sacrifice the effectiveness of my narrative; but let my readers imagine the nebulous sentences which clouded that night.

Ireneo began by enumerating, in Latin and Spanish, the cases of prodigious memory cited in the *Historia naturalis:* Cyrus, king of the Persians, who could call every soldier in his armies by name; Mithridates Eupator, who administered justice in the twenty-two languages of his empire; Simonides, inventor of mnemotechny; Metrodorus, who practiced the art of repeating faithfully what he heard once. With evident good faith Funes marveled that such things should be considered marvelous. He told me that previous to the rainy afternoon when the blue-tinted horse threw him, he had been—like any Christian—blind, deaf-mute, somnambulistic, memoryless. (I tried to remind him of his precise perception of time, his memory for proper names; he paid no attention to me.) For nineteen years, he said, he had lived like a person in a dream: he looked without seeing, heard without hearing, forgot everything—almost everything. On falling from the horse, he lost consciousness; when he recovered it, the present was almost intolerable it was so rich and bright; the same was true of the most ancient and most trivial memories. A little later he realized that he was crippled. This fact scarcely interested him. He reasoned (or felt) that immobility was a minimum price to pay. And now, his perception and his memory were infallible.

We, in a glance, perceive three wine glasses on the table; Funes saw all the shoots, clusters, and grapes of the vine. He remembered the shapes of the clouds in the south at dawn on 30 April 1882, and he could compare them in his recollection with the marbled grain in the design of a leather-bound book which he had seen only once, and with the lines in the spray which an oar raised in the Río Negro on the eve of the Battle of the Quebracho. These recollections were not simple; each visual image was linked to muscular sensations, thermal sensations, etc. He could reconstruct all his dreams, all his fancies. Two or three times he had reconstructed an entire day. He told me: *I have more memories in myself alone than all men have had since the world was a world.* And again: *My dreams are like your vigils.* And again, toward dawn: *My memory, sir, is like a garbage disposal.*

A circumference on a blackboard, a rectangular triangle, a rhomb, are forms which we can fully intuit; the same held true with Ireneo for the tempestuous mane of a stallion, a herd of cattle in a pass, the ever-changing flame or the innumerable ash, the many faces of a dead man during the course of a protracted wake. He could perceive I do not know how many stars in the sky.

These things he told me; neither then nor at any time later did they seem doubtful. In those days neither the cinema nor the phonograph yet existed; nevertheless, it seems strange, almost incredible, that no one should have experimented on Funes. The truth is that we all live by leaving behind; no doubt we all profoundly know that we are immortal and that sooner or later every man will do all things and know everything.

The voice of Funes, out of the darkness, continued. He told me that toward

1886 he had devised a new system of enumeration and that in a very few days he had gone beyond twenty-four thousand. He had not written it down, for what he once meditated would not be erased. The first stimulus to his work, I believe, had been his discontent with the fact that "thirty-three Uruguayans" required two symbols and three words, rather than a single word and a single symbol. Later he applied his extravagant principle to the other numbers. In place of seven thousand thirteen, he would say (for example) *Máximo Perez;* in place of seven thousand fourteen, *The Train;* other numbers were *Luis Melián Lafinur, Olimar, Brimstone, Clubs, The Whale, Gas, The Cauldron, Napoleon, Agustín de Vedia.* In lieu of five hundred, he would say *nine.* Each word had a particular sign, a species of mark; the last were very complicated. . . . I attempted to explain that this rhapsody of unconnected terms was precisely the contrary of a system of enumeration. I said that to say three hundred and sixty-five was to say three hundreds, six tens, five units: an analysis which does not exist in such numbers as *The Negro Timoteo* or *The Flesh Blanket.* Funes did not understand me, or did not wish to understand me.

Locke, in the seventeenth century, postulated (and rejected) an impossible idiom in which each individual object, each stone, each bird and branch had an individual name; Funes had once projected an analogous idiom, but he had renounced it as being too general, too ambiguous. In effect, Funes not only remembered every leaf on every tree of every wood, but even every one of the times he had perceived or imagined it. He determined to reduce all of his past experience to some seventy thousand recollections, which he would later define numerically. Two considerations dissuaded him: the thought that the task was interminable and the thought that it was useless. He knew that at the hour of his death he would scarcely have finished classifying even all the memories of his childhood.

The two projects I have indicated (an infinite vocabulary for the natural series of numbers, and a usable mental catalog of all the images of memory) are lacking in sense, but they reveal a certain stammering greatness. They allow us to make out dimly, or to infer, the dizzying world of Funes. He was, let us not forget, almost incapable of general, platonic ideas. It was not only difficult for him to understand that the generic term *dog* embraced so many unlike specimens of differing sizes and different forms; he was disturbed by the fact that a dog at three-fourteen (seen in profile) should have the same name as the dog at three-fifteen (seen from the front). His own face in the mirror, his own hands, surprised him on every occasion. Swift writes that the emperor of Lilliput could discern the movement of the minute hand; Funes could continuously make out the tranquil advances of corruption, of caries, of fatigue. He noted the progress of death, of moisture. He was the solitary and lucid spectator of a multiform world which was instantaneously and almost intolerably exact. Babylon, London, and New York have overawed the imagination of men with their ferocious splendor; no one, in those populous towers or upon those surging avenues, has felt the heat and pressure of a reality as indefatigable as that which day and night converged upon the unfortunate Ireneo in his humble South American farmhouse. It was very difficult for him to sleep. To sleep is to be abstracted from the world; Funes, on his back in his cot, in the shadows, imagined every crevice and every molding of the various houses which surrounded him. (I repeat, the least important of his recollections was more minutely precise and more lively than our perception of a physical pleasure or a physical torment.) Toward the east, in a section which was not yet cut into blocks of homes, there were some new unknown houses. Funes imagined them black, compact, made of a single obscurity; he would turn his face in this direction in order to sleep. He would also imagine himself at the bottom of the river, being rocked and annihilated by the current.

Without effort, he had learned English, French, Portuguese, Latin. I suspect, nevertheless, that he was not very capable of thought. To think is to forget a difference, to generalize, to abstract. In the overly replete world of Funes there were nothing but details, almost contiguous details.

The equivocal clarity of dawn penetrated along the earthen patio.

Then it was that I saw the face of the voice which had spoken all through the night. Ireneo was nineteen years old; he had been born in 1868; he seemed as monumental as bronze, more ancient than Egypt, anterior to the prophecies and the pyramids. It occurred to me that each one of my words (each one of my gestures) would live on in his implacable memory; I was benumbed by the fear of multiplying superfluous gestures.

Ireneo Funes died in 1889, of a pulmonary congestion.

Translated by Anthony Kerrigan

Note

1 The Eastern Shore (of the Uruguay River); now the Republic of Uruguay.

Victorian Fathers

Victoria Ocampo

*Victoria Ocampo (1890–1979), founder and director of the sophisticated literary jour-
nal* Sur *(1933–70) and member of a well-known landowning family, opposed Perón and
his administration from a strongly elitist position. As a woman, Victoria Ocampo was
Eva Perón's aristocratic opposite. Victoria was very well educated, had traveled extensively, spoke several languages, and at times partook of the sexual freedoms enjoyed by
those protected by aristocratic discretion. Although both were concerned with women's
issues, there were important differences between their positions. Eva, who used her
power and influence to improve labor conditions for female workers and encouraged
women to get involved in politics through voting and party work, advanced—at least
in her public statements—an image of the ideal woman whose defining role was to
be a loyal companion, always standing by her man. By comparison, although within
a narrower social range, Victoria's position regarding women's freedom appears more
consistent. Inspired by Virginia Woolf's feminist writings, she demanded a room of
their own for all educated and ambitious Argentine women constrained by the Victorian mores of their bourgeois families. But, when it came to Peronism, her feminist
views were not free from contradiction. In 1947, when women's suffrage was finally
won under Peronism, for reasons still difficult to understand, she opposed the new
legislation.*

Reading Sophocles, Virginia Woolf compares Electra with Emily Brontë. She
sees the same kind of feminine heroism in Greece as in England. But Electra
suffered under a more oppressive burden and more suffocating customs than
those that the Victorian taboos imposed. Nevertheless, some Greek prohibitions were the exact equivalent of the one Virginia sums up by the phrase "a
maid and a hansom cab." The daughter of a prominent man had to be married
before she could walk alone through Piccadilly and before she could go out
by herself in a cab. She wouldn't have dreamed she could do so daring a thing
without stirring up her whole family. Like most of my contemporaries, I have
gone through this experience. It always seemed grotesque to me.

Victoria Ocampo at age seventy-seven, at the bookstore El Ateneo (1967). Courtesy Archivo General de la Nación, Buenos Aires.

The maid, Virginia observes in *Three Guineas,* had an important role in the life of the English upper classes (and the same was true in Argentina) until the onset of the war in 1914. The maid escorted, not only young girls, but also married women. I have known some women who felt secretly flattered because their husbands would not permit them to go out in a taxi without taking a maid along as a chaperone. An interesting book could be written on the theme: "The role of the maid in the leisure classes." . . . I am referring here to the services that the fathers or husbands entrusted to the maids and not to those that the maids rendered according to their own judgment and character. Virginia sarcastically emphasizes that after a certain time the protection of chastity by maids becomes too costly an item for the bourgeois budget.

In order for a young girl to "preserve her body intact for her future husband" (whatever that may mean), who generally didn't restrain from wild escapades; in order for a wife to avoid the risk of being unfaithful to a husband who rarely devoted his fidelity to her, nothing better was found than to put those females (this is the name that squares with such treatment) under the custody of another female in whom, one doesn't know by what characteristic aberration of masculine logic, one had more confidence.

Virginia Woolf felt passionately about this matter, and thanks to this she was able to give her writing full measure of her satirical spirit, of her sense of the comical, just as she revealed her love for fairness and her blessed indignation in the face of all dictatorial attitudes. *A Room of One's Own* and *Three Guineas* are the true history of the Victorian struggle between the victims of the patriarchal system and the patriarchs, between the daughters and the fathers and brothers. Virginia ended up by telling these despots: Consider, reason, reflect for a moment. Our struggle, the one of women against the tyranny of the patriarchal conditions imposed by you, is analogous to the struggle that you were later to engage in against the tyranny of the fascist, Hitlerist state.

Our struggle was not merely about "a maid and a hansom cab" nor the prohibition of smoking cigarettes (things that became important, disquieting, as symptoms, because of the prohibition itself). Our struggle also concerned the right to choose a husband and a career. The case of the Reverend Patrick Brontë was not an isolated case, nor did it in any way provoke the censure of the society of its time. This Anglican minister became famous only because Charlotte Brontë, the victim, was famous. It was a common case. When the author of *Jane Eyre* wanted to marry Nicholles (another minister, a respectable man in the sense in which the elder Brontë understood respectability, consequently making Nicholles acceptable as a son-in-law), her father forbade the marriage. There was no motive other than caprice, beyond the desire to keep Charlotte for himself, for his exclusive service. For months the poor girl submitted, suffered, debated with herself. She didn't dare rebel for fear that her father's health might be jeopardized, for fear that an act of unusual insubordination might be a mortal blow to him. (Oh, such innocence. The Reverend finally died of old age. She was the one who was to die in the full bloom of youth when the stubborn patriarch finally consented to her marriage, which lasted less than a year.) Society of the Victorian era remained undaunted by the conduct of the Reverend Brontë. However, as Virginia notes, if he had publicly tortured a dog or stolen a watch, his reputation would have suffered. . . .

The Victorian and post-Victorian fathers who acted in ways similar to Patrick Brontë today form a great multitude of anonymous and forgotten shadows. If their hardness of heart and their infantile egotism (in which psychiatrists today would detect some fixation) have been forgiven in heaven, so much the better. Here on earth Virginia Woolf has settled accounts with them in *Three Guineas,* without ever abandoning her enchanting and implacable smile.

She never underestimated, as other ungrateful and ignorant women have, what the woman of today owes to her heroic sisters of the past, the suffragettes, the feminists, who were treated with contempt, reviled, ridiculed. Their battle, our battle, was long and fierce.

This is what happened to us in Argentina around 1935: a reform of the Civil

Code threatened the limited rights that had already been won by women. With respect to the economic aspects of life, married women were to share the fate of minors and the insane. Without authorization from her husband, according to the projected reform, a woman would not be able: first, to work in any profession, industry, or business; second, to freely dispose of the product of her labor; third, to administer her property (the husband was to be its responsible, legal administrator); fourth, to become a member of any society, civil, commercial, or etc.; fifth, to make or receive donations.

The matter appeared to us so senseless and serious that some friends and I decided to protest to the magistrates who were to decide on the reform. It fell to me to visit two of these magistrates, one of them an important person. This last man felt it was reasonable and healthy, for example, for a woman to need the consent of her husband, not only to work outside her home—of course, in her house she could break her back from sunrise to sunset—but also to carry on a professional career, It is necessary, the magistrate said, that there be a head of the family, just as there is a captain on a ship. Otherwise, there would be confusion in the home. What would happen if a woman got it into her head to work in an office as a typist? She would leave her children in the hands of hired help; she would neglect the household chores; she would abandon her husband since there wouldn't be time for watching over his material well-being. I answered him that the ladies who spend their lives in dress shops, in movies, in theaters, at cocktail parties, at bridge tournaments (canasta was still unknown), also left their children in hired hands. To make matters worse, the magistrate added, the typist would expose herself to temptations. The magistrate seemed to believe that an office (the boss, male employees at all levels) was a cauldron of dangers for a woman determined to earn her own living. He was obsessed by that image.

As I insisted on defending the rights of women to work and to live on an equal footing with men, he concluded by saying: "But, Madam, remember your parents, the way they have educated you. What have you seen in your own family? Was your father the head or not? What role did your mother have?" I responded that, although I loved my parents very much, I had never shared their ideas on that point, nor even on others, which of course was neither original nor exceptional. The generations that succeed each other rarely agree with one another. Especially these days. The magistrate heard me as one hears the rain.

We went from that subject to the subject of children born out of wedlock and those born of adultery. It is obvious that I found it absurd that those recently come to our vale of tears would be condemned to expiate for the sins—if they were sins—of their fathers. Naively—according to the judge—I thought that all children were natural and that only the parents could be accused of being unnatural. This assertion infuriated the magistrate.

He responded that, if a man were tempted beyond his strength, he shouldn't be exposed to the possibility of falling into the trap of some adventuress who might break up his home. What wouldn't a woman without scruples do to get money from him if the law didn't intervene? If children were all equal before the law, the tranquillity of the home would be forever compromised, threatened, and destroyed. I asked him then if there wasn't some advantage in that men might learn to resist temptations and to realize the kinds of situations to which these temptations might expose them. The magistrate smiled at me with paternal indulgence. "Men, Madam, are often weak when confronted by temptation. The law must take this into account and protect them." The reply came by itself. "And women?" No. Women, if they were respectable, knew how to avoid those temptations that for men were not resistible (and for that reason itself were excusable). If the law gave them the chance, the adventuresses, experts in masculine weakness, would take even more advantage of such situations than they had already.

For the magistrate in question, it was always the woman who offered the fruit of the tree of good and evil. As he talked of all this, he spoke in clipped tones. Legitimate children, born of legal marriages, had to be protected. And the other kind? Their situation was to be lamented, but what could one do? There are such sad fates in life. "No," I shouted. "That is precisely the case in which sad fate does not come into play; it is rather a case of men's egotism." In response, he again asked me what I had observed in my own family.

Finally he said to me: "Madam, you are a widow, are you not? And independent, from the economic point of view?" I answered yes for the first time in that interview. "Then," he went on, "why do you bother yourself with problems that are not yours?"

Since there was talk of giving the husband the power to annul his marriage if he could prove that his wife was not a virgin, we discussed the subject of virginity with another magistrate. First, I asked if the woman could annul the contract for the same reasons. With that smile of commiseration that I already knew well, the magistrate answered: "Naturally not." I asked if virginity in the widow was also required. New smile — they are a different case, he assured me. (The magistrate thought, no doubt, that he was dealing with an idiot or a shameless woman.) I asked then if he and those other gentlemen found it just as easy to pronounce judgment on similar questions. If their analysis of virginity might not be used to support deplorable abuses and every kind of blackmail. I asked if that clause about causes for annulment was not humiliating and intolerable from the woman's point of view. The magistrate did not show that he had very clear ideas on the point.

In England it is not until 1916 that Asquith stops opposing the political rights of women. And only in 1919 do they remove the barriers to entry into the professions. The same year the first woman, Lady Astor, sits in the British House of Commons. Even today, 1954, women are not admitted in the House of Lords. In that respect, what John Stuart Mill wrote in his *The Subjection of Women* continues to be true: "But Queen Elizabeth or Queen Victoria, had they not inherited the throne, could not have been entrusted with the smallest of the political duties, of which the former showed herself equal to the greatest."

A Room of One's Own appears in 1929, *Three Guineas* in 1938. As impossible as it may seem today, the struggle for women's rights was not completed, even though, thanks to World War I, the movement had gained decisively. Virginia writes in her diary, on the eve of launching *A Room of One's Own*: "I am afraid it will not be taken seriously. Mrs. Woolf is so accomplished a writer that all she says makes easy reading. . . ." But she has written that book with passion and conviction. What she longs for are not praises for her skill as a writer. And, as for *Three Guineas,* page after page have sprung from her pen, she tells us, "like a physical volcano."

In the years between the Victorian era and ours, how many forms of reactions have there been against the patriarchal dictatorship, against that male right to treat "respectable" women as obedient nurses and chained virgins, and to treat the other women, those who aren't "respectable," as vile cattle. We only have to look around to find the answer.

If we could study the intimate life, the infancy, the adolescence of famous women — those who for one reason or another have excelled in the last hundred years — we would discover the preponderant role played in those lives by the rebellion against feeling themselves the eternal nurse, the eternal virgin, the eternal flock of sheep. We would realize then the humiliation of enduring the arbitrary masculine dictatorship, whether it came from the most affectionate of fathers or from the most altruistic brother. For, if our century is that of recognizing the rights of the proletariat, it is also, with greater reason, the century of the emancipation of women. (The *feminine proletariat* embraces all classes, equally suppressed by male tyranny, while the *proletariat* only applies to one class.) That is to say that this is the century in which women begin to be treated equally, as people and not as objects, however sacred that object might be. And it matters little that men placed "the object" on an altar, a place that made vigilance all the easier.

Translated by Patricia Owen Steiner

The Foreign Gaze

Witold Gombrowicz

The Polish writer Witold Gombrowicz (1904–69) arrived in Buenos Aires for a short visit in 1939, just one day before World War II began. Unable to return to his country, he remained in Argentina for twenty-four years. Since he did not master Spanish and could not join the cultural elite, Gombrowicz formed groups of young marginal intellectuals with whom he discussed Argentine society with a sense of parody and detachment. His Diaries *offer a simultaneously critical and admiring evaluation of the country where he initially felt imprisoned but that eventually became his home. In these two entries from 1953 and 1954, Gombrowicz evaluates the cultural and social dimensions of the ongoing antagonism between the local educated elite and the popular classes who supported Perón.*

Thursday

Concert in Colón.

What is the significance of the best virtuoso compared to the disposition of my soul, which today, this afternoon, was permeated through and through with a melody, badly hummed by someone so that now, this evening, it pushes away the music served on a golden platter (along with the meatballs) by a *maître* in tails. The food does not always taste best in first-class restaurants. To me, art almost always speaks more forcefully when it appears in an imperfect, accidental, and fragmentary way, somehow just signaling its presence, allowing one to feel it through the ineptitude of the interpretation. I prefer the Chopin that reaches me in the street from an open window to the Chopin served in great style from the concert stage.

This German pianist galloped along accompanied by the orchestra. Rocked to sleep by the tones, my mind wandered in some sort of daydream—reminiscences, things that I had to get done the next day, Bumfili, the fox terrier. In the meantime, the concert continued, the pianist galloped on. Was he a pianist or a horse? I could swear that this had nothing to do with Mozart but rather with whether or not this nimble steed would wrestle the bit away from Horowitz or Rubinstein. The folks present were concerned with the question: of what class is this virtuoso? Do his *pianos* measure up to those of Arrau's? Are his *fortes* attaining the heights of Gulda's? I imagined, therefore, that this was a boxing match and I saw how he drove Brailowski down the ropes, how he punched Gieseking with the octaves, and aimed a knockout trill at Solomon. A pianist, a horse, or a boxer? It also seemed to me that he was a boxer who had mounted Mozart, who was riding Mozart, pounding and hitting him, jangling and jabbing him with his spurs. What's that? He's reached the finish line? Applause, applause, applause! The jockey got off his horse and bowed, wiping his forehead with a handkerchief.

The countess with whom I was sitting in the loge sighed: Oh how wonderful, wonderful, wonderful!

Her husband, the count, added: "I am not an expert, but I had the impression that the orchestra had a hard time keeping up."

I looked at them as if they were dogs! How upsetting when the aristocracy does not know how to behave! How little we demand of them, and then they can't even do that! These people ought to have known that music is only a pretext for a social get-together, of which even they were a part along with their manners and manicures. Yet instead of remaining in their territory, in their aristocratic-social world, they wanted to take art seriously, they felt obliged to pay it timid homage, and so, jolted out of their count- and countessness, they bumbled into sophomorism! I would have gladly agreed to purely formal platitudes, expressed with the cynicism of people who know the weight of compliments, but they tried to be honest—poor things!

After which we moved into the foyer. My eyes rested on an excellent little crowd that circulated, dispensing bows. Do you see the millionaire X, Y? Look, look, there is the general and the ambassador, and over there, the chairman is buttering up the minister, who is simpering in the direction of the professor's wife! I had the feeling, therefore, that I was among Proust's characters, who went to the concert not to listen but to grace it with their presence, where the ladies stuck Wagner into their hair as they would a diamond pin. Where the sounds of Bach accompanied the parade of names, ranks, titles, money, and power. But what's this, what's this? When I joined their ranks, I encountered the twilight of the gods, all the greatness and power were gone. I overheard them sharing their impressions of the concert, which were timid, humble, full of respect for music and worse than what an "aficionado" from the gallery could have said. This is what they had been reduced to. It seemed to me that these were not presidents but fifth-grade pupils, and because I return to my school days reluctantly, I left this timid youth.

Alone, in the loge, I, a modern person, deprived of superstitions, I, an anti-salon man, I out of whose head the whip of defeat had knocked the sulks and airs, thought that a world in which man adores himself with music is more convincing than a world in which man adores the music itself.

After which, the remainder of the concert got under way. The pianist, sitting down to Brahms, galloped on. No one really knew what was being played because the perfection of the pianist did not allow one to concentrate on Brahms, and the perfection of Brahms drew attention away from the pianist. But he got there. Applause. The applause of the knowledgeable. The applause of amateurs. The applause of the ignorant. The applause of the herd. Applause incited by applause. Applause feeding on itself, piling onto itself, exciting, creating applause. And no one could *not* clap because everyone was clapping. We went backstage to give our regards to the artist.

The artist was shaking hands, exchanging courtesies, and accepting compliments and invitations with the wan smile of an errant comet. I looked at him and his greatness. He himself seemed quite pleasant, yes, sensitive, intelligent, cultured, but his greatness? He wore that greatness the way he wore his tails, and, really, hadn't they been tailor-made? At the sight of so many eager kudos it might have seemed that there was no difference between his fame and Debussy's or Ravel's, after all, his name was on everyone's lips, too, and he was an "artist" as they had been. Yet . . . yet . . . was he famous like Beethoven or famous like Gillette blades or a Waterman pen? What a difference between the fame for which one pays and the one from which one makes a profit!

But he was too weak to oppose the mechanism that was exalting him, one could not expect resistance on his part. Quite the contrary. He danced to the tune. And he played for those who were dancing around him.

Friday

With the Spanish painter Sanza in Galeón. He came here for two months, sold paintings for a few hundred thousand, knows and values Lobodowski. In spite of the fact that he has made a ton of money in Argentina, he speaks about it without enthusiasm. "In Madrid, a person can sit at a table in a street café, and even though nothing specific awaits him, he knows that anything can happen: friendship, love, adventure. Here you know nothing will happen."

Sanza's discontent is quite restrained compared with what other tourists say. These foreigners pouting over Argentina, their lofty criticism and summary judgments don't seem to be of the highest category. Argentina is full of miracles and magic, but this charm is discrete; wrapped in a smile that does not want to express too much. Here we possess decent enough *materia prima* (raw material) even though we cannot yet afford manufactured products. We have no Nôtre Dame or Louvre, nevertheless, one does often see dazzling teeth, fabulous eyes, and the shape of harmonious, graceful bodies on the street. When from time to time cadets from the French navy visit us, the Argentine woman inevitably goes into raptures, as if she had seen Paris itself, but then she always says: What a shame they are not nicer looking. French actresses impress Argentineans with their Parisian perfume, but they also say: There isn't a single one with everything in the right place. This country, satiated with youth, has a certain aristocratic serenity, specific to creatures that move easily and don't need to be shy.

I am speaking mainly of the young people because it is characteristic of Argentina that its beauty is young and "low," earthy, you will not find it in larger amounts in the higher or median strata. Only the common people are distinctive. Only the common people are aristocratic. The young people alone are impeccable in every detail. This is a reversed country where the young strip-ling who sells the literary *revista* has more style than all of its collaborators put together; where the mediocrity of the plutocratic and intellectual salons is appalling; and where a catastrophe occurs when one turns thirty — the utter transformation of youth into uninteresting maturity.

Argentina, together with the rest of America, is young because it dies young. Yet its youth, in spite of everything, is ineffectual. At the parties here you can spot a twenty-year-old worker who is a Mozart melody, approach a girl who is a Benvenuto Cellini vase, and see how nothing results from this meeting of two masterpieces. This then is a land in which poetry does not become reality, yet precisely because of that one feels even more strongly its awful silent presence behind the curtain.

One should not really speak of *masterpieces* as this word is out of place in Argentina. There are no masterpieces here, there are only works of art. Here not only is beauty something that is not abnormal, it constitutes the embodi-ment of ordinary health and average development. It is a triumph of matter, not a divine revelation. And that ordinary beauty knows that it is nothing ex-traordinary, which is why it does not value itself and is, therefore, an entirely secular beauty, deprived of grace. Nevertheless, because it is linked to grace and divinity by its very essence, it is all the more shocking as an abdication.

And now:

Just as with physical beauty in Argentina, so it is with form. Argentina is a country of early and easy form: there is not much here of the pain, degrada-tion, dirt, suffering that accompany a form that perfects itself only slowly and with great effort. Rarely is there a social blunder. Timidity is the exception. Outright stupidity is rare, and these people resort to neither melodrama nor sentimentality, to neither pathos nor buffoonery, at least they never resort to these altogether. As a result of this early and smoothly maturing form (thanks to which a child moves with the ease of an adult), which facilitates and paves, no hierarchy of values on a European scale has materialized in this country, and this, perhaps, may be what attracts me most in Argentina. They are not repulsed, they are not outraged, they do not condemn, and they are not ashamed to the extent that we are. They have not experienced form, and they have not tasted its drama. Sin in Argentina is less sinful, holiness less holy, revulsion less repulsive, and it is not just the beauty of the body but all virtue that is less lofty here and inclined to eat off the same plate as sin. There is something disarming in the air here: an Argentinean does not believe in his own hierarchies, or else he accepts them as something imposed on him. The resonance of the spirit is not convincing in Argentina, something that Argentineans themselves know best, and that is why two separate languages exist here: one public, serving the spirit that is ritual and rhetoric, and another, private one through which people make themselves understood behind the back of the first one. There isn't the slightest connection between these two languages, and an Argentinean presses a button in himself that turns on the lofty and then presses another button, which returns him to his everyday self.

What is Argentina? Batter that has not yet become cake, or something that is simply unshaped, or, perhaps, a protest against the mechanization of the spirit, the reluctant, devil-may-care gesture of a man who is removing himself from a too automatic accumulation — an intelligence that is too intelligent, a beauty that is too beautiful, a morality that is too moral? In this climate, in this constellation, a genuine and creative protest against Europe could arise if — if the softness found a way to make itself hard or if the indistinctness could become a program, a definition.

Translated by Lillian Vallee

Village on the River

Juan L. Ortiz

The other Argentina — the country of misery and squalor surrounded by large exten-
sions of fertile land — continued to haunt its modern counterpart. Juan L. Ortiz, a
poet from the northeastern province of Entre Ríos, whose commitment to artistic cre-
ation and philosophical reflection would turn him into a cultural hero, devoted his life
to translating into poetic language the subtle rhythms of his homeland and the quiet
perseverance of its people. In the poem "Village on the River" (1954), Ortiz invites the
reader to look through the layers of misery and see the gentle strength that enables the
children of a small village to endure the dark humiliations of those "that seem to sleep."

See that dark-skinned boy who seems to look out from another world,
the white of his eyes whiter, or maybe yellowish.
Ah, the little girl already wearing glasses, leading him or carrying him,
the lightest clay herself upon even lighter willow-sticks.
See the other girl in a little cart, so fragile,
the monstruous flower of her knees almost terminal,
led by brothers and sisters, smaller than her, to the edge of what star?
See, a ten-year-old, with the pale head of an impossible fish
that all but transfixes you through the very ears. . . .
See that old branch that survived "the quarries,"
bent back over another short branch stuck in the ground
with a cadence that quickens:
upon it and others like it, turned to anonymous ash, there,
and not upon stones,
a few winged houses sprang up and a few piles of banknotes . . .
and with their blood, ah, so red, a "mysterious" alchemy:
a few names were polished and in time became brass plates. . . .
See that dry, dry ghost emerging from a long night of glass . . .
sexless, in spite of the "skirt"

and the woolen cloth flowing over the line of the shoulders . . .
ah, the voice out of the deep cavern of age
and long resistance, perhaps, to exposure and hunger. . . .

Ah see, for all that, a tenacity in them
as the spikes of a thornbush push upwards or into someone between broken
    branches. . . .
But see, this metal canoeist with more oil on him than light
standing in the middle of the street, like Adam, as if giving rules to the after-
    noon. . . .
And this washerwoman dense but with feet of feathers
almost dancing with her washbowls upon the rug of her life. . . .
And those little girls who sometimes expose their smile like the water,
leaning lightly over an unbelievable river:
and only, only their dark years or the slightly twisted agate of their eyes,
or that waiting at the door when other jewels start to fly, suddenly. . . .
And these young men with nothing embracing the last ripples like their
    girls,
after wounding the other ones, all day long, among the islands. . . .
And this fisherman, silent, back from a fever of silence
still loitering, nocturnal, over fatty mother-of-pearl and embers,
then sleeping, finally, at first touch, like a water-lilly bloom. . . .
And these boys with their ark on dry land, traveling with their small animals,
in a counterpoint of glass and tin, that rises up . . .
until, upon nighttime grass, singing, from there
they too, holding hands, go round the world, barefoot. . . .
And this "granny" wrapped all over still looking for the veils of the instant
so as to bare its silver and dissolve it into soap lillies, squatting . . .
while her chickens, nearby, go crazy, blonde and blue. . . .
And this mother who carries stones from the riverbank until nighttime,
and crushes her life with them, to make the table less poor,
but not her smile, which is everyone's, in an offering composed of jasmine. . . .
And this other one, who is discrete and who tempers her own soul more than
    she does the oven,
and out of it comes a bloom of dough that "keeps you company," as they say
    around here. . . .

And these little devils, arrows over unknown negation,
summoned as wings by the smallest event,
with all the iridescence of amazement and all the faces of tea,

and the hair, all of it, more joyful, and the scant clothing even more fallen
   down. . . .

Where do they find, all these children of the coast,
in spite of everything, that gentle strength,
profoundly gentle, against the dark humiliations that seem to sleep?
Thrown against things by people who don't know,
things give them milk and breath like mothers.
(Oh, for sure, in the adventure of bread or silent nightmare,
at the mercy of the air's worst weapons and the earth's worst humors
and the strange, strange river that would like to rise up and take them back to
   the earth,
leaving them floating between two rejections, under the *Siriris*[1] of the
   night. . . .)
No one thought about the power of those laps,
rich with white rays in mysterious exhalation,
a god not to be invoked, an anointment not to be asked for, for the beings held
   close to them.

But could that have been taken away from them too?
And there they are, in the fluids of the river's time
in melodies that are not heard but that are pure and that give the order of
   rituals.
There they are, separate or fused with the delicate time of willows,
or with the love of that which is theirs, unbelievable in decorum or honor
   beneath the winds,
unbelievable in keenness of sense and in attention, even in the light of certain
   flowers. . . .
There they are, pure of pure soil, in line with canes of sunlight,
standing, in nothing itself, under the same deep sun. . . .
There they are, with blade of hidden steel and hidden coal,
at the "point of anguish, unspeakable and absurd," of the moment without
   exit. . . .
And there they are, in the great exit, which they will find,
with this blade aligned, ay! with all the rest, for the day without an end,
in the column that will march, enormous, to the other side of the star:
a bramble on fire this time, burning from itself, "upon the air of an accor-
   dion." . . .

Translated by William Rowe

Notes

The translator would like to thank Hugo Gola, Alejandro Kaufman, and Claudio Canaparo for their advice.
1 Siriri: a local, onomatopoeic name of a species of duck.

House Taken Over

Julio Cortázar

Julio Cortázar's early works tend to depict an oppressive atmosphere in which educated people from the middle class find themselves trapped in bizarre and incomprehensible situations. "House Taken over" is one of the most representative short stories from that period. It has been interpreted as a metaphor for Peronist Argentina, when an advancing faceless and threatening other (the poor, the racially mixed, the masses) takes over and finally destroys the balance of the bourgeois home. It was that very feeling of asphyxiation that would make Cortázar (1914–84) choose exile in 1951.

We liked the house because, apart from its being old and spacious (in a day when old houses go down for a profitable auction of their construction materials), it kept the memories of great-grandparents, our paternal grandfather, our parents, and the whole of childhood.

Irene and I got used to staying in the house by ourselves, which was crazy, eight people could have lived in that place and not have gotten in each other's way. We rose at seven in the morning and got the cleaning done, and about eleven I left Irene to finish off whatever rooms and went to the kitchen. We lunched at noon precisely; then there was nothing left to do but a few dirty plates. It was pleasant to take lunch and commune with the great hollow, silent house, and it was enough for us just to keep it clean. We ended up thinking, at times, that that was what had kept us from marrying. Irene turned down two suitors for no particular reason, and María Esther went and died on me before we could manage to get engaged. We were easing into our forties with the unvoiced concept that the quiet, simple marriage of sister and brother was the indispensable end to a line established in this house by our grandparents. We would die here someday, obscure and distant cousins would inherit the place, have it torn down, sell the bricks, and get rich on the building plot; or more justly and better yet, we would topple it ourselves before it was too late.

Irene never bothered anyone. Once the morning housework was finished, she spent the rest of the day on the sofa in her bedroom, knitting. I couldn't tell you why she knitted so much; I think women knit when they discover that it's a fat excuse to do nothing at all. But Irene was not like that, she always knitted necessities, sweaters for winter, socks for me, handy morning robes and bedjackets for herself. Sometimes she would do a jacket, then unravel it the next moment because there was something that didn't please her; it was pleasant to see a pile of tangled wool in her knitting basket fighting a losing battle for a few hours to retain its shape. Saturdays I went downtown to buy wool; Irene had faith in my good taste, was pleased with the colors and never a skein had to be returned. I took advantage of these trips to make the rounds of the bookstores, uselessly asking if they had anything new in French literature. Nothing worthwhile had arrived in Argentina since 1939.

But it's the house I want to talk about, the house and Irene, I'm not very important. I wonder what Irene would have done without her knitting. One can reread a book, but once a pullover is finished you can't do it over again, it's some kind of disgrace. One day I found that the drawer at the bottom of the chiffonier, replete with mothballs, was filled with shawls, white, green, lilac. Stacked amid a great smell of camphor—it was like a shop; I didn't have the nerve to ask her what she planned to do with them. We didn't have to earn our living, there was plenty coming in from the farms each month, even piling up. But Irene was only interested in the knitting and showed a wonderful dexterity, and for me the hours slipped away watching her, her hands like silver sea-urchins, needles flashing, and one or two knitting baskets on the floor, the balls of yarn jumping about. It was lovely.

How not to remember the layout of that house. The dining room, a living room with tapestries, the library and three large bedrooms in the section most recessed, the one that faced toward Rodríguez Peña. Only a corridor with its massive oak door separated that part from the front wing, where there was a bath, the kitchen, our bedrooms, and the hall. One entered the house through a vestibule with enameled tiles, and a wrought-iron grated door opened onto the living room. You had to come in through the vestibule and open the gate to go into the living room; the doors to our bedrooms were on either side of this, and opposite it was the corridor leading to the back section; going down the passage, one swung open the oak door beyond which was the other part of the house; or just before the door, one could turn to the left and go down a narrower passageway which led to the kitchen and the bath. When the door was open, you became aware of the size of the house; when it was closed, you had the impression of an apartment, like the ones they build today, with barely enough room to move around in. Irene and I always lived in this part of the house and hardly ever went beyond the oak door except to do the cleaning. Incredible how much dust collected on the furniture. It may be Buenos Aires is a clean city, but she owes it to her population and nothing else. There's too much dust in the air, the slightest breeze and it's back on the marble console tops and in the diamond patterns of the tooled-leather desk set. It's a lot of work to get it off with a feather duster; the motes rise and hang in the air, and settle again a minute later on the pianos and the furniture.

I'll always have a clear memory of it because it happened so simply and without fuss. Irene was knitting in her bedroom, it was eight at night, and I suddenly decided to put the water up for *mate*. I went down the corridor as far as the oak door, which was ajar, then turned into the hall toward the kitchen, when I heard something in the library or the dining room. The sound came through muted and indistinct, a chair being knocked over onto the carpet or the muffled buzzing of a conversation. At the same time or a second later, I heard it at the end of the passage which led from those two rooms toward the door. I hurled myself against the door before it was too late and shut it, leaned on it with the weight of my body; luckily, the key was on our side; moreover, I ran the great bolt into place, just to be safe.

I went down to the kitchen, heated the kettle, and when I got back with the tray of *mate*, I told Irene:

"I had to shut the door to the passage. They've taken over the back part."

She let her knitting fall and looked at me with her tired, serious eyes.

"You're sure?"

I nodded.

"In that case," she said, picking up her needles again, "we'll have to live on this side."

I sipped at the *mate* very carefully, but she took her time starting her work again. I remember it was a grey vest she was knitting. I liked that vest.

The first few days were painful, since we'd both left so many things in the part that had been taken over. My collection of French literature, for example, was still in the library. Irene had left several folios of stationery and a pair of slippers that she used a lot in the winter. I missed my briar pipe, and Irene, I think, regretted the loss of an ancient bottle of Hesperidin. It happened repeatedly (but only in the first few days) that we would close some drawer or cabinet and look at one another sadly.

"It's not here."

One thing more among the many lost on the other side of the house.

But there were advantages, too. The cleaning was so much simplified that, even when we got up late, nine thirty for instance, by eleven we were sitting around with our arms folded. Irene got into the habit of coming to the kitchen with me to help get lunch. We thought about it and decided on this: while I prepared the lunch, Irene would cook up dishes that could be eaten cold in the evening. We were happy with the arrangement because it was always such a bother to have to leave our bedrooms in the evening and start to cook. Now we made do with the table in Irene's room and platters of cold supper.

Since it left her more time for knitting, Irene was content. I was a little lost without my books, but so as not to inflict myself on my sister, I set about reordering Papa's stamp collection; that killed some time. We amused ourselves sufficiently, each with his own thing, almost always getting together in Irene's bedroom, which was the more comfortable. Every once in a while, Irene might say:

"Look at this pattern I just figured out, doesn't it look like clover?"

After a bit it was I, pushing a small square of paper in front of her so that she could see the excellence of some stamp or another from Eupen-et-Malmédy. We were fine, and little by little we stopped thinking. You can live without thinking.

(Whenever Irene talked in her sleep, I woke up immediately and stayed awake. I never could get used to this voice from a statue or a parrot, a voice that came out of the dreams, not from a throat. Irene said that in my sleep I flailed about enormously and shook the blankets off. We had the living room between us, but at night you could hear everything in the house. We heard each other breathing, coughing, could even feel each other reaching for the light switch when, as happened frequently, neither of us could fall asleep.

Aside from our nocturnal rumblings, everything was quiet in the house. During the day there were the household sounds, the metallic click of knitting needles, the rustle of stamp-album pages turning. The oak door was massive, I think I said that. In the kitchen or the bath, which adjoined the part that was taken over, we managed to talk loudly, or Irene sang lullabies. In a kitchen there's always too much noise, the plates and glasses, for there to be interruptions from other sounds. We seldom allowed ourselves silence there, but when we went back to our rooms or to the living room, then the house grew quiet, half-lit, we ended by stepping around more slowly so as not to disturb one another. I think it was because of this that I woke up irremediably and at once when Irene began to talk in her sleep.)

Except for the consequences, it's nearly a matter of repeating the same scene over again. I was thirsty that night, and before we went to sleep, I told Irene that I was going to the kitchen for a glass of water. From the door of the bedroom (she was knitting) I heard the noise in the kitchen; if not the kitchen, then the bath, the passage off at that angle dulled the sound. Irene noticed how brusquely I had paused, and came up beside me without a word. We stood listening to the noises, growing more and more sure that they were on our side of the oak door, if not the kitchen, then the bath, or in the hall itself at the turn, almost next to us.

We didn't wait to look at one another. I took Irene's arm and forced her to run with me to the wrought-iron door, not waiting to look back. You could hear the noises, still muffled but louder, just behind us. I slammed the grating and we stopped in the vestibule. Now there was nothing to be heard.

"They've taken over our section," Irene said. The knitting had reeled off from her hands, and the yarn ran back toward the door and disappeared under it. When she saw that the balls of yarn were on the other side, she dropped the knitting without looking at it.

"Did you have time to bring anything?" I asked hopelessly.

"No, nothing."

We had what we had on. I remembered fifteen thousand pesos in the wardrobe in my bedroom. Too late now.

I still had my wrist watch on and saw that it was 11:00 P.M. I took Irene around the waist (I think she was crying) and that was how we went into the street. Before we left, I felt terrible; I locked the front door up tight and tossed the key down the sewer. It wouldn't do to have some poor devil decide to go in and rob the house, at that hour and with the house taken over.

Translated by Paul Blackburn

Operation Massacre

Rodolfo Walsh

In 1955, General Francisco Lonardi led a military coup that ended Peron's second presidency. The coup's leaders called their action the "Liberating Revolution" and Perón "the tyrant." In 1956 a sector of the military loyal to Perón attempted to overthrow the new government and regain power. This counterrevolution's failure was followed by indiscriminate acts of repression against Peronist militants. After meeting a survivor, the journalist Rodolfo Walsh (1927–77) felt compelled to investigate the illegal detention and execution of several workers. The outcome of his inquiries was Operation Massacre *(1957)—a report that reconstructs this brutal act from the perspective of its dumbfounded victims. Years later, the critic Angel Rama would call Walsh's nonfictional account the first political* testimonio *in Latin America.*

Cast of Characters

THE EXECUTIONERS
Rodolpho Rodríguez Moreno, an army officer
Fulminea, a guard
Various anonymous policemen, serving as guards

THE VICTIMS (Peronist activists: workers and a noncommissioned officer):
Garibotti
Brión
Carranza
Carlitos Lisazo
Vicente Rodríguez
An anonymous noncommissioned officer

THE SURVIVORS
Juan Carlos Livraga
Miguel Angel Giunta
Horacio di Chiano

Workers' demonstration. Workers heading to the Plaza de Mayo to show support for Perón in the months prior to his overthrow by a military coup. Courtesy Archivo General de la Nación, Buenos Aires.

Gavino
Troxler
Benavídez
Rogelio Díaz

The Slaughter

TIME: 9 June 1956

PLACE: A dump, "a sea of tin cans and optical illusions," near a ditch and a stand of eucalyptus. Somewhere close to Buenos Aires.

The moment has come. A short, impressive dialogue marks the beginning.

"What are you going to do to us?" one asks.

"Walk straight ahead!" they respond.

"We're innocent!" various men shout.

"Don't be afraid," they answer them. "We're not going to do anything to you."

WE'RE NOT GOING TO DO ANYTHING TO YOU!

The guards herd the men toward the dump like a flock of terrified sheep. An army pickup truck stops, shining its headlights on them. The prisoners seem to float on an intensity of light. An officer, Rodríguez Moreno, gets out of the truck, pistol in hand.

From that instant on, the story fragments. It bursts into twelve or thirteen bits of panic.

"Let's make a run for it, Carranza," Gavino says. "I think they're going to kill us."

Carranza is sure of it. But the faintest hope of being wrong keeps him walking.

"Let's stay," he murmurs. "If we run, they'll shoot us for sure."

Giunta stumbles along, looking back, with one arm held up, protecting his eyes from the blinding lights.

Livraga begins wandering off to the left, cautiously. Step by step. Dressed in black. Suddenly, something that seems a miracle: the headlights leave him alone. He has left their shining field. He is alone and almost invisible in the darkness. Ten meters ahead he can make out a ditch. If he could only manage. . . .

Brión's white sweatshirt stands out in the dark, almost incandescent.

Troxler is still sitting on the van that brought them, leaning forward with his hands on his knees. Out of the corner of his eye, he's looking at the two policemen keeping watch over the exit. He's ready to jump. . . .

Across from him, Benavídez has his eye on the other gate.

Carlitos, astonished, only manages to mumble: "But, what. . . . Is this how they're going to kill us?"

Further on, ahead of them, Vicente Rodríguez is zigzagging through the rough, unfamiliar terrain. Livraga is five meters from the ditch. Horacio, who was the first one out of the van, has managed to veer off to the side of the ditch.

"Stop!" a voice orders.

Some of them stop. Others keep going for a few more steps. The policemen begin to pull back, keeping their distance. They keep their hands on the triggers of their Mausers.

Livraga does not look back, but he hears the click as the trigger is cocked. There's not enough time to get to the ditch now. He's going to throw himself on the ground.

"Straight forward and shoulder to shoulder!" shouts Rodríguez Moreno.

Carranza, his face contorted, turns around. He drops to his knees in front of the firing squad.

"For my sons . . . ," he sobs. "For my s . . . ."

A violent vomiting cuts short his cry.

In the van, Troxler is poised, ready to spring. His knees are almost touching his jaw.

"Now!" he yells, and jumps at the two guards.

He grabs each of their rifles. And now they are the ones who are afraid, imploring:

"Not the weapons, please! Not the weapons!"

Benavídez is already on his feet, and he takes Lisazo by the hand. "Let's get going, Carlitos!"

Troxler smashes the policemen's heads together and tosses them aside, like puppets. He leaps up and is lost in the night.

The noncommissioned officer, also a prisoner, is slow to react. He gets halfway up. From the hood of the van a third policeman is covering him with a gun. A shot goes off. He goes "Aaaah!" and sits down again; just the way he was. But dead.

Benavídez jumps. He feels Carlitos' fingers slip from between his. With desperate helplessness he realizes that the boy has left him, buried beneath the three bodies thrown on top of him.

From below, the police hear the shot from behind, and, for a fraction of a second, they hesitate. Some of them turn around.

Giunta doesn't wait any longer. He runs! Gavino does the same.

The flock begins to scatter.

"Shoot them!" Rodríguez Moreno shouts.

Livraga throws himself on the ground. Further away di Chiano makes a dive for it too.

The shot stuns the night.

Giunta feels a bullet near his ear. Behind him he hears the impact, the muffled moan, and then the thud of a falling body. It's probably Garibotti. With impressive instincts, Giunta pretends that he's dead and stays still.

Carranza follows on his knees. They put the guns up to his neck and pull their triggers. They shoot his body full of holes.

Brión has little chance of escaping with that white sweatshirt of his shining in the night. We don't even know if he tried.

At one point Vicente Rodríguez pretends to be a body lying on the ground. Now he hears the guards running, getting closer. He tries to get up, but he can't. He's worn out from the first thirty meters of flight; it's not easy to move his more than one hundred kilos. When he gets himself up at last, it's too late. The second shot sends him toppling over.

Horacio de Chiano turns over twice and stays motionless, playing dead. Overhead he hears the whistle of bullets aimed for Rodríguez. One hits close to his face and covers him with dirt. Another pierces his trousers but doesn't wound him.

Giunta stays flat on the ground for about thirty seconds, invisible. Suddenly he jumps up, like a greyhound, staggering around. When he hears the gun go off, he throws himself on the ground again. Almost simultaneously he hears the searing whine of the bullets again. But now it is far away. Now he is safe. When he repeats his maneuver, they don't even see him.

Díaz escapes. We don't know how, but he escapes.

Gavino runs for two or three hundred meters before stopping. At this moment he hears another series of explosions and a terrifying scream that splits the night and seems to stretch out to infinity.

"God forgive me, Lisazo," he will later say, crying to one of Carlitos' brothers, "but I think it was your brother. I think he saw everything and was the last to die."

Over the bodies lying there in the dump, caught in the beams of the headlights where the acrid smoke of gunpowder is swirling, a few moans are floating. A new crackle of shots seems to put an end to them. But suddenly Livraga, who is still motionless and unseen where he fell, listens to the pleading voice of his friend Rodríguez:

"Kill me! Don't leave me like this! Kill me!"

And now, yes, they take pity on him, and they finish him off.

Time Stops

Horacio di Chiano doesn't move. He is lying on his stomach, his bent arms reaching up to his shoulder, his hands on the ground. By some miracle, they haven't broken the glasses he is wearing. He has heard everything—the shots, the screaming—and he is no longer thinking. His body is a mass of fear that penetrates to his bones. Every inch of his tissue is saturated with fear, in each cell the heavy weight of fear. Don't move. In those two words are condensed all the wisdom that humanity can treasure. Nothing exists aside from that ancestral instinct.

How long has he been like this, as if he were dead? He no longer knows. He will never know. He only remembers that at a certain moment he heard the bell of a nearby chapel. Six, seven rings? Impossible to say. Perhaps those slow sounds, so sweet and sad, that mysteriously fell in the shadows were something he dreamed. Surrounding him are the infinitely expanding echoes of the horrifying butchery, the running of the prisoners and guards, the explosions that madden the air and reverberate in the nearest trees and houses, the faint cries of the dying.

Finally, silence. Then the roar of a motor. The pickup truck begins to move. It stops. A shot. Silence once more. The motor starts again in a nightmare of advancing and backtracking.

In a burst of lucidity, Horacio understands. The coup de grace. They are going around, body by body, and putting an end to the men who give any sign of life. And now. . . .

Yes, now it's his turn. The pickup is getting closer. The ground under Horacio's glasses disappears, in a chalk-like incandescence. The guards are shining their lights on him, they are pointing guns at him. He doesn't see them, but he knows that they are pointing at his neck.

They are waiting for some movement. Perhaps not even that. Perhaps they'll shoot him no matter what. Perhaps it seems strange to them that he doesn't move. Perhaps they'll discover what is evident, that he isn't wounded, that there's no blood on any part of him. A sickening nausea rises up from his stomach. He manages to choke it back as it reaches his lips. One part of his body—his wrists, resting on the ground, his knees, the tips of his toes—would like to escape it all by becoming crazy. Another part—the head, the neck—repeats to him, "Don't move, don't breathe."

What to do to stay calm, to contain his breathing, not to cough, not to howl from fear?

But he doesn't move. Neither do the headlights. They watch over him, as in a game of patience. Nobody speaks in the semicircle of guns that surround him. But nobody shoots. And so seconds, minutes, years go by. . . .

And the shot never comes.

When he hears the motor again, when the headlights disappear, when he knows that they are leaving, Horacio begins to breathe, slowly, slowly, as if he were learning to do it for the first time.

Closer to the paved road, Livraga has also remained still, but, unfortunately for him, in a different position. He has fallen on his back, face to the sky, with his right arm stretched back, and his chin resting on his shoulder.

Besides hearing everything, he sees a lot of what is happening: the flashes of powder from the shots, the policemen running, the exotic dance steps of the pickup now slowly headed back to the road. The headlights begin to veer to the left, toward where he is lying. He closes his eyes.

Suddenly he feels an irresistible itch on his eyelids, a warm tickling sensation.

An orange light, where fantastic little purple figures dance, penetrates the hollow of his eyes. Because of a headlight that he can't block out, he blinks at the intense blast of light.

Fulminea bursts out with the order:

"Get that one who's still breathing."

Horacio hears three explosions. With the first one, a spurt of powder beside his head. Then he feels a lacerating pain on his face, and his mouth fills with blood.

The policemen don't bend over to make sure he's dead. It's enough to see his shattered, bloodied face. And they go away believing they have given him the coup de grace. They don't know that that shot (and another one to his arm) are the first bullets to hit him.

The ghoulish van and Rodríguez Moreno's pickup head back to where they came from.

"Operation Massacre" has ended.

Translated by Patricia Owen Steiner

VII

Revolutionary Dreams

As in many other regions of the world, the 1960s and early 1970s were times of engaging optimism in Argentina—an era when everything seemed possible. This generalized feeling of empowerment manifested itself in a series of cultural and political changes that would transform every aspect of social life. Among the most memorable changes was the development and internationalization of a highly irreverent youth culture, easily distinguished by its repeated violations of traditional norms, such as those concerning dress and speech. Jeans, miniskirts, long hair, and the use of expletives and certain types of lingo were the most obvious signs of young people's contempt for bourgeois values and morals. Experimentation centered on the body. Drug consumption and sexual freedom provided alternative ways of experiencing the physical and emotional worlds, while rock and pop music helped create a countercultural public sphere where the new generation could express itself. The emphasis on youth also modified accepted ideas about childhood and parenting. Childhood was no longer considered merely a preparatory stage for adult life but the repository of a singular state of mind that flourished before social conventions twisted and repressed the best characteristics of an individual's inner life. As is the case with the little people that made the comic strip *Mafalda* famous, kids would be credited with a previously unacknowledged wisdom and a talent for seeing through social conventions. Deepening interest in the personal and the new meaning of childhood led educated Argentines to embrace psychoanalysis as the dominant paradigm for explaining all sorts of conflicts.

For a significant number of youths, the reshaping of the personal was seen as only the starting point for greater revolutionary transformations. Driven by the irresistible promise of leftist utopias and the appalling injustice and misery caused by the social recipes of capitalism, many students, political activists, priests, intellectuals, and artists adopted even more radically dissident political stances. Given Argentina's weakening position in the international market and the steadily increasing foreign influence on its domestic affairs, they saw the future of Argentina and its popular classes as bound to the struggles for national liberation that were taking place elsewhere in the so-called Third World. The teachings of the legendary guerrilla leader Ernesto "Che" Guevara inspired the view that Latin America, along with Africa and Asia, was a peripheral region whose local economies had been distorted by the perverse designs of imperialism. The Cuban Revolution, in which poor peasants led by a band of young, educated idealists used guerrilla warfare to prevail over a dictatorship backed by American capital, served as a successful model of popular insurgency. Demanding the impossible became the guideline for political activity. There was a widespread perception that a new era was dawning and that, this time, it was the people's turn. Thus, when in 1969 a strike in Córdoba City unexpectedly turned into violent confrontations between demonstrators and the army—the labor leader Agustín Tosco would later recall—the students and workers involved thought that Argentine history was spontaneously following the correct path.

Revolutionary ideals were substantially reformulated by Argentina's own political traditions. After the military coup that overthrew Perón in 1955, Argentine political society remained profoundly divided between Peronists and anti-Peronists. The proscription of Peronism from the general elections created an atmosphere of distrust and acute frustration that tainted the legitimacy of any political agreement. For eighteen years, Perón's loyal followers fought for the return of their leader. But, if Peronism proved tenacious enough to withstand ostracism, its survival was not static. Thus, when Perón finally returned from Spain in 1973, he found that the political movement that bore his name had a very different constituency from the one he left behind nearly twenty years earlier. The nonconformist youths who had joined its ranks had significantly radicalized the populist agenda of old Peronism, pushing the whole movement further to the Left. Perón himself had been instrumental in these transformations. While still in exile, he had encouraged and manipulated the new radical forces as part of a general campaign to create the conditions for his return. From this unlikely marriage emerged the Montoneros—a left-wing organization of youthful Peronists that became famous for the daring and spectacular nature of its terrorist operations. In one of the few serious studies available on the group, the historian Richard Gillespie traces the ideological contradictions of Montonero rhetoric—a peculiar combination of Peronist populist slogans and a Marxist agenda. Afraid of the explosive situation that he had helped create, Perón tried immediately on his return to neutralize the influence exerted by radicalized groups like the Montoneros. His speech to the governors in 1973, included in this section, underscores Perón's desire to disassociate himself from the radical sectors within Peronism as well as his plan to transform an overgrown movement into a coherent political party. After Perón's death in 1974, the rapid deterioration of the economy, the escalation of guerrilla warfare, and the brutal repression carried out by paramilitary groups and the state during Isabel Perón's administration created a politically turbulent period ending in the military coup of 1976.

Cultural and artistic innovation went hand in hand with political upheaval, particularly in public universities. Radical thinking was especially intense in disciplines such as history, sociology, and philosophy, where professors and students alike reinterpreted Argentine realities through detailed readings of Marx, Freud, and Sartre. The number of printing houses multiplied, while new publications sought to satisfy an expanding middle-class readership. Journals like *Primera plana* fed the public's voracious appetite for novelty with reports on the most important artistic and intellectual developments at home and abroad. The Di Tella Institute — a center for the arts founded in 1963 — provided financial support and a well-located building in the city of Buenos Aires for all types of cultural experimentation, including pop art, happenings, and art cinema. Together with the renovated public university, the institute represented the artistic, intellectual, and political avant-garde of the period.

Art intervened in politics and politics in art. In 1968, a group of artists assembled a collective exhibition entitled "Tucumán Is Burning" in which they put their talent and technical skills at the service of the workers' social and economic demands. Calling attention to consumerist society's excesses amid poverty, the painter Antonio Berni incorporated actual garbage into a series of works that focused on the figure of Juanito Laguna, an imaginary kid growing up in the harsh reality of an urban slum. The disruptive potential of popular culture was also put to work. The folk singer Atahualpa Yupanqui reappropriated the old musical traditions of the Argentine countryside to denounce modern inequalities. In the field of sexual politics, women and gay writers exposed the limits of the revolutionary dreams that had captured the young generation's imagination. The poet Alejandra Pizarnik labored to find a language that could give voice to her transgressive self in a society that was severely restrained by the patriarchal prison of traditional sexual differences.

The Latin American Revolution

According to "Che"

Ernesto "Che" Guevara

In the 1960s, political utopia bore the face of Ernesto Guevara (1928–67), alias "Che," the revolutionary leader who defined guerrilla tactics for popular insurgency in Latin America. He was born in Rosario, Santa Fé, to an old and well-to-do Argentine family and attended medical school at the University of Buenos Aires. From early on he distinguished himself for his intellectual curiosity and social awareness, but in his formative years his rebelliousness never went beyond occasionally indulging in eccentric attire or voicing middle-class concerns regarding public welfare. In 1953 Guevara embarked on a series of trips throughout Latin America that eventually took him to troubled Guatemala, where he had his true political rite of passage. He gained international recognition in 1959, when he and Fidel Castro led the popular revolution that overthrew the loathed dictator Fulgencio Batista. After holding several official positions in the revolutionary government and leading a brief excursion to Africa, Guevara left Cuba for Bolivia, where he sought to create a revolutionary movement after the Cuban model. Killed by the Bolivian national army in 1967, he became an icon of the rebellious spirit of the 1960s. After his death, the generalized myth of Guevara as the young leader martyred for his ideals eventually overshadowed his advocacy of guerrilla warfare. In the following essay, entitled "Tactics and Strategy of the Latin American Revolution,"[1] written during the missile crisis of October 1962, Guevara openly argues that only tactical violence could level Latin America's deep economic inequities and that the struggle for national liberation would eventually set all the peripheral countries of the so-called Third World on the common path toward freedom.

Tactics show us how to use armed forces in combat, and strategy teaches us how to use combat encounters in order to obtain the war's objective.
—Karl Von Clausewitz

Ernesto "Che" Guevara in Uruguay (1962). Exporting the revolution: Che Guevara, drinking the Argentine infusion called *mate,* with Eduardo Víctor Haedo in Punta del Este, Uruguay (1962). Courtesy Archivo General de la Nación, Buenos Aires.

I began this work with a quotation from Clausewitz, the military author who fought against Napoléon and who theorized so brilliantly about war; Lenin loved to quote him because of the clarity of his thinking, in spite of the fact that he was, of course, a bourgeois analyst.

Tactics and strategy are the two main elements of the art of war, but war and politics are intimately related by a common denominator: the effort to reach a specific goal, whether it be annihilation of the adversary in armed conflict or the taking of political power.

But analysis of the essential tactics and strategies that rule political or military struggles cannot be reduced to a schematic formula.

The richness of each one of these concepts can be measured only by combining practice with the analysis of the complex activities that they imply.

There are no unalterable tactical and strategic objectives. Sometimes tactical objectives attain strategic importance, and other times strategic objectives become merely tactical elements. The thorough study of the relative importance of each element permits the full utilization, by the revolutionary forces, of all of the facts and circumstances leading up to the great and final strategic objective: *the taking of power.*

Power is the sine qua non strategic objective of the revolutionary forces, and everything must be subordinated to this basic endeavor.

But the taking of power, in this world polarized by two forces of extreme disparity and absolutely incompatible in interests, cannot be limited to the boundaries of a single geographic or social unit. The seizure of power is a worldwide objective of the revolutionary forces. To conquer the future is the strategic element of revolution; freezing the present is the counterstrategy motivating the forces of world reaction today, for they are on the defensive.

In this worldwide struggle, position is very important. At times it is decisive. Cuba, for example, is a vanguard outpost, an outpost that overlooks the extremely broad stretches of the economically distorted world of Latin America. Cuba's example is a beacon, a guiding light for all the peoples of America. The Cuban outpost is of great strategic value to the major contenders who at this moment dispute their hegemony of the world: imperialism and socialism. . . .

Relating this discussion to America, one must ask the necessary question: What are the tactical elements that must be used to achieve the major objective of taking power in this part of the world? Is it possible or not, given the present conditions in our continent, to achieve it (socialist power, that is) by peaceful means? We emphatically answer that, in the great majority of cases, this is not possible. The most that could be achieved would be the formal takeover of the bourgeois superstructure of power and the transition to socialism of that government that, under the established bourgeois legal system, having achieved formal power will still have to wage a very violent struggle against all who attempt, in one way or another, to check its progress toward new social structures.

This is one of the most debated and most important topics, and, possibly, it is a topic on which our Revolution disagrees the most with other revolutionary movements of America. We must clearly state our position and try to analyze its rationale.

Today America is a volcano. Although not in a state of eruption, it is shocked by subterranean vibrations that announce its coming. There are visible and audible signs everywhere. The Second Declaration of Havana is the concrete expression of those subterranean movements. It strives to achieve an awareness of its objective, that is, an awareness of the necessity and, even more so, the certainty of the possibility of revolutionary change. Evidently, this American volcano is not divorced from the revolutionary movements that have appeared in the contemporary world in this moment of crucial confrontation of forces between two opposing conceptualizations of history.

We could refer to our fatherland with the following words from the Declaration of Havana: "What is the history of Cuba if it is not the history of Latin America? And what is the history of Latin America if it is not the history of Asia, Africa, and Oceania? And what is the history of all of these peoples if it is not the history of the most merciless and cruel imperialistic exploitation in the modern world?"

America, like Africa, Asia, and Oceania, is part of a whole where economic forces have been distorted by imperialism. But not all the continents present similar characteristics; the forms of economic exploitation — imperialist, colonialist, or neocolonialist — employed by the European bourgeois forces have had to cope, not only with the liberation struggle of the oppressed peoples of Asia, Africa, and Oceania, but also with the penetration of U.S. imperialist capital. This has created different correlations of forces in different areas and has permitted peaceful transition toward national independent or neocolonialist bourgeois systems.

But in America such systems have not developed. Latin America is the parade ground of U.S. imperialism, and there are no economic forces in the world capable of supporting the struggle that the national bourgeoisies have waged against imperialism elsewhere; that is why these forces, relatively much weaker than in other regions, back down and compromise with imperialism.

The frightened bourgeoisie is faced with a terrible choice: submission to foreign capital or destruction by domestic popular forces. This dilemma has been accentuated by the Cuban Revolution; through the polarization created by its example, the only alternative left is to sell out. When this takes place, when the pact is sanctified, the domestic reactionary forces ally themselves with the most powerful international reactionary forces, and the peaceful development of social revolutions is prevented.

Pointing out the present situation, the Second Declaration of Havana states,

> In many Latin American countries revolution is inevitable. This fact is not determined by the will of anyone. It is determined by the horrible conditions of exploitation under which the American people live, the development of a revolutionary consciousness in the masses, the worldwide crisis of imperialism, and the universal liberation movements of the subjugated nations.
>
> Today's restlessness is an unmistakable symptom of rebellion. The entrails of the continent are stirring after having witnessed four centuries of slave, semislave, and feudal exploitation of man by man, from the aborigi-

nes and slaves brought from Africa to the national groups that arose later—whites, blacks, mulattoes, mestizos, and Indians—who today share pain, humiliation, and the Yankee yoke and share hope for a better tomorrow.

We can conclude, then, that when faced with the decision to bring about more socially just systems in America, we must think fundamentally in terms of armed struggle. There exists, nevertheless, some possibility of peaceful transition; this is pointed out in the studies of classical Marxist authors, and it is sanctioned in the declaration of the parties. However, under the current conditions in America, every minute that goes by makes a peaceful commitment more difficult. The latest events in Cuba are an example of the cohesion that exists between the bourgeois governments and the imperialist aggressor on the fundamental aspects involved in the conflict.

Remember this point we have continually emphasized: Peaceful transition is not the achievement of formal power by elections or through public opinion movements without direct combat, but rather it is the establishment of socialist power, with all of its attributes, without the use of armed struggle. It is reasonable, then, that all the progressive forces do not have to initiate the road of armed revolution but must use—until the very last moment—every possibility of legal struggle within the bourgeois conditions. . . .

On all of the exploited continents there are countries whose social systems have reached different levels of development, but almost all of them have strong social divisions with feudal characteristics and heavy dependence on foreign capital. It would be logical to think that in the struggle for liberation, following the natural process of development, one would reach national democratic governments in which the bourgeoisie more or less predominates. This has occurred in many cases. Nevertheless, those peoples who have had to use force to achieve independence have made greater advances in the path of social reforms, and many of them are building socialism. Cuba and Algeria are the most recent examples of the effects of armed struggle on the development of social transformation. If we conclude, then, that the peaceful road is almost nonexistent in America as a possibility, we can point out that it is very probable that the outcome of the victorious revolutions in this area of the world will produce regimes of a socialist structure.

Rivers of blood will flow before this is achieved. Algeria's wounds have not yet healed; Vietnam continues to bleed; Angola struggles bravely and alone for its independence; Venezuela, whose patriots identify with the Cuban cause, has recently demonstrated its high and expressive solidarity with our Revolution; Guatemala is waging a difficult, almost underground struggle. All of these are good examples.

The blood of the people is our most sacred treasure, but it must be used in order to save more blood in the future.

Other continents have achieved liberation from colonialism and have established more or less strong bourgeois regimes. This was accomplished without, or almost without, violence, but we must realize that following the logic of events up to this moment, this national bourgeoisie in constant development at a given moment will find itself in contradiction with other strata of the population. When the yoke of the oppressor country is removed, this national bourgeoisie is no longer a revolutionary force and transforms itself into an exploiting class, renewing the cycle of social struggle. It could advance or not on this peaceful road, but irrevocably two great forces will confront each other: the exploiters and the exploited. . . .

We cannot say when the struggle will take on these continental characteristics or how long it will last, but we can predict its coming, for it is the product of historical, political, and economic circumstances. Its advance cannot be stopped.

Faced with this continental tactic and strategy, some people offer limited formulas: minor election campaigns, an election victory here or there, two deputies, a senator, four mayors, a large popular demonstration broken up by gunfire; an election lost by fewer votes than the preceding one; one labor strike won, ten strikes lost; one step forward, ten steps back; one sectoral victory here, ten defeats there. And then, at that precise moment, the rules of the game are changed, and one has to start all over again.

Why these formulas? Why the weakening of the people's energies? There is only one reason: Among the progressive forces of some Latin American nations there exists a terrible confusion between tactical and strategic objectives. Small tactical positions have been interpreted as great strategic objectives. One must credit the reactionary forces with the success of having forced their class enemy to make these minimal offensive positions their fundamental objective. . . .

Latin America offers a contradictory picture. There are progressive forces that are not up to the level of those whom they lead; people who rise to unknown heights, people who boil with a desire to act, and leaders who frustrate those desires. The hecatomb is almost here, and the people have no fear; they try to move toward the moment of sacrifice, which will mean the definitive achievement of redemption. The educated and prudent ones, on the other hand, put all available brakes on the movement of the masses, attempting to divert the irrepressible yearnings of the masses for the great strategic objectives: the taking of political power, the annihilation of the army, and the destruction of the system of exploitation of man by man. The picture is contradictory but full of hope because the masses know that "the role of Job is not for the revolutionary," so they prepare for battle.

Will imperialism continue to lose one position after another, or will it, in its bestiality, as it threatened not long ago, launch a nuclear attack and burn the entire world in an atomic holocaust? We cannot say. We do assert, however, that we must follow the road of liberation even though it may cost millions of atomic victims. In the struggle to death between the two systems we cannot think of anything but the final victory of socialism or its relapse as a consequence of the nuclear victory of imperialist aggression.

Cuba is at the brink of an invasion, threatened by the most powerful imperialistic forces of the world, and, as such, threatened with atomic death. From its trench, refusing to retreat, Cuba issues a call to arms to all of Latin America. This is a struggle that will not be decided in a few minutes or an hour of terrible battle. The end of the struggle will take years of bitter encounters causing atrocious suffering. The attack of the allied imperialist and bourgeois forces will time and again force the popular movements to the brink of destruction, but they will always come back strengthened by the support of the people until total liberation is achieved.

From here, from its lonely vanguard trench, our people make their voice heard. This is not the song of a revolution headed for defeat; it is a revolutionary anthem destined to be sung eternally from the lips of Latin American fighters. It will be echoed by history.

Translated by Rolando Bonachea

Note

1 According to the Cuban government, this article was written during the missile crisis of October 1962 but not published until Guevara's death (see *Juventud rebelde* [Havana], 2 October 1968).

Are We All Neurotic?

Anonymous

Psychoanalysis entered Argentina's intellectual circles in the early 1930s, but for several decades it existed almost exclusively as an alternative therapeutic practice. After 1958, its influence broadened, achieving over time a popularity unprecedented in Latin America. Its vocabulary, its sexual interpretations of private life and experience, as well as the professional codes regulating the relationship between patient and therapist became essential components of middle-class culture and language. Not surprisingly, Buenos Aires is one of the most renowned centers of psychoanalytic thinking in the world today. This journalistic piece, published on 13 November 1962 by the influential Primera Plana, *is an unequivocal indication of the rapid spread and popularization of psychoanalysis in the 1960s. Quoting actual reports and using psychoanalytic jargon, the anonymous author parodies the fashionable use of psychoanalytic theories to explain all sorts of problems, from the personal to the political.*

Last week an Argentine psychologist found himself observing drivers' faces in Buenos Aires as they came around the circle at 9 de Julio Avenue and Corrientes. When he was interviewed by one of our reporters, he stated that these fleeting images of drivers gave the best X-ray of the mental state of our population: the shouts, the fury registered on their faces, the dejection of people who couldn't move ahead as fast as they wanted, the cynical remarks. But one can question the young psychologist's objectivity because he himself appeared disturbed by the sole fact that he was having so much difficulty crossing the avenue and because he was a little dazed by the din of all the cars.

In any case, this simple anecdote was the beginning of an investigation conducted in 1959 by a group of *Primera plana* reporters concerning the mental state of the Argentine people. The conclusions are alarming.

The Picture

. . . According to the latest psychological studies, Buenos Aires suffers from a widespread state of mental illness, ranging from neurosis to acute schizophrenia. The city, and indeed the entire country, is gripped by a kind of paralysis that prevents us from assuming our responsibilities and at the same time forces us to turn to small pleasures that are quickly and easily satisfied: eating in a good restaurant, going to the movies, watching TV. Unconsciously we deny problems and fall back on the hope for a paternal or authoritarian "hero" who will emerge to solve our problems and get everything back on track. We are a nation with "no tomorrow"; we want everything today, we look for instant, irrational solutions. This all makes for a neurotic portrait of the Argentines that disturbs the psychologists . . . provided that they themselves are free of the generalized "denial." . . .

Society is made up of many individuals. Our first step will be to ask ourselves how any particular person comes to have mental illness. Can we say how many Argentines can be considered mentally ill? Experts distinguish various levels of manifestation for the basic states of mind. They say that all of us are a little obsessive, a little phobic, hysterical, or paranoid. In normal people these traits occur without characterizing their behavior. But when one trait becomes very typical of someone, they speak of *character*. The individual who controls everything, who tries to put things in order, has an obsessive character. The person who feels that the world is dangerous and is frightened by it has a phobic character. When we unconsciously believe that we are very fine and that everyone else is about to attack us, we reveal a paranoid character, while the hysterical character is the person who is always playing a role, who assumes theatrical behavior so that other people will think he is better than he is in reality. There can come the moment, however, when the trait is so strong that it dominates all other traits. Psychology then speaks of the *obsessive personality* or the *hysterical personality*, depending on the case. . . .

A Fad

Neurosis is the sickness of the moment. It is reasonable to suspect that not all the people who are being psychoanalyzed today need it very much but that there is a lot of fad and snobbishness involved. . . . There are reliable indices to determine the incidence of neurosis in Buenos Aires: the undeniable success of publications on the subject, the healthy financial situation of psychoanalysts, and a tremendous interest in the effectiveness of psychotherapy.

The Investigations

For experts, there are many studies of collective psychology that are sufficiently conclusive. The desire for a "strong government" would demonstrate, for example, the existence of animosity and the necessity for passive submission, the inability to resolve problems for oneself, and the anxious search for someone to whom to delegate responsibility.

In November 1959, the sociologist José Enrique Miguens directed a careful investigation in the major cities of Argentina. In this way he learned that seven out of ten Argentines believed that "we need a strong government that will put things back on track." Furthermore, the investigation revealed a crisis of confidence; the number of those who thought that there was no group, organization, or institution deserving their trust was about 60 percent of the population. . . . We are an unbelieving nation, in search of a charismatic leader who will take care of all our faults and obligations.

According to another investigation carried out in October 1959 by the specialists Floreal Ferrara and Milcíades Peña, Argentines are prisoners of an unconscious impulse to deny mental illness. The investigations found that nine out of ten people "forget" mental illness when they are asked to name the most feared illnesses. The average person here recognizes only the most violent forms of mental illness. . . .

Six in ten of all Argentines find very normal an individual who is evidently abnormal. The image of insanity surrounds us. . . . According to the psychologist Dr. Eduardo R. Colombo, the appeal of authoritarian ideologies and the segregation of the mentally ill, like our denial of our own conflicts, are "mechanisms to cope with an overload of anxiety." In other words, they are already a pathological symptom.

Prejudices

The level of authoritarianism is easy to measure. In our country, three out of four people think that, "deep down, human nature doesn't change." And almost all the people who say this agree that, while human nature remains this way, "there will always be wars" and "the most important thing for a child to learn is to obey his parents" and "most people don't get ahead in the world because they lack willpower." These are precisely the responses that, according to psychology, help define the despot. Ferrara and Peña confirmed this in their research. They discovered that most authoritarian people are the very ones who deny the nature of mental illness of the neurotic person and yet would not accept a cured mentally ill individual as a neighbor. For his part, Colombo discovered that eight out of ten Argentines consider that a child who disobeys his parents and superiors is "worse" than some other child who persecutes and abuses younger children.

At times it is thought that the neurotic or the psychopathic person is just not adjusted to society. Dangerous error! There could be a repressive organization whose members feel very "happy" and show no visible conflicts but that could not be characterized as "normal." For that reason, Ferrara and Peña have affirmed:

"The normal embraces the pathological, and one must be very careful to avoid the mistake of people who do not realize that full adjustment to society, by living with an absence of struggle and conflicts, is an individual form of general alienation from the social world. Jaspers made a profound contribution when he spoke of the neurosis that encircles mental health. The complete unflappability of the ideal business leader is suspicious from the point of view of mental health.

"It is not conflict that defines the pathological person but rather the blocking of conflict and the impossibility of resolving it."

The Irony

One of the characteristics of all mental illness is the evasion of reality. The fact is that the Argentine society of today produces pathological denials that find their expression in ironic attitudes.

During the most recent military disturbance, an advance "red" guard posted along the road to Mar del Plata was found looking through a spyglass at the "blue" tanks of Colonel López Aufranc. Ready for action, they were some five kilometers away. A van belonging to an evening newspaper happened to pass by, and one of the reporters asked what had happened to six or seven "red" captains. The guard said that he knew only what he had heard on the radio (everyone there had transistor radios). Then one of the soldiers anxiously asked the reporter: "Did you read the papers this morning?" The reporter nodded yes. "Good. Then tell me, what's today's exchange rate on the dollar?"

And that is not the only example. In subsequent articles, *Primera Plana* took note of the impassivity of the onlookers who were contemplating the skirmish. At a gathering in Constitución Rail Station, there were hundreds of civilians who were making very satisfied comments about how a bullet had hit another of the casual spectators. We ourselves have observed identical reactions in Chacabuco Park.

Right now, during the Cuban missile crisis, the entire city is going wild over one of Landrú's cartoons about sending Argentine ships to Cuba. Nobody realizes that our fellow countrymen are actually going on those ships and that what is important is the state of belligerency and that it's not at all pleasant, in fact that it's terribly serious.

Depression

The well-known psychoanalyst Dr. Arnoldo Rascovsky agreed that Argentina is being worn down by "a wave of intense depression." He said that all governments are paternal images of the father and, in the language of psychoanalysis, that populations also have an id and a superego as essential components of their personality. When Peronism crumbled, the superego disappeared, and there was no substitute for it. This circumstance condemns us to a structural anarchy that manifests itself in worthless checks, in nonpayments, in changes in moral values.

However, this results in an intolerable lack of love and solidarity in society, in a general feeling of disharmony, and in a pervasive sense of mistrust. Man is "a neurotic animal who lives in permanent conflict; he has to feel compensated for his efforts; work is one means of channeling his aggressions and eroticism. The crisis comes when there are factors that no longer allow him to love his work." It is possible, however, that a major coming together of the population, born of necessity, will expand our limits for expressing love.

Immaturity

The Reverend Father Moyano, S.J., rector for the Psychology Department at the University of Salvador, finds an "immaturity" in the Argentine character. He suggests that it shows up in its intellectual underdevelopment, in the search for security at all cost, and in a mass mentality that has a minimum of creative imagination that reacts only to ready-made mechanical objects. Flight from problems turns into a geographic escape—an exodus of herds to all kinds of places—or a crowd that encourages a coup d'état (a government that will take care of everything in the dream) or having hopes but no goal.

The Atmosphere

Dr. Mauricio Goldenberg, head of psychiatry at the Lanús Polyclinic, observes a clear increase in neurotic influences among young people fifteen to twenty-five years old. He also finds that people of his own generation have been subjected to frustrating situations that have prevented them from producing leaders.

"They were born during World War I, an event that affected their families and, in turn, influenced them. When they were teenagers the downfall of Yrigoyen also left its mark. New hardships arrived with the economic depression of 1932. In 1939 World War II began in Europe. With the rise of Perón in 1945, that generation endured other complications. Then came another coup, Frondizi and his fall, the struggle between the 'reds' and the 'blues,' the Caribbean blockade. . . . As adults they feel greatly hampered in their attempts to communicate with each other, and the technological means of communication only made things worse.

"The other day I was talking with some friends as we were driving, and one of them turned on the radio. He learned about the situation in Cuba and was unable to go on speaking. Ours is a communication with catastrophe."

Translated by Patricia Owen Steiner

Tucumán Is Burning

María Teresa Gramuglio and Nicolás Rosa

In tune with the ubiquitous politicization of intellectual life, some artists began to question the bourgeois definition of art as a collection of autonomous works created to provide aesthetic pleasure and provoke metaphysical insights. In 1968, a group of painters, photographers, and filmmakers allied themselves with the peasants working in the sugar mills in the northwestern province of Tucumán and organized an itinerant exhibition entitled Tucumán Is Burning. *Properly speaking, there were no individual works. The exhibit consisted of a giant collective collage of photos, newspaper clips, recorded interviews, and nonfiction short films, assembled to inform the public of the real social conditions of the poor. Displaying their rejection of both official and avant-garde institutions devoted to art, such as the National Art Museum and the Di Tella Institute, the artists chose to exhibit their controversial works in the labor unions' various headquarters. The group's manifesto underscores the political content of all artistic creation and calls for revolutionary art committed to the proletarian cause.*

This year, 1968, a series of aesthetic acts has burst on the world of fine arts in Argentina. These acts have broken with the elitist attitudes of the artists who worked within the Instituto Di Tella, the institution that has claimed until now to be the sole arbiter of new modes of expression, not only for its own artists, but for all of the new artistic experiences that have been springing up across the country.

These new modes of artistic expression erupted in the midst of the overly exquisite aesthetic atmosphere of the false vanguards sheltered within the institutions of official culture. Initially these expressions outlined a fresh approach that would lead to seeing artistic acts as positive and real actions that tended to reshape the society that produced them.

This attitude aimed to make evident the implicit political content of every work of art. The idea was to put forth this content with a violent and active symbolic charge so that an artist's production would become part of reality with a truly vanguardist, and therefore revolutionary, intent. Aesthetic acts de-

Tucumán Is Burning (1963). Art exhibition. The province of Tucumán, traditionally called *the garden of the republic,* here is renamed *the garden of misery* by the participating artists.

nouncing the cruelty of the Vietnam War or the hypocrisy of American foreign policy plainly indicated the need to create, not just a relationship between the work and society, but an artistic object that could by itself produce changes just as a political act would.

The recognition of this new concept led a group of artists to postulate aesthetic creation as a *collective and forceful* act that would destroy the bourgeois myth of the individuality of the artist and the passive character traditionally assigned to art. Planned aggression became the form of the new art. To be aggressive is to possess and to destroy the old forms of art based on private property and the personal enjoyment of a unique work. Today, aggression is a creative act that produces new meanings: it destroys the network of official culture, opposing it with the subversive culture of the process of change, creating a truly revolutionary art.

This revolutionary art is born from the artist's political awakening to his present-day reality as part of the political and social context that surrounds him.

Revolutionary art proposes the aesthetic act as a focal point where all the elements that make up human reality are joined. This includes economic, social, and political elements, thus bringing together the contributions of distinct disciplines and eliminating the sense of separation between artists, intellectuals, and technicians. It is a unified action of all of those elements, propelled by the desire to change the total social structure. That is to say, it aims at *total art.*

Revolutionary art acts on reality by intervening in a process of harnessing the elements that compose it, starting with a clear ideological conception based on principles of materialist rationality.

Revolutionary art, in this way, is a partial form of the reality that is integrated into the total reality. It destroys the idealistic separation between the work and the world to the degree that it carries out a true transformation of social structures: that is to say, it is a *transforming art.*

Revolutionary art is the manifestation of political ideas that struggle to destroy the worn-out cultural and aesthetic underpinnings of bourgeois society, joining the revolutionary forces fighting against economic dependency and class oppression: that is to say, it is a *social art.* . . .

This collective work, called *Tucumán Is Burning,* bears directly on the present national crisis, which takes particularly radical form in one of our poorest provinces, Tucumán, which has long been subjected to a tradition of underdevelopment and economic oppression. The present Argentine government, embarking on a disastrous colonialist policy, has closed down most of the Tucumán sugar refineries, a vital resource of the provincial economy. This has caused the spread of hunger and unemployment, with all the social consequences that they produce.

An "Operation Tucumán" designed by government economists is trying to disguise this overt aggression against the working class with a false program for economic development based on the creation of new, hypothetical industries financed by capital from the United States. The hidden truth of the Tucumán operation is this: it aims to destroy a real and explosive trade union movement that reaches across Northeast Argentina. The plan is to do this by breaking up workers' groups, atomizing them into small industrial sites, and forcing them to emigrate to other regions in search of underpaid and unstable temporary work. One of the serious consequences of this is the breakup of workers' families, whose survival is left to chance and improvisation. The economic policy followed by the government in Tucumán Province is a kind of pilot program intended to measure the degree of resistance of the worker population so that, after the neutralization of trade union opposition, this program can be applied to other provinces with similar economic and social profiles.

"Operation Tucumán" is reinforced by a campaign of silence, organized by government institutions so as to confuse, distort, and hush up the serious situation in Tucumán, a campaign that the so-called free press has joined out of shared common class interests.

Faced with this situation, taking up their responsibility as artists committed to the social reality that includes them, the avant-garde artists have responded to this "campaign of silence" by producing this work, *Tucumán Is Burning*.

This work consists of the creation of an information overload network, to bear witness to the underhanded misconstruing of events in Tucumán by the information and diffusion media in the hands of official power and the bourgeoisie. The communication media are powerful mediating forces that can be filled with varied contents; the positive influence that those media exercise on society depends on the reality and veracity of those contents. Information about what has been happening in Tucumán has been controlled by the government and the official media. They tend to keep silent the serious social problems unleashed by the closing of the sugar refineries and to provide a false image of economic recuperation of the province that the actual facts scandalously belie. So as to gather facts and to put in evidence the fallacious contradictions of the government and of the class that sustains it, the avant-garde artists, accompanied by technicians and specialists, traveled to Tucumán. They verified the social reality that exists there. The process culminated in a press conference where the artists made a public and violent repudiation of the actions of the authorities, of the complicity of the cultural media in keeping the workers of Tucumán in a shameful and degrading social state. The artists' action was carried out in collaboration with student and worker groups who united with them to show support for their efforts.

The artists went to Tucumán with abundant documentation concerning the economic and social problems of the province as well as detailed information about the stories that the media had produced about the problems in Tucumán. These findings were then analyzed in order to weigh the degree of distortion and adulteration of the facts. Later, artists and technicians wrote up the information that they had collected, which will be used for the show in the union halls. And, finally, the information that the media have produced on the artists' actions in Tucumán will be incorporated into the first stage of the information network.

The second part of the artists' efforts will be the actual presentation of all the information gathered about the situation in Tucumán. Part of this will be circulated in trade union halls and student and cultural centers. The full show with audiovisuals and performances will be carried out at the Argentine CGT [Confederación General del Trabajo] union hall in Rosario and later will be brought to Buenos Aires.

Our information overload network, whose basic aim is to discredit the image of reality in Tucumán produced by the mass media, will have its culmination in a third and ultimate stage, where all the third-degree information (reports on reports on reality) that has been sparked will be collected in a publication that will show all the processes of conceiving and carrying out the work, together with all the documentation produced, as well as a final evaluation.

The protesting artists demand that their works not be incorporated into official, bourgeois institutions, but be placed in a different context; that is why this show is taking place in the Argentine CGT because this is the body that represents the class that is at the vanguard of a struggle whose final objectives are shared by the authors of this work.

Translated by Patricia Owen Steiner

Antonio Berni, *Juanito sleeping* (1974). Courtesy Lily Berni, and Inés and José
Antonio Berni.

The Cordobazo

Agustín Tosco

The so-called Cordobazo—a set of violent riots that shocked the city of Córdoba in May 1969—was the first in a series of extreme political clashes that would characterize the following decade. For several days, radicalized union workers, university students, and practitioners of liberation theology demonstrated against the damaging economic programs and the repressive policies carried out during General Juan Carlos Onganía's dictatorship (1966–70). Paradoxically, the protests were staged in a city famous for its conservative history. Sparked by a strike organized by autoworkers, the conflict quickly expanded to other sectors of society, eventually becoming a broad, popular demonstration. As it headed downtown, the swelling mass of protesters built barricades and damaged the property of several multinational companies. Following the governor's orders, the army harshly repressed the riots, wounding sixty civilians and making at least one hundred arrests. Agustín Tosco was one of the main union leaders involved in the riots. In this personal account, he gives his version of the confusing events leading to the Cordobazo and what he saw as the spontaneous convergence of popular forces.

"The Cordobazo" is the militant expression of the highest quantitative and qualitative order, born from the conscience in action of an oppressed people who want to free themselves in order to build a better life. The people know that it is possible to have a better life, but they also realize that standing in the way of it are those who simply speculate and benefit from its postponement and thus, day by day, frustrate all the people's efforts.

And why Córdoba precisely? Because Córdoba was not deceived by the so-called Argentine Revolution. Córdoba did not share the "hopeful expectations" of other cities. Córdoba never believed in the plans for modernization and transformation that Onganía's dictatorship promised. . . .

In the middle of August in 1966 our local union, the Córdoba Federation of Power and Light, issued a public statement entitled "Negative Signs." It was the first trade union stand in Córdoba against the series of purely repressive measures that the dictatorship was initiating. That declaration had widespread repercussions, not just locally, but nationally. Almost alone it took the lead in the rebellious opposition to the policies of Onganía and his team.

The death of Santiago Pampillon at the hands of the repressive regime gave proof of historic student resistance. Nobody could forget the struggles, the protest demonstrations of the entire student group, and the hunger strikes nor the hour-long work stoppage carried out by the Córdoba workers' movement in solidarity with their university comrades. . . .

In February 1967, in connection with a general strike planned for March, the workers organized large demonstrations in Córdoba. . . .

As repression grew, so did resistance. A minor demonstration revealed different ways of repudiating the regime and its accomplices. . . .

I want to transcribe here a paragraph from a document of 23 February 1967 because it gives a premonition of the Cordobazo. It said: "History is marked by milestones like the one yesterday that was heroically led by the workers' movement of Córdoba in their workshops and factories and in the streets of our city. Yesterday's landmark actions signaled a day of progress written with vigorous strokes and powerful expressions that go beyond the usual limits. These protests were then kept alive in the press and on television, in the mind's eye and in the spirits of thousands of heroes and heroines and spectators who lived through the sequence of actions planned by the CGT [the Confederación General del Trabajo, the national labor union organization) and the confederated labor unions of Córdoba. It was a lucid, committed day of accomplishment that brings us a little closer to the crucial solution to our problems, problems that are the inevitable outcome of the situation into which the Argentine people have been dragged. We workers now have a clear, concrete, and irreducible position."

The repression that followed the general strike of 1 March 1967 and the disastrous leadership of the national CGT produced an obvious vacuum characterized by the increasing split between the local trade unions and their leaders and the national CGT and its "collaborationist" leaders. . . .

What was the clear conscience of the people of Córdoba all about at the end of 1967? What was our accusation? What was our stand?

We expressed our ideas in a brief synthesis: "Under the heading of modernization and transformation, the government established an economic plan whose philosophical-political foundation apparently rested on the most crude and orthodox liberal economics, on the resurrection of the notion of 'laissez-faire,' on the practice of an extreme version of free trade that would allegedly

Working-class neighborhoods (1967). The deficiencies of working-class neighborhoods became the focus of radical politics. Courtesy Archivo General de la Nación, Buenos Aires.

encourage the stability and greatly increase the economic well-being of the country. However, this so-called economic freedom is nothing but a scheme destined to make the country submit, to make it part of the monopolistic, capitalistic system and of the ever more pronounced deterioration of that system."

We pointed out: "For some time now the version of liberalism that is peddled here has ended in all the nations of the world. The industrial powers — monopolies that work out of the great metropolises — practice crude economic management: internally, by protecting their domestic products and consumer goods by means of tariffs and other such trade barriers; externally, by creating international organizations that impose policies of unregulated economic penetration and exploitation on underdeveloped countries. This 'economic freedom' is imposed on us and directed from afar, especially by American monopolistic concentrations of power that excessively favor the United States and its allies. These actions provoke in Argentina the sharpening of the crisis and the deepening of its recessive effects." . . .

As to the ultimate details of our accusation against the promotion of this reactionary policy, we declared: "The government pretends to have a tacit consensus of public opinion and yet makes no attempt to test whether it is right in its understanding of public opinion. At the same time, it justifies its refusal to have a public debate by saying that such a debate would be detrimental for the country. With the logical perseverance of their retrograde proposals, the government approves the Civil Defense Law, which militarizes the entire population over fourteen years of age, under the pretext of maintaining internal security, but with the objective of suppressing every legitimate defense of the economic, social, and political interests of the workers. Soon afterward it approves the so-called Law against Communism, affecting all people and institutions that protest or engage in any action to protect their rights. This law even surpasses the repressive program of a Joseph McCarthy, leaving it to the Argentine Information Service to determine which people, for 'ideological, Communistic motivations,' might be a danger to the government. A punishment of up to nine years in prison is added for those who qualify as enemies of the state.

"The national universities are taken over by the government, thus nullifying the force of the Argentine students. The government is making plans for restrictive regulations and doing away with student organizations. It violates the concept of privacy of communication, just like modern inquisitors who are jealous of every opinion that is adverse to official dogma. In the international arena, it proposes (though it was happily voted down) the institutionalization of the Inter-American Junta of Defense as the modern police of Latin American cities where people are fighting for their complete emancipation. The government's intent is to lock these people into a stage of underdevelopment, to keep them at a standstill and in a state of neocolonial dependence."

Accusations were made that might be superficially known but that were still not understood by all people. It was delegations from Córdoba for the most part that planted these ideas. . . .

The Rebellion of the Local Trade Unions

The national CGT tried by every means to organize a congress to support the principles of a sort of "collaborationism" that would echo the government's policies and would bring about worker participation in the process. All of this clearly contradicted the workers' demands and deserved to be rejected by the people. . . .

The local trade unions repudiated the whole shameful program of collaboration with Onganía. A wave of demonstrations and other public acts, all organized by the dissident members of the CGT, made for a true celebration on 1 May 1968.

In Córdoba more than five thousand people crowded onto the premises of the Córdoba Sport Club. Labor leader Ongaro spoke, again denouncing and repeating once more what we had seen coming ever since 1966: that the dictatorship was destroying the country.

On 28 June 1968 the CGT of Córdoba organized a demonstration in front of its headquarters to express their total displeasure with the second anniversary of the dictatorship. The resulting repression, as happened repeatedly, dealt severe blows to the entire workers' organization, which recorded that 322 of the demonstrators had been taken prisoner. The workers' movement, the student body, and groups from the general population all demonstrated in the streets to express their protest. They were successively repressed.

But we did not rest. Some people now maintained that it was no longer possible to stage "political actions" since the police wouldn't allow them and the public was getting worn out. But the majority took the opposite position. We did not want to give up our right to express ourselves, to protest, to demand solutions. Over and over government forces broke up our groups, sending workers and students to jail.

In September 1968, the local CGT and the Student Frontline group planned a week of protests in memory of "the people's martyrs." The date for this demonstration coincided with the anniversary of the death of Santiago Pampillon. . . .

The Week of the People's Martyrs was violently repressed. A young student, Aravena, was shot down and today is still completely disabled by that treacherous attack. The "actions" were broken up. A demonstration by trade union leaders, students, and an organization called Priests of the Third World (whose members were coming out of a mass for Santiago Pampillon) was attacked. Various activists, trade union representatives, and students were arrested and, without any legal justification, held in prison for a month.

At the end of 1968, the CGT organized another "action" that was put down in the same way. We all experienced solid indignation; our condemnation of the regime was beginning to reflect signs of our fury. It was not possible to do anything. Repression was in evidence at every moment. The government continued to support the national CGT leadership. The national federation of Power and Light censored our Córdoba trade union because we had sympathized with the CGT of Argentina. . . .

The Caldron Explodes

The metalworkers, the transportation workers, and people from other Córdoba trade unions declared a general strike for 15 and 16 May because of firings in the district and the lack of recognition of workers' seniority when they changed jobs. The mechanical workers held a meeting; they were attacked as they left. The workers defended their rights in a pitched battle in the center of the city on 14 May. The attacks, the oppression, the refusal to acknowledge a long list of rights, the shamefulness of all the government's actions, the problems of the student body and neighborhood centers: all these grievances are mounting.

The city is totally paralyzed on 16 May. No one works. Everyone is protesting. The government represses.

In other places in the country, student conflicts erupt because of the privatization of the university dining rooms.

In Corrientes a student, Juan José Cabral, is killed, and that fact has serious repercussions throughout Córdoba. The university is closed down. All the student groups protest and prepare to take part in "actions" and demonstrations. They work in common accord with the CGT.

On 18 May, a student, Adolfo Ramón Bello, is killed. With students and the Priests of the Third World we carry out, in silence, a march in homage to the fallen.

On 20 May, I am detained, incommunicado, in the police station while they did a background check on me. I am freed the following day.

On 21 May, students disrupt classes and interfere with university activities. A series of communications from the workers' movement supports their actions. Another victim—the student and metallurgical apprentice Norberto Blanco—is killed in Rosario. The government establishes councils of war.

On 22 May, the students of the Catholic University declare that they are in a "state of alert." They are supported by the rest of the student movement.

On 23 May, the Medical School clinic is taken over by the students. Héctor Crusta, a student, is gravely wounded by a bullet from the police. Bonfires and clashes are the outcome. The police are overwhelming, and the clashes become more and more serious.

On 25 May, I speak at the Catholic University of Córdoba, and I severely criticize, to the point of condemning, the bloody police assaults as well as the arbitrary procedures of the Council of War in Rosario.

On 26 May, the workers movement of Córdoba, after two meetings, resolves to hold a general work stoppage of thirty seven hours beginning at 11:00 A.M. on 29 May and to stage public protest demonstrations. The students support all the resolutions of the Córdoba CGT.

Everything is ready for the great work stoppage. The sense of indignation is now out in the open, obvious and eloquent at all levels of the population.

There is nothing spontaneous about it. Neither is it improvised. Nor does it depend on support from other groups. The local trade unions organize, and so do the students. They decide on places to concentrate their action and how they will lead the marches. The major concentration of people is opposite the CGT office on 137 Vélez Sársfield.

Thousands and thousands of flyers inundate the city. They all demand the reinstatement of rights that have been trampled down. Meetings of the trade unions and of the students who support the work stoppage and the protest take place, one after the other.

The twenty-ninth of May dawns tense. Some workers begin to abandon the factories even before eleven o'clock. At that hour the government orders that public transportation come to a halt in the downtown area. Workers at the Power and Light attempt to organize an "action" at the summit of Rioja and General Paz, but they are attacked with tear gas. Once again: repression in action. Indiscriminate repression. The violent prohibition of the right to assembly, the right to protest.

Meanwhile, long lines of workers from the automobile factory are arriving in the city. They are attacked with the intent to disperse them. Businesses are closing their doors; the streets begin to fill with people. There is notice of the death of a comrade, Máximo Mena, of the Mechanics Union.

Then a popular "explosion" erupts, a rebellion against so many injustices, against the killers, against the attacks. The police pull back. Nobody controls the situation. It is the people, the trade unions, and the students who, inflamed, fight on. Everyone helps. There is total support from the entire population, both in the center of the city as well as in outlying neighborhoods.

This is the conscience in action of everyone, making itself evident in the streets, against so many prohibitions. We've had enough of the guidance of the usurpers of power and their union accomplices! The payoff of the battle of Córdoba — "the Cordobazo" — is tragic. Dozens of deaths, and hundreds of wounded. But the dignity and the courage of a people have flourished and written a page in Argentine and Latin American history that will never be erased.

The policy of foreign exploitation burns in the bonfires set in the streets. They burn with the light, the heat, and the force of the workers and the students, of both young and old, of men and women. That fire is one of the spirit — of the principles and great aspirations of the people. It will never be extinguished.

In the midst of this struggle for justice, liberty, and the sovereign will of the people, I was taken off in handcuffs on an airplane, worried about the years in prison to which I had been unjustly sentenced. But these years in prison turned out to be a little less than seven months, thanks to the ongoing protest that is freeing our people, especially in Córdoba, and that has rescued me from the distant prisons of the South. Now I hope that all of us together, workers, students, men of all ideologies and all religions (yet with our doctrinal differences), may learn how to unite to build a society that is more just, a society where man will no longer be a wolf to his fellow man but a *compañero* and a brother.

Translated by Patricia Owen Steiner

The Words of Silence

Alejandra Pizarnik

The poetry of Alejandra Pizarnik (1936–72) has frequently been read as the disturbing expression of a life thwarted by excruciating emotional and physical pain and ending in suicide. A lesbian Jewish woman who suffered from schizophrenia, Pizarnik certainly experimented with language to trace the open wounds of her daring choices and the contradictions that tormented her inner self. However, the formidable beauty of her poetry exceeds the bounds of the merely biographical. The insurmountable difficulties of writing and the permanent gap between words and things endow Pizarnik's verses with their shocking strength and allow the reader to hear the collective murmur of other women laboring to translate into words an existence circumscribed by silence.

FRAGMENTS FOR DOMINATING SILENCE

I

The strengths of language are the solitary ladies, desolate, who sing through my voice, which I hear in the distance. And in the distance, on the black sand, a girl lies down dense with ancestral music. Where is true death? I have tried to illuminate myself in the light of my lack of light. Branches die in memory. The girl nests inside me with her mask of a wolf. She who couldn't go on any longer and begged for flames and we burned.

II

When the roof flies off of the house of language and words offer no shelter, I speak.

The ladies in red got lost inside their masks but will still return to sob among the flowers.

Death is not mute. I listen to the song of the mourners sealing the cracks of silence. I listen to your sweet cry flowering my gray silence.

III

Death has restored to silence its bewitching prestige. And I will not say my poem and I have to say it. Even though the poem (here, now) makes no sense, has no destiny.

Translated by María Rosa Fort and Frank Graziano

WORDS

We wait for the rain to stop. For the winds to come. We speak. For the love of silence we utter useless words. A pained, painful utterance, without escape, for the love of silence, for love of the body's language. I would speak; language has always been an excuse for silence. It's my way of expressing my unspeakable weariness.

This fatal order of things should be reversed. Words should be used to seduce the one we love, but through pure silence. I have always been the silent one. Now I used those mediating words I have heard so much. But who has so often praised lovers over those loved? My deepest leaning: to the edge of silence. The mediation of words, the lure of language. This is my life now: self-restraint, trembling at every voice, tempering words by calling upon all the cursed and fatal things that I have heard and read about the ways of seduction.

The fact is I enumerated, analyzed, and compared the examples gathered from my readings or from mutual friends. I could show that I was right, that love was right. I promised him that if he loved me, a place of perfect justice would be his. But I wasn't in love with him; I only wanted to be loved by him and no one else. It's so hard to talk about. When I saw his face for the first time I wanted it to turn toward mine out of love. I wanted his eyes to fall deeply into mine. Of this I wish to speak. Of a love that's impossible because there is no love. A love story without love. I speak too soon. There is love. There's love in the same way that I went out the other night and observed: there's wind tonight. Not a story without love. Or rather, a story about substitutes.

There are gestures that pierce me between the legs: a fear and a shuddering in my genitals. Seeing his face pause for a fraction of a second, his face frozen for an immeasurable moment, his face, such a dead stop, like the change in one's voice when saying *no*. That Dylan Thomas poem about the hand signing the page. A face that lasts as long as a hand signing a name on a sheet of paper. I felt it in my genitals. Levitation: I am lifted, I fly. A *no*, because of that *no* everything comes undone. I have to give an orderly account of this disorder. A disorderly accounting of this strange order of things. While *no* goes on and on.

I speak of an approaching poem. It comes closer as I am held at a distance. Weariness without rest, untiring weariness as night—not the poem—approaches and I am beside him and nothing, nothing happens as night draws near, passes by and nothing, nothing happens. Only a very distant voice, a magical belief, an absurd, ancient wait for better things.

Not long ago I said *no* to him. An unspeakable transgression. I said no, when for months I've died waiting. When I begin the gesture, when I began. . . . A shaking shudder, hurting, wounding myself, thirsting for excess (thinking sometime about the importance of the syllable *no).*

Translated by Susan Jill Levine

The Muleteer

Atahualpa Yupanqui

*With the massive influx of European immigrants and Argentina's rapid urbanization
in the early twentieth century, traditional music and dances from the countryside lost
ground to tango and other musical forms that were emerging from cultural intermingling in the eastern cities. In the 1960s, folk music regained its vitality as a new wave
of composers politicized the original popular genres through their innovative lyrics.
Among them was a man from the northwestern province of Santiago del Estero who,
evoking the Amerindian rebellions against the Spaniards and the struggles of all subaltern groups, adopted the pseudonym Atahualpa Yupanqui and wrote songs that have
remained anthems of political resistance to the present day. From his work we have
selected "El arriero" (The muleteer), a song protesting the injustice of a world in which
the majority takes care of the cattle owned by a few. The power of its condemnation
has not weakened with time. In 1989 the song was recorded again by a rock band.*

Wind devils dance in the sand
Bright sun glistens on the stones
And dressed for the magic of the road
The muleteer presses on . . . the muleteer presses on. . . .

His poncho a windblown banner of clouds,
Flutes greet him from grassy fields.
And boldly, on paths through those hills,
The muleteer presses on . . . the muleteer presses on. . . .

Troubles and pretty cows go with him
Troubles and pretty cows go with him
The troubles are ours
The cows belong to someone else.

As evening slowly beheads the sun
The lights on the stones fall asleep.

And still driving his herd (git along there!)
The muleteer presses on . . . the muleteer presses on. . . .

May night bring him soft memories
to make him feel less all alone.
Like a shadow in the shadow of those hills
The muleteer presses on . . . the muleteer presses on. . . .

Troubles and pretty cows go with him
Troubles and pretty cows go with him
The troubles are ours
The cows belong to someone else.

Translated by Patricia Owen Steiner

Montoneros: Soldiers of Perón

Richard Gillespie

The rise of several guerrilla organizations, angered by what they considered to be the failure of democracy in Latin America and the increasing gap between rich and poor, was in part inspired by significant political developments abroad, such as the Cuban Revolution and the uprisings of May 1968 in France. In Argentina, clandestine forms of armed struggle developed their own unique features. For example, the Montoneros had a greater popular appeal than the Trotskyite Revolutionary Army of the People (ERP), probably because they combined the social objectives of the Left with the strong nationalistic slogans so dear to Peronism. This double orientation explains the group's ambiguous status, which lay somewhere between legality and clandestinity. The Montoneros developed a military hierarchy and used guerrilla warfare to achieve their political objectives. Beginning in 1973, they were challenged by the Triple A — another paramilitary organization of the Peronist Right. In the following selection, the historian Richard Gillespie accounts for this violent decade in Argentine history through an analysis of the ideological and political ambivalence that traversed the Montoneros' history.

Montonero Peronism

In drawing together radical Catholicism, nationalism, and Peronism into a populistic expression of socialism, the Montoneros brought together a whole wealth of historical legitimacy into something that attracted civilians of diverse political denominations: Catholic militants, popular nationalists, authoritarian but populistic nationalists, recruits from the traditional Left, combative Peronists. The original group contained no outstanding theoretician, yet its very pragmatism was as often a source of strength as of weakness in the early years, facilitating tactical flexibility and the forging of political alliances. Emphases differed: some members saw the goal as a national variant of socialism; others envisaged it as a socialist form of national revolution. All, however, saw the "principal contradiction" affecting Argentina in terms of imperialism versus the nation and the latter's interests as represented by a popular but multiclass

Montoneros in the 1970s. Courtesy Archivo General de la Nación, Buenos Aires.

alliance. Indeed, due to their relegation of class struggle to a secondary plane and their devotion to a leader who had in power sponsored class harmonization, it can be said that the Montoneros were less "leftist" to the extent that they were Peronist, and vice versa. They presented their organization as a champion of the people, *el pueblo,* because they were not working class themselves; and, rather than seek the "workers state" aspired to by the non-Peronist revolutionary Left, their central commitments were to national development, social justice, and "popular power." Vague in their notions of what *socialismo nacional* signified, some agreed with José Pablo Feinmann that it and justicialism were "equivalent concepts," that it was not some new fourth Banner of justicialism but "the most profound synthesis of the political project which has animated Peronism since its origins." Others, concurring with Juan Pablo Franco and Fernando Alvarez, did not project *socialismo nacional* so forcibly back into the 1940s and instead asserted the proletarianization, dialectical development, and Social Darwinization of Peronism since 1955. All, though, created a Perón in their own image and proved more willing to listen to rhetoric than study political history.

As would-be revolutionaries, the Montoneros' most damaging illusion was that Peronism was a specifically Argentine revolutionary movement, owing its dynamism to an intimate bond between Perón and the masses. Perón's monologues addressed to his followers at mass rallies in Plaza de Mayo were ingenuously imagined to have formed part of a symbiotic dialogue: "Perón spoke with the workers, explaining to them the principal problems of the Fatherland, and listened to the masses' proposals and desires." If at times Perón had appeared weak or made tactical mistakes, if the Peronist process had run into crisis in the early 1950s, it was largely, in Montonero minds, because the revolutionary darling of the Peronist Left, the nexus binding Perón and the masses together, had died in 1952. Their evitismo, their acceptance of the Eva Perón cult, extended even to believing the claim that she, not the union leaders, deserved the credit for the big 17 October 1945 mobilization that ensured Perón's release from detention—a claim belied by all historical investigation of the event.

Evita's posthumous reputation was greatly enhanced by the fact that her political career coincided with the "golden years" of Peronism. She was associated with the general benefits made possible by the late 1940s economic boom, especially the handouts to the poor from her Fundación Eva Perón. Allegations that she had invested Fundación money in her vast wardrobe were dismissed as slanders spread by an embittered Radical Party. But it was her diatribes against the oligarchy and impassioned denunciations of social injustice that really endeared her to the Peronist Left. She preached death to the oligarchs: "With or without bloodshed, the race of oligarchs, exploiters of man, will undoubtedly die this century"; and she also provided the Left with ammunition for use in their battle against the Peronist Right and Vandorist bureaucracy: "I am more afraid of the oligarchy within than the one we defeated on 17 October," Eva wrote. She warned against "the Pilots within our cause" and maintained that "the official who uses his station to serve himself is an oligarch. He does not serve the people but his own vanity, pride, egoism, and ambition."

Yet these same personality traits speak out from under the cover of that false humility that permeated Eva Perón's writings. She presented herself as "only a humble woman," but the message was that she was really a modest heroine whose whole life was bound up with the popular cause, a saintly figure who had dedicated her life to "serve my people, my Fatherland, and Perón." Her hatred of the oligarchs, who snubbed her throughout her short life, was undoubtedly sincere, but many of her postures were hypocritical. She adopted a plebeian self-image, true only to her origins, yet loved to dress in the most glamorous minks and expensive jewelery, weakly explaining to her *descamisados,* "I am taking the jewels from the oligarchs for you . . . one day you'll inherit the whole collection"—but it was invariably "one day" or during "this century," not right now. She posed as a dedicated and selfless servant of Perón and his people, yet her career as the "greatest social climber since Cinderella" involved the acquisition of an ever-expanding bureaucratic empire. And she set herself up as a revolutionary, as a banner of the proletariat, yet had no qualms about visiting fascist Spain, receiving the Grand Cross of Isabel the Catholic from Franco, and reciprocating Falangist salutes at reception rallies during her 1947 Rainbow Tour.

The Montoneros, however, on "discovering the people," were only too ready to share their adoration of her, to embrace the myth of Evita the jacobin, for their desire for acceptance by Peronists overrode their critical faculties. For them, she was a symbol of combativity, the woman who had tried to create a "workers militia" in the early 1950s. She had made an arms deal with the Dutch royal family for its munitioning: five thousand .45 pistols were ordered, of which only one hundred were distributed before the plan was shelved. In fact, its membership was to have included junior army officers as well as trade union contingents, and it was to have been essentially a defense mechanism for activation only when a military coup seemed likely. Nevertheless, the Montonero Dardo Cabo (who derived his knowledge of it from his father, the trade union leader Armando Cabo) was to compare it with "the Cubans' armed defense scheme," failing to differentiate between what was to be defended in each case. If Perón had vetoed the plan in 1952, this could be understood in terms of army pressures on him, an unfavorable balance of forces, and so on; if the exiled leader who was telling the Montoneros to hit the regime until it fell had been feted by notorious dictators—Alfredo Stroessner in Paraguay, Marcos Pérez Jiménez in Venezuela, Rafael Trujillo in the Dominican Republic, and Francisco Franco, generalissimo of the armies of land, sea, and air, by the grace of God[1]—well, one had to remember that Perón had been a military man and so was "naturally" predisposed to friendship with other military men. After years of isolation from the working people of Argentina, the middle-class militants now accepted Peronist mythology lock, stock, and barrel, for whatever criticisms had been raised against the Peróns, they could not believe that the people's unwavering faith in them could be misplaced. Hence the Montonero slogans were not intentionally insincere, nor merely self-legitimating, when they read "Evita—Perón—Revolution!"; "Evita, Present, in Every Combatant!"; and the favorite of all, "If Evita were alive today, she would be a Montonero." . . .

The Nature and Effects of Montonero Activity

To understand the growing popularity of the Montoneros in these years, it is essential to examine the nature of their guerrilla activity. Most of their actions were examples of "armed propaganda" rather than military operations. Even the June 1971 takeover of the small rural town of San Jerónimo Norte, forty miles from Santa Fé, was a case of psychological warfare rather than an attempt to engage in an armed confrontation with enemy units. As at La Calera eleven months earlier, Montonero aims were partly to seize resources ($10,000 from a bank; twenty-seven rifles, other weapons, and uniforms from a police station; documents, identity cards, and driving licences from the law courts) and partly to encourage popular combativity by demonstrating the vulnerability of the military regime. By exploiting the classical guerrilla advantages of surprise and mobility a force of twenty-five could occupy a town of five thousand people for two hours and thus make the government appear weak and incompetent in the eyes of the public, foreign investors, and international bankers. Even in small-scale actions during these years, the accumulation of financial, military, and logistical resources and the stimulation of popular sympathy and support were the prime Montonero motives. There were no assaults on military garrisons and no instances of Montonero *comandos* deliberately setting out to do battle with the army or police.

A sympathetic response to Montonero activities was carefully cultivated by means of a minimal use of offensive violence and extreme discrimination in the selection of targets, as opposed to random terrorism. The guerrillas paid special attention to symbolic operations that all Peronists could relate to. Early in 1971 their Evita Fighting Unit occupied the historic Casa de Tucumán, where Argentine Independence had been declared in 1816, as "an act of homage and a reminder of the economic independence that Perón declared in 1946" in the same place. Bombs inevitably exploded in all the major cities on important Peronist anniversaries such as those of the 1956 military revolt and of Eva Perón's death on 26 July 1952. Over one hundred bombs went off, destroying foreign businesses, on the twentieth anniversary of the demise of "Evita Montonera." And, whether they applauded or not, the public at least grasped the political significance of these explosions; far fewer spectators realized that the regular Guevarist 9 October blitzes were intended to record the death of Che. Favorite Montonero targets in these early years were symbols of oligarchic privilege and opulence, such as the numerous Jockey Clubs, golf course buildings, and luxurious country clubs that were blasted. And it was all performed with a lot of verve and style, in such a way as to facilitate the growth of a romantic aura around the authors. While the clubs of the wealthy were being detonated, approach roads were invariably closed off with signs reading "Danger! Dynamited Zone."

By killing no army conscripts and very few policemen, most of these being of plebeian origin, the Montoneros in their first three years of public life denied their enemy the boon of being able to successfully present them through the media as "bloodthirsty terrorists." They displayed their potential and also their self-control when, for instance, the *comando* Chacho Peñaloza in February 1971 disarmed police guards outside the West German embassy, without harming them or proceeding to spray machine-gun bullets inside the embassy. It was only very occasionally that violence was employed less discriminately: when Montoneros placed a bust of Evita in the central plaza of San Isidro in July 1972, together with a sign reading "Plaza Evita—Montoneros," they also laid booby-trap bombs that injured three policemen, blinded a fireman, and killed another. And of course Montoneros at times got themselves into "them or us" situations and left enemy corpses behind them as they shot their way out of trouble. At the end of June 1971 the *comando* Juan José Valle, composed of eleven Buenos Aires Montoneros, "expropriated" $88,000 from the Banco de Boulogne in Villa Ballester after disarming two police guards. The leader of the organization, José Sabino Navarro, knew nothing about the plans for this operation and quite by chance drove into that area from Córdoba on the same day. Two police patrol-car men spotted the suspicious character waiting on a dark corner in his car; they tried to search him, opened fire when he pulled a gun on them, and were both shot dead. As in this incident, most of the people killed by Montoneros died only when they posed a fatal threat to the guerrillas, though the latter patently engaged in activities that dictated that such eventualities were certain to occur from time to time.

Foreign companies and executives were especially singled out for punishment, but here too assassination was not yet on the Montonero agenda. Discouragement of foreign investment in Argentina came in the form of blowing up executives' houses but not executives: property, not people, was the prime target of Montonero violence.[2] On several occasions, executives involved in industrial disputes learned that their homes had been set on fire by Montoneros, and in February 1971 the Eva Perón Combat Unit occupied and blew up a new police station under construction in Santa Fé. Nine months later, in solidarity with the struggles of militant car workers, another unit invaded a car plant in Caseros, sprayed thirty-eight Fiats with petrol, and then sent merchandise valued at $98,000 up in smoke.

There were few kidnappings, that of Vicenzo Russo, production manager of Standard Electric Argentina (an IIT subsidiary), in December 1972, being a 1 million dollar exception to the general rule. One reason for this may have been that the only two other publicized Montonero kidnap attempts both resulted in unforeseen deaths: in March 1972, Roberto Uzal, a leading member of the extreme right-wing Nueva Fuerza, was killed after he had himself slain the Montonero Jorge Rossi and wounded two others; and, in April 1973, Colonel Héctor Iribarren, head of the Third Army Corps' intelligence service, was gunned down when resisting a kidnap bid by the Mariano Pujadas and Susana

Lesgart Units of the Montoneros. Altogether, even if one includes joint operations, no more than a dozen deaths could be attributed to the Montoneros
during these years of military rule. Although they were never quite as successful as the early Tupamaros in presenting a Robin Hood image to the public,
lessons about the politically counterproductive nature of terrorism seemed to
have been learned from precedents such as the "kill a cop a day" campaign
waged in the early 1960s by the Venezuelan Tactical Combat Units (UTCS) in
Caracas.

By helping to create a climate of insecurity and social disorder, Montonero
guerrilla activity certainly became a factor in the military decision to return to
barracks and attempt a political solution to the Argentine crisis. But it was by
no means the only factor. The change in military tactics was motivated just as
much, if not more, by the semi-insurrectional challenges that had shaken the
regime from 1969. In March 1971, it was the Cordobacito (little Cordobazo)
that was primarily responsible for the military junta's decision to oust the pretentious Levingston and appoint the electorally minded Lanusse as president
in his stead. On that occasion, it had taken the occupation of Córdoba by thirty-
five hundred troops to put an end to a provincial general strike, street demonstrations, and barricade fighting, after Governor José Camilo Uriburu had
threatened to "cut off the snake's head" of rebellion there; over fifty vehicles had
been burned and several businesses destroyed in the fighting, and the damage
bill ran into millions of dollars. April 1972 saw more mass violence, this time
in the Andean city of Mendoza, sparked off by the raising of electricity prices.
This Mendozazo subsided only after the regime agreed to suspend the increase
and after intervening troops had killed three demonstrators and imprisoned
five hundred. During the next three months, further rioting, demonstrations,
and strikes in San Miguel de Tucumán and General Roca maintained the momentum of popular revolt. In the course of the Rocazo, the local population
went so far as to expel their mayor and run the town themselves.

All these mass challenges to military rule, complemented by a series of national and regional CGT [Confederación General del Trabajo] strikes in support of economic claims, persuaded General Lanusse that the regime's position
was untenable. Though the guerrillas themselves were considered more of a
scourge than an immediate military threat, he and his minister of the interior,
the Catalan Arturo Mor Roig, clearly feared the prospect of a growing incorporation of plebeian oppositionists into guerrilla ranks. In memoires published
in 1977, Lanusse justified his behavior during his twenty-six-month presidency
on the grounds that "left totalitarianism can flourish naturally where there are
reactionary dictatorships." "Democracy" had to be restored "to deprive the
subversives of all their arguments," and the aging Perón had to be brought back

to Argentina if his myth were to be exploded. Otherwise, "Perón in Spain, deprived of an alternative, would have ended his days as the commander-in-chief of subversion, without running any risks." Back home, Perón would seek a more solid power base than his "special formations" could offer him. Lanusse feared that the general situation would worsen and military divisions deepen unless the "legitimacy of power" were restored. Almost cynically he described his electoral plan as an "escape valve" but did not, it would appear, consider that Peronism would be the prime beneficiary of it.[3]

Perón's Justicialist Party was recognized by the military regime as a legal political grouping in January 1972, but, by stipulating that presidential candidates had to be permanently resident in the country from 25 August of that year, Lanusse virtually ensured that Perón himself would not stand. The Peronist leader could not afford to be seen fulfilling military conditions by returning in time, especially when no guarantees had been offered with regard to his personal security — Lanusse seems to have calculated that the Peronist-led Frejuli alliance would obtain something less than 50 percent of the votes on 11 March 1973, thus necessitating a runoff ballot for the presidency that would then be won by non-Peronist forces; the latter would sink their differences and rally round the Radical Party candidature of Ricardo Balbín. It was a gamble that failed to come off. Though Lanusse was accurate in his estimation of the electoral might of Peronism, he underestimated Perón's capacity to put together a broad electoral front that he could dominate: an achievement consolidated only during Perón's November 1972 visit to Argentina. As it turned out, Frejuli presidential candidate Héctor Cámpora, with 49.59 percent of the poll, was to come so close to attracting the 50 percent required for election on 11 March that there was no point in the military enforcing their own second-ballot regulations.[4] In this way Lanusse lost control of the process that he had been instrumental in initiating, and the military were left incapable of conditioning the behavior of the incoming government.

While pursuing his Great National Agreement, Lanusse did not call a halt to his government's repressive treatment of popular opposition forces. Death squads operated, political prisoners were tortured, and the homes of left-wing lawyers were bombed. Yet to some degree repression was tempered by military divisions over the junta's strategy and by Lanusse's desire to reach agreements with the largest of the civilian parties. Lanusse was politically unable to order a "no-holds-barred" drive against the Peronist guerrillas, for, given the widespread sympathy and support for them within the Peronist movement, this would have entailed such an offensive against Peronists in general that military deals with even the most conciliatory Peronist leaders would have been rendered impossible. According to Montonero records, about one hundred people were killed and five hundred imprisoned for political reasons by the agents of the 1966–73 "Argentine Revolution"; far more were to lose their lives or liberty during the first *year* of the post-1976 Videla regime.

Notes

For complete references and notes, consult Richard Gillespie, *Soldiers of Perón: Argentina's Montoneros* (Oxford: Clarendon, 1982), 70–75, 110–16.

1 The only other country to provide Perón with hospitality during his 1955–73 exile was Panama. There in 1956 he met his third wife, María Estela Martínez (Isabel), thirty-five years younger than he and working as a nightclub dancer in the Happy Land Bar. Its manager was Raúl Lastiri (provisional president of Argentina, July–October 1973), the son-in-law of José López Rega, who himself became Perón's private secretary in Madrid, social welfare minister (1973–75), and organizer of the Triple A death squad. Perón's residence in Spain lasted from January 1960 until June 1973, though there was an attempted return to Argentina, which got as far as Río, in December 1964 and an officially tolerated return visit in November–December 1972.

2 It is difficult to assess the impact of such activities prior to 1973. However, *Time* of 14 January 1974 estimated that 60 percent of foreign businessmen left Argentina during 1973, prompted by over 170 business kidnappings in that year.

3 There were three general strikes in 1970, five regional strikes in Córdoba in 1971, and three regional strikes in Córdoba, one in Mendoza, and one in San Juan during 1972.

4 Out of 11,911,832 valid votes, the Frejuli formula for the presidency and vice-presidency attracted 5,907,464 votes; the radical (UCR, or Unión Cívica Radical) ticket headed by Balbín gained 2,537,605 votes (21.3 percent) and came in second.

Antirevolutionary Peronism

Juan Domingo Perón

On 12 March 1973, while most Argentines danced in the streets, others foresaw unavoidable disaster. Both were reactions to the electoral victory of a Peronist coalition under the umbrella of the Frejuli (Justicialist Front of Liberation). The elected president, Héctor Cámpora, resigned only a few months later in order to make room for Perón, newly returned with his third wife, Isabel. In new elections, Perón won 61.9 percent of the vote, returning Peronism to power for the third time. Despite his eighteen-year exile, most citizens believed that he still had the answers to Argentina's problems. Inflation, unemployment, social and political antagonisms, and guerrilla activity were some of the challenges facing the new government. As before, Perón applied a mixture of reformist ideas, avoiding radical solutions. Although support for Perón was initially strong, the worsening economic crisis led the most radicalized groups — university students and guerrillas — to reject the Peronist approach to national liberation. In response, Perón began to attack the Left. In this speech to the governors on 2 August 1973, he openly criticized radical Argentine youths for what he considered a lack of political maturity. Feeling the burden of his advanced age, Perón called for order and political stability as well as an effort to define the Peronist movement within the institutional limits of a traditional bourgeois party. After Perón's repeated attacks on the revolutionary wing of Peronism, the Montoneros went underground.

I have the immense pleasure of seeing once again all the *compañeros* who now have the responsibility of governing our provinces. I have especially asked President Cámpora to permit me to talk with you, although only for a few moments, because the doctors still won't let me do much talking. But, at the very least, I would like to express some of the ideas that will begin to characterize our party activity. After eighteen years in which we have had to sustain a difficult and bitter struggle under all kinds of circumstances and in all parts of the country, the Peronist movement needs organization.

There is an old principle of struggle that declares, "Live alone, but fight together." For many years, we have not provided a political direction but led a

Perón delivers an angry speech against the Montoneros' radical demands (1974). Courtesy Archivo General de la Nación, Buenos Aires.

political struggle. This struggle demanded centralized leadership, which is the form of leadership par excellence.

But the struggle has now come to a conclusion, at least in its most basic aspect. That bitter, difficult, and at times violent struggle has ended. We must now begin a more unified struggle, together with all political groups, to defend the interests and objectives of the nation.

We are the ones who, by popular decision, have the responsibility of leadership. Therefore, so does our movement, which is what really won, not so much because of the struggle and all those matters, but because we have also acted truthfully on behalf of a cause that, in the end, is always the winner. And our grave responsibility falls, not on one man, or on a few men, but on the entire justicialist movement, across the country. Because of this, I believe it is essential that we begin by institutionalizing our movement, institutionalizing it with all seriousness and all commitment.

Ever since we fell from power in 1955, I have thought about trying to institutionalize the movement. But it was not an easy thing to do because all our energies were taken up with carrying on a struggle that demanded centralized leadership.

But the present circumstances will allow us to transform that great movement, lacking in ideas until now, into a true political institution, concerned not only with political struggle but also with the political culture that our country needs.

Our country is politicized, but it has no political culture.

And everything that is happening to us, even within our movement, is due precisely to that lack of political culture. Our function within the movement is no longer just one of indoctrination—something we have worked on a great deal and has brought politicization—but is also a matter of cultivating methods that will carry our movement to the highest level of political culture. This will be of immense benefit to the country, not only because of what it represents for the justicialist movement, but also because it will induce other political forces to acquire that same level of political culture.

Nowadays, politics no longer means two trenches, each occupied by a man ready to fight his opponent. This modern world has created social needs, and the people cannot afford the luxury of dabbling in politics. Those times have passed. A time is coming of integrated democracy, in which everyone will struggle toward a common purpose, keeping his individuality, his ideas, his doctrines, and his ideologies, but all working toward a common goal. Nobody can try to keep up systematic and negative opposition because countries can no longer put up with such political attitudes. One can see how this is coming all over the world.

Perhaps our arduous and difficult struggle over these eighteen years has been the very last; a new era is beginning for us, in which the organization and elevation of political culture of our masses will make all the work that we have to do easier. For that reason we have ordered that the Peronist movement begin to be structured as an institution. I will stop being the factotum because we no longer need factotums. We now need organizations; we need to create a High Council that will truly be in charge of the direction and the leadership of the Peronist movement. . . .

We must remember, gentlemen, that, while popular movements die with their inventor, institutional movements go on living even after all those who created them have disappeared. Because man cannot conquer time; only organization can conquer time.

I am old now, and the fact that my end is approaching ought to make us realize that this movement must institutionalize itself so that it can continue in time and space, even without me. And, from this moment on, it should begin to do without me so that it can be managed by the Peronists that Peronists themselves designate.

That was the first thing I wanted to say to you, so that each one of the governors can carry this concept back to his province. If we do this completely all across the country, in a short while, we will have managed to institutionalize our movement. . . .

Another matter that I should mention to the governors has to do with our new administration, which fortunately has gotten off to a constructive start. These first sixty or more days of the government have allowed us to clearly realize what is happening and what has happened in the country. This is the first step: opening up the package to see what's inside. These sixty days have been sufficient for all of us to see what the situation in the country is. And we think that the country can move forward if all the people of Argentina join together to work for it.

I believe that this is an extraordinarily important moment to accomplish this action, which would be decisive and definitive for the country.

I was in Europe at the time of the reconstruction. In each country where I visited and talked to the people, I saw the effort and the great feeling of unity with which all, conservatives and Communists alike, worked together to rebuild their country. No one even thought of taking a closed, oppositional political stance. That is to say, thanks to the circumstances, they came to form an integrated democracy in which each one was part of a great organism that worked toward a single objective: to rebuild the country.

We are coming out of a civil war, acknowledged or not, but a civil war nonetheless. In that war everything that could be destroyed in the country was destroyed, beginning with the Argentine people itself, which is the most terrible of all the destructions that could have been carried out.

Juvenile delinquency has flourished in a spectacular way in our country, and this is one of the most telling indices of what has happened to the destruction of man. Administrative procedures, with all the deformities that each governor must have encountered in his province, indicate another sector of the decomposition. Ideological deviation and the growth of the far Left are no longer tolerated even on the far Left. I have visited countries behind the Iron Curtain, and even there the far Left has died out. For Communist countries, the far Left is produced for export only. All of these are signs of the decay of man, which is the most serious thing that could have happened in our country. . . .

We have to educate a people who are headed in the wrong direction; we also have to set the younger generation on the right path. What happened at Ezeiza makes us question the young people who took part. We question those young people. Our young people are marvelous, but watch out because they could head off in the wrong direction! Making sure they don't is our obligation, our task.

This has nothing to do with limiting the aspirations or the thoughts of man. It has to do with educating man and giving him the sense of balance without which we'll never get anywhere. We have to return to the Greece of Pericles, where there was a sign on the facade of every building that read: "All things in harmony and moderation." We are a left-wing movement. But the Left that we defend is a justicialist Left above all else. It is not a Communist or an anarchist Left. It is a justicialist Left that wants to establish a community where every Argentine has the possibility of fulfillment; nothing more.

We have seen individualist capitalism break down, but we have also seen state capitalism fail. Both systems have been condemned by evolution, and not just here, but in Budapest and all over. Let's not follow these procedures or processes that have been condemned; let's follow what we have kept alive for thirty years, what has given success to the justicialist movement. . . .

Self-criticism is necessary. In the past, during the two justicialist governments, we hurried things a bit and created an opposition, justified or not, but an opposition that finally overcame us. We had not done "all things in harmony and moderation." Today there are many *gorilas* [opponents] who say: "Now we agree, we have learned." Back then, they were wrong because they were too slow, and we were wrong because we were too fast. In the future, what we have to do is put an end to both extremes and do "all things in harmony and moderation."

This is what the government of our day and the justicialism of our times bids us to do. We are revolutionaries because we are aiming for structural changes that will make the Argentine people happier and make our country greater and more prosperous.

What we do in harmony and moderation will be constructive. Whatever we might like to do violently, quickly or slowly—that is not the path that we should choose. I believe that it is not hard to govern in these times and in this Argentina, despite the chaos they have left us. It is not hard if we call on all men of goodwill who, as Argentines, want to struggle for the grandeur of our land and for the happiness of our people. I believe that no well-intentioned heart can reject these premises, for they are premises for all times.

Gentlemen: I do not wish to go on and on, discussing other matters further. I believe that these two points I have referred to are the fundamental ones.

I am undertaking a political task: calling all politicians, whatever their orientation, to set themselves to this work. That will be the common task. I have already spoken with those who have been our comrades in the struggle on the Justicialist Front of Liberation. I have talked with Dr. Balbín, the leader of the Radical Party; I am going to speak tomorrow with those who formed "The

Hour of the People." Afterward I will do so with our remaining opponents, whatever their ideology.

I will even talk with the Communist Party, which, if it stays within the law, we will protect and even defend. But within the law. (Be careful what you do; if not, we will have to throw the book at you.)

We do not permit guerrillas because I know perfectly well what their origins are. Communist Parties in other countries saw that staying "within the law" led to their destruction, so they went outside the law in order to defend themselves better. That is not possible in a country where the law will be fully in effect. Because the only way not to be enslaved is to be slaves to the law; and that is something that we have to impose, in whatever way we can.

I know the origin of all this. I have been in Paris, on the very barricades, and I have spoken with many people who were there and had gone there for that, for the barricades. And I well know which procedures they want to set in motion and that they put in action in what they called the "Second French Revolution." On 30 and 31 July 1968, they hung on the facade of the Sorbonne a huge sign that said: "You guerrillas will liberate us from what they want to sell us: Air-conditioned death in the name of the future. The Industrial Order must go. The marketplaces of consumption must die a violent death. *We want a government with half an imagination.*" Thus the sign read. But the bottom line was to form the guerrilla movement. Guerrillas whom we have seen at work everywhere.

Well: that is a matter that the law cannot tolerate, and that, consequently, we cannot tolerate. We have no objection if a political party—whether called Communist, ERP, or whatever—wants to operate within the law, as we are doing. Neither do we have any fears if it operated outside of the law, but it is not the proper thing for a government. We have already seen guerrillas function in other places, and they do not behave properly. When something happens outside the law, it is a matter for the courts and the police.

If we can persuade all Argentines of all these things, I believe that it will be a great triumph for the government. To govern is not to give orders; that is the mistake that we military people often make, for we are accustomed to command.

To command is to require, to govern is to persuade. And it is better to persuade a man than to require him to do something. That is our task, the one of persuading all Argentines to start kicking the ball toward the same goal, that is to say, to work toward the objectives of our country and the needs of our people. . . .

I have always had much more faith in businessmen; they are the ones who

Perón's funeral (1974). Courtesy Archivo General de la Nación, Buenos Aires.

have demonstrated convincingly that they know how to do things. The country is one big business writ large; a person who can manage a big business can also manage this other great business. Technique is important because there are always fiscal matters involved. In my opinion, the overall planning should be left to those with a broader understanding, and the details should be left to managers who know how to handle the daily execution of its affairs. For that reason, the two complement one another: the businessman comes up with ideas, and the technical manager carries them out. And, if we can manage to bring these two qualities together, we can rest easy. The national economy is in good hands, as I see it has been during the time we have been governing so far.

Other matters will resolve themselves in the same way. Social order will reestablish itself when, through popular education, we take away all hope from the troublemakers and the infiltrators, and we will give true meaning to the social concerns of our country, bringing, through the state and through institutions of all kinds, the concept of social life as in modern countries.

As for political action, I believe that I have already given my opinion.

If, gentlemen, we accomplish all this in accordance with the old dictum of the Greeks, "all in harmony and moderation," we can guarantee that success will be ours.

I ask God every day that this miracle might be realized and that one day the Argentines will thank us the way people used to thank men, back in the time when men not only were honored by the political office but also knew how to ennoble those political offices.

Translated by Mark Alan Healey

VIII

State Violence

After Perón's death in 1974, the antagonistic political forces contained under the umbrella of the Justicialist Party were unleashed. The increasing chaos within Isabel Perón's administration and mounting political violence led to a military coup in 1976 and the beginning of one of the bloodiest periods of Argentine history. The persecution of political dissidents—which began at least two years before the coup—was institutionalized and expanded to create a systematic killing machine. Scholars have found no easy explanation for the degree of cruelty and indifference to human life shown by the military and its supporters. Although old political rivalries played a role, the political scientist Guillermo O'Donnell has argued that the harshness of the military regimes characteristic of the 1970s was primarily the product of the requirements of a new wave of modernization throughout Latin America and of a shift in the professional profile of the armed forces. At the time, however, the military justified organized repression as absolutely necessary to put an end to guerrilla activity and defended state violence as the only means of guaranteeing political stability. The ideology behind all military operations was the doctrine of national security—a program backed by U.S. anti-Communist foreign policy, which supported authoritarian regimes against leftist movements. During the eight years of the dictatorship, thousands of people mysteriously "disappeared" at the hands of death squads, which, acting with total impunity, kidnapped union leaders, writers, journalists, students, and political activists. Cultural life was meticulously screened by a censorship committee, and all universities and unions came under government control. Efforts to maintain a repressive security state were complicated by an economic model that generated unemployment, corruption, and inflation. With the return to democracy in 1983, President Raúl Alfonsín decreed that an extraordinary trial bring to justice all the members of the military juntas that had governed the country between 1976 and 1983 as well as many high-ranking officers who had collaborated with the regime.[1] The public trials brought to light the horrifying

experiences of thousands of illegally confined prisoners who, after being kidnapped, had been taken to clandestine concentration camps, where they were
savagely tortured and ultimately killed. Survivors' testimonies were essential
for the prosecution of those responsible for human rights violations and were
collected in the official report *Never Again*.

The art and literature produced under the dictatorship bear the scars of
political brutality. Although some artists openly denounced state violence,
others cloaked their opposition in hidden messages of muffled despair. In the
novel *Artificial Respiration* by Ricardo Piglia, convoluted metaphors circumvent forced silence through oblique allusions to the unspeakable depravities
and the pervasive violence that shattered the lives of Argentine citizens. In *The
Mute*—a disturbing sculpture from 1973 that uncannily prefigured what was
coming—Juan Carlos Distéfano froze in acrylic the unbearable helplessness
of a dehumanized tortured body, while the painter Carlos Alonso engraved
in his series of prints on torture the contorted gesticulation of a pain that defied representation. In 1982, after six devastating years of dictatorship, the poet
Néstor Perlongher cataloged in "Corpses" what remained of a society that had
become utterly suffused with death. Just as art provided the tools for protest,
it also created a locus of resistance. Defending the revolutionary ideals embraced by the political activists, artists, and intellectuals that the dictatorship
was methodically annihilating, the poet Juan Gelman crafted his poems with
the language of hope.

After seeing many of their friends disappear or return to their homes emotionally and physically scarred by brutal interrogations, or after themselves
being persecuted and threatened by the military regime, hundreds of Argentinians were forced into exile and spent several years in countries such as
Mexico, Spain, and France. Although usually free from danger, the experience
of exile was neither comforting nor serene. Tununa Mercado re-creates the
underlying agony of living a divided existence in Mexico, where she and other
exiles remained in a permanent state of memory, continuously grieving the
loss of their country.

The extreme measures adopted by the regime to silence and control dissident voices did not prevent the emergence of organized forms of protest. Confronted with a judicial system deaf to their claims, the mothers of those who
had disappeared began to assemble every Thursday at the traditional Plaza de
Mayo, in front of the presidential palace, demanding to be told their children's
fate. Like their sons and daughters, they were the victims of police abuse and,
in some cases, ended up joining the thousands of disappeared. But, by stressing their condition as suffering mothers, they managed to survive and have
their complaints heard by the foreign press and international human rights

organizations. Arm in arm with them were the "grandmothers of the Plaza de Mayo" — women who sought to recover their grandsons and granddaughters who, kidnapped with their parents or born in concentration camps, were given away, in many cases to the very officers who had been instrumental in their parents' deaths. The mothers and grandmothers of the Plaza de Mayo were the only visible oppositional presence during the dark years of the dictatorship; and, toward its closing, they would become the main protagonists in the transition to democracy. In the testimony that we have selected, Hebe de Bonafini recounts the uncertain beginnings of the organization that she helped found.

In 1982, the dictatorship began to crumble. In March, the unions organized a national strike that paralyzed the country. The police and the army harshly repressed public demonstrations in downtown Buenos Aires, triggering popular riots. Images of wounded protesters, burning cars, and police brutality were broadcast and published worldwide. On 2 April, a confounded citizenry learned from the media that Argentine troops had landed on the Malvinas Islands (Falklands) in defiance of British occupation. Unexpectedly, Argentina was going to war for the possession of territories that had been under dispute for centuries. Although it initially rallied broad public support, the act of aggression was soon revealed as a desperate and foolish attempt by General Galtieri to counter the military regime's decline in credibility. Personal accounts by soldiers and officers who were sent to the front indicate that the government initiated the war with neither a clear plan nor the necessary supplies for an armed confrontation in the South Atlantic. The embarrassing defeat that immediately followed precipitated the end of the military dictatorship. In October 1983, general elections were held, and Raúl Alfonsín, the candidate of the old Unión Cívica Radical (UCR), was elected president. Democracy had finally returned.

Note

1 In contrast with the Chilean case, the Argentine dictatorship was not organized around the figure of a strong military man but consisted of a series of military juntas formed by members from the three armed forces.

Modernization and Military Coups

Guillermo O'Donnell

After the military coup of 1976, many asked themselves whether Argentina was indeed an authoritarian society, unable and unwilling to defend its democratic and republican institutions. The recurrence of military coups with some degree of civil support, along with the strong ties that party politics of many colors had with certain sectors of the army, suggested an affirmative answer. The political scientist Guillermo O'Donnell has developed one of the most complex and convincing explanations of Argentine dictatorial relapses after 1955. Far from being the necessary outcome of national character, he contends, military coalitions were shaped by local and international trends. In a context of rapid modernization and weak institutional mediations, a newly professionalized military sought to suppress "excessive" popular demands and to promote capitalist development while engaging in the international war against communism launched by the United States. In O'Donnell's view, the last Argentine dictatorship followed a political pattern—the authoritarian-bureaucratic state—inaugurated by the military regime of General Onganía in 1966.

First Structural Level: The Argentine Social Context, 1955–66

The period 1955–66 marked the worsening of a crisis that embraced—and embraces—numerous facets of Argentine society. The complex manifestations of this crisis make it impossible to attempt a satisfactory summary within the confines of this study. I will limit myself to stating briefly those factors that appear to have exerted the most significant and direct influence on the political behavior of the military. Thus, the criterion used is somewhat arbitrary, and this summary does not pretend to substitute for a detailed study of the Argentine social context during the 1955–66 period.

Argentina does not fit the stereotype of the "underdeveloped country." The Argentine case is one of high modernization.[1] Argentina is a dependent society, marked by an imbalanced productive structure and spatial configuration. It is subject to many social rigidities, a high concentration of economic and political power, and a low level of creativity directly applicable to productive processes.

The great influence of more economically advanced societies on institutions, roles, and social practices, particularly in the more modernized sectors (especially the large urban centers), is reflected in patterns of dependence. These are linked to other structural characteristics of high modernization: a high degree of industrialization, high urban concentration, a high level of social differentiation and of political activity, and a relatively solid and autonomous organizational base (especially among trade unions) in the popular sector.

Argentine industry operates at high cost, with multiple inefficiencies, a combination of high oligopolistic concentration and numerous small producers, and a growing need for raw material imports, capital goods, and technological know-how. These characteristics, combined with stagnant agricultural production, produced a chronic balance of payments deficit, which contributed to the limited economic growth and high inflation of the 1955–66 period. After the overthrow of Perón, the prevailing viewpoint was that controlling inflation and increasing exports were requisites for Argentine economic growth. To attain these objectives, it seemed indispensable to contain demands for goods and services in order to transfer income to the producers of agricultural exports. Because it was felt that excess demand originated in the consumption expectations of the popular sector, these socioeconomic policies tended to worsen the situation of the very same sector that maintained a strong loyalty to Peronism. Consequently, the socioeconomic cleavage between the "popular sector" and the "rest of society" tended to coincide with the political cleavage between "Peronists" and "anti-Peronists." This situation was accentuated by the vindictiveness of numerous public decisions during the period 1955–58 and by the various attempts to destroy and to weaken the unions. It was inevitably consolidated by the exclusion of Peronism from the electoral process, whether by direct and open proscription or through the annulment of elections of Peronist candidates.

It is necessary to mention some aspects of the economic situation during the 1955–66 period. Per capita income grew at an annual rate of only 1.3 percent, and from year to year great fluctuations occurred within this low average.[2] The annual inflation during the period was 32.67 percent, but the average inflation in the negative-growth years was 39.68 percent.[3] Deflated wages surpassed the level of 1947 only in 1958 and 1965, declining again the following year. After reaching a maximum of 46.9 in 1952, the percentage of the gross national product represented by wages and salaries had fallen to 39.8 in 1965, despite the fact that as early as 1961 productivity per worker exceeded the rate in 1953 by 23 percent.[4] The low productivity of the agrarian sector and the deficient structure of the industrial sector generated a massive demand for imported goods in years of resurgent economic activity. This further worsened the economic strangulation that originated in the balance of payments deficits. This led to drastic devaluations, generally accompanied by measures to reduce internal demand, to eliminate "marginal" producers, and to transfer income to agrarian producers. The devaluations fed inflation by raising the price of imports and exportable foodstuffs intended for domestic consumption, while the associated recessive policies markedly diminished production and demand. This resulted in negative growth, inflation, and a large negative redistribution of income. . . .

Inflation and zero-sum conditions also determined that for each sector the time spent "catching" inflation was of critical importance. As time passed, real losses increased, and it became more unlikely that one would attain sufficient new monetary income to compensate for that already lost through inflation. This situation produced strong politicization and concentration of socioeconomic demands. Politicization occurred for three reasons. First, the most efficient means for the competitors to effect a reallocation of resources was to influence the choice and implementation of public policies. Second, the coercive apparatus of the state represented the means necessary to impose these reallocations on the sectors that would have to "pay" for them with a real decline in their income levels. Third, it was impossible to channel demands through government institutions (such as Parliament, the political parties, or the provincial and municipal governments) because they played a very secondary role in the allocation of socioeconomic resources. It also became increasingly improbable that other institutions would achieve any real influence in the expression and resolution of conflicts.

This situation maximized the importance of channels of political access that allowed one to exercise power over the presidency directly. Since the armed forces were the most effective channel for exercising power over the presidency, competing civilians tried to persuade military factions to articulate sectoral demands. These patterns of demand formulation implied for governments the explicit threat of being overthrown. The credibility of this threat was reinforced by numerous *planteos* and by various coups d'état (successful and unsuccessful) during the period 1955–66. This gave an obvious advantage in the race against inflation to those sectors that could initiate threats of coups d'état by the armed forces.

The better organized urban workers counted on a strategy that, although more indirect and costly, could produce similar results. The promotion of high levels of social protest, such as paralyzing production by means of strikes and occupying buildings, placed governments in the position of being unable to maintain "law and order" and, for that reason, in imminent danger of being toppled. With this base, the better organized workers could aspire (although at a cost sometimes high in terms of repression) to obtain an improvement in wages and working conditions from governments already chronically pressured by military factions and their civilian allies who saw in the persistence of high levels of social protest the best justification for the overthrow of the government.

The threats of a coup d'état were very real, and any government that valued its survival could not afford to ignore them. Therefore, governments tended to adopt the public policies demanded by the most threatening sector at a given moment. The conditions of zero sum, however, meant that these same decisions created new threats from other sectors that possessed direct or indirect means of exerting power over the government. Frequent and apparently erratic changes of public policies resulted from these circumstances.

The resulting situation is related to the concept of "mass praetorianism" proposed by Samuel Huntington. Accentuating a notable historical tendency, the norms for political behavior and for the implementation of demands became farther and farther removed from those institutionally prescribed. Norms tended to be transformed into naked power strategies. All those sectors that were capable of using the strategy of formulating threats against the government did so, for to be more threatening than the other sectors was the most effective means available to each sector for the attainment of its demands. This resulted in a marked tendency to escalate the level of threats and to convert the presidency into the focal point of a veritable agglomeration of demands, which existing conditions made particularly urgent and hardly compatible.

Meanwhile those sectors and regions lacking the organizational power to threaten the government effectively became increasingly marginalized in the allocation of resources. In addition, the government's resources markedly diminished during the period. Under these conditions, government personnel were limited in their ability to make and implement decisions other than those demanded by the most threatening sectors at any given moment. In turn, this incapacitation of the government and its steadily declining political resources worsened the larger social situation and consolidated the zero-sum conditions. . . .

. . . It became evident that almost everyone was losing and only a few winning—and then only to see part of their winnings annulled shortly thereafter. This perception of the situation led to the questioning of the very rules of the "game" and of the political institutions that had been unable to guide the game more efficiently. This generalized perception of the sterility of the "political game" corresponded to a similar perception of the inadequacy of the socioeconomic criteria that had shaped both the ostensible content of demands and the implementation of policies. Increasingly, participants from very different ideological viewpoints proposed drastic changes in the existing distribution of political power and socioeconomic resources and the introduction of a new political regime, presumably capable of carrying out and institutionalizing the changes.

Toward the end of the period 1955–66, the majority of the participants reached what might be termed a *consensus of termination*: the existing political regime had exhausted its resources and had to be replaced. Naturally, the "consensus" was strictly limited to the replacement of the existing regime. The participants remained in disagreement regarding the new rules to be introduced and the new distribution of power and resources they should reflect. But, despite this, the "consensus of termination" eliminated the few points of support remaining to the existing regime. From this point on, the principal question became how long it would take for a winning coalition to form among the participants that had arrived at the so-called termination consensus. A question of equal importance to the theme of this study was the time that would elapse before the advent of military intervention, an intervention that would represent a radical change from the existing political regime.

Second Structural Level: The Argentine Armed Forces, 1955–66

The Argentine armed forces have a long-standing tradition of coups d'état and intense participation in national politics. Following the overthrow of Juan Perón in a climate of intense social protest, the armed forces and the Peronist unions became the most visible opponents in an intense conflict. The reconstruction of the national government and the ascent of Frondizi to the presidency after an electoral "pact" with Perón produced vehement dissatisfaction in the military. Also, as expressed by the commander-in-chief of the army, General C. Toranzo Montero, the armed forces felt they were charged with the protection of "the republican way of life against all extremism or totalitarianism" and were ultimately responsible, due to the "failure of the civil authorities," to "restore the values of national unity and of public order," for resolving the problems "caused" by Peronism.[5] This "custodial function" of the military opened the way for a long series of plots and coups.

This definition of the armed forces' role left to their unilateral interpretation the meaning of the "values" to be protected and the conditions under which they would be threatened. On this basis they opted for the electoral exclusion of the supposedly "totalitarian" Peronism. In addition, since it could be argued thta those "values" were compromised by practically any government decision, their custodial function permitted the armed forces to become a channel for numerous and changing sectoral demands. The armed forces became a reflection of the praetorian competition of the non-Peronist sectors of Argentine society. This situation, together with the frequent coup threats in support of sectoral demands, resulted in the severe factionalization of the armed forces. This factionalization, in turn, resulted in several internal putsches, the destruction of vertical patterns of authority, and the abrupt end of careers for numerous officers.

When Frondizi was overthrown in 1962, the *golpista* officers attempted to reestablish a prolonged dictatorship to restore "order and an authentic democracy." However, by this time, an important reaction had taken shape within the army and the air force. Many officers argued convincingly of the disastrous effects—for both military organization and their own careers—of the intense politicization and the resultant factionalization of the military. These officers argued for a return to their "specific duties" and opposed political participation, including any installation of a prolonged military dictatorship. Today it appears evident that this argument was fostered by an acute concern for the survival of the organization itself, which seemed threatened by internal division and by growing levels of social protest. This argument favoring organizational survival and the preservation of careers had great impact within the military. Likewise, its obvious implication (a "return to the barracks") found immediate support among the numerous civil sectors frightened by the possibility of a *golpista* dictatorship.

The organizational motivation for the "return to the barracks" policy was the conflict between the dictatorial *golpistas* and a new breed of legalist, professional officers. These groups confronted each other twice, in September 1962 and April 1963, resulting in a decisive victory for the "legalists." This "legalist" victory did not benefit the first plurality of the electorate, however; in spite of their professed support for professional "apolitical" armed forces, after some internal debate the "legalists" decided to continue the electoral exclusion of the Peronists.

After the "legalists" attained firm control of the armed forces, a series of important organizational changes took place. Under the direction of General Onganía, "legalists" conducted a successful process of professionalization that merits detailed examination. First, they reestablished patterns of authority more in keeping with vertical lines of command. Second, they established new methods of military training that emphasized the study of modern technology and "contemporary social problems." Third, in 1964 a "program of military assistance" was signed with the United States that played an important role in armaments modernization and adaptation to the type of warfare foreseen by the new "Doctrine of National Security." Fourth, a clear sense emerged of the distinction between belonging to the military organization and belonging to the rest of society. In summary, these occurrences produced a marked advance in the professionalization of, and in U.S. influence over, the Argentine armed forces. These factors, in turn, generated consequences of great importance.

The first and perhaps most important of these consequences was a clear recognition of the organizational achievements of the military and the need to preserve them through a high degree of internal cohesion. Still fresh was the memory of the organizational damage wrought by the type of political participation characteristic of the *golpista* period, particularly the internal factionalization resulting from the channeling of sectoral demands through the military in the praetorian game. Consequently, the "legalist" officers insisted on adopting a position supposedly "above politics," which among other things meant that the political plots, which were so commonplace in previous years, disappeared in the period 1963–66. Of course, a position "above politics" did not indicate disinterest in national politics, nor did it signify that the new military leaders entirely dismissed the possibility of new coups d'état. Rather, as General Onganía stated repeatedly, the armed forces should not interfere with the normal official activities of civilian authorities but should and could intervene in "cases of extreme seriousness," as determined by the armed forces in each concrete case.

A second and closely related consequence was the redefinition of the position and functions of the armed forces in Argentine society. To quote General Onganía,

> [The armed forces] exist to guarantee the sovereignty and territorial integrity of the nation, to preserve the moral and spiritual values of Western and Christian civilization, to maintain public order and domestic peace, to promote the general welfare, to sustain the enforcement of the constitution, of its rights and essential guarantees, and to maintain the republican institutions in which they are established legally.[6]

The functions of the armed forces became much broader than those postulated by the *golpista* officers, who tended to define their role as preventing "totalitarian parties" from attaining government power. But, more importantly, for the armed forces to fulfill their vast "mission," their organizational power and Argentine socioeconomic development were postulated as necessary conditions. Therefore, any problem that would hinder establishment of these conditions could be interpreted as an impediment to the fulfillment of the armed forces' mission. According to this concept, the functions of the armed forces are so extensive and essential that any problem affecting these conditions has to be interpreted as an attack on the most "vital" interests of the nation. Since by action or inaction governments can impede the fulfillment of the "fundamental premises," it is obvious that within this conception government authorities can receive only conditional loyalty.

This conception should be understood from the perspective of a third consequence: the armed forces' adoption of the so-called Doctrine of National Security. U.S. authorities supported the adoption of this "doctrine" by the Latin American armed forces as the best safeguard against the impact of the Cuban Revolution and the revolutionary potential of the area. According to this "doctrine," the local armed forces, in addition to the "traditional aim" of preparing for foreign wars, must include among their "specific duties" the execution of "internal warfare" against "subversive" agents who attempt to wrest the "underdeveloped" nations from the sphere of "Western civilization" and to bring them under "Communist" control.[7] Since the "enemy" is multifaceted, "internal warfare" can be "ideological, economic, or political."[8] Consequently, multiple strategies are needed to fight him. In addition, the description and definition of the enemy are not always clear. "Here is where the combat experience of the armed forces and their special preparation for warfare make them indispensable in the securing of the objective — in the characterization of the enemy, in the determination of his capabilities and modes of operation, in the selection of strategy, and in assuring that the appropriate course of action is taken to achieve desired ends." "Victory" in this "war" will mean the attainment of a satisfactory state of "national security" — defined as "the situation, certainly classifiable, in which the vital interests of the nation are safe from interferences or disturbances — internal or external, violent or nonviolent, open or surreptitious — that can neutralize or delay development and consequently weaken the very existence of the nation or its sovereignty."[9]

"Subversion" flourishes "in an underdeveloped socioeconomic environment." Therefore, without a prosperous, highly integrated society with a low level of conflict, "national security" will not be attained, and the armed forces will not have accomplished one of their fundamental goals. From this it naturally follows "that development is the very essence of national security."[10] It also follows that "there consequently does not exist a doctrine or a strategy of the armed forces that differs from that of the entire society."[11] "Security" is confused with "development," and both become part of the "specific functions" of the armed forces. This ideology permits, at least potentially, the militarization of any social problem that for whatever reason is considered important by the officers of the armed forces.

The persistence of the social processes alluded to in the first section of this study could be interpreted as an indication that the "fundamental premise" of "socioeconomic development" was not being fulfilled. In addition, the combination of this with high levels of social protest led to the diagnosis of the growing probability of an extensive diffusion and final victory of "subversion." According to the national security conception, poor government management and the strangulation of development interacted to facilitate "subversion." Therefore, the underlying logic of the national security conception indicated that it was part of the "specific duty" of the armed forces to eliminate these two "authentic causes" of "subversion."

But these conclusions are valid only if a fourth consequence has also resulted from the efforts at professionalization: the military officers must be convinced that their capabilities are clearly superior to those of the civil sectors and that these capabilities are sufficient to solve a wide range of social problems. That conviction resulted, in part, from the continuation of socioeconomic problems and the persistence of mass praetorianism. However, it is my impression that it resulted principally from the very success of the attempt at military professionalization. As the military officers saw it, they had resolved "their" problem, while the civil sectors and the government continued in a state of total crisis. This feeling of organizational accomplishment led to the belief, however illogical, that the military possessed a superior capacity to confront the social problems that the civil authorities evidently could not solve. But, in my opinion, the military's perception and evaluation of the social structure and of its own role were not consciously justificatory pretexts for taking over the government. The majority of these officers were acutely aware of their organizational accomplishments and were sincerely convinced of their superior ability to attain "socioeconomic development" and to eliminate "subversion." Not only were the armed forces the "last hope" for a situation viewed as bordering on acute social crisis—as the *golpista* officers had also claimed—but they were also an organization that had acquired technical skill, training in "social problems," and sufficient internal unity to involve themselves directly and successfully on the socioeconomic battlefront. . . .

By 1965, indications were abundant that numerous civil sectors had reached the "consensus of termination" and were pressing strongly for a new military intervention. The high level of social protest, marked by strikes and the occupying of businesses, seriously worried the more established sectors. In addition, President Illía was noted for his lassitude and his ineffectiveness in making decisions, and the Parliament seemed reduced to a forum for personal quarrels. Given this stimulus, the internal evolution of the military, and the continuation of the processes mentioned in the first section of this study, it is no exaggeration to say that in 1965 the major question was simply the date of the new coup d'état.[12] The choice of the date seems to have been largely determined by an attempt to limit the risk of reintroducing military factionalization over what attitude to adopt toward the elections coming in 1967. The military continued to be divided over the electoral participation of the Peronists, who still retained a plurality within the electorate. To deal with this problem effectively, the "legalist" officers had to execute the coup late enough for the risk to be clearly perceived in the military, but not so late that the electoral campaign of 1967 had already begun. In this way the "legalist" leaders optimized the probability of strong military cohesion in support of the coup d'état and minimized the possibility of civil opposition.

On 28 June 1966, a revolutionary junta, made up of the commanders-in-chief of the three branches of the armed forces, deposed President Illía and designated General Onganía as president. The new government dissolved the institutions of the former political regime, enunciated the wide-ranging "goals of the Revolution," and stated their willingness to stay in power for the indefinite (but doubtless long) period of time required to achieve these goals. With very few exceptoins the social sectors and public opinion expressed their support for the coup. . . .

The real advance in military professionalism, the feeling of organizational accomplishment and of superior capability, the high degree of corporate identification, and the ideology of "national security" characterized a military process that produced enough objective capacity and subjective confidence to execute a coup d'état that sought a drastic and definitive change from the existing political regime. In order to do this, and despite the fact that various civil sectors had reached the termination consensus well before June 1966, it was necessary for the armed forces to have completed the process of professionalization (with four consequences already indicated) and for the social structure to have presented new dangers of factionalization in the armed forces. The *golpista* military officers intervened several times, but with much more specific demands and with the expressed purpose of restoring government power to "appropriate" civilian rule. When, in 1962, the *golpistas* tried to take over the government directly and for an extended period of time, they failed because of their precarious control of the seriously divided military and the absence of a justifying ideology. In contrast, the new "legalist" military leaders did not intervene until, strongly united, they could take direct control of the government with the intention of maintaining power indefinitely to accomplish much more ambitious goals. For what occured in 1966, two necessary conditions had to exist that were absent in 1962: (1) variables in the social structure that were expressed in the termination consensus and (2) variables within the military organization resulting from its process of professionalization. The professionalization of the armed forces in a praetorian context raises the critical point for military intervention. But, once the critical point is reached, military intervention takes place with more internal cohesion, with a comprehensive justificatory ideology, and with the purpose of achieving goals much more ambitious than those of the coups undertaken by less professional armed forces. Contrary to what many governing officials and experts have supposed, professionalization of the armed forces does not resolve the endemic problem of militarism. All it does is exchange a higher critical point for the probability of a much more comprehensive military intervention directed toward the establishment of much more complete domination.

What has been said up to this point permits us to propose generalizations that available information suggests should be applicable to other nations whose social structures have similar characteristics of high modernization and mass praetorianism. The next section will be devoted to comparing these propositions with prevailing interpretations in political sociology, with which they differ in several important respects.

Comparative Theoretical Focuses on the Political Behavior of the Military

The social and organizational processes described in the preceding sections support propositions applicable to the political behavior of the military in social contexts of high modernization.

Proposition 1: The "highly modernized" nations have distinct characteristics that tend to generate equally distinctive patterns of political behavior. Specifically, (*a*) a prolonged process of industrialization that fails to acquire either a sufficient level of vertical integration or a scientific-technological structure capable of generating innovations and of applying them continuously to the uneven productive processes typical of this form of industrialization and (*b*) the existence of large and complex urban centers with a politically active and highly organized popular sector. Furthermore, high modernization tends to consolidate historically inherited problems (particularly external dependence and inequitable distribution of resources) and to generate high rates of inflation, irregular economic growth, and limited government capability.

Proposition 2: If this historical legacy also includes a high level of popular alienation from the political regime and its authorities as well as little conformity between real and institutionally prescribed behavior, it is highly probable that nations experiencing situations of high modernization will undergo prolonged periods of mass praetorianism. In a situation of high modernization and mass praetorianism, political competition tends to establish intersectoral violence and threats against the government as the most effective means of formulating and articulating demands. This leads to a decline in the role played by formally democratic institutions, to an even greater diminution of government capability for resolving social problems, and to the consolidation of conditions of zero-sum competition between sectors. These consequences reverberate, aggravating mass praetorianism.

The logic of the situation of high modernization and mass praetorianism leads to diminishing socioeconomic returns and to growing political activity on the part of the urban popular sector. In turn, this heightened political activity is perceived by a substantial part of the more established sectors as a serious threat to their control. This perception provokes defensive reactions aimed at closing direct access to the political process for the popular sector and its leaders as a requisite for the implementation of public policies that, by favoring an even greater concentration of resources in large public and private organizations, will supposedly generate higher and more stable rates of economic growth. But the form the defensive reaction will take depends in great measure on changes in the military organization.

> *Proposition 3:* Given the conditions specified in the previous propositions, there exists a strong probability of frequent interventions by the armed forces, as much by threats of force (*planteos*) as by taking over government power. The motivation, and a fundamental effect, of these interventions was the closing of direct political access to the popular sector and the denial of its public policy demands. In these interventions, the armed forces express and execute the defensive reaction of the more established sectors to the growing levels of political activism by the popular sector, to the conditions of zero sum that characterize the competition for the distribution of resources, and to mass praetorianism generally.

The preceding proposition coincides with an important current in the study of the political behavior of the military. José Nun has argued that, in contemporary Latin America, political interventions by the military were expressions of the ambiguities and fears aroused in the middle class (from which a good part of the army officers are drawn) by processes of social change that had mobilized the working class and had placed in question the viability of capitalist development in the more economically advanced nations of the continent. Much later, Samuel Huntington continued this line of argument in more general terms: the armed forces tend to fulfill a "progressive" role in promoting the entry of the middle class into a political arena previously monopolized by traditional oligarchies; but, once this objective is reached, its principal preoccupation is to impede the political participation of what Huntington calls "the lower class."[13]

With certain reservations, it seems clear that the Latin American case supports the interpretation of these two authors. In those cases (such as Argentina and Brazil) in which, through an extended period of industrialization, a substantial part of the middle sectors has secured various agreements with the traditionally dominant sectors, the motivation and effects of military interventions have been in the direction implied by this structuralist focus. In other cases—Argentina during the Perón era, Brazil under Vargas, and modern-day Peru—where the aspirations of numerous middle sectors were to a large extent blocked by still dominant traditional sectors, and where industrialization, density of urban concentration, and the degree of political activism of the urban popular sectors were considerably lower, the armed forces fulfilled the more "progressive" role also foreseen by these authors. But, although the structuralist focus points in the correct direction, it leaves various outstanding problems that should be carefully considered.

First, it pays little or purely circumstantial attention to the consequences that military organizational factors can have on the political behavior of the military. Accordingly, this focus refrains from studying over time empirical variations in the form and degree of the closure of political access for the popular sector that military interventions may produce. As the Argentine case illustrates, these different forms of military intervention hold different consequences for the society and for the political regime.

Second, this conception may be sufficient as a generic description of military behavior under different kinds of social structures, but it cannot in reality explain variations in this behavior in similar kinds of societies. One possible solution to this problem, which is utilized by these authors, is to postulate that the middle-class background of the majority of the armed forces officers leads them to "express" or to "represent" the attitudes and interests of the middle class. But the presumption of this linkage as the principal factor explaining the political behavior of the military ignores the factor of military organization itself. It also overlooks the ambiguity of the terms *express* and *represent* and, above all, the extreme heterogeneity of the so-called middle class in highly modernized societies.

Proposition 4: The different ways in which the armed forces close political access to the popular sector, and reject its public policy demands, depend to an important extent on the nature of the military organization. The state of the military organization is a variable whose empirical changes should be studied over time because they are a fundamental factor for explaining and predicting the political behavior of the armed forces.

This proposition should be stressed strongly. It is the basis for important differences in the interpretation of military behavior that I am proposing from those that come from the "structuralist" focus and from the "neorealist" focus, which I will analyze next. One important difference with the "structuralist" authors is the emphasis on the explanatory role of the level of organization. A second and more important difference is on the level of military organization as a variable that should be studied empirically over time. One can apply the term *army* to the forces in nineteenth-century Prussia, in nineteenth-century Argentina, and in present-day Argentina, but it is deceptive to imply that the concept *army* has the same meaning in these various applications. To mention only two very basic matters: for most of the nineteenth century the Argentine army had no clear supremacy in the control of the means of violence inside the national territory, and most of its members did not dress in a way that distinguished them from the civilian population. It makes no sense to designate as *army* entities that differ in fundamental respects or to hope that by some magic effect of names they will conduct themselves in similar ways. The state of the military organization varies from one national unit to another and within the same national unit over time. And these variations should be empirically determined and theoretically weighed for the purpose of explaining or predicting the political behavior of the military.

"Neorealist" interpretations of military behavior are derived from characteristics of "the military in the developing countries" inferred from the probable consequences of transferring the organizational forms of the military in Western countries to transitional societies.[14] On the basis of these presumed characteristics, "neorealists" deduce that the capabilities of the military are significantly superior to those of the civilian sectors in terms of technological qualification, efficient and rational decisionmaking and implementation, of "modernizing" motivations. In turn, this presumed superiority endows the military with special abilities, markedly superior to those of the civilian sectors, to conduct and attain the "development" of their nations. From this conception, it follows easily (although not always in an explicit way) not only that is it probable that the military will directly assume government power in the "underdeveloped countries" but also that they should assume it for the sake of "development." The least that can be said about the evidence this interpretation offers in support of its arguments is that it is completely unsatisfactory. But it is worth the effort to analyze some of its aspects and implications. . . .

Proposition 5: In a praetorian context, the armed forces will tend initially toward a low level of professionalism. Under such conditions they will participate directly in the praetorian game, channeling the demands and threats posed by the civilian sectors and maintaining a low critical threshold for attempting the overthrow of the government (civilian or military). In this way the armed forces become important factors contributing to the high political instability (from cabinet crises to coups) that characterizes the praetorian periods. The weak professionalism of the armed forces (especially their weak internal cohesion) prevents them from espousing important goals or from effecting significant changes in the state of the social context. Political interventions by scarcely professional armed forces tend to hand over or return government power to their civilian allies after short periods of direct government control. Although some military factions may wish to attain more ambitious and comprehensive objectives, the weak internal cohesion and the lack of a justificatory ideology generally accepted among the members of the armed forces impede the realization of these designs.

Proposition 6: The persistence of praetorianism at the societal level and of factionalization at the military organizational level implies great costs for the military officers, including threats to the survival of their organization, uncertainty in their personal careers, and the severe reduction of their possibilities of power over the national political processes. Furthermore, the high levels of social conflict and the high degree of political activism by the urban popular sector (both characteristics of mass praetorianism in high modernization) induce well-established sectors and actors (including foreign interests) to view the armed forces as an indispensable guarantee for the preservation of the country's existing social structure and its international alliances. The perception of corporate interest on the part of the military officers, together with civilian persuasions to strengthen the military organization, generate a military reaction directed at rapidly and drastically raising existing levels of professionalism. One condition necessary for achieving this goal is a temporary military retreat from its direct and immediate participation in the praetorian game.

Proposition 7: The professionalist reaction enjoys a good probability of success either by completely displacing those officers most compromised in the praetorian game (the Argentine case) or by attaining control over the military academies, elite units, and contacts with the military in the more developed nations by the officers that concern themselves with the process of professionalization (the Brazilian and Greek cases). In both instances marked progress occurred in internal cohesion, combat capabilities, and

corporate identification. At the same time, the withdrawal from direct political participation by the armed forces does not impede the continuation
of mass praetorianism among the civilian contenders.

Proposition 8: The organizational gain involved in the significantly higher
level of professionalization tends to be contrasted by part of the military to
the continuation of the social crisis. This contrast foments a very low opinion of the capability and the motivations of the civilian sectors and a feeling
of superior military ability for resolving not only its present organizational
problems but also the wide range of salient societal problems.

The military tends to see itself as the only sector that has been able to provide a solution to "its" problem. Simultaneously, the greater internal cohesion, technical capabilities, and corporate identification attained by the military allow it to act more effectively within a certain range of problems (internal
conduct of its organization, training for various forms of combat, and use of
armaments). This superior ability does not imply a similar progress in the military aptitude for solving problems external to its organization, as "neorealists"
argue, but it does seem to have a marked influence on the military officers'
extrapolation from one context to the other. This is a crucial point in the evolution of the political attitudes of the military officers.

During the period in which the professionalization of the armed forces is
weak, it is not credible to view the military officers as possessing the superior
capabilities necessary to resolve the social problems of high modernization.
For that reason, the officers of the scarcely professionalized armed forces tend
to divide themselves into coalitions in which the civilians play a decisive role,
and in their interventions they do not pretend to do much more than to hand
government power over to their civilian allies. Further, in the period of low professionalization, it is improbable that an ideology justifying military interventions guided by much more ambitious and comprehensive goals will emerge
and be generally accepted. But the situation changes radically with the successful professionalization of the armed forces. The old allies are looked on with
resentment, new civilian contacts are established, and the level of the military's
corporate identity rises rapidly. In turn, this heightened identity stimulates
further growth of the military's perception of its marked superiority over the
civilian sectors.

Proposition 9: The consequences of military professionalization (in particular, of greater internal cohesion and corporate identification), combined
with the feeling of superiority with respect to the civilian sectors, facilitate
and, in turn, are facilitated by military adoption of political ideologies that

will potentially militarize all of society's salient social problems. Adoption of such ideologies also places the preservation of the achieved professionalization (especially the high degree of internal cohesion) at the level of the highest national interest—as defined and interpreted by the military.

In the nations located within the U.S. sphere of influence, the "doctrine of national security" fulfills this role. As mentioned previously, this ideology (or any "functional equivalent") legitimizes a military political intervention aimed at a much more ambitious and comprehensive domination than that which the officers of factionalized and scarcely professional armed forces could formulate. One fundamental aspect of this ideology is the preeminence it gives to the corporate interest of the armed forces. Military cohesion is a prerequisite for "victory" in the "internal wars." Therefore, everything should be subordinated to the preservation and augmentation of the internal cohesion of the armed forces. In addition, the structural position of the armed forces, especially its control over the means of organized violence, permits—if and when the professionalist impulse has been successful—the elaboration or adoption of an ideological justification for political domination in which the corporative interest is identified with "the highest interests of the nation."

The change in the political ideology of the military officers and its close connection with the organizational changes encompassed in the shift from a low state to a relatively high state of professionalism is of utmost importance. The content of the military officers' political ideology, its changes and connections with the organizational changes, should be contrasted with a third component of the "neorealist" attitude, which attributes a particular ethos to the military, resulting from education in military institutions. This ethos is composed of a strong devotion to duty, intense national identity, a certain indifference toward civilian sectoral interests, a "puritan" attitude, and a tendency toward corruption weaker than that of the civilian sectors. This "neorealist" attribution implies taking at face value another ostensible aspect of the military organization—the self-image of the military officers. . . .

Proposition 10: Given the conditions stipulated in the preceding propositions, internal cohesion of the armed forces is converted into the most highly valued organizational achievement and its preservation into the dominant preoccupation of its members. The persistence of mass praetorianism implies an inevitable risk for the preservation of internal cohesion and/or for the very survival of the military institution. The corporate interest in guaranteeing the preservation of cohesion raises the critical point at which military intervention and the assumption of government power become probable. But, insofar as praetorianism is perceived as (and effectively is) a grave menace to cohesion and survival, it creates strong impulses in favor of new military intervention. In contrast to the previous ones, the coups executed by professional armed forces aim at a radical transformation of the social context, in ways that would supposedly eliminate threats to the military organization and to its professional achievements.

This proposition underscores the importance of the perception of corporate military interest as an explanatory factor in the promotion of new coups and in the ends to which they are directed. The professional interests of the military officers (including involvement with their own careers), the expansion of potential political power implied by professionalism, and the emergence of justificatory ideologies cause the preservation of internal cohesion and the survival of the organization to predominate the thoughts of the military leaders. In praetorian conditions, civilians quickly recognize the efficacy of the armed forces as a channel for their demands and seek from them limited actions to satisfy these demands. But for the professional military leaders it is clear that to continue taking frequent part in civilian conflicts fatally reintroduces factionalization. This results in a temporary withdrawal by the military from political participation, creating a "political vacuum" in the last stages of mass praetorianism and high modernization. Praetorianism continues in full force, aggravated by the persistence of social problems and by the increase in the rates of political activity of movements and sectors (particularly the popular sector) that are no longer contained by military interventions. But eventually praetorianism, as well as the characteristics of growing conflict that tend to accompany the "withdrawal" of the military, ends by being perceived as the most serious threat to internal cohesion and to the survival of the military organization. Whether by means of national problems on which the armed forces cannot avoid taking positions that will divide them (the case of the electoral participation of the Peronists in Argentina) or by means of the emergence of mass movements that seem resolved to eliminate the armed forces or at least reconstruct them profoundly (the Brazilian and Greek cases), a context of mass praetorianism cannot fail to generate strong inducements in favor of a coup on the part of the professional armed forces. . . .

Proposition 11: Once they are in direct control of the national government, leaders of professionalized armed forces remain preoccupied with the preservation of internal cohesion. This preoccupation permeates their criteria for decisionmaking and is hardly congruent with the attribution to the military of superior capabilities for rapid and efficient decisionmaking.

The sharing of an ideology of "national security" (or its equivalent) and a social utopia of harmony and integration does not prevent daily dissension on problems as fundamental as the criteria by which public and private goods should be allocated among diverse regions and sectors. The military's concern not to carry these disagreements to the point of provoking internal factionalism leads to dysfunctional consequences: a marked slowness in decisionmaking; an inhibition of initiative in government decisionmaking due to the veto power of various military strata; the application of criteria of military seniority in assignments to government positions (including president of the nation); the arbitrary allocation of certain government functions and areas of competence to particular service branches; immense difficulties in coordinating the actions of functionaries who are, in reality, responsible to their respective branches. The classic discovery is made that government problems are much more complex than had been imagined and much less amenable to resolution through vertical patterns of decisionmaking and command.

Proposition 12: Government by professionalized armed forces once again generates the serious risk of rupturing their internal cohesion. If their governance is "successful," this risk can be temporarily controlled but at the cost of high levels of repression and a marked isolation of the military government from many political actors. If their governance "fails," internal cohesion is inevitably ruptured. The principal cleavage within the military organization emerges between those who maintain that an even more right-wing radicalization is necessary ("deepening the Revolution") and those who maintain that a quick "exit" from the most salient position of power would be the lesser of evils given the circumstances.

In the case of Argentina, real social explosions demonstrated that the government had failed to politically deactivate the popular sector and its most important organizational support, the unions. The government also "failed" to guarantee "order and authority," raise and stabilize rates of economic growth, diminish inflation, alleviate balance of payments problems, and carry out other measures required by the technocratic conception of *development* that is attempted to implement and that its civilian allies demanded. . . .

Although the basis for my opinions on this matter is highly speculative, it seems clear that the principal component of the new internal cleavage remains the perception of corporate interest. But, whereas in the past the effort at professionalization and coup d'état seemed the most "obvious" means of protecting the interest, today it is far from obvious which side of the option between "continuism" and "exit" can best serve it. "Exiting" implies elections — mass praetorianism has reemerged; the government is clearly unpopular and cannot obtain enough guarantees that the "appropriate" candidate will be elected. On the other hand, the indefinite continuation of the current regime presupposes a degree of military cohesion currently nonexistent. Government failure has eroded the military's confidence in the authority of its "developmentalist" aptitudes, and an enormous degree of government coercion, probably too disruptive to the interests under protection, would have to be exercised.

This essay has focused on one aspect of the political behavior of military institutions: their formulation of demands via "threat" tactics and, more especially, their execution of coups d'état against national governments. This is also the focus of most of the literature on the military in politics, but I hope to have demonstrated the flaws in the currently prevailing emphases and the potential for alternative foci. The Argentinian armed forces of 1960, 1965, and 1970 were nominally the same. Nevertheless, their political behavior differed in many very fundamental ways. Processes of change of the larger social context and within the organizations themselves determined and were influenced by differences in the political behavior of the armed forces—their objectives, their political ideologies, the means and aptitudes at their disposal (and those that they thought they had) for the attainment of objectives, the public policies that they proclaimed, and, later, the public policies that they constructed and attempted to implement.

The resulting framework is one of complex interactions over time, between two structural levels, the larger social level and the organizational level, and between those levels and the military's political behavior. Simplifying, one can affirm that a high level of modernization tends, on the one hand, to result in mass praetorianism and, on the other, to introduce "professionalizing" changes in military organization. These, in turn, effect critical changes in the means and objectives with which the armed forces attempt to affect the social context of which they are a part. In a first stage, concerns centered on the military organization itself induce a successful attempt at professionalization. In a second stage, that same motivation contributes toward the execution of a new coup d'état, which inaugurates a "bureaucratic" type of political authoritarianism. This coup d'état implies a level of political participation by the military and a militarization of social problems that greatly exceed what could have been attempted by officers of a less professionalized institution. Therefore, in conditions of high modernization, a relatively high level of military professionalization is achieved that in short order induces the most intense and comprehensive type of military politicization. This is a paradox built into the very logic of the situation, to which a second paradox is added: the high probability that this politicization will destroy a fundamental component of military professionalization, whose preservation powerfully contributed to the decision to assume government power — the internal cohesion of the armed forces. Therefore, mass praetorianism and military factionalism can easily emerge in the political regime that the military implanted precisely in the hope of eliminating both. Should this occur, "the politicians" may return to the scene, but it would be risky to guarantee them an incumbency longer than that required for the concretizing of a new professionalist attempt by the armed forces.

Notes

For complete references and notes, see the original version of this essay in *Armies and Politics in Latin America,* ed. Abraham F. Lowental and J. Samuel Fitch (New York: Holmes and Meier, 1986), 97–133.

1 In using the concept *modernization* and its related term *high modernization,* I follow David E. Apter, *The Politics of Modernization* (Chicago: University of Chicago Press, 1965), and *Choice and the Politics of Allocation* (New Haven, Conn.: Yale University Press, 1971).

2 Statistics from Banco Central, *Boletín estadístico* (various issues).

3 Alejandro C. Díaz, *Essays on the Economic History of the Argentine Republic* (New Haven, Conn.: Yale University Press, 1971).

4 CEPAL, *El desarrollo económico y la distribución de ingreso en la Argentina* (Buenos Aires, 1968). This is a work of primary importance for the study of the sociopolitical dynamics of the period.

5 Taken from *La Prensa,* 9 April 1959.

6 The complete text of the speech can be found in *La Prensa,* 6 August 1964.

7 The phrases in quotations correspond to the definition of *internal warfare* according to the official doctrine of the Argentine army: "Conducción para las Fuerzas Terrestres," anexo I, inciso F, número 37 (El Instituto Geográfico Militar, 1968).

8 The quotations are from an article by General J. Guglialmelli, "Función de las fuerzas armadas en la actual etapa del proceso histórico argentino," *Estrategia,* no. 1 (May–June 1969): 8–19. For a similar vein of thought, consult General O. Villegas, *Guerra revolucionaria comunista* (Buenos Aires: Pleamar, 1963), and *Políticas y estrategias para el desarrollo y la seguridad nacional* (Buenos Aires: Pleamar, 1969).

9 The quote is from the definition of national security found in a document of the Superior War College, "La seguridad nacional: Un concepto de palpitante actualidad," *Estrategia,* no. 4 (November–December 1969): 132–34. For a similar definition, see the "Ley de seguridad nacional," no. 16.970. Also see Villegas, *Guerra revolucionaria comunista* and *Políticas y estrategias.*

10 J. Guglialmelli, who points out that "development as an essential factor of national security constitutes a basic part of our military doctrine" ("Fuerzas armadas y subversión interior," *Estrategia,* no. 2 [July–August 1969]: 7–14). Also see Villegas, *Guerra revolucionaria comunista;* and the Superior War College, "La seguridad nacional."

11 Guglialmelli, "Fuerzas armadas."

12 Carlos Astiz ("The Argentine Armed Forces: Their Role and Political Involvement," *Western Political Quarterly* 22, no. 4 [1969]: 862–78) has compiled publications that openly discussed the coup d'état before its actual occurrence.

13 Samuel Huntington, *Political Order in Changing Societies* (New Haven, Conn.: Yale University Press, 1968). This focus, which will be called *structuralist* for its emphasis on ordered factors situated at the global social structural level, is synthesized clearly in the following passage from the cited work: "[The military] become the guardians of the existing middle-class order. They are thus, in a sense, the door-keepers in the expansion of political participation in a praetorian society: their historical role is to open the door to the middle class and to close it to the lower class" (p. 222). Other authors have expressed similar points of view, either on Latin America (M. Needler, *Political Development in Latin America: Instability, Violence, and Revolutionary Change* [New York: Random House, 1968]) or on "underdeveloped" countries (E. Nordlinger, "Soldiers in Mufti: The Impact of Military Rule upon Economics and Social Change in Non-Western States," *American Political Science Review* 64, no. 4 [1970]: 1112–30). Nordlinger's article contains a good critique of the "neorealist" or "militarist" conception, which I will analyze.

14 The quotation is from R. Price, "A Theoretical Approach to Military Rule in New States: Reference Group Theory and the Ghanaian Case," *World Politics* 23, no. 3 (1971): 399–430. This author adds some interesting alternatives to his critique of the "neorealist" focus. See also Alfred Stepan, *The Military in Politics: Changing Patterns in Brazil* (Princeton, N.J.: Princeton University Press, 1971), 7, 253.

Artificial Respiration

Ricardo Piglia

Owing to the dictatorship's restrictions on political activity and public debate, the risks of speaking out were enormous. Although ever present, repression could be acknowledged only in private, far from watchful eyes and untrustworthy ears. Thus, resistance was practiced from behind the protective cover of silence. In 1980, Ricardo Piglia published Artificial Respiration—*a novel that metaphorically discussed state violence and censorship through allegory. The book immediately became a channel through which a community of survivors could tacitly shed light on the possible causes of a shared national ordeal. The novel tells the story of a writer, Renzi, who sets out in search of his uncle, Professor Marcelo Maggi—a nonconformist historian with unorthodox ideas—who has mysteriously "disappeared." Piglia uses this central anecdote as a pretext for digression into a discussion of national cultural traditions and the history of violence that has haunted Argentina from its inception. In the following passage, Renzi converses with Vladimir Tardewski, a Polish intellectual who may or may not have the key to Professor Maggi's location. What begins as an inquiry rapidly becomes a long and erudite debate on the role of Europeanism in Argentina's literary self-perception. Like Piglia, his characters believe that the explanation and possible redemption of an age intolerant of intellectual freedom are encrypted in the politics of literature.*

That, more or less, is what I explain to Renzi when we meet at the club at six that afternoon. And then? he says to me. Nothing, I say. Let's wait for him. As soon as he arrives, I'm sure he'll come here. If he arrives, he says. Of course, I tell him, if he can return today. So then, he says. It's strange. From one day to the next. He seemed to know exactly, I tell him, what he was doing. On the other hand, I say to him, he was not the sort of man interested in explaining very much. And why, after all, should he explain anything? He decided to go away, I tell him. That's all. I see, he says. But why that night, Marcelo? Renzi starts to say. Maybe a way, I interrupt, of having company. To have someone with whom to talk as morning approaches. We were good chess mates, the

Juan Carlos Distefano, *The Mute* (1973) (front).

Juan Carlos Distefano, *The Mute* (back). Courtesy Juan Carlos Distefano.

Professor and I, during all those years. He did not have many friends; he taught his classes, sometimes met up with his students, they went to visit him. For some time, I tell him, he had been living at a hotel, one that is on the riverbank, on the other side of the square; perhaps you saw it when you came here. He seemed to want to forget himself; he did not like sharing intimacies. On the other hand, who could want to share intimacies at times like these?

Renzi thought that in any case I must have some hunch. What did I think had happened? I am not the most appropriate person, I want you to know, I tell him, to have hunches or gave explanations for the behavior of others. I live — how shall I put it? — a bit removed. Sometimes I even think that he cultivated my friendship, if we can call it that, I tell him, that he cultivated my friendship all of this time because he was preparing for this departure and needed me, Vladimir Tardewski, or someone like me, an exile, a foreigner. For years now no one has paid much attention to me, and—to tell the truth—you are the first person to visit me, to put it that way, since the consul came to see me and asked that I become a naturalized citizen, which I refused.

Afterward I told him that I was not like him, like the Professor; I, I told him, do not like to change. Besides, changing is very difficult, don't you think? Things should change, be transformed, but oneself? I told him that changing was much more difficult and risky than people could ever imagine.

Then Renzi wanted to know what we had talked about, that night, the Professor and I. He thought that perhaps that night Marcelo had said or hinted at something that would help us, he said, understand why he decided to go away. I also think, said Renzi, that he knew from the start what he was doing, what he wanted to do, and that if he began writing to me it was because in a sense he was also preparing me, Renzi said, for his departure and that he wanted me, at that moment, when that happened, to be here, as I am here now, he said, with you, ready, intent on waiting for him. That is why he believed that if it were possible to reconstruct, even if only in part, what we had said that night, perhaps some clue could be found, or at least, he said, the beginning of an explanation. . . .

Renzi then told me that the Professor was not like that. He was not sure that he knew him well, he said, but he could imagine exactly how he thought. And how did he think—I ask him—according to you? Against himself, always against himself, Renzi said; that method seemed to him like an almost infallible guarantee of lucidity. That's an excellent method of thinking, he said to me. To think against, I tell him, yes, that's not bad. Because he, Marcelo, Renzi told me, mistrusted himself. They train us for so long to be stupid, and finally it becomes second nature to us, Marcelo would say, Renzi says to me. The first thing that we think is always mistaken, he would say, it's a conditioned reflex.

One must think against oneself and live in the third person. That—Renzi says—is what Professor Maggi told him in his letters. Let's drink to him then, I say. To Professor Marcelo Maggi, who learned to live against himself. Cheers, says Renzi. Cheers, I say.

And yet you see the Professor also did what he could, like the rest of the world, I tell Renzi now. One day, it seems, he decided to go away on a trip, to change his life, to begin again—who knows?—somewhere else. And what's that, after all, I tell him, if not a modern illusion? It happens to all of us eventually. We all want, I say, to have adventures. Renzi told me that he was convinced that neither experiences nor adventures existed any longer. There are no more adventures, he told me, only parodies. He thought, he said, that today adventures were nothing but parodies. Because, he said, parody had stopped being what the followers of Tynianov thought, namely the signal of literary change, and had turned into the very center of modern life. It's not that I am inventing a theory or anything like that, Renzi told me. It's simply that I believe that parody has been displaced and that it now invades all gestures and actions. Where there used to be events, experiences, passions, now there are nothing but parodies. This is what I tried to tell Marcelo so many times in my letters: that parody has completely replaced history. And isn't parody the very negation of history? Ineluctable modality of the visible, as the Irishman disguised as Telemachus would say during the Trieste carnival, in the year 1921, said Renzi cryptically. Afterward he asked me if I had *really* met James Joyce. Marcelo told me that you met Joyce, it seemed so incredible, Renzi told me. I met him, I say, or at least I saw him a couple of times; he was extremely nearsighted and quite surly. A lousy chess player. He would, I suppose, have accepted your idea that everything is parody (because in fact, to insert a parenthesis, what was he but a parody of Shakespeare?), but he would have rejected your hypothesis that adventures no longer exist. I myself, I should confess, I confess to Renzi, I myself resist that hypothesis. Might that be because I am European? The Professor said of me that I was here to bring to a close the long line of Europeans acclimated to this country. I was the last of a line that began, according to him, with Pedro de Angelis and reached as far as my compatriot Witold Gombrowicz. Those Europeans, the Professor said, had managed to create the greatest inferiority complex that any national culture has ever suffered since the occupation of Spain by the Moors. . . . The clearest example was, for the Professor, that of Groussac. He in fact saw Groussac as the most representative of those transplanted intellectuals, above all because he came into action at the precise moment when Eurocentrism became dominant. Groussac is the intellectual of 1880 par excellence, the Professor would say; but above all he is the European intellectual in Argentina par excellence. That is why he was able to fulfill that role as arbiter, judge, and true cultural dictator. This implacable critic, to whose authority everybody submitted, was irrefutable because he was European. He had what we might call an authenticated European perspective, and from that vantage point he judged the achievements of a culture that was trying to appear European. An authentic European amused himself at the expense of these dressed-up natives. He laughed at all of them; they seemed mere South American literati to him. And in turn he, Groussac, was nothing more than a pretentious little Frenchman who thanks to God had ended up at these shores of the Río de la Plata, because without a doubt in Europe he would not have had any other fate than ending up in laborious anonymity, the victim of his meritorious mediocrity. What would have become of Groussac had he stayed in Paris? A journalist of the fifth rank; here, in contrast, he was the arbiter of cultural life. This character, not merely unpleasant but paradoxical, was actually a symptom: in him were expressed all the values of a culture dominated by Eurocentric superstition. But nonetheless Borges, Renzi says to me, laughs at him. At Groussac? I ask him, I don't think so. Of course it doesn't look like that, Renzi says. For, on the one hand, Borges sings the praises that we all know, *says* things about Groussac. But the truth of Borges has to be found elsewhere: in his fictional texts. And "Pierre Menard, Author of *Don Quixote*," whatever else it might be, is certainly a cruel parody of Paul Groussac. I don't know if you are familiar, Renzi says to me, with a book by Groussac on the apocryphal *Don Quixote*. That book—written in Buenos Aires and in French—by this pedantic and fraudulent man of learning has a double objective: first, to announce that he has liquidated forever all of the arguments of all of the specialists who have ever written on this subject before he himself; second: to inform the world that he has been able to discover the identity of the real author of the apocryphal *Quixote*. Groussac's book is called (with a tide that could be applied without difficulty to Borges's "Pierre Menard") *Une énigme littéraire*, and it is one of the most incredible gaffes in our intellectual history. After labyrinthine and toilsome demonstrations, in which he makes use of every imaginable kind of proof, among others an anagrammatical argument derived from one of Cervantes's sonnets, Groussac arrives at the inexorable conclusion that the true author of the false *Quixote* is a certain José Martí (a homonym of the Cuban hero altogether alien and even hostile to the spirit of the latter). Groussac's arguments and conclusion have, like his style, an air at once decisive and deceptive. It is true that among the conjectures about the author of the apocryphal *Quixote* there are all sorts of things, said Renzi, but none of them has the merit of Groussac's of being physically impossible. The candidate favored in *Une énigme littéraire* had died in December 1604, from which fact it becomes obvious that the supposed plagiarist and author of a sequel to Cervantes could not even have read the printed version of the first part of the real *Quixote*. How can one fail to see in this blunder of the Gallic man of learning, Renzi says to me, the seed, the basis, the invisible plot from which Borges wove the paradox of "Pierre Menard, Author of *Don Quixote*"? A Frenchman who writes in Spanish a sort of apocryphal *Quixote* that is, nevertheless, the real one, a pathetic and yet shrewd Pierre Menard, is nothing but Borges's transfiguration of the figure of this Paul Groussac, author of a book that demonstrates, with a deathless logic, that the author of the apocryphal *Quixote* is a man who died *before* the publication of the authentic *Quixote*. If the writer discovered by Groussac had been able to compose an apocryphal *Quixote* before reading the book of which his own is a mere sequel, why shouldn't Menard succeed in the great deed of writing a *Quixote* that is at once the same as and different from the original? It was Groussac, then, with his discovery of a posthumous author of the false *Quixote* who, for the first time, employed that technique of reading that Menard has done nothing but reproduce. Groussac was really the one who, to say it with the words most appropriate to the case, by means of a new technique enriched the halting and rudimentary art of reading: the technique of deliberate anachronism and of erroneous attribution.

. . . [I]t starts with the first page of *Facundo*. The first page of *Facundo*: foundational text of Argentine literature. What does it consist of? asked Renzi. A phrase in French: that's how it starts. Which is as if to say that Argentine literature begins with a phrase written in French: *On ne tue point les idées* (memorized by all of us in school, already translated into Spanish). How does Sarmiento open his *Facundo*? By telling how in the first moments of his exile he writes a slogan in French. The political gesture is not in the content of the phrase, or not only in that content. It is, above all, in the fact of writing it in French. The barbarians arrive, look at those foreign words written by Sarmiento, fail to understand them: they have to get someone to come and translate them. And then? asked Renzi. It's clear, he said, that the line between civilization and savagery runs right there. The barbarians don't know how to read French; better still, they are barbarians precisely *because* they don't know how to read French. And Sarmiento makes a point of it: that is why he begins his book with that anecdote; it's perfectly clear. But it turns out that that phrase written by Sarmiento ("Ideas can't be killed," in the school version), and which for us is his own, isn't his at all but a quotation. So Sarmiento writes a quotation in French, attributing it to Fortoul, although Groussac hastens to clarify, with his usual generosity, that Sarmiento is mistaken. The phrase is not by Fortoul but by Volney. So, Renzi says, Argentine literature begins with a phrase written in French, which is a false, mistaken quotation. Sarmiento misquotes. At the moment he wants to show off, to call attention to his familiarity with European culture, everything collapses, undermined by savagery and a lack of culture. And from that moment we could see the proliferation, in Sarmiento, but also in those who follow him, including Groussac himself, as we were saying a little while ago with Tardewski, says Renzi, the proliferation of an ostentatious and fraudulent erudition, a forged bilingual encyclopedia. That is the first of the threads that constitute the fiction of Borges: texts that are chains of forged, apocryphal, false, distorted quotations; an exasperating and parodic display of secondhand culture, constantly invaded by a pathetic pedantry: that's what Borges makes fun of. He—I mean Borges—exaggerates and carries to extremes, almost parodic extremes in fact, the line of cosmopolitan and fraudulent erudition that defines—even dominates—the greater part of the Argentine literature of the nineteenth century. But there's something else besides, says Renzi. Do you want some gin? asks Marconi. Sure, says Renzi. Volodia? With a bit more ice, I tell him. But there's something else, another line: what we could call Borges's populist nationalism. I mean, says Renzi, Borges's attempt to synthesize in his work another current, a current opposed to Eurocentrism, that is built on the gauchesque tradition, taking as its model *Martín Fierro*. Borges proposes to bring to a close a tradition that in a way defines Argentine literature in the nineteenth century. What does Borges do? asks Renzi. He writes a sequel to *Martín Fierro*. Not only because he writes, in "The End," an ending for that poem. A cigarette? says Renzi. A bit later. Not only because he writes an ending for it, he says now, but also because he makes the gaucho, by now turned into a suburban thug, the hero of a series of stories that Borges intentionally sets in the decade from 1890 to 1900. But it's not only that, says Renzi, it's not only a thematic question. Borges does something different, something essential, to wit, he understands that the literary basis of the gauchesque tradition is the transcription of the voice, of popular speech. . . . All of which is no more than a manner of saying, says Renzi, that Borges should be read, if you want to understand what he's about, from within the system of nineteenth-century Argentine literature, the fundamental lines of which— with its conflicts, dilemmas, and contradictions—he comes to complete, to bring to an end. So that Borges is anachronistic, bringing things to an end, looking back at the nineteenth century. The one who opens things up, who initiates, is Roberto Arlt. Arlt begins over again: he is the only true modern writer that Argentine literature has produced in the twentieth century.

Translated by Daniel Balderston

The Madwomen at the Plaza de Mayo

Hebe de Bonafini and Matilde Sánchez

The women who began to gather weekly at the Plaza de Mayo in 1977 to silently protest clandestine repression were brought together by the agony and controlled fury that only a mother whose children have been taken away could feel. In most cases, they were housewives who lacked ties to the traditional political parties and political experience. Since their collective protest was based on their condition as suffering mothers, the military government found it difficult to repress them as easily as they had other points of opposition. Thus, in order to deny the legitimacy of their claims, military officials called them las locas *(the madwomen) and mocked their despair by arguing that they had been driven mad by misbehaved children who had most likely left the country because of their subversive activities. In return, the women called themselves "The Mothers of the Plaza de Mayo" and wore white shawls around their heads bearing the names of their sons and daughters and the date of their disappearance. In this moving personal narrative, Hebe de Bonafini, who lost two sons to repression, recalls the painful and confusing events that led her to join the group and traces the beginnings of a long, collective struggle for justice that is still going on.*

24 March 1977, Humberto Bonafini

I hereby inform you that because of the terms of Book I of the Code of Criminal Procedures in Case No. 26,271, which includes the petition for the writ of Habeas Corpus on behalf of Jorge Omar Bonafini, the following resolution has been handed down: La Plata, 24 March 1977. Considering proceeding and pronouncements, I deny the petition for Habeas Corpus on behalf of Jorge Omar Bonafini. Written, notified, and filed. Leopoldo Russo, Federal Judge of La Plata.

I enter the bar at Constitución Bus Station. I have just arrived in Buenos Aires, and it must be about three in the afternoon. María Elena and Raúl came to the city early in the morning, and we agreed to meet here. I know they might be late, and I should make myself comfortable. I look around: everyone in the bar is just passing through. Nobody would think of meeting here unless it had to do with something sad. I look at the long line of buses. People get off them in waves and quickly head for the station. The young people I'm waiting for are not among them. I reach into my purse for some paper, and I find a small pad advertising the printer La Platense. Almost without thinking I begin to write:

I am sitting at the window of a bar, I see all kinds of people passing by. Each of them obviously has his problems. They are dressed in the strangest clothes and are sad, pensive, lifeless, alone even in the middle of the crowd. I am also alone. I am waiting. While I wait, I drink coffee. I watch some pigeons around the buses nibble the crumbs that a boy has dropped. The child's mother holds him by the other hand.

I am thinking, thinking. Where are you, my son? You are out there somewhere, perhaps closer than I imagine? I think, and I wait for María Elena and Raúl who don't come. But I am with you; I imagine you thin, bent over, absent. Every day, and even more at night, I see you arrive, or I hear knocking on the door. I open it, and there is nothing but silence, silence for everything.

Outside, the changing scene, people constantly passing by. From the window of the bar I always see young couples. I envy them, and I think about you. Your image stands out among all the others, brilliant, luminous. What are you thinking about, my dear, you who were always doing so much thinking? Who occupies your thoughts now? How hard everything is, son. No matter how much you imagine it, it's never the same in reality. I know that your great intelligence will help you get through this trance more easily. Close your eyes, as I do now, and think of me. I'm sure if you do everything will go by very quickly.

I was beginning to notice that the faces were repeating themselves in the courts and police stations of La Plata. But I didn't say hello to the other women. And it was obvious that what had happened to me had happened to them because after a time I had exhausted all the possibilities in La Plata and absolutely had to go to Buenos Aires, where I began to run into those same faces in the courts, in the Ministry of the Interior, which was located at the time in the Casa Rosada itself. But we gave each other only shy, sideways glances. For my part, at first there was only a disguised effort to fish for a little information. Since we were all standing in the same lines, there was no need to ask questions. Each of us had to repeat her own story of the crime dozens of times to the changing faces at the little windows.

It was in April, I believe, when I first started to talk with some of the women. Our conversations were limited to the habeas corpus petitions and the best way of writing them and of identifying the judges that weren't granting them. But I didn't give any of the women my name or my telephone number. We were anonymous, distrustful people, united by the paperwork and the lives we were trying to recover. Faces of mothers without children, wives without husbands or brothers. Women looking for other people, we were a precarious company in the aloneness of bureaucracy.

As I walked the few meters to the side door of the Casa Rosada, I wasn't thinking about Videla, or the junta, or the Doctrine of National Security. I only wanted to reach the hope I got from that little window where a nice police woman, almost syrupy, would wait on me with the promise of interceding and would preoccupy herself personally with my business. "Leave me your telephone number and your address, and I'll let you know. I'll try to do everything possible; I promise you. Poor soul! Your case is so moving. . . ." And all of us left our addresses, and we secretly clung to that promise, believing it was true. Of course, nobody cared about us personally: it was a trap they used to get a lot of information to put into that evil filing system where they kept our information and home addresses — our X-rays.

On the train from La Plata to Buenos Aires, one of those faces that I used to see in those days in the offices of the capital was already approaching its dreadful destiny. That afternoon my steps and my itinerary matched those of that gray-haired woman with the dark circles under her eyes whom I had spotted days before on the train when I went to the First Army Corps. We both made the change to the subway at Constitutión and rode together to the Plaza de Mayo, to the offices of Interior Minister Albano Harguindeguy. I greeted her. We didn't meet again for two weeks.

"We could go back on a bus if that seems like a good idea to you," the woman finally said one afternoon when we saw each other again. "It's a little more expensive, but it's a much more comfortable ride."

I agreed. We sat down in the back of the bus. We were silent. Then I began to ask myself why I had accepted her invitation if I intended to remain mute. In reality, I was wondering if she had a child missing. Perhaps her child might be sharing the cell and some meals with my son while we were sharing the bus seat, mute, not knowing how to get to know each other under such circumstances. She was the one who spoke. She didn't give her name. She was looking for her twenty-four-year-old daughter. They had taken her away five months ago. She was pregnant.

I was overwhelmed by astonishment: her case seemed unbelievable. How could that woman go on living if her daughter was a prisoner and about to give birth? I refused to believe that things were really so harsh, so crude. I didn't know the woman's name, but I began to feel a tremendous sense of solidarity with her pain. I was beginning to think that my case was not as serious, although it was my own case that was hurting me. Yet as the bus sped along — probably late because it was leaving lines of passengers standing at every stop — I felt a bond of sisterhood with that woman. I felt understood. She went on talking about her daughter, about the paperwork she had done. But although she sounded sad, she seemed a little released from her own suffering, as if she had gotten past the moments of confusion that I was now living through myself. "We are many more than you believe," she finally said, "and we are beginning to work."

"To work?" I asked. I had no idea what that could mean in this case. The woman responded that a group of mothers were doing their paperwork together and were arranging for interviews with influential people who could help them. I asked her if my presence would do any good. ("I feel alone; every day it gets harder and harder to keep on with all this paperwork. I'm beginning to get the feeling that they're pulling the wool over my eyes, that in reality this is all for nothing.")

The woman smiled; that initial distance between us had evaporated. She said that next Thursday afternoon a group of mothers would be getting together at the Plaza de Mayo. They were going to sign a petition or meet with a priest. It wouldn't be a bad idea to come—"the more mothers, the better." I said that I'd think it over (something in me was still asking if we weren't creating too much of a scandal over nothing, over some confusion that would surely be cleared up sooner or later). The woman stood up and shook hands with me and began to walk down the aisle of the bus.

"Don't forget. Thursday at two, on the dot." . . .

I walked around; it wasn't two o'clock yet. I hadn't seen the woman from the train with the dark circles under her eyes. I was feeling nervous; I wanted to be sure she would be in the Plaza before I arrived. Suddenly I asked myself why I was afraid: what was wrong, when you came right down to it, with my joining those women? The billboards on Bolívar Street proclaimed the official slogan, "The country is advancing," in sky-blue letters on a white background, like the national flag. I followed that street back to the Plaza.

Some women were already there, near the obelisk, on the right, standing together beside a bench. There were no more than ten: the woman from the train hadn't arrived yet, but another woman walked toward me. She had brown hair and strong, attractive features. She was short, with strong arms and workers' hands, and her body made you think of a great fortress. The weather was cool for April, but she was wearing a loose cotton T-shirt. I tried to explain who I was and how I happened to be there: "A lady from La Plata told me on the bus." It was all very vague, but the woman began to smile. "Ah! Yes." she said at last. "She mentioned you. She said you'd be here. Come on over."

They all appeared extremely rushed. They were talking quickly, softly, their voices bumping into one another. They were passing around a piece of paper.

"By chance we managed to get hold of a typewriter," the woman whispered to me. "We wrote a letter to President Videla pleading for our children. Now we're signing it, before we deliver it to the secretary. Sign it if you want."

She—"call me Azucena"—was talking with the others while a second woman took two pens out of her bag and a third woman came up to me: "You've gone to the League, haven't you? The League for Human Rights. No? Ah! And I suppose you didn't go to the Permanent Assembly or to Emilio's group either." "Wait," I said. "I think I know him. I saw him in the Batallion." She told me that Emilio Mignone, that bald and patient man, was trying to organize other parents and that he was a lawyer. But she and the other women wanted to do this on their own. "As mothers, it seems to me that we feel differently and other groups don't understand us. We think that it's better to negotiate alone, by ourselves. I don't know."

Then she told me that she and Azucena had gone various times to speak with Father Emilio Gracielli, chaplain-general of the navy and a friend who has an "in" with the people who call all the shots. "Several of us went, Azucena, María Adela, Dora, Juanita, but he didn't pay us any attention. You go, and he makes another appointment for the next week, but he doesn't find out anything. At times it seems like he's giving us the runaround." . . .

The women continued passing around the paper and explaining what it was about to the latest women to arrive. Behind us, the city kept on at its rhythm; it didn't seem to realize that we were there. Men were hurrying because the banks were closing; some retired men, completely indifferent, were lying in the sun. We women might well be alumnae of some school, meeting to arrange another reunion. Most of us were about my age or somewhere in their fifties; Azucena moved quickly, like a young woman, but she was a little older. She and I became friends. I agreed with the petition, and I signed. I did it with a large, clear signature so that the president would read my name and it would be engraved on his eyes. Also, so that he would know that my son's name gave me no shame.

We left saying that we would see each other again the following Thursday in the Plaza. At that time, none of us thought that our waiting without children would be longer than a couple of months or that the initial search would someday be transformed into this painful story. Not one of those women took any notes about the small things we were doing. Who could have guessed what would happen? . . .

I went on being my same old self who, little by little, got back to my household routine: I fed on it, that was my true life. Nevertheless, my two worlds came irremediably into conflict: the outside world wasn't really an enlarged replica of my neighborhood, nor were the courts and government offices as diligent as the neighborhood council we ran entirely on our own. It was hard to accept the idea that there were people so different from you and that this difference often implied an infinite capacity for evil. There was another way of talking, of dressing, that I would never adopt for myself but that I had to learn to struggle against, to live with, and to confront. And that was what we learned to do in the Plaza.

We countered the horror and our own naïveté with meetings that were more and more organized. On Thursdays we went to the Plaza at 3:30, we told each other the results of our collective paperwork. Azucena had ideas. (She was from Sarandí, bore the name and the activist tradition of the Villaflor family, and had a son and a daughter-in-law "disappeared.") Little by little, I start to take charge of our connections with the mothers of La Plata. Only a few of them dare to go to the obelisk in Buenos Aires; they prefer the quiet cathedral of their own city.

Toward the end of September 1977, we are already more than fifty women, and our feelings grow closer with our growing numbers. Every time there are more of us. Every time we feel stronger and less afraid. Every time we feel safer together. But every time there are more children missing. At the benches on the side of the Plaza we feel defiant, almost invincible for a few minutes. The truth is, they don't know what to do with us. If there is anything left in their hearts, it is the line from all those macho tangos about "my poor old lady." That keeps us safe for the moment. They think that we are crazed by grief, that we'll last until we get tired of standing there with all our varicose veins or until one of us has a heart attack.

It is sad that there are more of us every time, but now we can see the balcony of the Casa Rosada more clearly. There are so many things we'd like to ask the assassin, President Videla. We are beginning to bother him: a crowd of fifty old women can't be the alumnae group from any school. Every day when leaving work, the bank clerks look at those Thursday faces; we are always waiting for someone to ask.

They dispatch the police. "This is a demonstration, and the country is under a state of siege. Move on, ladies, move on." We begin to walk together in pairs, arm in arm. Then they make us walk separately.

The Plaza is big, the pairs break up, nobody can make us out from the other women who are just out for a walk. We know that the most important thing is to keep closing the circle, but imperceptibly, a little closer to the obelisk each time, so that they don't have time to realize it. There are more of them all the time; but every Thursday there are more of us, and the police bring reinforcements. They stand in front of the obelisk and keep us from getting close to it.

We walk around talking in pairs, watching the necks of the pair of mothers in front of us. Now I see the neck of the French nun, Alice Domon, walking arm in arm with Mary Ponce. I see her smiling, childlike face, and I feel like I have the same God as that nun. Further ahead I see the strong figure of Azucena in the spring chill, with her sturdy arms and a light pullover.

The ridiculous and clumsy way the police treated the Mothers would reach its highpoint a few years later when that first forced circling around the obelisk had become our weekly ritual. Since they couldn't beat us up or put us in prison, they opted for building a fenced-in area in the middle of the Plaza. We had to show them our white kerchiefs before they would let us in. Isolated from the Plaza—to avoid that contamination that they feared so much—we made our walk around the obelisk, and then they let us leave. . . .

September 1977: in a week the Catholic community of Buenos Aires is planning a march to Luján. The small group of mothers who were working the hardest got together for tea at the Las Violetas sweet shop. (It's an ideal place because it's always full of women having tea and pastries.) Azucena said it would be a good idea for all of us to join the annual pilgrimage to Luján "because people talk a lot on the way and we can stand out." We agreed: besides, there were also many Catholic mothers with us who wanted to go to pray the rosary. The problem is that not all of them wanted to go on foot: some would meet in Haedo, others in Moreno or Castelar. "We all have to agree clearly on where we'll meet."

"I know," said Eva, a mother who usually preferred to keep quiet. "We have to wear something that can be spotted from far away so we can find each other. A kerchief on our heads, for example."

"Or a mantilla. But we don't all have mantillas. Better a kerchief."

"Yes," says another woman. "Or better still a baby diaper; it looks like a kerchief, but it'll make us feel better, closer to our children." A baby's diaper on our heads: we've all kept some, we'll iron one carefully before the procession. We're just waiting for the moment. We have to spread the word in La Plata and all over so there'll be plenty of us. We have to drag out the mothers who are waiting, just sitting in their armchairs, and we have to convince them to come with us.

The husbands come along that day, but they always keep a little to the side. As soon as they enter the crowd, they see many other white-headed women like their wives. The diapers leap out at the sun in the sea of people walking along: we begin to come together, first two, then three. Further on, we come across another small group. The diapers multiply and stun the rest of the pilgrims who have already ceased to see them as a coincidence. When we get to the plaza across from the basilica in Luján, we're a good-sized group. Fifteen or twenty of us come together, and, standing in a circle, we pray the rosary for the children who no longer are. For the children who have disappeared.

Naturally the word *disappeared* bursts out. What does it mean? someone asks. The term is explicit: only someone who didn't want to understand could fail to understand. The word is multiplied many times by our mouths. It is repeated with the Ave Marias of the rosary. It embraces all the impunity of the situation. One woman, then another, comes over to talk with us. Their children are also "disappeared," they want to see us again, to pray with us, even with diapers on their heads. People look on, listening to the rosary in the plaza. In the basilica, in front of the altar, some of the devoted women are taking communion or praying for world peace. We are, in some way, the horrible worm that has wriggled out of a shining Argentina "that is advancing." Advancing toward what? Toward those graves without crosses. Toward the bottom of the river.

. . . A week after the procession, all of Luján is still talking about the women "with the white kerchiefs." Azucena and the others and I talk about it, and we decide that this is what identifies us, makes us visible. It's a sign. But we'll have to forget about the diapers; they wear out, and anyway we want to save them. With a half meter of cambric we'll make our own kerchiefs. . . .

We knew it was going to be a hard year. The frenzy of the soccer World Cup was already heating up. Some rumor we got from the useless office of some high-up priest told us that "they are planning to cleanse the country very thoroughly of disturbing elements before the first tourist sets foot in Argentina. Our country is going to show the world its capacity for recuperation." Translated, this meant that they would exterminate dissent at any cost.

The World Cup was in full swing. Just as they put up walls to hide the misery of poverty and moved entire shantytowns, they also needed to cover up all of us and the children a few of us still had because we were a stain on the country. Too many eyes were turned on Argentina for those women to go right on making a big hullabaloo and broadcasting their demands. Wasn't that their plan? For our rulers to be seen and yet to prove themselves able to conceal the horror, to be applauded and to turn the lie into reality.

A few days before the World Cup, a final blow struck "our family." On 25 May, in the afternoon, military forces abducted a group of women in a pastry shop in Lomas de Zamora. One of them was María Elena Bugnone, who was looking for her husband, her brother-in-law Raúl, her sister, and her sister's husband. Not one of that group of women ever returned. Later information from released prisoners indicated that María Elena was held for two years in the prison at Ezeiza. . . .

We know that the World Cup will fill the country with tourists and media professionals from all over the world. I said, "The question is how do we take advantage of those TV cameras for our own cause, to ask for our children and produce a juicy scandal for the government."

"But we don't know how to talk very well, Hebe. We know how to keep house, and we have learned how to do the paperwork, but what are we going to answer if they ask us something in English?"

"It's easy, Clarita," said a mother who had just joined but had plenty of energy. "You look at the journalist, and you say, 'We want our children. We want them to tell us where they are.' "

Our slogans and our rallying cries were being born: later on, they would shatter our silent circling of the obelisk at the center of the Plaza. But for the month of May they wouldn't let us circle: the police were there waiting punctually at three o'clock and charged whenever they saw more than three women together. But we fought them as long as we could. They threw us out one side, and we slipped back in the other. They dragged us out of one flower bed, and, after going around the block, we turned up next to the other. This game of cat and mouse that so exasperated them had for us the almost symbolic objective of occupying the obelisk, the center of the Plaza. From there people would see us better.

And the World Cup began: Argentine flags, confetti thrown from every office window. This meant the indifference of others, of all those Argentines who didn't want to know anything about death but preferred to celebrate to the end the mad fiesta power had offered them, stuffing themselves full with the four TV channels until they were sick or thoroughly brainwashed.

Meanwhile, we women worked to spread the news about our group. We sent hundreds of letters to foreign politicians, and we sought interviews with different world TV networks. Those men listened to us wide-eyed, some became indignant, and all considered us news. We had made it.

The first of June at 3 o'clock. The opening day of the World Cup. While local channels like ATC were showing the joyous flight of hundreds of doves in the stadium, most of the journalists were with us in the Plaza de Mayo, covering the flip side of the Argentine coin: "Boycotting the World Cup." The police, so used to charging us without any need for orders, are held back by a superior just as we were waiting for their attack. All this to the glee of Dutch TV, which decided to send footage of the Mothers instead of the simultaneous shots of the opening. The TV networks interview us; they cover our march around the obelisk. Half protected by the soccer tournament, we extend other bridges to the outside world through the words of the correspondents who are covering the championship.

As if the World Cup wasn't enough for the government, they had ensured more successful fanfare with the International Congress on Cancer. We went there: the doctors listened to us. Three days later, two doctors came to support us in our march in the Plaza. They wore their credentials hung over their neatly tailored suits, and no one could touch them. The police had taken over the Plaza; we circled around in front of City Hall. The doctors stepped out to the front of the line, defying the police.

One of the mothers, protected by the doctors, shouted at the police: "Our children were taken alive; we want them back alive." She repeated it, and the rest of us took up the chant: "Our children were taken alive; we want them back alive." Minutes later, the march had broken up, and we vanished down the Avenida de Mayo. But another rallying cry had just been born. It was nothing, and yet it was everything. It managed to bring together what we felt: it denounced. That cry of ours had shaken us and perhaps, we thought, had awakened from their worker-ant life some complacent passerby lost in his flood of dollars, soccer goals, and trips abroad. . . .

After Azucena was kidnapped by the government, the vacuum she left was gradually filled with new strength. Our strategies had effect, and, although it sounds brutal, because it is, we found a certain happiness. In the midst of the terror, of the lost children who every day seemed further away, a little laughter grew timidly, the paradoxical happiness that came from all of us supporting one another.

In the face of increased persecution, we felt obliged to be in church more than ever. "Hail, Mary, full of grace (Monday at 5:30; we'll meet at the Ideal) the Lord is with thee. . . ." That's what our rosaries were like, messages infiltrated in the prayers that were passed along the bench and inevitably became distorted. That meant we often went to the wrong place, some of us ending up in one tea house, the rest of us in others.

We had energy and a lot of commitment, but I must admit that, as spies, we were a disaster. Our security system was transparent. If we wanted to disguise a meeting place when threatening ears were close, we used childish signals. Sweet shop the Roses or the Carnations instead of the Violets; the Little Boat instead of the Frigate. No one would have to spend much time to figure out the place. . . .

When Jorge first disappeared, I felt a tremendous void, a desperation, a bewildering shock. I remember that one mother who had come to meet me at the house in City Bell told me she had spent seven months waiting in a rocking chair, rocking back and forth like some grandmother, paralyzed. I myself had to react with an almost frenetic activity, to recuperate quickly from the loss by doing things. The search was transformed into a dizziness that kept me from thinking, but sparked my inner strength and pro-

pelled me out into the street, to the ministries, to write letters. Working was the only way not to feel dead, humiliated, and empty.

One woman would say, "My children are prisoners, they are 'disappeared,'" but those words didn't mean a thing. One never knew the exact weight of the burden they concealed. There wasn't time to ask, "How are they? How are they holding up under blows?" You didn't think; you acted. And behind the action was always hope. Not to take action was to surrender the children. To abandon them.

I never sat down and cried, I never screamed or shut myself in for days to sniff the clothes that my child had left behind. Action was multiplied by the number of mothers. We wouldn't say, "They beat them, they torture them, they drag them off, they make them faint." We would say, "We have to send a letter to Laghi. We must see Prima-testa." We had to work until we dropped, until we were completely spent. That way we could sleep at night.

Translated by Patricia Owen Steiner

Never Again

National Commission on the

Disappearance of Persons

According to some estimates, the death toll from military repression totaled approximately thirty thousand people. Most were kidnapped by paramilitary forces and later killed in clandestine concentration camps — their bodies disposed of in anonymous mass graves or in the waters of the Río de la Plata. By a perverse twist, the dictatorship coined the term desaparecidos *(disappeared) to refer to those who were conspicuously missing due to kidnappings. However, there were a few who survived to tell the horror stories of kidnapping, confinement, and torture. In 1983, the newly elected democratic president Raúl Alfonsín created the* CONADEP *(National Commission on the Disappearance of Persons), which was in charge of gathering information from and about the people who had "disappeared" during the dictatorship. Survivors' testimonies like the ones that follow were the core of an official report entitled* Nunca más *(Never again) that was to be published as an unpleasant reminder of what could happen again.*

Sometimes the victims not only were taken to the limits of endurance but did not even understand what they were being asked — as could happen to anyone who was totally unfamiliar with the jargon used by the torturers. Antonio Horacio Miño Retamozo (file no. 3721) was abducted from his workplace in Buenos Aires on 23 August 1976. It was the usual sequence of events. First they took him to Police Station no. 33. Then he tells us:

> In the station, things began normally. I was first questioned about my full name, *nom de guerre* (I didn't know what that was), my rank in the *orga* (again, I didn't know what they were talking about), and then I was offered a passport, flight ticket, and a thousand dollars to leave the country. Not knowing what they were asking me about and refusing to reply, the dia-

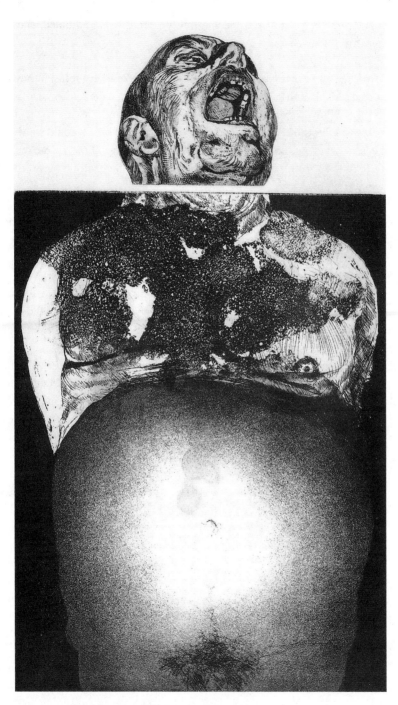

Carlos Alonso, *Vital Space* (1977). Courtesy Carlos Alonso.

logue came to an end and, "persuasion" began. I was blindfolded, and the beatings started.

Three or four people surrounded me, and blows and kicks started raining down all over my body. When I remained firm in my refusal, they resorted to sticks and rubber truncheons. They repeated the sequence of questioning followed by blows until they lost patience and, in order to achieve better results, took me, wrapped in something thick, which could well have been a carpet, to the Federal Security Headquarters. They put me on the floor in the back of a police car. Two or three people trod on me so that I wouldn't move.

At the headquarters I was taken straight to the *parrilla* [grill]. That is, I was tied to the metal frame of a bed, electrodes were attached to my hands and feet, and they ran an electric prod all over me, with particular savagery and intensity on the genitals.

Despite the bonds, when on the "grill," one jumps, twists, moves about, and tries to avoid contact with the burning, cutting iron bars. The electric prod was handled like a scalpel, and the "specialist" would be guided by a doctor who would tell him if I could take any more. After a seemingly endless session they untied me and resumed their questioning.

They would plague me with questions about the *cap of the mir.* I hadn't the faintest idea what *cap of the mir* could be. I couldn't understand any of their jargon. And immediately I was on the "grill" once again, and the questioning–electric prod–grill sessions recommenced. They would repeat the same questions, changing the order and wording to obtain answers and find contradictions.

It was only a year later that I learned from another prisoner that *cap of the mir* referred to the capture of the Twenty-ninth Rural Infantry Regiment, which occurred on 5 October 1975 in Formosa, a town I had lived in all that year.

The interrogation sessions later became shorter, but the electric prod was more intense, savagely seeking out the sphincter. The worst was having electrodes on the teeth—it felt as if a thunderbolt was blowing your head to pieces—and a narrow string of beads, which they put in my mouth and which were very difficult to swallow because they induced retching and vomiting, thus intensifying the ordeal, until finally they forced one to swallow them. Each bead was an electrode, and, when they worked, it seemed like a thousand crystals were shattering, splintering inside one, and moving through the body, cutting everywhere. They were so excruciating that one couldn't even scream or groan or move. They produced convulsions that, if one hadn't been tied down, would have forced one into a fetal position. This left one shaking for several hours with all one's insides one huge wound and an unbearable thirst, but the fear of more convulsions was stronger, so for several days one didn't eat or drink, in spite of their trying to force one to do so.

Every day they invented new things as collective punishment. Once it was really horrific. A person calling himself "Lieutenant" came and said that he was giving us military training, which wasn't true — we were tightly blindfolded and couldn't talk. There were nearly always guards there, and they were always coming and going, bringing people in and taking them away.

They took us to what I imagine was a large room; they surrounded us and began to hit us all over, but especially on the elbows and knees; we would crash into each other, blows were coming at us from all sides. We would trip and fall. Then, when we were completely prostrate on the floor, they started throwing ice-cold water over us, and with electric prods they would force us to our feet and take us back to the place we had come from. They left us all together, shaking, wet, shivering, huddling together for warmth.

We could hear them playing cards, their voices raised to drown out the constant screams of somebody being tortured. When they finished the game, they would amuse themselves by ill treating us.

When they took us from the "lion's cage" to the questioning-torture room, we would have to climb three steps and go down two, or vice versa, go up two and down three, and they would make us turn round so as to disorientate us.

The night of Wednesday, 1 September, was transfer night for some, and with it came additional fear and insecurity, for in those days it was well-known that they would kill prisoners during the transfers, inventing "shoot outs."

We were taken to a transit camp, for "softening up" before being disposed of. There the torture was such that we had no name or surname but a number. Mine was number 11. It was like a cellar, there were fifteen of us; I recognized Puértolas's voice by its high-pitched intonation, which still haunts me.

The punishment was brutal. On Thursday they took me for two sessions, and on Friday I received the most horrific beating I've ever had. There was somebody on the "grill"; it sounded like Puértolas, although it was very difficult to recognize his voice, we were in such a sorry state. They put me on the bed on top of him, and, when they applied the electric prod to me, he would jump too. My feet were close to a wall, and, if I touched or dirtied it or moved at all, they would beat me on the legs.

Following continuous illtreatment and death threats, Miño Retamozo was taken to the Twenty-ninth Rural Infantry Regiment.

> I arrived with a star billing since in their view I was the one who had planned the attack on the regiment.
>
> They began to work on me early on Monday and continued morning, noon, and night. For the first few days, in between sessions, I was tied naked to a bed, with a guard beside me and without food. At night I would be taken to a corridor and thrown down alongside the other prisoners, who didn't know what to do, wanting to move away from me through fear of being mistaken for me and taken away in my place. At night the "female voice" would arrive, a well-known officer of the Gendarmería who spoke in falsetto. The first thing he would do was to stroke one's testicles in anticipation of the pleasure of his task.
>
> This went on for three weeks. They suffocated me with plastic bags or by putting my head under water. They tore me apart with the "helmet of death" (a horrendous device full of electrodes placed over the head), which doesn't even allow you to say no. Your body is racked with screams.
>
> One night they amused themselves with a boy from Las Palmas (Chaco Province) and myself. The soldiers were whiling away the time listening to the radio; the local team Patria and Rosario Central were playing football. Throughout the match they used the helmet on the boy, which left him crazy for about two weeks afterward. Then it was my turn. During the interrogation sessions there was always someone who would smash the joints of one's hands and feet with a piece of wood.

Regarding his subsequent transfer to Formosa, Miño Retamozo adds:

> As Formosa was a town with a population of about 100,000, most of those there knew the identity of the torturers, such as Sergeant or Top Sergeant Eduardo Steinberg, Second Commander Domato, and the man known as "Death with a Female Voice," also Second Commander of the Gendarmería.
>
> When the guards were a little more lenient, we would ask for a bucket of water so we could wash. I nearly died the first time I had a bath. When I took off my blindfold, I could hardly recognize myself. I was black with marks, as if I'd been rolling in barbed wire, covered in burns from cigarettes and the electric scalpel; I was the picture of misfortune. The "electric scalpel" cuts, burns, and cauterizes. They hardly used it on me, compared with Velázquez Ibarra and other prisoners. I still have scars from it on my back. Electrodes or scalpel? As my back was raw, my shirt would stick to

it. With the heat and dirt it had started to fester, and I hadn't noticed. My companions, who took such care of me, called a soldier from the infirmary to disinfect the wound.

One day I finally understood the reason for my misfortunes, if one can use the word in these cases. At breaktime, someone from the cell opposite told me that Marta Infran had talked. They had caught her and her husband. First they tortured her husband until he was completely broken and then killed him. Then they started on her. At some stage she cracked, tried to save herself, or was driven to the edge of insanity and began to invent the most far-fetched things. She sent over fifty people to prison. She said that I had planned the attack on the regiment, that I was active in the "Montoneros" organization, and that they had offered me logistic backing.

I had met Marta Infran in 1975, when she was nineteen and working in a law court. We both attended the same course, in the first year of forestry technology, and we were casual acquaintances.

I was released on 6 June 1977.

C.G.P., Argentine, married (file no. 7372), was abducted outside her workplace in the center of Buenos Aires at 5:00 P.M., the time she usually leaves work. The usual procedure followed—car without markings . . . blindfolded . . . , ending up in an unknown place . . . tied to a bed . . .

. . . and five men proceeded to question me for about an hour, roughing me up and insulting me. They obtained my in-laws' address and decided to go there, leaving me alone for several hours.

When they returned from my in-laws' house, they were furious. They tied me with my arms and legs spread out and interrogated me again with worse treatment and insults than before. They said they had taken my two-year-old son prisoner so that I would cooperate: soon afterward they took that back.

Then they proceeded to insert what I afterward knew to be a police truncheon into my vagina. Then they took me to another room, where they tried to force me to eat handcuffed to a table. When I refused, they moved me again, and they stood me in a corner while they interrogated me once more, hitting me on the head and threatening to stick the truncheon into my anus.

Within what could be called the daily routine, I remember the door of the room was locked from the outside. We were fully dressed all the time, even when we slept. In the sleeping quarters, on trips to the bathroom and to the kitchen, my eyes were uncovered. They would make some or all of us wear a blindfold—"wall up"—whenever members of the force other than the usual guards came in. In these cases it was routine for them to intimidate us with their guns, pushing them into our bodies, neck, or head.

On two occasions they took me blindfolded to another building, where I was made to strip against a wall. Shouting abuse, they pushed me down on the metal frame of a bed and tied me with my limbs apart. Then they "prodded" me in the lower abdomen and vulva while questioning me. On the second occasion they told me they had A.G.P. with them, who worked in the same department as me and was office representative. She had been abducted on 28 March 1977, outside the institution.

After these sessions they would make me dress, and politely, with words of consolation, they would take me to the sleeping quarters and tell another woman prisoner to come and comfort me. This they also did when they brought one of the other woman prisoners from their sessions. I asked for medical attention, and they did give me some treatment for my palpitations . . .

One day they took me blindfolded from the dormitory to a room I recognized as the place where I had been "prodded." They made me take off my blindfold, and I was left alone with a man who, offering me cigarettes, politely asked me to tell him everything they had done to me.

As I described the events to him, he pointed out one I had missed, which showed that he had witnessed all the interrogation and torture sessions or, at least, that he was fully aware of them. At the same time, he tried to instill in me the idea that nothing that had happened to me there had really been that serious, nor had the blows been as heavy as I imagined. He told me they would release me and that I wasn't to tell anybody what had happened to me during that time.

Blindfolded once again, they took me back to the dormitory. At midnight on 14 June they announced that they would let me go and gave me back some of the belongings (watch, bracelet, money) I had had with me at the time of my abduction. They took me blindfolded out of the building and put me in a car in which there was only the driver (who turned out to be the same person who had kindly tried to show me that all that had happened was trivial) and myself.

After driving over a rough, potholed terrain, he stopped the engine. He told me he had orders to kill me, guiding me with his gloved hands to touch the guns he had in the glove compartment. He offered to save my life if in exchange I would agree to have sexual relations with him.

I agreed to his proposal, in the hope of saving my life and of having the blindfold removed. . . .

He started the car, and after we got on to an asphalted surface he told me to remove the blindfold. He drove the car to a motel: he told me that he was taking a big risk and that if I did anything suspicious he would kill me immediately.

We entered the motel. I carried out his demands under threat of death, so I felt and consider myself to have been raped. On leaving, he drove me to my in-laws' house.

Still Harboring

Juan Gelman

The capacity to imagine and hope for a better future, when pain would be redeemed by justice, was as important for survival as denouncing the atrocities committed by the military regime. In celebrating life at the epicenter of death, the poet Juan Gelman sought to sustain the dreams of liberation that writers like Rodolfo Walsh, Paco Urondo, and Haroldo Conti—all of them kidnapped and murdered during the dictatorship—had helped shape with their viscerally gripping works. His coupling of justice and beauty never fails to make the reader uneasy. As the essayist Eduardo Galeano has aptly put it, "To read Juan Gelman with impunity is impossible."

STILL HARBORING

still harboring little words / haroldo
studies his unbeing / rodolfo is silent for the first time
in his death before the assembly of *compañeros*
exiled / desolate / unfired by

the air / the time of combat / little *compañeros*
once our vital organs / flickering out already /
paco is passing into the mineral state / or the higher waters
of the soul / where reign

the love children / dignities committed
against capitalism / against selfishness /
stones they sold us for light /
us the poor who fed on patience

IN PRISON

my rings have fallen off / but not my fingers /
my splendor is not made of jewels /
my faith / my dignity I have

my soul which shines / the name
my father was named / and already
in this prison I hear a voice singing /
whether it be dove or swallow /
it asks that birds fly
to the window of the beloved / and
leave there the light of the tortured one /
that they return to the beloved the image of her /
which is life / which is he / which is untouched /
no steel can burn it /
the jailer cannot break it /
with thirst / with hunger / the prisoner
drinks the beloved in his tears /
the salt of her tenderness /
eats nights of love that burn on still /
the unfortunate one hides himself
in the night of solitary confinement
like an untimely bird /
the teeth of the rats make sounds /
fleas / other faceless beasts /
besiege him body and soul / he
thinks of time / sees
the word *perhaps* /
sees the word *tomorrow* /
under another sun / the sun /

Translated by Joan Lindgren

In a State of Memory

Tununa Mercado

Since the nineteenth century, political exile has been a common practice among Argentinians. The political exiles who moved to Chile and Uruguay to escape Rosas's authoritarianism began a tradition followed by opponents of twentieth-century dictatorial governments. The ruthlessness of the 1976–83 dictatorship forced hundreds of people into exile to avoid political persecution and intellectual censorship. As Tununa Mercado states in this compelling text on her experiences in Mexico, exile did not provide a sanctuary free of worries. Feelings of nostalgia and rootlessness were both troubling and recurrent. Waiting for a return long delayed, the exiles lived in an extended state of memory, isolated in islands of Argentineness where they meticulously relived the everyday rituals of a ghostly country.

My life in exile appears before me like a huge mural by Rivera, composed of protagonists and extras, leaders and buffoons, the living and the dead, the sick and the dispossessed, the corroded and the corrupted; the mural is the dense color of lead, with heavy and thick brushstrokes. There is anguish in the evocation, and, though I genuinely try to find some moment of collective happiness in the tableau (for there must have been some), a sense of melancholy predominates, nothing escapes the melancholy feeling of this gray, albeit intense, memory. This mural has a width and a height, a beginning and an end, and what stands out most in this delineated canvas, what undeniably vibrates in the landscape, is melancholia.

Nothing could be more anodyne and stupid than to say: "The exiles had it good." This trivial remark, as a sort of excuse, is all too often passively accepted, like its counterpart of the same suit, "Those who stayed in Argentina had it worse," and other simplistic variants that can only cause offense by comparing, as if it were a competition, situations that neither admit to, nor resist, placating classifications such as exile/interior exile, which are intended to differentiate and qualify the substance, the dough, so to speak, that has never been broken down or torn apart, never been truly explored, but has been maintained very neat and compact even though it embodies those destructive and devastating years from 1974 until the restoration of democracy, not to mention the aftereffects that even today evoke terror.

Time spent in exile has a trajectory like a great sweeping brushstroke, it has a broad open rhythm, its curves are like the ocean waves far from the coasts where there are no breakers and where they blend into the horizon; time takes place in the far beyond, in some other place, it is heard in the silence of the night, but it is brushed aside, one prefers not to perceive it because one assumes that the banishment will end, that it has all been some kind of parenthesis unrelated to the future.

Time is provisional, passing week by week on a train of successive stops; one reads the news, one considers events, one thinks in terms of options, in the imagination one confronts the adversary that has interfered with the passage of time, one imagines accumulating force with which to confront the superior enemy who occupies, also week by week and with constantly increasing firepower, the terrain that exiles have lost by being absent.

Discussions are endless, suspicions are endless; in the thickets and density of that timeless jungle there are no embankments to hold back the flow, the leaves do not fall, the cold does not come, the present never passes into the future. Events are illuminated as if in a theater, their significance exalted; paranoia has never had such a sibilant body as in this seasonless sojourn.

One could not have imagined then that once the parenthesis had ended, if in fact it were ever going to end, what had ended would be perceived as a dense and variegated whole, as one single massive entity coursed through with multiple labyrinths whose cross sections would provoke such a gnawing sensation; the layers or strata thus exposed, in effect, rise up like ancient anthills, now abandoned, yet producing the same sensation of terror as if they were still teeming with life.

Terror is also provoked through evocation of the way in which 70 percent of our time was spent fretting over conditions in Argentina, that wretched country that had expelled us and of whose situation we never stopped talking—the sun never set, there were no new dawns—filling the cracks and hollows of our reality, so to speak, with Argentine substance, plugging all possible perforations with Argentine putty, stuffing the body and soul with that substance that produced neither pleasure nor fond memories, that only added a quota of death by entering or exiting our conscience (and still more while we slept, this quota entered our unconscious mind, yielding immediate and magnified results, ever more powerful and horrible than while awake).

One almost always dreamed of death; one's dreams were constantly invaded by images of eviction and destitution; the sleeper would experience nights without end, naked, exposed, persecuted by invincible forces, tumbling into swirling torrents, missing one's train, leaving the house barefoot, losing one's documents, being driven in cars to unnamed destinations; a person lost stature, returned to an infancy immersed in clouds and layers of gauze, to rooms lit by distant ceiling lights and suddenly transformed into forests of shadows; people, in short, did not have sweet dreams. And in one's waking hours the effect of these dreams would recur like gusts of wind, interfering with any form of transitory happiness.

Very naively, many exiles in Mexico continued to believe that, in spite of everything, they were the world's best, and, thus, they failed to mix into or merge with the population at large—their neighbors, colleagues, or the like—but persisted in maintaining very national traits and gestures that tended to provoke a kind of vicarious shame felt by other exiles who, out of fear or timidity, had opted to be as inconspicuous as possible. At government offices, the immigration office, for example, they might speak arrogantly or insistently, inciting a sudden obstinacy or defensiveness in response to their petulance by the Mexican official attending them. The civil servant's expression would suddenly change, as if drawing an internal curtain and at the same time closing the gates leading either in or out; he or she would neither listen nor respond to the arguments of the claimant; he or she would withdraw into a shell, playing possum, which is a common strategy, learned through the ages, among many species of animals in response to external threats.

This ability to play dead, which a fair number of psychoanalysts have adopted following Lacanian rules in an anecdotal and reproductive fashion, is part of the Mexican culture and bureaucracy, almost part of its nature, and thus it is neither anecdotal nor affected but, rather, inherent to the spirit. Confronted with an arrogant Argentine, the Mexican's eyes go blind, the ears become deaf, and the lips are sealed, leading to a sense of absolute impotence on the part of the claimant. It can take an Argentine years to learn this method of distancing oneself from the exaggerations and vanities of one's fellows, and, if indeed the method is learned, it is not unlikely that it will carry with it a certain connotation of disdain, something that the Mexican avoids; taking the liberty to generalize, it seems to me that the Mexican puts into practice, perhaps unwittingly, a method for protecting one's mental health or one's proverbial dignity. In its extreme form, this weapon can be very effective and destructive; thus, there are many Argentines who, sure of themselves and their social position, have suffered this type of attack and have been overwhelmed by it, which logically engenders bitter commentaries against the aggressor, that is to say, their host.

Our bond to the country we were forced to leave conditioned our lives; there were even some who were never able to bear the sum of their losses, who passed their days remembering their old neighborhoods and idealizing customs that, one might wonder why, were considered paradigmatic of a lost paradise; that substance of Argentina that they missed seemed to be embedded in mythologies of little interest. Viewed today, both from near and afar—prior to the period of exile and after having returned to the country—that "iconography" and worshiping of objects that pervaded our fantasies, judged unemotionally, would seem insignificant, a patrimony with neither intellectual nor imaginary value.

There were affirmations of Argentine faith that were nothing but farces of patriotism, as, for example, the rapacity that could be produced by the Argentine flag as it hung from the wall together with the so-called Mexican *labarum patria* in the "house" of exile, which was twice brought forth with fervor and excitement. The first time being after the Argentine victory in the World Cup soccer championship when an emotionally charged group paraded the flag through the streets of the city raising their voices in victory chants; the other occasion was when this same group surrounded the British embassy, waving the flag, after the Argentine military regime waged a war, with which they identified, to recover the Malvina Islands.

Those longings for Argentine substance gave no respite, they adhered to one's body, suffused the mind, absorbed the bodily liquids, and left behind a desert wasteland; whoever could escape them, whoever could diminish their longings, did so with an iron will and determination to integrate themselves into their new environment. They had to learn a different way of life, that is, they had to learn to say hello to their neighbor, to yield the right of way, not to pass between two people who were engaged in conversation, not to pass plates in front of people at the table; to say *please* if they wanted something, and the corresponding conventions, *allow me* and *excuse me,* to express gratitude when necessary and even more than was necessary, responding to someone's *thank you* with *you're welcome;* not to interrupt people engaged in conversation, and, when in control of the floor, to tone down as much as possible their verbal theatrics; to say *bless you* when someone sneezed and *enjoy* when others started to eat; to offer one's own food to a recent arrival with a simple *care to join?* (practices that fell out of use long ago in Argentina by consensus of the haughty middle class); they had to learn to express hospitality with the courtesy form consisting in saying: *We'll be expecting you in your house,* which Mexicans used when inviting to their home an Argentine, who at first believed that the Mexicans were announcing a visit to the Argentine's home; the misunderstanding could go on for quite some time, repeating the phrase *your house,* or with the attempted clarification, *your own house,* with which phrase the Mexican wished to reaffirm the generous offer of his home to the foreigner; this generosity was never quite understood by the Argentine, whose interpretation was that the Mexican was assuming ownership of the Argentine's home, and the phrase *here you have your home* was never quite recognized, nor responded to with corresponding courtesy, which left the Argentine in poor standing and confirmed his inability to listen to others unlike himself.

These misunderstandings were like springboards that required the rapid and urgent learning of civility, and, after several years, it may be said with a degree of justice that some Argentines indeed learned to incorporate these laws of coexistence into their behavior, and they could be seen in friendly get-togethers with Mexicans making special efforts to allow others to speak, yet with expressions on their faces of arduous restraint of their natural impulses to fill the silent spaces with the sound of their own voices, and with an air of intense frustration at finding themselves obliged to give up the floor and employ more prudent tones.

At times they had to humbly eliminate certain linguistic forms from their own manner of speech, such as the use of *che* and the informal *vos* form of address; so, there they were, humbled even in the way they spoke the Spanish language, though it was almost impossible for them to completely erase their *porteño* accent, that of Buenos Aires, so clearly distinctive. The humiliation included having to replace the rigorous Buenos Aires street-tough pronunciation of the *ye* with a kind of *iod,* which people from Córdoba and northward can do with such ease but, on the lips of a *porteño,* causes extreme discomfort because it simply does not conform, and even when the speaker believes that he has it mastered, in no way does it resemble the Mexican *elle* and, even less, the *ye;* thus could be heard some very meager and starved *poios/pollos* (chickens) and *gainas/gallinas* (hens), hungry for a sense of belonging, which were like dropped stitches in the fabric of conversation.

It cannot be denied that the implantation of an Argentine in Mexico is indeed a rare historical phenomenon. And it continues to be a rather ridiculous spectacle, as seen over the years, as if through some secret vengeance Mexico was constantly resisting all attempts at appropriation by foreigners. The Argentines arrived and, with great care, erected their conglomerate living quarters, the so-called condominiums, where, for gregarious as well as financial reasons, they grouped together, accommodating themselves in Argentine style while, at the same time, declaring how much they loved Mexican arts and crafts. I always felt ashamed of myself, as I have said before, but particularly ashamed of others, every time I heard such phrases in the mouths of the recently arrived in Mexico, a kind of litany that deferred for a few moments the lament of the exile. I believe that, viewed from a distance, always from a distance, we knew very little about Mexican art and that the massive, if relative, acquisition of those cultural goods in the various markets was hardly governed by a criterion for quality. This may not sit well with those who read this, but there was incredible homogeneity in the furnishings of the houses of Argentines in Mexico; in almost every case, one encountered Taxco furniture or, more generally, rustic colonial-style furniture; acrylic tapestries with designs of Chiapaneca communities, serapes from Oaxaca, also synthetic, and the almost obsessive persistence with which they ate, at least in the early stages, from crockery containing lead; all of this created the sensation of being perpetually in the same house, whether one's own or someone else's, of always sitting in the same seats, drinking from the same blown-glass tumblers, seeing the same palm-leaf placemats and Michoacán tablecloths, and using the exact same leather seats, as if there were no differences in taste or intentions from one family to another, and as if they all inhabited the same space.

These houses, in which a legitimate art object would only rarely appear, were very often transported to Argentina, exactly as they were, in enormous freight containers. This mark of uniformity, recognizable in many homes, has a melancholic effect because, although it may have been part of a defensive ideological unity while living in exile, in Argentina it serves no clear purpose but, rather, gives rise to nostalgia and longing, and one feels somewhat silly for believing that these small rituals of settling back onto Argentine soil will save one from the din of lost identity.

It makes me laugh now to see how we all arrange our temples, virtual Mexican altars to the dead, with offerings that include crocks without mole, fictional flour of *nixtamal* and chiles, and the perfunctory conversations about where one can get chiles or tomatillos strike me as pathetic with everyone saying that it is possible to find cilantro when everyone, yes everyone, knows that, in fact, cilantro makes Argentines sick, and the corn tortillas used to frustrate everyone because they preferred those made from wheat flour, and only very few Argentines ever really enjoyed eating frijoles; also, it truly upsets me to hear my compatriots, now called *Argenmex*, asking anyone who is traveling to bring back some chile chipotle because, for some unknown culinary reason, it is the only kind they allow on their meat; it seems a great pity to me that their relation to chile is suddenly much greater than it ever was in situ, and that they lost so many years during which they could have appreciated it and could have learned to discern between the *pasilla* and the *árbol,* the *morita* and the *mulato,* without abandoning their traditional hot ground pepper. I get impatient when I hear them say that it is possible to get *chile serrano* for sauces in Buenos Aires, when what Bolivian women sell in the market—seated on the ground like Mexican women, as is the manner of their race, and having a startling mirage effect on the Argenmex—is really *chile árbol* and cannot even remotely add the same flavor to a salsa verde; and it bores me to hear others and myself engaged in long dull conversations about Mexican eating habits with people who, I suspect, never ate anything other than breaded fried veal scallopini and fried potatoes, and it seems incredible to me when they pronounce the letter *y* in the Mexican way while complaining of how much they miss the papaya/papaia from their table, a fruit whose memory they cherish but in fact rejected, and even more tedious do I find the fact that there is nothing with which we can diminish our nostalgia today, just as we could not diminish our nostalgia then with our *dulce de leche*[1] and other ploys of outcasts.

Translated by Peter Kahn

Note

1 *Dulce de leche* is an Argentine caramel spread.

Corpses

Néstor Perlongher

Néstor Perlongher (1949–92) was a sociologist, gay activist, and one of Argentina's best and most prolific poets. In a style that mixes the most convoluted neobaroque tropes with the profanity of sensual sordidness, his poetry registers the main cultural and political transformations in Argentina's recent history—from the revolutionary dreams of the 1960s and 1970s and the unspeakable crimes of the dictatorship to the triumph of neoliberalism and the explosive spread of AIDS. In 1981, on a bus from Buenos Aires to São Paulo, Brazil, Perlongher wrote "Corpses," a long poem about the dictatorship. By invoking the myriad places touched by pervasive political violence, "Corpses" depicts a society whose most intimate acts are tainted by the rotting memories of death.

Beneath bushes
In scrub
On bridges
In canals
There are Corpses

In the track of a train that never stops
In the wake of a ship that sinks
In a ripple that vanishes
On quaysides railway halts trampolines piers
There are Corpses

In fishermen's nets
In stumbling in crabswamps
In she whose hair is pulled
With hairclasp hanging undone
There are Corpses

In the necessity for this absence
In what underlines that speech

In your godly presence
Commander, in your line
There are Corpses

In the warm sleeves of the woman with the passport who
    Throws herself out of the boat with a baby in her arms
In the muffin man compelled to roast peanuts
In the peanut man who gets coated
In liver, in straw, there
There are Corpses

Precisely there, and in the happiness
of she who unravels, and
in that sideways glance of the woman you had best not
    say, and
in the scorn of the woman you must not say does not
    think, maybe
in she who you do not say it should be known . . .
There are Corpses

Notwithstanding, in the tongue of that shoe that's tied,
    secretly, in the mirror, in the
strap of that buckle pulled tight, without wanting, on the
    upturned roof of
that purse that deflates, like a fat owl, and, nevertheless,
in that c . . . that, how do you spell it? c . . . for what? But,
    Cunsidering Everything
Above All
There are Corpses

In the shawl of she who decompresses herself, feverishly,
    in the
waggle of she who lizards herself in that ivy, defenseless,
    in the
gutspill of she who has only a small jacket to cover herself,
and in the big trunk full of jackets, and old
    mannequins, past
fashions like dead shells from which
There are Corpses

They can be seen, they've had their bellies cut floating
    descriable in the swamp:

in the butt of the trousers mucked, similarly;
in the hem of the train of the silk gown of the bride, who
    never gets married
        because her fiancée has
. . . . !
There are Corpses

In that below-the-belt punch, in the lowness
of that cheek, in the ambiguous
disguise of that vulture, the z of
those azaleas, on fire, in that darkness
There are Corpses

It's full: in the little jars of sow's milk with which
    peasant girls
fete their pimps, in the
fiords of the port women who wake up, secretly,
    with their pants full;
in the
damp of those little bags, balls, that get rolled flat in the
    movement from which
There are Corpses

It looks residual: in the hobble
of those gauchos, in the hair of
that wild herd, in the canefields (rough straw), in that
vagrant's wine jug, that sheriff's smell of weeds
There are corpses

. . .

In the subtlety of the seamstress attaching ribbons where
    a hole was,
In the delicacy of the manicurist's hands electrifying
    nitrous nails, in the
cuticles she exposes, as in a dressing room; on the dressing
    table, so . . . indecisive . . . , where she
sticks pins charmingly, in the queen's hips and
the princess's little notebooks, which in the sound of a
    falling monarchy, *oui*
There are Corpses

Yes, in the camphorated bag on that pretty teacher's breast
Ecco, in the charcoal where that pretty teacher traces the
    embers of that incense;
Da, in the throat of that bracelet, or in the gizzard of
    that bruise
run through by a ring, petticoat, in
Ya
There are Corpses

In the thing that pushes
that sticks in the throat.
In what swallows
what prostitutes
In what amputates
what impales,
In what whores
There are Corpses

It cannot be sustained: the handle
of the spade that nails its rosary of mosses in the earth
the rosary
of the cross that impales in the wall of the earth of a nail
the current
that fixes to the rushes of the piss — tin, tin . . . — of the
rattle in the sputum that's spat
There are Corpses

In the mucous that also curdles in the throat; in the likewise
glacial tonsil; in the staff that can't be sucked with pleasure
because it's fringed with shit; in the sputum
imprinted on a prick,
in the saliva an elephant penetrates, in those jokes
    about ants,
There are Corpses

In the canals of slags
In the shaft of a southern gladiator, a dream
In the florin of a debauchee who winds himself, in some
breaches, in the shroud of the client
who's paid an exorbitant price for a screw
in the screw
There are Corpses

In the desert of consulting rooms
In the dust of "unconscious" couches
In the ceaselessness of that business, that "process" in
   hospitals
where the dead circulate, in the corridors
where the nurses say SHHH! With a needle in their ovaries,
in the holes
in the displays behind orchestral glass where surgeons
dress up as "draped man,"
the opossums of rubbish, where a palate is tattooed, or
slashed
(or palated), in lathes
There are Corpses

In mama's shopping bags alternately filled and
   emptied with
emeralds, tubes, in the pleats of that
binding that girdles—a bit too much—those corsets, in
   moon-blue hair,
seaglory, in the suck of that tit as expressed, in the
salami reclining against a mandolin, full of smooth pipes
. . .
There are Corpses

In those circumstances, when the mother
washes the plates, the son his feet, the father his belt, the
sister the pus stain getting bigger under the
armpit, or
There are Corpses

Impossible to count any more: in the small line of ash
that my horse leaves smoking in the fields (fields, huh . . .),
   or in
the pastures, eh, you'll see it's not
There are Corpses

When the horse steps on
cracked polders,
it sinks plumed
into the forage;
when the swallow, *tera, tera,*
flies in circuits, like a cock, or when the tram

like a cobra's milk serpent dis-
sipates itself,
observers reach the following
conclusion:
There are Corpses

In the country where the miller sweats
in the state where the butcher sells his steaks, for cash,
and where all occupations have a name . . .
In the regions where a tart flicks her nylon fox,
they smell her from far off, from long ago
There are Corpses

In the province where no truth is told
In the places where no lie is spoken
— This will not go beyond these four walls —
In the sites where drunks piss and a red spot appears on
       the flies of one who urinates — this will not stop
       here — against the
tiles, in the doorway of the number 14 or 15 police stations,
       at the corner of
Corrientes and Esmeraldas
There are Corpses

And becomes immediately the Captive,
the Indian chiefs her an enema,
open her c . . . to take out the boy,
the husband keeps the baby girl,
but she manages to keep a scapular with a faded photo,
       of a room where . . .
There are Corpses

       . . .

In   the country
In the country
In the house
In the hunt
There
There are Corpses

In the decline of this writing
In the smudging of these inscriptions

In the blurring of these legends
In the conversations of lesbians who show surrender
marks to each other,
In that elastic cuff,
There are Corpses

Is it not a miracle to say "in"?
A presumption of centering?
A centering of the centered, whose forward
dies at dawn, decomposed by
The tunnel
There are Corpses

An area where the foremost graves?
A parrot where caged edges?
A pavilion of fun girls?
A pip, broken up, in cubism
of frivolous surfaces . . . ?
There are Corpses

. . .

Allegorical coffins!!
Metaphoric basements!
Metonymic coffee cups!
Ex-plicit!
There are Corpses

Exercises
Campaigns
Consortiums
Condominiums
Contracts
There are Corpses

Yermos or *Luengos*
Pozzis or *Westerleys*
Rouge or Eyeshadow
Flounces or Pleats
There are Corpses

—None of this just happens
—Why not?

—Don't tell me you're going to talk?
—Don't you think so?
—When did you qualify?
—Was he a party member?
—Are there Corpses?

You went out alone
In the cool of the night
When the storm caught you
Without a jacket
And
There are Corpses

Does it make sense?
Was it clear?
Was it not a bit too much for nowadays?
Blue fingernails?
There are Corpses

Translated by William Rowe

War in the South Atlantic

Graciela Speranza and Fernando Cittadini

In 1982, the dictatorship's political apparatus began to weaken. Serious allegations of human rights violations and the steady deterioration of the economy led to a series of public demonstrations. These gained momentum in the general strike of March 1982, which was savagely repressed by the police. Four days later, the military junta in power announced that Argentine troops had retaken the Malvinas Islands from British hands and that the country was consequently at war with the United Kingdom. Within a few weeks, the Argentine armed forces would suffer a humiliating defeat at the hands of an enemy remarkably superior in both military and financial resources. For years, the true circumstances of the defeat and the conditions of surrender were not made public. The war divided the Argentine people. Although most opposed the dictatorship, many supported the country's national claims to the islands. The emotional testimonies of officers and drafted soldiers published by Graciela Speranza and Fernando Cittadini in 1997 attest both to the heroism of those who fought on the front and to the sense of betrayal that they felt once the war was over.

Juan José Gómez Centurión

In 1982 I was a lieutenant in the Twenty-fifth Infantry Regiment in General Sarmiento, Chubut, a place in the middle of Patagonia. Beginning with the first days of March we shared the agitation that everybody was experiencing in Argentina because of the problem in the Georgian Islands. But we only participated in a very distant way. Ever since 1978, because of our geographic location, all our activity was concentrated on Argentina's problems with Chile. Early in March, as was usual, all of us who were officers in the regiment left to take part in a reconnaissance on the Andean border, with the idea of bringing up to date a tactical defense plan in case of Chilean aggression.

We spent a week in the thick of the cordillera without any kind of contact with the regiment. When we returned, we found a rather strange atmosphere. That morning, the chief officer of the regiment had a meeting with all the officers. He sat us down in front of a blackboard covered by a sheet, and he swore us to secrecy about the orders we were going to receive. We looked at each other in silence, intrigued, until the sheet was pulled away and the map of the Malvinas appeared, along with all the situation maps. The map of the Georgias was more or less expected; the map of the Malvinas was a surprise. Right then he gave us the full plan of operations: our regiment, together with the armada, was going to be part of an action to take back the islands. This was, if I remember it right, the morning of 21 March. That same night my company was to leave by plane for the Espora Base on Puerto Belgrano. There we would embark on the *Santisima Trinidad* and the *Admiral Irizar* the next day and become one of the stepping stones for the amphibious assault on the Malvinas. The rest of the regiment stayed in General Sarmiento, and the night before the operation began they mobilized in Comodoro Rivadavia to be transported on the *Hercules* the following day, once the first landing forces had secured the airport area. That was more or less the concept of the operation, although we weren't absolutely sure whether it was all a fiction or if it was for real. It might be just an exercise, but swearing us to secrecy made us doubt that it was. Besides that, we were given a scenario for deceiving our families. This was hard to do because the barracks and our homes were very close to each other and our families virtually lived inside the military base. To make matters worse, I had returned to the regiment in January right after my honeymoon and had gone straight off to the field with the troops and then to the frontier. By the way our leader described the situation, I would now have to tell my wife that I was going away again, this time to take part in an exercise in Río Gallegos, at the far end of continental Patagonia. Anyway, we got the company ready in just a few hours. With only the supplies we put together that day we managed to get along until we returned to the continent; we didn't have even the slightest shred of logistical support in the Malvinas.

We left that same evening. It was a very difficult good-bye, very happy but very difficult. We left with drums and cymbals and with the secret circling around us. None of those outsiders understood the elation that we felt for a mere exercise that was going to spoil Holy Week. Our feelings were rather a mixture of euphoria and surprise. We viewed the Malvinas as a lost treasure — which should have been ours — with a sentimental longing that everybody shared in Argentina. Admittedly our idea of the islands was closer to the patriotic symbolism instilled by schoolteachers and folklore than it was to the real concerns of recent military history.

We didn't all feel the same way. I remember Roberto Estevez, a friend who was a year older than me, who said to me: "Look, I have a letter here for my father, and I would like to leave it with your wife in case something happens to me." They were two completely different outlooks. I, twenty-three years old and possibly more immature, let myself be carried along by enthusiasm, without completely analyzing the situation. He saw everything more clearly. In fact, the letter was left with an officer in the barracks, and after the war it was delivered to his parents.

Oscar Poltronieri

It was more or less a week after our troops had taken over the islands that we were lined up on the parade ground, facing the large flag, and the regimental commander asked which of us soldiers was inspired to go to the Malvinas. He said it like this: "Any soldier who volunteers to go to the Malvinas should step forward." No one stepped forward.

Then I say to the chief: "My chief, I will go." "No, you be quiet and just stay where you are," he says to me. Then I say to him: "I will go," and I took three steps forward. Then the regimental commander calls me over and says to me: "Soldier, what is your name?" "Poltronieri," I tell him. Then he says: "Stay where you are." And then he asks: "Who else wants to go to Malvinas with Poltronieri?" But no one came forward, no one came forward. Then they made everyone march around the parade grounds until, finally, everyone had to go.

I don't know why I stepped forward—whether I did it because nobody else volunteered or because I wanted to. I had already been in the army for a year, and I had learned a lot of things in the barracks. I didn't know how to read or write, and they sent me to school. I loved military life so much that even though I had the chance to avoid military service I didn't.

Once I was inducted and was in the regiment, I got an ear infection. Then one of the captains who was the chief medical officer says to me: "Soldier Poltronieri, we are going to have to discharge you." "No," I tell him, and I start to cry. "I want to stay." So all right, then he says to me, "Are you sure you want to?" I repeated my answer four or five times. "Yes, I want to stay. My ear still hurts a little, but when the swelling goes down, I'll feel better."

I lost something like forty days of training, but I made it all up afterward, and I learned almost faster than the others. And everything I learned I put to use in the Malvinas.

The thing was that one Saturday in April they sent us home and told us that we had to be back at the regiment by six the next morning—on Sunday— and that the family could come visit that afternoon. But that we shouldn't tell them we were going to the Malvinas. Three men in our family have been in military service, and all of us had faced similar problems. I was in the Malvinas, a cousin was in a unit involved with the crisis on the Chilean frontier, and an uncle had been in Tucumán during the "Dirty War."

So I didn't tell either my mother or my father about the Malvinas. Only that I had to wash my clothes and have them ready to wear in the morning and that they should come to the barracks on Sunday. And what happened was that Sunday arrived and they didn't come, they didn't come, they didn't come.

Then a boy, a friend from my neighborhood, came, and I say to him: "How about doing me a favor and ask my old lady to come visit me, at least today?" Then he went, and he asked her. And my mother said that she couldn't, and she didn't come. My father was in Roque Pérez working with the harvesters. He didn't know anything about it, he didn't know that I went to Malvinas. He learned about it two years later when they gave me the medals.

Italo Piaggi

By late in the afternoon on 28 May our situation was desperate. On the north-ernmost line of Goose Green, First Lieutenant Manresa's Company A, plus the supporting troops of Second Lieutenant Colombo, had been totally over-run, and they fell back in disorder without their heavy weapons. The unit at Boca House surrendered, and the second lieutenant in charge, Aliaga, was seri-ously wounded. Second Lieutenant Peluffo was also gravely wounded, and his troops retreated from Darwin Hill. Second Lieutenant Estévez, who had at-tempted to reinforce that position, had died in combat, and Second Lieutenant Gómez Centurión, after suffering numerous losses during the counterattack, also had to retreat. There was insufficient information about which companies had fallen, and the lack of radio communication at the command level impeded all possibility of reorganization. There was no longer any antiaircraft or artil-lery support, and, except for some small, scattered amounts, there was no am-munition. We had approximately three hundred losses between the wounded, the dead, and prisoners — half of our entire outfit. Our line of defense was bor-dered by a group of houses, and the enemy was able to destroy our position with continuous bombardment from both the land and the ships. It is what I would have done in their place.

Late at night the enemy fire was less intense, and I decided to call a meeting to talk about our overall strategy and an immediate plan of action. My logistics officer and chief of staff weren't around, so I made decisions mostly by con-sulting with Major Frontera, my assistant chief of operations. More than once I had to leave him to make decisions at the command post; because of our lack of communication, I felt obliged to go over to our position on the front so I could lead the combat. In any case, I decided to ask for the opinions of the commander of the air base and of my superior officer, to see if they could figure out any solution. I knew that it was absolutely impossible to go on fighting with any hope of success, but perhaps I could find an Alexander the Great who would come up with some saving idea.

The truth is that I heard only words of desperation. The men who didn't want to consider a surrender had no suggestions for a viable course of action, and, as if I wasn't truly conscious of what it meant, they limited themselves to making me realize the indignity and shame of surrendering. But the situation didn't allow for the luxury of hysterical heroics.

From Puerto Argentino I had been told of the impossibility of any immediate support, and I was given the responsibility of the decision. The loneliness of command is terrible. Over and over again during the night I analyzed the situation. On one side was my job, my situation as a professional soldier who wanted to fight to the very end. But on the other side were the hundreds of soldiers who had been drafted and who had already fought under the most adverse conditions, and I was reluctant to sacrifice their lives. As long as the possibility of fighting on still existed, I kept firing, even when it endangered the lives of those of us who had been taken prisoner by the British. After that I wasn't disposed to go on spilling blood needlessly. From Puerto Argentino they told me that the condition of our fort didn't warrant continuing operations. If they had told me that they needed to have me hold out for fifteen hours more, I would have answered that we couldn't last another fifteen hours. I would have said good-bye to everyone, and I would have ordered the soldiers to hold their defense down to the last man. But they told me that I was the one who knew what was going on at the front and so the final decision was mine.

Nothing is a greater challenge to firmness of character or moral courage than the fear of military men who, having the means and justification to continue the battle, give an order — because they are afraid, because they are negligent, or because they are looking out for their own glory — that means the annihilation of a combat unit, without any consideration for the lives sacrificed. I could have made the "heroic" decision to wipe out my regiment, but I was not ready to be decorated for climbing to the top on a pile of cadavers.

By about three in the morning I had come to a decision. I gave orders to bring in the flag of Regiment 12, and we set it afire in the burner with a fire made from the peat on the island. It was one of the most dramatic moments of my life. If we had fought under equal conditions with a corresponding armed unit and they had overcome us, perhaps I would have handed over the regimental flag. But, having fought under the conditions we were fighting, I thought that those British soldiers didn't deserve the flag of the Twelfth Regiment. It was the only flag in the war that was burned. The rest of the units surrendered theirs to the enemy.

Gustavo Pedemonte

I remember that as we were about to set off for the Malvinas I was sitting in the bus with Ronconi and behind us came a Citroën with his girlfriend, his brother, and his mother. They went along with us as far as Palomar. Somewhere in my memo book I have the address of Ronconi's parents and of other soldiers who were with me, but I never could talk to them. I couldn't imagine just going up and ringing their doorbells and introducing myself. They sought me out, but I never could bring myself to tell them how their sons had died. The families found out about it only through other people whom I did manage to talk to. I have the addresses, and I tell myself someday I'm going to go, but I don't feel like it. I'm not cured yet.

In the beginning I was six months in the psychiatric ward of the military hospital. Afterward I was almost two years going in for checkups, and the doctor I talked to helped me a lot. I went in, and I just cried. The business of having gotten out of the situation and never having returned stayed with me. From my company six men died: Ronconi, Petruchelli, Ferdigaldo, Pascual, Díaz, and Maidana. Three of them in the same trench where I was. Even today many things still are painful to me. Things that I could've done, or that I did and shouldn't have, things the Army should have done for us but didn't. For example, they always told us that in front of our defensive position we should plant land mines so that when the English appeared their bodies would be flying through the air; but we didn't have any mines or wire or anything that would hold back their advance. If, on that first night, we had been able to hold our position until the sun came up, we might have made mincemeat of the British. But they advanced and rolled right over us. We had courage, we had valor, we had everything. Because it isn't true that we offered no resistance to the British, that our guns didn't work and all the rest, like some say. That is all a lie. What we didn't have was leadership, information, trust. They never officially said to us, "Good, gentlemen, the English made a beachhead on San Carlos, and they are advancing on us here, but from here they are to go no further." They never said that to us. When they sank our ship the *General Belgrano*, stories reached us that it was a cruiser full of cadets that was sailing out of Buenos Aires to go on an expedition in Africa or something like that. Blah, blah, blah.

In spite of all of this, when the English were coming at us, we faced them and shouted "Viva Argentina! Come on you sons of bitches—we're going to kill you all." And suddenly three men died on me, six men died on me. How could I not be sick? How could I have felt otherwise when I came back? And, even today, nobody recognizes us, and we have to go on fighting that war, and the books tell you one story, and the newspapers tell you another. Then I say: "And I was there, was this what I saw my friends die for?"

I don't want them to put up a monument for us, even though I lived through it and I'm proud and would do it again. But at times I think that my friends died for nothing. I was in the army, I went into it as a job, and I have no right to ask for anything. If I had to die for my country, I would die fighting because that's the way they taught me. But the kids, Ronconi, Petrocelli, Maidana, the ones who died? No. It is different. They went because of a law, they were part of the compulsory military service, and even so they took part because, for them, it was a noble, just cause. I saw them die without weakening at all, without leaving their positions.

Many of them had made the mistake of thinking that we and our fellow officers were the only Argentine soldiers in the Malvinas. However, there were over ten thousand men there. Perhaps what saved my life was a fellow officer who was three hundred or so meters away and shot at an English soldier who was aiming his gun at my head.

In the hospital I realized that we weren't the only ones there and that there were other kids on San Carlos, on Tumbledown, fighting the same way we were fighting. And this helped me, and I was able to come out of it. Others have never come out of it. There are others who are still shut away in hospitals or who went back home and just got worse. More than two hundred committed suicide. Six kids died on me in combat, but Juan Pinto, who was another soldier in my group, committed suicide a couple of years ago. His suicide was number 100.

Translated by Patricia Owen Steiner

IX

Democracy and Neoliberalism

In 1983, a devastated Argentina returned to democracy. As the first constitutional president after seven years of corrupt dictatorship, Raúl Alfonsín's main goal was to instill democratic thinking in a country where only three free presidential elections had been held in fifty years. Argentina's recurring cycle of weak civilian governments succeeded by dictatorships was partially rooted in a widespread distrust of democracy. For both Peronists and the Left, which together constituted the majority, the democratic system was a facade that disguised the persistent exploitation of workers and therefore could be easily sacrificed for the sake of social justice. Since "true" democracy was identified with economic equality, the preservation and defense of political institutions had never been a priority. For their part, the armed forces and certain sectors of the bourgeoisie believed that democracy created fertile ground for subversive ideologies that threatened Argentina's progress. After years of unprecedented brutality, the citizenry under Alfonsín was more willing to assume the civic responsibilities implied in maintaining a democratic system, with greater tolerance and respect for ideological disagreement. The revolutionary dreams of the 1960s and 1970s gave way to a politics of negotiation and consensus. This change in attitude was instrumental in bringing about new political agencies. Restructured political parties and nongovernmental organizations channeled the new forms of civic participation during this difficult but hopeful period. Alfonsín's democratic crusade included putting the military on public trial for crimes against humanity. For the first time in Latin American history the disruption of the democratic system would be penalized.

But, despite the sense of jubilation and new civic duty that accompanied the restoration of institutional legitimacy, Argentines were soon overwhelmed by the dictatorship's harsh legacies. In 1987, defiant military officers threatened to overthrow Alfonsín's government if their demands for lenience were not met. Fears of a coup attempt prompted a series of pardons. First came the so-called Punto Final Law, which held that, after 23 February 1987, no more claims of human rights abuses would be heard by the courts. Three months later, the Due Obedience Law, which absolved all officers beneath the rank of lieutenant colonel of any responsibility for crimes they might have committed, curtailed justice even further.

The deplorable economic situation posed another difficult challenge. The dictatorship's economic policies had left the country with a foreign debt of $45 billion that slowed productivity and generated inflation. Despite Alfonsín's administration's repeated efforts to push the economy in a new direction, all plans proved ineffective. In 1989, inflation spun out of control. As the writer Osvaldo Soriano reveals in his ironic recording of those frenetic days, living under inflation shattered the lives of millions of Argentine citizens.

Under the pressure of unrestrained hyperinflation, and with his political credibility severely weakened, Alfonsín called elections before his term was legally over. For the fourth time, Peronism took power with the election of Carlos Saúl Menem. Under Menem's leadership, the political movement founded by Perón would go through yet another surprising metamorphosis. Although during his electoral campaign Menem had resorted to old populist slogans and embraced Perón's political ideals, his version of Peronism would follow a very different path. Against all expectations, once in power Menem surprised everyone by implementing economic and social policies that favored fiscal austerity, economic liberalization, and massive privatization. The effects of Menem's neoliberal program on the national economy were striking. The rate of inflation dropped sharply, the budget was balanced, and defense spending was cut in half. The restoration of the country's financial credibility abroad facilitated the renegotiation of the foreign debt and new international loans. Economic stability was not without high social costs. Real wages fell drastically, and unemployment more than doubled. The adjustments hit particularly badly the interior, where the termination of trade protections and federal subsidies would push unemployment up to 35 percent in some areas.

More aligned with Peronist tradition was the search for political alliances between antagonistic sectors of society and a tendency to manipulate the law. While generally respecting free speech and political liberties, Menem frequently used his presidential power to circumvent Congress and avoid political debate. To secure support of the armed forces, he granted pardons to all the military officials involved in past repression, excepting only the members of the juntas. But, overall, what was decisive in Menem's political success was his ability to build and maintain an extraordinary level of consensus among the population—a political talent that allowed him to go ahead with economic policies that would have been unthinkable just a few years before. Thus, despite the high social costs of the political and economic stability that he help secure,

Menem was reelected president in 1995. Eradicating inflation had turned him into the savior of democracy. The essay by Palermo and Novaro included in this part analyzes Menem's new style of politics and his reformulation of traditional Peronism.

Reform of the welfare state and the privatization of services reshaped the Argentine citizenry's relationship with the national state. The new political dynamics spawned new patterns of popular protest by groups and minorities who, rejecting traditional forms of political organization such as the party, sought to occupy public spaces to confront neoliberalism. Revealing the lack of galvanizing political utopias, circumscribed political acts — in which particular groups defended their own agendas — replaced the mass demonstrations of the past. Again, Buenos Aires provided the public stage where most of the new political and cultural trends were put on display. Impoverished retirees, teachers, and workers from across the country would take over its plazas to make their complaints heard. Yet, notwithstanding these groups' political resourcefulness and tenacity, their achievements were always limited, if not null. It was not until late in Menem's second administration, when corruption became untenable and international events thwarted economic growth, that popular discontent gained momentum. The rapid spread of violent protests in the provinces in 1997 provoked the writer Rodolfo Rabanal to reflect on the limitations of a democracy that was deaf to the common people's demands.

Probably the most controversial aspect of Menem's administration was the degree of corruption that permeated all levels of government, including the presidential family. The tragic death of Menem's only son, Carlos Menem Jr., in an accident in 1995 immediately raised suspicions that it was retaliation for dealings in international drug traffic. Also suspicious were the shady connections of the industrialist Alfredo Yabrán with government officials as well as the circumstances of his suicide after being indicted. The law was inexplicably slow and inefficient in solving these cases. Some even argued that the judicial system protected the interests of those close to Menem by covering up irregularities and even criminal activities. To counter the sense of overreaching corruption, the press became the people's detective, denouncing and investigating illegal activities, interviewing witnesses, and collecting evidence for the prosecution. The assassination of José Luis Cabezas is an example of the risks that some journalists were willing to take in the pursuit of truth. In his analysis of the then leading newspaper *Página/12,* Horacio González traces the stylistic and political origins of the new press to the tradition inaugurated by Rodolfo Walsh's investigations of political crimes in the 1950s.

Teaching the Republic

Raúl Alfonsín

When Raúl Alfonsín took the podium to give his first presidential address to Congress on 10 December 1983, he instilled the occasion with a foundational meaning. The new administration's task would not be limited to solving the severe financial and social ills plaguing the country. Its greater public mission was nothing less than to shore up the democratic institutions of the Republic. With a strong didactic tone, Alfonsín's inaugural speech is a lecture on the virtues of democracy. Purposely rejecting the authoritarian methods of both the oligarchic Right and the revolutionary Left, Alfonsín insists that only suffrage can guarantee a better society, where it will be possible to enjoy political freedom without giving up social justice.

Honorable Congress of the Nation:

I come to express before you, the honorable representatives of the nation, the principal objectives of the new administration in the various areas where it must act: national and international politics, defense, the economy, labor relations, education, public health, justice, the infrastructure, public services, and all other issues that require the attention of the people, administrators, and legislators.

But I also want to say that there should be a deep, fundamental connection between all these areas and that a common strength should nourish the life of each of the acts of the newly born democratic government, namely, the rectitude and morality of its actions.

There are many problems that will not be solved immediately, but today the atmosphere of public immorality is over. We are going to build a decent government. Yesterday a despairing, melancholy, and unbelieving country could exist: today we convene the Argentine people in the name, not just of the legitimate origins of the democratic government, but also of the ethical feeling that sustains such legitimacy.

This ethical feeling is one of the most noble movements of the soul. The ob-

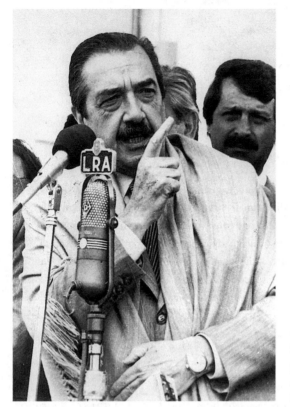

Raúl Alfonsín delivering a
public speech. Courtesy
Archivo General de la
Nación, Buenos Aires.

jective of establishing national unity should be completely understood through
ethics.

This ethical feeling, which accompanied the struggle of millions of Argentines who fought for liberty and justice, signifies that the end can never justify
the means.

Those who believe that the end justifies the means assume that a marvelous
future will erase any blame due to ethical failings and crimes. Justifying the
means by the end implies admitting that other human beings could be hurt,
that they could be starved, and that they could be exterminated under the
illusion that such a terrible price might make for a better life for future generations. The logic of pragmatic cynics always refers to a distant future. But
our obligation is here and now, basically an obligation to our contemporaries,
whom we have no right to sacrifice in the service of the hypothetical glories
of future centuries.

We are going to work for the future. Democracy works for the future, but
it is a tangible future. Only by working toward a tangible future can one estab-

lish a positive correlation between the ends and the means. There can be no government without memory, there can be no government without hope, but hope for a conceivable time, not an indeterminate future. . . .

We are going to fight for an independent state. We have established that this means that the state cannot subordinate itself to foreign powers and to international financial groups, but neither can it subordinate itself to powerful local groups. Private property plays an important role in the development of societies, but the state cannot be the private property of the economically privileged sectors. Oligarchies tend to always think that the business owners or those who control the nation's capital must necessarily be the owners of the state. We have witnessed this once again in the past years. Others, meanwhile, believe that the state should be the owner of all national businesses. We believe that the state must be independent: neither the property of the rich, nor the sole proprietor of the mechanisms of production.

The independence of the state presupposes two fundamental conditions.

First of all, popular leadership. If this did not exist, where else would the state get the strength to maintain its independence? From the beginning, democracy will be a mobilizing force. Democracy will always mobilize, while [oligarchic] regimes demobilize. . . .

Second, it requires administrative morality, regarding the conduct of the administrators. We shall be more than just ideology or ethics. The struggle against the corrupt, against immorality and decadence, reinforces the need for popular leadership. In reality, they both go together: there can be no struggle against corruption, which comes forth from the depths of the [oligarchic] regime, without recourse to popular leadership, but popular leadership cannot be preserved without maintaining a politics of openness, an ethics that will assure its own survival. . . .

Suffrage has many different, simultaneous meanings. On the one hand, the right to vote makes it possible for the people to govern and for the state to be free. On the other hand, it enforces a system of rules to obtain legitimacy since the people are not able to express themselves on their own and any so-called spontaneity never exists in real life. By means of suffrage, the people have a means of electing their administrators and their representatives. They cannot elect them by means of insurrection. It is impossible for violence to be the permanent method to spark change. . . .

The way we have chosen to challenge the monopolizing possession of the state and the nation by economic or financial powers, and also to fight against the monopolizing possession of the state and the nation by armed groups, no matter what their excuse for taking power, is suffrage.

Suffrage, by definition, constitutes a means to limit the privileged sectors, and, as an instrument of the majority, it generally achieves greater distributive justice.

Suffrage makes possible the peaceful resolution of societies' controversies, and, by providing the only possible legitimacy for the state, it allows for the continuity of republican institutions and their corresponding principles. In Argentina, we have proved up to what point the dissolution of the people's rights to elect their own government has always implied the transfer of sovereignty to foreign powers, to unemployment, misery, immorality, decadence, improvisation, the lack of public liberties, violence, and disorder. Many people are unaware of what it means to live under the rule of law and the constitution, but we all know what it means to live outside the boundaries of the law and the constitution.

Honorable Congress:

The will of the people through their representatives is manifest today in these venerable quarters, testifying to the birth of a new era in our national life. The possibility that the people could be the protagonists of this definitive new beginning inspires in all of us a sense of responsibility in keeping with the effort that we undertake together today and infuses in us the strength to confront the mass of problems that afflict our fatherland.

These difficulties are many and immense, as well we know, but we are going to push forward with the necessary faith and force because we undoubtedly have the resources, will, and passion required. And, above all, because we are all united in this struggle. . . .

Translated by Desirée Martin

Living with Inflation

Osvaldo Soriano

In 1989, before President Raúl Alfonsín stepped down, prices reached extraordinary levels. In a matter of days, hyperinflation made food and housing unaffordable for hundreds of thousands of people. The deteriorating economy was yet another manifestation of the dictatorship's harsh legacy, one that democracy seemed unable to control. In this ironic essay, the writer Osvaldo Soriano highlights the almost surrealistic everyday experiences of citizens living with extreme levels of inflation.

Ever since 1975 Argentina has been eaten away by an inflation that at its most dramatic, around 1985, reached 100 percent per month and at its most benign (in 1980, during the military dictatorship) was 90 percent annually. Under the government of Raúl Alfonsín, money was devaluated by 86 percent. This past spring, aware that at such a rate of economic disintegration the ruling party would lose the May 1989 elections to the Peronists, the government implemented a structural adjustment plan that reduced the rise to 6 percent per month.

This country has gotten used to living with inflation just like people live with hurricanes in the Caribbean, with drought in Lima, and with smog in Mexico. When all is said and done, this way of life, so inexplicable to others, doesn't keep the cats from meowing, the dogs from barking, or the sun from setting on time.

As the Dew to the Sun

The day before my departure for Brussels, in June 1976, I went to a travel agency to change into dollars all the "legal pesos" (that until 1969 had been "national money") that I had obtained that very day by selling my car and some other trifles. I remember that the line at the exchange window was very long and that, no matter how much the cashier hurried, the price of the dollar went up faster than his fingers could count the bills. Behind that little gray man, with his mustache trimmed in the 1940s style, there was another man, slimmer and quicker, who had a telephone pressed between his jaw and his shoulder. With his free hand, he was turning a handle to change the exchange rate posted on a display like a taxi meter. With each step the line advanced, the value of the bills that I had in my pockets evaporated like the dew when the sun begins to shine.

With the dollars I got that day, I managed to survive a few months in Brussels in a group house I rented with some friends near the European Economic Community building. For a long time I was amazed that Belgian money would maintain its value unchanged, or almost; that cigarettes, tea, and typewriter ribbons always cost the same amount. At times I was surprised—and I wrote to my friends in Buenos Aires about it—that some products actually went down in price. There were times when I published articles in *El diario de Caracas* and the honorarium sometimes was in bolivars, sometimes in dollars, because for the Venezuelans it was all the same.

Then I went to France, and for six years inflation was measured in cents. It was a new world, to which I adapted easily, because my life with galloping inflation back in Argentina had lasted only a few months. The real blow came when I went back.

In Buenos Aires in 1985, it was no longer possible to buy anything at night for what it had cost in the morning. In the cafés, the cashiers went crazy between the orders of clients and the demands of the boss, who spent his time listening to the escalation of prices on the radio. Rents, salaries, everything in life was—and still is—indexed. Your pockets filled up with worn-out bills, full of holes and all stuck together, and the face of General San Martín got washed out in between love notes, surly messages, and requests for help written by people with stronger ink than they used at the central bank.

Wallets were not a good present for anyone. There was no room in their compartments to keep paper with a value of 100,000, of 500,000, of 1 million pesos. Popular ingenuity rebaptized the numbers: the million was the *palo* (it still is, and, if it's in dollars, it's a green *palo*). Anyone coming from overseas—like me, just back from Europe—was driven crazy trying to distinguish between the millions and hundreds of millions necessary to pay for a simple taxi ride. "Six *palos* 120,000," said the taxi driver when he looked at the taxi meter. And at times, just to increase the confusion, he would add: "If you give me 2 *lucas,* I'll give you back a *colorado.*"

The *luca* had been the thousand-peso bill that my father dreamed of in vain in the 1950s, when he was earning, I think, 140 national pesos per month. The comic books my mother bought for me every week cost twenty cents, and a package of soccer trading cards and the movies cost five and stayed that way all through my youth.

The five-cent piece was a nice coin, fairly heavy, with the face of the Liberator on one side and the number 5 on the other. When we played soccer, we had to ask a neighbor or some passerby to loan us one so we could flip it up in the air to see who went first or to figure out the direction of the wind. Now you can find these coins in stamp museums next to stamps featuring Eva Perón or the ones with General Manuel Belgrano, which reappeared in 1955 when the first Perón government fell.

We'll Settle Up Tomorrow

Back then at school they gave us accounts with the National Postal Savings Bank; we deposited our cents in those accounts, using little passbooks to keep track with a new stamp pasted below the others to represent that week's savings, building up a pool of money we couldn't touch until we were eighteen. Needless to say, no one from my generation ever managed to turn that passbook into hard cash. In the 1960s inflation in Argentina was the way it is now in Uruguay and Venezuela, between 30 percent and 40 percent annually. Viewed from the perspective of here and now, that wasn't really inflation.

Meanwhile, the "national money" peso was converted to the "Argentine peso," then to the "legal peso," and in 1985, with the implementation of the first adjustment plan of the current government, to the *austral*. This new monetary unit was supposed to exchange at 0.85 *australs* per dollar, but by November of 1988 the dollar bought 15.6 *australs*.

The monetary chaos began in 1975, during the government of Isabel Perón. An ephemeral minister of economics, Celestino Rodrigo, immortalized his name one winter day when he produced what is still known as the *rodrigazo*. I remember that day because I was in a bar with some friends, discussing the latest news, and, when we were ready to leave, we called the waiter over so we could pay the bill.

"How much do we owe you?" one of us asked. And the waiter, throwing his arms in the air, said to us: "I don't know. The owner doesn't even know. Whatever you give me that isn't less than ten thousand pesos is fine. If that's not right, we'll settle up tomorrow."

The convulsion of that day would become, over the next three years, an exercise of childish everyday economics. All Argentines are small or big speculators, used to putting their money in a bank for seven days in an interest bearing account and then running to take it to a "money table," that speculative circuit where the financiers earn thousands in a single day. There are enormous masses of money that are deposited for interest for a single night, between the closing and the opening of the banks, because the banks need to fulfill the requirements for cash flow set by the national treasury.

In November 1988, money deposited for a fixed time in any bank produced earnings of 8 percent monthly in dollars. This phenomenon brought in capital that only came to pass through the financial circuit and then returned, considerably fattened up, to its safe shelter back in New York or Switzerland. It is calculated that $10 billion came in from overseas, passed through the banks, and was multiplied by speculation, all at the state's expense.

The operation was simple. . . . If someone has at his disposal something like $100,000 — and there must be people who have — he would change it into *australes,* and he would deposit it for a fixed time in the bank at 10 percent (or in the black market at 14 percent), with interest paid every seven days. Since the price of the dollar stayed constant, at the end of a month the first $100,000 could buy, if the person had been cautious, things worth $108,000. And, if he had been risky and invested in the "bicycle," as the parallel financial market is called, he could have earned much more. Rates of interest and yields were announced all through the day by radio and television, before the weather report.

Many Heart Attacks

Of course, there were many heart attacks because this financial wager depended on the government keeping the exchange rate frozen, by whatever means. When the system broke down, as it did six months after the Austral Plan was implemented in 1985, almost all the small, inattentive savers were left with useless paper. But that also forms part of the culture of inflation, just like the multitudes of lotteries, races, sport competitions, and raffles sponsored by the state, the provinces, private enterprises, and television.

Language changed with the currency and the sense of disenchantment. Any reasonably well educated young Argentine today dreams of "being bailed out," that is to say, of earning a fortune in one fell swoop, or else of "splitting," "hitting the road," "jumping ship," or whatever other linguistic variation means leaving the country before it's too late. The Uruguayans had circulated a joke that said that the last man to leave the country should turn off the lights. In the Argentine version, that last act of civility would be impossible because, before that, someone would have stolen the map — or cut off the electricity.

Yet that word *inflation,* which is in all the newspapers and on the lips of all the politicians, is not a term that is used in the streets. The shopkeeper says that "there's no dough," the butcher that "there isn't any money," but I have not heard many people blame their ills on inflation. The labor unions are still struggling to get higher salaries for their workers, no matter how devalued the money is when they get it at the end of the month. In November 1988, the economy minister set wage increases at only 4 percent, supposedly to keep from feeding inflation, and the result was paralysis of all government activities—from the mail, to the railroads, to customs, and even to providing gas, power, and electric service.

Strikes had a justification that is evident in growing poverty and also in the statistics: in five years of constitutional government, the value of salaries has diminished by 42.7 percent, according to sources of the Confederación General del Trabajo.

In daily life, the deterioration is spectacular, except in the neighborhoods of the upper middle class and the haute bourgeoisie. When the *austral* was launched three years ago, the largest and most coveted bill in the new currency was the red 100 *austral,* which was worth $85.00. A little more than twelve months later, the 500 *austral* bill appeared, which was at first hard to get change for, and finally, by October 1988, the brand-new 1,000 *austral* bill went into circulation, worth barely $70.00.

Precautions?

While I am writing this article, the cigarettes that I smoke as I sit here in front of my typewriter went from eleven to thirteen and then to fourteen *australs.* This movement does not disturb us because we know it is inevitable. To estimate the value of an automobile, one has to figure in the cost of the insurance policy, which is renewed every four months and itself anticipates the inflationary index. In all the bills for public service—water, light, gas—the computer signals the price to pay on the due date and another, with the added charge also calculated, after a grace period of ten days.

No one sets the price of a contract for services in *australes* but in dollars. As the law obliges us to use Argentine money, at least in appearances, any agreement to pay within six months will include a clause that says, for example: "This will be paid in *australes* equivalent to *x* dollars in Bonex value [the name of a public money exchange that pays in U.S. money] according to the current price on that day in Uruguay."

And woe to anyone who doesn't take precautions! Among the most frequent victims of inflation are the tenant who has to pay an indexed rent, the doctor who sees patients from workers' comp (which pays him seventy days after he has rendered his services), or the writer, whose editor pays him royalties every six months. The very few who are able to set their own terms are paid in advance and arrange to be paid every three months, but, in any case, all compensation—beginning with salaries—deteriorates before becoming effective.

You live with inflation like you live with the landscape. The businessman accepts Argentine money in order to get interest, and he doesn't consider reinvesting it. Thus, the only profitable businesses are those that get paid immediately: supermarkets, transportation services, shows, prepaid savings schemes to finance cars and housing. In some cases, products bought wholesale at low prices are sold below cost—especially in supermarkets—because the ability to put the money into speculation immediately means that losses can be recovered in two days and profits can be accumulated in the following five.

Everyone knows the usual excuses for delaying a payment, and that is part of the rules of the game. Postdated checks abound, at times they bounce, and even casinos, whose clientele had been shrinking, have begun to accept the idea of buying chips by check, which signifies a barely disguised way of giving credit to the player.

In view of the presidential and legislative elections coming up in May 1989, the government has set out to lower inflation in order to provide an image of order and efficiency that might give the radical Eduardo Angeloz some chance against the Peronist Carlos Menem, who is leading in the polls. That is why the central bank has set such high interests rates and kept the dollar frozen. As a result, inflation has fallen to 6 percent monthly, but nobody knows what will happen when this policy runs out.

Perspectives

In any case, the printers at the treasury never stop. The designers of bills, who have chosen the faces of constitutional presidents to decorate the bills, are already preparing 5,000 and 10,000 *austral* bills. Maybe even before this government finishes its term, at the end of 1989, we might see the portrait of the radical Hipólito Yrigoyen, the first head of state elected by universal male suffrage. And, if things continue the way they're going, long before we enter the twenty-first century we will have in our pockets bills with the face of the smiling General Perón. But it is risky to predict just when we will see, printed on the 1,000,000 *austral* bill, the austere, chastened face of Raúl Alfonsín.

Translated by Patricia Owen Steiner

Menem: A New Style in Politics

Vicente Palermo and Marcos Novaro

For ten years, Carlos Menem governed Argentina in a style that puzzled traditional politicians. By applying presidential decrees in a manner that some saw as authoritarian, Menem was in a few years able to impose neoliberal economic and social policies that nobody considered viable in a country with Argentina's political history. The virtual elimination of inflation and the reform of the welfare state were among his achievements — unemployment and corruption among his grave failures. Despite the negative social effects of his policies during his first term, Menem won reelection in 1995. In this widely respected analysis of Menem's political style, Palermo and Novaro try to explain the paradox of an elected president who, despite his unpopular programs, was seen by the majority as the only political option for the 1990s.

Above all, Menemism is a reformist strategy of government. By analyzing the content and means of implementing its policies for transforming the state, the economy, and society in general, we can find the keys to understand its nature. To understand, that is, Menem's particular style of accumulating power, producing consensus, and facing conflicts. Within this broad and complex set of issues, we can pose the question, Have Peronist identity and traditions blocked or aided the development of Menemist policies?

Perhaps they did both at the same time. Menem made use of more than a few typically Peronist gestures to justify his audacious plan of reforms and to secure the support of his voters and his party. He overcame his initial credibility problems by drawing on the Peronist trust in the leader as the supreme guide in rebuilding the nation and unifying the people. He attacked the "political class" and politics as usual, a strategy that had served Perón so well in his day, in order to justify recruiting figures from other political groups, even artists and businessmen. He dismissed his adversaries and "disciplined" his own legislators to follow the course of reforms. And he absorbed the talk of free markets and alliance with the United States without too many problems, thanks to the traditional pragmatism of Peronists. In sum, if Menem were not a Peronist, he would hardly have been able to convince his followers and allies to support him on the path he undertook in those years.

But being a Peronist was not enough. His party origins and his markedly populist and traditional record as governor of La Rioja aroused distrust among businessmen and other actors with economic power and also among more middling sectors. They were especially concerned whether he could avoid the factionalism of Peronism in the past. How could he stop history and tradition from becoming insurmountable obstacles that would keep him from governing? Menem's answer to this dilemma had effects that were immediate and — even for him — surprisingly successful.

From the beginning, Menem set out to remake tradition itself, redefining the role and character of the allies and "internal forces" who would join him in the government. He did this partly because circumstances forced him to and partly because he was genuinely convinced of its benefits. This was why he sparked the break within the CGT ([Confederación General del Trabajo], the Peronist-dominated labor central) and the political and institutional weakening of labor unions. He forged a watertight alliance with the most powerful economic actors, with U.S. foreign policy, with international financial institutions, and, perhaps most strikingly of all, with free market politicians until then considered the most recalcitrant of anti-Peronists. On the other hand, his first steps toward carrying out structural reforms of the state and the economy showed his willingness to abandon the protectionist, redistributionist, and statist policies that had previously dominated — although not always with the same intensity — the Peronist imaginary.

The fact is that, in July 1989, Menem faced a very difficult choice. If he stayed within tradition — as he had done as governor of La Rioja between 1983 and 1989 and as many of his supporters suggested he still should — he would have a difficult time controlling the hyperinflation that was plaguing the country, much less establishing the solid alliance with dominant economic figures that would enable him to govern. But, if Menem took his distance from historic Peronism, his electoral support might become too fragile, and he ran the risk of losing control of the wide range of institutional spaces controlled by Peronist leadership, which were crucial in consolidating his political power. As Menem himself said, he was obliged to prove that Perón would have done the same things he was doing and that what needed to be done had little to do with old-time Peronism.

Menem has been compared with Fujimori, with Collor de Melo, and with other leaders who appeared around the same time on the political scene of various Latin American countries, running as *outsiders*. But the similarity is rather superficial: none of these leaders emerged from a populist movement strongly rooted in the political life of their countries, as did Menem. For that reason, perhaps, it would be more exact to compare him with Carlos Salinas de Gortari, who faced a similar dilemma to his in 1988, as the head of the Revolutionary Institutional Party (PRI) and the government of Mexico. Like Menem, he used a strong populist tradition to bring about reforms that affected his historic social base but also provided him with a new one. In this way, he could govern without being obliged to openly renounce his prior identity. For both men, the strategic management of the tension between continuity and rupture was the key to their success.

However, there exists a fundamental difference between the two men that should not pass unnoticed. Menem took power in the last days of a long period of crisis that rotted away the financial and institutional resources of the state, fragmented and disorganized the structural bases of the once vigorous Peronist movement, and weakened not only labor unions but also business groups and other social organizations. Peronism had ceased to be a coalition of organized, articulated, and mobilized interests years before, and there was little chance that it would become one again, even if it could win the elections. The Mexican PRI, on the other hand, faced the reforms at the end of the 1980s strongly in control of the still-solid state apparatus, foreseeing the imminent and otherwise inevitable political debacle that would follow the economic crisis already under way. The situation that Menem had to confront was infinitely more delicate than the one that Salinas encountered since Menem had far fewer government resources and much less maneuvering room in launching a reform plan and a political strategy.

Menem had to make up for this relative weakness with a larger dose of imagination and audacity, although it is true that he did have one resource in abundance that was quite scarce in Mexico. The political legitimacy of the Mexican president was in doubt. Chosen in elections suspected of fraud, Salinas lacked full democratic legitimacy, while the traditional legitimacy of the PRI was falling apart—although not so much as traditional Peronism—owing to internal divisions, increasing electoral competition, modernization, and the economic crisis. By contrast, Menem could count on the backing of an indisputable democratic legitimacy that, even in the times of economic and state crisis of 1989, did not seem to be greatly affected. That legitimacy would be a fundamental weapon in Menem's hands. . . .

At the beginning of 1989, riding along with hyperinflation, Argentina entered the terminal phase of a crisis that had already lasted fifteen years and had profoundly affected, not only the economy, but also the state—which had been practically frozen by exhausted finances, weakened authority, and administrative chaos—as well as interest groups and political parties. Peronism was not immune to this situation. As we have already said, its social base was falling apart, turning into an impoverished, dispersed, and uneven mass. The labor movement, small businessmen, and the redistributive state, once the pillars of the populist regime, could be considered by then "endangered species."

Yet, just when the depth of the crisis showed the impossibility of reestablishing a governing coalition like those of traditional populism, Peronism reversed the decline that had begun with its electoral defeat by Alfonsín in 1983 — or even earlier with Perón's death in 1974. Disproving repeated predictions of its imminent disappearance, by 1988 Peronism had completed its renovation and institutionalization as a national party, given birth to a leadership capable of reuniting the country after fifteen years of violent internal conflicts (known as the Renovators), and prepared to occupy the government vacuum left by the collapse of Alfonsín's government. Given the context of the crisis in which it took place, one understands why the scope and meaning of this apparent political recovery was not immediately clear. Would this be Peronism's final, tragic death rattle before its disappearance or its incorporation at last, after a long march, into a "postpopulist" democratic political system? Only time would tell.

Menem's strategy bet on a simultaneous transformation of his allies and of the political setting in which the democratic transition had taken place. Menem understood that he could be both the gravedigger and the victim of a Peronism that was, curiously enough, structurally collapsed but electorally vibrant. But, at the same time, he had a relatively open field in which to try something new. Above all, this was because of the legitimacy that the reestablished democratic regime gave him, but it was also because all his potential opponents — including labor unions and other "historic" Peronists, his ex-partners in the Peronist Renovation, and supporters of Alfonsín — were in worse shape than he to offer a way out and because the crisis itself demanded a tremendous amount of innovation, predisposing society to accept changes, even changes that were painful and hardly respectful of traditions. Based on that, Menem took up the double challenge that he was facing. In between the terminal crisis under way and the sense of emergency that it had instilled in society, Menem reshaped the terms of the democratic transition, which until then had featured Peronism in a secondary and hostile role and had left the implementation of economic, fiscal, and administrative reforms in a swampy terrain of ambiguities and delays. In so doing, he redefined the character and objectives of his party, laying out a new political, economic, and social program to organize his own forces and alliances around. It was a matter, in short, of avoiding the double danger of being tied to tradition or diluting his reputation. For this, he aimed both to

"Peronize" democracy and to bring Peronism up to date—because, from his point of view, it was already democratic enough.

Even though the specific instruments and courses of action to resolve each problem did vary, and in many of them a persistent improvisation and inconsistency was evident, the overall strategic course was adopted decisively and remained constant over time. This was another of the merits of Menem's strategy.

From the beginning, Menem proved himself ready "to do whatever it takes," even if that meant breaking promises, abandoning or redefining principles, and negating the most deep-rooted practices of the Justicialist Party (the legal name for Peronism) and its voters. He didn't encounter any great resistance in those areas, probably owing to the severity of the crisis that those values and traditions had been experiencing ever since the death of Perón. The very identity and interests of these actors seemed to have been falling apart with the passing of the years, with successive frustrations, and, above all, with the pressure of the situation of economic emergency. This left people ready to consider a political strategy that was sufficiently daring and original to yank them out of their sense of defeat and decline.

It was no coincidence that, shortly after assuming the presidency, Menem blamed the crisis on "the traditional model of party action and public administration," including historic Peronism within the accusation. This diagnosis was somewhat partial, perhaps, but not completely off base, and very convenient for his own practical ends.

During the first years of the transition, this "model" had been caught in the crossfire between statist, redistributionist, and nationalist mandates and the demands and pressures of various interest groups that tried to speed up, sidetrack, or hold back the inevitable remaking of the state and the economy. This had generated a pronounced ideological confusion and a growing practical stagnation among both Peronists and radicals. This led both parties to adopt ambiguous, if not contradictory, stances toward privatization, the role of the market, the crisis of the welfare state and the protectionist model, and other matters of fundamental importance. These stances, in turn, made it more and more clear that traditional Peronism and radicalism could not be dependable instruments for mediating interests and making decisions in the new democratic Argentina. Anyone within those parties who wanted to face up to the new situation would find himself obliged to loosen ties to party history and discard inherited social and ideological commitments.

Years before Menem came to power, Alfonsín's followers within radicalism and Renovators within Peronism had tried to do all of this. Whether because conditions did not favor them or because they acted too timidly, their reform proposals came up against internal and external resistance, forcing them to abort their plans. Alfonsín, who dreamed of giving birth to a new political regime, thought that he could do it by democratizing the actors and institutions of the old Argentina. But those actors and institutions did not take long to turn against him, taking advantage of his weak spots and his ambiguities. The result was tragic for the radical administration and instructive for the social and economic actors involved: the depth of the crisis demanded a decisive and unbiased approach from those in power.

Menem took the opposite path from Alfonsín. Taking up a much more pragmatic and decisive attitude, and taking advantage of the already advanced disintegration of the political field and of his own party, he shamelessly drove forward this disintegration, thus affecting his own powers as much as those of his adversaries. Making a sharp break between the "old politics" and the "new" (his), he cut back the role of labor unions and his own party in making decisions, ignored protests about historic rights and faithfulness to tradition, and liquidated publicly owned companies, public employees, and basic public services without any compunction. With this, he deepened the crisis of inherited identities, the fragmentation of interest groups, and the loosening of the electorate's feelings of party loyalty. Thus, Menem presented himself as the only politician who was truly "up-to-date" and "decisive." Relying on a surplus of public confidence, Menem took the initiative to shape a majority that would back his politics of reform. For this reason, there is little point in speaking of Menem's "betrayal of his mandate," of his abandonment of the key points of his campaign program and speeches, or of the costs of his policies to certain interest groups. Society had already paid the "material" cost of those policies many times over during hyperinflation, while the cost of ideological and programmatic renovations could easily be covered by his surplus of public confidence. Given the absence — whether apparent or real — of alternatives, public opinion was more than willing to accept the idea that the past had to be left behind as soon as possible, and at whatever price, and that this required letting go of customs, tradition — and publicly owned companies.

This route was in any case extremely risky. Before 1991, Menemism came very close to disaster several times: its economic policy was not yet producing any palpable results, and its strategy of remaking Peronism was on the verge of sparking a break whose consequences, if it had taken place, would have been irreversible for the party and perhaps tragic for Menem himself. . . .

After a first period of disaffection and fragmentation of identities (which took place between 1989 and 1991), broad sectors within and outside Peronism that had been left politically "available" began to be brought in by new bonds of consent and identification. This political realignment resulted mostly from Menem's very dynamic strategy, which appealed to "available" groups, giving new meaning to the remaining components of their identities in crisis. This would explain why many of those who voted for Menem in 1989 for one reason voted for him again in 1991 and 1993 for the opposite reason and why others vote for him now, contradicting their earlier actions. It also explains why many trusted in him, granted him a great deal of authority to act and centralize power, and considered him a way of achieving economic progress, renewing the political system, consolidating institutions, and even democratizing them, even though their "historic" interests or immediate sectoral demands were not being listened to. The emergency situation generated by a crisis that everyone experienced as "terminal" had opened the way to Menem's call for a "new era." Because he was different from traditional politicians, he could channel his appeal for authority and for recovering the effectiveness of politics into a wager on a "new politics" that broke with the past by invoking the common good, as opposed to individual interests, and offering an unorthodox combination of republican, liberal, and populist values and principles. . . .

As already suggested, political networks of identity, solidarity, and community were already in crisis before Menem came to power. Menem simply proposed that society come to terms with the irreversible nature of this crisis, which in turn allowed him to convince society that it should resign itself to losing its former political ideals, replacing them with the new ones that he was offering. Instead of the classic oppositions between Peronists and anti-Peronists and between nationalism and liberalism, he proposed a choice between change and decay. Direct appeals to workers were replaced by diffuse calls to "brothers and sisters," while free enterprise and the market supplanted the Peronist ideals of organized community and the welfare state. Along the way, this turned the values of success and effectiveness, which had already spread into all corners of society, into practically the only criterion for judging the behavior of public figures, including political ones.

This truly epochal change meant that democratic politics were frustrating much of what they had promised in terms of values, rights, and principles formulated at the beginning of the transition. But had they ever really been honored by traditional politics? What should we object to in the "new politics," and what should we miss about traditional politics? Is Menemism in this sense a step backward for the political culture of Argentine democracy? These questions demand that we look at the wide variety of results, not all of them similar, of Menem's strategy in political life. We should examine the functioning of institutions (what the scholarly literature calls the *democratic consolidation* that supposedly should follow every transition), and that terrain includes a wide range of aspects, from government efficiency and the distribution and balance of powers to the respect for rights and procedures. We must also look at social practices and social representations, at how interests are articulated and identities formed, as well as at tolerance, respect for pluralism, citizen participation in public affairs, and social equity.

Translated by Mark Alan Healey

The Journalist as the People's Detective

Horacio González

In 1985, soon after the return of democracy, the newspaper Página/12 *began publication. Directed by the young journalist Jorge Lanata, the newspaper emerged onto the public scene marked by a discourse critical of the traditional media. Through the use of ironic headlines and a cynical tone, it consciously displayed the political positioning implicit in any news coverage. As a voice for the middle classes,* Página/12 *grew steadily by offering information about local politics and giving expression to the cultural tastes of a modern, informed audience. From its inception, the newspaper featured a weekly column on political analysis by the journalist Horacio Verbitsky. His work soon turned to investigating cases of corruption that the state court and the police were unable or unwilling to solve. Journalism began to occupy the vacuum left by an inept judicial system. In the following essay, entitled "Legal Dramas and Hard-Boiled Detective Novels," the sociologist Horacio González identifies the features of the new journalism's unconventional style in the context of a political system riddled with corruption.*

A chronicle that investigates a massacre and a novel about a detective who hides his puritanism behind perfectly acid wisecracks: these are the foundations of modern critical journalism in Argentina. Legal dramas and hard-boiled detective novels: Rodolfo Walsh in *Operation Massacre* and Raymond Chandler in *The Long Good-Bye* explored the two similar genres that are now the instinctive basis of the journalism we read in *Página/12*. These dramatic genres present conflicts much larger than the poor creatures who plunge into them with open-eyed resignation. The drama takes place in institutional labyrinths, on long corridors paced by judges, lawyers, and policemen who modestly, violently, and fatally embody evil.

Tragedy is a narrative that demands the unexpected appearance of proof. That is why, as has been said so often, tragic tales follow — at a gentle distance — the same course as a court trial.

Such legal dramas do not require a standing court of justice. As the critic

Angel Rama noted with compelling simplicity, Walsh was heir to a literary tradition that presented the victims of history as denied the aid of established justice. For the persecuted, the law was no protection. On the contrary, the legal system was a force that had turned against them.

Walsh presented the legally unprotected as fallen men, escapees from a thoroughly arbitrary order built on complacent laws. None of those courts or judges could offer protection to a fugitive who himself offered the living—or, rather, the surviving—proof that laws are written in the language of deceit. But Walsh took his judicial proof to the courts of the reading public, the true judges. These readers would know how to weigh the tragic paradox of a law that existed in order to destroy rights, not to guarantee them. The text of the law code was turned against the authorities themselves by an investigative journalist willing to step out into the darkness. Terror shrouded in fraudulent legality: that was the darkness.

Every proof demanded that he put himself on the line. As a lone investigator, he had to find hidden texts. Walsh searched for unknown traces that might later bring the law back to its intended meaning. But when would that "later" be? He had to take legal structures back to their original adherence to truth. But when? At some later time, longed for and utopian, but remote. Not visible on the horizon. As a lawyer, the journalist-investigator would have found no courtroom to expound his case. Walsh proved his truth by putting his own body into the account. The truth was to be found in each step of his investigation into the essential injustice sheltered in institutions that had betrayed their purpose. And, finally, the investigation was carried out against a guilty party, the diabolic synthesis of hidden everyday horror.

Página/12 was possible only when people could once again think of justice as a present possibility. To achieve this, justice had to be turned on itself, using a mirror to examine its dark and abject side. The harm that the courts did to society could be contemplated in the mirror of a journalism that made its efforts to renew justice in those very courts. This was a circular movement to rescue justice in public, without the lone detectives or hermit journalists who trusted only the written documents that have taken the place of a disappeared body.

From Rodolfo Walsh to Horacio Verbitsky, we can glimpse a chance at renewing the independent power of justice through the denunciations of the journalist-lawyer. This move from the journalist-investigator to the journalist-lawyer draws a dramatic arc across Argentine journalism, with *Página/12* at one of its extremes. . . .

Horacio Verbitsky and *Página/12* have taken over the present chapter of social struggles in Argentina, written in journalistic style. Their sole subject is denouncing the crimes protected by those worn-out tablets of the law. But the investigator now speaks to democratic public opinion and has an audience who reads him. This is no solitary exercise in justice but an exploration of the possibilities of public communication — with no holds barred. Verbitsky pursues symptoms, he captures signs: he identifies the deformed tendencies that bubble to the surface of the political life of the state, of power groups, of fortunate or archetypal people. Those tendencies emit facts: infinite transmissions chaotic in meaning and hieroglyphic in appearance. Within the power grid, there are constant crossed cables, short-circuits, and sudden drops in judicial and economic currents.

The hard core of truth that sparks all this agitation, all these biographical connections, these obscure actions and dark fates, must be revealed by the sieve that filters out the facts. Verbitsky's writing style has given way to his greater effort to put together the facts that spurt out in bursts. In a newspaper whose dominant style comes from the mocking burlesque spirit that it uses to criticize officialdom, Verbitsky plugs an inexhaustible series of facts into satiric pigeonholes. But these facts are always charged with the aura of having been extracted from a secret magma, the product of being immersed in the fog of hidden information longing to speak for itself. The naked fact as the agent of the story. This is what is left of the hard-boiled detective novel produced by the journalism of denunciation in the 1960s. . . .

For Walsh, reaching the heart of darkness was a matter of a stroke of destiny in the life of a journalist. This is very different, naturally, from the struggle for speed in transmitting the latest news from the underworld of corruption. *Clarín, Noticias, Página/12.* . . . Which was the first to reach into the inner circle of hell to cast that kind of light that amazes all in our present times? The political heart of this present moment is revealed in the sudden appearance of something previously hidden, something that now bursts open as a shining star in the news firmament. In Walsh's day, there was no reliance on the market for news or on journalism thought of as an "estate," that "fourth estate" of corporatist-democratic theories that now seem to be coming true much more convincingly than when they were advanced by superficial liberal thinkers years ago. Today, in some way, we can glimpse the outlines of the party of the mass media, the party that substitutes for politics in this satellite age yet does take up the great causes of open information and the fight against censorship. Walsh's idea of investigative journalism stood guard over a different moment, a time when there was no stable public sphere and newspaper readers had traditional political loyalties.

Walsh read each puzzle piece and made them fit together, and he paid for it by finding himself inside the danger zone that he himself had shaped. While the secret plots in Walsh were strictly military and political (and only legal in a secondary sense), in Verbitsky they are legal and economic. With this the reporter's story loses some of its drama but wins a greater ability to intervene in the criminal plot itself. Each kind of story permits a different kind of hero. Walsh's heroes are fragile creatures who reach heroics starting out from a transparent frankness. These are Hegelian heroes who only *afterward,* as darkness falls, reach their conclusions and valiantly rule: guilty! . . .

Once tragedy has left everyday life — that invisible tunnel that links the two extremes of living — the course that remains is the one that, much later, will take the form of *Página/12*. Everyday life is no longer weighed down by absurdity. It becomes a site to observe anthropologically the entangling or unraveling of powers that produce our living world. In the absence of tragedy, everyday life turns into a place for journalism to reflect on new lifestyles, the uses of pleasure, self-improvement, and ethical and therapeutic matters derived from more or less crude reinterpretations of psychoanalysis. *Página/12* ends up producing an extensive chronicle of different lifestyles, shot through with a sense of lyrical abandonment (Quino's comic strip *Mafalda* was gently skeptical, Rep's strip *Socorro* mixes neurosis, abandonment, and sharp wit). The media's rediscovery of hidden cameras and parodies of the mass media have rendered the everyday world, not an absurd place, but a comically unreal one. Tragedy has become an optional part of reporter's stories, and power flows toward all kinds of mass media scenes. This allows for the kind of view of the presidency that the cartoonists Rudy and Paz offer: power is embodied in a creature who lives outside the usual political discourse and is forever absentmindedly unraveling plots that have been so carefully spun by others, with punchlines worthy of *The Three Stooges*.

Tragedy has also become sordid. A multitude of slender judicial threads trap lives for ever. Tragedy, in short, becomes corrupt. Accusations of corruption are drums beaten with loud drumsticks. Horacio Verbitsky justifies this as the new limit of political reason. In the introduction to his book *Robo para la corona* [Stealing for the crown], Verbitsky presents his approach in quick brushstrokes. In the past, what was in question was how the government came to power against the popular will; now, he suggests, what is in question is how the government exercises that power.

Democracy is no longer in danger. What is in jeopardy is the quality of its use and expression. What is important now is finding the means of perfecting democracy. A magnificent opportunity for doing just that lies in the rediscovery of crimes not described by legal codes and the unearthing of the invisible actions of the "shadow parliaments" of society. The investigation and denunciation of this illicit network makes Verbitsky's book an anthropological study of the secret actions and schemes of the transdemocratic economy. But it is also a veritable treatise on morals. While there is indeed talk of the internationalist bourgeoisie and big companies as the center of the new strategies of domination, the true subject is how political ties take conspiratorial form. Debts, favors, covert ties, personal subterfuges, hidden manipulations. The shadowy language of the business of trafficking in the ritual functions of democracy. . . .

Legal dramas, as a style of journalism and fiction, reflect a shift in critical writing, which now deals almost exclusively with the failures of the law or its use in the service of illegal actions. Before the investigator was a journalist with an open political identity; now he has become a journalist who is an expert in the complex and fictitious world of the law.

Legal dramas are a genre with a central place before audiences worldwide (from *JFK* to *Cape Fear,* from *Law and Order* to *X-Files*), and they make for a kind of eyewitness democracy. An omniscient narrator sees everything that happens in the unearthly solitude of power. But in these lonely places plots are hatched—plots of bewildering complexity—that end up defining the era and bringing obscure life histories to light. . . .

Translated by Mark Alan Healey

Roadblocks, Detours, and Crossroads

Rodolfo Rabanal

In December 1994, the so-called Tequila Effect, caused by the devaluation of the Mexican peso, severely affected the Argentine economy, triggering recession. By making major corrections in the national economy, Menem was able to avoid the worst and maintain enough credibility to win the elections in 1995. Soon thereafter his popularity began to decline. The most clear signs of a breach in consensus came from the interior. Since 1993, the extreme austerity measures forced on the provinces by the Menem administration had been producing an escalating series of protests that climaxed in 1997, when hundreds of protestors blocked national roads and organized riots in Patagonia and the Northwest. The crisis unleashed by the outbreaks of popular violence was deepened by the continuing political fallout from the assassination in January 1997 of the journalist José Luis Cabezas, who was investigating the illegal activities of Alfredo Yabrán — an industrialist with obscure connections to government officials and one of the main beneficiaries of Menem's privatizing programs. In this contemporary piece, which appeared in the newspaper La nación on 19 June 1997, the writer Rodolfo Rabanal uses the roadblock as a metaphor for the obstacles that a fragile democracy faces under a corrupt neoliberal administration.

One commonplace saying refers to the solitude of power, another, just as well-known, to the fascination that power produces. Those who govern Argentina today surely have known both extremes, and, judging by their present incompetent responses to what is going on, they seem to be trapped underneath a bell of polarized glass. But there are notable cracks in the glass, and unsettling flashes of reality are beginning to filter through them.

Without the government being able to do anything to stop it, social discontent has deepened, spreading like a shadow across Menem's hopes for this October's elections. The unjust death of Teresa Rodríguez on a picket line in Patagonia, the dangerous situation at Cutral-Có, and the constant clashes between police and demonstrators are the living embodiment of a painful statistical fact: every day more and more people are being socially and economi-

Roadblocks (1997). Courtesy *La Nación*.

cally excluded from Argentine society, without anyone so far having even the vaguest idea how to stop it.

An Anachronistic Explanation

When the roadblocks began, the government thought it opportune to blame them on a return of political subversion. To be sure, this was an anachronistic idea: it has now been at least two decades since subversive organizations disappeared from the country, along with the worldwide historical moment that accompanied them. By dusting off a political scenario from the 1970s, the president was trying to shift the blame for present-day social disorder onto old-fashioned troublemakers. He was unable — or unwilling — to understand that each roadblock was the material and symbolic expression of the standstill his administration has come to.

The "return of subversion" argument was worn out before Menem even came up with it, and, after a few weeks, he found it more appropriate to get indignant about his ministers' failure to pay any attention to the economic and social situation of the provinces. And so the official explanation passed, with virtually no transition, from one rhetorical accusation derived from conspiracy theories to another that was equally conspiratorial. After all, without a conspiracy, how could the president be indignant about the behavior of his ministers when he himself maintains that we live in the best of all worlds?

Sinister Suspicions

While the excluded build roadblocks, the government sets up detours, trusting in the unlikely virtues of shortcuts, and refusing to recognize that, in reality, it finds itself at a crossroads. Surely this government has not faced any moment more difficult than this one. Along with the outbreaks of violence in the provinces and the heated struggle over education—which is itself quite serious and intractable—there is the accusation that a third passenger was on the helicopter when Carlos Menem Jr. died two years ago. This last accusation only feeds the sinister suspicions of Menem's ex-wife, Zulema Yoma, that the "accident" that killed her son was no accident.

Of course, in the severity of its potential consequences, nothing could equal the assassination of the photographer José Luis Cabezas. This case has been deliberately made complicated, with its own roadblocks and detours, in order to hide the identity of those responsible for the murder. Yet all the ominous plots surrounding the case *could not avoid scandal* or prevent suspicions from cascading down on Alfredo Yabrán and his shadowy ties to political power. Surprisingly, none of those who carried out this atrocious crime imagined on that summer night beneath a full moon the wild, uncontrollable chain of events that they would set in motion. It was like picking up a stone to discover underneath it a burrow that connected back, through a labyrinth of paths and branches, to tunnels that led to the most luxurious palaces of the kingdom. Suddenly this evil that had remained perfectly hidden was made evident and multiplied before the eyes of all.

Vices and Myths

It is curious to discover once again how well man's worst vices can still be explained by the most ancient and enduring myths.

At the unreachable center of the labyrinth in Crete roared a powerful monster, devourer of the innocent. The legendary King Minos held this secret power to be his greatest weapon since power always wishes to be invisible, shielded by the mystery that its secrecy produces. But one day, with the aid of the king's daughter Ariadne, who was disloyal to her father out of a higher loyalty to justice, a hero named Theseus managed to penetrate the darkness, reach the forbidden center, and finally slay the minotaur.

From that point on, one of the most important distinctions in Western culture began to emerge, the difference between those two concepts that are so easily confused, power and authority. Authority can guide the behavior of others without threats or punishments, thereby proving itself legitimate and sovereign. But power's only recourse is to its crushing force.

The Trap of the Labyrinth

In today's Argentina, people have come to see the labyrinth for what it is and come to realize how mixed up power and authority are. It is very likely that Menem is irritated with those cracks in his polarized glass bell because he is coming to the same conclusion but worrying that he may be reaching it too late.

With each passing day, with each detour of justice, and with each one of the seemingly endless lies and omissions used to muddy the case in order to conceal those truly responsible, it seems more and more like we have stepped into a hall of mirrors. But these are dangerous mirrors, and they may reflect precisely the image that power is looking to conceal.

We undoubtedly find ourselves at a very complex and confusing crossroads, with roadblocks marking off the directions we cannot turn. Looking beyond politicians and the government, people cannot help but ask themselves, Who are the minotaurs of today, who are those who, without any authority, wield a power that terrifies leaders and corrupts institutions?

From Plato to Today

On returning from his long exile in Syracuse, the young Plato went back to his beloved Athens, where democracy had been restored after the cruel tyranny of the Thirty. Full of hope, he wanted to join the government. But, watching the behavior of the leadership, he discovered to his dismay that the new democracy had been surprisingly moderate and even generous in its treatment of those who had abolished it.

The result did not take long to unfold before his eyes: the same characters who had thrived under the tyranny now benefited from the restored institutions, corrupting democracy and making a mockery of justice. Plato concluded bitterly that it is very difficult to restore public life once it has been undermined. More than two thousand years separate us from those events, but the distance seems insignificant.

Translated by Mark Alan Healey

X

Argentina in the Age of Globalization: New Citizenships and the Politics of Memory

Since the triumph of Menem's new Peronism in 1989, Argentina has gone through a far-reaching transformation comparable only to the profound changes brought about by modernization a century ago. But, although these two colossal historical shifts are somewhat analogous in scope, the consequences and the expectations that they have so far raised in the majority of Argentines are, to put it mildly, quite dissimilar. The implementation of a neoliberal economic model stopped inflation by impoverishing further the already stricken lower classes while also laying waste the traditionally proud and upwardly mobile middle classes. This has produced a drastic reappraisal of the dreams of social progress and personal betterment that were always at the core of modern Argentina, ever since millions of immigrants poured onto its shores searching for an earthly promised land. The complementary phenomena of falling wages and drastically limited workers' rights, in particular, have put a halt to the long history of political struggles to improve the standard of living for laborers, struggles that began with the spread of popular mobilization and union activism by immigrant workers in the late nineteenth century.

In the eyes of a dispirited majority, the Western, progressive, middle-class country imagined by the nation's founding fathers resembles more and more its less fortunate Latin American partners, enduring like them the dangers of insecurity, high unemployment, and economic stagnation. Pervading pessimism has created the suspicion that a curse now governs the destiny of the Argentine people. This sense of futility is especially prevalent among society's most marginalized groups. In his study of one of the oldest and largest slums in the country, paradoxically named Villa Paraíso (paradise village), the sociologist Javier Auyero echoes the despair of poor residents who, isolated and abandoned by the state, regard their daily life as an unending struggle. In a different context, Eduardo Archetti sees social impotence expressed in the sexist imagery of the chants of today's soccer fans. Parallel to this culture of despair and resentment has been the diffusion of an ideology of consumerism. The rapid spread of malls and shopping centers displaying imported goods and the promise of happiness embedded in certain brands constitute the bright, if hollow, side of neoliberal Argentina.

In art the crisis has inspired symbolic activism. Acknowledging the rage hidden in disillusionment without giving up the language of hope, the experimental group Escombros (the name means "rubble") has occupied what they see as the urban ruins of a defeated society in order to create collective art. Considering themselves the survivors of a fragmented culture, these artists advance an "ethics of disobedience" that challenges indifference. Among the group's most memorable public interventions in abandoned areas of Buenos Aires was the open convocation to found a "city of art," during which more than ten thousand people put together the work *Suture* by sewing a deep, natural crack in the ground with enormous ropes. Again pointing to the possibilities of cultural recycling and collective creativity, in the 1993 exhibition *Art in the Street in the Museum,* the group presented the installation MAR, consisting of five hundred black garbage bags, each labeled with the word *corruption,* piled inside and outside the walls of the National Museum of Art.

The artists' call for peaceful civic participation is intrinsically related to the vigor of democratic values that have emerged after twenty years of uninterrupted institutional stability. Democracy has become a common arena where old and new political actors seek recognition and representation. To remedy past discrimination under the country's legal codes, Congress has passed several laws redefining the traditional limits of citizenship. The effects of these laws have varied from the symbolic to the significant. In 1985, during Alfonsín's administration, the national Congress passed resolution 23302, which granted, for the first time in Argentine history, legal status to all remaining indigenous communities. The passage of several laws concerning women's rights underscores important modifications in the country's sexual politics. Improvements in women's rights and the prominence that women's issues now have in many political debates have not translated into meaningful growth for the feminist movement. As the historian Marcela Nari shows in her essay, the constituency of Argentine feminism today remains fairly small and divided.

As many new nongovernmental organizations have begun to make demands that did not find proper means of expression in the past, unprecedented forms of civic participation are emerging to deal with issues of impunity, corruption, discrimination, and insecurity. Marta Dillon, a member of the organization HIJOS, formed by the children of those "disappeared" during the dictatorship, is also an HIV-positive woman actively involved in the struggle to protect AIDS victims from discrimination. Her advocacy work is emblematic of many of the challenges that those making politics in a globalized Argentina must meet.

Central to all the new patterns of engagement are the politics of memory. For those who refuse to forget, the act of remembering is vital for the durability of a true democracy. As the Mothers and Grandmothers of the Plaza de Mayo and HIJOS continue their relentless quest for justice, other groups are following their lead to confront a still corrupt and inefficient judicial system. Frustrated by the lack of official action to track and bring to justice those responsible for terrorist attacks against the Argentine Jewish community, victims' relatives have founded Active Memory — an organization whose main goal is to prevent the public and the government from forgetting those who, now dead, cannot speak for themselves.

Globalization and neoliberalism are also shaking the foundations of Argentina's long-standing cultural and political traditions. The predominance of the market and the increasing commodification of culture appear to many as the first stages of a dark technocratic age, marked by the fall of intellectual thinking and political dissent and the rising influence of media-driven spectacles. As an apocalyptic prophet, Beatriz Sarlo, a prolific writer and scholar, campaigns against what she sees as the likelihood of a senseless future characterized by political indifference and cultural alienation.

As in many previous moments in Argentina's history, literature has provided a fundamental space for reflection. César Aira, perhaps one of the most enigmatic and original writers of the last two decades, explores the present through paradoxical fictions that combine the most enduring elements of the country's cultural traditions with themes and images from the culture industry and mass media. In "Infinity," one of Aira's recent fictional pieces, the remembrance of a lost childhood provides his narrator with an excuse to digress about time, money, and disinterested playfulness.

The 1990s represent a period of radical transformations whose main cultural manifestations we have tried to bring together in this concluding section. As with any interpretation of a confusing present, our choices have been tentative and inconclusive. Rather than aspiring to complete closure, we chose to emphasize the loose ends of Argentina's continuing history. While some are seeing through apocalyptic eyes the end of a promising dream and others still find promise in neoliberalism, their reflections are always set against the backdrop of an unpredictable society: a society that has survived the worst of times through the endurance and the imagination of its people.

Escombros, *Mar* (1993). Courtesy Juan Carlos Romero.

We Are All Cursed

Javier Auyero

Since the 1930s and early 1940s, when the quickening pace of industrialization multi-plied their numbers around Argentina's largest cities, slums have been the symbol of many hopes and fears. They have been portrayed as the ultimate proof of the failures of Peronist populism in the 1950s, as nests of revolutionary activism in the 1970s, and as obstacles to progress during the dictatorship. For the migrant poor looking for a home in a new environment, the slums were once an ordeal to be endured temporarily before moving on to better areas. In the last two decades, economic recession has transformed the dream of moving up into a futile illusion. Today, slums have become permanent locations of despair. Combining statistical data with the voices of people who live in Villa Paraíso, one of the oldest and largest slums in Buenos Aires city, the sociologist Javier Auyero presents the everyday experiences of common men and women enduring the curse of misery in neoliberal Argentina.

"See those guys over there?" Eloísa, an old-time resident of a shantytown called Villa Paraíso, asked me. "They always steal cars." They were parking a new car in front of the neighborhood association. Eloisa looks at them with resig-nation and wonders, "I don't know . . . here, as time goes by, we are more and more isolated . . . cabdrivers don't want to come into the slum . . . they say that they don't want to be robbed."

Villa Paraíso is located in the southern part of the Conurbano Bonaerense[1] bordering the federal capital of Argentina. It is one of the oldest and largest slums in the country (approximately fifteen thousand inhabitants according to the last population census). By official standards, more than 50 percent of its population have unmet basic needs, and approximately 70 percent have in-comes below the official poverty line.

"The men who sell milk, soda, and bread do not enter this area any more because they get robbed. . . . They stole my bicycle . . . the ones who come to buy drugs stole it," Hugo, another long time resident, tells me. During the last decade, armed robbery and violent mugging have become, in fact, quite common in the slum. Today, under democracy, slum dwellers are afraid not so much of the military or the police–as they used to be during the military dictatorship—but of their own neighbors, mostly of the young ones. Themselves victims of socioeconomic exclusion, streetcorner youth groups find their way to contest their vulnerability and redundancy by setting the tone of the slum's public life. "The guy next door sells drugs. You can't denounce him anywhere because he might rob you or, even worse, hurt you. Every night they smoke pot or fire guns right outside my window . . . we are cursed," Hugo recounts with an expression of grief on his face.

Drugs, distrust, and interpersonal violence become locked in a self-perpetuating cycle that, having neither clear purpose nor clear origin, pervades the whole atmosphere of the slum's life and affects basic everyday routines such as taking the bus for work. Juan's depiction encapsulates this feeling of dread: "I head to work early in the morning, at that time it is kind of dangerous here. I already changed my bus stop three times because the youngsters on the corner . . . are always doing drugs . . . and they began to 'charge me a toll,' you know, a coin or a cigarette . . . if I didn't have it, they wouldn't let me pass. . . . The other day they robbed me the two pesos I had for the bus, and they even got angry with me because that was all the money I had at the time."

It is probably Alejandra who best summarizes the pathos that suffuses much of the slum: that of being socially isolated, alienated from those institutions and services that middle- and upper-class neighborhoods take for granted, abandoned by the state, and at the mercy of drug addicts and dealers who terrorize them: "During the weekend this is like the Wild West, there are a lot of gun shots . . . at night you can't sleep . . . there are tons of drugs around."

Although the violence that dominates the daily experience and routines of most of the residents of Villa Paraíso comes from other residents, state violence is still present in the slum, taking the form of sporadic and fiercely brutal raids targeted at youngsters. Daily interpersonal violence, intermittent state repressive violence, *and* the structural violence of unemployment (52 percent of the economically active population had no stable jobs) dictate the pace of everyday life in Paraíso as well as in most poverty enclaves in contemporary Argentina.[2]

These different kinds of violence and fear are interconnected manifestations of deeper socioeconomic and institutional changes that took place during the past two decades. In the first part of this report, I briefly describe the most important transformations in the country's economic and social structure during the last twenty years, namely, a sectoral shift from a manufacturing to a service economy, the growing relevance of unemployment and poverty, and the dismantling of the welfare component of the state. In the second part I examine the way in which these structural forces affect the living *conditions* of shanty-town dwellers and the *relationships* (or the lack thereof) that the slum has with larger society. Attention to connections together with conditions shows that the story of Villa Paraíso (and most poor neighborhoods and squatter settlements in Argentina) contains elements of both continuity and discontinuity. There is continuity in the sense that these enclaves have experienced the cumulative effects of disadvantage since their inception. During the late 1930s and early 1940s, as the industrialization of Buenos Aires quickened, Villa Paraíso began receiving huge contingents of migrants from the provinces. As standard housing was scarce and extremely expensive given the low income of the new migrants becoming industrial proletarians, deserted lands around the central city and close to newly installed factories, like Villa Paraíso, became natural squatting grounds for thousands of migrants' families. Since then, the shanty-town has been an area of concentrated, chronic poverty. "What was the first thing that caught your attention as soon as you arrived in Villa Paraíso?" I asked Victoria, who came to the slum in the 1960s: "It was horrible, you know? It was dreadful. . . . I used to ask to my husband: 'Is this Buenos Aires?' Because when you live in the province, you think Buenos Aires is the best thing, you think that it is beautiful. When he brought me here, I thought to myself: Am I gonna live here? But, you know, necessity . . . and I had to stay. This street was a garbage dump. . . . I didn't even dare go outside my home because I was very shocked . . . stepping in the mud and seeing all that garbage."

The story of poverty enclaves also has elements of discontinuity because these areas suffered the devastating effect of the mass growth of un- and under-employment (and the subsequent increase in the *vulnerability of their residents*) during the 1980s and 1990s. There is a new marginality spreading within these old territories. "Nowadays the slum is almost an inferno," the Catholic priest Farinello says about the slum where he works. Since the early eighties the population of poverty enclaves such as Villa Paraíso has been increasingly confined into what Mingione aptly describes as "highly malign circuits of social marginalization."[3]

Unemployment and Dismantling of the State

Neoconservative reforms and structural adjustment policies have held devastating effects on enclaves of urban poverty. The dismantling of the state not only increased the number of poor people but also made life in poverty more precarious and vulnerable. As UNICEF warned more than ten years ago, the market-oriented policies and austerity programs (increased exports and reduced internal expenditure) required of developing nations by the World Bank and the International Monetary Fund in exchange for their lending became the major driving forces behind the dramatic increase in poverty throughout Latin America.

In September 1998, the Ministry of Justice and Security of the Province of Buenos Aires announced that 3,700 new prisoners would be temporarily placed in the storage spaces of once-active industrial plants. "There's no room for the new prisoners, jails are full, and so are the precincts," the ministry admitted. There should be no problem in housing the increased prison population in former factories. In the ten years since 1988, the Conurbano Bonaerense lost 5,508 industrial plants, and manufacturing jobs decreased by 22 percent. As in the United States, the disappearance of work hits the poor, unskilled, and uneducated harder. Today, the harmful consequences of the privatization drive and export-oriented economic strategy can be seen in Argentina's current, record-high 16 percent unemployment rate. Since 1991, there has been a 300 percent increase in unemployment.

At present, job creation is circumscribed to the service sector of the economy, where part-time, flex-time, and temporary work tends to predominate. From 1994 to 1999 there has been a 27 percent increase in the number of jobs "off the books" (jobs that have 40 percent less salary than those in the formal sector); there has also been a 50 percent increase in the number of underemployed people.

Rising poverty and inequality are the result of this veritable hyperunemployment. In the 1980s and 1990s *income disparity* has dramatically increased. In 1974, the richest ten percent held 28.2 percent of the national wealth (GNP), while in 1999 they held 37.3 percent. The holdings of the poorest 30 percent dropped from 11.3 percent to 8.1 percent. In 1991 a person in the richest 10 percent earned, on average, fifteen times more than someone in the poorest 10 percent; in 1999 he or she earned twenty five times more. *Poverty rates* also skyrocketed. In 1980, 11.5 percent of households were below the poverty line in Greater Buenos Aires. In 1995 one out of four households were below the same line (25.8 percent).

At the root of this increased poverty and inequality have been the destruction of manufacturing jobs, the sharp rise in the number of temporary, intermittent, menial, devalued, and unprotected jobs (those traditionally at the core of poverty reproduction throughout Latin America), *and* a dismantling of state welfare services. A week after the "factory-into-jails" announcement, the Argentine Ministry of Economy sent its budget proposal for approval to the National Congress. A member of the congressional majority (the Peronist party) outlined the budget in quite explicit terms: "This is a budget that cuts social services in order to increase security spending and to meet the foreign debt payments." The new 1999 budget, negotiated with and approved by the IMF and the World Bank, was passed into law weeks later; it included considerable cuts in education, health, social security, job programs, and housing, while increasing expenditures on domestic security (the already inadequate welfare programs suffered a $37 million cut and the military had $110 million added to its budget). The new budget demonstrated in quite explicit form that the state — which, in principle, could make a difference in remedying the effects of unemployment — did not care to cushion the devastating impact of worklessness.

De-industrialization and State Retrenchment Seen from the Slum

After their emergence in the urban landscape in the 1950s as transitory phenomena typical of a "stage of development," slums have become a permanent part of the geography of most Latin American cities. During this fifty-year period, slums have captured the imagination of Argentine filmmakers such as Lucas Demare (1957), novelists such as Bernardo Verbistky (1957), and social scientists such as Hugo Ratier (1971). *Las villas* have also been the sites of intense political, religious, and social activism.

One can hardly think of an urban form that was (and still is) the repository of so many (mis)representations, of so many hopes in the past and so many fears in the present. Slums were portrayed as the ultimate example of the failure of Peronist populism during the 1950s, as project sites for the modernizing dreams of the 1960s, as hotbeds of revolution during the "glorious 1970s," as obstacles to progress during the dictatorship of the 1980s, and as places of immorality, crime, and lawlessness in contemporary Argentina. Today, hardly a conversation about public security avoids mentioning the *villa* or the *villeros* (a label that is equally applied to people living in poor areas, irrespective of whether or not they live in slums) as a symbolic threat (but no less real) to be avoided. In today's fragmented and polarized Argentina, shantytowns are no-go areas, patches of crime to be feared and averted. Media accounts periodically refer to the fear incited by slums and their inhabitants, overwhelmingly focusing on the reactions that people from outside feel toward these "refuges (*aguantaderos*) of criminal activities."

The slum population skyrocketed in the 1980s and 1990s. Between 1983 and 1991, the slum population of the capital city grew 300 percent (from 12,500 to approximately 50,900).[4] Since 1991, there has been a 65 percent increase in the slum population in the city of Buenos Aires from 52,472 to 86,666 slum dwellers. In a city that has only increased its population by 2.5 percent, this slum growth can mean only one thing: a displacement of people from poor neighborhoods into slums. As of 1981, there were 300,000 slum dwellers in the province of Buenos Aires, with the highest concentration in the southern districts. Since 1983, the slum population has been growing in other districts as well.

Overcrowding in extremely precarious and unhealthy houses is, fifty years after the first residents began to massively populate the area, the dominant and defining feature of Villa Paraíso. More than half of its population live in substandard housing and over a third live in houses with more than three persons per room. Twenty-five percent of the dwellings do not have piped-in water, and almost 98 percent of the houses get their gas for cooking and heating from pressurized containers (tank gas) that dwellers purchase periodically and that imply higher risks of house fires, contact burns, and noxious fumes.[5] As a former resident of Villa Paraíso (now a resident in another slum in the capital city) puts it: "Yes, [a lot of children die] because of the accidents. There are a lot of accidents because we live very close to each other (*encimados*). A frying pan might fall down, or they might fall down into one of the holes we make to put garbage or to put what comes out of the toilets."[6]

Almost 70 percent of the dwellings' roofs are made of metal sheets. Houses are cold in winter, usually damp, and without adequate ventilation which — together with their zinc roofs — make them extremely hot during the summer. Outside their houses, the environment that dwellers confront daily is not much better. Household wastewater and rainwater run in open ditches through many areas of the slum, producing a stench that can, at times, be nauseating even for residents. Located in the flood zone adjacent to a stream killed by industrial and sewer dumping (the Riachuelo) and close to a huge garbage dump, the damp environment of the slum is extremely unhealthy. Slum dwellers suffer high degrees of respiratory illnesses (such as asthma), gastrointestinal and parasitic diseases, and epidemic skin diseases (scabies and lice infestation). In 1984, 80 percent of the cases of infantile tuberculosis and measles in the country were found among shanty children.

A municipal truck brings water on a daily basis to huge areas of Villa Paraíso; from the truck the water is carried in buckets into the houses with obvious risks of contamination. Those who are served by a water network drink contaminated water served by a clandestine grid connected to the city water supply. The majority of pipes are plastic, and the defects in the joints and the countless breaks in the hoses make bacteria and parasites a common presence in the officially defined "potable" water. This defiled water is responsible — according to the physicians of the local health center — for the prevalence of diarrhea as the most common disease among children and adults during summer. During winter, bronchitis, angina, and pneumonia greatly affect slum dwellers. Obviously, these diseases are not restricted to the slum population. Yet, according to physicians of the local health center, they are overrepresented among the slum population. "There are the same germs, yet the conditions are different," another physician of the local health center asserts. "People who do not eat well are prone to any kind of sickness," she summarizes. More than half of the population of Villa Paraíso do not have any health insurance coverage (54 percent according to the last 1991 census, and nowadays probably more due to the general state of unemployment). This makes them dependent on the crumbling public health sector.

Widespread unemployment is the single, most significant defining characteristic of Villa Paraíso. Fifty-two percent of the population between eighteen and sixty years old is currently unemployed or underemployed. Long-term unemployment is rampant: more than half of those unemployed have been without a steady job during the last year. Most of them rely on casual, temporary odd jobs as a source of (always scarce) monetary income.

Exclusion and Violence

Overcrowding, unhealthy habitat, higher-than-average rates of un- and underemployment, rampant and stigmatized misery: these living conditions in the slum are hardly products of the two decades of neoconservatism. Present since the slum's inception, they were slowly beginning to recede during the 1960s and 1970s. Yet the two "lost decades" of the 1980s and 1990s (lost for the poor, that is) have intensified the already-present marginality of slum dwellers to a point at which *social exclusion becomes the defining characteristic of the slum population*. As Gazzoli asserts, unknowingly agreeing with the resident of Paraíso quoted in the introduction: "During the seventies the shantytown was perceived as a transitional place (*un lugar de paso*) where someone could get a job, [become] integrated, and then leave. Today it is a place to stay, *no hay chance de zafar;* besides there were not so many drugs. There used to be clear rules: no one would steal in the slum. If and when they stole, they would do it outside the slum. Now, they rob you in the slum and everywhere; they charge you a toll (*te cobran peaje*)."[7]

The surrounding landscape of the slum and the internal makeup of the alleyways are probably the best indicators of the fate of Villa Paraíso. In the southeastern part of the slum stands the huge abandoned skeleton of the Fabricaciones Militares factory, and the household-appliances factory where many inhabitants of Paraíso used to work is now a storage facility with no industrial activity whatsoever; in the northwest, the metallurgic factory has been significantly downsized. These empty factories are an illustration of the state of the slum and its inhabitants, and of the way in which the withering away of the wage-labor economy is being inscribed in the urban landscape, visible in abandoned buildings and desolate fences. Villa Paraíso, once the place of the newborn working class, is now the space where the *un*-population (unemployed and uneducated) survives.

The internal makeup of the alleyways is also an unconventional sociological indicator of the changes the slum has suffered in the last twenty years: the walls of the houses facing the alleyways have been substantially elevated. Once, the alleyways were roads from which the interior of the houses could be seen, and neighbors could talk across them. Now the alleyways look like veritable tunnels: the elevated front walls serve as a defense against the social predators (drug dealers and addicts) that—although a tiny minority—intimidate slum dwellers. As Adela puts it: "This is terrible . . . on the corner, many kids get together and they smoke . . . weird things . . . you can't take your kids to the sidewalk because of the smell. And at night it is terrible, they fire their guns at the police." Drug trafficking and diverse addictions (mainly alcohol, marijuana, and cocaine) are having devastating consequences on the life-world of slum inhabitants. Their feelings about dealers and consumers point not only to the insecurity they feel—their fear of being mugged or assaulted—but also to the abandonment and the impotence they experience. The state is viewed as both *impotent* in solving this problem and *suspect* in arrangements with dealers. Most people are afraid to complain about the dealings or see no point in denouncing dealers because the police and state officials "are with them."

> You can't trust the police. (Juan)

> No one cares if you denounce people selling drugs. . . . I cannot say that it is true, but I heard that the councilwoman knows about the drug problem, and doesn't do anything about it. (Adela)

Changes in poor enclaves are not caused solely by the spread of joblessness (that is, by the dynamic of the market); state inaction is also a second fundamental driving force. Truly, Villa Paraíso has received a plethora of "social programs," the largest one being the Plan Vida (literally, Life Plan). This program is organized around block delegates who distribute milk and eggs to every pregnant woman and child below age six on a daily basis. The PROMIN (the Progama Materno-Infantil, also targeted at pregnant women, with the supervision and funding of the World Bank), the Plan Asoma (funded by the national state, targeted at the elderly without social security), and the distribution of food by the grassroots offices of the government Peronist party are other social programs that help some slum dwellers make ends meet. However, the meager assistance received (mostly) by the women and children of the slum should be carefully distinguished from an actual concerted effort by the state to solve the problems generated by both female and male unemployment. A daily supply of half a liter of milk and one egg per pregnant woman and/or child below age six cannot possibly work as a support system against the ravages of joblessness. The percentage of population covered by unemployment insurance is negligible (less than 5 percent), particularly in Greater Buenos Aires, the region most affected by unemployment. During nine months of fieldwork, I could not find a single slum dweller covered by this insurance. Public programs for the unemployed (Trabajar, Servicios Comunitarios o Barrios Bonaerenses) are temporary and provide workers with derisory wages and no social security, thus reproducing the pattern of "flexible" (a euphemism for more exploitable) jobs that have become increasingly prevalent in the labor market. Many of these employment and food programs are subject to clientelist manipulations that personalize the always-meager benefits and present them as gifts or favors of local politicians. One resident from the slum of Bajo Flores probably best expresses the official indifference and sustained stigmatization that slum dwellers experience:

x: Do you think that the government should help the slum dwellers?

w: I don't know. If it [the aid] is as it has been until now, they better not. Because each time they come, there are problems. . . .They throw mattresses, or they invite us to eat, and then there's not enough food.

x: Do you think that the government should install the water system, the light, and the gas?

w: Did the people who don't live in the slum install the gas system or did they find it installed? Did they install the sewage system?

x: And why do you think they don't install it here?

w: Because they want us to leave. Or they think we don't need that, because we are *villeros*.

Notes

1 The Conurbano Bonaerense is the area comprising the nineteen districts in Argentina's industrial heartland surrounding the federal capital. The names of people and places have been changed to ensure anonymity.

2 Survey based on a stratified random sample of three hundred cases, conducted in October 1996.

3 Enzo Mingione, ed., *Urban Poverty and the Underclass: A Reader* (Cambridge, Mass.: Blackwell, 1996), 9.

4 "Las cuatro chapas del desamparo," *Ciudad Abierta* 9 (bulletin published by the Defensoría del Pueblo of the city of Buenos Aires): 9.

5 Eileen Stillwaggon, *Stunted Lives, Stagnant Economies: Poverty, Disease, and Underdevelopment* (New Brunswick, N.J.: Rutgers University Press, 1998).

6 Gazzoli quoted in ibid., 8.

7 Ibid., 13.

Soccer and Masculinity

Eduardo Archetti

The weekly soccer game offers players and fans an autonomous world of male comrade-ship free of accustomed societal and ideological distinctions. Partly at odds with this experience of commonality and equality, however, is the stylized aggression of players and fans toward the opposing team. Over the last decade, sexual innuendo has become more prominent in the verbal sparring of spectators. The combination of economic in-stability and political cynicism has produced a sense of insecurity and powerlessness among many men and an accompanying exacerbation of physical and symbolic vio-lence in the stadium. In his analysis of soccer chants, Eduardo Archetti documents the common use of the threat of sexual subordination to demonstrate one's virility.

One of the secrets of soccer is that it can still, despite its critics, be defined as a game. Games are generally associated with the exercise of imagination and the gratuitous search for difficulty. That is why the ultimate reward of soccer is always a reward for difficulties and rarity. The maximum event is seen as an aesthetic work, as a creation, as if the final product were the result of impro-visation, intuition, and risk. At the same time, football creates conditions of equality among the players, in theory eleven on one side against eleven on the other, all with the same capacities and powers.

This condition of equality in the soccer stadium undoubtedly permits a rup-ture of the hierarchies of daily life and social structure. Furthermore, it is valid not only for the "central" players but also for the "peripheral" actors, the fans. Every Sunday soccer match creates a special world in clear contrast with the world of factory, office, or family. Because it allows the suspension of a certain social order, participants are granted a certain license. Football as a game has the power to decenter authoritarian rules and to recenter basic egalitarian feel-ings. The stadium thus offers men and those about to be men, the adolescents and children who accompany their fathers, a site where they can construct an order and a world that are strictly masculine. There an explicit moral discourse takes place, one that establishes boundaries between what is allowed and what is not allowed, between good and evil, and finally between the positive and negative aspects of what is ideally defined as masculine.

In the symbolic world of Argentine fans there are traditional verses called *hijos nuestros* (our sons) chanted for expressing the superiority of one team over the other. This chant is not a modern invention and has certainly existed since the first stages of the game in Argentina. What is the significance of this chant? Undoubtedly, "our sons" refers to a relation of paternity: son refers to father, whether known or unknown. When one group of fans refers to another in this way, alluding to the nature of the relationship between the two clubs, the effect of contempt and disdain is secured through the symbolic transformation of the other into child or son.

These chants presuppose the loss of the opponents' autonomy and the fact that they cannot act like real men. One does not expect rebellion or victory from a son: the son has to accept the authority, power, and orders of the father. At the same time, converting a person into a father means awarding a status of authority, respect, and power. The relationship between father and son does not refer to a symmetrical relationship where understanding and mutual respect prevail; instead, the central point comes to be subordination. This chant from the River Plate fans summarizes this type of relationship: "Calamar, calamar, calamar / ya sabemos que te vas para la B / te lo dice tu papá / que se llama River Plate" (Shellfish, shellfish, shellfish / We know you go to the B [the second division] / Your father tells you so / And he's called River Plate).[1]

The automatic response to an alleged relation of paternity is usually the traditional "sons of bitches" (*hijos de puta*), chanted loudly until "our sons" is drowned out. It is interesting to note that in these cases the insulted fans will never reply with an "hijos nuestros" unless this is substantiated by the statistics of the matches played. Accordingly, "hijos nuestros" expresses a relation of paternity and subordination that can be proved statistically.

The condition of being a child does not appear in many chants at present, and I do not think it did much in the past either. In the past Boca Juniors fans used to chant to River Plate fans: "River tenía un carrito / Boca se lo quitó / River salió llorando / Boca salió campeón" (River had a little cart / Boca took it away / River got up crying / Boca became champion) and "Vea, vea, vea / qué cosa tan fulera / ahora los de River / toman leche y mamadera" (Look, look, look / What a clumsy lot / Now the River boys / Suck a baby's bottle). Obviously, it does not allude to a filial relationship but, rather, to the condition of childhood or to the lack of maturity, autonomy, and independence. The disqualification comes about by converting the other into a child; his condition as an adult, as an independent, autonomous man, is thereby denied. At present one of the favorite chants of the rival groups of fans against San Lorenzo de

Almagro fans runs as follows: "Aquí está la famosa barra de San Lorenzo / la que no tiene cancha / la que se fue al descenso / ahora le pusieron un supermercado / y la mandan los domingos / a hacer los mandados" (Here's the famous San Lorenzo gang / Who haven't got a field / Who were pushed aside / So they set up a supermarket / And they send them on Sundays / To do the shopping). Presumably, no one but children would go shopping on Sundays, a day when "real men" are at the football stadium.

The short presentation of an event will serve to bring out one of the main concerns of contemporary militant fans. In 1984 in a match for the Libertadores Cup between Olimpia de Paraguay and Independiente of Argentina, played at level pegging, cleanly and with no violence, almost at the end of the second half it was a draw, 2=2. In those short, dramatic final minutes Independiente took the third goal and the victory. After the shout for the goal, and while the ball was going back to center field for what was to be a pointless further kickoff, the stands and the terracing of the red side of Independiente joined in a stentorian, unanimous shout: "Y ahora, y ahora / me chupan bien las bolas" (Now, now / They're really sucking me off properly). This was said with the typical jumps and fists raised toward the area of the stands occupied by five thousand or so Paraguayans, who, it should he mentioned, had arrived at the stadium with posters praising Argentine democracy and condemning the Stroessner dictatorship.

The immediate question is why in the moment of victory did the fans choose to offend the losers, to humiliate them? The affirmation of masculinity depends on depriving the other of his masculinity. The conquered, the weak, in other words the one who is not a "real man," has to do, or be supposed to do, things that go against his nature. The fans have created a vast repertoire where the construction of sexuality and a world divided between men and fake men, that is, homosexuals, comes to be the central aspect.[2] One example among many: "Cordobés, cordobés / limpiáte bien el culo / que te vamos a coger" (Cordoban, Cordoban / Wipe your bottom well / Cordoban we're coming to screw you). This relation looks more personal in the following chant: "Sol y luna, sol y luna / sol y luna, sol y luna / la poronga de Armando / en el culo de Labruna" (Sun and moon, sun and moon / Sun and moon, sun and moon / Armando's dong / In Labruna's ass).

The famous "Bambino Veira case or incident" has in recent years become the privileged context for creating chants.[3] Veira was accused of molesting a boy, making his nickname "Bambino" sound somewhat ironic. The rival fans of San Lorenzo shouted: "Compañero, Bambino, zapatero / la concha de tu madre / le pagaste al portero / le pagaste a la cana / te cogiste al pibe / hijo de la puta madre" (Mate, Bambino, cobbler / Your mother's cunt / You paid off the doorkeeper / You paid off the cop / You were screwing a boy / You son of a bitch).

In all these chants what seems clear is that the fans of one team or particular central actors (a trainer, a player, or a manager) are the real machos, the real men, able to force the other fans or social actors to play the homosexual. It is interesting to note that the homosexuals are those who let themselves be humiliated, those who do not defend their masculine identity with sufficient force. A popular chant, sung by many fans in three recent seasons, is a clear threat against the players if they do not win, warning them of what might happen to them: "Vamos, vamos a ganar / que si no, los vamos a vejar" (Come on, come on, we're going to win / Otherwise we're going to take them). Those who do the taking are the strong, the real men, and in no case see themselves as homosexuals. This distinction between the passive and the active role is illustrated clearly in the rhymes alluding to the "Veira case": for the rivals of San Lorenzo, Bambino is downgraded into a "son of a bitch," and the San Lorenzo fans reclaim his role as macho. In no case is there an explicit moral sanction on behavior judged as abnormal. The rival fans do not say that Bambino is a homosexual.

The field of sexuality is in turn a world of rules and prohibitions that refer to morality, to what is permitted and accepted in a particular society, to a range of expectations in which it is possible to play and experiment with unsatisfied fantasies and desires. Similarly, the sexuality displayed in a particular relationship is bound up with sensual and sentimental aspects that articulate both individual and gender identity. The fans, by choosing the field of discourse of sexuality, call on all these levels and therefore transform the traditional content of the discourses. The explicit introduction of sexuality into the public arena of football is a recent change that is worth stressing. In doing this, the fans are in a way breaking a taboo, a set of rules: sexuality is being converted into a public, open discourse (many would say an expression of the coarseness and "bad taste" of the popular classes). My hypothesis is that the "conversation" set up between rival groups of fans takes place at the level not of the comic but of the tragic.

The "tragic" effect is secured by breaking a rule, namely the norm of heterosexuality. This breach, it is worth stressing, is done by a person (individual, player or trainer, or a social being, a particular group of fans) with whom people sympathize and can identify. From the viewpoint of the San Lorenzo fans, Bambino is not repulsive but at the same time not so good that one cannot identify with him. If Bambino were entirely evil as a character, this positive identification would not exist. The same could be said of the other personalities mentioned in the chant. However, the presence of transgression does not eliminate the rule that defines *normality,* namely, that normal sexuality is that between persons of different sexes. Tragic themes are usually related with the type of existential dilemmas that may be particularly prominent in the field of sexuality. This observation does not imply that the normality of heterosexuality is not considered. However, the chants referring to it are very much in the minority, and those I have compiled have to do with the traditional grudge against the English. When they lost against England in the 1966 World Cup, the fans of River later chanted: "Y si la Reina / se baja su tapado / el viejo Onega / le clava su poronga" (And if the Queen / Gets down on all fours / Old Onega / Will nail her yam). When there was a win over England in the 1986 World Cup, one of the most popular chants during the celebrations was "Thatcher, Thatcher, Thatcher / ¿Dónde estás? / Maradona te anda buscando / para metértela por detrás" (Thatcher, Thatcher, Thatcher / Where are you? / Maradona's looking for you / To screw you from behind). How is the meaning of this type of obsession by militant fans to be interpreted? I think the interpretation invites an obvious psychoanalytic interpretation: the chants display protective inversion mechanisms because they combine the sadistic fantasies of the macho with his deep doubts as to his own masculinity. These doubts evidently stimulate the making of this type of affirmation. This interpretation assumes, without much discussion, that all the psychological symbols have a special meaning at the motivational level. I do not deny that this may be true for many fans, but it is hard to know it without interviewing every one of them. I think that the examples I have given can be treated not as personal symbols but as symbols that constitute a public field of discourse where there is no need to operate with the hypothesis of profound motivation. This enables us to distinguish the origin of the chants, which may be in the unconscious or even form part of the dream repertoire, from their operational meaning, that is, the creation of a public tragic effect. The conversion into an element of public discourse is a feature of a general attitude and not of the free expression of individual emotions, as I have sometimes emphasized in this text.

Clearly, homosexual relationships, in the case we are concerned with, refer to a public arena where symbols operate at a collective level. The fans dramatize these relationships, and their ritual use refers on the one hand to a sensual aspect, in this case sexual relations, the anus and the penis, and on the other to an ideological aspect where what is affirmed is strength, omnipotence, violence, and the breaking of the other's identity. In this process what appears as the central concern is the construction of a certain type of masculinity, a sort of prototype of the militant fan. What is important about this tragic effect is that it makes it possible for intrapsychic conflicts to be expressed in a cultural idiom and through the license of a ritual such as football. . . .

Soccer allows perception of a world as socially constructed by its various actors, especially by the peripheral players, the fans, and their vanguard. In this cultural world, the idioms of masculinity tell us something about the way in which packages of social and individual identity are constructed through the dramatization that can be found in linguistic codes. At the same time the actors appear as "moral actors" in the sense that they assign value to particular objects and particular actions. It is, accordingly, a world full of explicit and implicit meanings. It is a world in which symbolic frontiers appear clearly, starting with thoughts about a set of important social relations: father/son, adult/child, and "real man" / homosexual. On these, obviously, the actors ponder in other less public contexts, with less show, and without the smell of police tear gas. Thus, relations between men can partially be understood in terms of dominance, control, and power.

Notes

For complete references and notes for this piece, see Eduardo Archetti, "Multiple Masculinities," in *Sex and Sexuality in Latin America,* ed. Daniel Balderston and Donna J. Guy (New York: New York University Press, 1997), 200–16.

In the original piece, the word *football* was used instead of soccer.

1 Or when, appealing to tradition, they chant: "Vamos, vamos los villeros / vamos a ganar / que nacieron hijos nuestros / hijos nuestros morirán" (Come on, come on slum lads / We are going to win / They were born our children / Our children they will die). Many of the *cantitos* do not rhyme, but some do. They are usually sung to the tune of a current hit song. The use of very current hits is taken as a sign of ingenuity on the part of the fans because what is a popular song one day may be forgotten the next.

2 My analysis is mainly focused on "key" teams of the Argentine first divisions—Boca Juniors, River Plate, San Lorenzo de Almagro, Independiente, and Racing, called the *five great teams*—and on important but less "legendary" teams such as Huracán, Estudiantes de La Plata, Gimnasia y Esgrima, and Newell's Old Boys. The five great are from different suburbs of Buenos Aires. These clubs, well-known internationally because they have exported outstanding players to European soccer since the 1920s, can also be seen as the only "national teams" with supporters all over Argentina.

3 Veira was a famous San Lorenzo de Almagro player in the 1960s. A brilliant technical striker, he was also well-known for his flamboyant "playboy" life. He later became a coach. In 1980 he was accused of raping a young boy who approached him asking for an autograph and was put into prison for a short period. While the trial continued, he became a successful coach in Argentina, Colombia, and Spain. Finally, in May 1992, he was sentenced to four years in prison. He appealed and in 1994 was declared innocent.

Amerindian Rights

State Law of Indigenous Rights

Until they were virtually annihilated by the national army in 1879, Argentina's Amerindian populations were always seen by the state as a stubborn obstacle to modernization. The arrival of millions of European immigrants and the canonization of the gaucho as the embodiment of national identity established the image of an overwhelmingly white, European Argentina. During this century, the remaining Amerindian communities suffered bitter economic, cultural, and political marginalization. For all practical purposes, they were invisible. In 1985, as part of the democratization process initiated by President Raúl Alfonsín, the congress passed the Law of Indigenous Rights, granting legal status to all Amerindian communities within national territory. The political symbolism of the new law, which later became part of the newly drafted constitution of 1995, was remarkable since it signaled the official acknowledgment of cultural difference in a country that has seen itself predominantly as a homogeneous national society.

I. Objectives

ARTICLE 1. Let it be acknowledged that it is in the national interest to take responsibility for the support of aboriginal and indigenous communities existing in the country as well as for the protection and development of their full participation in the social, economic, and cultural processes of the nation by respecting their values and ways. To this end, programs will be implemented that will permit indigenous peoples to own land and that will encourage their development of this land, whether it be as farmers, cattle tenders, foresters, miners, industrial workers, or artisans, that will preserve their cultural values in educational programs, and that will ensure the protection of the health of their constituents.

II. Concerning the Indigenous Communities

ARTICLE 2. By this law legal status is granted to the indigenous communities in the country.

Indigenous communities will be understood to be the collection of families that are recognized as such by the fact of their having descended from peoples who were inhabiting national territory during the times of conquest and colonization and indigenous people or Indians who are members of this community.

Each community will acquire legal status once registered in the Register of Indigenous Communities. Such status will be terminated only by public cancellation. . . .

IV. Concerning the Adjudication of Lands

ARTICLE 7. Property shall be awarded to those indigenous communities that are officially registered. Such property shall consist of lands suitable and sufficient for the development of farming, animal husbandry, forestry, industry, or crafts, according to the ways appropriate to each community. The land should be located where the community lives or, if necessary, in nearby areas more suitable to their development. In awarding land, preference should be given to the communities that are lacking land or have insufficient land; the same could be done with individual properties, for the benefit of those indigenous people not integrated into the community, giving preference to those who form part of family groups.

The authorities responsible for implementing this law will also deliver legal title to those who have land with only temporary or faulty titles. . . .

ARTICLE 9. The awarding of such land will be carried out with free titles. The organization in charge will request such tax exemptions from the provincial and community governments. The procedure for awarding land will question doubtful exemptions before the provincial and community governments. The executive power will arrange for opening lines of preferential credit for those being awarded land for the development of their respective economic undertakings; such money is intended for the acquisition of the tools of their trade, seeds, livestock, buildings, and improvements and includes whatever else might be useful or necessary for their better development. . . .

ARTICLE 14. A first priority is the intensification of educational and cultural services wherever indigenous communities have settled. The plans that are implemented to carry out these services should recognize and protect the historic and cultural identity of each aboriginal community, assuring at the same time their egalitarian integration into the national society.

ARTICLE 15. In accordance with the methods of social organization foreseen in article 4 of this law, the educational and cultural programs should also do the following:

a) teach modern techniques for the cultivation of the land and the manufacture of their products and promote demonstration or community orchards and farms;

b) promote the organization of workshops for the preservation and diffusion of the techniques of craftsmanship; and

c) teach the theory and practice of the cooperative movement. . . .

Translated by Patricia Owen Steiner

Feminist Awakenings

Marcela Nari

In twentieth-century Argentina, women's rights were on many parties' agendas, but not all struggles for the improvement of women's lives were labeled as feminist. Only in the 1970s did groups of middle-class, educated women who identified themselves as radical feminists begin to emerge in the public eye. In Marcela Nari's historical account, the feminism of the 1990s is both a continuation of and a break with earlier approaches. Whereas women in the 1970s sought to identify issues that would unite them under a common identity, today they must acknowledge diversity in order to avoid fragmentation. At a time when women's demands are receiving increasing attention from state and party organizations, the feminist agenda has become more diversified. The meaning of being a woman and the role of the state in sexual politics are some of the issues under revision.

In Argentina in the 1970s, after a long period of apparent slumber, groups of women who identified themselves as feminists emerged into public view. Whether they knew it or not, they were recovering the struggles of other women for rights and liberation between the late nineteenth and early twentieth century. . . .

Feminists were in the 1970s a small, limited group mostly made up of middle-class women. Thanks to their social position, their intellectual work, or their political activities, these women had dreamed that they could be seen as equals by men, by their brothers, and by their *compañeros*. At first, they had seen the "woman problem" as a problem for "other women," those of the "second sex": women workers, battered women, women overburdened with children, and women "back then" (including their own mothers). Previous struggles found new ideological frameworks and social contexts in the 1970s: feminist consciousness-raising groups. They spoke of consciousness because they wanted to set themselves apart from other leftist groups; they were not imposing some outside way of thinking but developing one out of women's own experience. Although for most of these women Simone de Beauvoir's

The Second Sex had been a fundamental text in their development, they also read Anglo-American radical feminist writings, like Kate Millett, Shulamith Firestone, Carla Lonzi, and Juliet Mitchell.

In 1970, a small group of women decided to found UFA (Unión Feminista Argentina, or Argentine Feminist Union). At the same time, the Alianza Feminista (Feminist Alliance) appeared on the political scene and, in 1974, began to publish the journal *Persona*. This group would later become the MLF (Movimiento de Liberación Femenino, or Women's Liberation Movement). Another contemporary group was Nueva Mujer (New Woman), which focused on studying, translating, developing, and publishing theoretical works. *Las mujeres dicen basta* (Women say that's enough) was also published at the time, as was J. Gissi's *La mitología de la femineidad* (The myth of femininity).

The tensions and conflicts between these groups have to be seen within the broader Argentine context of repression and political authoritarianism, guerrilla groups and revolutionary practices, and the return to Perón after almost twenty years of proscription. Some of the women in feminist groups had started out in leftist organizations but had left them disillusioned with the contradictions between their theory and their practice, between their public and their private ethics. Others kept up a double activism in both kinds of groups. For example, one faction of the Partido Socialista de los Trabajadores — Muchachas (Socialist Workers' Party — Young Women) took part in the UFA from the beginning, although under its own name.

This double leftist and feminist activism generated conflicts between women. For feminists, leftist parties were interested only in "women's rights" just before elections, and they subordinated issues of women's oppression to the class struggle since their parties continued to be patriarchal organizations in structure and operation. Their feminism was just a facade. Feminists suspected that many of these leftist activists were sent to infiltrate feminist groups as spies and to win converts. The women who belonged to political parties had other experiences and concerns. Not only were they rejected by feminists, but they were also frequently rejected by their male fellow activists. They were at a crossroads: while they had firsthand experience of how leftist organizations discriminated against them and ignored women's concerns, they also saw the feminists as too isolated, too distanced from the social and political context.

After an internal split in 1973, UFA began a second phase. One year later, ALMA (Agrupación para la Liberación de la Mujer, or Women's Liberation Group) was founded by breakaway factions from other groups. Other groups were also organized: the Grupo de Política Sexual (Sexual Politics Group) was made up of heterosexual and homosexual men and women, and the Asociación de Mujeres Socialistas (Association of Socialist Women) was formed to create a Frente de Lucha por la Mujer (Women's Struggle Front) to support the International Year of the Woman in 1975. Many connections tied women together, and many thought that it was possible and worthwhile to struggle for change from within and/or come to some minimum agreements between them.

Double activism was not the only obstacle that feminist groups faced during the first half of the 1970s. They debated absolute horizontality — that is, equal political authority — within groups, although this generated conflicts, since not everyone shared the same perspective on leadership, coordination, and organization. The issue of *writing* was seen as a difficult obstacle to overcome; to this day, almost none of the material produced by these groups has been collected or published. There were also inhibitions in the *oral narratives* of personal experience, and not only having to do with "silenced matters" like lesbianism.

Civil society received this feminism with ignorance or indifference; it inspired "neither echoes nor sympathies" in its social reception. Some of the public actions that were carried out, such as the campaign for abolishing the 1974 law prohibiting the free distribution and sale of contraceptives, were unsettling to even the police, who had no idea who these feminist groups were or where they came from. At the same time, the feminist groups drew mockery, sarcasm, and ridicule: the mass media presented them as "bra burners" and "fat old ladies," forever ugly and alone. For the Left, they were "proimperialist" bourgeois women, but they were politically harmless. Feminist campaigns on behalf of contraceptives, as well as their ties to homosexual men (who belonged to the Frente de Liberación Homosexual, or Homosexual Liberation Front), were viewed by the Right as clear signs of the threat that they posed to the family and the traditional order. By 1975, the political climate had turned more violent, and there were death threats. The right-wing label *agents of world subversion* also came to include feminists. In this context, 1970s feminism has been, for some women, a totally forgotten experience, concealed by the military dictatorship. Others perceive this movement as the basis on which feminism was built in the 1980s.

The Long Winter of the Dictatorship, 1976–83

The 1976 coup d'état began a period of paralysis, retreat, and silence. The majority of feminist groups disbanded and abandoned their public actions. Nevertheless, at the same time new forums arose for smaller, more private and intimate gatherings dedicated to conversation, reading, and reflection. In this manner, a *feminism of the catacombs* was founded: deep, clandestine, underground. Eventually, some of these gatherings evolved into more formal organizations, such as the Agrupación de Mujeres Argentinas or Argentine Women's Group in 1977 (which later became the Asociación de Mujeres Alfonsina Storni, or Alfonsina Storni Women's Association) and the Asociación Juana Manso (Juana Manso Association) in 1978. Also during these years, other women began to organize, namely the Madres de Plaza de Mayo (Mothers of the Plaza de Mayo).

Paradoxically, the dictatorship offered some women (those who were not "disappeared" or forced into exile) a period of monastic calm for study, research, and writing. Alone or with women, they reread the classics, critiqued their influences, debated, and confronted one another. Toward the end of the decade, women's studies began to attain a certain legitimacy in some settings outside the university.

With the slow decompression of the climate of terror, some of these shared experiences began to emerge. Toward the end of 1979, a group of professional women organized an interdisciplinary conference on "the role of women in today's society." A direct consequence of this event was the foundation of the Centro de Estudios de la Mujer (CEM, or Center for Women's Studies). At the same time, the Unión de Mujeres Socialistas (Socialist Women's Union) was reestablished under the leadership of the feminist historian Dr. Alicia Moreau, as part of the Confederación Socialista Argentina (Argentine Socialist Confederation). In 1981, the MLF was reborn as OFA (Organización Feminista Argentina, or Argentine Feminist Organization), while another group, LIBERA, came together to study and discuss feminist theory, and a year later, the Asociación de Trabajo y Estudios de la Mujer "25 de Noviembre" (ATEM, "25 November" Labor and Women's Studies Association) established itself with its journal *Brujas* (Witches). In 1982–83, DIMA (Derechos Iguales para la Mujer Argentina, or Equal Rights for Argentine Women), which had been founded prior to the 1976 coup, returned to political activism in order to fight for equal parental rights, an objective that they saw as achievable and socially relevant. The act and experience of writing was also crucial, and several texts attest to this. In 1983, Lugar de Mujer (Women's Place) was established to organize and unite these experiences.

Many of the women who came together in these years were new to the feminist agenda; they were young women coming to feminism for the first time as well as older women who had not previously identified themselves with the movement. Some were just returning from exile; others had followed solitary paths during the dictatorship. For many, the period of forced exile sparked a turn toward feminist readings and practices while also opening a space to think over and evaluate their political experiences, their participation as women, or simply the social meaning of their gender. At the same time, not all those interested in the "woman question" had a feminist perspective.

The climate and sensibilities of Argentine society were also changing: the "woman question" (not feminism) found a larger and more favorable place in public opinion, the mass media, political parties, and certain centers for social research. Finally, toward the end of the dictatorship, women began to lead important social movements, most notably the Mothers of the Plaza de Mayo but also the many others who took to the streets to fight for *their* children, discriminated against this time by poverty.

Democracy and Feminism

. . . The return of democracy presented a challenge to Argentine feminism. Many women believed that, for the first time, they faced a state with which they could and should enter into dialogue. They believed that the process of democratization should reach beyond formal politics, in parties and institutions, into everyday life. By participating in the system, they hoped to drive democratic change in all social relations, including those of gender.

The "woman question" became relevant for political parties as well, partly stimulated by the demands of activists, who, whether in exile or in Argentina, had rethought their public and private pasts. Also within trade unions spaces began to be developed, sometimes formal ones, "for women." Feminists and "political" women politicians (in parties and trade unions) founded the "Multisectorial de la Mujer" (Women's Multisectorial Alliance, parallel to the Multisectorial of Political Parties). When International Women's Day was first celebrated in Argentina, and on 8 March 1984, they presented a basic plan of reforms: in addition to calling for equal parental rights, they demanded equal rights for children (i.e., between "illegitimate" and "legitimate" children), equal pay for equal work, supervision of child-care centers, retirement benefits for housewives, the creation of a government secretary for women's affairs, and the ratification of the 1979 UN Convention on the Elimination of All Discrimination toward Women.

From the beginning, there were also doubts and misgivings about these patriarchal institutions that were suddenly receptive to women's demands. The state's greater involvement in the "woman question" and greater participation in state organizations by women and feminists generated tensions between the two groups.

In the last two decades of the twentieth century, government bodies were established at the national, provincial, and municipal level in order both to formulate and coordinate public policies in general and to concentrate on specific questions, such as education, labor, and violence (among the first were a sec- retary of women's affairs in 1987 and a women's council in 1991). At the same time, some of the historical demands of Argentine feminism were achieved: divorce, legal equality for children born in and out of wedlock, and shared (not individual) paternal rights. Furthermore, in 1985 the UN convention was adopted, and, one year later, the ILO (International Labor Organization) con- vention on equal opportunity and treatment for male and female workers was also passed.

Violence against women was also a focal point for the resurgence of femi- nism in the 1980s. But, in contrast to legislative reforms, this matter found less social resonance. Even so, some forms of sexual violence (especially domestic violence) have gradually become legitimate issues for public debate over the last two decades, thanks mostly to the tenacity of feminist activism.

By the late 1980s, hopes for the gradual achievement of equal political repre- sentation for both sexes dwindled in the face of the truth: throughout the first decade of democracy, the percentage of women in the Chamber of Deputies never rose above 5 percent. As a result, women members of political parties created a network and supported "affirmative action." In 1991, they achieved the passage of law 24.012, which required at least 30 percent of each party's candidates in every national election to be women. Few feminists openly re- jected the law, although many disagreed with at least some of its political and philosophical implications. Did women have the right to increase their politi- cal presence because they were like men or because they were different from them? What would women contribute to politics? How would the various po- litical parties handle this quota? And would the women elected through this law have a specific moral obligation to their female constituents and their par- ticular problems?

In the 1990s, reproductive rights (including the legalization of abortion) have become an important part of the feminist agenda. But even basic agree- ments don't indicate any kind of theoretical, political, or philosophical unity on this issue. So the argument has been made as much on a "women's bodily rights" basis as on a class basis, decrying the unequal economic ability of women to have abortions (i.e., rich women can afford to do them quietly or to travel to other countries where they are legal). Although the reality of abor- tion has made this discussion something that stretches beyond feminism or even the women's movement, no mainstream political group has committed to legalizing it.

Lesbian feminism has begun to slowly open a path for itself. Among the feminist groups of the 1970s, lesbianism was always a silenced experience. The first workshop on the subject took place at a National Encounter of Women

(Córdoba, 1987), although its organizers feared a "scandal." Following this experience (which attracted many women) were other conferences, workshops, publications, and lesbian and gay pride marches. Nevertheless, the relation between feminism and lesbianism is neither easy nor harmonious. Many heterosexual women who consider themselves feminists fear being confused with lesbians, while not all lesbians are feminists.

Another arena for the development of feminism was the university. Both "women's studies" and taking "sex" into account in social science research had started out in the 1970s outside formal university structures. After the return of democracy, these kinds of studies not only started to take place inside the university but also began to be carried out especially inside the university, particularly in the 1990s, with the creation of specialized research centers, areas, programs, and institutes. These studies do not take a unified position, and they are also involved in the conflicts over what *feminist practice* means even within women-centered institutions.

The women's social movements that emerged during the dictatorship did not collapse along with it. On the contrary, these groups reached their peak in the 1980s, especially those struggling against the economic crisis. Most of these women did not identify themselves as feminists: they had become politicized, not against traditional femininity but against injustice in general. The economic crisis and structural adjustment policies had struck especially hard against working-class women.

Yet the state also intervened, during the 1980s and especially during the 1990s. This deepened the tensions between feminist groups and women's social movements. As I have already noted, the latter generally did not want to identify themselves as feminists because they saw feminists as middle-class intellectuals who were very distanced from their problems and lives. For their part, feminists often saw these other women as passive instruments of vote-buying aid campaigns of each successive government. The government's strategy for "administering poverty"—providing aid to voters and allies—not only fails to question the existing economic model but also frequently reinforces gender inequalities and increases the exploitation of women.

Women's movements for human rights had a different relation with feminism. While feminists found a space for common dialogue and struggle with some groups, they took a different, and even opposed, path from others—especially the most important of all, the Mothers of the Plaza de Mayo. On the one hand, there are those who support the Mothers' politicization of the private sphere. Some feel that they laid the foundation for an alternative women's politics. Yet others accept these transformations but maintain that there were not enough to overcome democratic party politics or to take an active role in it. Even more, they point out the political dangers of reinforcing the idea that women are naturally mothers.

The emergence and growth of these women's movements has sparked hopes, challenges and conflicts for feminism. Since 1986, several national women's conventions have been organized with the specific objective of experiencing, including, and confronting issues of diversity: conventions with feminists and nonfeminists, housewives and workers, political, labor, and human rights activists, and so on. But these conventions have had a limited presence in the press, and most of their resolutions have had no direct impact on national politics. At the Quinto Encuentro Feminista Latinoamericano y del Caribe (the Fifth Latin American and Caribbean Feminist Encounter) in Argentina in 1990, there was analysis of this tension between identity/equality and diversity/fragmentation that in large part characterizes Latin America as a whole. Participants reflected on the growth of feminism, its possibilities, and its limits.

Feminism in the 1990s is very different from that in the 1970s. If before women looked for issues that would unite them, a common identity, today it seems necessary to reflect on diversity in order to prevent it from becoming mere fragmentation. Instead of small, isolated groups, there are now stronger, more clearly defined groups, legally established, that seem to demand less of an emotional commitment from activists. Relations have also changed with the state and with revolutionary practice. For many women, equality is an attainable goal within present society.

Many of the feminist demands of the 1970s today seem more fully developed, more socially acceptable, and even, in some cases, more fully incorporated throughout all of society. However, this expansion of feminism is not without conflict. While the transformation of many groups into nongovernmental organizations, the funds and subsidies received, and the paths opened into institutions (the state, international organizations, universities) have helped spread feminist ideas and practices, they have also produced confrontations and splits. As a result, it seems that the movement has taken "shadow" form: it appears suddenly at certain events or supports certain slogans, only to later disappear into long periods of dormancy.

No one within feminism rejects diversity or the need for plurality. Moreover, in theory, they are associated with growth, richness, and vitality. But in daily practice things work out differently. Difference produces more splits than debates. While we can find a desire to build links and connections with difference throughout feminist publications, the persistence and repetition of such calls testify to their frustration. There are few debates, and, when there are debates, they leave little room for differences of opinion, slipping into reproaches of those "other women" for claiming that they represent the whole movement.

These conflicts and splits are not just with other women. They are also expressed within, and in, everyday life. Becoming feminist, as a way of living and thinking, exacts and has always exacted a high price, one that has not always diminished over time. Again and again, the problems of work, friends, family, and partners arise. But these internal conflicts have not generally led women to abandon feminism because it also has its benefits: understanding relationships and things better, including one's own life, feeling less of a sense of obligation and more joy in being a woman. Despite everything, feminism in Argentina remains a lonely path, threatened by a society that, despite certain changes, is not supportive.

Translated by Desireé Martin

Escombros, *Suture* (1993). Courtesy Juan Carlos Romero.

The Children of Death

María Moreno and Marta Dillon

While the Mothers of the Plaza de Mayo were the first to petition in public for the gov-
ernment to account for the "disappeared" in the late 1970s, in the 1990s it is the children
of the disappeared, as members of the organization HIJOS *(Hijos por la Identidad y la*
Justicia, contra el Olvido y el Silencio [Children (of the Disappeared) for Identity and
Justice, against Oblivion and Silence]), who have kept up a politics of memory that
refuses to let Argentina forget the atrocities committed during the last dictatorship.
Extremely active in their political mobilization, this group has developed innovative
ways of demonstrating in the streets. For example, escraches *(a slang term alluding to*
the action of making a person's secret transgressions public) are public performances
in which a group of people goes to the home of someone involved in the repression and
informs passersby of their neighbor's illegal past, either by talking to them or by spray-
painting slogans on the streets and walls. Many of these "children" were recovered by
the Mothers and Grandmothers of the Plaza de Mayo from the hands of their military
captors; others were raised by the families of the officers who illegally "adopted" them
after their parents were killed in underground prisons. In this interview with journal-
ist María Moreno, Marta Dillon explains how her being the daughter of a victim of
the dictatorship—a leftist political activist—affected all her subsequent political and
personal choices.

Marta Taboada, my mom, became a revolutionary activist in MR 17. But she
started out as a Christian Democrat. She was just a girl from Salta who studied
at a top Catholic school in Buenos Aires and then married the president of
Catholic Youth of Argentina, my dad. Only after having four kids and splitting
up did she stop to say: what is this world about? Then she got radicalized, while
my dad ran off with the secretary. I was eight years old.

That was when we got really close. My brothers—three boys—would go
off with my dad, with my aunts, but not me. The tie between us was very
strong, maybe because of what came later. . . .

Her real commitment began when activists from the MR 17 began to show up in Buenos Aires after the repression in Tucumán. She told me: look, these people need somewhere to be, if we take them in we're in danger, there are risks, you know what could happen. I didn't know much, but I knew that my mom had worked with Ortega Peña, and they had killed him. I said yes, of course, let them come, I don't think I had any other choice. . . .

My mom was really sharp. I remember one day we were in a bar with a *compañera* and the police came in. She had a bag full of pamphlets because they were doing a propaganda stunt. They had planned to cut off the street with some molotov cocktails and then cover everything with pamphlets. The cops came over to ask for documents. The other girl turned pale. When the cops gave them back their documents, my mom asked: "Would you like me to show you the bag?" And she opened it. One of the cops said, "No, that's all right, thanks girls."

For me, it was all a big adventure. Sometimes we went out to eat, and when it came time to pay, the kids would slip out to the door, ducking under the tables. Then the adults would get up and run. After she split up with my dad, there were money problems. We had a house—the place in Moreno where I live now—but it was a family inheritance; we had a car, but not enough to buy gas. Living in hiding, my mom got a little out of hand. She was really bourgeois, and she didn't want to give up the small pleasures, like buying earrings, using French perfume, and eating out. I think it was only then that she realized she was really alive, just like it's only now that I realize I am.

The night she disappeared I hadn't given her a good-bye kiss. It must have been because I was mad because she had gone out with her boyfriend, Juan Carlos Arroyo, an MR 17 leader who had broken out of the Villa Urquiza prison in Salta. And the rest of us had stayed behind, waiting for a *compañero* who was coming down from Córdoba. I woke up because I heard the voice of someone from Córdoba, and we were waiting for someone from Córdoba, but he was totally a cop. Then the girl who was working in the house—who was in on the thing—said to me: "Stay quiet, and remember the girl named Porcel." Because this *compañera,* who was six months pregnant, had a father who was a policeman in Tucumán. She didn't want to give out her married name because they had already disappeared her *compañero.*

The operation had started out downtown, at the corner of Santa Fé and Talcahuano. That was where they murdered Kela, another activist. They found the address of my dad's office in his pockets. And he brought them to Moreno. The cops came in, saw that they weren't around, and waited for them. They moved their cars out of sight, but when my mom and her man showed up, they still kept on going. There were shots. I don't know. There are different stories. But in the end, my mom and Arroyo came back. I heard them being interrogated for hours. I pushed the door to get out of my room because I wanted to see my mom, but they wouldn't let me. A cop grabbed me by the arm, and I bit his hand. He hit me, threw me on the bed, and told me, "We're going to kill you first because you're subversives from when you're kids."

I know she was in [torture center] El Banco and later in El Vesubio. I spent many years thinking that I was going to run into her on the bus, that she had been tortured so much she had lost her memory. In my fantasy, I would find her really old. Later on, when I was part of HIJOS, I discovered that almost all of us thought the same thing.

I remember the last present she gave me: a book dedicated "to little Marta, my *compañera,* who has already learned to live the joys and struggles of the Latin American people as her own."

Being in hiding gives you an identity, a sense of belonging. And the same kind of hiding happens in the world of drugs. During the dictatorship drugs were a space of resistance. They had taken everything away from us. All that was left was smoking a joint with friends and having a good time; that's why in the 1980s people who took drugs became the new focus of repression.

When you're an activist or a drug user, you are in a context of holding back, where you learn to share certain codes, a certain language. It's a kind of family. When you start taking drugs, you can't talk to anyone who isn't taking drugs, just like, when you become an activist, it gets hard to talk to people who aren't activists. Drugs, like activism, let you exercise your freedom, live a fantasy, break through the walls the system puts up. When I was girl, I went to the *villa* [slum] with my mom to do politics. Later on, I went back to buy dope. When I started going to Hidden City [a slum], they met me at the entrance. Later I started going in, until finally I would stick around for a barbeque. In the world of drugs, if they bring it to your house, you're nobody, but, if you go to buy it in the *villa,* you're the Man. Later on, we organized rock shows there, with the magazine *El libertino.*

Although this analogy between the world of drugs and the world of political activism might seem scandalous, for my generation it is valid. From our parents—who were all middle class—we kept a spirit of adventure, of having the guts to go there, to the *villa,* to see how those without privilege lived, to take on their lives, to tell the system "No pasarán."

My interest in AIDS began when, during the Eroziarte show in 1993, I met the artist Liliana Maresca. We starting talking, inventing, dreaming, brought together by great complicity and passion. A little while after she died, I woke up with these tremendous stains on my feet. The first thing I thought was, it's

AIDS, but they went away after two hours. But, later on, it happened again: I woke up, and I looked like a Dalmatian. So I went out on the terrace of my house thinking, "I must have been bitten by a spider." And I also thought, "If I have AIDS, I'm repeating my mother's history, I'm going to leave my daughter all alone because I am going to die at thirty five. Why, for all of my life, have I had to give my body? Why is everything so obvious, so graphically obvious?" I left Eroziarte in 1995 because they didn't want to give any place to AIDS. We had these super chic meetings with cell phones and the most important patron of art in Buenos Aires, we thought of having a show for businessmen, then they decided that AIDS was just not compelling. Why mix up screwing and death? So I split. When I went to the show, as if I were just another visitor, I saw that the works by Maresca and Schiliro — the two who died of AIDS — didn't have the artist's names and didn't appear in the catalog. Later on, there was a protest ad with a big impact in the press. . . .

We ended up destroyed. I wore a T-shirt that said "I have AIDS." That was like saying, "It doesn't matter if I do or don't," it was militant, a little like the business of "We are all German Jews." By the second Eroziarte show I had some nodules, like little knobs on my legs, that I couldn't help but see. And at the same time [Army Chief of Staff] Balza was apologizing on TV [for the army's role in the Dirty War]. I felt like my body was bursting out at the same time as the social body. Not just the social body like Balza but also the ghetto I was part of, where AIDS had just become really visible. For me, it was all the same.

Today, I am an AIDS activist from my column in *Página/12*.

In political activism the people responsible for keeping memory alive are still the victims and in AIDS activism those directly affected. And it should be something for all of us to do.

When I was thirteen, I met a classmate who had a brother who had disappeared. It was only then that I started to talk about it. And that was when I told it for the first time — because I had known that this was not something you could tell. It was very powerful putting into words everything I had lived through and not talked about. So powerful that she and I wrote a song for the disappeared and went to Plaza Francia with a guitar to sing it. The police came and took us to the Santa Rosa asylum because they claimed they could not find our parents.

For a long time, I was burdened by guilt because I hadn't done anything to look for my mom. I thought, if I go to HIJOS, they'll ask me where I've been all these years. (There was a habeas corpus petition, a protest to the OAS, nothing else.) I never could join any marches until the Resistance march in 1995, when

I had already been diagnosed with AIDS, and I saw the group from HIJOS. I walked up to the banner with the pictures, and there was one of my mother. Then I began my double activism; the two now run through my body.

HIJOS is starting to take on a structure to intervene in national politics. Lots of people fantasize about taking up our parents' struggle again, opting for socialism. I think that, if you are opting for socialism, you need to be an activist in the Socialist Party. HIJOS has to be something else: the place where your history becomes something real. Where we can transform the place they left us, a place of silence and guilt, into the space we want. Because the day they disappeared our parents, the day of the kidnapping, should have been a day of mourning. But our families said: "Don't get sad because they'll show up soon." "When your mother gets back!" It was a way of keeping memory and hope alive. But it meant that we were slow to do the mourning that the Mothers [of the Plaza de Mayo] had done a long time before. And that should be the space of HIJOS, a space where you can get sad and cry.

Now they're giving us this line about how we have to be ready to kill or die like our parents, and that is not right for HIJOS. I always tell them: "Don't give your body because I already did."

. . . I think my interest in eroticism comes from my mom; for her, activism was very tied to her erotic awakening. She went from being a mom to being a sexual person, separated from me and from her kids. In our house in Moreno, we talked about screwing, about smells, about fluids. Since that was where the MR 17 kept the girls and the kids, we were all girls. All the kids laughed a lot, and the *compañeras* laughed too. And my mother had this great seductive power that she knew how to use.

That is why I don't think that my activism in HIJOS and my AIDS activism— above all my column in *Página/12*—are opposed to each other.

The right to pleasure remains to be won. We have to work so that people discover their capacity for pleasure. It hasn't been uncovered yet. When a man and a woman discover that ability, it belongs only to them, and it is not likely that anything can be imposed on them.

. . . We are a broken generation. And the place they've taken from us with the "specter of AIDS" is pleasure because we've gone so far backward on sexual matters that nothing will change with the good news of a cure. Now there's Magalí Moro on the TV telling us: Watch out! Watch out for your toothbrush, your hairbrush, your shaving razor! In other words, watch out for everyone else! In all these campaigns, being careful means being abstinent. Even with your computer, it's dangerous to stick in something we don't know. "Don't bring me any unknown diskettes, they might contaminate my computer." It's no coincidence we call it a *virus*.

I know I have AIDS, I chose to know it, and I refuse to give up my sexuality. Not only because I don't have to, but also because denying the possibility of exploring other bodies would be degrading. I am going to take on the possibility of living and not keeping myself in formaldehyde until some laboratory takes the risk to say, "This is the definitive cure." Maybe we would rather weep for the dead than celebrate the advances of treatment. Maybe it's more romantic to become eternal Penelopes who spin webs between their legs until the cure arrives instead of demanding our right to pleasure without guilt, with condoms, and with imagination.

If the disappeared "must have done something" and the victims of AIDS "must have done something," then we have to rethink never again. Say never again to repression, never again to genocide, never again to dictatorship. But also say never again to pleasure, to changing the world, to struggling? Everyone be quiet, careful, obedient? That would be the easiest way to cover up what happened, and to that too we must say, Never again.

Translated by Mark Alan Healey

Active Memory

Laura Ginsberg

On 17 March 1992, a car bomb exploded in front of the Israeli embassy in Buenos Aires, completely destroying the building and leaving a death toll of twenty five. On 18 July 1994, another bomb tore apart the Argentine Israeli Mutual-Aid Association (AMIA), killing eighty-six people, including employees and passersby. To this day, neither of the terrorist attacks has been cleared up. Although some evidence points to a possible collaboration between members of the Buenos Aires police and international anti-Israeli terrorist organizations, the official investigation has yet to deliver any breakthroughs. Frustrated and angered by official apathy, the victims' families founded Active Memory, a group that, following a pattern created by the Mothers of the Plaza de Mayo, meets every Monday in front of the courthouse in Buenos Aires City to demand justice and prevent historical amnesia. Laura Ginsberg, one of its main leaders, whose husband was killed in the second explosion, delivered this speech in 1997 during a public ceremony honoring the victims.

I close my eyes, and I imagine that it is 18 July 1994 at seven o'clock in the morning. Like any Monday, we all get up to begin another week. Parents have breakfast with their children, and we all say "I love you" before we leave the house. But many of us didn't do this because we never thought that it would be for the last time.

I close my eyes, and I imagine that it is the same day, 18 July, at ten in the morning. Mónica and Félix go to work; Romina attends classes at the university, Jorge brings coffee to a customer, and Sebastián, with all of his five years, goes walking along Pasteur Street with his mama. None of them will ever arrive at their destinations.

I open my eyes, and the image of the horror invades my being: smoke, firemen, police, people pushing, people crying, people screaming, people praying, people who are not able to do anything, neither cry, nor scream, nor even swear. At seven minutes to ten the building belonging to the Jewish Center has been blown up.

The Argentine Jewish community is one of the largest in the world. Here, Jews in Retiro Park in Buenos Aires celebrate the creation of the state of Israel in 1948. Courtesy Archivo General de la Nación, Buenos Aires.

I close my eyes, and I imagine that it is eleven o'clock on the morning of that day, 18 July. The people who work at the Jewish Center go on doing what they usually do: Marisa smiles at the people coming into the building; the young women from social service help worried people; everyone waiting in the employment office hopes to find work instead of dying. Rita and the boys from the funeral office help Luis, Fabián, Pablo, and Elías, who are going to bury their grandfather, while Néstor keeps on testing the air-conditioner and the bricklayers plaster the walls that are still standing.

But, when I open my eyes three years later, I find myself listening to the pronouncements of the minister of the interior, Carlos Corach, in words that heap glory on himself for having found the economic resources for the reconstruction of the Jewish Center and for having helped the families of the victims — as if this bears any relation to solving the crime.

I close my eyes, and I imagine that it is four in the afternoon of that day, 18 July. The children are getting out of school; they have a snack. They turn on the TV and the programs are the usual programs, no rubble, no death.

But, when I open them, it is three years later, and still nothing has been done about the famous, inconclusive investigation of the Iranian connection. President Menem has done nothing about it, and nothing has been done about

The AMIA in ruins after a terrorist explosion (1994). Courtesy *La Nación*.

the four Iranian diplomats who never were able to be interrogated, and nothing, absolutely nothing, has been done about the early alert from the Brazilian Wilson dos Santos, who warned the Argentine consul in Milan of the coming attack early in July 1994.

I close my eyes, and I imagine that it is eight o'clock at night on that day, 18 July. Just like any other day, the family is waiting impatiently for the sound of the keys in the door because it is Andrés who is arriving and his coming always lights up their lives.

But, when I open my eyes, it is three years later, and I am with other victims of the same type of unpunished crime: the twenty-nine dead in the attack on the Israeli embassy and the photographer, José Luis Cabezas, assassinated six months earlier. Their families, grieving and anguishing like us, watch in astonishment as a procession of witnesses complicates the investigation. And all the while the assassins surely glory in the crime and trust in the national government that covers their backs. . . .

I close my eyes, and I imagine that it is ten at night on that day, 18 July. Kuky kisses her children and puts them to bed; Silvana nurses her baby; Yanina and Verónica go off with their boyfriends; and Jaime plays with his granddaughter. Dorita goes out for dinner. Fabián comes back from the movies and Naomi talks with her daughters who are almost teenagers.

But, when I open my eyes and I listen, I don't hear the laughter of those we've lost; I hear threats. The families, I repeat, the families of the victims, are threatened by people who keep up the parody of fear in a country where darkness and impunity are the controlling forces. One of us is threatened with death, his car followed by unknown men; others receive intimidating phone calls that make accusations that seem of no importance to anyone. Active Memory is threatened with being the victim of an attack during a Monday ceremony, the Jewish Hospital is evacuated because of threats, Jewish schools have to be abandoned, Jewish cemeteries are profaned all over the country, right in front of the astonished eyes of the community. . . .

All the crimes and attacks, committed and yet to be committed, have a common denominator. I accuse the government of Menem and Duhalde of consenting to the impunity, of consenting to the indifference of those who know and yet keep silent, of consenting to a lack of security, of exhibiting a lack of skill and a sense of ineptitude. I accuse the government of Menem and Duhalde of covering up the local connection that killed members of our family.

I close my eyes, and I imagine that it is twelve midnight on 18 July. We are all deep in dreams, our families are still whole, and we all make plans for the following day with the irreverent madness of living, the defiant thought of living, the illusory desire to live.

But, when I open them, I find myself three years later with the irreverent madness of longing for justice, with the defiant thought of demanding justice, with the illusory desire of "never again."

Today is 18 July, and three years, three years, have gone by, and, as on each anniversary and on each day of our lives, we go on without having any answers. For that reason, we say:

> Today we are here, at the final corner of their lives, on the first corner of the long road that it falls to us to travel, demanding justice. Because exactly three years ago their laughter, our laughter, and all the shared laughter that now will never be has been silenced. Because their dreams, our dreams, and endless shared dreams all went up in smoke, in clouds of explosives and horror.
>
> And because that morning they left their houses, just as they did every morning, and never returned, they deserve justice. And because we will not forget, we demand justice. And because the law of life says that fathers do not bury their children, we demand justice. And for all those who will never see their children grow up, we seek justice. And for all those who will never grow old with their loved ones, we demand justice. And because we love them, we cry out for justice. And because they loved us, they deserve justice. And because they believed they lived in a free, safe country, we de-

mand justice. And because their voices cry out from the center of the land, we demand justice. And because we repudiate terrorism and violence and hatred between peoples and discrimination, in all their many guises, and because to shine light on the attack is an inescapable responsibility, we fight for justice.

And they deserve justice because, wherever they are in the universe or within ourselves, only when there is justice will our dead be able to rest in peace. Those who died at the Jewish Center: present!

Translated by Patricia Owen Steiner

Infinity

César Aira

One of neoliberalism's most important effects on Argentine society is how it has trans-formed people from citizens into consumers. At a time when the dynamics of global capitalism have pervaded all social spheres and even political debates are shaped by market strategies, political choices have become inextricably tied to the power to buy. Throughout the 1990s, despite the middle classes' deepening financial insolvency, both the government and the media encouraged rampant consumption. Returning to a lit-erature more prone to fictional fantasy than to realistic representation or personal nar-rative, César Aira's curious stories reenact—from an ironically naive perspective—the loss of past social worlds where the desire to play and the enjoyment of nonsense were cherished values.

As a child I played some of the most peculiar games. When I tell about them, they seem invented, and really they were an invention of the self that I am, except that it was many years ago, when I was in the process of evolving into the person I am now. My invention, or my friends' invention, it's all the same because those boys were all a part of what I turned out to be. If now I have proposed to myself the idea of describing those games and explaining them in writing, it is precisely because they have told me more than once that they deserved to be recorded so that they won't die with me. I am not so sure of that appraisal of peculiarity; boys used to say the craziest things. But the cata-log of these expressions is not limitless; I could swear, based on intuition, and on the law of probabilities, that the same thing, or something like it, occurred to others, once, somewhere. If that's so, if some reader into whose hands this happens to fall should be one of those boys, for him these descriptions will be a reminder, perhaps a resurrection, of a forgotten past. I believe that it will be necessary to go into details with a certain amount of complication, and it is possible that the tediousness will prove to be excessive. But I set about the task with high spirits to find out what my early years had in common with those of others who are far away and unknown to me. The common link must be in small things, in trifles. As I don't know in which trifles, in which details, I have no other solution than to spread out all the details. There's also a more practical motive—intelligibility. Even the most insignificant details have importance in order to complete the explanation of the strategy that at first sight might seem absurd. You have to go through the entire foolish ins and outs so that only the one with the magic power of making sense of the whole thing does not escape.

I begin by considering a mathematical or pseudomathematical game that was played by two people and simply consisted in saying a number larger than the one the opponent had just said. If one person said "four," the other person had to say "five" to stay ahead. (As his lowest number, he could also say "one thousand.") And thus the game continued. That said, there is nothing more to add with respect to the essence of the game; as can be seen, it was extremely simple. Obviously, given the nature of the series of numbers, the only person who could win was the person who didn't commit the error of saying a number less than the one announced earlier. But it is also obvious that such a victory was accidental and didn't affect the proclaimed essence of the game, which was that the person who finally said a number so high that his opponent could find none higher was the winner. We actively worked together on the essence of the game. We never made mistakes, and, if one of us might have made one, the other person would have been more than ready to let it pass and just keep on playing. It is difficult to imagine, then, how the full dimension of the game could be realized. There seems to be a contradiction in the very idea. But I believe that all the difficulty resides in the adult who wants to understand the theory of the whole business and would like to reconstruct a round of the game. For us it wasn't difficult to understand. To the contrary, it was almost too easy (and for that reason we complicated it a little). The difficulties, which others might find hard to understand, we found diverting and absorbing; they were on another plane, as I will try to demonstrate. As for the game itself, it was completely natural for us.

Before getting into it, I will make a few clarifications that have their raison d'être. In the first place: age. We would have been ten or eleven (or perhaps eleven and twelve). Omar was a year older than I: we were in primary school, but far along, not in the earliest grades. That is to say, we were not just learning to count, fascinated or astonished by the miracle of arithmetic. Not at all. Besides, at that time, thirty-five years ago, learning was not a game; one didn't waste time, there was no daydreaming. Even in the country school we went to (school no. 2 of Colonel Pringles, which still exists), the intellectual level was notably high; today its demands would seem excessive. And all the children, the majority of whom came from huts and from illiterate parents, kept up to pace. Indeed, yes, they did keep up to pace.

The characters: Omar and me. I never played this game with anyone else. I don't remember if I ever tried to, but, if I did, it didn't work. It was the type of game that has to find its player, and it is almost miraculous that it does find him. It had found the two of us, and we had adapted so much to its intricate, crystalline convolutions that we had made ourselves part of it. And it became a part of us in a way that excluded the rest of the world. . . .

And lastly: the scene. Colonel Pringles, the town, was then more or less what it is today; a little smaller, less urbanized, with more dirt roads; Alvear Street, where we lived, was the last asphalt street; one hundred meters further on was the beginning of vacant lots (whole blocks of them). Then the big estates, the countryside. On our block there were five houses, all on the same side: the Urunuela's on the corner, my Aunt Alicia and María's, our house, the one of Gonzalo Barba, my father's nephew and business partner, and the Berruet's house. On the other corner, the storage yard and offices of my father's business, Aira and Barba. Gonzalo and the Berruets rented their houses from Padelli whose home on the corner you could get to through the backyard. Out front, back of the sidewalk, there was a long wall. Behind it was the land belonging to the houses on the corner, the Astutti's on the left, the Perrier's on the right. . . .

Nothing happened on the street: an automobile every half hour or so. We had immensity of free time; we went to school in the morning, the afternoons lasted an entire lifetime. We had no extracurricular activities (that wasn't the way then), there was no television, our houses had open doors. To play at numbers we got into the red cab of Omar's father's small truck that was almost always parked out in front of the door. . . .

It is incredible that, being as covetous of things as we were, it never occurred to us to add the name of an object to the numbers. Because such naked numbers were nothing and we wanted everything. In reality, there's no contradiction between the description I have given of the two semisavage young boys, in a society that today seems archaic and primitive, and the fact that we were covetous. We wanted everything, even Rolls Royces, even things that had no use for us, like diamonds or centrifuge machines for subatomic particles. And how we wanted them! With an anxiety that borders on the distressing. There is no contradiction. The life of our parents was supernaturally sober; it seemed to have reached its goal. Perhaps its goal was us. The rents were frozen. Automobiles lasted eternities, the mania for electrified appliances would be late in coming to Pringles, the furniture was still what had been purchased to get married.

There's more: we ourselves always had the money we needed for the little that there was on sale that might interest us: cards, magazines, marbles, chewing gum. I don't know where we got the money, but we never lacked for it. But we were insatiable, avaricious, desirous to the highest degree. We wanted a ship with silken sails and a sculptured figure of pure gold at the stern. If we fantasized that we had found treasure, doubloons, and gold ingots and emeralds, we weren't so imprudent as to waste it on this thing or the other but insisted that we convert it into money. We put it in the bank, and, with the money that we got as compound interest, we bought statues from the island of Pascua, from the Taj Mahal, race cars, and slaves. We were still not satisfied. We wanted the philosopher's stone or, better yet, Aladdin's lamp. Midas's fortune didn't intimidate us: we had already thought of wearing gloves.

Numbers were numbers and nothing more. And the big numbers still more. Eight could still be eight automobiles, one for each day of the week and one extra with special tires for rainy days. But a billion? And an infinity? And an infinity of infinities? That couldn't be anything else but money. I don't understand why we didn't mention it. Perhaps it was implicit.

Translated by Patricia Owen Steiner

Postmodern Forgetfulness

Beatriz Sarlo

*In this fin de siècle Argentina, as in many other Latin American countries, the glob-
alization of politics and the economy has been accompanied by the ascent of a new
type of culture, described by some as the styles of postmodernity. Fifty television channels, video games, cyberspace, fast-food restaurants, retro fashion, etc. are some of the
technological developments and commercial habits characteristic of this global phenomenon. Faced with this new reality, many intellectuals are asking themselves about
the social consequences of such cultural experiences in peripheral countries like Argentina. In her search for answers to these fundamental questions, Beatriz Sarlo, one of
the most influential intellectual figures in today's Argentina, has written several pieces
on the subject. In this essay from her book* Instantáneas (Snapshots) (1997), *she questions the fatuous celebration of postmodernity by arguing that it poses a threat to
historical memory. In a neoliberal world that has a tendency to dismiss the political
struggles of the past as irrelevant, she argues that "remembering what happened" is a
political duty.*

We only seek a little order to shield us from chaos. There is nothing sadder nor more disturbing than a thought that escapes, ideas that flee or vanish completely almost as soon as
they appear, gnawed at by our habit of forgetting or being pushed on to other ideas we can't
control.
—Gilles Deleuze and Félix Guattari

Postmodernity is no stranger to ideas that fail to achieve a concrete life and
are always on the verge of vanishing. Certainly we are not now overwhelmed
by the weight of history: time goes by quickly, almost unnoticed, devouring
the innovations it brings and, at the same time, devoured by them.

In this climate the passion for cultural recycling is not surprising: the novelty
of the past is nourished by our habit of forgetting.

This year all the fashion magazines inaugurate the arrival of spring with
covers that announce the deification of the miniskirt and bell-bottoms, a style

of sincere and acknowledged inspiration of the 1960s. Things "retro" are the last cry of summer. But, in this, the summer that comes is no different from the previous one, nor from any other. There was retroromanticism, retrogothic, retroAfro, retropunk, retrorock. We had a new Woodstock, Paul McCartney's world tour, the discovery, no less, of blues music and the revival of the tango (retro, retro, retro), and a victorious world tour of the Rolling Stones. There was retro "femme fatale" and even the latest transformation of Madonna that also cultivates the retro of erotic uses of religious images. *New Age* is a kind of acceptable retrohippie for television, with natural foods instead of marijuana, flower pots on the balcony in place of sunsets over the bays of California or in the El Bolsón valleys of northern Patagonia, and campaigns in defense of the nutria instead of denunciations of racism. A retro in the measure of Nacha Guevara, she herself a turn of the retro screw, who went from an easygoing diva to an emotional counselor for her electronic friends.

Truly, "there is nothing sadder nor more disturbing than a thought that escapes, ideas that flee or vanish completely almost as soon as they appear, gnawed at by our habit of forgetting or pushed on to other ideas we can't control." Style recycles the past, and, through style, the past goes right on flying away just when we want to cling to it. The retro style presents the past as the last gasp of the present. It takes its character from something that was definitely of another time and that tranquilizes us in some way. Nostalgia has its own marketing, and the past can return without threatening us. In the retro the past becomes softened because it appears to be divided into pieces and reassembled. What does a very brief miniskirt matter after the topless? Who is going to be preoccupied by the vitamin supplements he takes when he becomes forty and has decided that those supplements are healthier than marijuana or whiskey? Who will be scandalized by the crucifixes hanging from Madonna—except for an overreactionary bishop? Yet, next to the crosses of Madonna that some people consider a blasphemy, the gates of a bazaar of new confessions are opened wide.

The aesthetics of postmodern life are based on disappearance more than on invention. To be precise, modernity had at its center the invention of the new; postmodernity has no center. It flows and carries everything in its current: the past and the future are comfortably interlaced because the past has lost its density and the future has lost its certainty. Save for the futurologists who believe that they know very well what awaits us in ten years (more interactive computers, more television where we can learn about everything, more virtual reality), people have less and less of an idea of what the future holds. It is enough to listen to high school students whose skepticism about the future is caused by the liberation from rigid ideologies but also by the uncertainty in which they live.

Everything combines with everything in a situation where everything changes at maximum velocity. We recklessly fling ourselves from "some ideas gnawed at by our habit of forgetting to others that we can't control." The retro style is the aesthetic face of a gaseous atmosphere that is extremely volatile. We live on a deposit of compressed gas, meaning not necessarily that social eruptions will be set off but rather that society has now begun to burst at its weak or inorganic points. The exaltation of speed, of which the modern age has made a true civic religion, has exposed all kinds of problems.

But, when a significant and dense relationship with the past is lost and is converted into a storehouse of entertaining recyclings, the past may come back to haunt us. It is not too important that the style might be retro, as long as it is not converted into the spirit of the time.

Some while ago, Carlos Menem made the most bombastic retro remark. He said that, if demonstrations by young people persisted in the public plaza, the Mothers of the Plaza de Mayo would return. The threat of recycling violence sounded as repugnant as it was incredible. However, it was uttered and survived, despite its general repudiation, in the same way as other such utterances survive.

The retro style has nothing to do with Menem's sentence, and to think otherwise would be simply absurd. However, to turn the past into something of no consequence is dangerous except when it comes to something like miniskirts or slacks. "We only need a little order to shield us from chaos": this doesn't have anything to do with order imposed by force, or with the order of great ideologies or traditional morals, or with the established version of history. Instead, it concerns the reestablishment of links with the past that are not just anecdotal or picturesque, like the pronouncements that TV programs make about the decades of the 1960s or 1970s.

A "retro" relationship with the past diminishes its meaning: the miniskirt no longer speaks of the sexual liberation of the 1960s; the decorative little rings that punks used to pierce into their ears and noses with gestures of insulting defiance no longer evoke the reactions that they did in the past; the bland ecology movement has forgotten the old libertarian vindication of nature and the body; the *New Age* does not remember the days when the business of expanding the senses went through physical, psychological, and moral experimentation that touched on all the limits. These forgotten things blot out some of the pages from our history that are really moving, heroic, or fanatic and others that show how far some people went astray. It is of no importance how these pages are judged; they are there, but not just so that the "retro" style may encounter new material.

It is impossible to hang a sign from each miniskirt that says, "Invented by Mary Quant at the same time as the Beatles were inventing 'Let It Be.'" But perhaps it is worth the trouble to reconstruct some histories so that all the ideas don't disappear, "gnawed away by our habit of forgetting."

Translated by Patricia Owen Steiner

Suggestions for Further Reading

I. At the Margins of the Empire

Azzara, Félix de. *Viajes por la América Meridional*. 1809. 2 vols. Reprint. Buenos Aires: El Elefante Blanco, 1998.

Baucke, Florián. *Iconografía colonial rioplatense, 1749–1767: Costumbres y trajes españoles, criollos, e indios*. Buenos Aires: Elche, 1973.

Cunninghame, Graham R. B. *The Conquest of the River Plate*. New York: Doubleday, Page, 1924.

Galvez, Lucía. *Mujeres de la conquista*. Buenos Aires: Planeta, 1990.

Gillespie, Alexander. *Gleanings and Remarks Collected during Many Months of Residence at Buenos Ayres, and within the Upper Country*. Leeds: B. Derhirst, 1818.

Groussac, Paul. *Mendoza y Garay: Las dos fundaciones de Buenos Aires, 1536–1580*. Buenos Aires: J. Menéndez, 1916.

Iglesia, Cristina, and Julio Schvartzman. *Cautivas y misioneros: Mitos blancos de la conquista*. Buenos Aires: Catálogos, 1987.

Lynch, John. *Spanish Colonial Administration, 1782–1810*. London, 1978.

Madero, Eduardo. *Historia del puerto de Buenos Aires*. Buenos Aires: Ediciones Buenos Aires, 1939.

Malaspina, Alessandro. *Viaje al Río de la Plata en el siglo XVIII*. Buenos Aires: Librería la Facultad, 1938.

Mörner, Magnus. *The Political and Economic Activities of the Jesuits in the La Plata Region*. Stockholm: Victor Petterson, 1953.

Socolow, Susan M. *The Merchants of Buenos Aires, 1778–1810: Family and Commerce*. New York: Cambridge University Press, 1978.

II. To Build a Nation / III. Frontiers

Andrews, George Reid. *The Afro-Argentines of Buenos Aires, 1800–1900*. Madison: University of Wisconsin Press, 1980.

Bemberg, María Luisa. *Camila*. Los Angeles: Embassy Home Entertainment, 1985. Videorecording.

Brown, Jonathan. *A Socio-Economic History of Argentina, 1776–1860*. Cambridge: Cambridge University Press, 1979.

De la Fuente, Ariel. *Children of Facundo: Caudillo and Gaucho Insurgency during the Argentine State-Formation Process (La Rioja, 1853–1870). Durham, N.C.: Duke University Press, 2000.

Ferns, H. S. *Britain and Argentina in the Nineteenth Century*. Oxford: Oxford University Press, 1960.

Goldman, Noemí, and Ricardo Salvatore, eds. *Caudillismos rioplatenses: Nuevas miradas a un viejo problema*. Buenos Aires: EUDEBA, 1998.

Goodrich, Diana Sorensen. *Facundo and the Construction of Argentine Culture*. Austin: University of Texas Press, 1996.

Halperín Donghi, Tulio. *Una nación para el desierto argentino*. Buenos Aires: CEAL, 1982.

Head, Francis Bond. *Rough Notes Taken during Some Rapid Journeys across the Pampas and among the Andes*. Boston: Wells and Lilly, 1827.

Ludmer, Josefina. *The Gaucho Genre: A Treatise on the Motherland*. Durham, N.C.: Duke University Press, 2002.

Lynch, John. *Argentine Dictator: Juan Manuel de Rosas, 1829–1852*. Oxford: Clarendon, 1981.

MacCann, William. *Two Thousand Miles' Ride through the Argentine Provinces, Being an Account of the Natural Products of the Country, and Habits of the People; with a Historical Retrospect of the Río de la Plata, Monte Video, and Corrientes*. London: Smith, Elder, 1853.

Mansilla, Lucio. *[Los] Siete platos de arroz con leche*. Buenos Aires: EUDEBA, 1960.

Mármol, José. *Amalia*. 1851. Reprint. Buenos Aires: El Elefante Blanco, 1997.

Masiello, Francine. *Between Civilization and Barbarism: Women, Nation, and Literary Culture in Modern Argentina*. Lincoln: University of Nebraska Press, 1992.

Paz, José María. *Memorias*. Buenos Aires: EUDEBA, 1960.

Ramos, Julio. *Divergent Modernities: Culture and Politics in Nineteenth-Century Latin America*. Durham, N.C.: Duke University Press, 1999.

Rodríguez Molas, Ricardo. *Historia social del gaucho*. Buenos Aires: CEAL, 1968.

Romero, José Luis. *A History of Argentine Political Thought*. Stanford, Calif.: Stanford University Press, 1963.

Rosa, José María. *Rosas nuestro contemporáneo: Sus 20 años de gobierno*. Buenos Aires, 1970.

Shumway, Nicholas. *The Invention of Argentina*. Berkeley and Los Angeles: University of California Press, 1991.

Slatta, Richard. *Gauchos and the Vanishing Frontier*. Lincoln: University of Nebraska Press, 1983.

Szuchman, Mark D. *Family, Order, and Community in Buenos Aires, 1810–1860*. Stanford, Calif.: Stanford University Press, 1988.

Szuchman, Mark D., and Jonathan C. Brown, eds. *Revolution and Restoration: The Rearrangement of Power in Argentina, 1776–1860*. Lincoln: University of Nebraska Press, 1994.

IV. Splendor and Fin de Siècle

Biagini, Hugo E., ed. *El movimiento positivista argentino*. Buenos Aires: Editorial de Belgrano, 1985.

Botana, Natalio. *El orden conservador: La política argentina entre 1880 y 1916*. Buenos Aires: Hyspamérica, 1986.

Cambaceres, Eugenio. *Sin rumbo*. Buenos Aires: Editorial Estrada, 1971.

Cortes Conde, Roberto. "The Growth of the Argentine Economy, c. 1870–1914." In *The Cambridge History of Latin America*, vol. 5, ed. Leslie Bethell. Cambridge: Cambridge University Press, 1986.

Gorelik, Adrián. *La grilla y el parque: Espacio público y cultura urbana en Buenos Aires, 1887–1936*. Buenos Aires: Universidad Nacional de Quilmes, 1998.

Gori, Gastón. *Inmigración y colonización en la Argentina*. Buenos Aires: EUDEBA, 1964.

Guy, Donna. *Sex and Danger in Buenos Aires: Prostitution, Family, and Nation in Argentina*. Lincoln: University of Nebraska Press, 1991.

Jitrik, Noé. *El mundo del Ochenta*. Buenos Aires: CEAL, 1982.

Martel, Julián. *La bolsa: Estudio social*. Buenos Aires: Editorial Huemul, 1891.

McGann, Thomas F. *Argentina, the United States, and the Inter-American System*. Cambridge, Mass.: Harvard University Press, 1937.

Prieto, Adolfo. *El discurso criollista en la formación de la Argentina moderna*. Buenos Aires: Sudamericana, 1988.

Rojas, Ricardo. *La restauración nacionalista*. Buenos Aires: Ediciones Centurión, 1909.

Rossi, Vicente. *Cosas de negros*. Buenos Aires: Hachette, 1958.

Salessi, Jorge. *Médicos, maleantes, y maricas*. Rosario: Beatriz Viterbo Editoras, 1995.

Solberg, C. E. *Immigration and Nationalism: Argentina and Chile, 1890–1914*. Austin: University of Texas Press, 1970.

Terán, Oscar, ed. *José Ingenieros: Pensar la nación: Antología de textos*. Madrid and Buenos Aires: Alianza, 1986.

Vezzetti, Hugo. *La locura en Argentina*. Buenos Aires: Paidós, 1984.

Viñas, David. *Literatura argentina y realidad política*. Buenos Aires: CEAL, 1982.

Zimmerman, Eduardo A. "Racial Ideas and Social Reform: Argentina, 1890–1916." *Hispanic American Historical Review* 72, no. 1 (February 1992): 23–46.

V. Modern Times

Arlt, Roberto. *The Seven Mad Men*. London: Serpent's Tail, 1998.

Armus, Diego, ed. *Mundo urbano y cultura popular*. Buenos Aires: Sudamericana, 1990.

Barrancos, Dora. *Anarquismo, educación, y costumbres en la Argentina del fin de siglo*. Buenos Aires: Contrapunto, 1990.

Carlson, Marifran. *Feminismo! The Woman's Movement in Argentina from its Beginnings to Eva Perón*. Chicago: Academy, 1988.

Deutsch, Sandra McGee. *Counterrevolution in Argentina, 1900–1932: The Argentine Patriotic League*. Lincoln: University of Nebraska Press, 1986.

Dickman, Enrique. *Recuerdos de un militante socialista*. Buenos Aires, 1949.

Discépolo, Enrique Santos. *¿A mi me la vas a contar?* Buenos Aires, 1973.

Fernández, Macedonio. *Papeles de recienvenido*. Buenos Aires: Editorial Proa, 1930.

Godio, Julio. *El movimiento obrero argentino (1910-1930): Socialismo, sindicalismo, y comunismo*. Buenos Aires: Legasa, 1988.

Güiraldes, Ricardo. *Don Segundo Sombra: The Great Novel of the Argentine Pampa*. Translated by Patricia Owen Steiner. Pittsburgh, Pa.: Colección Archivos, 1995.

Ivereig, Austen. *Catholicism and Politics in Argentina, 1810-1960*. New York: St. Martin's, 1995.

Lange, Norah. *Cuadernos de la infancia*. Buenos Aires: D. Viau, 1937.

Lavrín, Asunción. *Women, Feminism, and Social Change in Argentina, Chile, and Uruguay, 1890-1940*. Lincoln: University of Nebraska Press, 1995.

Luna, Félix. *Yrigoyen: El templario de la libertad*. Buenos Aires: Editorial Raigal, 1964.

Newton, Ronald. *The "Nazi Menace" in Argentina, 1931-1947*. Stanford, Calif.: Stanford University Press, 1992.

Olivera, Héctor. *La Patagonia rebelde*. Buenos Aires: Aries Cinematográfica Argentina, 1974. Videorecording.

Oved, Iaácov. *El anarquismo y el movimiento obrero en Argentina*. México: Siglo XXI, 1978.

Sarlo, Beatriz. *Una modernidad periférica: Buenos Aires 1920 y 1930*. Buenos Aires: Nueva Visión, 1988.

Savigliano, M. *Tango and the Political Economy of Passion*. Boulder, Colo.: Westview, 1995.

Scalabrini Ortiz, Raúl. *El hombre que está solo y espera*. Buenos Aires: Editorial Reconquista, 1941.

Walter, R. J. *The Socialist Party of Argentina, 1890-1930*. Austin: University of Texas Press, 1977.

VI. Populism and New Nationalism

Borges, Jorge Luis. "The Argentine Writer and Tradition." In *LabyrinthS: Selected Stories and Other Writings,* ed. Donald Yates and James E. Irby. New York: New Directions, 1964.

Borges, Jorge Luis, and Adolfo Bioy Casares. "La fiesta del monstruo." In *Nuevos cuentos de Bustos Domecq*. Buenos Aires: Ediciones Librería la Ciudad, 1977.

Brennan, James P., ed. *Peronism and Argentina*. Wilmington, Del.: SR, 1998.

Bruce, James. *Those Perplexing Argentines*. New York, 1953.

Caimari, Lila. *Perón y la iglesia católica: Religión, estado, y sociedad en Argentina, 1943-1955*. Buenos Aires: Ariel, 1995.

Carril, Hugo del. *Las aguas bajan turbias*. 1952. Memories Video Home, 1992. Videorecording.

Ciria, Alberto. *Política y cultura popular: La Argentina peronista, 1946-1955*. Buenos Aires: Ediciones de la Flor, 1983.

King, John. *Sur: A Study of the Argentine Literary Journal and Its Role in the Development of a Culture, 1931-1970*. Cambridge: Cambridge University Press, 1986.

Mallea, Eduardo. *History of an Argentine Passion.* Pittsburgh: *Latin American Literary Review* Press, 1983.

Marechal, Leopoldo. *Adán BuenosAyres.* 1948. Reprint. Buenos Aires: Editorial Sudamericana, 1999.

Meyer, Doris. *Victoria Ocampo: Against the Wind and the Tide.* Austin: University of Texas Press, 1990.

Molloy, Sylvia. *Signs of Borges.* Durham, N.C.: Duke University Press, 1994.

Page, Joseph. *Perón: A Biography.* New York: Random House, 1983.

Pauls, Alan. *Lino Palacio: La infancia de la risa.* Buenos Aires: Espasa Humor Gráfico, 1993.

Perón, Eva. *My Mission in Life.* New York: Vantage, 1953.

Perón, Juan Domingo. *Perón Expounds His Doctrine.* New York: AMS, 1973.

Plotkin, Mariano. *Mañana es San Perón: Propaganda, rituales políticos y educación en el régimen peronista (1946-1955).* Buenos Aires: Ariel, 1993.

Reyes, Cipriano. *La farsa del peronismo.* Buenos Aires: Sudamericana/Planeta, 1987.

Sábato, Ernesto. *On Heroes and Tombs.* 1961. Reprint. Boston: Godine, 1981.

Sebreli, Juan José. *Los deseos imaginarios del peronismo.* Buenos Aires, 1983.

Steiner, Pat Owen. *Victoria Ocampo: Writer, Feminist, Woman of the World.* Albuquerque: University of New Mexico Press, 1999.

Taylor, Julie. *Eva Perón: The Myths of a Woman.* Chicago, 1979.

Torre, Juan Carlos. *El 17 de Octubre de 1945.* Buenos Aires: Ariel, 1995.

Walsh, Rodolfo. "Esa mujer." In *Los oficios terrestres.* Buenos Aires: Jorge Alvarez, 1965.

VII. Revolutionary Dreams

Anguita, Eduardo, and Martín Caparrós. *La voluntad: Una historia de la militancia revolucionaria en Argentina.* Vol. 1, 1966-1973. Buenos Aires: Grupo Editorial Norma, 1997.

Baily, Samuel L. *The Durability of Peronism.* Buffalo, N.Y.: Council of International Studies, State University of New York at Buffalo, 1975.

Balán, Jorge. *Cuéntame tu vida: Una biografía colectiva del psicoanálisis argentino.* Buenos Aires: Planeta, 1991.

Bonasso, Miguel. *Diario de un clandestino.* Buenos Aires: Planeta, 2000.

Brennan, James P. *The Labor Wars in Córdoba: Ideology, Work, and Labor Politics in an Argentine Industrial City, 1955-1976.* Cambridge, Mass.: Harvard University Press, 1994.

Castaneda, Jorge G. *Compañero: The Life and Death of Che Guevara.* New York: Vintage, 1998.

Cortázar, Julio. *Hopscotch.* New York: Pantheon, 1987.

Favio, Leonardo. *El dependiente.* 1967. Buenos Aires: Blakman, 1991. Videorecording.

Germani, Gino. *Política y sociedad en una época de transición.* Buenos Aires: Paidós, 1971.

Giunta, Andrea. *Vanguardia, internacionalismo y politica: Arte argentino en los años sesenta.* Buenos Aires: Editorial Paisós, 2001.

King, John. *El Di Tella y el desarrollo cultural argentino en la década del sesenta.* Buenos Aires: Editorial Gaglianone, 1985.

Lamborghini, Osvaldo. *El fiord.* Buenos Aires: Ediciones Chinatown, 1969.

Massotta, Oscar, et al. *Happenings.* Buenos Aires: Jorge Alvarez, 1967.

Moyano, María José. *Argentina's Lost Patrol: Armed Struggle, 1969–1979.* New Haven, Conn.: Yale University Press, 1995.

Naipaul, V. S. *The Return of Eva Perón.* New York: Alfred A. Knopf, 1980.

Piazzola, Astor. *Soul of the Tango: The Music of Astor Piazzolla.* New York: Sony Classical, 1997. Sound recording.

Plotkin, Mariano. *Freud in the Pampas: The Emergence and Development of a Psychoanalytic Culture in Argentina.* Stanford, Calif.: Stanford University Press, 2001.

Pontoriero, Gustavo. *Sacerdotes para el Tercer Mundo: "El fermento en la masa," 1967–1976.* Buenos Aires: Centro Editor de América Latina, 1991.

Quino. *10 años de Mafalda.* Buenos Aires: Ediciones de la Flor, 1973.

Rizzo, Patricia, ed. *Instituto Di Tella: Experiencias '68.* Buenos Aires: Fundación Proa, 1998.

Sigal, Sylvia. *Intelectuales y poder en la década del sesenta.* Buenos Aires: Punto Sur, 1991.

Solanas, Fernando. *La hora de los hornos.* Berkeley, Calif.: Tricontinental Film Center, 1968. Videorecording.

Solanas, Fernando, and Octavio Getino. *Perón: Actualización política y doctrinaria para la toma del poder.* 1971. Buenos Aires: Blakman, 1990. Videorecording.

Terán, Oscar. *Nuestros años sesenta: La formación de la nueva izquierda intelectual en la Argentina, 1956–1966.* Buenos Aires: Punto Sur, 1991.

Vezzetti, Hugo. *Aventuras de Freud en el país de los Argentinos.* Buenos Aires: Paidós, 1996.

VIII. State Violence

Balderston, Daniel, et al. *Ficción y política: La narrativa argentina durante el proceso militar.* Buenos Aires: Alianza, 1987.

Barón, Ana, Mario del Carril, and Albino Gómez. *¿Por qué se fueron? Testimonios de Argentinos en el exterior.* Buenos Aires: Emecé, 1995.

Cerisola, Roberto Amigo. "Aparición con vida: Las siluetas de detenidos-desaparecidos." *Arte y violencia: Actas del XVIII Coloquio Internacional de Historia del Arte.* México: UNAM, 1995.

Corradi, Juan E., Patricia Weiss Fargen, and Manuel Antonio Garretón, eds. *Fear at the Edge: State Terror and Resistance in Latin America.* Berkeley and Los Angeles: University of California Press, 1992.

Feitlowitz, Marguerite. *A Lexicon of Terror: Argentina and the Legacies of Torture.* New York: Oxford University Press, 1998.

Fisher, Jo. *Mothers of the Disappeared.* London: Zed, 1989.

Gambaro, Griselda. *Bad Blood.* City: Woodstock Dramatic Publications, 1994.

Graziano, Frank. *Divine Violence: Spectacle, Psychosexuality, and Radical Christianity in the Argentine "Dirty War."* Boulder, Colo.: Westview, 1992.

Gusmán, Luis. *Villa*. Buenos Aires: Alfaguara, 1995.

Mignone, Emilio Fermín. *Witness to the Truth: The Complicity of Church and Dictatorship in Argentina, 1976–1983*. New York: Orbis, 1988.

Monaghen, David. *The Falklands War: Myth and Countermyth*. New York: Macmillan, 1998.

Muñoz, Susana, and Lourdes Portillo. *The Mothers of Plaza de Mayo*. Los Angeles: Direct Cinema Limited, 1986. Videorecording.

Partnoy, Alicia. *The Little School: Tales of Disappearance and Survival*. San Francisco: Cleis, 1998.

Potash, Robert. *The Army and Politics in Argentina*. 3 vols. Stanford, Calif.: Stanford University Press, 1969–96.

Puenzo, Luis. *La historia oficial*. New York: Fox Lorber Home Video, 1995. Videorecording.

Ramírez, Mari Carmen, ed. *Cantos paralelos: Visual Parody in Contemporary Argentinean Art*. Austin, Tex.: Jack S. Blanton Museum of Art, 1999.

Rock, David. *Authoritarian Argentina: The Nationalist Movement, Its History, and Its Impact*. Berkeley and Los Angeles: University of California Press, 1993.

Rouquié, Alain. *Poder militar y sociedad política en Argentina*. Buenos Aires: Emecé Editores, 1981.

Taylor, Diana. *Disappearing Acts: Spectacles of Gender and Nationalism in Argentina's "Dirty War."* Durham, N.C.: Duke University Press, 1997.

Timerman, Jacobo. *Prisoner without a Name, Cell without a Number*. New York: Alfred A. Knopf, 1981.

IX. Democracy and Neoliberalism / X. Argentina in the Age of Globalization

Burns, Jimmy. *Hand of God: The Life of Diego Maradona*. London: Bloomsbury, 1996.

Casaravilla, Diego. *Los laberintos de la exclusión: Relatos de inmigrantes ilegales en Argentina*. Buenos Aires: Lumen-Humanitas, 1999.

Cavarozzi, Marcelo. *Autoritarismo y democracia, 1955–1996: La transición del estado al mercado en la Argentina*. Buenos Aires: Ariel, 1997.

Cerruti, Gabriela. *El jefe: Vida y obra de Carlos Saúl Menem*. Buenos Aires: Planeta, 1998.

Dubatti, Jorge. *Batato Barea y el nuevo teatro argentino*. Buenos Aires: Planeta, 1995.

Godio, Julio. *Economía de mercado, estado regulador, y sindicatos*. Buenos Aires: Legasa, 1993.

Guillermo Prieto, Alma. "Buenos Aires, 1991." In *The Heart That Bleeds: Latin America Now*. New York: Alfred A. Knopf, 1994.

Jelin, Elizabeth, ed. *Los nuevos movimientos sociales*. Buenos Aires: CEAL, 1985.

Landi, Oscar, ed. *Medios, transformación cultural y política*. Buenos Aires: Editorial Legasa, 1987.

Lejtman, Roman. *Narcogate*. Buenos Aires: Editorial Sudamericana, 1993.

McGuire, James W. *Peronism without Perón: Unions, Parties, and Democracy in Argentina*. Stanford, Calif.: Stanford University Press, 1997.

O'Donnell, Guillermo. *Counterpoints: Selected Essays on Authoritarianism and Democra-tization*. Notre Dame, Ind.: University of Notre Dame Press, 1999.

Oszlack, Oscar, et al. *"Proceso," crisis, y transición democrática*. Buenos Aires: CEAL, 1984.

Salinas, Juan. *AMIA: El atentado*. Buenos Aires: Planeta, 1997.

Sarlo, Beatriz. *Escenas de la vida postmoderna: Intelectuales, arte, y videocultura en la Argen-tina*. Buenos Aires: Ariel, 1994.

Sawers, Larry. *The Other Argentina: The Interior and National Development*. Boulder, Colo.: Westview, 1996.

Verbitsky, Horacio. *Robo para la corona*. Buenos Aires: Planeta, 1992.

Acknowledgment of Copyrights

"National Identity in a Cosmopolitan Society" from *El Payador* by Leopoldo Lugones, 1916. Reprinted by permission of Jorge O. Castellani.

"Simón Radowitzky" from *Los anarquistas expropiadores: Simón Radowitzky y otros ensayos* by Osvaldo Bayer (Buenos Aires: Galerna, 1975). Copyright 1975 by Osvaldo Bayer. Reprinted by permission of the author.

"The Unión Cívica Radical" from *Politics in Argentina, 1890–1930: The Rise and Fall of Radicalism* by David Rock (Cambridge: Cambridge University Press, 1975). Copyright 1975 by Cambridge University Press. Reprinted by permission of Cambridge University Press.

"ExVoto" and "Milonga" from *Poemas para leer en el tranvía* by Oliverio Girondo (Buenos Aires: Editorial Martín Fierro, 1924). Copyright 1924 by Oliverio Girondo. Reprinted by permission of Susana Lange and Nora L. Kindal.

"Modern Women" by Alfonsina Storni from *Rereading the Spanish American Essay: Translations of Nineteenth and Twentieth Century Women's Essays,* ed. Doris Meyer (Austin: University of Texas Press, 1995). ©1995. Courtesy of the University of Texas Press.

"X-Ray of the Pampa" from *X-Ray of the Pampa* by Ezequiel Martínez Estrada, translated by Alain Swietlicki (Austin: University of Texas Press, 1977). Copyright 1971 by Agustina M. de Martínez Estrada. Reprinted by permission of Fundación Ezequiel Martínez Estrada and the University of Texas Press.

"Soccer and Popular Joy" from "Ayer ví ganar a los argentinos" in *Nuevas aguafuertes porteñas* by Roberto Arlt (Buenos Aires: Librería Hachette, 1960). Copyright 1960 by Librería Hachette. Reprinted by permission of Editorial Losada.

"Cambalache" by Enrique Santos Discépolo. Copyright 1942 Warner/Chapell Music Argentina. Reprinted by permission of SADAIC (Argentine Society of Authors and Composers of Music).

"Perón and the People" from *Resistance and Integration: Peronism and the Argentine Working Class* by Daniel James (Cambridge: Cambridge University Press, 1988). Copyright 1988 by Cambridge University Press. Reprinted by permission of Cambridge University Press.

"Saint Evita" by Tomás Eloy Martínez from *Santa Evita,* by Tomás Eloy Martínez (New York: Alfred A. Knopf, 1996). ©1996 by Alfred A. Knopf, Inc. Used by permission of Alfred A. Knopf, a division of Random House, Inc.

"Ramona's Revenge," two comic strips by Lino Palacio. Copyright by Lino Palacio. Reprinted by permission of Jorge Palacio.

"Funes, the Memorious" from *Ficciones* by Jorge Luis Borges (New York: Grove Press, Inc., 1962). Copyright 1962 by Grove/Atlantic, Inc. Reprinted by permission.

"Victorian Fathers" by Victoria Ocampo from *Victoria Ocampo: Writer, Feminist, Woman of the World,* edited and translated by Patricia Owen Steiner (Albuquerque: University of New Mexico Press, 1999). Copyright 1999 by the University of New Mexico Press. Reprinted by permission.

"The Foreign Gaze" from *Diary* by Witold Gombrowicz, translated by Lillian Vallee,

Index

Gabriela Nouzeilles is Assistant Professor of Latin American Studies
at Duke University and Graciela Montaldo is Professor of Language
and Literature at Universidad Simón Bolívar.

Library of Congress Cataloging-in-Publication Data
The Argentina reader : history, culture, politics / [edited by]
Gabriela Nouzeilles & Graciela Montaldo.
p. cm. — (The Latin America readers; Latin America in
translation/en traducción/em traduçao)
Includes bibliographical references.
ISBN 0-8223-2885-2 (cloth : alk. paper)
ISBN 0-8223-2914-X (pbk. : alk. paper)
1. Argentina—Civilization.   I. Nouzeilles, Gabriela.
II. Montaldo, Graciela R.   III. Series.
F2810 .A646   2002
982—dc21   2002004447